THE MEDIEVAL ENGLISH UNIVERSITIES:
OXFORD AND CAMBRIDGE TO *c*.1500

THE MEDIEVAL
ENGLISH UNIVERSITIES:
OXFORD AND CAMBRIDGE
TO *c.* 1500

ALAN B. COBBAN

Reader in Medieval History in the
University of Liverpool;
Past Fellow of Trinity College,
Cambridge

THE UNIVERSITY OF CALIFORNIA PRESS
Berkeley   Los Angeles

University of California Press
Berkeley and Los Angeles

First published in 1988 by
SCOLAR PRESS
Gower Publishing Company Limited
Gower House, Croft Road
Aldershot GU11 3HR

Reprinted 1990

Library of Congress Cataloging in Publication Data
Cobban, Alan B.
   The medieval English universities: Oxford
   and Cambridge to c.1500/Alan B. Cobban.
      p. cm.
   Bibliograpy: p.
   Includes index.
   ISBN 0–520–06244–2
   1. Universities and colleges—England—History. 2. University
of Oxford—History. 3. University of Cambridge—History. 4.
England—Intellectual life—Medieval period, 1066–1485. I. Title.
   LA636.3.C6 1988
   378.42–dc19   88–19839
                        CIP

To the memory of
PROFESSOR WALTER ULLMANN

Contents

Contents

Contents

Contents

Preface

Since the appearance in 1895 of Hastings Rashdall's monumental work *The Universities of Europe in the Middle Ages* an impressive amount of research on the medieval English Universities has been completed. Of particular importance have been the combined publications of the Oxford Historical Society and the Cambridge Antiquarian Society, which, beginning in the nineteenth century, comprise a kaleidoscopic array of monographs and editions of source material bearing on the history of the English Universities and of their colleges, halls and hostels, and also embracing associated institutions and features of life within the two university towns. In the closing years of the nineteenth and opening years of the twentieth century, the series of Oxford and Cambridge Histories attempted to survey the collegiate history of the English Universities. While these were modest productions, and although they were not properly integrated into English academic history, they retain a residual value. Updated short studies of the Universities of Oxford and Cambridge and their colleges formed the third volume of the *Victoria History of the County of Oxford* (1954) and the *Victoria History of the County of Cambridge and the Isle of Ely* (1959). Although these accounts are useful, they are more in the nature of quarries for factual reference than interpretative contributions to university history. A now indispensable tool of research has been forged in the shape of A. B. Emden's magisterial Biographical Registers of the alumni of Oxford and Cambridge, in the case of the former extending in four volumes to 1540 and in the case of the latter forming a single volume to 1500. All five volumes were published between 1957 and 1974. These Registers have furnished the basic data for the computerized analysis of the personnel of medieval Oxford and Cambridge which has been a salient research activity since the 1970s and which is represented below in chapter 6.

If, for more than half of the twentieth century, historical evaluation of Cambridge's standing has set it immoderately low, the university being generally seen as a mere derivative and insubstantial version of Oxford, the balance has to some extent been redressed from the late 1950s. This reappraisal of Cambridge's standing was inaugurated by two pivotal articles by W. Ullmann relating to the Cambridge chancellor's authority and to Cambridge and the Great Schism, and published in 1958 in the *Historical Journal* and the *Journal of Theological Studies* respectively. This reassessment was further developed in my article in the *Bulletin of the John Rylands Library* of 1964 concerning Cambridge's legal status, and in my book *The King's Hall within the University of Cambridge in the Later Middle Ages* (1969) and in M. B. Hackett's *Original Statutes of Cambridge University: the Text and its History* (1970). During this regenerative period research into Cambridge University's history was facilitated by the publication in 1962 of *The Archives of the University of Cambridge*, a valuable historical introduction by the then Keeper, Miss Heather Peek, assisted by Mrs Catherine Hall. This professional historical interest in Cambridge University and its collegiate development has been vigorously maintained throughout the 1970s and 1980s, although nothing comparable to *The History of the University of Oxford* Project, currently underway, has been undertaken for Cambridge.

The Oxford Project, conceived in eight chronologically arranged volumes under the General Editorship of the late T. H. Aston, will deal with the evolution of Oxford University from its origins in the twelfth century down to the late twentieth century. When all eight volumes have been published, it will probably be true to say that no university will have been so evenly portrayed over such a lengthy period. Clearly, this is a notable collaborative venture. Of necessity, however, an enterprise by so many hands must assume the form of a multi-volumed work of specialist reference and cannot have the character of a unitary interpretative history. In terms of thematic coverage and chronological extent, *The History of the University of Oxford* Project will undoubtedly supersede all previous surveys of Oxford University, of which the most successful is arguably the three-volumed *A History of the University of Oxford* (1924-7) by the gifted amateur, Sir Charles Mallet. The Oxford Project is, however, closely confined to Oxford history, drawing but lightly upon comparative Cambridge or continental material. Consequently, it does not have the aim of encompassing Cambridge University's history to any significant degree. The only extensive survey of Cambridge University yet essayed in the modern period is the three volumes of J. B. Mullinger's *University of Cambridge* (1873–1911). However, Mullinger's work, it has to be said, is frequently rambling and is amateurish in tone. The first volume, which purports to take Cambridge's history down to 1535, is largely made up of extraneous matter relating to Paris and Oxford, and to currents of intellectual life. As a guide to the history of medieval Cambridge University, it is only of marginal use.

It is therefore clear that despite the large number of particular studies, both professional and amateur, which have been produced in the period following Rashdall's coverage of Oxford and Cambridge in the 1890s, there is no single volume on the medieval English Universities which has attempted either to take cognizance of the substantial amount of research completed since that time or to give a due prominence to the perspectives and themes which have acquired significance in the second half of this century. The present book has been written in an endeavour to grapple with these objectives. In so far as the evidence will allow, the English Universities are here comparatively assessed throughout so that English university history may be viewed as an integrated whole and not, as has so often been the fashion, seen through the separate eyes of either Oxford or Cambridge. Within the compass of a single volume the medieval English Universities are analysed with reference to their origins and early development, their government and organization, their colleges, halls and hostels, their teaching structures, their academic concentrations, their relations with the town and ecclesiastical authorities, the composition of their academic communities and the contribution of their personnel to Church and State, and with reference to many diverse features of student academic and social life. The intellectual achievements of the English Universities *per se*, which belong to the historical vastness of European thought, are not the concern of this volume.

I began my researches within the sphere of medieval English academic history in 1961 as a protégé of Professor Walter Ullmann.

Since then my research projects have alternated between the English and continental Universities. In a general sense, I wish to express my gratitude to the late Professor Ullmann and to Dr A. B. Emden for their encouragement and counsel in the early stages of my career. I would also like to thank the archivists and librarians of the many Oxford and Cambridge college libraries in which I have worked over a quarter of a century. My particular thanks are due to Miss H. E. Peek, the former Keeper of the Cambridge University Archives, and to her successor, Dr D. M. Owen, for their unfailing help and kindness; to the late Dr W. A. Pantin, the former Keeper of the Oxford University Archives; and to the late Mr T. H. Aston, his successor in this office and, since its inception until his death, the Director of *The History of the University of Oxford* Project, in which I am involved as a contributor. I am indebted to the editor of the *Bulletin of the John Rylands Library* for permission to reproduce table 1, which was originally appended to my article 'Theology and Law in the Medieval Colleges of Oxford and Cambridge', *B.J.R.L.*, lxv (1982), pp. 57 ff. at p. 77. Finally, I wish to thank my colleague Elizabeth A. Danbury for valuable assistance given with some of the illustrative material.

University of Liverpool   ALAN B. COBBAN

Abbreviations

A.H.R.	*American Historical Review*
Annals	C. H. Cooper, *Annals of Cambridge* (4 vols., Cambridge, 1842–53)
B.A.	Bachelor of Arts
B.C.L.	Bachelor of Civil Law
B.Cn.L.	Bachelor of Canon Law
B.I.H.R.	*Bulletin of the Institute of Historical Research*
B.J.R.L.	*Bulletin of the John Rylands Library*
B.R.U.C.	A. B. Emden, *A Biographical Register of the University of Cambridge to 1500* (Cambridge, 1963)
B.R.U.O.	A. B. Emden, *A Biographical Register of the University of Oxford to A.D. 1500* (3 vols., Oxford, 1957–9)
B.Th.	Bachelor of Theology or Divinity
Cal. Close R.	Calendar of Close Rolls
Cal. Pat. R.	Calendar of Patent Rolls
Camb. Docs.	*Documents relating to the University and Colleges of Cambridge* (3 vols., ed. by the Queen's Commissioners, London, 1852)
C.A.S.	*Cambridge Antiquarian Society*
Chartularium	*Chartularium Universitatis Parisiensis* (4 vols., ed. H. Denifle and E. Chatelain, Paris, 1889–97)
CUL/UA	Cambridge University Library/University Archives
D.C.L.	Doctor of Civil Law
D.Cn.L.	Doctor of Canon Law
D.Th.	Doctor of Theology or Divinity
Econ. Hist. Rev.	*Economic History Review*
E.H.R.	*English Historical Review*

J. Eccles. Hist.	*Journal of Ecclesiastical History*
M.A.	Master of Arts
Mediaeval Archives	*The Mediaeval Archives of the University of Oxford* (2 vols., ed. H. E. Salter, Oxf. Hist. Soc., lxx, lxxiii, 1917–19)
Munimenta Academica	*Munimenta Academica: Documents illustrative of Academical Life and Studies at Oxford* (2 vols., Rolls Series, ed. H. Anstey, 1868)
Oxf. Hist. Soc.	Oxford Historical Society
Oxford Formularies	*Formularies which bear on the History of Oxford c. 1204–1420* (2 vols., ed. H. E. Salter, W. A. Pantin and H. G. Richardson, Oxf. Hist. Soc., new series, iv-v, 1942)
Registrum Cancellarii	*Registrum Cancellarii Oxoniensis 1434–1469* (2 vols., ed. H. E. Salter, Oxf. Hist. Soc., xciii-iv, 1932)
Snappe's Formulary	*Snappe's Formulary and other records* (ed. H. E. Salter, Oxf. Hist. Soc., lxxx, 1924)
Statuta Antiqua	*Statuta Antiqua Universitatis Oxoniensis* (ed. S. Gibson, Oxford, 1931)
Statutes	*Statutes of the Colleges of Oxford* (3 vols., ed. by the Queen's Commissioners, Oxford and London, 1853)
Statuts	*Les Statuts et Privilèges des Universités françaises depuis leur fondation jusqu'en 1789* (3 vols., ed. M. Fournier, Paris, 1890–2)
The King's Hall	A. B. Cobban, *The King's Hall within the University of Cambridge in the Later Middle Ages* (Cambridge Studies in Medieval Life and Thought, third series, vol. 1, Cambridge, 1969)
The Medieval Universities	A. B. Cobban, *The Medieval Universities: their development and organization* (London, 1975)
The Register of Congregation 1448–1463	*The Register of Congregation 1448–1463* (ed. W. A. Pantin and W. T. Mitchell, Oxf. Hist. Soc., new series, xxii, 1972)
T.R.H.S.	*Transactions of the Royal Historical Society*
Universities	H. Rashdall, *The Universities of Europe in the*

	Middle Ages (3 vols., 2nd ed., F. M. Powicke and A. B. Emden, Oxford, 1936)
V.C.H. Camb. ii	*Victoria History of the County of Cambridge and the Isle of Ely*, ii (ed. L. F. Salzman, London, 1948)
V.C.H. Camb. iii	*Victoria History of the County of Cambridge and the Isle of Ely*, iii (ed. J. P. C. Roach, Oxford, 1959)
V.C.H. Oxon. iii	*Victoria History of the County of Oxford*, iii (ed. H. E. Salter and M. D. Lobel, London, 1954)
V.C.H. Oxon. iv	*Victoria History of the County of Oxford*, iv (ed. A. Crossley, Oxford, 1979)
Welsh Hist. Rev.	*Welsh Historical Review*

All other abbreviations are considered self-explanatory

Chapter 1

The Medieval University: The European Context

The medieval university was primarily an indigenous product of western Europe.[1] It is true that the Greek, the Graeco-Roman, the Byzantine and the Islamic worlds had produced centres of higher education in rich profusion, and that these may have prefigured features of the medieval universities, such as regular curricular arrangements, and produced tentative forms of organization among teaching staff,[2] but they nowhere paralleled the medieval universities as privileged corporate associations of masters and students with their statutes, seals, administrative machinery and degree procedures.[3] There appears, therefore, to have been no significant organic continuity between the universities which evolved in western Europe in the twelfth century and previous institutions of advanced learning. However much the universities

[1] On the concept of the medieval university, see A. B. Cobban, *The Medieval Universities: their development and organisation* (London, 1975), pp. 21–36; H. Rashdall, *The Universities of Europe in the Middle Ages* (3 vols., 2nd ed., F. M. Powicke and A. B. Emden, Oxford, 1936), i. ch. 1; H. Denifle, *Die Entstehung der Universitäten des Mittelalters bis 1400* (Berlin, 1885), ch. 1.

[2] For academic arrangements at the philosophical school of Athens, dating from the fourth century BC, at the law school of Beirut, which flourished between the early third and mid-sixth century, and at the imperial university of Constantinople, founded in 425 and functioning intermittently until 1453, see M. L. Clarke, *Higher Education in the Ancient World* (London, 1971), pp. 55 ff., 116–17, 130 ff., 136; see also S. S. Laurie, *Lectures on the Rise and Early Constitution of Universities* (London, 1886), pp. 15–16. On Islamic institutions of learning, see G. Makdisi, *The Rise of Colleges: Institutions of Learning in Islam and the West* (Edinburgh, 1981), esp. ch. 4: the author's conclusion that 'the university, as a form of organization, owes nothing to Islam' is given on p. 224.

[3] See the comments of S. Stelling-Michaud, 'L'histoire des universités au moyen âge et à la renaissance au cours des vingt-cinq dernières années', *XIe Congrès International des Sciences Historiques, Rapports*, i(Stockholm, 1960), p. 98; also C. H. Haskins, *The Rise of Universities* (New York, 1923), pp. 3–4.

owed to Graeco-Roman and Arabic intellectual life, their corporative character was a novel educational development, born of the need to expand the resources for professionally oriented education in an increasingly urbanized European society.

The terminology concerning the medieval universities is a complicated issue. Only by accident did the Latin term *universitas* come to be specifically associated with university institutions.[4] In the twelfth, thirteenth and fourteenth centuries, *universitas* was commonly applied in such a way as to denote several types of corporate bodies such as craft guilds or municipal councils.[5] When used in relation to universities the term for long referred to the guild of masters or of students or of masters and students combined, that is to say, to the academic personnel and not to the university as a complete entity. It was only from the late fourteenth century that *universitas* began to be associated particularly with universities as distinct from other modes of corporation. And it came to be used increasingly, in less formal documentation, to designate the university structure as a whole and not merely its guild constituent.[6] Before the fifteenth century, however, the abstract term which most frequently and formally rendered the medieval concept of a fully-fledged university was *studium generale*.[7]

The *studium* part of the expression *studium generale* indicated a school with organized facilities for advanced study, and the *generale* component referred not to the general or universal nature of the subjects taught but to the ability of the school to attract students from beyond the local region. A school lacking this drawing power

[4] On *universitas*, see Denifle, op. cit., pp. 29 ff.; Rashdall, op. cit., i. 4 ff., 15.

[5] See e.g. P. Michaud-Quantin, *Universitas: expressions du mouvement communautaire dans le moyen âge latin* (L'Eglise et l'Etat au Moyen Age, 13, Paris, 1970), *passim*, and Michaud-Quantin, 'Collectivités médiévales et institutions antiques', *Miscellanea Mediaevalia*, i(ed. P. Wiepert, Berlin, 1962), pp. 239 ff.

[6] Denifle, op. cit., esp. pp. 34 ff.; Rashdall, op. cit., i. 16–17.

[7] On the notion of *studium generale*, see Denifle, op. cit., ch. 1; Rashdall, op. cit., i. 6 ff., and ii. 2–3; Cobban, *The Medieval Universities*, pp. 23 ff.; Stelling-Michaud, 'L'histoire des universités . . .', art. cit., pp. 99–100; and G. Ermini, 'Concetto di "Studium Generale"', *Archivio Giuridico*, cxxvii (1942), pp. 3 ff., where the divergent views of H. Denifle, F.C. von Savigny, A. Pertile, F. Schupfer and G. Kaufmann on the essential features of the *studium generale* are summarized.

and serving only the needs of a town or a limited area was, by contrast, labelled a *studium particulare* or 'particular school'.[8] There was no definitive view as to the range of attraction which a school had to exhibit before it was to be recognized as a *studium generale*. It is true that a *studium generale* would normally draw students from more than one country, and indeed it might evolve into a markedly cosmopolitan centre such as Bologna, Paris, Montpellier or Salamanca. But a *studium* which recruited mainly from different parts of the same country and catered for only a small number of foreign students might nevertheless be ranked as a *studium generale* — as was the case with the Universities of Oxford and Cambridge. Apart from its drawing strength, a *studium generale* was distinguished by a regime which, in addition to or sometimes in place of arts,[9] offered instruction in at least one of the superior faculties of law (canon or civil or both), theology or medicine, and which maintained a sufficient core of regent or teaching masters to meet its diverse academic requirements. Before legal precision in such a matter was achieved, the final arbiter of whether or not a centre was to be classified a *studium generale* as opposed to a *studium particulare* was informed educational opinion. This meant that in the early stages of the university movement, when universities were not specifically founded but arose haphazardly, the status of *studium generale* was of a customary nature and not of a strictly legal character. But in the late thirteenth and fourteenth centuries, legal definition permeated the university scene. Italian jurists fashioned the term *studium generale ex consuetudine (studium generale* by custom) and applied it retrospectively to centres such as Paris, Bologna, Montpellier, Padua, Orleans, Oxford and Cambridge to describe their customary standing in the period before formal validations were sought.[10]

[8] For the concept of *studium particulare*, see Cobban, op. cit., pp. 34–5.

[9] Some of the universities which specialized in law did not establish arts faculties until the later medieval period, and even then, as in many of the Italian and French provincial universities, they were relatively insignificant, providing an elementary grounding in arts for future law students. At Orleans, civil and canon law were the only disciplines to acquire full faculty status in the pre-Reformation era.

[10] See the comments of Rashdall, op. cit., i. 10.

From the second half of the thirteenth century, the validating source thought necessary for the endorsement of a centre of learning as a *studium generale* was either the papacy or the emperor because they alone were deemed capable of conferring an ecumenical authority. Indeed, earlier in the century the papacy and the imperial power had helped to promote the notion of the planned as distinct from the spontaneously evolved university. Following upon what appears to have been the first university to be established by a definite act — the Castilian University of Palencia, founded by Alfonso VIII of Castile in 1208-9 — the Emperor Frederick II instituted the University of Naples in 1224, Pope Gregory IX created the University of Toulouse in 1229, and Innocent IV established a *studium generale* in the papal curia at Rome in 1244 or 1245.[11] By the third quarter of the thirteenth century the idea that the authority to erect universities was vested in papal or imperial prerogative, and especially in the former, had taken such firm root that an attempt was made to rationalize the university landscape by encouraging those universities whose status was based upon custom to seek a formal authentication. Although this process of rationalization was not entirely completed or without its anomalies[12] (one such involving the University of Oxford)[13] it is generally true that the old-established universities, in tandem with the new creations, were, from the close of the thirteenth century, brought within the orbit of a distant papal or imperial tutelage.

This move towards the creation of an international university system rooted in an ecumenical authority helped to advance the theoretical notion of the *ius ubique docendi*, that is, the right of a

[11] For Palencia, see e.g. Rashdall, op. cit., ii. 65, and J. San Martín, *La Antigua Universidad de Palencia* (Madrid, 1942); for Naples, see e.g. Rashdall, op. cit., ii. 21-6, and F. Torraca et al., *Storia della Università di Napoli* (Naples, 1924); for Toulouse, see e.g. Rashdall, op. cit., ii. 160-73, and C. E. S. Smith, *The University of Toulouse in the Middle Ages* (Milwaukee, Wisconsin, 1958); and for the University of the Papal Court of Rome, see e.g. Rashdall, op. cit., ii. 28-31, and Denifle, op. cit., pp. 301-10.

[12] It seems probable that several centres of learning with some claim to be regarded as 'customary' universities, such as the schools at Lyons and Rheims, were subsequently denied the legal attestation of *studium generale*: see Cobban, op. cit., p. 34.

[13] See below, pp. 61-3.

graduate of one university to teach in another without undergoing further examination.[14] By the fourteenth century, the *ius ubique docendi* had become one of the cardinal legal hallmarks of the status of *studium generale* and was normally included in the foundation charters of new universities and conferred retrospectively on the old-established universities which had previously claimed this status as a prescriptive right. If the *ius ubique docendi* had been universally implemented, the untrammelled mobility of university teachers would have become a reality, bringing into being a European-wide academic commonwealth which transcended race and provincialism in the collective pursuit and dissemination of learning.

It would be misleading, however, to regard the *ius ubique docendi* as a reliable model for the actual pattern of relationships between medieval universities. In reality, university particularism tended to prevail against the supranational implications of the *ius ubique docendi*. It has to be remembered that the *ius ubique docendi* was an artificial device designed to mask the natural inequalities which existed among universities with respect to institutional maturity and degree of community recognition. It is therefore not surprising that the old-established universities were often less than willing to participate in a levelling system which detracted from their position in the upper rank of the university world.[15] But it was not only between the older universities and the newer foundations that the principle of the *ius ubique docendi* proved difficult to operate. Even within the ranks of the former, the code requiring mutual recognition of degrees was accorded only a minimal observance. For

[14] On the *ius ubique docendi*, see Cobban, op. cit., pp. 27–32; Rashdall, op. cit., i. 9–15; Stelling-Michaud, 'L' histoire des universités. . .', art. cit., p. 100.

[15] For example, when Gregory IX granted the privileges of Paris, including the *ius ubique docendi*, upon the University of Toulouse in 1233, he had to mollify the Parisian masters with the assurance that no interference with their own privileges was intended: *Chartularium Universitatis Parisiensis* (4 vols., ed. H. Denifle and E. Chatelain, Paris, 1889-97), i. no. 101. Paris was able to insist upon the examining of Toulouse graduates even after the award of the *ius ubique docendi* to Toulouse University: see C. E. S. Smith, op. cit., p. 58. See also the general comments of M.W. Strasser, 'The Educational Philosophy of the First Universities', *The University World, A Synoptic View of Higher Education in the Middle Ages and Renaissance* (ed. D. Radcliff-Umstead, Pittsburgh, 1973), pp. 1ff. at pp. 4–5.

example, while Oxford and Cambridge operated reciprocal degree arrangements, something akin to an academic tariff war raged between Paris and Oxford in the early fourteenth century, each university refusing to accept and license the graduates of the other without fresh examination.[16] And Montpellier, Angers and Orleans vigorously asserted the right of examination of all potential regent masters from other universities.[17] In the absence of written examinations, there were few fixed criteria by which one university could properly evaluate the academic standards of graduates of another without staging its own investigation.[18] This provided an additional reason to that of the retention of status for the reluctance to honour the code of the *ius ubique docendi*. Moreover, in some universities, the chief motive for the repudiation of the *ius ubique docendi* was the desire to maintain a self-perpetuating oligarchy of teaching masters in order to maximize incomes for small circles of established lecturers.[19] Although the medieval universities were indeed international institutions in terms of the common core of studies pursued and taught in Latin, the *lingua franca* of European scholarship, they nevertheless retreated from the full implications of a supranational university system by imposing these restrictions on the appointment of lecturing staff.

In general, and contrary to popular belief, the university ethos was antithetical to a wandering academic population in the sense in which it had existed in the pre-university age of the urban and

---

[16] See *Statuta Antiqua Universitatis Oxoniensis* (ed. S. Gibson, Oxford, 1931), *De resumentibus* (*a*. 1313: revised dating of G. Pollard), pp. 53–4.

[17] See the statutes of Montpellier of 1220, *Les Statuts et Privilèges des Universités françaises depuis leur fondation jusqu'en 1789* (3 vols., ed. M. Fournier, Paris, 1890–2), ii. no. 1194; for Angers, see the statutes of 1373 and 1398, ibid., i. nos. 396, 434; and for Orleans, see the statute of 1321, ibid., i. no. 78.

[18] For the examination system at medieval universities, see e.g. Cobban, *The Medieval Universities*, pp. 209 ff.

[19] This was the situation in many of the French provincial universities of the pre-Reformation era. Useful information on this point is contained in A. J. Scarth's unpublished Ph.D. thesis, *Aspects of the History and Organisation of the French Provincial Universities of Orleans, Angers, Avignon and Cahors, from their Origins to c. 1450* (Liverpool University, 1979), pp. 27–8, 116–22, 189–91, 234–5, 268–9.

cathedral schools.[20] What mobility there was on the part of students and teaching masters tended to be far more controlled and specifically directed than in the era of the transient schools which had played host to a scholarly army that was engaged in a restless quest for knowledge. This academic protectionism, which acted as a brake on the free interchange of personnel and which became such a marked characteristic of Europe's university order,[21] had an especially important bearing upon the English Universities. For it meant that their natural insularity as outposts of the continental university movement was reinforced by the self-imposed limitations on the interflow of university teachers. Their relative lack of cosmopolitanism rendered Oxford and Cambridge less prone to the turbulent upheavals which so often afflicted their continental counterparts. (The identification of Oxford with Wyclifism,[22] which had traumatic consequences for that university, and the involvement of Cambridge as a victim in the events of the Peasants' Revolt of 1381,[23] furnish two of the more celebrated exceptions to the broad stability of English university life.)

Of the more concrete privileges associated with the status of *studium generale*, one of the most far reaching was the right of beneficed clergy to receive the incomes of their benefices while non-

[20] For the cathedral schools, see G. Paré, A. Brunet and P. Tremblay, *La renaissance du xii͏ᵉ siècle: les écoles et l'enseignement* (Paris and Ottawa, 1933); E. Lesne, 'Les écoles de la fin du viii͏ᵉ siècle à la fin du xii͏ᵉ', *Histoire de la propriété ecclésiastique en France*, v (Lille, 1940); S. d'Irsay, *Histoire des universités françaises et étrangères des origines à nos jours* (2 vols., Paris, 1933–5), *passim*.

[21] Not all historians appear to appreciate the extent to which academic mobility between universities might be circumscribed and seem to assume that the *ius ubique docendi* was in accord with what actually occurred: see e.g. P. Delhaye, 'L'organisation scolaire au xii͏ᵉ siècle', *Traditio*, v (1947), pp. 211 ff. at p. 268, and H. Perkin, 'The Changing Social Function of the University: A Historical Retrospect', *CRE-Information Quarterly*, new series, no. 62(1983), pp. 117 ff. at pp. 120–1. In the same publication, H. de Ridder-Symoens, in a valuable article, 'La migration académique des hommes et des idées en Europe, xiii͏ᵉ – xviii͏ᵉ siècles', ibid., pp. 69 ff., discusses the patterns of academic migration between universities within the same country or geographical area and on the international plane, but she does not take sufficient cognizance of the teaching oligarchies which became entrenched in many university centres.

[22] See below, pp. 131–3, 235–7, 284–7, 298–9, 406–7.

[23] See below, pp. 264–7.

resident at a university for the purposes of study or teaching. This privilege had crystallized in its mature form by the mid-thirteenth century.[24] As a result, beneficed clergy formed significant groupings in most of the universities of continental Europe and in the academic populations of Oxford and Cambridge. In addition to those already mentioned, a *studium generale* might harbour further privileges, but a distinction has to be drawn between those rights which were inherent in the concept of *studium generale* and those which were specifically conferred upon individual universities. It is clear that the particular relationships between universities and external bodies, whether episcopal, archiepiscopal, civic, regal or imperial, were so diverse that they could not be subsumed under the umbrella title of *studium generale*. For example, emancipation from episcopal or archiepiscopal authority was not a right which could be extrapolated from the notion of *studium generale*. For such a right, a university was required to have a specific papal award,[25] as is amply demonstrated in the cases of Oxford and Cambridge set out in chapter 7.

In the midst of all the discussions of legal forms and privileges, however, it must never be forgotten that the essence of the medieval university was the academic guild organized for the mutual defence of its members and for the supervision of the teaching regime. Until the late medieval period, universities functioned without the benefit of purpose-built accommodation[26] and with only a rudimentary administrative apparatus.[27] Unencumbered as they were by material plant and its attendant cares, the universities, including Oxford and

---

[24] See Cobban, op. cit., pp. 26–7.

[25] On particular and common privileges of the *studium generale*, see ibid., p. 33; also Cobban, *The King's Hall within the University of Cambridge in the Later Middle Ages* (Cambridge Studies in Medieval Life and Thought, third series, vol. i, Cambridge, 1969), p. 107.

[26] On the advent of purpose-designed buildings in medieval universities, see e.g. J. Verger, *Les universités au moyen âge* (Paris, 1973), pp. 181–2, 187 ff.

[27] In the medieval universities, the administration was undertaken by academics — either by members of the teaching staff or by students, depending upon the constitutional form of the university — and was usually assisted by a number of common university servants, the number and variety of whom varied from university to university.

Cambridge, can be described as having been in their initial phase, intellectual occasions rather than highly structured administrative organizations. As such, the energies of the majority of the teaching staff could be concentrated upon the primary academic task with only the minimum of administrative distraction,[28] a consideration which must have had a salutary effect upon the life of both the teaching masters and the students. Against this, it has to be recognized that the universities had to contend with all manner of uncertainties and hardships before they acquired a more cohesive and sedentary character in the later Middle Ages.[29] The universities had their genesis in conflict, and struggle punctuated every stage in their evolution and rapid expansion as they fought first to win and then to defend an acceptable degree of autonomy *vis-à-vis* a range of ecclesiastical and secular authorities.[30] It could be argued, however, that the unsettled conditions, potential or actual, within which university life had perforce to operate, tended, if anything, to emphasize the precious and desirable nature of advanced education. There can be little doubt that among Europe's earliest wave of universities the academic life was infused with much infectious dedication, which made possible the realization of the highest intellectual standards, especially in those universities which enjoyed a significant degree of freedom from authoritarian repression.[31]

[28] Only a small proportion of academics would have been involved in administrative tasks at any one time. Offices were generally held for relatively short periods and were rotated with some frequency.

[29] Universities in the thirteenth and fourteenth centuries were subject to periodic cessations of lectures and migrations of colonies of teachers and students to rival cities. These arose, for example, from conflict with the municipal or local ecclesiastical authorities or as a reaction to unwelcome royal or papal policy. In addition, academic disruption might be caused by visitations of plague or by military operations in the vicinity. For the many cessations of lectures, migrations and plague stoppages which occurred at Bologna in the thirteenth and fourteenth centuries, see P. Kibre, *Scholarly Privileges in the Middle Ages* (Mediaeval Academy of America, London, 1961), ch. 2.

[30] No comprehensive study has yet appeared on the drive for university autonomy in the medieval period, but for universities in northern Europe, see e.g. A. B. Cobban, 'Episcopal Control in the Mediaeval Universities of Northern Europe', *Studies in Church History*, v (Leiden, 1969), pp. 1 ff.; also Cobban, *The Medieval Universities*, pp. 75–6.

[31] See e.g. the comments of J. B. Williamson, 'Unrest in Medieval Universities', *The University World, A Synoptic View of Higher Education in the Middle Ages and*

The roots of the medieval university phenomenon were formed in utilitarian soil. Europe's earliest universities were institutional responses to the need to harness the expanding intellectual forces of the eleventh and twelfth centures to the ecclesiastical, governmental and professional requirements of society. In this sense, the universities were the systematic continuators of the cathedral and urban schools.[32] Although these schools had intermittently promoted educational ideals which went beyond practical community wants, their essential purpose had been to augment the number of trained personnel to meet the demands of secular authorities, the Church and the organized professions. These cathedral and municipal schools, which were widely dispersed throughout Europe, aided the transformation of a monastically dominated culture into one in which professional concerns became one of the mainsprings of advanced education. Nevertheless, the facilities which could be provided by these schools were necessarily limited, patchy and frequently ephemeral. The long-term solution was to be found in the more rational deployment of teaching personnel and resources which characterized the universities, Europe's first collectivized educational ventures on any scale.

The universities were conceived during a period of intense and eclectic intellectual activity. In a sense, they were the eventual product of the manifold intellectual developments which had gathered momentum in the course of the eleventh and twelfth centuries.[33] Of prime importance here were the discovery and assimilation of the heritage of the Greek and Graeco-Roman worlds and the subsequent efforts made to reconcile a vast corpus of pagan

---

Renaissance (ed. D. Radcliff-Umstead, Pittsburgh, 1973), pp. 56 ff. at pp. 76–9.

[32] See above, n. 20.

[33] For these intellectual developments see e.g. C. H. Haskins, *Renaissance of the Twelfth Century* (Cambridge, Mass., 1927) and Haskins, *Studies in the History of Mediaeval Science* (New York, 1924; reprinted 1960); D. Knowles, *The Evolution of Medieval Thought* (London, 1962), esp. chs. 6–12; and the collection of specialist essays in *Renaissance and Renewal in the Twelfth Century* (ed. R. L. Benson and G. Constable, with C. D. Lanham, Oxford, 1982).

material with Christian learning.[34] From the conflation of selected ingredients of classical and Christian thought there arose the synthesis of Christian humanism, which had reached a stage of some maturity in the eleventh and twelfth centuries.[35] In its literary and less profound sense, this humanist movement implied the cultivation of classical literature and the stylistic imitation of the ancient authors.[36] On a deeper level, however, Christian humanism involved a set of beliefs and values which came to be firmly embedded in Europe's universities. Prominent among these were the belief in the dignity of man, who, even in his fallen state, was capable of impressive mental and spiritual growth; the belief in an ordered universe which was open to rational understanding; and the belief in the prospect of man's mastery of his environment through his intellect and in his mounting knowledge and experience. The buoyant optimism which such beliefs engendered, the prospect of a fundamental revivification in the human condition and the intoxicating awareness of the capacity of man's reasoning powers, amounted to a reorientation in Europe's intellectual life. Although some of the early enthusiasms were tinged with naivety, and although some of the pristine freshness waned as time advanced, the essential beliefs and values were perpetuated to form part of the thought structure underlying the intellectual life of Europe's universities.[37] By contrast, the more superficial level of literary humanism was accorded only a subordinate niche in the curricula of Europe's earliest universities. At Paris and the English Universities,

[34] See the elaborate exposition by R. R. Bolgar, *The Classical Heritage and its Beneficiaries from the Carolingian Age to the end of the Renaissance* (New York, 1964), esp. chs. 1–5; also Knowles, op. cit., *passim*.

[35] For the main features of Christian humanism, see R.W. Southern, *Medieval Humanism and other Studies* (Oxford, 1970), pp. 29–33; see also C. Morris, *The Discovery of the Individual 1050–1200* (Church History Outlines 5, London, 1972), *passim*.

[36] See the discussion by J. Martin, 'Classicism and Style in Latin Literature', *Renaissance and Renewal in the Twelfth Century*, pp. 537 ff.

[37] See Cobban, *The Medieval Universities*, pp. 13–14.

for example, the study of classical literature was commonly regarded as preparatory to the arts course proper.[38]

Among the reasons for the sharp contraction of interest in literary humanism was the powerful counter-attraction of the professionally geared studies of law, theology and medicine.[39] The prospect of financial reward and a secure position within the established order was enticing to the student of high ability, and there were strong pressures on the universities to limit the arts course to ingredients considered a suitable groundwork for more advanced professional study. It was partly because a prolonged literary appreciation of the classical authors was deemed too static a pursuit for the careerist ambitions of the age, that this area of study fell victim to vocational priorities. Another palpable reason for the ousting of classical studies from the new universities derived from the primacy attained by logic in the arts course.

Until the first half of the twelfth century only fragments of Aristotle's system of logic were known in western Europe, through transmission by Boethius in the fifth century. But in the hundred years or so between *c*. 1150 and *c*. 1250, the main body of Aristotle's logic, as well as his physical, metaphysical, ethical, political and literary works, with their Arabic and Jewish commentaries, were made available in Latin versions.[40] The rediscovery of Aristotle's 'New Logic', as it came to be termed, set the seal upon the commanding position which logic had been acquiring in the twelfth-century schools. Initially, there had been no inevitable antagonism between the attraction of Aristotelian logic and the claims of the classical authors. The situation changed, however, when, in the twelfth century, logic had advanced with such

---

[38] Loc. cit. The erosion of classical literature within the arts course did not prevent the unofficial promotion of classical learning by univeristy lecturers in the thirteenth and fourteenth centuries: see Bolgar, op. cit., p. 222.

[39] The reasons for the minimal emphasis on classical studies in the curricula of Europe's earliest universities are extensively analysed by L. J. Paetow, *The Arts Course at Medieval Universities* (Illinois University Studies, iii. no. 7, Urbana-Champaign, 1910), *passim*.

[40] On the rediscovery of Aristotle's works, see Knowles, op. cit., ch. 15; see also G. Leff, *Paris and Oxford Universities in the Thirteenth and Fourteenth Centuries* (New York, 1968), esp. pp. 119–37.

meteoric pace that it had begun to displace established classical norms of education.[41] For its disciples, logic furnished the key whereby order and system could be wrested from a seemingly chaotic world. Logic, or dialectic, was projected as the indispensable instrument for the deep penetration of all branches of learning, including theology, law, medicine, the natural sciences and grammar. As such, logic had emerged at the dawn of the university experience as the subject which, for a veritable army of teachers and students, was the quintessence of all that was forward-looking and creative. The study of classical literature, on the other hand, stood out as a conservative calling, a memorial to a dead culture, an indulgence out of tune with the sharper educational objectives of the age.[42] This recession of the literary aspects of the classical heritage had a profound effect upon the nature and direction of European education. For the dominance achieved by logic as the centrepiece of the arts curriculum marked a radical transition from an educational system founded on a passive attachment to an inherited culture to one in which a questioning, analytical approach to both classical and contemporary material was in the ascendant. This extension of the analytical faculty was a prerequisite for the rise of university institutions with their

---

[41] Critics, such as John of Salisbury, cogently denounced those logicians who tended to regard logic as almost an education in itself and who spurned the need to equip themselves with a broadly based education in the liberal arts and classical authors. John and his followers were not antithetical to logic, only to excessive claims on its part, and they argued that logic had a useful function if grouped within a broad educational programme: see John of Salisbury, *Metalogicon* (ed. C. C. J. Webb, Oxford, 1929), bk. 1. ch. 3, pp. 9–12; bk. 2. ch. 9, pp. 76–7 and ch. 11, p. 83; bk. 4. ch. 28, p. 194, and the translation by D. D. McGarry, *The Metalogicon of John of Salisbury* (Berkeley and Los Angeles, 1955), pp. 13–16, 93–5, 100–1, 244–5.

[42] The contest between classical studies and logic was dramatically embodied in *c.* 1250 in the French allegorical peom by the trouvère Henri d'Andeli, *Battle of the Seven Arts*, in which grammar, championed by Orleans and supported by the Christian humanists and the classical authors, does battle with logic of Paris and is decisively defeated. The poet's expressed hope for a revival in the fortunes of the classics in the near future was not to be realized, and even at Orleans, one of the bastions of humanist studies well into the thirteenth century, law had emerged as the primary subject by the time of the poem's creation.

commitment to a critical and thrusting outlook and their accessibility to new and invigorating modes of thought.

Given that they were urban phenomena, the spread of universities was facilitated by the European urban revival of the twelfth and thirteenth centuries and, indirectly, by the quickening in communications resulting from the expansion of international trade and from Crusading enterprises. And whilst the pursuit of scholarship by an intellectual élite as a contribution to an understanding of the ordered universe and man's place within it was reckoned to be one of the perennial functions of the universities, they were also viewed, in an increasingly urbanized milieu, as service agencies catering for a hierarchy of social needs.[43] Medieval university education was assumed to provide a range of intellectual skills of direct community value.[44] A rigorous training in logic and the art of the disputation was thought to be a suitable general preparation for most types of professional activity. In a society with an intricate maze of competing rights and privileges, that exactitude of mind, honed by dialectical and disputational expertise, proved to be a prized marketable asset at the disposal of graduates in arts, in the superior disciplines of law or theology or even in medicine.[45] Whether the graduate was destined for one of the myriad posts available within the governmental, judicial or ecclesiastical structures, for a position within a lay or clerical household, for a teaching post in a school or university or as a private tutor, for royal

[43] That medieval universities were susceptible to changing social and professional needs is graphically illustrated by the fact that, in some universities, curricular adaptations occurred to meet developing community requirements: for instances embracing the Italian and English Universities, see Cobban, *The Medieval Universities*, pp. 220–5.

[44] See the reflective essay on this theme by F. M. Powicke, 'The Medieval University in Church and Society', *Ways of Medieval Life and Thought* (London, 1949), pp. 198 ff.

[45] A training in logic was an integral feature of medical courses in many medieval universities. The earliest documented example of the close curricular link between logic and medicine appears to be an enactment of the Emperor Frederick II of *c*. 1241 which set out a curriculum of study for medicine. This enactment, which would have applied to the medical school at Salerno, prescribed three years of training in logic prior to five years spent in medical instruction: see *Historia Diplomatica Friderici II* (7 vols., ed. J. L. A. Huillard-Bréholles, Paris, 1852–61), iv. 235–7.

or papal service abroad, or for employment as one of the legion of polemicists helping to fuel the ideological warfare waged between the secular powers and the papacy, dialectical training, allied to a knowledge of relevant procedures, could be applied successfully over a wide range of intricate administrative, litigious, educational, diplomatic and propagandist affairs.[46] In general, contemporaries evaluated the training in the arts course as no less utilitarian than that in the more professionally oriented disciplines.[47]

The persistent charge, deriving from humanist critics of the late fifteenth and sixteenth centuries, that before the onset of humanist educational ideas, the basic product of the universities had been one trained in an arid form of mental gymnastics with little or no social relevance is now seen to be a serious distortion. It may well be the case that at the time of the humanist impact the Aristotelian based logical exercises had come to occupy an excessively prominent place in the curriculum and had come to impede rather than facilitate invigorating lines of scholarly pursuit.[48] But for the greater part of the medieval period, the sound dialectical training seems to have been in conformity with the oral and written requirements of professional life. Medieval European society had at its disposal only limited finances for the purposes of higher education. Returns of a concrete nature were expected, no less in England than on the Continent, from investment in university concerns. Scarce resources were not available for the subsistence of ivory towers.

However much the concept of study *per se* operated at rarefied university levels, and however much the universities were engaged in seeking a unified view of the world order through a reconciliation between the polarized elements of classical and Christian thought, the essential truth remains that medieval society expected its universities to be vocational institutions responding to vocational needs. To that extent, it may be said that a symbiotic relationship existed between the medieval universities and their surrounding societies. Of intellectual necessity, university education will always

[46] See e.g. the discussion by Cobban, op. cit., pp. 219–20.

[47] Emphasized e.g. by Perkin, 'The Changing Social Function of the University: A Historical Retrospect', art. cit., p. 121.

[48] E.g. Rashdall, *Universities*, iii. 453–4.

have an élitist character. But the medieval universities were for a long time open-access communities in the sense that they would admit any male applicant who had the required Latin expertise and supportive finances. In the universities of northern Europe the typical student was probably of intermediate social status,[49] although, from the fifteenth century, aristocratic recruitment assumed significant proportions, with the corollary that academic populations became more divisively stratified. In southern Europe, on the other hand, significantly large aristocratic contingents were present in universities in the thirteenth and fourteenth centuries.[50] Despite the constraints of the medieval situation, the absence of a groundwork for mass education, the lack of a state-funded system of student grants, and the random pattern of student recruitment, the universities met the professional expectations of a broad spectrum of contemporary society. In no sense were the universities of the pre-1500 era the monopolistic agencies of any one privileged section of the community. In England, the aristocracy remained largely aloof from the universities until the fifteenth and sixteenth centuries. It is only as they were in the post-Reformation period that Oxford and Cambridge can to some degree be described as vehicles of class privilege.

The universities which evolved at Paris and Bologna in the course of the twelfth century acquired the status of archetypes which generally determined the twofold pattern of university organization in the Middle Ages. The Parisian archetype gave rise to the concept of the magisterial university whose affairs were directed by a guild of masters and whose students were in the nature of academic apprentices devoid of *de iure* rights of participation in university government. Bologna, which started life as a magisterial university,[51] soon developed into the archetypal student-controlled

---

[49] Ibid., iii. 408. Analyses of the personnel of individual universities, some of them by computerized means, have tended to reinforce Rashdall's conclusions on the intermediate social status of medieval students in the universities of northern Europe.

[50] See Cobban, op. cit., pp. 201–2.

[51] Ibid., p. 56; also G. Rossi, '"Universitas Scolarium" e Commune', *Studi e memorie per la storia dell'università di Bologna*, new series, i (Bologna, 1956), pp. 173 ff. at p. 175.

university. The idea of guilds of students directing the business of a university and keeping the lecturing staff in a state of subservience has been alien to European thinking for about six hundred years.[52] But as we have just seen, Bologna, one of the two original universities, was, shortly after its inception, a student-dominated university and the prototype for a large family of universities either partially or mainly controlled by students. Although Paris and Bologna remained the ultimate models for university organization, with the passage of time many universities produced either their own adaptations[53] or mixed forms of constitutions representing a fusion between the patterns of Paris and Bologna. These considerations apply to all the main groupings of universities, whether those of provincial France, Italy, Spain, Portugal, Germany, the Low Countries, Bohemia, Hungary, Poland or Scandinavia. The three fifteenth-century Scottish Universities of St Andrews, Glasgow and Aberdeen were magisterial in form, but they incorporated interesting and colourful features from the Bolognese model, including the office of rector, which still survives, albeit in an attenuated and much altered form.[54] By contrast, the Universities of Oxford and Cambridge appear to have owed little to the inspiration of the Bolognese constitution. They were magisterial universities in the Parisian mould, but like so many universities of this genre they both made notable constitutional adaptations from the parent source and, furthermore, they exhibited important differences the one from the other.[55]

Although the precise dating of Europe's earliest universities is often problematical, it is apparent that Oxford, firmly established by the close of the twelfth century, can be reckoned among the first

---

[52] On the whole subject of student power in the medieval period, see Cobban, 'Medieval Student Power', *Past and Present*, no. 53 (1971), pp. 28 ff., and Cobban, *The Medieval Universities*, chs. 3, 7.

[53] The extent to which the Italian Universities departed from the Bolognese model is discussed by P. Denley, 'Recent Studies in Italian Universities of the Middle Ages and Renaissance', *History of Universities*, i(1981), pp. 193 ff. at pp. 198–9.

[54] Rashdall, *Universities*, ii. ch. 11.

[55] See below, ch. 3.

wave of universities, and that Cambridge, which emerged as a university soon after 1209, can be accounted a member of the second wave.[56] It is perhaps noteworthy that in *c.* 1209, the putative date for the first stirrings of a university at Cambridge, there were, in addition to Oxford, only seven other centres which could reasonably be classified as universities: that is to say, Paris, Montpellier, Palencia, Bologna, Reggio, Vicenza and Salerno,[57] although Salerno never measured up to the fully-fledged concept of a medieval university, remaining basically a specialist centre of medical study which acquired some of the attributes of a university.[58] For a small country with a modestly sized population, England, by engendering two universities, made an unexpectedly prominent contribution to the initial phase of European university development. That these two universities should have originated at Oxford and Cambridge was by no means predictable within the context of English academic life in the twelfth and early thirteenth centuries. It is this apparent enigma which will now be considered.

---

[56] The dating of Oxford and Cambridge is discussed below in ch. 2.

[57] See Rashdall's table of universities in op. cit., i. xxiv. Rashdall was in error to include Salerno as a twelfth-century university without making the necessary qualifications.

[58] For the position of Salerno as a proto-university, see Cobban, *The Medieval Universities*, pp. 37–47.

Chapter 2

The English Universities: Origins and Early Development

In the eleventh and twelfth centuries, the focus of higher education in Europe migrated from the monasteries to the cathedral schools and to other forms of urban school.[1] Just as Paris University, the *premier* university of northern Europe, was, in a sense, a product of the cathedral-school movement,[2] so a parallel university development might have been expected to occur in England. But the Parisian sequence of events was not reproduced in England. Although several cathedral schools came near to achieving the transmutation to university status,[3] in the event, no English cathedral city succeeded in creating a durable *studium generale;* and the Universities of Oxford and Cambridge were established in towns which were innocent of cathedrals.[4] In partial explanation it may be said that cathedral schools were not as prominent on the English educational landscape as they were on that of the Continent. Monasticism in England was for long so much in the ascendant that the secular cathedrals tended to be less opulent and less commanding than their European equivalents. While some of the English cathedral schools expanded their curricula to meet the needs produced by growing urbanization, which were insufficiently served by monastic education,[5] they probably made a

[1] See e.g. D. Knowles, *The Evolution of Medieval Thought*, pp. 84–6. For the cathedral schools, see the reference cited above, p. 7, n. 20.

[2] On the origins of Paris University, see e.g. Rashdall, *Universities*, i. 269 ff.; Cobban, *The Medieval Universities*, pp. 75 ff.; Leff, *Paris and Oxford Universities in the Thirteenth and Fourteenth Centuries*, pp. 15 ff.

[3] See below, pp. 27–9.

[4] Oxford, within Lincoln diocese, was some 122 miles from the cathedral at Lincoln, and Cambridge, within Ely diocese, was about 16 miles from the cathedral at Ely.

[5] K. Edwards, *English Secular Cathedrals in the Middle Ages* (2nd ed., Manchester, 1967), p. 323

smaller contribution proportionately than those made by cathedral schools in the rest of northern Europe such as Paris, Orleans, Rheims, Chartres, Laon, Liege and Tournai. Indeed, however influential a number of cathedral schools were to become in England in the twelfth century, it is not at all easy to distinguish a neatly defined cathedral-school period as a transitional phase between monastically dominated education and the university era.

The origins of the Universities of Oxford and Cambridge have been overlaid with the mythological imaginings of antiquarian scholarship.[6] Although, in essence, these conceits had been established by the late medieval period, they were further elaborated and refined in the late sixteenth and seventeenth centuries by rival antiquaries of Oxford and Cambridge. The earliest trace of the notion that Oxford University was founded by Alfred the Great in *c.* 873 is to be found in fourteenth-century chronicle material, and especially in the *Polychronicon* of Ranulf Higden, the Benedictine monk of Chester, whose work was begun in the 1320s and was still in progress when he died in 1363/4.[7] Higden asserted that, on the advice of the abbot of St Neots, Alfred was the first to initiate public schools of diverse arts at Oxford *(scholas publicas variarum artium apud Oxoniam primus instituit).*[8] This claim would appear to have no historical corroboration. It was further embellished by the Warwickshire antiquary John Rous, in his *Historia Regum Angliae,*

---

[6] On the mythological origins of Oxford and Cambridge Universities, see the lengthy treatment by J. Parker, *The Early History of Oxford 727–1100* (Oxf. Hist. Soc., 1885), ch. 2, pp. 5 ff., and appendix A, containing passages from contemporary sources, pp. 305 ff.; C. H. Cooper, *Annals of Cambridge* (4 vols., Cambridge, 1842–53), i (1842), 1–3; also Rashdall, op. cit., iii. 5–6, 276; T. D. Kendrick, *British Antiquity* (London, 1950), pp. 25–6, 76–7; M. McKisack, *Medieval History in the Tudor Age* (Oxford, 1971), pp. 70–1.

[7] On the dating of the *Polychronicon*, see J. Taylor, *The Universal Chronicle of Ranulf Higden* (Oxford, 1966), pp. 2, 89, and A. Gransden, *Historical Writing in England c. 1307 to the Early Sixteenth Century* (London, 1982), p. 44.

[8] *Polychronicon Ranulphi Higden Monachi Cestrensis* (9 vols., Rolls Series, ed. C. Babington and J. R. Lumby, London, 1865–86), vi. (1876), 354 (translation of John Trevisa on p. 355); Parker, op. cit., p. 47 and appendix A, pp. 313–14; Taylor, op. cit., p. 45. For the Alfredian legend, see further B. A. Lees, *Alfred the Great* (New York and London, 1915), pp. 450–1, and the detailed discussion by V. A. Huber, *The English Universities* (transl. and ed. by F. W. Newman, London, 1843), n. 4, pp. 373–85.

completed between 1485 and 1491,[9] and received a later influential promotion by the historian and topographer William Camden, in the fourth edition of his *Britannia* of 1600.[10] Camden cited as his authority a seemingly spurious passage attributed to Asser, the putative author of the *Life of Alfred*, allegedly written in 893, and this passage was reproduced in Camden's edition of Asser's *Life*, published in 1602–3.[11] Not only was Alfred widely projected as either the founder or the restorer of Oxford University, he was also appropriated by University College, Oxford, as its founder.[12] This latter invention was harnessed to meet the needs of law suits involving University College in 1378/9 and in 1427.[13] It was given a literary fixation in Rous's *Historia Regum Angliae*,[14] and in 1727, the claim to Alfred as founder was upheld in the court of the King's Bench.[15]

If the Alfredian legend of the foundation of Oxford University could be discussed in at least pseudo-historical terms, the other

[9] J. Rous, *Historia Regum Angliae* (2nd ed., T. Hearne, Oxford, 1745), p. 76; Parker, op. cit., pp. 49–51 and appendix A, p. 315; Kendrick, op. cit., p. 25.

[10] W. Camden, *Britannia* (4th ed., London, 1600), p. 331.

[11] For Camden's interpolated passage, see Asser's *Life of King Alfred together with the Annals of Saint Neots* (ed. W. H. Stevenson, Oxford, 1904: new impression, with article on recent work on Asser's *Life of Alfred*, by D. Whitelock, Oxford, 1959), p. 70 (in both impressions), and for Stevenson's comments on Camden's interpolation, see pp. xxiii–xxxi; Parker, *The Early History of Oxford*, pp. 40 ff., and appendix A, pp. 312–13. See also *Alfred the Great: Asser's Life of King Alfred and other contemporary sources* (transl. and introduction and notes by S. Keynes and M. Lapidge, Penguin Books, 1983), p. 47.

[12] Parker, op. cit., pp. 52–7, 62; A. Oswald, 'University College', *Victoria History of the County of Oxford*, iii (ed. H. E. Salter and M. D. Lobel, London, 1954), 61 ff. at 63; Lees, *Alfred the Great*, pp. 450–1; C. E. Mallet, *A History of the University of Oxford* (3 vols., London, 1924–7), i. 2.

[13] For these law suits, see Parker, op. cit., pp. 54–5, 57 and appendix A, pp. 316–17. The late fourteenth-century case is discussed by H. C. Maxwell-Lyte, *A History of the University of Oxford* (London, 1886), pp. 244–5, and by Oswald, 'University College', cit., p. 63, and by W. Carr, *University College* (College Histories Series, London, 1902), pp. 37–48.

[14] J. Rous, *Historia Regum Angliae*, ed. cit., p. 76; Parker, op. cit., appendix A, p. 315.

[15] Oswald, 'University College', p. 69; V. H. H. Green, *A History of Oxford University* (London, 1974), p. 1; Carr, *University College*, pp. 173–4.

mythical accounts of the origins of the University were of a wholly fantastical nature. These fantasies were of a more distant chronology than ninth-century England, and owed their inspiration to the imagined inception of British society by exiles from Troy led by King Brutus, the entire saga being set out in richly textured vein in Geoffrey of Monmouth's *Historia Regum Britanniae* in 1135/6.[16] To this tissue of myth there was added the fable that a number of Greek philosophers had accompanied Brutus and his Trojans and had established an academy of learning at Greeklade or Cricklade in Wiltshire which was subsequently transferred to Oxford.[17] The earliest version of this conceit is to be found in the *Historiola*, the account of the origins of Oxford University prefaced to the Chancellor's Book (*Registrum A*), the oldest official register of the University, which may be ascribed tentatively to *a.* 1313.[18] The *Historiola* not only made this claim for the antiquity of the University, but also advanced the claim that Oxford was the oldest university in Latin Christendom.[19] As in the case of the Alfredian legend, the Greeklade myth was incorporated into Rous's *Historia Regum Angliae*.[20] Beginning by this route, the scenarios of the Greek professors and Alfred, either as sole founders or founder or as sequential founders, were perpetuated by numerous writers in the sixteenth and seventeenth centuries, and could still produce echoes as late as the nineteenth century.

[16] See Geoffrey of Monmouth, *The History of the Kings of Britain* (transl. with an introduction by L. Thorpe, Penguin Books, 1966) and *The Historia Regum Britanniae of Geoffrey of Monmouth* (ed. A. Griscom, London, 1929). The main features of the work are discussed by Kendrick, *British Antiquity*, pp. 4–17 and *passim*, and by A. Gransden, *Historical Writing in England c. 550 – c. 1307* (London, 1974), pp. 201–9.

[17] Parker, op. cit., pp. 10 ff.; Kendrick, op. cit., p. 25.

[18] The *Historiola* is printed in *Munimenta Academica: Documents illustrative of Academical Life and Studies at Oxford* (2 vols., Rolls Series, ed. H. Anstey, 1868), ii. 367–9, and in *Statuta Antiqua Universitatis Oxoniensis*, ed. cit., pp. 17–19.

[19] 'Omnium autem inter Latinos nunc extantium studiorum universitas Oxonie fundatione prior . . .': *Munimenta Academica*, ii. 367; *Statuta Antiqua*, p. 17.

[20] Rous, *Historia Regum Angliae*, ed. cit., p. 21; Parker, op. cit., appendix A, pp. 305–6.

A series of parallel myths grew up surrounding the origins of Cambridge University. This cumulative mythology pertaining to the English Universities is a striking demonstration of the extent to which inter-university rivalry was prevalent from as early as the fourteenth and fifteenth centuries. In his *Historia Regum Angliae*, John Rous provided a spirited account of the lore on the town and University of Cambridge circulating in the fifteenth century. Building upon an episode outlined in Geoffrey of Monmouth's *Historia Regum Britanniae*, Rous recorded that both the town and University had been founded by a Spanish prince, Cantaber, an exile from Spain, who had been granted land in East Anglia by a certain British king, Gurguntius Brabtruc, whose son-in-law he had become.[21] Rous indicated that he relied for his information upon the writings of Cambridge scholars, but it is not certain that he had seen the Cambridge *Historiola*, the dramatic equivalent of Oxford's fabled narrative of origins. The Cambridge *Historiola* has generally been attributed to the Carmelite friar Nicholas Cantelupe or Cantelow, who was a master of theology at Cambridge and died in 1441.[22] Although the Cambridge *Historiola* is anterior to Rous's account of the inception of Cambridge, it does contain additional features. These include the bringing of philosophers from Athens to Cambridge by Prince Cantaber (in obvious emulation of the similar Oxford myth), the granting of charters to the University by King Arthur in 531, by King Cadwallader in 681 and by King Edward the Elder in 951, and a list of prominent personages said to have attended the University, such as Theodore of Tarsus, Aidan and Bede.[23]

---

[21] Rous, op. cit., ed. cit., p. 25; Parker, op. cit., p. 9 and appendix A, p. 307.

[22] The *Historiola de Antiquitate et Origine Universitatis Cantabrigiensis* of the Carmelite friar Nicholas Cantelupe is appended to *Thomae Sprotti Chronica* (ed. T. Hearne, Oxford, 1719), pp. 262–80. Richard Parker's *History and Antiquities of the University of Cambridge*, completed in 1622 and published in London in 1721(?), included an English version of the *Historiola*.

[23] The spurious charters of King Arthur, King Cadwallader and King Edward the Elder are contained in the *Historiola* in *Thomae Sprotti Chronica*, ed. cit., pp. 268, 272, 279, and are printed by G. Dyer, *The Privileges of the University of Cambridge* (2 vols., London, 1824), i. 55–6, 56–7, 57–8. For the eminent figures alleged by the author of the *Historiola* to have attended Cambridge University, see Kendrick, *British Antiquity*, p. 26. John Lydgate, the English

Another myth relating to the foundation of Cambridge University, which, in the event, proved to be less popular than that of Cantaber, was the claim that the University had been established by Sigebert, a seventh-century king of the East Angles. The inspiration for this was a vague passage in Bede's *Ecclesiastical History* referring to the founding of a school in East Anglia by King Sigebert with the assistance of Felix, bishop of the East Angles.[24] The location of the school is not further specified, but a number of writers through to the sixteenth century made the assumption that in this school lay the genesis of the Univeristy of Cambridge. The antiquity of the University was supposedly reinforced by two awards of the seventh-century popes Honorius I and Sergius I which purported to confer on Cambridge University a full exemption from all ecclesiastical authority.[25] It seems that these papal bulls were forged in *c*. 1400 to provide documentary evidence to serve in the University's drive for independence from episcopal and archiepiscopal jurisdiction, a matter which was finally resolved in 1432/3.[26]

The debates over the relative ages of Oxford and Cambridge reached a climax in the writings of the Elizabethan antiquaries John Caius, the refounder of Gonville Hall as Gonville and Caius College, Cambridge, of which he was the master from 1559 to

poet of the late fourteenth and early fifteenth centuries, produced a verse account of the antiquity of Cambridge University which features the fable of the Athenian philosophers, some years before it appeared in the *Historiola*. The poem seemingly had the propagandist purpose of projecting Cambridge as a university free from the current heretical entanglement of Oxford: the poem is printed by J. B. Mullinger, *The Univesity of Cambridge* (3 vols., Cambridge, 1873–1911), i (1873), 635–7, and a truncated version by Dyer, *Privileges*, ii. 146–7.

[24] See Bede's *Ecclesiastical History of the English Nation* (Everyman's Library, 1958), book iii, ch. xviii, p. 131; see also Parker, *Early History of Oxford*, pp. 34–7, and Cooper, *Annals*, i. 2.

[25] The alleged bulls of Honorius I of 624 and of Sergius I of 689 are preserved in Cambridge University Archives: Cambridge University Library/University Archives, Luard, no. 115. They are contained in the Cambridge *Historiola* in *Thomae Sprotti Chronica*, ed. cit., pp. 253, 255, and are printed by Dyer, *Privileges*, i. 58–60.

[26] For this matter, see Cobban, *The King's Hall*, pp. 109–11.

1573, and his namesake, Thomas Caius, at one time registrar of the University of Oxford and a fellow of All Souls.[27] The Elizabethan controversy, which brought together all of the mythical strands described above, arose during the Queen's visit to Cambridge in 1564, when the Cambridge orator claimed that the University was of greater antiquity than Oxford. In response to this, Thomas Caius presented to the Queen during her visit to the University in 1566, in manuscript, his counter-case for the prior chronology of Oxford. In 1568, John Caius published anonymously his *De Antiquitate Cantabrigiensis Academiae*, [28] an elaborate defence of Cambridge's entitlement to seniority. Bound up with this, he published, without naming the author, Thomas Caius's work of 1566. A second edition of John Caius's history was published in 1574, a year after his death, in which the author's name appears for the first time. This work also incorporated the *Historiae Cantabrigiensis Academiae*, another treatise by John Caius, which had the objective of summing up the whole question of the prior antiquity of Cambridge University.[29] Following his initial tractate of 1566, Thomas Caius spent the last few years of his life preparing a comprehensive reply to the arguments of his namesake, but the outcome was not published until 1730, when it appeared under the general title of *Vindiciae Antiquitatis Academiae Oxoniensis*.[30] The defence of the mythological origins of Oxford University was continued into the early seventeenth century by the Oxford antiquary Bryan Twyne, was perpetuated in the second half of the century by his more orderly and more coherent successor, Anthony Wood,[31] and found a scattered embodiment in the eighteenth

---

[27] This controversy is discussed at some length by J. Parker, op. cit., pp. 20–33; see also Kendrick, *British Antiquity*, pp. 76–7, and M. McKisack, *Medieval History in the Tudor Age*, pp. 70–1.

[28] J. Caius, *De Antiquitate Cantabrigiensis Academiae* (London, 1568) (published anonymously).

[29] J. Caius, *Historiae Cantabrigiensis Academiae ab urbe condita, Liber primus* (London, 1574).

[30] *Vindiciae Antiquitatis Academiae Oxoniensis* (ed. T. Hearne, Oxford, 1730).

[31] See B. Twyne, *Antiquitatis Academiae Oxoniensis Apologia* (Oxford, 1608) and A. Wood, *The History and Antiquities of the University of Oxford* (2 vols. in 3, ed. J. Gutch, 1792–6), i (1792).

century in various works of the indefatigable editor and antiquary Thomas Hearne. By contrast, it is to the credit of Thomas Fuller that, in his *History of the University of Cambridge*, published in 1655, he studiously avoided any discussion of the myths about the origins of Cambridge despite the fact that John Caius was one of his major authorities.[32]

The extent and durability over several centuries of the foundation myths of Oxford and Cambridge are symptomatic not only of propagandist rivalry but also of a deep-seated need to endow English academic life with a past so remote as to render the English Universities unequivocally the earliest in European history. There is here a parallel with Geoffrey of Monmouth's *Historia Regum Britanniae*, which had inspired aspects of the fabled university origins. Just as Geoffrey had aimed to provide a glorious past for the British race comparable to that of the Greeks, Romans or Jews,[33] so, through mythology, Oxford and Cambridge were to take their rightful place of chronological primacy among the universities of the world, even if avowedly they were surpassed in size and as intellectual centres by a galaxy of universities throughout Europe.

Reverting to the historical plane, it is clear that Oxford and Cambridge, like Bologna and Paris, were not specifically founded but came into being over a period of time. Oxford was established, apparently, as a fully-fledged university or *studium generale* towards the close of the twelfth century, while Cambridge, it seems, emerged as a university shortly after 1209. As already indicated, on the basis of this suppositional dating, Oxford may be assigned to the first grouping of European universities and Cambridge may be reckoned to belong to the second.[34] A twelfth-century observer, however, would have been singularly prescient if he had designated either Oxford or especially Cambridge as the location of a future English university. There were a number of educational centres in

---

[32] T. Fuller, *The History of the University of Cambridge from the Conquest to the year 1634* (ed. M. Prickett and T. Wright, London and Cambridge, 1840), pp. 1–2.

[33] On Geoffrey's motivation, see Kendrick, op. cit., pp. 9–11, and H. A. MacDougall, *Racial Myths in English History* (Montreal and Hanover, New Hampshire, 1982), pp. 7 ff.

[34] See above, pp. 17–18.

twelfth-century England from which a *studium generale* might have evolved.[35] For in England, as all over Europe, the demands of an increasingly urbanized society for literate and numerate officials for the service of government, the Church and the landowning aristocracy were a powerful stimulus to the growth and multiplication of schools at various levels.[36]

The cathedral school of Lincoln probably came very close to developing into a university.[37] By 1176, Lincoln had a reputation for legal study, for in that year, in a letter of Peter of Blois, it was ranked as a centre for law along with Paris, Bologna and Oxford. Towards the end of the century, however, theology seems to have surpassed law as the principal discipline in Lincoln. Gerald of Wales (Giraldus Cambrensis), the voluminous writer and early topographer who spent several years at Lincoln in furtherance of his theological studies, declared in the 1190s that it was more renowned for theology than was any other centre in England.[38] However, Gerald's witness was not always of a reliable character. The cathedral school of Exeter also had considerable attraction for students of theology and law in the twelfth century, and teaching in these subjects was still active there in *c*. 1200.[39]

Hereford cathedral school is particularly interesting. According to the poem of *c*. 1195–7 of Simon du Fresne, canon of Hereford, written as an invitation to Gerald of Wales to come to the city, all seven liberal arts were taught there, along with legal studies and

[35] See R. W. Hunt, 'English Learning in the late Twelfth Century', *T.R.H.S.*, 4th series, xix(1936), pp. 19 ff., *passim*, reprinted, with revisions, *Essays in Medieval History* (ed. R. W. Southern, London, 1968), pp. 106 ff.; also N. Orme, *English Schools in the Middle Ages* (London, 1973), pp. 167 ff.

[36] See e.g. the comments of R. W. Southern, 'From Schools to University', *The History of the University of Oxford* (to be published in 8 vols., general editor, T. H. Aston, Oxford, 1984–), i (*The Early Oxford Schools*, ed. J. I. Catto, 1984), 1 ff. at 1–2.

[37] Hunt, art. cit., pp. 21–2 (*Essays in Medieval History*, pp. 107–8); see also K. Edwards, *English Secular Cathedrals in the Middle Ages*, ed. cit., pp. 185–6.

[38] *Giraldi Cambrensis Opera* (8 vols., Rolls Series, ed. J. S. Brewer and others, London, 1861–91), i(1861), 93–4.

[39] Hunt, art. cit., p. 28 (*Essays in Medieval History*, p. 114); Edwards, op. cit., pp. 186–7.

geomancy.[40] If the information in this poetic invitation is accurate, Hereford would appear to have been one of the few English cathedral schools, or even the only one, to place an equal emphasis on each of the subjects of the *trivium* (grammar, rhetoric and logic) and *quadrivium* (arithmetic, geometry, astronomy and music), which together made up the seven liberal arts.[41] In the twelfth century, Hereford was probably one of the main centres in England for the scientific and mathematical pursuits which came under the umbrella heading of *quadrivium* studies.[42] As such, Hereford may be seen as a temporary institutional reflection of the activities of a number of English scholars who participated in the twelfth-century scientific movement. Some of these had journeyed to Spain, southern Italy, Sicily and the eastern Mediterranean area generally in the quest for Greek and Arabic scientific and mathematical data.[43] This English scientific tradition was to find a permanent home in the University of Oxford in the first half of the thirteenth century. There are, however, sporadic indications of a degree of continuing interest in *quadrivium* subjects at Hereford well beyond *c*.1200.[44]

The cathedral school of York appears to have been noted in the twelfth century for the study of law.[45] The three principal schools of London, which were attached to St Paul's Cathedral and the

[40] The poem is edited (but not translated) by Hunt, art. cit., pp. 36–7 (*Essays in Medieval History*, pp. 121–2). For the main features of the Hereford school, see Edwards, op. cit., pp. 189–91.

[41] For a detailed exposition of the seven liberal arts, see *The Seven Liberal Arts in the Middle Ages* (ed. D. L. Wagner, Indiana, 1983).

[42] See e.g. the career and works of Roger of Hereford, the teacher and writer on astronomical and astrological subjects, who, in *c*. 1178, adapted Arabic astronomical tables for use at Hereford, in Haskins, *Studies in the History of Mediaeval Science*, pp. 124–6.

[43] For the activities of these English scholars, see Leff, *Paris and Oxford Universities in the Thirteenth and Fourteenth Centuries*, pp. 128–9, 143; R. W. Southern, 'The Place of England in the Twelfth-Century Renaissance', *Medieval Humanism and other Studies* (Oxford, 1970), pp. 167–71; R. M. Thomson, 'England and the Twelfth-Century Renaissance', *Past and Present,* no. 101(1983), pp. 3 ff. at pp. 5–7.

[44] Edwards, op. cit., p. 190, n. 6.

[45] Ibid., pp. 187–8.

churches of St Martin-le-Grand and St Mary Arches and which were described by William FitzStephen *a.* 1183, specialized in arts, including both written and spoken rhetoric.[46] While not recorded by FitzStephen, there is some evidence to indicate that one or more schools of law operated in the city, that evidence being that all schools of law in London were suppressed by order of Henry III in 1234, the reason for the prohibition being unspecified.[47] It is surprising that the vigorous school life of the capital did not produce a university in the medieval period.[48] The fact that it did not serves to underline the haphazard nature of the initial phase of university development. It would seem that the English monarchy was less attuned than its Capetian counterpart in France to the intellectual, social and economic benefits to be derived from the establishment of a university in the political heart of the country.[49] There is no record of an attempt made by an English king to deflect either or both of the emergent universities at Oxford and Cambridge to the capital, and London had to wait until the nineteenth century for its university foundation.

None of the schools discussed in the last three paragraphs progressed to university status. But for a short time late in the reign of Henry II and early in that of Richard I the schools of Northampton probably constituted a *studium generale* which, for a time, was just as important as Oxford or even more so.[50] The Northampton *studium*, however, of which more will be said below,[51] had accorded the primacy to Oxford by the end of the

---

[46] See William FitzStephen's *Descriptio Londoniae* in *Materials for the History of Thomas Becket* (7 vols., Rolls Series, ed. J. C. Robertson and J. B. Sheppard, London, 1875–85), iii(1877), 4–5, 9.

[47] *Cal. Close R.*, 1234–7, p. 26.

[48] On St Paul's Cathedral as an intellectual centre throughout the twelfth century, see C. N. L. Brooke assisted by Gillian Keir, *London 800–1216: the Shaping of a City* (London, 1975), pp. 355–8.

[49] See e.g. the comments of Cobban, *The Medieval Universities*, p. 79, and of J. W. Baldwin, 'Masters at Paris from 1179 to 1215: A Social Perspective', *Renaissance and Renewal in the Twelfth Century*, ed. cit., pp. 138 ff. at pp. 140–2.

[50] This thesis is unfolded by H. G. Richardson, 'The Schools of Northampton in the Twelfth Century', *E.H.R.*, lvi(1941), pp. 595 ff.

[51] See below, pp. 33–4.

twelfth century. Although in the thirteenth century a *studium* of some kind was intermittently maintained at Northampton, to which scholars from Oxford migrated in 1238 and 1263 and scholars from Cambridge in 1261,[52] it failed to achieve a permanent recognition as a *studium generale*. In 1261, Henry III had permitted the settlement of a university at Northampton,[53] but this permission was revoked in 1264 after the migrant scholars from Oxford and Cambridge had during Henry's seige of the town supported the barons opposed to the king.[54] The capture of Northampton by Henry III probably marked the end of the attempt to launch a university in the town. Similar efforts on the part of a number of disaffected Oxford scholars, mainly northerners, to originate a university at Stamford in Lincolnshire in 1334–5 were defeated following requests from the chancellor and masters of Oxford, by a series of royal interventions, designed to safeguard the monopolistic position of Oxford and Cambridge.[55] The Stamford episode appears to have been the last significant bid to create a third university in England in the medieval era.

The size of England's population in the fourteenth century could

[52] Rashdall, *Universities*, iii. 86–8; Mallet, *A History of the University of Oxford*, i. 36, 52–3.

[53] *Cal. Pat. R.*, 1258–66, p. 140.

[54] *Cal. Close R.*, 1264–68, pp. 92–3. Although the official reason given for the revocation of the permission for the Northampton *studium* was the injury being done to Oxford (Cambridge is not mentioned), there can be little doubt that Henry's suppression was provoked by the military opposition he encountered from the students when laying seige to the town.

[55] On the secession to Stamford and the efforts of Edward III to quash the nascent university, see A. F. Leach, 'Stamford University', *Victoria History of the County of Lincoln*, ii (ed. W. Page, London, 1906), pp. 471–3; Mallet, *A History of the University of Oxford*, i. 157; Maxwell-Lyte, *A History of the University of Oxford*, pp. 134–6; H. E. Salter, 'The Stamford Crisis', *E.H.R.*, xxxvii (1922), pp. 249 ff.; C. H. Lawrence, 'The University in State and Church', *The History of the University of Oxford*, i. 97 ff. at 131–2; and J. M. Fletcher, 'University Migrations in the Late Middle Ages, with particular reference to the Stamford Secession', *Rebirth, Reform and Resilience: Universities in Transition 1300–1700* (ed. J. M. Kittelson and P. J. Transue, Columbus, Ohio, 1984), pp. 163 ff. esp. pp. 175 ff. See also *Cal. Close R.*, 1333–7, p. 330; *Cal. Pat. R.*, 1334–8, p. 140; *Snappe's Formulary and other records* (ed. H. E. Salter, Oxf. Hist. Soc., lxxx, 1924), pp. 294–5.

not easily justify a third university, especially when it is considered that both Oxford and Cambridge offered instruction in all four faculties — arts, law, theology and medicine — and, moreover, were empowered to award degrees in theology at a time when, on the Continent, only Paris was accorded this privilege. Hence, compared with many regions of Europe in the first half of the fourteenth century, England was already well furnished with university facilities. In these circumstances, Edward III would have seen no strong need to break the monopoly of Oxford and Cambridge by sanctioning a more northerly university, which, conceivably, might become an intellectual focal point of northern resistance to a southern-based monarchy.

Hastings Rashdall advanced the thesis that Oxford owed its principal position among English schools especially to a migration of English masters and students from Paris in 1167 arising from an incident in the Becket controversy.[56] He argued that, before this date, although there was a succession of individual masters teaching in Oxford, there is no evidence of several masters teaching concurrently; and that until a plurality of masters can be proven to have existed, Oxford cannot be designated a *studium generale*. The known existence soon after 1167 of a group of masters teaching in more than one faculty and attracting students from a considerable distance led Rashdall to the conclusion that the effective beginnings of Oxford as a *studium generale* date from the settlement there of the English scholars who had quit the Parisian schools.

This celebrated interpretation was based on two main documentary sources: a letter of *c.* 1167 of the exiled John of Salisbury which refers, somewhat vaguely, to events realized in accordance with an astrological prophecy, one such event being the expulsion of alien scholars from France; and a series of ordinances of Henry II directed against Becket's supporters which, among other provisions, enacted that royal permission was required for the passing of English clerks to and from the Continent, and that beneficed English clerks should return home within three months if

---

[56] For this thesis, see Rashdall, *Universities, iii.* 11 ff.: A. F. Leach's criticisms and Rashdall's response are printed ibid., iii. appendix i, 465 ff. The thesis is also discussed by Cobban, *The Medieval Universities*, pp. 97–9

they were to secure their incomes.[57] Rashdall argued speculatively that the edict relating to the beneficed clerks could probably be assigned to 1167 and that it was one of the principal reasons for the exodus referred to by John of Salisbury. It was assumed by Rashdall that English scholars studying in Paris, including English beneficed clerks, would have formed a significant proportion of the scholars who left Paris in *c.* 1167 and that the majority of them would have returned to England.

This thesis may be challenged on several counts. Rashdall may well have exaggerated the number of English beneficed clerks studying in Paris in the mid-twelfth century.[58] Moreover, the assigning of the date 1167 to the edict concerning their return to England does not easily relate it to any particular event in the Becket dispute which would explain its promulgation at this juncture.[59] It may also be averred that Rashdall too conveniently surmised that the majority of the returning scholars would have been absorbed by Oxford, some perhaps after a temporary stay in other towns, instead of being distributed among the sundry centres of learning in England or resorting to their benefices. But even if Oxford had absorbed all of the returning scholars, which is inherently unlikely, the numbers involved were probably insufficient to have elevated the Oxford schools to a position of unambiguous ascendancy. By the dramatic linkage of the Parisian exodus with the emergence of Oxford as a university, Rashdall seems to have unduly minimized the gradual nature of the process by which Oxford became a *studium generale*. Impressed by the apparent alacrity with which Oxford leapt into prominence after *c.* 1167, Rashdall was led to propose an external cause. The early phase of university development is alive with examples of *studia generalia* inaugurated by academic

---

[57] *Materials for the History of Thomas Becket*, ed. cit., i(1875), 53–4; vi(1882), 235–6; see also Rashdall's discussion of these sources, *Universities*, iii. 12–16, with qualifying notes.

[58] See H. E. Salter, 'The medieval University of Oxford', *History*, xiv (1929–30), pp. 57 ff. at p. 57, and A. F. Leach's trenchant criticism of this point in Rashdall, op. cit., iii. 467–8, 469, and Rashdall's reply, p. 472.

[59] Leach ascribes this edict to 1169 and denies any connection with the Becket controversy: see Rashdall, op. cit., iii. 466–7.

migrations.[60] Rashdall contended that Oxford afforded one of the earliest of such instances in European history. The fact that Oxford, with adaptations, followed the broad organizational mould of Paris University was an added reason for Rashdall to doubt that the Oxford *studium generale* was attributable entirely to an insular evolutionary process.

Although valuable in focussing attention upon the possible impact of the Paris exodus upon the Oxford schools, Rashdall's thesis does not easily fit with the vicissitudes of educational life in twelfth-century England. In particular, insufficient cognizance is taken of the Northampton schools, which, as previously noted, appear to have acquired a temporary reputation as a *studium generale* in the period after the Paris migration. The available evidence, set out by H.G. Richardson, seems to show that in the latter years of the reign of Henry II and into the early years of the reign of Richard I the Northampton *studium*, which was subject to the jurisdiction of the bishop of Lincoln, rivalled or even eclipsed the Oxford schools. Between 1176 and 1193 a protégé of Henry II's daughter, the queen of Spain, was maintained by the English monarchy in the schools of Northampton in preference to those of Oxford. From 1193, however, clerks supported academically by the king were sent to Oxford. Richardson explains this change in status by reference to the insecurity of the Northampton scholars, who, because of Richard I's absence on crusade and his subsequent period of captivity, were unable to ensure adequate protection against the town authorities. In the light of this, it is reasonable to suppose that it may have been considered preferable to transfer in some numbers to the comparative safety of Oxford, a provisional date for this migration being *c.* 1192.[61] If Richardson's conclusions are valid, it becomes clear that the Parisian exodus of *c.* 1167 did not immediately raise Oxford to the position of a *studium* surpassing all

---

[60] E.g. the Italian Universities of Vicenza (1204), Arezzo (?1215) and Padua (1222) all seemingly owed their existence to migrations from Bologna, while Vercelli (1228) evolved from a Paduan migration: see conveniently Rashdall, op. cit., ii. 6–7, 8, 10, 26–7

[61] For Richardson's thesis, see Richardson, 'The Schools of Northampton in the Twelfth Century', art. cit., pp. 595 ff.: for more specific points raised, see pp. 597, 603–4.

others. Even if the Paris migration provided some kind of boost to the Oxford schools, that from Northampton a quarter of a century later was perhaps no less significant in helping to establish the durability of a *studium generale* at Oxford. It would therefore seem mistaken to seek a single decisive event which would explain the emergence of Oxford as a university. Rather, the migrations from Paris and from Northampton are best seen as important links in a chain of desultory development extending over the whole of the twelfth century.

Favourable siting may be adduced as one component in the rise of the Oxford schools which coalesced around St Mary's parish church,[62] although it needs to be affirmed that teaching personnel and academic specialisms were often of greater significance than situation in determining the location of the earlier *studia generalia*. Only when universities came to be specifically founded did considerations of site become crucial in the founding process: only then could features such as sufficient accommodation, plentiful food supplies, a healthy climate, the availability of supportive finance and a reasonably stable environment be assessed rationally prior to the selection of the university venue.[63] In the case of Oxford, it is presumably only in retrospect that aspects of the site appear especially conducive to the emergence of a *studium generale*. But it is clear that Oxford was a congenial anchorage for university development. Although Oxford was not the seat of a bishopric, only of an archdeaconry, it was strategically placed in the centre of the kingdom, midway between Northampton and Southampton, and it was a meeting point of routes between a variety of important towns, including London, Bristol, Winchester, Bedford,

---

[62] Rashdall, op. cit., iii. 10. See further Southern, 'From Schools to University', *The History of the University of Oxford*, i. 28: 'St Mary's was only a small parish, but it lay in the centre of the later schools of the university, and it is highly likely that several of them were already in existence before 1200'.

[63] On general prerequisites of university foundations, see P. Classen, 'Die ältesten Universitäts-reformen und Universitätsgründungen des Mittelalters', *Heidelberger Jahrbücher*, xii (1968), pp. 72 ff. at pp. 79–80. For a particular case, see the importance of geographical considerations in the decision to found a university in Hungary at Pécs (papal bull of foundation issued 1367) in A. L. Gabriel, *The Mediaeval Universities of Pécs and Pozsony* (Frankfurt am Main, 1969), pp. 15 ff.

Buckingham, Worcester and Warwick. It was also within easy reach of the south coast and the Continent.[64] Oxford's position on the Thames was probably not as advantageous for river traffic as might be supposed. It had serious navigational difficulties, and barges did not usually proceed beyond Henley.[65] As a result, Oxford, it seems, relied mainly upon the road network for most of her essential supplies. The building of the royal palace of Woodstock by Henry I in *c*. 1100 only a short distance away, the establishment of three Augustinian institutions — namely, the college of the secular canons of St George-in-the-Castle in 1074, the Priory of St Frideswide, begun in 1121, and Oseney Abbey (a priory in 1129) in *c*. 1154 — and the foundation of the Benedictine Nunnery of Godstow (dedicated as an abbey in 1139) in *c*. 1132 a few miles north of the town, would all have rendered Oxford open to increased political and ecclesiastical influence.[66] Moreover, Oxford's central position within the province of Canterbury made it a suitable meeting place for ecclesiastical courts and councils. This circumstance enlarged her floating population, brought much legal business to the town, and presumably stimulated the teaching of law in the Oxford schools and established a close connection, as in other continental university towns, between academic instruction in law and practical court procedure.[67] The commercial activity of Oxford in the twelfth century is attested by the existence of guilds of weavers and leather

[64] For Oxford's situation, see Rashdall, op. cit., iii. 8–9; H. E. Salter, *Medieval Oxford* (Oxf. Hist. Soc., c. 1936), pp. 90–1; J. I. Catto, 'Citizens, Scholars and Masters', *The History of the University of Oxford*, i. 151 ff. at 158.

[65] Salter, op. cit., p. 17; A. L. Rowse, *Oxford in the History of the Nation* (London, 1975), pp. 9–10.

[66] For the royal palace of Woodstock, see Salter, op. cit., p. 30; for the college of the secular canons of St George-in-the-Castle, the Priory of St Frideswide, Oseney Abbey and Godstow Abbey, see *Victoria History of the County of Oxford*, iv (ed. A. Crossley, Oxford, 1979), 11, 364–5, 381, and Southern, 'From Schools to University', *The History of the University of Oxford*, i. 4, 15–16.

[67] See the discussion of R. W. Southern, 'Master Vacarius and the Beginning of an English Academic Tradition', *Medieval Learning and Literature: Essays presented to R. W. Hunt* (ed. J. J. G. Alexander and M. T. Gibson, Oxford, 1976), pp. 257 ff. at pp. 270–1, and Southern, 'From Schools to University', *The History of the University of Oxford*, i. 15–17.

[68] *V.C.H. Oxon.* iv. 312–13, 316; Salter, *Medieval Oxford*, pp. 31–2, 60–2.

workers[68] and by the presence of a substantial Jewish business community. The earliest definite evidence for the presence of this Jewish settlement dates from 1141. The livelihoods of its members were derived mainly from the lending of money at certain rates of interest and were supplemented by trading in imported precious commodities.[69]

It has been reckoned from the Domesday Survey of 1086 that Oxford comprised 946 houses inside and outside her walls, of which 478 or about 51 per cent either were dilapidated or had inhabitants who were not liable for taxation on the grounds of poverty.[70] Even allowing for a measure of urban revival in the twelfth century, when Oxford may have grown to be the eighth or ninth largest town in England,[71] these figures indicate a very mixed property scene. They suggest only a moderate housing capacity, in no wise comparable to the capacious accommodation of university towns such as Paris.[72] Although convenient, Oxford's situation was not, it seems, notably superior to that of several of the other academic centres in England already mentioned. In the first half of the twelfth century, Oxford does not appear to have possessed the magnetic pull to attract a steady flow of students, and what academic progress was made is likely to have been arrested by the civil war of Stephen's reign, which between 1139 and 1145, perturbed parts of the Midlands and East Anglia especially. Indeed, Oxford was very much in the centre of hostilities when captured by Stephen in 1142.[73]

Although there is no proof of sustained academic activity at Oxford in the first half of the twelfth century, there is tentative evidence that during that period individual teachers taught there, though intermittently and without consolidating anything in the

[69] See C. Roth, *The Jews of Medieval Oxford* (Oxf. Hist. Soc., new series, ix, 1951), p. 2. Roth covers all facets of Oxford Jewry until the expulsion of the Jews in 1290; see also *V.C.H. Oxon.* iv. 27–8.

[70] Salter, op. cit., pp. 21 ff.; Parker, *Early History of Oxford*, pp. 221 ff.

[71] Salter, op. cit., p. 31.

[72] On the attractions of twelfth-century Paris, see e.g. R. W. Southern, 'The Schools of Paris and the School of Chartres', *Renaissance and Renewal in the Twelfth Century*, pp. 113 ff. at pp. 119–20.

[73] *V.C.H. Oxon.* iv. 11.

way of a permanent school tradition. The earliest recorded teacher is Theobald of Etampes,[74] who described himself as a master of Oxford in three of his extant letters.[75] He had previously taught at Caen,[76] and he began to teach at Oxford before 1100 and perhaps as early as 1094.[77] On the basis of four of his extant letters, which deal with theological matters, it has been generally assumed that he taught theology at Oxford. But a contemporary critic, who responded to one of his letters, refers to Theobald only as a master of the liberal arts, one of a large number commonly found in towns and villages throughout France, Germany and England.[78] Whatever the exact nature of Theobald's teaching, which seems to have continued at Oxford until the 1120s,[79] it is unlikely that when Robert Pullen, the eminent theologian and one of John of Salisbury's masters at Paris, began to teach in Oxford in 1133 he fell heir to a strongly rooted theological school.[80] On the contrary, according to the Oseney Annals, Robert came to teach a subject which had fallen into desuetude throughout England.[81] He

[74] On Theobald of Etampes, see Southern, 'Master Vacarius and the Beginning of an English Academic Tradition', pp. 267–9, and Southern, 'From Schools to University', *The History of the University of Oxford*, i. 5–6; A. B. Emden, *A Biographical Register of the University of Oxford to A.D. 1500* (3 vols., Oxford, 1957–9), iii (1959), 1754; T. E. Holland, 'The University of Oxford in the Twelfth Century', *Collectanea*, ii (ed. M. Burrows, Oxf. Hist. Soc., xvi, 1890), 137 ff. at 141-2, 151-9; Rashdall, *Universities*, iii. 16–18.

[75] Theobald's six extant letters are printed by Holland, op. cit., pp. 151–6: he describes himself as *magister Oxenefordiae/Oxinfordie* in letters 4, 5 and 6 (pp. 152–3).

[76] He describes himself as *doctor Cadumensis* and *magister Cadumensis* in letters 1 and 2: Holland, op. cit., p. 151.

[77] For these dates, see Southern, 'From Schools to University', *The History of the University of Oxford*, i. 5, and Holland, op. cit., p. 159.

[78] The response of Theobald's critic is printed by Holland, op. cit., pp. 156–8 (see esp. p. 158).

[79] Southern, 'From Schools to University', p. 6.

[80] For Robert Pullen, see ibid., pp. 6–7, and Southern, 'Master Vacarius and the Beginning of an English Academic Tradition', p. 269; Holland, op. cit., pp. 142, 159–60; Rashdall, *Universities*, iii. 18–19.

[81] Oseney Annals, *Annales Monastici* (4 vols., Rolls Series, ed. H. R. Luard, London, 1864–9), iv (1869), 19, and Holland, op. cit., p. 189.

returned to Paris after only five years, and the fact that nothing is known of Oxford disciples suggests that the teaching of theology may have declined at Oxford after his departure. In addition to Theobald of Etampes and Robert Pullen, the romance writer and historical poseur Geoffrey of Monmouth was resident in Oxford between 1129 and 1151, and it was probably there that he wrote his *Historia Regum Britanniae*.[82] Geoffrey may have been a secular canon of the college of St George-in-the-Castle, one of whose provosts was Walter of Coutances, archdeacon of Oxford between *c.* 1112 and *c.* 1151, a patron to Geoffrey and a scholar of repute.[83] There is no evidence to suggest that either Geoffrey or Walter taught in the Oxford schools, but their presence in Oxford for so long suggests that it was an attractive, learned environment, even if it was as yet devoid of permanent academic institutions. Mention should also be made of Robert Cricklade, who became prior of St Frideswide's in *c.* 1141 and who was a conspicuous theologian who, tangentially, produced an abridgment of Pliny's *Natural History*.[84] He was a teacher in the earlier part of his career but it is not known for certain where his teaching was concentrated: it may have been at Cricklade rather than at Oxford.[85]

Of primary interest is the traditional view that Vacarius, the celebrated Lombard jurist, brought the new scientific study of the Roman law from Bologna to England and lectured in this subject at Oxford in *c.* 1149, his textbook, the *Liber Pauperum*, being used in Oxford well into the thirteenth century.[86] While accepting, with

[82] See H. E. Salter, 'Geoffrey of Monmouth and Oxford', *E.H.R.*, xxxiv (1919), pp. 382 ff.

[83] Salter, *Medieval Oxford*, p. 92.

[84] For Robert (of) Cricklade, see Holland, op. cit., pp. 142, 160–5; Thomson, 'England and the Twelfth-Century Renaissance', art. cit., p. 13.

[85] See the comments of Southern, 'From Schools to University', p. 8, n. 2.

[86] For the traditional view of the career of Vacarius, see F. de Zuluetta, *The Liber Pauperum of Vacarius* (Selden Soc., 44, London, 1927), pp. xiii-xxiii. More-recent assessments include Southern, 'Master Vacarius and the Beginning of an Academic Tradition', pp. 257 ff., and 'From Schools to University', pp. 8–10; P. Stein, 'Vacarius and the Civil Law', *Church and Government in the Middle Ages: Essays presented to C. R. Cheney* (ed. C. N. L. Brooke, D. E. Luscombe, G. H. Martin and D. Owen, Cambridge, 1976), pp. 119 ff.

reservations, the essentials of this account, Rashdall was inclined to date Vacarius's teaching twenty years later,[87] which would more aptly fit Rashdall's own version of the emergence of Oxford as a *studium generale* following the Parisian migration of 1167. A main difficulty about the claim that Vacarius was a teacher at Oxford is that this episode is mentioned by only one chronicler, Gervase of Canterbury — in his *Actus Pontificum Cantuariensis Ecclesiae*, compiled after 1205 and perhaps in *c.* 1210.[88] Professor R.W. Southern has argued that the passage in Gervase's work relating to Vacarius and Oxford is a later interpolation of unknown authorship, and consequently has a most uncertain historical status.[89] If Vacarius did not teach at Oxford, a long gap is seen to exist between Robert Pullen's departure in the late 1130s and the presence there of those masters known to have taught at Oxford towards the close of the century. Given the fragmentary nature of the evidence, however, the matter of Vacarius's teaching in England must remain problematical.

For a considerable part of the twelfth century, Oxford's academic life was of a decidedly tenuous character, especially with regard to the higher disciplines of theology and law. There may have been greater continuity in the teaching of arts subjects, although that this was so is speculative. Since many of the abler English students, such as John of Salisbury, Thomas Becket and Stephen Langton, were motivated to study in the cosmopolitan schools of France and Italy,

---

[87] Rashdall, *Universities*, iii. 21: F. de Zulueta was prepared to accept Rashdall's later dating of Vacarius's teaching at Oxford, *The Liber Pauperum of Vacarius*, p. xvii.

[88] Gervase of Canterbury, *Actus Pontificum Cantuariensis Ecclesiae, The Historical Works of Gervase of Canterbury* (2 vols., Rolls Series, ed. W. Stubbs, London, 1879–80), ii (1880), 384–5.

[89] Southern, 'Master Vacarius and the Beginning of an English Academic Tradition', pp. 279–82. De Zulueta argued that 'to doubt whether Vacarius ever taught at Oxford is to doubt against the evidence': *The Liber Pauperum of Vacarius*, pp. xvi-xvii. P. Stein concludes that 'Vacarius may never have set foot in Oxford, but there is evidence that he did teach the civil law academically in England, and he managed to set a tone, which was recognised later as what was needed': Stein, 'Vacarius and the Civil Law', p. 123. J. L. Barton, 'The Study of Civil Law before 1380', *The History of the University of Oxford*, i. 519 ff. at 524, is convinced that wherever Vacarius may have taught in England 'he was the teacher of the first generation of English-trained civilians'.

there was necessarily a limited demand for advanced education in England, which, in turn, made teaching in the English schools a doubtful proposition for teachers from the Continent. In the last quarter of the twelfth century, however, the situation was palpably transformed, and the main lines of a *studium generale* at Oxford can be discerned.

The earliest specific evidence for the existence of several faculties, in the sense of loosely organized branches of learning, and of a sizeable concourse of masters and students at Oxford is traceable to the report by Gerald of Wales of his reading at Oxford in *c.* 1185–8 of his recently completed *Topographia Hibernica*, a feat which was spread over three days. On the first day, he read part of his work to all the poor scholars of the town; on the second day, he continued his reading before the doctors of the various faculties along with their more distinguished students; and on the third day, he completed his bombastic reading in the presence of the rest of the scholars and some of the townsfolk and military personnel.[90] As we have seen, academic numbers were probably boosted by an influx of scholars from Paris in *c.* 1167 and from Northampton in *c.* 1192. There is definite evidence that in the last decade of the century theology and law were being regularly taught. With regard to law, for example, it is recorded that just before 1200 Thomas de Marleberge, later abbot of Evesham, lectured on civil and canon law at Oxford and Exeter.[91] Proof of the existence of trades dependent upon the Oxford schools and established in the area of the schools in the vicinity of St Mary's Church occurs in a document of *c.* 1200 concerning the transfer of property in Cat Street. Among the names of the witnesses to the transaction are those of a bookbinder, a writer, three illuminators and two parchment-makers, all occupations supportive of a university.[92] In *c.* 1190, Oxford was described as a *studium commune* by Emo, a Friesland student then

[90] *Giraldi Cambrensis Opera*, ed. cit., i. 72–3; Holland, 'The University of Oxford in the Twelfth Century', pp. 173–4; Rashdall, op. cit., iii. 25.

[91] *Chronicon Abbatiae de Evesham ad annum 1418* (Rolls Series, ed. W. D. Macray, London, 1863), p. 267.

[92] Printed by Holland, op. cit., pp. 178–9.

studying in Oxford.[93] It is known that before the term *studium generale* acquired a technical precision *studium commune* was used as one of several alternatives.[94] Consequently, it would be accurate to regard Oxford as it was towards the close of the twelfth century as a fully-fledged *studium generale ex consuetudine*, recognized as a *studium generale* not by formal validation but by customary acclaim, as was the case with the other twelfth-century universities of Bologna, Reggio, Paris and Montpellier.[95]

Oxford's position as a nascent *studium generale*, specializing, apparently, in arts, civil and canon law, and theology, was reinforced in the last decade of the century by the presence of a group of prominent scholars. These included Daniel of Morley, a student of Arabic science who had spent some time at Toledo working under Gerard of Cremona,[96] and Alexander Nequam, the theologian and Aristotelian enthusiast, who had been a master of arts at Paris and who from *c.* 1190, was resident in Oxford, where he seems to have lectured for several years in theology.[97] It is of some remark that Nequam associated Oxford with Salerno, Montpellier, Bologna and Paris in his treatise *De Naturis Rerum* (written before 1200).[98] That he did so suggests that Oxford was beginning to reach out for a place within the world of European scholarship. Among the scholars who are known to have taught at

---

[93] Ibid, p. 175.

[94] In the thirteenth century, the terms *studium generale, studium universale, studium commune* and *studium solempne* (or *sollemne, solenne*) were used with much the same connotations: see Cobban, *Medieval Universities*, p. 24.

[95] See above, p. 3.

[96] For Morley, see e.g. Leff, *Paris and Oxford Universities in the Thirteenth and Fourteenth Centuries*, pp. 77–8, 143; J. A. Weisheipl, 'Science in the Thirteenth Century', *The History of the University of Oxford*, i. 435 ff. at 435, 436.

[97] On Alexander Nequam, see e.g. Leff, op. cit., pp. 78, 143–4, 273; Southern, 'From Schools to University', pp. 22–5. Southern (p. 22) and J. I. Catto, 'Theology and Theologians 1220–1320'. *The History of the University of Oxford*, i. 471ff. at 479, are definite that Nequam was a lecturer at Oxford: Leff (p. 273) argued in 1968 that there is no clear evidence that Nequam lectured in the Oxford schools, but this view would now appear to have been superseded.

[98] *Alexandri Neckam De Naturis Rerum Libri Duo* (Rolls Series, ed. T. Wright, London, 1863), p. 311; also printed by Holland, op. cit., pp. 185–6.

Oxford in the opening years of the thirteenth century and who promoted in England the logical, metaphysical and scientific works of Aristotle were Robert Grosseteste, the future chancellor of Oxford and bishop of Lincoln,[99] who may have been lecturing at Oxford from *c*. 1190[100] and who was probably the most original and influential of the thirteenth-century Oxford scholars with regard to Aristotelian-inspired scientific and mathematical achievement; Edmund Abingdon, later archbishop of Canterbury, who taught arts at Oxford from *c*. 1202 to *c*. 1208 and who, according to Roger Bacon, was the first to lecture on Aristotle's *Sophistici elenchi*, one of the treatises of the New Logic; a certain Master Hugh, who was credited by Bacon with having realized the first commentary on Aristotle's *Posterior Analytics*, another portion of the New Logic; and John Blund, who was a master at both Paris and Oxford and who lectured at the latter in arts from *c*. 1207 to *c*. 1209 on the *libri naturales*, Aristotle's writings on natural philosophy.[101] As a result of the temporary suspension of Oxford University which began in 1209, Grosseteste, Edmund of Abingdon and probably John Blund migrated to Paris,[102] all three later returning to Oxford.

Despite this hiatus, the activities of these and other scholars at Oxford in the early years of the thirteenth century indicate that, in addition to conventional arts subjects, theology and law, Oxford was becoming a conspicuous focus for those areas of Aristotelian science and philosophy which were prohibited at the University of

---

[99] For the multifarious career of Grosseteste, see e.g. *Robert Grosseteste: Scholar and Bishop* (ed. D. A. Callus, Oxford, 1955) and R. W. Southern, *Robert Grosseteste: The Growth of an English Mind in Medieval Europe* (Oxford, 1986); see further J. A. Weisheipl, 'Science in the Thirteenth Century', *The History of the University of Oxford*, i. 435 ff. at 440–53.

[100] D. Knowles, *Evolution of Medieval Thought*, p. 282, states that Grosseteste 'was teaching in Oxford as early as 1190', but this point has not been proven: see D. A. Callus, 'Robert Grosseteste as Scholar', *Robert Grosseteste*, pp. 1 ff. at p. 3, and Southern, 'From Schools to University', p. 36, n. 1.

[101] For Edmund Abingdon, see Leff, op. cit., pp. 144, 272, 273; for Master Hugh, see ibid., p. 144; and for John Blund, see ibid., pp. 144, 272, 273–4, and Southern, 'From Schools to University', p. 24.

[102] Leff, op. cit., pp. 145, 273.

Paris in 1210 and 1215, and which were not taught openly at Paris until the 1230s.[103] The ecclesiastical ban on Aristotle's physical and metaphysical works applied only to Paris, and this enabled Oxford to forge ahead in these invigorating intellectual spheres, giving a distinctive cast to the University's academic contribution in the first half of the thirteenth century. Such a development helped Oxford to strike out independently of the Paris schools and to generate confidence in itself as a university capable of participating in some of the foremost activities of European scholarship.

The rapid burgeoning of Oxford from the late twelfth century is corroborated by the chronicler Richard of Devizes, who, in 1192, referred to Oxford as so crowded with clerks that the city could scarcely support them.[104] The growth in the University's population would have been sustained by the state of war between England and France in the years following 1193. The intensity and wide-ranging nature of the hostilities made it extremely difficult for English students to study on the Continent, a predicament commented on by Gerald of Wales.[105] Oxford was now emerging as a natural venue for the abler and wealthier indigenous students, who, in earlier generations, would have gravitated towards centres such as Paris and Bologna. And although it became less easy for English students to attend continental schools in the last decade of the twelfth century, there was nonetheless some traffic the other way and Oxford was capable of attracting a stream of students from abroad. For example, in *c.*1190 two brothers from Friesland, Emo and Addo, studied rhetoric and canon and civil law at Oxford, using in their studies and indeed making a copy of the *Liber Pauperum* of Vacarius.[106] And the evidence of the Pipe Rolls reveals that between 1193 and 1196 Richard I maintained the clerk Nicholas of Hungary

---

[103] See Knowles, op. cit., pp. 226–8, and Leff, op. cit., esp. pp. 191–205.

[104] *Chronicles of the reign of Stephen, Henry II and Richard I* (3 vols., Rolls Series, ed. R. Howlett, London, 1884–6), iii (1886), 437; see also Holland, op. cit., p. 183.

[105] *Giraldi Cambrensis Opera*, ed. cit., i. 93–4.

[106] Holland, op. cit., pp. 175–6; Southern, 'From Schools to University', pp. 17–19; de Zuluetta, *The Liber Pauperum of Vacarius*, p. xvii, n. 13.

in the Oxford schools,[107] and that a certain Robert of Vermeilles was supported in the schools in 1198 by the archbishop of Canterbury.[108] Since the ability to draw students from a wide geographical area was one of the attributes, however imprecisely defined, of a centre of learning that possessed the status of *studium generale*, the presence of foreign students in Oxford from the last decade of the twelfth century is an important consideration in cementing the notion of Oxford as a fully extended university as that was understood within the international academic community.

The growing organizational cohesion and academic distinction of the Oxford *studium* suffered a severe setback when the University was voluntarily suspended between 1209 and 1214–15. This arose from the hanging of two or three of the scholars by the mayor and burgesses in retaliation for either the murder or manslaughter of a woman by a scholar.[109] The fact that King John had apparently endorsed the action of the burgesses and that the event occurred during the Interdict laid upon England by Pope Innocent III made the prospect of early retribution for the scholars remote. In tandem with their brethren at Paris, the Oxford scholars claimed to enjoy a privileged clerical status rendering them immune from the jurisdiction of secular judges, an immunity which had been so spectacularly violated by these summary and ruthless hangings. Clerical immunity for the Parisian scholars had been implied in a bull of Pope Celestine III of 1194,[110] and this was explicitly affirmed by the charter of privileges granted to the scholars at Paris by Philip II in 1200.[111] In 1209, the Oxford scholars were prepared to adopt an extreme course in order to achieve specific recognition of an

---

[107] *Pipe Roll Society* (New Series, ed. D. M. Stenton), iii (1927), 122; v (1928), 88; vi (1929), 142; vii (1930), 70: see also D. M. Stenton's comments on Nicholas of Hungary, iii. p. xxiii.

[108] Ibid., ix (1932), 190.

[109] For the events leading to the closure of the Oxford schools, see Rashdall, *Universities*, iii. 33–4; Mallet, *A History of the University of Oxford*, i. 31; Maxwell-Lyte, *A History of the University of Oxford*, pp. 16–18.

[110] *Chartularium Universitatis Parisiensis*, ed. cit., i (1889), introduction, no. 15; Rashdall, op. cit., i. 291, n. 1; P. Kibre, 'Scholarly Privileges: Their Roman Origins and Medieval Expression', *A.H.R.*, lix (1954), pp. 543 ff. at p. 551.

[111] *Chartularium*, i. no. 1.

equivalent status. Given the immediate hostility of the English monarchy and the disarray into which the Interdict had thrown the senior ecclesiastics from whom support might otherwise have been forthcoming, the majority of the Oxford masters decided upon a suspension of lectures. As a consequence, parties of masters and students migrated in some numbers to centres such as Paris, Reading and Cambridge. Although a few of the masters remained in Oxford, the University must have been virtually in abeyance until King John's reconciliation with Innocent III in 1214. In that year, the papacy was enabled to redress the grievances of the scholars through an award made by the papal legate, Nicholas, cardinal bishop of Tusculum. It was this legatine ordinance which paved the way for the reopening of the Oxford schools.

The award of the papal legate of June 1214 was tantamount to Oxford University's first charter of privileges.[112] Among the various clauses requiring the burgesses to make recompense to the scholars was the enactment that for ten years the former were to take only half the rent, assessed at pre-cessation levels, for all accommodation, which had previously been rented by scholars, and that for another ten years they were to charge no more than the rent customary before the closure of the schools. The rents of accommodation which had not previously been inhabited by scholars were to be assessed in the future by a joint commission of four masters and four burgesses, a fresh assessment being made every ten years. The burgesses were also required to give 52s. yearly for the benefit of the scholars, a sum which can be construed as the University's first annual income.[113] They were further obliged to

---

[112] The version of the award of 25 June 1214, collated with that of 20 June 1214, is printed by H. E. Salter, *The Mediaeval Archives of the University of Oxford* (2 vols., Oxf. Hist. Soc., lxx, lxxiii, 1917–19), i. 2–4, and other associated documents are printed i. 4–10; a version is printed in *Munimenta Academica*, ed. cit., i. 1–4. The award is discussed by Rashdall, *Universities*, iii. 34 ff.; Mallet, op. cit., i. 32–4; Maxwell-Lyte, op. cit., pp. 18–21; P. Kibre, *Scholarly Privileges in the Middle Ages* (Mediaeval Academy of America, London, 1961), pp. 268–9; Leff, *Paris and Oxford Universities in the Thirteenth and Fourteenth Centuries*, pp. 78–9; Southern, 'From Schools to University', pp. 29 ff.

[113] The distribution of this income of 52s. was to be made by the abbot of Oseney and the prior of St Frideswide acting on the advice of the bishop of Lincoln or

provide the scholars with a yearly feast on St Nicholas's Day and to promise to sell food and other necessities to them at just and reasonable prices. It was further stipulated that the burgesses were to swear to maintain the clerical immunity of the scholars from arrest by the lay authorities. It is arguable that in this explicit recognition of the status of the scholars as clerks, exempt from the normal processes of secular jurisdiction, lay the central importance of the award. For it defined Oxford's academic body as a privileged corporation set apart from the citizenry and encircled by a distinct system of legal protection. The Oxford townspeople were not always willing to acquiesce in the full implications of the privileged position of the academic community. Repeated disputes arose over the University's interpretation of its protected clerical status; an interpretation which necessitated, in certain circumstances, the extension of its jurisdiction over laymen.[114] Although this recurrent problem, common in university towns throughout medieval Europe, was a destabilizing factor, it is nonetheless clear that the award of 1214 made a substantial contribution towards securing the permanency of Oxford University following the period of closure. When universities were unfettered by property and purpose-made buildings,[115] it was still a feasible proposition for an emergent university facing major problems and lacking the requisite

one of his agents: but this responsibility was soon assumed by the abbot of Eynsham. It seems that the University made no regular provision for the distribution of this annual payment until 1240, when Robert Grosseteste, then bishop of Lincoln, framed ordinances for the administration of this fund. The money was to be placed in a chest in St Frideswide's priory, and this was to be operated as a loan-chest, the first of many to be established in the medieval University: see T. H. Aston and R. Faith, 'The Endowments of the University and Colleges to *c.* 1348', *The History of the University of Oxford*, i. 265 ff. at 266–8.

[114] More-detailed information regarding the periodically strained relations between Oxford University and the citizenry is provided by Kibre, *Scholarly Privileges in the Middle Ages*, ch. 9, and by Rashdall, *Universities*, iii. 79 ff.

[115] On purpose-made buildings in universities in the later medieval period, see e.g. J. Verger, *Les universités au moyen âge*, pp. 181–2. So far as Oxford is concerned, even as late as the mid-thirteenth century the University had virtually nothing in the way of property holdings or capital assets: see Aston and Faith, 'The Endowments of the University and Colleges to *c.* 1348', p. 269.

ecclesiastical or secular support to uproot itself completely and seek an alternative and safer location. In this regard, the papal intervention in favour of the Oxford scholars was crucial in ensuring the long-term survival of the Oxford *studium*. But while what amounted to Oxford's first charter of privileges emanated from the papacy, it was not, generally speaking, to the pope so much as to the English king that the scholars of both Oxford and Cambridge became accustomed to turn for the confirmation and extension of their privileges and immunities. From the reign of Henry III, each king confirmed the existing privileges of the English Universities, adding to them as appropriate.[116]

The degree to which the Oxford *studium* had acquired a sense of corporate identity in the early thirteenth century may be extrapolated from some of the provisions of the award of 1214. The sentence of suspension from lecturing for three years imposed upon the minority of masters who had irreverently continued to lecture at Oxford during the cessation[117] indicates that a measure of formal decision making, regulating the conduct of members of the teaching guild, had been in operation for some time previously. Moreover, the stipulation that the rents of all accommodation to be newly inhabited by scholars were to be assessed by a joint commission of four masters and four burgesses reveals the organizational capacity of the guild to negotiate with civic officials through its own appointed representatives. This office of university assessor or taxor, which had an early being in most university towns in both northern and southern Europe, was perhaps the oldest university office at Oxford, along with the chancellorship, and may

---

[116] See e.g. Kibre, *Scholarly Privileges*, pp. 269 ff.

[117] That there was a need to impose this severe sentence proves the erroneous nature of Roger of Wendover's statement that not a single clerk, master or scholar remained in Oxford during the cessation: Roger of Wendover, *Flores Historiarum* (Rolls Series, 3 vols., ed. H. G. Hewlett, London, 1886–9), ii (1887), 51. Wendover's estimate of the academic population at this time at almost 3,000 (p. 51) appears to be manifest exaggeration: it is probable that in 1209 before the cessation the academic population numbered several hundreds and that it was a good deal less than 1,000: see the conclusions of M. B. Hackett, based upon a computerized analysis, 'The University as a Corporate Body', *The History of the University of Oxford*, i. 37 ff. at 37–8.

have been in existence before 1209.[118] The first reference to the Oxford chancellorship, which came to embody the corporate personality of the masters' guild, occurs in the award of 1214. Indeed, the award contains no fewer than three references to a chancellor. They are so framed, however, that it is unclear whether the office of chancellor was already in existence but vacant, or was being actually established by this award, or was being mooted as a possibility for future establishment. The balance of probability seems to be that the chancellorship was being proposed as a formal office to which the bishop of Lincoln was soon expected to make an appointment.[119]

It is not certain when the first chancellor was instituted but there is evidence to suggest that Master Geoffrey de Lucy became chancellor at some point between June 1214 and August 1216, and probably by September 1215, and that he was one of the earliest chancellors, and perhaps even the first.[120] Cognizance must be taken, however, of a reference in a letter of Innocent III of 1201 wherein Master John Grim is described as a *magister scolarum Oxonie*. Another letter of Innocent III, of 1210, was addressed to

---

[118] Rashdall, *Universities*, iii. 47, 172. The number of university taxors was later reduced from four to two: ibid., iii. 56, n. 1.

[119] On the inception of the Oxford chancellorship, see Rashdall, op. cit., iii. 37 ff.; Leff, op. cit., pp. 79–81; Cobban, *The Medieval Universities*, p. 102; Southern, 'From Schools to University', pp. 31 ff.; Hackett, 'The University as a Corporate Body', pp. 43 ff.; M. G. Cheney, 'Master Geoffrey de Lucy, an early chancellor of the University of Oxford', *E.H.R.*, lxxxii (1967), pp. 750 ff.; G. Pollard, 'The Legatine Award to Oxford in 1214 and Robert Grosseteste', *Oxoniensia*, xxxix (1975), pp. 62 ff.; C. H. Lawrence, 'The Origins of the Chancellorship at Oxford', *Oxoniensia*, xli (1976), pp. 316 ff.

[120] M. G. Cheney, art. cit., p. 735, argues that Geoffrey de Lucy was made chancellor between June 1214 and August 1216, and G. Pollard concludes that Geoffrey must have become chancellor by September 1215 at the latest, art. cit., pp. 62, 63, 70. Pollard (pp. 63, 70) allows that Grosseteste may have been head of the University from about October/November 1214 to the appointment of Geoffrey de Lucy as chancellor by September 1215: but he denies that Grosseteste was ever chancellor, only master of the schools (*magister scolarum*), having been refused the title of chancellor by the bishop of Lincoln, Hugh of Wells. Lawrence, art. cit., p. 322, concurs with the main conclusions of Cheney and Pollard. Southern's claim that Grosseteste's association with the chancellorship was after 1225 is inherently improbable: 'From Schools to University', pp. 34–6, 36, n. 1.

the prior of Oseney, the dean of Oxford and Master Alard, *rector scolarum*.[121] It is conceivable that the masters who had reassembled at Oxford in 1214 had tried to elect Robert Grosseteste as their 'chancellor', but had been frustrated in their attempt to confer that title upon him by the bishop of Lincoln, Hugh of Wells, who would permit only the title of *magister scolarum*.[122] These designations imply antecedents of the chancellorship, and from analogy elsewhere the *magister* or *rector scolarum* may have conferred the teaching licence under the jurisdiction of the bishop of Lincoln, although equally, this function may have been vested in the archdeacon of Oxford.[123] Whatever the case, it is plausible that the office of chancellor had some kind of shadowy existence before 1209 and that it was more fully instituted in the years immediately following the legatine award of 1214 and fully so after an ambiguous phase during which the bishop of Lincoln was unwilling to accord the chancellorship a plenary recognition. The difficulty over the nomenclature of the headship of the masters' guild is an early pointer to the jurisdictional feuding which was to divide the masters and the bishop of Lincoln over the independent position of the chancellorship.[124] Originally, the chancellor was the official of the bishop and exercised delegated episcopal powers. At an early stage, however, the chancellor came to be elected by the masters' guild. From being an officer set above and apart from the masters, the chancellor was rendered one of their number and became the embodiment of the autonomy of the guild. It is this identification of the Oxford chancellor with the aspirations of the masters' guild, a situation paralleled exactly at Cambridge, which above all demarcates the chancellorship in the English Universities from that in the University in Paris. Whereas the latter was largely external to

---

[121] For these letters of 1201 and 1210, see C. R. Cheney and M. G. Cheney, *The Letters of Pope Innocent III (1198–1216) concerning England and Wales* (Oxford, 1967), no. 279 (p. 46) and no. 865 (p. 143); see also the notice in *Snappe's Formulary*, ed. cit., pp. 318–19.

[122] *The Rolls and Register of Bishop Oliver Sutton, 1280–1299* (7 vols., ed. R. M. T. Hill, Lincoln Record Society, 1948–75), v (1965), 60.

[123] See the comments of Rashdall, *Universities*, iii. 38–9.

[124] See below, pp. 276 ff.

the magisterial guild and at times seemed a major impediment to its autonomous growth, the English chancellors were the personifications of their universities in their dealings with external authorities, both secular and ecclesiastical.[125]

It is evident that after a lengthy period of evolutionary growth, especially marked from the late twelfth century, the Oxford *studium* had, by the end of the reign of King John in 1216, acquired a recognizable measure of corporate cohesion. It seems clear that the bitter interlude of the closure of the Oxford schools helped in important ways to crystallize the need for more assertive organizational strength on the part of the disaffected masters. Paradoxically, this lengthy disruptive episode, by the very reaction it provoked, appears to have done much to reinforce the standing of the masters' guild and, by extension, the stability of the Oxford *studium* in its entirety. Thus, the aftermath to the Oxford cessation was a phase of vigorous rebirth for England's first fully evolved university, and that same cessation was instrumental in setting in motion the train of events which gave rise to England's second university. For it seems that Cambridge emerged as a *studium generale* only after the migration of a party of the Oxford masters and scholars to Cambridge following the virtual demise of their schools in 1209.

Of Europe's earliest universities which evolved and were not specifically founded, Cambridge furnishes one of the best instances of a university which came into existence in a less than ideal environment. It is true that, having been successively a Roman, Saxon and Danish settlement, Cambridge was evidently a centre of some strategic significance.[126] It was also a natural focus of regional trade. The River Cam was a principal artery for traffic through the Fenland area, enabling Cambridge to act as a clearing house for the agricultural produce, most importantly the corn, of the surrounding districts.[127] The Domesday account of the town,

---

[125] On the English university chancellors, see e.g. Cobban, *The Medieval Universities*, pp. 102–3.

[126] See e.g. H. M. Cam, 'The City of Cambridge', *V.C.H. Camb.* iii (ed. J. P. C. Roach, Oxford, 1959), 2–3.

[127] Ibid., pp. 86–7.

though incomplete, reveals Cambridge as a sizeable borough taxed at about ten times the rate of the average Cambridgeshire village.[128] In the mid-twelfth century, Cambridge, like Oxford, housed a business community of Jews, until they were expelled in the 1270s,[129] and the lists of contributors to royal tallages in 1211 and 1219 yield proof of the existence in Cambridge of a substantial group of wealthy burgesses.[130] In the twelfth and early thirteenth centuries, many of the burgesses had given liberally of their wealth in the form of endowments to religious institutions, such as Barnwell Priory (*c.* 1092–1112) and the Priory of St Radegund (*c.* 1133–8). The majority of the Cambridge churches appear to have been founded in the twelfth century or earlier by burgesses, either individually or collectively.[131] An indication of the commercial liveliness of the town may be deduced from the fact that no fewer than four fairs were in existence on the eve of the birth of the University, including Sturbridge (Stourbridge) Fair, which was granted by King John in *c.* 1211, and which was to become a fair of international proportions.[132] But despite these positive features, Cambridge was, in some ways, an unprepossessing venue for a university. Low-lying and on the frontier of the Fen country,

[128] Ibid., pp. 3–5; F. W. Maitland, *Township and Borough* (Cambridge, 1898), p. 54.

[129] On Cambridge Jewry, see Cam, 'The City of Cambridge', pp. 95–6; also C. N. L. Brooke, 'The Churches of Medieval Cambridge', *History, Society and the Churches: Essays in Honour of Owen Chadwick* (ed. D. Beales and G. Best, Cambridge, 1985), pp. 49 ff. at pp. 58–60; M. Rubin, *Charity and Community in Medieval Cambridge* (Cambridge Studies in Medieval Life and Thought, fourth ser., vol. 4, Cambridge, 1987), pp. 108–9, 218–21, 224–6.

[130] For these lists, see Maitland, op. cit., pp. 167–70.

[131] See Cam, op. cit., pp. 6–7. For the Priory of Barnwell and the Priory of St Radegund, see D. M. B. Ellis and L. F. Salzman, 'Religious Houses', *V.C.H. Camb.* ii (ed. L. F. Salzman, 1948), 197 ff. at 234–49, 218–19.

[132] For the Cambridge fairs, see Cam, op. cit., pp. 91–5. Accounts of Sturbridge (Stourbridge) Fair are given by J. E. T. Rogers, *A History of Agriculture and Prices in England* (7 vols., Oxford, 1866–1902), i (1886), 141–4; C. Walford, *Fairs, past and present* (London, 1883), pp. 54–163; L. F. Salzman, *English Trade in the Middle Ages* (Oxford, 1931), pp. 144–5, 157. The fair, which was opened on 18 September and lasted three weeks, was held under the authority of the corporation and town of Cambridge.

Cambridge was not a particularly healthy setting for an academic population.[133] Moreover, it was subject to periodic flooding throughout the medieval era and beyond. It cannot, therefore, be supposed that Cambridge would have attracted a community of scholars because of any peculiar advantages which the site could offer.

As already discussed, there were, in addition to Oxford, a variety of favourably situated and already recognized centres of learning in England in the twelfth and early thirteenth centuries. Any one of these would have seemed more likely than Cambridge to produce a *studium generale*.[134] In addition to the dubious nature of the site, there is no definite proof that Cambridge produced schools of advanced learning at any point in the twelfth century. It is true that a verse life of Robert Grosseteste of 1503 by the monk Richard of Bardney alleges that Grosseteste studied and taught logic and rhetoric at Cambridge before 1199.[135] Although this claim should not be altogether discounted, the matter has not been corroborated.[136] It has also been suggested that the scholar Daniel of Morley may have moved to Cambridge from the Northampton *studium* in the early 1190s, with the implication that he may have

---

[133] See the sixteenth-century description of Cambridge by William Harrison, who had studied at both Oxford and Cambridge: 'Cambridge . . . standeth verie well, saving that it is somewhat neere unto the fens, whereby the wholesomeness of the aire there is not a little corrupted', *William Harrison's Description of England AD 1577-1587* (ed. from the first two editions of Holinshed's chronicle, AD 1577, 1587, by F. J. Furnivall, New Shakespeare Society, series vi, i, London, 1877), 72; reproduced in Cooper, *Annals*, ii (1843), 349.

[134] See above, p. 26-9.

[135] See J. C. Russell, 'Richard of Bardney's Account of Robert Grosseteste's Early and Middle Life', *Medievalia et Humanistica*, ii (1943), pp. 45 ff. esp. pp. 51-4.

[136] Callus, 'Robert Grosseteste as Scholar', *Robert Grosseteste: Scholar and Bishop*, p. 5, concludes that 'although the possibility of his (i.e. Grosseteste) going to Cambridge is not to be altogther excluded, we need a better founded authority than that of Richard of Bardney to render it acceptable'. M. B. Hackett's statement that 'the evidence that Grosseteste lectured at Cambridge *c*.1199 is so flimsy and late as to be almost worthless' is excessive: M. B. Hackett, *The Original Statutes of Cambridge University: The Text and its History* (Cambridge, 1970), p. 44, n. 1.

taught at Cambridge.[137] This contention is tenuously based and no confirmation has been adduced. As in other towns of any size, Cambridge possessed grammar schools in the second half of the twelfth century.[138] There is no firm evidence, however, that these were fostered and augmented, as has been claimed, by the activities of the monks of Ely Cathedral, Croyland Abbey and Barnwell Priory so as to constitute the kernel of the subsequent university.[139] In the absence of a satisfactory and alternative explanation, it is probable that the decisive factor in the rise of the *studium generale* at Cambridge was the exodus of masters and scholars from Oxford in 1209, one colony of whom, encamped in Reading and another in Cambridge, according to the sole authority for this episode, the chronicler Roger of Wendover.[140]

It may well be that the Reading contingent, being within easy distance of Oxford, intended to return as soon as normality was restored. The motives of the Cambridge party were probably more mixed. A proportion of the exiles returned to Oxford after the issue of the award of the papal legate in 1214.[141] This suggests that for some of the Cambridge party the migration had always been of a temporary character. Concerning those who remained, it is unclear whether the aim from the outset was to establish a rival university or whether this became an objective only after the experience of the Cambridge settlement. Whatever the case, the question arises as to why Cambridge was selected as a migration point rather than say Northampton, which had been a prominent *studium* from the late twelfth century and continued to flourish at certain stages in the thirteenth century.[142] A possible clue may be found in the

---

[137] Richardson, 'The Schools of Northampton in the Twelfth Century', art. cit., p. 602.

[138] See e.g. Orme, *English Schools in the Middle Ages*, p. 170.

[139] For this thesis see G. Peacock, *Observations on the Statutes of the University of Cambridge* (London, 1841), pp. 14–15, n. 1, and Mullinger, *The University of Cambridge*, i. 334. The theory is rejected by Rashdall, *Universities*, iii. 277 and nn. 1, 3, and by Cobban, *The Medieval Universities*, pp. 110–11.

[140] Roger of Wendover, *Flores Historiarum*, ed. cit., ii. 51; Cooper, op. cit., i. 34.

[141] Hackett, *The Original Statutes of Cambridge University*, pp. 44, 47.

[142] See above, pp. 29–30, 33–4.

circumstance that some of the migratory masters seem to have been natives of Cambridge and some of East Anglia;[143] this would have provided a reason for the choice of Cambridge by a section of the Oxford exiles in 1209. Among the Oxford masters who dispersed to Cambridge was John Grim. He was a member of a leading Cambridge family and had held the office of master of the schools at Oxford in 1201,[144] an office which was a forerunner of the position of chancellor. It is conceivable that such an influential figure, with powerful, Cambridge connections, may have been a principal organizer of the party which migrated to Cambridge. Another consideration stems from the notable number of *magistri* attached to the entourage of Eustace, bishop of Ely between 1197 and 1215. Some of them had definitely been Oxford masters, and these may have used their influence with the bishop to secure his support for the academic settlement within Ely diocese.[145] The presence of these Oxford *magistri* in the Ely episcopal household may therefore have a bearing on the selection of Cambridge by one group of the Oxford exiles.

Although a proportion of the masters and scholars would doubtless have returned to Oxford from Cambridge in 1214–15, a sufficient number of teaching masters remained after that year to ensure the continuity of the schools which had been firmly entrenched during the period of the Oxford closure. It would consequently appear that the years immediately following the reopening of the Oxford schools witnessed the emergence of Cambridge as a *studium generale ex consuetudine*, a university whose standing derived from customary approbation and not from formal validation. Initially, it seems, Cambridge specialized in arts, theology and canon law, there being no faculty of civil law until the mid-thirteenth century and no faculty of medicine until *c.* 1270–80.[146] Considering that civil law was taught at Oxford from the late twelfth century, the delay in instituting the faculty

[143] Hackett, op. cit., p. 46.

[144] See above, p. 48.

[145] Hackett, op. cit., p. 47.

[146] Ibid, pp. 29–33, 30, n. 3.

organization of and degrees in this discipline at Cambridge is difficult to explain. The study of canon law required an admixture of civil law, and in Cambridge some lectures in civil law were given as part of the course in canon law in the first half of the thirteenth century. It is highly improbable that Honorius III's ban on the teaching of civil law at Paris in 1219[147] had any bearing on the situation at Cambridge, for this prohibition was confined to Paris University. The slowness with which Cambridge came to encompass civil law as an independent study is a problem which remains largely unresolved.

Cambridge's academic population, in parallel with that of Oxford, was apparently augmented and diversified in 1229 when Henry III gave an open invitation to the dispersed masters and scholars of Paris who had quit that city following a conflict with the civic authorities.[148] It is to be presumed that some of the Parisian refugees gravitated towards Oxford and Cambridge as they certainly did towards Angers, Toulouse and Orleans.[149] The injection of a contingent of scholars from Paris can only have strengthened the standing of the English Universities, and was particularly opportune for Cambridge, which had so recently aspired to a place within the international university order. In 1231, Henry III testified to the large concourse of students from diverse parts of the country and from overseas which had converged on Cambridge.[150] And the entrenchment of the Franciscans and Dominicans at Cambridge over the period *c.* 1224–38[151] added a further cosmopolitan dimension; one which was especially productive of the exchange of ideas, treatises and scholars between the mendicants of Cambridge and those of Paris and later those of other continental universities. From these indications, it would

---

[147] *Chartularium*, i. no. 32; see also W. Ullmann, 'Honorius III and the Prohibition of Legal Studies', *Juridical Review*, lx (1948), pp. 177 ff.

[148] *Cal. Pat. R.*, 1225–32, p. 257; see also Fuller, *The History of the University of Cambridge*, ed. cit., pp. 21–2.

[149] Rashdall, *Universities*, i. 336–7.

[150] *Cal. Close R.*, 1227–31, p. 586.

[151] *V.C.H. Camb.* ii. 146. The Franciscans settled in Cambridge as early as 1224 or 1225, and the Dominican settlement probably dates from 1238.

appear that within twenty years of the Oxford migration of 1209 Cambridge had established itself as a university capable of attracting students from a geographical range sufficient to satisfy, at least minimally, the criterion for broad recruitment implicit in the concept of *studium generale*.

In the case of Europe's earliest *studia generalia*, such as Bologna, Paris, Montpellier, Oxford or Palencia, it is not at all easy to discern exactly when their constituent guilds either of masters or of students acquired a legal corporate standing. Among the characteristics of the legal corporation, as then understood, were the right to elect officers, the right to frame statutes and enforce obedience to them, the right to sue and be sued in a court of law as a fictive 'person' and the right to possess property and a seal in common.[152] The realization of these rights was, for the spontaneously developed universities, a gradual process. It has been argued that the Parisian masters formed a legal corporation by 1215 at the latest.[153] But the situation with respect to the English Universities is less certain. Although the legatine award of 1214 for Oxford indicates a measure of corporate cohesion, there is nothing in the phraseology of the document to imply that Oxford was then regarded formally as a legal corporation. A letter of 11 March 1217 or 1218 from the cardinal legate, Guala de Bicheriis, and addressed to all masters and scholars living in Oxford, refers to them collectively as a *universitas*. Whether this nomenclature was meant in the formal sense of a legal corporation or was used in an unofficial context is not at all clear.[154] In one of three writs issued by Henry III on 3 May 1231 — a writ which refers to disciplinary matters and

---

[152] On the concept of the *universitas* or legal corporation, see e.g. P. Michaud-Quantin, *Universitas: expressions du mouvement communautaire dans le moyen âge latin, passim*, and Michaud-Quantin, 'Collectivités médiévales et institutions antiques', *Miscellanea Mediaevalia*, i. 239 ff. The legal definition of the *universitas* as a corporation crystallized only in the course of the thirteenth century.

[153] G. Post, 'Parisian Masters as a Corporation, 1200–1246', *Speculum*, ix (1934), pp. 421 ff. See also J. Verger, 'Des Ecoles à l'Université: la mutation institutionelle', *La France de Philippe Auguste: Le Temps des Mutations* (Colloques internationaux CNRS, no. 602, Paris, 1980), pp. 817 ff.

[154] This letter is printed by Salter, *Mediaeval Archives of the University of Oxford*, i. 16–17.

rented accommodation in the English Universities — the assumption appears to be that the chancellor and masters of both Oxford and Cambridge would act as legal corporations.[155] From this, it might be plausibly argued that the magisterial guilds of the English Universities had received royal recognition as legal bodies by 1231 and that presumably, especially in the case of the Oxford masters, they had received it some years before that date.

The growing corporate maturity of Cambridge is evidenced by the rapid appearance of the office of chancellor, first recorded on 4 June 1225,[156] only sixteen years after the Oxford migration. It is to be supposed that the Cambridge chancellorship was instituted in direct imitation of that of Oxford, which seems to have been in operation by September 1215.[157] The earliest known Cambridge chancellor was the canonist Richard de Leycestria or Wethringsette, who may have been appointed by *c.* 1222,[158] although the point cannot be proven. Originally, the Cambridge chancellor was conceived of as an episcopal agent, exercising delegated powers of the bishop of Ely, and this paralleled the relationship between the Oxford chancellor and the bishop of Lincoln. From the ecclesiastical standpoint, the inception of the Cambridge chancellorship signified that the University was seen as a strictly defined institution within Ely diocese and that, like any

---

[155] *Cal. Close R.,* 1227–31, pp. 586–7. See also Hackett, 'The University as a Corporate Body', *The History of the University of Oxford,* i. 49. J. H. Baker, 'The Inns of Court and Chancery as Voluntary Associations', *The Legal Profession and the Common Law: Historical Essays* (London and Ronceverte, 1986), pp. 45 ff. at pp. 48–9, argues that the English Universities were not formally incorporated until 1571: whatever the finer points of this technical subject, there can be no doubt that the English Universities were regarded as legal corporations from the thirteenth century.

[156] *Curia Regis Rolls,* xii, 1225–26, pp. 139–30, no. 646: the item concerns a property dispute involving the archdeacon of Bedford, the chancellor of Cambridge and the precentor of Barnwell. H. E. Salter, 'The Beginning of Cambridge University', *E.H.R.,* xxxvi (1921), pp. 419–20, advances documentary evidence to establish that the chancellorship was in existence by Midsummer 1226: but, clearly, this dating must now be revised to 1225 at the latest.

[157] See above, p. 48.

[158] Hackett, *The Original Statutes of Cambridge University,* pp. 48–9, 49, n. 1.

other diocesan unit, it was subject to the force of episcopal jurisdiction.

The earliest known papal recognition of Cambridge University as an academic corporation was contained in an indult of Gregory IX of 14 June 1233.[159] This was addressed to the chancellor and university of scholars at Cambridge, and it granted to Cambridge the crucial judicial privilege of the *ius non trahi extra*, whereby scholars could not be summoned to ecclesiastical courts outside Ely diocese as long as they were willing to have their cases adjudicated in the court of either the chancellor or the bishop. This was an exceedingly important privilege: it was described by Rashdall as *the* characteristic university privilege for universities in northern Europe.[160] It is of considerable interest that Paris was granted an equivalent right only in 1245 and Oxford only in 1254 — the first recorded papal recognition of Oxford University as an academic corporation, granted some twenty-one years after that accorded to Cambridge.[161] As the privilege of the *ius non trahi extra* was applied to Paris and Oxford, scholars were not to be summoned to ecclesiastical courts beyond the town, whereas for Cambridge, the diocese of Ely was the prescribed area. This difference probably redounded to the advantage of the Cambridge scholars. The privilege was essentially the same, however, in all three institutions. From this, it would appear that Cambridge was the first university to acquire this valued privilege of the *ius non trahi extra*. This is only one indication that Cambridge was a more prominent university in the thirteenth century than Rashdall's estimate would lead us to believe.[162]

The direction of recent research has made apparent the need for a reassessment of the status of Cambridge University during the first

---

[159] *Register, Gregory IX* (ed. L. Auvray, Paris, 1896), i. 779, no. 1389.

[160] Rashdall, *Universities*, i. 342.

[161] For Paris, see *Chartularium*, i. no. 142, and Rashdall, op. cit., i. 342, 418 and n. 5; for the award to Oxford of 27 September 1254, see *Les Registres d'Innocent IV* (3 vols., ed. E. Berger, Paris, 1884–97), iii (1897), 519, no. 8082: on 6 October 1254, Oxford received a papal confirmation of its immunities, liberties and customs, ibid, iii. 519, no. 8081. See also Rashdall, op. cit., iii. 55.

[162] See Rashdall's disparaging remarks, op. cit., iii. 284.

hundred years of its existence. A traditional view has been that Pope John XXII officially conferred the status of *studium generale* upon the Univerity of Cambridge by a bull of 9 June 1318, and that before this date Cambridge had not attained a rank equal to that of Oxford, which had been recognized as a *studium generale ex consuetudine* from the late twelfth century.[163] But a reappraisal of the papal bull of John XXII, based on a more accurate text than had been previously used,[164] proves that the papal award, which was issued in response to a petition of 18 March 1317 from Edward II,[165] was nothing more than a confirmation of the status of Cambridge as a *studium generale*. That is to say, the pope in 1318 merely strengthened an already existing *studium generale* without, in any way, improving upon its status. This has important implications for the history of medieval Cambridge. For it clearly means that at no time did the papacy confer, even officially, the status of *studium generale* upon Cambridge University. At the request of Edward II, an apostolic confirmation was obtained in 1318 in order to reinforce the position of a well-established academic centre which had been recognized as a *studium generale ex consuetudine* throughout most of the thirteenth and in the early fourteenth century. It is appropriate to mention here that even before the issue of John XXII's bull in 1318 Cambridge University had been described as a *studium generale* in an incidental reference in a letter of Pope Nicholas IV of 9 June 1290 addressed to the canons of the Order of Sempringham, who had members attending the University.[166]

[163] See e.g. Denifle, *Die Entstehung der Universitäten des Mittelalters bis 1400*, esp. pp. 352–3; Rashdall, op. cit., iii. 283; Roach, 'The University of Cambridge', *V.C.H. Camb.* iii. 154.

[164] The letter of John XXII is re-examined by A. B. Cobban, 'Edward II, Pope John XXII and the University of Cambridge', *B.J.R.L.*, xlvii (1964), pp. 49 ff. at pp. 68 ff.: the revised edition of the letter is printed as an appendix, pp. 76–8.

[165] This petition is printed by T. Rymer, *Foedera* (ed. A. Clarke, London, 1818), II. i. 357; see also *Documents relating to the University and Colleges of Cambridge* (3 vols., ed. by the Queen's Commissioners, London, 1852), i. 6, and Cooper, *Annals*, i. 76.

[166] *Les Registres de Nicolas IV* (9 Fascs., ed. E. Langlois, Paris, 1881–93), Fasc. 4 (1890), 455, no. 2731: see also Hackett, *The Original Statutes of Cambridge University*, p. 178.

Although this *de facto* recognition of Cambridge as a *studium generale* did not preclude the need to obtain a bull in 1318 specifically concerned with the matter, it demonstrates that Cambridge had been acknowledged by the papacy as a university of primary rank at some point in the thirteenth century and by 1290 at the latest.

It has already been seen that Cambridge had fulfilled the customary criteria for recognition as a *studium generale* within twenty years of the Oxford migration of 1209. That is, it harboured a plurality of masters teaching in arts and the superior faculties of theology and law, and it had the ability to recruit from a broad geographical area. There can now be little doubt that even if Cambridge University was considerably smaller than Oxford in the thirteenth century and did not possess an international reputation as influential as that of its more prominent English partner, it was nevertheless recognized as ranking equal in status to Oxford. Indeed, there is every justification for ranging the Cambridge *studium* with all those other *studia*, such as Paris, Bologna, Montpellier, Oxford, Padua and Orleans, which had owed their positions as *studia generalia* originally to custom and not to official enactment.

Edward II's petition of 18 March 1317 to John XXII seeking a papal confirmation of Cambridge's status as a *studium generale* has to be seen as part of the movement in which, from the late thirteenth century, universities whose standing rested upon the strength of custom were encouraged to acquire a formal sanction from the ecumenical authority of either the pope or the emperor. As mentioned in the preceding chapter, the aim was to supersede the phase of haphazard university growth by a more rational process of development by bringing both the old-established and new foundations within the papal or imperial directional sphere.[167] One of the supposed advantages accruing to an established university from obtaining a confirmation of its status as a *studium generale* by pope or emperor was deemed to be a buttressing of its claim to award the *ius ubique docendi*, which theoretically enabled its graduates to teach in another university without undergoing further examination and which previously had been advanced as a

---

[167] See above, p. 4.

prescriptive right.[168] Although the principles of the *ius ubique docendi* were honoured more in the breach than in the observance, it was nevertheless thought desirable for established universities in the late thirteenth and early fourteenth centuries to secure ecumenical endorsement for this alleged right. In 1289, Pope Nicholas IV formally recognized Montpellier as a *studium generale* and conferred upon its doctors the *ius ubique docendi*.[169] Similar bulls were issued by the same pope for Bologna and Paris in 1291 and 1292 respectively,[170] and by Clement V for Orleans in 1306.[171]

This is the context within which Edward II successfully negotiated the bull of John XXII for Cambridge in 1318. It is, however, a striking anomaly that Oxford seems never to have procured a papal bull which specifically confirmed its position as a *studium generale*, with the concomitant *ius ubique docendi* — a negative condition which Oxford was to share in the medieval period with the French provincial university of Angers'.[172] The papacy was petitioned regarding the status of Oxford on several occasions. In 1296, both the bishop of Lincoln, Oliver Sutton, and the bishop of Carlisle, John Halton, sent letters to Boniface VIII requesting that Oxford be accorded full equality of privilege with the other major universities, especially with those in France.[173] A further plea may have been sent in the 1290s, by Edward I himself, although this tantalizing matter is not altogether certain.[174] But it is

---

[168] On the *ius ubique docendi*, see e.g. Cobban, *The Medieval Universities*, pp. 27–32, and Rashdall, op. cit., i. 9–15.

[169] The bull is printed in Fournier, *Statuts*, ii. no. 903.

[170] The bull for Paris is printed in C. E. Bulaeus, *Historia Universitatis Parisiensis* (6 vols., Paris, 1665–73), iii (1666), 449–50, and in *Chartularium*, ii (1891), no. 578; that for Bologna in M. Sarti, *De Claris Archigymnasii Bononiensis Professoribus a saeculo xi usque ad saeculum xiv* (Bologna, 1769–72), i. pt. i (1769), 59.

[171] The bull for Orleans is printed in Fournier, *Statuts*, i. no. 19.

[172] For the case of Oxford, see G. L. Haskins, 'The University of Oxford and the "ius ubique docendi"', *E.H.R.*, lvi (1941), pp. 281 ff., and for Angers, see Rashdall, op. cit., ii. 154.

[173] See Haskins, art. cit., p. 283: the letters are printed, pp. 288–9.

[174] This letter, presumed to be from Edward I to Pope Nicholas IV, is printed by Haskins, art. cit., pp. 290–1; see also the comments of Haskins, p. 286.

certain that Edward I in 1303–4 and Edward II in 1317, 1320 and 1321 petitioned the pope concerning the privileges for Oxford, stressing firmly its prior antiquity over Paris University.[175] All these efforts were of no avail, and this consistently negative response is not easy to understand unless it is thought that the dispute between the secular masters and the mendicants, especially the Dominicans, which began at Oxford in *c.* 1303 and lasted in a serious form until 1320, and which involved the masters in litigation with the friars at the papal court at Avignon,[176] rendered the University an object of papal disfavour. However, even if this was so, the period of odium would only have been temporary and, in any case, would not, it seems, have embraced the last decade of the thirteenth century, when the first series of petitions had been sent. The suggestion that Oxford was denied a full equivalence of privilege with the French Universities because of Oxford's rivalry with Paris and the papacy's predilection for the latter is not very convincing.[177] Cambridge's equivalence received unambiguous papal acknowledgement even though, to some degree, Cambridge could be reckoned a competitor to Paris, particularly in the theological sphere.

Whatever the precise reason for the withholding of papal ratification for Oxford's status, the practical effect was minimized, for the operation of the *ius ubique docendi* was in reality severely restricted. In these circumstances, Oxford was not to be disadvantaged in any tangible sense. It is nonetheless of some remark that Oxford was, it seems, discriminated against in this manner by the papacy and that Cambridge was afforded a plenary validation

[175] A letter accredited to Edward I and assigned to 1303–4 and which is, with a few slight differences towards the end, identical to that assigned to the 1290s by G. L. Haskins (see previous note) is printed in *Formularies which bear on the History of Oxford c. 1204–1420* (2 vols., ed. H. E. Salter, W. A. Pantin and H. G. Richardson, Oxf. Hist. Soc., new series, iv-v, 1942), i. 6. The letter of Edward II to Pope John XXII of 26 December 1317 is printed by Haskins, art. cit., pp. 289–90, and in *Chartularium*, ii. no. 756: for the attempts of 1320 and 1321, see Kibre, *Scholarly Privileges in the Middle Ages,* p. 290.

[176] For this dispute, see M. W. Sheehan, 'The Religious Orders 1220–1370', *The History of the University of Oxford*, i. 193 ff. at 205–8.

[177] See F. M. Powicke, *Ways of Medieval Life and Thought* (London, 1949), p. 159.

without undue difficulty. This is only one pointer to the need to dispel the old notion that Cambridge was a derivative and insubstantial version of Oxford. On the contrary, by the early fourteenth century it was an accepted member of Europe's primary university league. The degree to which it is necessary to differentiate the English Universities will be illustrated further with respect to their government and organization, the subject of the next chapter.

Chapter 3

Government and Organization

In a general sense, the Parisian constitution provided the model for the English Universities, for Paris was the archetypal point of reference for most of those universities of northern Europe which were organized along magisterial as opposed to student lines.[1] Nevertheless, there were important areas of difference between Paris and the English Universities, and these indicate a measure of indigenous growth in the latter. The most singular of these lay in the position of the chancellor.[2] As mentioned in the previous chapter, the chancellors of Oxford and Cambridge originated as the officials of the bishops of Lincoln and Ely respectively, and wielded delegated episcopal authority.[3] From the early thirteenth century, however, the chancellors came to be elected by the masters of the academic guild, who presented their chancellors-elect for

---

[1] For the general influence of Paris's constitution on Oxford's, see Rashdall, *Universities*, iii. 49 ff., and Cobban, *The Medieval Universities*, pp. 101–7. Mullinger, *The University of Cambridge*, i. 343, asserted that 'the statutes of both Oxford and Cambridge had originally been little more than a transcript of those of Paris': this, however, is a most inaccurate judgement and needs to be firmly rejected. For the possible impact of Parisian customs and statutes upon the Cambridge constitution, see the detailed arguments of Hackett, *The Original Statutes of Cambridge University, passim*.

[2] On the Oxford chancellor, see Hackett, 'The University as a Corporate Body', *The History of the University of Oxford*, i. 69–81, and Lawrence, 'The University in State and Church', ibid., i. 106–110; Rashdall, op. cit., iii. 41–7, 49–54, 81–7 and *passim*; Gibson, *Statuta Antiqua*, pp. lxx–lxxiv; *Registrum Cancellarii Oxoniensis 1434–1469* (2 vols., ed. H. E. Salter, Oxf. Hist. Soc., xciii–iv, 1932), i. xiii–xliv. For the Cambridge chancellor, see Hackett, *The Original Statutes*, esp. pp. 104–18; Peacock, *Observations on the Statutes of the University of Cambridge*, pp. 17–18 and p. 18, n. 4; Roach, 'The University of Cambridge', *V.C.H. Camb.* iii. 156–7. The English chancellors are discussed by Cobban, op. cit., pp. 102–4.

[3] See above, pp. 49, 57.

confirmation by the bishop.[4] This need for episcopal confirmation
was not dispensed with until 1367/70 in the case of the Oxford
chancellor and not until 1401 at Cambridge. It was only in 1395, by
a bull of Boniface IX, that Oxford, apparently, acquired a complete
emancipation from ecclesiastical jurisdiction. However, this was
not accepted by the king or the archbishop of Canterbury and it was
revoked by Pope John XXIII in 1411. Exemption was not
unambiguously attained until 1479 at Oxford and until 1430/3 at
Cambridge.[5] While the bishops retained their legal rights over the
English Universities as institutions within the diocese for more than
two hundred years, throughout most of that time the chancellors
were the *de facto* heads of their universities and the elected
personifications of guild autonomy.

It is this rapid conversion of the English chancellors from their
situation as vicegerents of the diocesan to that of the highest
embodiment of university interests which above all differentiates
the English chancellorship from that of Paris and from the
equivalent episcopally dominated office of *scholasticus* or *primicerius*
found at many of the French provincial universities, such as
Orleans, Angers, Toulouse and Avignon.[6] It is true that there may

---

[4] For relations between the chancellors and the bishops of Lincoln and Ely, see
below, pp. 274 ff.

[5] For Oxford's dispensation of 1367 from the need for episcopal confirmation of
the chancellor-elect, see *Cal. Papal Registers (Papal Letters)*, iv (1362–96), p. 66,
with further confirmation of 1370, p. 83; for the equivalent dispensation of
1401 for Cambridge, see ibid., v (1396–1404), pp. 370–1. Oxford's contested
claim to complete exemption from ecclesiastical dominion derives from a bull of
Bonifacii IX of 1395, printed in *Snappe's Formulary*, pp. 144–6: the bull of Sixtus
IV of 1479, which conferred an unchallenged exemption, is printed by Wood,
The History and Antiquities of the University of Oxford, ed. cit., i. 632–5. For the
papal investigation into Cambridge's claims to ecclesiastical exemption set up in
1430 by Martin V and conducted by the prior of Barnwell as papal delegate, see
*Processus Barnwellensis ex mandato Martini Papae V cum bullis Johannis XXII et
Boniface IX*, dated 10 October 1430, CUL/UA, Luard, no. 108: a printed
translation is provided by J. Heywood, *Collection of Statutes for the University and
Colleges of Cambridge* (London, 1840), pp. 181 ff. Cambridge's claim to
exemption was upheld by the prior of Barnwell, and this conclusion was
confirmed by Pope Eugenius IV on 18 September 1433: this papal confirmation
is preserved in CUL/UA, Luard, no. 114; see also *Cal. Papal Registers (Papal
Letters)*, viii (1427–47), pp. 484–5.

[6] For the extent to which the Universities of Angers, Orleans and Avignon were
subject to the local bishops and their representatives, the *scholasticus* or

be some parallel between the Oxford and Cambridge chancellors and the medical chancellor of Montpellier. For the latter was not connected with a cathedral body, operated at a distance from the centre of episcopal power at Maguelone, and owed his election in part to the masters, being jointly elected by the bishop and three masters, of whom one had to be the senior.[7] In the event, however, the authority of the Montpellier chancellor was much more circumscribed than that of the English chancellors being largely confined to civil matters, while criminal and spiritual jurisdiction over masters and scholars and the granting of the teaching licence remained with the bishop.[8] It is apparent that among the officers of Europe's earliest universities the English chancellorship was *sui generis*. It combined in one person the headship of the university with some of the powers associated with a cathedral chancellor and some of the functions normally pertaining to the jurisdiction of an archdeacon.[9]

The Cambridge chancellorship seems to have been modelled largely upon that of Oxford. Both chancellors came to exercise an impressive array of spiritual, civil and criminal jurisdictions. This endowed them with a far more extensive authority than that enjoyed by their continental counterparts, including the chancellor and rector of Paris, the chancellor of Montpellier and the student rectors of Bologna.[10] Their spiritual jurisdiction was derived from the bishop of the diocese and was translated into the ecclesiastical

primicerius, see Cobban, 'Episcopal Control in the Mediaeval Universities of Northern Europe', art. cit., pp. 9–13; see also Rashdall, op. cit., ii. 155–8, 144–6, 175–8, and for the situation at Toulouse, where the *scholasticus* of the cathedral was to be styled chancellor, ibid., ii. 166, 170.

[7] See Rashdall's discussion, op. cit., ii. 123–4. For the electoral procedure of 1220, see Fournier, *Statuts*, ii. no. 882.

[8] Rashdall, op. cit., ii. 124; Hackett, *The Original Statutes of Cambridge University*, pp. 91–2.

[9] E.g. Hackett, op. cit., pp. 105, 108, and 'The University as a Corporate Body', pp. 70 ff., and Lawrence, 'The University in State and Church', pp. 106–10.

[10] On the authority of the English university chancellors, see the references in n. 2 above.

powers of the chancellor's court, which was conducted along canonical lines.[11] Through this court, the English chancellor exercised ordinary jurisdiction as judge ordinary (*iudex ordinarius*) of the bishop over all members of the academic community. These comprised clerical, lay and religious members and categories of 'privileged persons', who were university and college servants, the servants of masters and students, and certain tradesmen who served the university such as stationers, parchment-dealers, illuminators and bookbinders.[12]

A distinctive feature of both chancellorships is that their holders were invested with some of the capacities of an archdeacon — capacities which were presumably conferred upon them by the diocesan when these offices were first instituted.[13] Their archidiaconal powers over the scholars as clerks embraced such matters as discipline, the correction of morals, and probate of the wills of members of the university who died within its precincts. This aspect of the chancellor's authority did not entirely pass without challenge from the archdeacons of Oxford and Ely. But matters of contested jurisdiction at Cambridge in 1276 and at Oxford in 1346 were resolved largely in favour of the chancellors.[14]

[11] See e.g. Hackett, 'The University as a Corporate Body', p. 78, and *The Original Statutes of Cambridge University*, p. 109; Salter, *Registrum Cancellarii*, i. xxi.

[12] On 'privileged persons' at Oxford, see Lawrence, 'The University in State and Church', pp. 141–2; W. A. Pantin, *Oxford Life in Oxford Archives* (Oxford, 1972), p. 59; Salter, *Mediaeval Archives*, i. 92, and *Registrum Cancellarii*, i. xxxi-xxxiii; Kibre, *Scholarly Privileges in the Middle Ages*, pp. 280, 297. For 'privileged persons' at Cambridge, see H. E. Peek and C. P. Hall, *The Archives of the University of Cambridge* (Cambridge, 1962), pp. 47, 57–9; Dyer, *The Privileges of the University of Cambridge*, i. 86–8, 97–9. The concept of 'privileged persons' was common throughout the medieval universities.

[13] For the Oxford chancellor's archidiaconal powers, see e.g. Salter, *Registrum Cancellarii*, i. xv-xvii; for the equivalent situation at Cambridge, see Hackett, *The Original Statutes of Cambridge University*, pp. 108–9. On the office of the archdeacon of Ely, see *Vetus Liber Archidiaconi Eliensis* (ed. C. L. Feltoe and E. H. Minns, *C.A.S.*, Octavo Publications, xlviii, 1917), pp. xiii-xviii.

[14] For the Cambridge dispute, see Roach, 'The University of Cambridge', *V.C.H. Camb.* iii. 152–3: the terms of the settlement are printed in *Vetus Liber Archidiaconi Eliensis*, pp. 20–3, and in Fuller, *The History of the University of Cambridge*, ed. cit., pp. 47–51, and with an English version in Cooper, *Annals,*

It is probable that the archdeacon of Oxford had initially exercised jurisdiction over the town's grammar schools. After the establishment of the chancellorship, however, these schools and their masters and students came under the direct supervision of the chancellor, two salaried masters of arts being elected annually by the University for this directorial role from at least 1306.[15] At Cambridge, on the other hand, the archdeacon of Ely retained jurisdiction over the grammar schools, through his appointee, the master of glomery, who was the head or superintendent of the grammar schools, an office which persisted into the sixteenth century.[16] The master of glomery had cognizance of most cases where both parties were grammar students (*glomerelli*) and of most cases involving grammar students and townsmen. However, disputes between grammar students and members of the university were heard in the chancellor's court, as were cases involving the rents of houses and cases involving serious crimes.

As part of their commission, bestowed originally by the bishop and later regarded as inherent in their office, the chancellors of Oxford and Cambridge had, as one of their foremost prerogatives in imitation of cathedral chapters, the right to confer the teaching licence, that is, the licence to proceed to a degree which was completed by the fulfilment of academic exercises prescribed and supervised by masters of the relevant faculty. The chancellors could grant the licence only after the regent masters in the appropriate faculty had registered their consent by means of individual depositions as to the intellectual and moral suitability of the

---

i. 56–8. The Oxford altercation is discussed by Hackett, 'The University as a Corporate Body', p. 75: the text of the settlement of 1346 is printed in *Munimenta Academica*, i. 148–52. See also Rashdall, *Universities*, iii. 120–1, and Gibson, *Statuta Antiqua*, p. lxxi.

[15] The statute of 1306 is printed by Gibson, op. cit., p. 22: see also ibid., p. lxxxvi, and Rashdall, op. cit., iii. 346.

[16] On the master of glomery, see H. P. Stokes, 'The Mediaeval Hostels of the University of Cambridge', *C.A.S.*, Octavo Publications, xlix, 1924), pp. 49–56; *Vetus Liber Archidiaconi Eliensis*, pp. 289–91; Peacock, op. cit., pp. xxxii-xxxvi; Rashdall, op. cit., iii. 288. The few instances of archdeacons appointing schoolmasters to English grammar schools in the medieval period are discussed by Orme, *English Schools in the Middle Ages*, p. 146.

candidate for the degree.[17] This circumstance emphasizes the concord which existed between the chancellors and the regent masters over the awarding of degrees — a concord which ensured that the English Universities avoided the lengthy and often vitriolic conflicts which arose between, for example, the chancellor and the masters of Paris, especially in the first three decades of the thirteenth century.[18]

In addition to the ecclesiastical authority derived ultimately from the bishop, the English chancellors came to exercise a considerable amount of civil and criminal jurisdiction. This was built up intermittently from the reign of Henry III and was registered in a series of royal charters.[19] The chancellors thus became authorized to hear all civil suits, with the exception of cases dealing with freehold, not only between scholars but also between scholars and parties who were not university members, whether clerical or lay. Moreover, during the thirteenth century, the chancellors gradually acquired cognizance of all criminal cases arising within Oxford and Cambridge where one or both parties were scholars, with the exception of cases of murder and maiming, which were to be heard before the royal judges. At Oxford in 1406, however, even this exception was waived for lay servants and other dependants of the scholars who could now be tried for felonious crime by a special

[17] For the statutory regulations governing depositions at Oxford, see Gibson, *Statuta Antiqua*, pp. 28–31; for Cambridge, see Hackett, *The Original Statutes of Cambridge University*, pp. 121–2, 277, and *Camb. Docs.*, i. 360–1, 361–2, 375–8.

[18] See e.g. Cobban, *The Medieval Universities*, pp. 82–4; Leff, *Paris and Oxford Universities in the Thirteenth and Fourteenth Centuries*, pp. 20–34.

[19] For royal charters granting privileges to Oxford University to *c*.1500, see Kibre, *Scholarly Privileges in the Middle Ages*, pp. 268–324, and Lawrence, 'The University in State and Church', pp. 125–50. Many of the charters issued by the crown to Oxford University between the thirteenth and sixteenth century are printed by Salter, *Mediaeval Archives*, i. 1–274. Some of the texts of royal charters granted to Cambridge from the reign of Henry III to that of James I are printed by Dyer, *The Privileges of the University of Cambridge*, i. 5–53. The earliest extant document in Cambridge University Archives is the grant of Henry III of 7 February 1266 to the chancellor and scholars allowing an assessment every five years of the rents of houses to be inhabited by scholars to be made by a joint committee of two masters and two burgesses: CUL/UA, Luard, no. 1.

court presided over by a university seneschal or steward appointed by the chancellor.[20] Clerks accused of a felony were to continue to be tried by royal judges before being handed over to the bishop for ecclesiastical sentence. After the Reformation, when clerks could no longer claim the privilege of lenient ecclesiastical sentencing following conviction in a secular court, the provisions which had been made in 1406 in favour of lay members of the university were extended to cover the whole academic population with respect to charges of felony and treason.[21] Similar arrangements existed at Cambridge and these were fully endorsed by Elizabeth in 1561.[22] This combined civil and criminal jurisdiction rendered the English chancellors a powerful judicial presence within their university towns and caused considerable friction with the burgesses throughout the medieval period. The entrenchment of the Universities in urban affairs was further extended when the chancellor of Oxford in 1355 and the chancellor of Cambridge in 1382, after a phase of limited involvement, attained sole custody of the assize of bread, wine and ale, the supervision of weights and measures and the general regulation of market trading in the town and suburbs.[23] The control of the Oxford and Cambridge markets may have worked to the protective advantage of ordinary clerical and lay consumers.[24] It also realized a useful university income

[20] The charter of 1406 is printed by Salter, *Mediaeval Archives*, i. 231–4: see the comments of Rashdall, op. cit., iii. 103–5; Lawrence, 'The University in State and Church', p. 141.

[21] Rashdall, op. cit., iii. 105.

[22] Peek and Hall, *The Archives of the University of Cambridge*, pp. 48–9.

[23] The royal charter of 1355 for Oxford University is printed by Salter, op. cit., i. 152–7; the royal charter of 1382 for Cambridge University is printed by Dyer, op. cit., i. 82–4, and is summarized in English by Cooper, *Annals*, i. 124–5. See also Salter, *Registrum Cancellarii*, i. xv, and Peek and Hall, op. cit., pp. 55–7. Salter, *Mediaeval Archives*, ii. 130–267, has printed the rolls of the courts held in Oxford between 1309 and 1351 which dealt with the assize of bread and ale along with one roll for the assay of weights and measures. Although these rolls belong to the period before the Oxford chancellor assumed complete control over these matters, they presumably give a good insight into the nature of the business with which the chancellor was concerned after he acquired sole custody of the assize.

[24] This at least is the verdict of Salter, *Medieval Oxford*, p. 57.

through the collection of fines for infringements of trading standards. But the dominant economic function of the English chancellors, as with their judicial role, gave rise to long-term difficulties with the mayor and burgesses. It is probable that the English Universities were the most economically protected of the medieval universities. This is symptomatic of the continuous solicitude of the English monarchs for the detailed well-being of their academic subjects — a solicitude which was not easily matched in continental Europe.

The chancellor of an English university had at his disposal a formidable armoury of weapons for the enforcement of the university statutes and the decisions of his court.[25] At both Oxford and Cambridge, the chancellor could deprive academics of their degrees or prevent them from taking them or withdraw the licence from regent masters and bachelors. For clerks and laymen alike, he could impose an impressive hierarchy of fines. He also had the power of expelling miscreants from the university town and suburbs for a specified duration, ranging from one or two months to a number of years. For more serious offenders, and especially those who contumaciously refused to appear before his court, the chancellor could authorize the penalty of banishment. In addition, as an ecclesiastical judge, the chancellor, with the aid of the secular arm and with certain restrictions, was empowered to pass sentence of excommunication on recalcitrant members of the university and on recalcitrant townspeople.[26] Committal to prison was another option available to the chancellor. He used for this purpose in Oxford and Cambridge either the town prison or the castle, although it should be emphasized that the terms of imprisonment were generally confined to one or several days.[27] As a guardian of

---

[25] On the range of penalties available to the Oxford chancellor, see e.g. Salter, *Registrum Cancellarii*, i. xv-xxvi; for the similar penalties at Cambridge, see Hackett, *The Original Statutes of Cambridge University*, index under *Chancellor, University, powers*.

[26] For the Oxford chancellor and the procedure of excommunication, see *Snappe's Formulary*, pp. 22–9.

[27] Unlike the Paris chancellor, who possessed his own prison until prohibited to do so in 1231 (Rashdall, op. cit., i. 338), the English chancellors always had to rely upon prison accommodation provided by the king or by the town.

moral standards within the university town, the chancellor had the right to inquire into the lives of scholars and citizens suspected of immorality. Because immoral behaviour was often closely linked with disturbances of the peace — one of the chancellor's principal areas of concern — much attention was paid to keepers of immoral houses and the activities of prostitutes. These were liable to a range of penalties, including expulsion from the town for a stipulated period, complete banishment, imprisonment, or even a spell on the pillory.[28] Given the remarkable range of the chancellor's responsibilities, embracing civil, criminal, economic and moral offences, it is understandable that the ecclesiastical and secular sources of his authority became increasingly blurred. A stage was reached in the later medieval period when the chancellor's multifarious authority came to be regarded as an indivisible whole rather than as a mere aggregate of a series of separate jurisdictions.

From one point of view, the growth of the English Universities may be monitored with reference to the establishment and extension of the chancellor's jurisdiction at the expense of episcopal and archiepiscopal authority and the common-law system as represented by the royal justices and the borough courts of Oxford and Cambridge. In this expansionist drive, the English chancellors were firmly advanced by the piecemeal support of both the crown and the papacy. Protection necessary to ensure the continuance of the universities while they were in their unstable state in the early thirteenth century resulted in the creation of a highly privileged headship unique in the medieval universities.

As has been said, from an early stage the English university chancellors were elected by the masters' guild. There were, however, differences in procedure as between Oxford and Cambridge. At Oxford, according to a statute of *a*. 1313,[29] the chancellor was elected normally from the doctors of theology and canon law[30] by an indirect system of voting: that is to say, he was

[28] An illuminating view of the Oxford chancellor's activities as a guardian of morals in the fifteenth century is supplied by Salter, *Registrum Cancellarii*, i. xvii-xix: there appears to be no source for Cambridge comparable to this valuable register of the acts of the Oxford chancellor.

[29] Gibson, *Statuta Antiqua*, p. 64: see also pp. xxxvii, lxxii-lxxiii.

[30] There were exceptions: see ibid., p. lxxii, n. 16.

elected by the majority decision of a committee of two proctors and eight regent masters, the latter, one from each of the four superior faculties and four from the faculty of arts, being nominated by the proctors. At Cambridge, on the other hand, by *c.* 1250, the chancellor was elected by the direct vote of all the regent masters or at least a majority of them.[31] In the fourteenth-century statutes, this procedure was refined to the extent that the chancellor was to be elected by all the regents as long as there were twelve regents in arts. Failing this, the chancellor was to be elected by the majority of all the regents and non-regents.[32] Although not stipulated, it seems that, as at Oxford, the Cambridge chancellor was usually a doctor of canon law or theology.[33] It is of some remark that having set up the chancellorship at Cambridge in imitation of Oxford the Cambridge legislators proceeded to devise an electoral system unlike that of Oxford and, in some ways, more democratic than it. By a statute of 1322, the tenure of the Oxford chancellorship was limited to two years,[34] although this restriction was not always observed. An equivalent statute for Cambridge is no longer extant, but it can be deduced that before 1337 at the latest the tenure of the Cambridge chancellorship was likewise limited to a two-year period.[35] From the second half of the fifteenth century, however, the English chancellorships were radically transformed by virtue of the fact that chancellors became non-resident dignitaries, and were increasingly selected for the political influence which they could exercise in the university's favour. Their term of office came to extend well beyond the statutory limit and this resulted eventually in its becoming a life tenure.[36]

The first non-resident chancellor of Oxford was George Neville, who, at various times, was bishop of Exeter, archbishop of York

[31] Hackett, *The Original Statutes of Cambridge University*, pp. 79, 197.

[32] *Camb. Docs.*, i. 309–10.

[33] Hackett, op. cit., p. 106.

[34] Gibson, op. cit., pp. 121–3.

[35] Hackett, op. cit., pp. 247–8.

[36] See e.g. M. H. Curtis, *Oxford and Cambridge in Transition 1558–1642* (Oxford, 1959), p. 23; also Mallet, *A History of the University of Oxford*, i. 328–32.

and Lord Chancellor, and whose second period as university chancellor lasted from 1463 until 1472. John Russell, Lord Chancellor and bishop of Lincoln, was elected Oxford chancellor in 1483 and was the first to hold the office for life. At Cambridge, Thomas Rotheram, who at various times was bishop of Rochester, bishop of Lincoln, archbishop of York, keeper of the privy seal, and Lord Chancellor from 1474 until his deprivation in 1483, was university chancellor from 1469 to 1471 and from 1473 to at least 1492 and was the first non-resident holder of the office. John Fisher, bishop of Rochester, was elected to the Cambridge chancellorship in 1504 and was the first to hold that position for life.[37]

The change in the character of the English university chancellorships which began in the second half of the fifteenth century proved to be a two-edged sword. The change presumably came about because it was advantageous to have as chancellor a prominent personage close to the centre of political power, but in the sixteenth century the chancellorship was to be one of the several instruments whereby the crown was to subject the universities to a substantial measure of direct royal control,[38] a process which Paris University had undergone in the fifteenth century.[39] Perhaps nothing so marks the transition of the English Universities from their evolving position as autonomous corporations before *c.* 1500 to their more straitened position as agents of the centralist Tudor state than the externalization of the chancellorship. From being the very symbol of academic autonomy over almost three hundred

---

[37] For Neville, see Emden, *B.R.U.O.*, ii. 1347–9, and Salter, *Registrum Cancellarii*, i. xxxviii, and for Russell see *B.R.U.O.*, iii. 1609–11, and Mallet, op. cit., i. 331. Russell died in 1494. For Rotheram, see Emden, *A Biographical Register of the University of Cambridge to 1500* (Cambridge, 1963), pp. 489–91. On Fisher's election to the chancellorship and his execution in 1535 while chancellor, see Mullinger, *The University of Cambridge*, i. 441–2, 628–9. Much information on Fisher and Cambridge is provided ibid., i. 423–629; see also Emden, *B.R.U.C.*, pp. 229–30.

[38] See e.g. Curtis, op. cit., pp. 23–9.

[39] Cobban, *The Medieval Universities*, pp. 94–5, and J. Verger, 'The University of Paris at the End of the Hundred Years War', *Universities in Politics: Case Studies from the Late Middle Ages and Early Modern Period* (ed. J. W. Baldwin and R. A. Goldthwaite, Baltimore, 1972), pp. 47 ff.

years, the chancellors became in the sixteenth and seventeenth centuries, in general, appointees closely identified with the interests of the crown, which stamped its authority upon the universities as royal institutions through direct interventions in university affairs and by means of the control of university appointments and promotions. For the implementation of such a policy of conditioning the universities to the royal will, the need to secure a succession of pliable chancellors was clearly of fundamental concern.

The growing absenteeism of the chancellors from the second half of the fifteenth century increased the importance of the office of vice-chancellor, which, from this time, began to be established as the office of the permanent *de facto* heads of the English Universities.[40] From the early thirteenth century, the chancellors were empowered to delegate their authority to deputies. At Oxford before *c.* 1500, there could be several of these deputies or commissaries. From *c.* 1520, however, there seems to have been only one commissary or vice-chancellor.[41] The title of 'vice-chancellor' was in fairly common usage from *c.* 1450, although it was not officially adopted in Oxford until 1549.[42] If the Oxford chancellorship became vacant before the occupant had completed his term of office, his responsibilities were assumed not by a commissary, but by the senior regent in theology, or failing this, the next in seniority, the acting chancellor being styled the *cancellarius natus*.[43] Apart from his commissaries (or, after *c.* 1520, his commissary), the Oxford chancellor had lesser deputies, in the form of the *hebdomadarii*.[44] These officials were originally drawn from the regents in law: later they were taken from the ranks of the law bachelors. The *hebdomadarii* deputized for the chancellor or his commissary in his weekly court for the purpose of hearing minor

---

[40] Salter, *Snappe's Formulary*, p. 335; Hackett, op. cit., p. 114.

[41] Salter, *Registrum Cancellarii*, i. xxxviii-xxxix: for statutory references to commissaries, see Gibson, *Statuta Antiqua*, pp. 84, 277–8.

[42] Gibson, op. cit., p. lxxiv.

[43] For the *cancellarius natus*, see Salter, *Registrum Cancellarii*, i. xlii-xliv; Gibson, op. cit., p. lxxiv.

[44] Gibson, op. cit., pp. lxxviii, 90. The *hebdomadarii* were functioning by 1267: Salter, *Mediaeval Archives*, i. 27.

judicial cases. The bachelor judges were organized on a rotational basis, each bachelor sitting for a week and the choice alternating between a canonist and a civilian. In order to expedite the judicial process, the *hebdomadarii* were required to decide cases within three days, under penalty of fine. They did not, however, have competence to hear cases involving regents, which were reserved for the chancellor or his commissary. At Cambridge, the chancellor's substitute or vicar had been formally designated 'vice-chancellor' by 1275 or 1276.[45] The Cambridge vice-chancellor had the full authority of the chancellor during his absence. His court had the same standing as that of the chancellor. He could excommunicate, award the teaching licence and preside over the important assemblies of the university.[46] The Cambridge vice-chancellor was, in effect, a near equivalent of the Oxford commissary. The term 'commissary' was also employed at Cambridge, but there it referred to the official who looked after the routine of the chancellor's court and whose functions bore some affinity to that of the Oxford *hebdomadarii*.[47] As already indicated, the vice-chancellorship became a permanent office at both English Universities from the late fifteenth century in response to the vacuum created by the phenomenon of non-resident chancellors.

In association with the chancellor, the proctors were the chief executive officials of the medieval English Universities.[48] They

---

[45] See W. Ullmann, 'The Decline of the Chancellor's Authority in Medieval Cambridge: a Rediscovered Statute', *Historical Journal*, i (1958), pp. 176 ff. at p. 182: the term used for vice-chancellor in this statute is *vicecancellarius*.

[46] Hackett, *The Original Statutes of Cambridge University*, pp. 113–14.

[47] Ibid., p. 112.

[48] On the Oxford proctors, see Gibson, op. cit., pp. lxxiv-lxxvii; Rashdall, *Universities*, iii. 53–4, 57–60, 62, 145–7; Hackett, 'The University as a Corporate Body', *The History of the University of Oxford*, i. 82–5; Mallet, *A History of the University of Oxford*, i. 175; Leff, *Paris and Oxford Universities in the Thirteenth and Fourteenth Centuries*, pp. 100–1; P. Kibre, *The Nations in the Mediaeval Universities* (Mediaeval Academy of America, Cambridge, Massachusetts, 1948), pp. 161–3; Pantin, *Oxford Life in Oxford Archives*, pp. 76–84. For the Cambridge proctors, see Hackett, *The Original Statutes of Cambridge University*, pp. 152–8, and index under *Proctors, University* and *Rectors (Proctors), University; Grace Book A* (ed. S. M. Leathes, *C.A.S.*, Luard Memorial Series, i, Cambridge, 1897), pp. xxxiv-xxxv; Rashdall, op. cit., iii. 280, n. 1, 286; Mullinger, *The University of Cambridge*, i. 144.

were initially known as 'rectors'. At Oxford, this nomenclature was largely superseded by 'proctor' from the mid-thirteenth century, but it was still fairly common at Cambridge until the late fourteenth century.[49] In both Universities, the office of proctor appears to have originated in that of taxor, which was probably the earliest of the university offices.[50] At some point before the mid-thirteenth century at Oxford and between *c.* 1255 and *c.* 1268 at Cambridge, the office of taxor was separated from that of proctor.[51] Subsequently, the proctors acquired a vast array of functions and became the principal administrative officers, second in importance to the chancellor.

It may be that the office of proctor in the English Universities was suggested by that of Paris University, where the proctors were the elected heads of the four nations of the faculty of arts.[52] There is no clear evidence that the proctors of Oxford were the constitutional heads of the rather amorphous two nations which certainly persisted there until amalgamated in 1274, although they were elected on a north–south basis, in conformity with the regional division of the nations.[53] At Cambridge, there does not appear to have been a constitutional division into nations, but a natural sense of cleavage prevailed between northerners and southerners and the basis of the election of the proctors, as at Oxford, may have reflected this scission.[54] The fundamental difference between the proctors of Paris University and those of England, however, is that whereas the former were essentially officers of the faculty of arts the English proctors were executive

---

[49] Hackett, 'The University as a Corporate Body', p. 82, and *The Original Statutes of Cambridge University*, pp. 152, 204-7. The earliest statutory reference at Oxford to 'proctors of the university' dates from 1252: Gibson, op. cit., p. 86; the terms 'chancellor and proctors' are, however, used in a grant of privileges made to the University by Henry III in 1248, *Mediaeval Archives*, i. 18–19.

[50] Rashdall, op. cit., iii. 47, 172.

[51] Hackett, *The Original Statutes of Cambridge University*, p. 153.

[52] Rashdall, op. cit., iii. 56 ff.

[53] Hackett, 'The University as a Corporate Body', p. 65, n. 3.

[54] Hackett, *The Original Statutes of Cambridge University*, p. 154.

agents for the university as a whole. As in the case of the chancellor, there was a difference in the mode of election of the proctors as between Oxford and Cambridge. At Oxford, the proctors were elected by the regents in arts using an indirect voting procedure. That is, the senior northern regent in arts and the senior southern regent in arts nominated six electors, who then elected the two proctors. One of the proctors was known as the senior proctor and the other as the junior proctor, the distinction being apparently based upon academic seniority. This procedure had been modified by 1313 to the extent that all the regents in arts were now to elect two nominators of electors, who were to elect six masters, whose task was to elect the two proctors.[55] It has often been remarked that the senior proctor at Oxford was generally a southerner.[56] There is, however, no known statutory requirement for his being so.[57] Cambridge avoided such a convoluted system of indirect election, and the two proctors were elected from among the masters of arts by means of a method of direct voting. For at least part of the thirteenth century, the voting constituency comprised not only regents in arts but also the regents in theology and canon law. This means that from the start the Cambridge proctors, or rectors as they first were, were very pointedly the executive agents of the entire university corporation.[58] By the early fourteenth century, the voting constituency had contracted and typically comprised only the regent masters in arts, although the non-regents in arts were to assist in the election if the number of regents in arts fell short of twelve or if the regents in arts reached an electoral impasse.[59] The

[55] For the original and revised method of election of the proctors, see Gibson, *Statuta Antiqua*, pp. xxxix, lxxvi, 64–6. On the distinction between the senior and junior proctor, see A. B. Emden, 'Northerners and Southerners in the Organization of the University to 1509', *Oxford Studies presented to Daniel Callus* (Oxf. Hist. Soc., new series, xvi, 1964), pp. 1 ff. at p. 18.

[56] E.g. Gibson, op. cit., p. lxxiv, n. 11 and Pantin, *Oxford Life in Oxford Archives*, p. 77.

[57] Emden, op. cit., p. 18. Kibre, *The Nations in the Mediaeval Universities*, p. 162, states that a statute of 1304 provides evidence for the seniority of the southern proctor: this appears to be an error, for no such statute seems to exist.

[58] Hackett, *The Original Statutes of Cambridge University*, pp. 153–4, 204–5.

[59] *Camb. Docs.*, i. 338–9.

title of 'senior proctor' at Cambridge was bestowed upon the regent who received the most votes in the election, the designation of 'junior proctor' being conferred on his less-successful companion.[60] According to fourteenth-century material, the proctors at both Universities held office for a year and were eligible for re-election.[61]

The activities of the proctors were exceedingly heterogeneous, and they were manifestly omnipresent figures in the daily life of the English Universities.[62] In an overall sense, they were responsible, along with the chancellor, for the execution of the whole range of their university's public business. They supervised the academic regime, including the timetable and the ordering of lectures, disputations and inceptions; they organized university ceremonies and the funerals and liturgical functions of members of the masters' guild; they enforced university discipline, reported offenders to the chancellor and kept the names of disturbers of the peace, murderers, and anyone who had been excluded from the town or sent to prison by order of the chancellor's court; and, on behalf of the chancellor, they helped in the regulation of business relations between the townspeople and the scholars in an effort to defend the latter against economic malpractices, such as the use of inaccurate weights and measures, the sale of inedible victuals and the maintenance of

---

[60] Ibid., i. 339.

[61] For the annual election of proctors at Oxford, see Gibson, *Statuta Antiqua*, pp. 64–5, and for the possibility of re-election, pp. 133–4; for the annual election of proctors at Cambridge and the limitation of tenure to two consecutive years, see *Camb. Docs.*, i. 338–9. A list of the Oxford proctors who held office between 1267–8 and 1509–10 is printed in Emden, 'Northerners and Southerners in the Organization of the University to 1509', pp. 19–28: a list of Cambridge proctors from 1451–2 to 1488–9 is printed in *Grace Book A*, ed. cit., pp. xxxv–vi, and a list of proctors from 1488–9 to 1510–11 is printed in *Grace Book B Part i* (ed. M. Bateson, *C.A.S.*, Luard Memorial Series, ii, Cambridge, 1903), p. xxii.

[62] For the statutory duties of the Oxford proctors, see Gibson, op. cit., pp. lxxv–vi, 66, 67, 197–8; further references to their duties are scattered throughout the early fourteenth-century statutes, for example, at pp. 28–30, 57–9, 68, 73, 88, 96, 107, 123–6, 182, 187, 195–6, 211–12. For the statutory duties of the Cambridge proctors, see *Camb. Docs.*, i. 340, 341, 342, 343–5, 345–6, 346–7, 348–9.

artificially high prices arising from an assortment of monopolistic practices.

At Oxford, the proctors played a major role in the conduct of university assemblies, even though there is some statutory divergence as to whether the chancellor or the proctors had the exclusive right to summon the congregation of regents.[63] It is probable that at Oxford the right to call a congregation of regents was normally the combined concern of the chancellor and the proctors,[64] the latter summoning a congregation after consultation with the chancellor and advising him on the agenda.[65] A statute of 1322 demonstrates that in certain circumstances the chancellor or the proctors alone could summon a congregation if they could not agree to do so jointly.[66] The statute enacted that if a dissension arose among the regent masters which necessitated the calling of a congregation and either the chancellor or the proctors refused to comply, then the willing party was obliged unilaterally to summon the assembly. The statute further enacted that if the matter was so grave that a congregation of the regents and non-regents, that is, of the sovereign body, was required, then the proctors alone had the authority to summon such a meeting if the chancellor proved unwilling and vice-versa. It would seem, therefore, that at Oxford the chancellor and proctors held a watching brief over each other with respect to the calling of congregations, but that, typically, the proctors took the leading role in the matter. The situation was very different at Cambridge, where, in normal circumstances, the chancellor alone summoned all congregations.[67] It is true that by a

---

[63] A statute of 1257 suggests that the proctors had the right to summon congregation, but in a statute of *a.* 1313 this appears to belong to the chancellor: Gibson, op. cit., pp. 57, 108.

[64] Congregations in 1434 and 1460 were summoned by the chancellor and proctors combined: Gibson, op. cit., p. 256; *The Register of Congregation 1448–1463* (ed. W. A. Pantin and W. T. Mitchell, Oxf. Hist. Soc., new series, xxii, 1972), p. 357.

[65] In a statute of *a.* 1313, it is clearly stipulated that the proctors must explain to the chancellor the need for the summoning of congregation: Gibson, op. cit., p. 67.

[66] Gibson, op. cit., p. 123

[67] Hackett, *The Original Statutes of Cambridge University*, p. 144.

statute of 1275 or 1276, already referred to in connection with the office of vice-chancellor, the proctors were authorized to convoke the regents if the chancellor failed to deal with certain offences committed against regent masters.[68] And the argument has been advanced that this statute marked a fundamental change in the balance of power within the University, whereby the previously sole jurisdictional authority of the chancellor was now vested in the assembly of regents, which henceforth, through its representatives, the proctors, exercised supreme dominion within the University.[69] But the impact of this statute was, in effect, far more limited. It merely provided the regents with a remedy against a chancellor who did not adequately assure their protection. Throughout the medieval period, the chancellor continued, in normal circumstances, to summon meetings of the regents and non-regents, a right reinforced by statutory authority in the early fourteenth century.[70] Although the Cambridge proctors were similar to those of Oxford with regard to the range and nature of their functions, they did not have an equivalent standing in the matter of the preliminaries attendant upon the summoning of university assemblies.

In the absence of professional administrators specializing in university finance, the proctors served as the principal financial officers of the English Universities and they had to render annual account of income and expenditure. Only fifteen audited proctors' accounts are extant for medieval Oxford, extending from 1464 to 1496,[71] although an informal list of payments and gifts received by the junior proctor John Arundel has survived for the period between April 1426 and April 1427.[72] For Cambridge, the extant

---

[68] Ullman, 'The Decline of the Chancellor's Authority in Medieval Cambridge: a Rediscovered Statute', art. cit., p. 181.

[69] Ibid., pp. 176–80.

[70] Hackett, op. cit., pp. 144–5, 315.

[71] These accounts are edited by Salter, *Mediaeval Archives*, ii. 272–358.

[72] A. B. Emden, 'The remuneration of the mediaeval proctors of the University of Oxford', *Oxoniensia*, xxvi/vii (1961/2), pp. 202 ff.: Arundel's accounts are printed, pp. 205–6.

proctors' accounts are virtually continuous from 1454.[73] They are contained in the 'proctors' books', and they differ from those of Oxford in so far as they are not final accounts as processed by the university auditors, although statements of the auditors have been occasionally inserted in them.[74] As a result, the Cambridge accounts are less systematized and more detailed than the Oxford accounts. They sometimes contain material, such as letters or statutes, not strictly germane to the business of accounting.[75] It is only for about half the period covered that any kind of reliable overview of income and expenditure can be obtained.

It is not possible to make accurate assessments of the income and expenditure of the English Universities before these earliest extant proctors' accounts of the fifteenth century. For several decades after they came into being, Oxford and Cambridge, as corporations, had little in the way of endowments and only a meagre income and modest expenditure. In the 1240s, Oxford still had no real property, and its annual income was probably less than £5.[76] From the 1250s, it acquired, in piecemeal fashion, urban property within Oxford and its suburbs in the form of academic halls, tenements and rents, mostly given by donors who had some connection with the University.[77] In the last quarter of the thirteenth century, the University's income rose to about £20 per annum.[78] In *c.* 1320, the University was in the position to erect its first purpose-built structure, the congregation house, which was financed by money given by Thomas Cobham, bishop of Worcester. Cobham also bequeathed to the University his manuscript collection, and this

---

[73] The accounts for 1454–5 to 1487–8 are printed by Leathes, *Grace Book A,* and for 1488–9 to 1510–11 by Bateson, *Grace Book B Part i.*

[74] *Grace Book A,* pp. 131–2, 156–7.

[75] E.g. see the letters in *Grace Book A* to Richard, duke of Gloucester, pp. 158–9, 171–2, and to the chancellor of England, pp. 157–8; and for a statute of 1458, see pp. 13–14.

[76] T. H. Aston and R. Faith, 'The Endowments of the University and Colleges to *c.* 1348', *The History of the University of Oxford,* i. 268.

[77] Ibid., pp. 270 ff.

[78] Ibid., p. 273: see also Salter, *Mediaeval Archives,* i. 314, 323–4.

was to be kept in the upper room of the congregation house and was to form the basis of a university library. Because of unforseen difficulties, the library did not come into regular use until 1412.[79] From the 1420s to the 1480s the University was much preoccupied with raising money for an exceedingly elaborate scheme, the building of the Divinity School, which when built incorporated in its upper chamber the bequest of just under 300 manuscripts given by Humphrey, duke of Gloucester. Many of these manuscripts were of primary importance for Greek and Latin humanist learning. They were received in instalments between 1435 and 1450.[80] This new library was designed to supersede Cobham's library, although they coexisted as complementary for some considerable time. The building of the Divinity School and of permanent accommodation for schools in other faculties, including the range built in *c.* 1440 containing seven schools for the liberal arts and three for the separate philosophies — moral, natural and metaphysical[81] — is a pointer to the transformation of the University from one functioning in scattered premises to one operating in purpose-built structures concentrated according to need.[82] While these building enterprises depended upon subscriptions from individual benefactors made in response to appeals,[83] the University still had to

[79] On Cobham's bequest and his plan for a library, see Aston and Faith, op. cit., pp. 272–3: for the statute of 1367 concerning the disposition of Cobham's collection, see Gibson, *Statuta Antiqua,* pp. 165–6, and for the regulations of 1412 governing the university library, pp. 216–21.

[80] On the building of the Divinity School and Duke Humphrey's bequest, see Mallet, *A History of the University of Oxford,* i. 314–21 and Pantin, *Oxford Life in Oxford Archives,* p. 35. Lists of the books given by Duke Humphrey are printed in *Munimenta Academica,* ii. 758–72, and *Epistolae Academicae Oxoniensis* (2 vols., ed. H. Anstey, Oxf. Hist. Soc., xxxv–vi, 1898), i. 179–84, 204–5, 232–7.

[81] Pantin, op. cit., p. 35.

[82] See the comments of Pantin, 'The Conception of the Universities in England in the period of the Renaissance', *Les Universités Européenes du xiv*ᵉ *au xviii*ᵉ *siècle* (L'Institut d'Histoire de la Faculté des Lettres de l'Université de Genève, 4, Geneva, 1967), pp. 101 ff. at p. 104.

[83] The University approached both individuals and corporate bodies in the quest for money and materials for the building of the Divinity School: see e.g. the letters to the Benedictine monks, the master of St Thomas's Hospital, London, Edmund Reed, Esquire, and Thomas Kempe, bishop of London, *Epistolae*

find a sizeable amount of money from its own resources. This implies rising levels of income and expenditure in the fifteenth century.

The fifteenth-century proctors' accounts for Oxford which survive, that is, those between 1464 and 1496, indicate that current income fluctuated from a peak of £98 9s. 3d. in 1469–70 to a low point of £35 0s. 10d. in 1492–3, and give an average in the region of £70 per annum.[84] It has to be affirmed, however, that in addition to current income the University had fairly substantial capital assets in the form of endowed loan-chests, at least twenty of which were established between 1240 and 1500.[85] Expenditure ranged from £87 18s. 3d. in 1469–70 to £34 3s. 7½d. in 1492–3,[86] suggesting an annual average of about £61.[87]

Of the sources of current university income, the most profitable was realized from the payment of degree fees, which averaged about £26 a year,[88] and which were surprisingly high, especially for doctoral degrees.[89] These fees, which varied according to the means

Academicae Oxoniensis, i. 20–2, 28–9, 321; ii. 429–30. Thomas Kempe gave 1,000 marks and this was the donation which made possible the completion of the Divinity School, the construction of which had been phased over fifty years.

[84] Salter, *Mediaeval Archives,* ii. 298, 346. I differ from Salter, who gives an average income of about £58 (ibid., ii. 272), which appears to be inaccurate. Salter's figure has been reproduced by several historians: e.g. Pantin, *Oxford Life in Oxford Archives,* p. 80.

[85] Aston and Faith, 'The Endowments of the University and Colleges to *c.* 1348', p. 283, estimate that the capital value of the University's loan-chests by 1360 was approximately £1,300.

[86] Salter, op. cit., ii. 300, 348.

[87] Salter states that the average annual expenditure was less than £45 (ibid., ii. 272), but, as in the case of his figure for average annual income, this estimate seems to be much too low: it is reproduced by Pantin, *Oxford Life in Oxford Archives,* p. 80. The University was in credit in twelve and in deficit in three of the fifteen years covered by the accounts: the years of deficit were 1471–2, 1474–5 and 1477–8.

[88] Salter, op. cit., ii. 274.

[89] On admission to the doctoral degrees in theology, 2 secular masters paid £20 each in 1469–70; 2 friars paid £10 each in 1472–3; 1 friar paid £10 in 1474–5; 4 friars paid a collective fee of £26 13s. 4d. in 1481–2; and 1 friar paid £6 13s. 4d. in 1496–7: see Salter, op. cit., ii. 298, 306, 314, 330, 355.

and status of the candidate, were mainly composition fees paid in lieu of giving a feast for the regents in the faculty, which was a statutory requirement for taking a degree.[90] In addition to the composition fees, a small amount of revenue was raised through the payment of degree fees known as 'commons' for those assuming a doctoral degree in any faculty and 'semi-commons' for those proceeding to the bachelor's degree in any faculty. The size of these sums, which varied, was apparently based upon the size of the weekly commons which a candidate for a degree had been accustomed to pay in his place of residence within the University.[91] Next in profitability to that of degree fees was the income from graces, which were dispensations from the statutory conditions for degrees, either by the omission or by the abridgement of requirements. Not all graces had monetary conditions attached, but the University generated a considerable sum from graces involving payment. For example, the University derived from this quarter just over £35 in 1469–70 and the same amount in 1478–9.[92] The

---

[90] Gibson, *Statuta Antiqua*, pp. 244–5, 290–1. Composition fees were usually paid by candidates for the doctorate in the superior faculties, masters of arts, it seems, preferring to provide the banquet: *The Register of Congregation 1448–1463*, pp. xxiii–iv.

[91] On this point, see Salter, op. cit., ii. 275: for receipts of degree fees known as 'commons' or 'semi-commons' in the proctors' accounts, see ibid., ii. 294, 298, 306, 310, 314, 317, 321, 326, 330, 336, 341, 346, 350, 355 (these receipts are recorded as composite sums and are not differentiated according to individual contributions). This type of degree fee also occurs in the mid-fifteenth-century register of congregation: *The Register of Congregation 1448–1463*, p. xxiii.

[92] Salter, op. cit., ii. 298, 321. Thomas Gascoigne, who was Oxford's chancellor in the early 1440s, in his *Loci e Libro Veritatum*, written between the 1430s and *c.* 1457, criticized the regent masters and proctors for abusing their power of dispensing from the statutes by granting graces too easily, for financial gain: T. Gascoigne, *Loci e Libro Veritatum* (ed. J. E. T. Rogers, Oxford, 1881), p. 3, and Gibson, op. cit., p. xxvi, n. 1. It is true that at the period of Gascoigne's writing the University was exploring every avenue to raise money for the building of the Divinity School, and that the revenue to be had from graces made a salient contribution: see *The Register of Congregation 1448–1463*, index under *Divinity schools, grace-money, assigned to*. Nonetheless, a study of the graces as set out in the Register of Congregation extending from 1448 to 1463 (*Registrum Aa*), where the graces are mostly given in full, does not altogether bear out Gascoigne's charge of excessive laxity: ibid., p. xxvi.

lesser sources of income itemized in the proctors' accounts were the rents of urban property; the payments of Eynsham and Oseney Abbeys; fines such as those for disturbances of the peace; moneys from the keepers of grammar schools in Oxford; and small sums from miscellaneous areas.[93]

The University's expenditure, as registered in the accounts, embraced a lavish annual entertainment for graduates; an annual distribution of money to the regent masters; a feast for the auditors of the accounts; sundry expenses and allowances for the chancellor, proctors and bedels; the payment of a number of rents; salaries paid to the registrar and to the chaplain-librarian; payments to the parish clerk of St Mary's Church; entertainment for visiting royalty; expenses in connection with the confirmation of the University's privileges; and payments towards the diverse building ventures.[94]

Estimates of the income and expenditure of Cambridge University are scarcely feasible for the period before 1454, when the series of extant proctors' accounts began. In parallel with Oxford, but a shade earlier, Cambridge launched a costly building programme, which extended from the late fourteenth century to the 1470s. This proved to be a severe drain on university finances. By 1400, the northern range of the Schools Quadrangle, containing the Divinity School and the Regent House, had been completed; the western range, comprising a school of canon law with a library above, had been built by 1438; the southern range, encompassing schools of arts and civil law and a library, was erected between 1458 and 1470 or 1471; and the eastern range, with rooms for legal and administrative purposes and another library, was built between 1470 and 1473.[95] As in the case of Oxford, much money for the Schools Quadrangle scheme was raised by private subscription.[96]

---

[93] Salter, op. cit., ii. 276–81.

[94] For an account of the University's expenditure, see ibid., ii. 281–93.

[95] For building at Cambridge in the fifteenth century, see R. Willis and J. W. Clark, *The Architectural History of the University of Cambridge and of the Colleges of Cambridge and Eton* (4 vols., Cambridge, 1886), iii. *passim; Grace Book A,* pp. xli–ii; *Grace Book B Part i,* pp. xxiii, xxv; Roach, 'The University of Cambridge', *V. C. H. Camb.* iii. 312–13.

[96] Roach, op. cit., loc. cit.

The series of extant proctors' accounts, however, which commenced in the midst of these building operations, intermittently records the contributions made from the University's own sources of income.[97]

It has already been remarked that the extant Cambridge proctors' accounts for the medieval period are less systematically arranged than those of Oxford because they are not the final audited accounts. Unambiguous figures for total receipts and expenditure are obtainable for only just over half of the years of account in the fifteenth century.[98] On the basis of this limited evidence, it can be asserted that current income fluctuated extensively, from a crest of £60 7s. 4d in 1465–6 to £4 12s. 8. in 1460–1,[99] and that the annual average was about £27. This average is less than two-fifths of the comparable Oxford average of about £70. As did Oxford, Cambridge had capital assets in the shape of loan-chests and often healthy reserves in the common chest of the University. The cash balance in the common chest was often sizeable, and when added to current income could make the total a substantial one.[100] The variations in expenditure matched those in current income: expenditure ranged from £55 2s. 4d. in 1478–9 to £7 2s. 6d. in 1490–1,[101] and indicates an annual average sum of about £21. This is just less than a third of that of Oxford at about £61.

The sources of Cambridge's income and expenditure are broadly similar to those of Oxford and need not be itemized in equivalent detail. There are, however, one or two points which are worthy of note. Whereas the proctors' accounts of Oxford usually record the degree fees known as 'commons' as one general entry for the year, at Cambridge the proctors normally listed each person by name

[97] E.g. *Grace Book A*, pp. 2, 3, 6, 19, 34, 38, 43, 44, 48, 131.

[98] Of the 46 years of account between 1454–5 and 1499–1500 reliable figures for income seem to be available for 26 years, and for expenditure for 23 years.

[99] Ibid., pp. 54, 27.

[100] For example, £87 9s. 2½d. in 1490–1, £76 9s. 2¾d. in 1493–4, £78 18s. 2¼d. in 1494–5 and £89 5s. 3¼d. in 1496–7: *Grace Book B part i*, 32, 56, 78, 101. For Cambridge loan-chests, see G. Pollard, 'Mediaeval loan-chests at Cambridge', *B.I.H.R.*, xvii (1939–40), pp. 113 ff.

[101] *Grace Book A*, p. 131; *Grace Book B Part i*, p. 32.

together with the amount paid by that person for the stipulated degree in arts or in one of the superior faculties.[102] The other type of degree fee, the composition fee, which was a prominent part of Oxford's annual income, was levied at a considerably lower rate at Cambridge.[103] Because this circumstance prompted some scholars to migrate from Oxford to Cambridge, Oxford was forced to moderate its composition fees in 1478.[104] One lucrative source of income found at Cambridge, but not at Oxford, was that realized from forfeited cautions (*cautiones*) or pledges. These cautions were exacted from candidates who intended to proceed to a degree, and were forfeited if they failed to do so or if they omitted to perform prescribed academic acts associated with admission to their degrees.[105] Since the forfeiting of cautions was a fairly regular occurrence, the University collected a solid annual income from this

---

[102] The 'commons' paid on becoming a quaestonist — a stage in the career of a student in the faculty of arts where he took part in the exercise of responding to the question as one of the requirements for the B.A. degree — was 1s.: from yearly entries, see e.g. *Grace Book A,* pp. 1, 3, 4, 9, 11, 16, 17, 21, 22, 26, 35, 36, 46, 47. The same rate was charged for admissions to the degree of master of grammar: e.g. ibid., pp. 1, 11, 83, 94, 110,145. The 'commons' rate for all other degrees was usually 1s. 8d.: e.g. ibid., 1, 4, 5, 9, 11, 12, 16, 17, 18, 21, 22, 26, 27, 35, 36, 41, 42, 46, 47, 53. Rates other than 1s. 8d. are occasionally found.

[103] E.g. in 1455–6, 1456–7 and 1458–9, friars, upon taking the doctoral degree, paid £2 each in lieu of providing the stipulated degree banquet; in 1455–6, however, a friar of the Augustinian Order had to pay £8 as a substitute for the feast. In 1461–2, a Franciscan friar and secular master paid £3 6s. 8d. and £5 6s. 8d. respectively, and in 1470–1, a friar paid £5 6s. 8d. in place of the banquet: *Grace Book A,* pp. 4, 9, 18; 5; 32, 84. In 1498–9, a monk was made to pay £6 13s. 4d. and 2 friars £5 6s. 8d. each: *Grace Book B Part i,* p. 118.

[104] Salter, *Mediaeval Archives,* ii. 274; *The Register of Congregation 1448–1463,* p. xxiii; Gibson, *Statuta Antiqua,* pp. 290–1.

[105] The caution might take the form of a sum of money, a book, an item of plate, or an article of dress: ibid., p. ix. A list of books deposited as cautions between 1454 and 1488 is printed ibid., pp. x–xvi, and for the period 1488–1511, in *Grace Book B Part i,* pp. viii–xiii. Books were less commonly deposited as cautions after 1500. The monetary value of these cautions varied with the status of the candidate. For example, a quaestonist's pledge was often worth about 13s. 4d., and that of a candidate proceeding to a degree in one of the higher faculties about £2: for the quaestonists' pledges, see e.g. *Grace Book A,* pp. 12, 35, 76, 83, 94, 108, 111, and for pledges in the higher faculties, ibid., pp. 2, 4, 9, 12.

quarter. At Oxford, the system of cautions did not prevail and a candidate admitted to a degree was bound to carry out all the duties pertaining to the taking of the degree not by the exaction of a caution, but by an oath.[106] Another point of difference concerning the income of the two Universities is that relatively few graces were granted for money at Cambridge between 1454 and 1488, the period covered by the first extant proctors' book, *Grace Book A*, although the sale of graces became a more significant item of receipt towards the close of the fifteenth and in the early sixteenth century.[107]

It is clear from the extant proctors' accounts that even by 1500 the English Universities, as corporations, and excluding the privately endowed colleges, were far from being wealthy institutions. The Universities certainly attracted valuable endowments through the medium of the loan-chests and thereby accumulated substantial capital assets. But current income and expenditure in the fifteenth century was on a modest scale. While the Universities probably maintained credit balances in most years, they were stretched to the utmost to finance their major building programmes. The financial situation must have been precarious throughout the medieval period. The available means for generating income from within the Universities were clearly limited. The Universities had to depend to an unhealthy degree upon the amount of external funding which they could attract, and this made forward planning a haphazard business.

It has been noted above that Cambridge's annual average income and expenditure levels in the fifteenth century were well below those of Oxford. It has been estimated that by the mid-fifteenth century the number of scholars at Oxford may have settled in the region of 1,700, while that of scholars at Cambridge, having risen from between 400 and 700 in the late fourteenth century, had reached about 1,300.[108] If these estimates are broadly reliable, they

---

[106] See Salter, op. cit., ii. 275.

[107] Bateson, *Grace Book B Part i*, p. xiii.

[108] See the estimates of T. H. Aston, G. D. Duncan and T. A. R. Evans, 'The Medieval Alumni of the University of Cambridge', *Past and Present*, no. 86 (1980), pp. 9 ff. at pp. 26–7.

show that the movement towards the equalization of the size of the populations of the Universities was well advanced by the period covered by the proctors' accounts — the second half of the fifteenth century. If the size of the academic population at Cambridge indeed approximated to that of Oxford by 1500, the differences in the financial capacities of the Universities are thrown into even stronger relief.

Despite its onerous nature, there was no salary attached to the office of proctor at either of the English Universities, although the proctors were entitled to a variety of fees, a proportion of fines and a generous allowance for expenses.[109] Two glimpses may be had into the divergent profits which a proctor at Oxford might receive in the fifteenth century. In 1426-7, John Arundel, who was the junior proctor, derived an income of at least £10 6s. 3d. in addition to gifts in kind.[110] On the other hand, in 1474, the income of one of the proctors, Richard Bradley, seems to have been only £5 17s. 1d.[111] While these sums are evidence that the office was remunerative to a certain degree, given the fundamental and multi-faceted role of the proctors in welding together the components of university government, the reward seems scarcely commensurate.

The proctors could not possibly attend to every detail in person. Apart from substitute proctors, or pro-proctors, they were assisted mainly by the university bedels, often known as the 'public' or 'common' servants or just the 'servants of the university'.[112] By 1346, there were six bedels at Oxford – three superior and three inferior bedels — the faculties of theology and arts and both faculties of law being each served by one superior and one inferior bedel. At

---

[109] Salter, op. cit., ii. 283; Hackett, 'The University as a Corporate Body', p. 85.

[110] Emden, 'The remuneration of the medieval proctors of the University of Oxford', art. cit., pp. 202-7.

[111] Salter, op. cit., ii. 283.

[112] For the Oxford bedels, see Gibson, *Statuta Antiqua*, pp. lxxviii–lxxviii, 68–70; Hackett, 'The University as a Corporate Body', pp. 86–7; Salter, *Registrum Cancellarii*, i. xlv–xlvii. For the Cambridge bedels, see H. P. Stokes, *The Esquire Bedells of the University of Cambridge from the 13th century to the 20th century* (*C.A.S.*, Octavo Publications, xlv, 1911); Hackett, *The Original Statutes of Cambridge University*, pp. 159–62, 206–9, 281–5; *Camb. Docs.*, i. 353–6, 359.

Cambridge, there were only two statutory bedels before the sixteenth century, one for the faculties of theology and canon law and the other for the faculty of arts. The shadowy figure of a third bedel, however, is apparent from the fourteenth century, although it was not until 1549 that a third bedel was given full statutory existence.[113]

In medieval universities, the office of bedel was a venerable one. In the English Universities, it may have predated even those of the chancellor and proctor. The manifold functions of the bedels were similar whether at Paris, Bologna, Padua, Oxford or Cambridge. The bedels of the English Universities served the chancellor and proctors in all manner of ways. They collected fees and fines; they kept lists of the names of those sentenced to imprisonment and of scholars who had received the licence; they read out proclamations and the texts of new statutes in the schools and gave notice of disputations; wearing the full ceremonial robes and carrying their staves of office, they were present at inceptions, masses, funerals and processions, and assisted at congregations; and they advertised the times of the sittings of the chancellor's court and served summonses and citations. In addition to doing these and other tasks, the bedels were, in effect, the caretakers of the university schools, supervising their cleanliness, seating arrangements and state of preparedness throughout the academic year. The bedels ranked as privileged members of the university, as indeed did their wives, and they identified themselves closely with the university which gave them prestigious employment and to which a proportion of them were appreciative benefactors.[114] The bedels were often men of substance in the university town, being either owners or tenants of lands or tenements. They sometimes became landlords to students, and they are found as agents for colleges, halls or hostels in the acquisition and transference of property. Bedels would act on occasion for both the town and the university and so

[113] See the discussion by Hackett, *The Original Statutes of Cambridge University,* pp. 283–5.

[114] See Aston and Faith, 'The Endowments of the University and Colleges to *c.* 1348', p. 272; Stokes, op. cit., pp. 1–3, 49 ff.; Stokes, 'Early University Property', *Proceedings of the C.A.S.,* xiii (new series, vii, 1908–9), pp. 164 ff. at p. 165.

helped to form a personal bridge between the two corporations.[115] The election of bedels, which ought to have been a wholly internal, university matter, could excite a more general interest. In the second half of the fifteenth century, Henry VI and Queen Margaret of Anjou, Edward IV and Henry VII all tried to bring royal influence to bear upon the outcome of the elections of bedels at Oxford.[116] The quantity of biographical material which has been assembled for the Cambridge bedels has revealed that until late in the fifteenth century these officials were non-graduates. From the close of that century and certainly from the 1530s, however, the position of bedel was always held by a master of the university.[117] This development brought the office of bedel entirely within the academic sphere.

Of the remaining university officials, the most notable were the registrars, chaplains, librarians and stationers. At Oxford, the office of registrar was in existence by 1447,[118] although it probably had a predecessor in that of the chancellor's scribe or clerk, first mentioned in 1428.[119] The main duties of the registrar at both Universities were to draft and to register degrees and graces, to record the proceedings of congregation and business transacted before the chancellor, to enter annually the names of the principals of halls in the chancellor's register, and to write out a fair copy of

---

[115] See the biographical detail assembled by Stokes, *The Esquire Bedells*, chs. vii, viii; also Catto, 'Citizens, Scholars and Masters', *The History of the University of Oxford*, i. 164–5, and *The Register of Congregation 1448–1463*, pp. 424–5.

[116] Mallet, *A History of the University of Oxford*, i. 176; see also C. I. Hammer, Jr., 'Oxford Town and Oxford University', *The History of the University of Oxford*, iii (*The Collegiate University*, ed. J. McConica, Oxford, 1986), 69 ff. at 75.

[117] Peek and Hall, *The Archives of the University of Cambridge*, pp. 44–5; Stokes, op. cit., p. 17.

[118] *The Register of Congregation 1448–1463*, p. xi and n. 2. The statute instituting the office of registrar and setting out his duties is printed by Gibson, *Statuta Antiqua*, pp. 285–6: Gibson dated the statute as *c.* 1470, but this is evidently a copy of an earlier statute, made perhaps in 1447, when John Manningham became the first holder of the office.

[119] *The Register of Congregation 1448–1463*, p. 426.

the proctors' accounts every year.[120] It is clear that this new office took over some of the functions previously performed by the chancellor and proctors. At Oxford, because of his legal responsibilities, the registrar was required to be not only an M.A. but also a public notary.[121] The position at Oxford was salaried, at £2 13s. 4d. a year,[122] and this was supplemented by fees received for the registration of degrees and graces. The office of registrar at Cambridge, where, perversely, it was called 'registrary', was a somewhat later development. It appears to have been instituted in 1506, when one of the bedels was made registrary, and from then until the seventeenth century the position was always held by a bedel.[123] Before 1506, the University seems to have employed a motley crew of letter writers, including, at different times, the Italian *poeta* Caius Auberinus, who was also a lecturer at Cambridge towards the close of the fifteenth century and at the beginning of the sixteenth,[124] a vicar or rector of Trumpington,[125] and the master of Clare College.[126] From the thirteenth century, both Universities had a chaplain, whose primary functions were to celebrate the statutory masses in the university calendar and to conduct services

---

[120] For the registrar's functions, see Gibson, op. cit., pp. 285–6; *The Register of Congregation 1448–1463*, pp. xi–xii, 427–8.

[121] Gibson, op. cit., p. 285; see also M. Underwood, 'The structure and operation of the Oxford Chancellor's court, from the sixteenth to the early eighteenth century', *Journal of the Society of Archivists*, vi (1978), pp. 18 ff. at p. 22.

[122] Gibson, op. cit., p. 286.

[123] Peek and Hall, *The Archives of the University of Cambridge*, pp. 7, 28.

[124] For payments to Caius Auberinus for writing letters on behalf of the University, see *Grace Book A*, pp. 185, 198, and *Grace Book B Part i*, pp. 10, 29, 50, 63, 64, 87, 88, 96, 104, 119–21, 136–8, 171–3, 183–4, 193–5. For payments to Auberinus for lectures delivered, see *Grace Book B Part i*, pp. 44, 51, 138, 159, 175, 196: on Auberinus as a Cambridge lecturer, see T. Warton, *The History of English Poetry* (3 vols., ed. R. Price, 1840), ii. 553, and R. Weiss, *Humanism in England during the Fifteenth Century* (2nd ed., Oxford, 1957), p. 163.

[125] See payments for writing letters, *Grace Book B Part i*, pp. 10, 69, 87, 88, 96, 97, 111.

[126] Ibid., p. 175.

for benefactors.[127] At Oxford, in 1412, the chaplain also acquired the new office of librarian, at a salary of £5 6s. 8d.[128] The care of the university library at Cambridge was similarly one of the duties of the chaplain in the fifteenth century.[129] In 1570, however, the office of university chaplain in Cambridge was abolished, and in 1577 the new position of university librarian was established at a stipend of £10 per annum.[130]

As in the case of the stationers of most of the old-established universities, the stationers of Oxford and Cambridge were subject to the chancellor's jurisdiction and were the authorized university agents for the conduct of the book trade within the town, and this probably entailed a general supervision over such constituent crafts as parchment- and paper-making, illumination and binding. They also had the duty of valuing books and manuscripts and other articles which had been offered as pledges against sums borrowed from loan-chests, and they acted as the university agents for the sale of forfeited pledges.[131] The Oxford stationers, of whom there were four in 1346,[132] from some point in the thirteenth until the mid-fourteenth century, were responsible for the management of the *exemplar-pecia* system, a cheap, utilitarian method of manuscript production which enabled multiple copies to be made of texts used

---

[127] On the Oxford chaplains, see Hackett, 'The University as a Corporate Body', p. 87, and Salter, *Mediaeval Archives*, ii. 286: the early fourteenth-century university calendar is printed by Gibson, *Statuta Antiqua*, pp. 1–14. On the Cambridge chaplain, see H. P. Stokes, *The Chaplains and the Chapel of the University of Cambridge 1256–1568* (*C.A.S.*, Octavo Publications, xli, 1906).

[128] Gibson, op. cit., p. 217.

[129] Roach, 'The University of Cambridge', *V. C. H. Camb.* iii. 313.

[130] Loc. cit.; Stokes, *The Chaplains and the Chapel of the University of Cambridge*, pp. 39, 40; Peek and Hall, op. cit., p. 45.

[131] For the Oxford stationers, see Gibson, op. cit., pp. 183–6, 211; Hackett, 'The University as a Corporate Body', p. 88; G. Pollard, 'The University and the Book Trade in Medieval Oxford', *Beiträge zum Berufsbewusstsein des mittelalterlichen Menschen* (Miscellanea Mediaevalia, 3, 1964), pp. 336 ff. The Cambridge stationers are briefly discussed by Leathes, *Grace Book A*, pp. xliii–xliv.

[132] *Munimenta Academica*, i, 150.

in degree courses.[133] The scale of the *exemplar-pecia* operation at Oxford and the extent to which it was exactly modelled upon the methods employed at Paris or Bologna are matters which are at present unclear. Nevertheless, it may be assumed that the stationers were required to maintain supplies of accurate *exemplars* which were approved copies of texts and commentaries used in teaching and sometimes embraced lectures and disputations as well. These *exemplars* were divided by the stationers into separate quires or *peciae* of varying length, and these portions or pieces were hired out to scholars who wished to have a copy made for their own use, the copying being done by professional scribes, or by the scholars themselves, or by undergraduates who wished to earn some money by scribal activity. It is rather peculiar that there is as yet no definite evidence that at Oxford the *pecia* system was applied to texts used in the arts faculty, only that it was applied to those used in the faculties of civil and canon law and theology, where students were obliged either to possess or to borrow the prescribed texts.[134]

As it did at several of the other universities in northern Europe, the *exemplar-pecia* system may have petered out at Oxford towards the mid-fourteenth century — for reasons which are obscure.[135] It lingered on in some universities in southern Europe until the fifteenth century. For example, it was still in existence at Bologna in 1476, five years after printing began in the city.[136] In all, the *exemplar-pecia* system is known to have functioned in at least eleven of the medieval universities. Curiously, however, there is no firm

[133] The *exemplar-pecia* system was illuminated in the pioneering study by J. Destrez, *La Pecia dans les manuscrits universitaires du xiii᷎ et du xiv᷎ siècle* (Paris, 1935); see also the important revisionary essay by G. Pollard, 'The *pecia* system in the medieval universities', *Medieval Scribes, Manuscipts and Libraries: Essays presented to N. R. Ker* (ed. M. B. Parkes and A. G. Watson, London, 1978), pp. 145 ff.

[134] See Pollard, op. cit., p. 150: for the requirement that students in the faculties of civil and canon law had to own or borrow the key texts, with their commentaries, see Gibson, *Statuta Antiqua*, pp. cvi, cviii, 43–4, 46. At Paris, the *pecia* system was applied automatically to the arts faculty, Pollard, op. cit., p. 151.

[135] See Pollard's views on the demise of the *pecia* system in northern Europe generally, and at Oxford in particular, op. cit., p. 149.

[136] Loc. cit.

proof for its operation in Cambridge.[137] While it was only a palliative, the system did ensure that in the pre-printing age a proportion of students at a number of universities who could not otherwise have afforded the high price levels for manuscripts had the opportunity of acquiring the relevant texts for a moderate outlay.

One of the most arresting features of the government of the medieval English Universities is the extent to which it was conducted by members of the teaching staff. It has to be remembered that even the chancellors and proctors had to combine the burdens of office with their duties as regent masters. There were, however, many other areas of involvement for teaching masters apart from the highest executive positions.[138] Regent masters might act as keepers of loan-chests or of the administrative chests which housed items such as muniments, vestments and the university seal and cross; they might serve as taxors; they might be appointed to the care of university houses and properties, being charged with the effecting of repairs and the collection of rents; they might assist the chancellor with the assize of bread, ale and wine, the maintenance of pavements and the cleanliness of the streets; they might aid the chancellor and proctors with investigations into disturbances of the peace and the state of immorality within the town; they might act as principals of halls or hostels; and they might be fellows of colleges and be engaged in internal government or in the business of estates. Even by 1500, the notion of a professsional administrative class was still only in embryonic form in the English Universities: registrars and bedels, stationers and chaplain-librarians, these provided only a minimal support to government by academic personnel. The degree to which teaching masters gave of their energies to university affairs at all levels must have helped preserve the supposition that the core of the university

---

[137] The *pecia* system is found to have been used in the Universities of Bologna, Padua, Vercelli, Perugia, Treviso, Florence, Salamanca, Naples, Paris, Toulouse and Oxford: there is no clear evidence of its operation at Salerno, Montpellier, Orleans, Angers, Avignon or Cambridge, Pollard, op. cit., p. 148.

[138] See conveniently Hackett, 'The University as a Corporate Body', pp. 89–92.

was the masters' guild. At the close of the fifteenth century, the English Universities were as yet innocent of any rigid bifurcation into academic and administrative sectors.[139] The Universities continued to be viewed as essentially founded on the activities of the guild of teaching masters and associated students, non-academic assistance occupying a decidedly subordinate niche within the time-honoured scheme of things.

Sovereignty within the medieval Universities of Oxford and Cambridge came to be located in the congregation of regents and non-regents,[140] composed of masters and doctors in all of the faculties. But this had not been the case for the best part of a century after the inauguration of the Universities. Initially, the congregation of regents was the supreme governing body at both Universities.[141] Its original function had been the admission of new masters by the act of inception into the teaching guild and, by extension, it came to regulate a series of matters, including the duties of the masters, the details of the academic regime, the approved dress, and attendance at the funerals of members of the guild and at other liturgical occasions. In this way, the congregation of regents became the statute-making body when the early university customs were reduced to a written form. In addition, the congregation of regents was responsible for the granting of graces or dispensations from the stipulated degree requirements, and for the staging of the elections of the chancellor,

---

[139] Oxford and Cambridge were here in broad conformity with the generality of medieval universities.

[140] The non-regents were masters who had ceased teaching. If they had been lecturers in arts, they would often be engaged in study in a higher faculty. Even if they had left the university, they would retain the title of non-regent and could return to teaching at a later stage.

[141] For Oxford, see Hackett, 'The University as a Corporate Body' pp. 55 ff. Both Rashdall, *Universities,* iii. 65, and Gibson, *Statuta Antiqua,* pp. xxi–xxii, assumed that the congregation of regents and non-regents was the supreme governing body of the University from the early thirteenth century: but this interpretation appears to be flawed. For the initial sovereignty of the congregation of regents at Cambridge, see Hackett, *The Original Statutes of Cambridge University,* pp. 102, 106, 144, 146, 225–6, 240–1, and the perceptive comments of Peacock, *Observations on the Statutes of the University of Cambridge,* p. 19 and n. 1.

proctors, bedels and other university officials.[142] One of the significant differences between the constitution of Paris and those of the English Universities concerns the standing of the non-regents. For in the latter the non-regents were eventually raised to the status of co-legislators with the regents, so that the congregation of regents and non-regents superseded the congregation of regents as the sovereign assembly.[143] At both Oxford and Cambridge in the thirteenth century, the non-regents occasionally met with the regents in extraordinary sessions, which were sometimes concerned with legislation.[144] Towards the close of the century at Oxford — the change had been formalized by *c.* 1303[145] — the non-regents acquired statutory powers coequal with those of the regents. At Cambridge the non-regents had won similar powers by 1304.[146] The dispute between the secular masters and the friars in the late thirteenth and early fourteenth centuries served to promote and then to cement the combined constitutional entity of regents and non-regents. Indeed, fear of the threat posed by the privileged position of the friars was probably the strongest single motive which impelled the regents of Oxford and Cambridge to share their sovereign power with the non-regents on a permanent basis.[147] As the supreme legislature of

[142] E.g. Hackett, 'The University as a Corporate Body', pp. 55–6; Peacock, op. cit., p. 19. The earliest surviving register of the Oxford congregation of regents has been printed as *The Register of Congregation 1448–1463*. There is no equivalent record of the congregation of regents at Cambridge before 1500, although *Grace Book A* and *Grace Book B Part i* contain, apart from the proctors' accounts, a list of the graces passed in congregation as well as other items of business which presumably had come before congregation.

[143] Hackett, 'The University as a Corporate Body', pp. 59, 61, and *The Original Statutes of Cambridge University*, pp. 240–1.

[144] Hackett, 'The University as a Corporate Body', pp. 58–60, and *The Original Statutes of Cambridge University*, p. 240.

[145] Gibson, op. cit., p. 109.

[146] *Camb. Docs.*, i. 308.

[147] On this matter, see e.g. Hackett, 'The University as a Corporate Body', pp. 59–61, and *The Original Statutes of Cambridge University*, pp. 241–4. The documentation of the dispute with the friars at Oxford, with an introduction, has been printed by H. Rashdall, 'The Friars Preachers v. the University AD 1311–1313', *Collectanea*, ii., ed. cit., 193 ff.; see also Sheehan, 'The Religious Orders 1220–1370', *The History of the University of Oxford*, i. 205–8.

the University, the congregation of regents and non-regents had the sole authority to make, repeal, or amend statutes,[148] and it constituted the highest court of appeal in the university. At Oxford, at any rate, it could be deployed to resolve an impasse which had strained relations between the chancellor and proctors, or to settle disputes which had arisen in the congregation of regents.[149]

Because of the rather unwieldy nature of the sovereign body, however, it was summoned at only infrequent intervals.[150] The routine of business in the English Universities in the fourteenth and fifteenth centuries was conducted by the congregation of regents, which continued to carry out the functions it had exercised before it had ceased to be the sovereign body, with the obvious exception of the formulation of statutes, although it claimed the right to interpret statutes where necessary.[151] In practical terms, it was this regular assembly of regents which was the effective hub of university government. Since arts was the largest of the faculties in both Universities, it follows that the regent masters in arts were in a numerical preponderance in the congregation of regents. This circumstance had implications for the character and even for the calibre of university government. For a proportion of the regents in arts were recently qualified masters in their early twenties and only a few of these would have envisaged university teaching as a life-long career. Oxford and Cambridge were among the last of the European universities to establish a nucleus of salaried lectureships.[152] Prior to this development, teaching, especially in arts, was not of a

---

[148] See the Oxford *Historiola,* or historical account of the University, of a. 1313, Gibson, op. cit., p. 18; for Cambridge, see the statute of 1304, *Camb. Docs.,* i. 308, which contained a saving clause that the regents retained the power to alter or dispense with statutes previously enacted.

[149] Gibson, op. cit., pp. 123, 124.

[150] See the Oxford *Historiola,* ibid., p. 18.

[151] For Oxford, see Gibson, op. cit., p. xxiii; for the rather complex situation at Cambridge, see Hackett, *The Original Statutes of Cambridge University,* pp. 235–6.

[152] A. B. Cobban, 'Decentralized Teaching in the Medieval English Universities', *History of Education,* 5 (1976), pp. 193 ff. at pp. 204–5. On the

particularly remunerative nature, and this must have led to the loss of many promising lecturers who sought more lucrative employment elsewhere. As a result, the faculty of arts depended a good deal upon the 'necessary regency' system, whereby every new master of arts had to teach for the remainder of the year in which the degree was taken and for one year further. In the governmental sphere, this meant that the congregation of regents contained a fair number of youthful and inexperienced masters[153] who would probably have no long-term stake in the university's future. There was criticism in fifteenth-century Oxford of the alleged irresponsibility of the congregation of regents with regard to their powers of granting statutory dispensations.[154] Whatever the case, the involvement of all the regents in the conduct of affairs characterized the open, democratic nature of government in the English Universities in their first three hundred years. During the course of the sixteenth century, however, this democratic constitution was gradually altered in favour of a more oligarchical structure, with power concentrated in the heads of the colleges, who, in turn, were expected to defer to the authoritarian demands of the Tudor monarchy.[155]

In this connection, mention need to be made of the distinctive Cambridge institution known as the 'Caput'.[156] This appears to have originated in the late fifteenth century as a council of the chancellor or vice-chancellor whose purpose was to assist with the selection of graces to be placed before congregation. This council

---

growth of the salaried lectureship in European universities, see Cobban, *The Medieval Universities*, pp. 154–7.

[153] See e.g. the comments of Pantin, *Oxford Life in Oxford Archives*, p. 20.

[154] See above, p. 85, n. 92.

[155] See above, pp. 74–5. See also G. D. Duncan, 'The Heads of Houses and Religious Change in Tudor Oxford 1547–1558', *Oxoniensia*, 45 (1980), pp. 226 ff.

[156] On the Caput, see Peacock, *Observations on the Statutes of the University of Cambridge*, pp. 21, n. 1 (extending to p. 23), 46–8; Leathes, *Grace Book A*, pp. xxxiii–xxxiv; Peek and Hall, *The Archives of the University of Cambridge*, pp. 29–30; Roach, 'The University of Cambridge', *V. C. H. Camb.* iii. 183–4; *Camb. Docs.*, i. 478–9.

then came to concern itself with matters other than graces, and eventually it seems to have prepared the agenda for congregation. The make-up of the membership of the council in the fifteenth century is obscure. It probably consisted, however, of one doctor from each of the superior faculties, one regent and one non-regent master in arts, one doctor in theology who belonged to a religious order, and as chairman of this august body, the chancellor or vice-chancellor. The Caput represented a range of sectional interests, and each member could veto an item proposed for discussion in congregation. In Elizabeth's reign, the nomination of members of the Caput was largely in the control of the heads of the colleges, who thereby retained a firm grip on the legislative business of the university. There appears to have been nothing comparable to the Caput at Oxford. It is probable that by means of this conciliar device Cambridge government lost something of its democratic character a shade earlier than did Oxford, although these processes cannot be monitored with chronological exactitude.

The numerical superiority of the artists was institutionalized at Oxford in a third assembly, the congregation of artists or Black Congregation, named after the colour of their habits. This body claimed the privilege when summoned by the proctors of deliberating separately on proposed legislation before it came before the sovereign assembly, the congregation of regents and non-regents.[157] There is no evidence of the existence of a similar assembly at Cambridge. The earliest specific reference to the right of prior deliberation by the Oxford artists dates from 1325. There is also an oblique reference to that right in a statute of 1322. But this claim on the part of a faculty which regarded itself as the fountain-head of all the others was ultimately based upon older custom.[158] In addition to this right of anterior deliberation, the artists claimed to have the power to veto any item proposed for discussion in the congregation of regents and non-regents.[159] This claim to possess a

---

[157] For the congregation of artists, see Gibson, *Statuta Antiqua*, pp. xxiii–xxiv, xxvi–xxxiv; *The Register of Congregation 1448–1463*, pp. 57–8, 227–8.

[158] Gibson, op. cit., pp. 124, 127–8, 142.

[159] Ibid., p. 179.

power of veto was firmly rejected by the faculties of theology and civil law and the non-regents in 1357.[160] While the claim seems never to have been fully endorsed, the artists did come to gain acceptance for the principle that no statute or interpretation of a statute or grace would be passed in the congregation of regents or of regents and non-regents if the whole faculty of arts objected.[161] The reality was sometimes different, and there are instances of statutes being passed without the consent of the artists, the non-regents combining with the regents in the superior faculties and voting against the arts faculty.[162] The Black Congregation declined in the late fifteenth century. This may have been a natural consequence of the growing powers of the congregation of regents, with its majority of artists. The Black Congregation was finally phased out in the course of the sixteenth century as authority within the University assumed a more centralist stamp.[163]

There can be no doubt that before 1500 the faculties of arts in the English Universities made a major contribution to university government. Apart from their decisive role in university assemblies, the artists elected the proctors and provided an imposing legion of regents in arts to serve as administrative officials. In this respect, the situation was similar to that of Paris, where the faculty of arts came to occupy the dominant position within the *studium*. There is, however, one crucial difference. The rector of the artists at Paris, by virtue of the numerical superiority of the regents in arts and the lead which they had taken in university affairs first against the chancellor and then against the mendicants, succeeded in emerging as the common head of the guild of masters, a position admitted *de facto* by the mid-thirteenth century and recognized *di iure* by the mid-

---

[160] Ibid., p. 156.

[161] See the comments of J. M. Fletcher, 'The Faculty of Arts', *The History of the University of Oxford*, i (*The Early Oxford Schools*, ed. J. I. Catto, Oxford, 1984), 369 ff. at 372.

[162] E.g. a statute of 1438 was passed with the consent of the non-regents and of the regents of all the faculties, with the exception of those of the faculty of arts: Gibson, op. cit., pp. 258–9.

[163] Ibid., pp. xxxi–xxxiv.

fourteenth century at the latest.[164] In the English Universities, by contrast, the chancellor was normally chosen from the doctors of theology and canon law, after an election in which the regents in all faculties were represented. But while it is true that the English artists did not furnish the chancellor and, from this standpoint, were not as influential as their Parisian colleagues, it is also undeniable that the faculties of arts at Oxford and Cambridge were for long the most advanced of the faculties at the English Universities in organizational terms. At Paris, while the faculty of arts had been the first to evolve a substantial organization, and had done so by the mid-thirteenth century, in the second half of the century the superior faculties were also moved to frame their own internal organization, with their deans, assemblies, statute-making powers and so on.[165] In the English Universities, the superior faculties do not seem to have developed the distinct corporate characteristics of their Parisian counterparts, and right through to the fifteenth century they appear to have lagged significantly behind the arts faculty in terms of institutional cohesion.[166]

A further basic difference between the constitutional development of the English Universities and that of Paris was the relatively peripheral standing of the nations at Oxford and Cambridge. In imitation of the Parisian model, magisterial nations were reproduced at Oxford as sub-divisions of the faculty of arts, and, for a period in the thirteenth century, they received official sanction.[167] Very little has been discovered about nation groupings at Cambridge.[168] It has been suggested that Cambridge never gave

---

[164] On the position of the faculty of arts and rector at Paris, see e.g. Cobban, *The Medieval Universities*, pp. 84–5; Kibre, *The Nations in the Mediaeval Universities*, chs. 1, 3, *passim*; Leff, *Paris and Oxford Universities in the Thirteenth and Fourteenth Centuries*, esp. pp. 60–7.

[165] The position and organization of the superior faculties at Paris are discussed e.g. by Rashdall, *Universities*, i. 321 ff.

[166] Rashdall, op. cit., iii. 78, 147.

[167] For the Oxford nations, see Kibre, op. cit., pp. 160–6; Cobban, op. cit., pp. 104–5; Leff, op. cit., pp. 98–100.

[168] Kibre, op. cit., pp. 166–7, can supply only one paragraph on the Cambridge nations.

constitutional effect to nation divisions, and there is certainly no evidence of their statutory endorsement.[169] In actual practice, however, nation groupings did materialize at Cambridge in the thirteenth century, even if not officially approved.[170]

Whereas the Parisian nations remained a vital force in the life of the *studium* until at least the mid-fifteenth century and, in a much-reduced and much-altered state, persisted until 1793, when they were abolished,[171] the English nations were stunted in their growth. In the more insular English situation, there was not the same need for defensive organizations as there was in large cosmopolitan universities such as Paris and Bologna. After the manner of Paris, Oxford may originally have had a fourfold nation division, though the evidence for this is not particularly strong. However this may be, the paucity of scholars recruited from outside the British Isles led to the stabilization at Oxford of a dual pattern based upon a geographical division between the northern and southern British. At Oxford, at any rate, English and Scottish masters from north of the River Nene[172] were classed as northerners or *boreales*, and those from south of the Nene as southerners or *australes*, the Welsh, Irish and foreign masters being grouped with the southerners. Judging from a serious fracas at Cambridge in 1260 involving northern and southern scholars, it is probable that similar regional and ethnic alignments applied in the Cambridge context.[173] The nations in the English Universities do not seem to have acquired much corporate autonomy, and no common head

---

[169] Hackett, *The Original Statutes of Cambridge University*, p. 154.

[170] In 1260, there were violent clashes between northern and southern masters at Cambridge which seriously disrupted the University and led to a temporary migration to Northampton: Cooper, *Annals,* i. 48 (the date is mistakenly given as 1261); see also the colourful account by Fuller, *The History of the University of Cambridge,* ed. cit., pp. 28–31.

[171] On the Paris nations, see Kibre, op. cit., chs. 1, 3; Cobban, op. cit., pp. 86–90; Leff, op. cit., pp. 51 ff.

[172] Emden, 'Northerners and Southerners in the Organization of the University to 1509', has shown that the River Nene, not the Trent, was taken as the point of division between north and south.

[173] See above, n. 170.

emerged — as it did at Paris, in the person of the rector. The involvement of the English nations in academic matters appears to have been negligible in contrast to that of the nations at Paris, where they maintained their own schools in arts, which provided the core of teaching in the faculty of arts until the second half of the fifteenth century. Perhaps only in the area of nation turbulence and inter-nation feuding had the English nations much in parallel with those of the faculty of arts at Paris. The very elaborate agreement of 1252 which followed a period of bitter strife between the *boreales* and the Irish scholars gives an indication of the scale of nation warfare at Oxford.[174] The special treaty settling the affray was drawn up by twelve commissioners from each party, and thirty or forty regent or non-regent masters from each side were by the terms of the treaty to be elected to take measures to preserve peace in the future. The recurrent nature of these gang-warfare activites led in 1274 to the abolition of the Oxford nations by amalgamation. It is abundantly clear, however, that even after 1274 the tensions between northern and southern scholars remained to disturb Oxford life until well into the sixteenth century.[175] An effort was made to ameliorate the situation, at least in so far as the administrative sphere was concerned, by ensuring an equal representation of northern and southern masters at most levels of internal government. A survey of holders of university offices to 1509 has shown that one of the proctors was always a northerner and the other a southerner; and that as many as thirty-four university offices, excluding that of the chancellor, the registrar, the chaplain and the bedels, had this geographical basis of appointment.[176] Such an equitable policy yields an interesting example of how a medieval university sought to harmonize regional antagonisms by translating them into constructive governmental channels.

All the evidence suggests, therefore, that the Oxford nations, and seemingly those of Cambridge too, in so far as they had crystallized,

---

[174] The agreement is printed by Gibson, *Statuta Antiqua*, pp. 84–7.

[175] See Pantin, *Oxford Life in Oxford Archives*, pp. 72–3.

[176] See Emden's analysis in 'Northerners and Southerners in the Organization of the University to 1509'.

were but pale imitations of those of Paris. They were pertinent neither to university government nor to the conduct of the academic regime. As there was no sustaining cosmopolitanism in the English Universities to lend them a permanent existence, they were eliminated as irrelevancies on the academic scene.

Before concluding this discussion of university government and organization, it is necessary to comment upon a series of claims advanced by Dr M.B. Hackett in 1970 which have important implications for the organizational maturity and degree of indigenous growth of Cambridge University in the thirteenth century.[177] Dr Hackett has claimed that the undated folios (fos. 54r – 55v) bearing the title *Constituciones Universitatis Cantebrigiensis* and contained in MS. 401 in the Biblioteca Angelica in Rome furnish the only surviving copy of the original statutes or constitution of Cambridge University, and that from this source it is possible to reconstruct the text of the earliest statutes. On palaeographical grounds, Dr Hackett dates the relevant folios of the Angelica manuscript to the third quarter of the thirteenth century, and, from internal evidence, he concludes that the text of Cambridge's original constitution was compiled *c*.1236–54 and advances 'by *c*.1250' as a convenient working date. It is firmly alleged that folios 54r – 55v of the Angelica manuscript make up neither a random nor a partial group of statutes but embrace a complete code, tantamount to a written constitution for Cambridge University which had been drawn up by *c*.1250. If this was so, these *Constituciones* would indeed be startling evidence for an integral statutory code which was not only earlier than that for Oxford but also the first of any European university. Oxford did not attempt to codify its statutes until the early fourteenth century,[178] and neither Paris nor Bologna nor Montpellier had a complete code of statutes in the thirteenth

---

[177] Dr Hackett's findings are set out in *The Original Statutes of Cambridge University, passim*.

[178] The earliest attempt at codification of the Oxford statutes appears to belong to *a*. 1313: G. Pollard, 'The Oldest Statute Book of the Univerity', *The Bodleian Library Record*, viii (1968), pp. 69 ff. This codification was not, however, executed without faults, such as the duplication of statutes and lapses in ordered arrangement.

century.[179] It would certainly be of moment for the history of European universities to discover that Cambridge alone of the *studia generalia* in operation by the mid-thirteenth century was possessed of a written constitution — a set of statutes forming an integrated body rather than the uncodified, piecemeal collection of statutes and customs which elsewhere appears to have been the norm.

The *Constituciones Universitatis Cantebrigiensis* of the Angelica text, thirteen chapters with rubricated titles, relate to such basic matters as a chancellor, rectors (i.e. proctors), regent masters, bedels, assemblies, judicial procedure, dress, discipline, hostels and the rents of houses, the commemoration of benefactors, and funerals of members of the university. Of particular note are the directives for the admission of scholars to the master's degree, regulations about lectures and disputations, and details of the terms of the academic session. The *Constituciones* do not include matter concerning curricular affairs or prescribed texts, and they refer only to the faculties of arts, canon law and theology. By comparing these *Constituciones* with the statutes of Oxford and of other thirteenth-century *studia generalia* and by tracing their evolution up to the sixteenth century, Dr Hackett has made available a wealth of detail illustrative of the constitutional and academic development of the University of Cambridge. He amply demonstrates that its constitution cannot be reckoned a mere derivative of that of Oxford or Paris, however influential these models may have been in certain respects.

It is fully recognized that Dr Hackett has added much new convincing material to support the view that Cambridge was a well-

---

[179] The Paris statutes do not appear to have been in any way codified before the fourteenth century: Denifle, *Chartularium*, i. xxxii–xxxiii. In the case of Bologna, it is known that in 1252 and 1253 the statutes of the law students were officially recognized by the commune of Bologna and the papacy respectively: these statutes, however, with the exception of a small fragment, have not survived. The earliest extant statutes of the law students are those of 1317, with additions up to 1347. These may be regarded as a code, even if incomplete, and they are very similar to the most extensive code of 1432: the statutes of 1317–47 were first printed in *Archiv für Literatur- und Kirchengeschichte des Mittelalters* (ed. H. Denifle and F. Ehrle, iii, Berlin, 1887): these statutes and those of 1432 were then printed in *Statuti delle università e dei collegi dello studio bolognese* (ed. C. Malagola, Bologna, 1888). The earliest statutes of Montpellier, those of the medical school were given by the cardinal

developed *studium generale ex consuetudine* in the thirteenth century and, from this point of view, his work is complementary to that on the legal standing of Cambridge discussed in the previous chapter.[180] What is not so clear, however, is that he has proved his thesis that these *Constituciones* measure up to a complete statutory code, the first among medieval universities.[181] There are undoubtedly early statutes here, but some of the other items are perhaps no more than written customs which only later acquired a statutory form. The absence of a preamble embodying a declaration of intent and imparting an official character or imprint, the terse economy of the text at several crucial points, the tangled textual, juristic, academic and dating problems, and the fact that the Angelica text had no official status and was probably privately commissioned, must make us hesitant about the unqualified acceptance of Dr Hackett's enticing thesis. What the exact significance of folios 54r – 55v of the Angelica manuscript for the history of Cambridge University is is likely to remain a contentious issue for some time to come. Whatever final view is taken on Dr Hackett's claim that the *Constituciones* form a complete statutory code, it is nonetheless clear that they depict Cambridge in the thirteenth century as a university of organizational maturity, encapsulating several indigenous features, and far removed from Rashdall's distorting image of it as an inferior and imitative version of Oxford, before it made in the late medieval period a measure of independent advance. This more balanced appraisal of the relative condition and status of Oxford and Cambridge in the thirteenth century is essential if English academic history is to be put into any kind of proper focus. The notion that, before the fifteenth century, Cambridge University could do little more than limp along within the shadow of Oxford is one which needs to be consigned to oblivion.

papal legate, Conrad, in 1220, but there is no sign of a complete code of university statutes in the thirteenth century: see Rashdall, *Universities,* ii. 123 and n. 2.

[180] See above, pp. 58 ff.

[181] See A. B. Cobban's review of Dr Hackett's book in *E.H.R.,* lxxxvii (1972), pp. 167–8; also the review by W. Ullmann in *J. Eccles. Hist.,* xxii (1971), pp. 134–9.

In reviewing the government and organization of the medieval English Universities, it would clearly be a simplification to regard the constitutions of Oxford and Cambridge as diluted replicas of the Parisian magisterial system. For the position and functions of the English chancellors, proctors, and nations, as well as the relative situations of the higher faculties within the university framework, differed markedly from those of Paris. On the other hand, the faculties of arts at Oxford and Cambridge enjoyed a prominence in the governmental affairs of the Universities almost as pronounced as that of the Parisian arts faculty in those of Paris. The absence of a cathedral-school origin and the relatively insular nature of the academic populations of the English Universities are only two of the factors which promoted indigenous growth. It is true that, with significant adaptations, the Parisian curriculum of studies and degree structure were broadly reproduced in Oxford and Cambridge, but this alone is insufficient to detract from the distinctiveness of the constitutional development of the English Universities before 1500. University government in medieval England was generally of an open democratic hue. It was concentrated in the hands of the regent masters, who were augmented by the non-regents when the infrequent sovereign assemblies were held. Given the numerical superiority of the regents in arts, government must have incorporated a high-spirited, youthful element, which may in certain circumstances have affected adversely the quality of decision making.

In *c.* 1500, after some three hundred years of their existence, the management of the English Universities was still overwhelmingly the concern of the masters' guild, there being only a skeletal professional administrative support. The extent to which the regent masters assumed responsibility for the various levels of university administration, from the olympian heights of the chancellorship to service as keepers of loan-chests, cannot but have reinforced the sense of corporate cohesion within the academic community.

As in most of the medieval universities, a separate administrative class was slow to evolve in Oxford and Cambridge and such a class would have seemed somewhat incompatible with the notion prevailing in northern Europe of a university as being, in essence, a masters' guild run by and for the benefit of its members and their associated students. It has been shown above that the English Universities, leaving aside the collegiate sector, were not wealthy corporations and enjoyed only modest levels of income and expenditure; and that during the elaborate building operations of the fifteenth century, their finances were strained to the point where much recourse had to be made to private donations. While the English Universities attracted a regular stream of solid endowments — for example, in the form of loan-chests and urban property — their financial condition was in no wise commensurate with the value placed upon them as centres of intellectual excellence and as producers of graduates for the myriad needs of Church and State.

In general, the tenor of life in the English Universities was less disturbed and less frenetic than that in some of the more cosmopolitan, continental universities, and was less prone to be disrupted by a European crisis, such as the Great Schism — although the impact of Wyclifism on Oxford and of the Peasants' Revolt on Cambridge, and the migrations to Northampton and Stamford, were traumatic enough exceptions to that relative stability, which typically allowed for quiet evolution. From the thirteenth to the sixteenth century, Oxford and Cambridge benefited from the positive support of the English monarchy and, intermittently, of the papacy. As a result, they became highly privileged corporations and the dominant forces within their university towns and surrounding areas, exercising a far greater degree of authority than did Paris University in relation to its own city and suburbs. The sustained concern of the English monarchy for the welfare, rights, privileges and immunities of the scholars of Oxford and Cambridge would be hard to find parallels for among the other universities of the medieval period. Finally, the fact of the constitutional advance which Cambridge had made by the mid-thirteenth century, its constitution incorporating features which were not in any way derived from that of Oxford, underlines the point that it is no longer tenable to view Cambridge as merely a lesser version of Oxford, even in the first half-century of its existence. The degree to which Cambridge continued to exhibit independent lines of growth is well exemplified in its collegiate scene, which is assessed, together with Oxford's, in the following chapter.

Chapter 4

Colleges, Halls and Hostels

I

THE COLLEGES

The European collegiate movement is a theme of seminal importance for the history of the medieval universities.[1] Within the earliest established universities of northern Europe, at Paris, Oxford and Cambridge, the secular colleges came to be the chief supports of the students in the superior faculties — law, theology and medicine. Along with the Franciscan and Dominican Orders, they maintained generations of the most talented postgraduate scholars in the universities, enabling those scholars to realize to a high level their academic and professional potential. In addition, the secular colleges at Paris, Oxford and Cambridge developed to the point where they had a fundamental impact on the evolution of their respective universities. For in the later Middle Ages, the Parisian and English colleges fell heir to the centralized public instruction of the university schools. By the mid-sixteenth century, the process was largely completed whereby teaching was centred in the colleges, rendering them self-sufficient educational units. This was the movement which above all transformed Paris, Oxford and Cambridge from being universities of a centripetal nature to being those of a centrifugal one. Moreover, several of the fourteenth- and fifteenth-century universities in Germany and Scotland would probably not have survived but for the stabilizing influences of the

---

[1] On European colleges, see Cobban, *The Medieval Universities*, pp. 122 ff.; for a detailed study of one important royal Cambridge college, see Cobban, *The King's Hall*.

111

college foundations in their midst. And when it is further considered that the wealth of extant collegiate material can provide illuminating and sometimes unique insights into the social and economic fabric of a crucial segment of university life, it becomes plainly justifiable that over the last two decades the colleges of the medieval universities have become conspicuous areas of historical study.

In its most mature state, the secular medieval college was an autonomous, self-governing legal entity, solidly endowed, and possessing its own statutes, privileges and common seal.[2] Many colleges, however, especially in continental Europe, did not progress far towards this fully-fledged model. As a result, the European collegiate scene subsumed a diversity of types, ranging from the self-governing, landowning structure usual in England to the unpretentious institution often found in France and Italy, which was, in effect, little more than a basic lodging house for students. The common factor underlying collegiate differentiation was the act of endowment made for educational purposes. It is this endowed status of the college which distinguishes it decisively from the rented hall or hostel, and which affords the only link associating organizationally sophisticated and wealthy societies, such as Merton College, Oxford, the King's Hall, Cambridge, or the College of Navarre, Paris, with the rudimentary boarding houses which were so numerous at the lower end of the collegiate hierarchy.

Although, in the main, the colleges of the medieval universities were designed to make available accommodation and financial support either for undergraduate students or for students capable of intellectual pursuits beyond the first-degree stage, or for students from both categories, the spiritual and charitable aims underlying collegiate enterprise should not be undervalued. To some extent, university colleges were born of that same milieu which produced the collegiate churches of secular canons with their accompanying schools of grammar and song. But whereas the *raison d'être* of the

---

[2] See the definition by A. L. Gabriel, 'Motivation of the Founders of Mediaeval Colleges', *Beiträge zum Berufsbewusstsein des mittelalterlichen Menschen* (Miscellanea Mediaevalia, 3, 1964), pp. 61 ff. at p. 61.

college of secular canons was a religious one, with education a secondary purpose, in the case of the academic college the functional emphasis was, by definition, reversed. Nevertheless, many secular colleges had an affinity with chantry foundations. Generally speaking, the founders of university colleges, whether kings, queens, high-ranking ecclesiastics or statesmen, or wealthy members of the lay aristocracy, regarded the establishment of a college as a charitable and pious venture which would enshrine their memory and which would result in a foundation in which masses would be said for their souls and for those of their relatives. Some colleges were more completely cast in the chantry mould than others. In England, for example, at King's College and St. Catharine's College, Cambridge, and at Queen's, New College and All Souls, Oxford, the fellows or scholars had onerous chantry duties to fulfil;[3] whereas at the King's Hall, Cambridge, only a minimal stress was laid upon the religious regime of the fellows.[4]

Whatever the extent of the chantry aspect in the intentions of a founder of a college, it was usually combined with his desire to help to supply a proven need of the academics. That help might take the form of the alleviation of the distress of genuinely poor students of varying ages and levels of attainment or of the support of stipulated courses of postgraduate study. This charitable ingredient of college-founding remained a constant throughout the Middle Ages, although the aims into which it was translated altered according to the prevailing social and intellectual climate. In the thirteenth century, the collegiate movement was directed especially towards the advancement of arts and theology; while in the fourteenth and

[3] For chantry arrangements at King's College, see *Camb. Docs.*, ii 564–6, 566–75; for St Catharine's, where about one sixth of the statutes relate to chantry aspects, see the original statutes, St Catharine's Muniments, XL/10, and the printed version in *Documents relating to St Catharine's College in the University of Cambridge* (ed. H. Philpott, Cambridge, 1861), pp. 11 ff. For chantry regulations at Queen's, New College and All Souls, see *Statutes*, i. ch. 4, 27–8, 35; i. ch. 5, 66–8; i. ch. 7, 11–12, 50, and the foundation charter of Henry VI of 20 May 1438 for All Souls, ibid., i. ch. 7, 4. An excellent discussion of this chantry theme in academic environments is provided by F. Ll. Harrison, 'The Eton Choirbook', *Annales Musicologiques*, i (1953), pp. 151 ff.

[4] See the King's Hall statutes in W. W. Rouse Ball, *The King's Scholars and King's Hall* (privately printed, Cambridge, 1917), p. 65.

fifteenth centuries the concentration was increasingly on civil and canon law,[5] even though, at Paris, this legal focus was inhibited by the prohibition of civilian studies by Pope Honorius III in 1219.[6] The Hundred Years War, allied to recurrent visitations of plague, led some college founders in France and England to place the emphasis upon the production of graduates to fill the depleted ranks of both the secular clergy and the teaching profession below university level.[7] In the late fifteenth and early sixteenth centuries, college founders made provision increasingly for branches of humanist culture. In England, for instance, Corpus Christi College, Oxford, and St John's College, Cambridge, were conceived in the early sixteenth century as the first comprehensive centres of humanist studies in the English Universities.[8] But whatever aims lay uppermost in the minds of medieval college founders at any particular period, the fusion of subjective spiritual motivation with objective educational purpose is an enduring characteristic of the collegiate movement.

The university collegiate system seems to have originated at Paris in so far as rudimentary colleges emerged there probably earlier than elsewhere. The initial group of Parisian college founders had no more elaborate aim than to furnish humble accommodation for poor students. The oldest European college about which there is definite evidence is the Collège des Dix-Huit, established at Paris in 1180.[9] This was a primitive foundation with, apparently, no arrangements made for internal government or for domestic economy. However, by virtue of its endowment, though that was a

---

[5] See e.g. A. L. Gabriel, 'The College System in the Fourteenth-Century Universities', *The Forward Movement of the Fourteenth Century* (ed. F. L. Utley, Ohio, 1961), pp. 79 ff. at p. 82.

[6] *Chartularium*, i. no. 32.

[7] E.g. Gabriel, 'Motivation of the Founders of Mediaeval Colleges', pp. 69–70.

[8] See M. H. Curtis, *Oxford and Cambridge in Transition 1558–1642*, pp. 70–2, 105–6; J. K. McConica, *English Humanists and Reformation Politics* (Oxford, 1965), pp. 76 ff.

[9] The foundation charter of this college is printed in *Chartularium*, i. no. 50. For a detailed discussion of this college, see J. M. Reitzel, *The Founding of the Earliest Secular Colleges within the Universities of Paris and Oxford* (unpublished Ph.D. thesis, Brown University, 1971), pp. 36–52.

modest one, it may be categorized a college or *collegium*, the progenitor of the collegiate family in Europe.

By the mid-thirteenth century, Paris had a cluster of colleges similar to or slightly more advanced than the Collège des Dix-Huit, all of which had only a minimal constitutional link with the University.[10] In general, most of these early Paris colleges were designed either for the support of grammar boys or for the support of youths who had completed their grammatical training and had embarked upon the arts course or for the support of both categories. That is to say, they were for advanced schoolboys or university undergraduates or both. A fundamental point of reference in European collegiate history was inaugurated with the College of the Sorbonne, founded in *c.* 1257/8 by Robert de Sorbon, chaplain to Louis IX.[11] The innovation *par excellence* of the Sorbonne was that it was confined to graduates — to scholars who had acquired the degree of M.A. and were destined to embrace the heavy course leading to the doctorate in theology. It was to be essentially a community of scholars with like-minded interests who, in theory at any rate, were to live together in harmonious amity and in an environment of stimulating intellectual exchange; a Christian society embodying spiritual, moral and academic excellence, and clearly very far removed from the unsophisticated colleges which had hitherto characterized the Parisian collegiate landscape. And it is this College of the Sorbonne which served as the most influential exemplar for the colleges of Oxford and Cambridge.

The English secular colleges had, as their original aim, the promotion of higher-faculty students in their universities. In an age without state support for postgraduates, it was often extremely difficult for the promising B.A. or M.A. graduate of slender means to remain at university to take a degree in one of the superior faculties — law, theology and medicine. Because of the length and expense of the courses in these disciplines, there was, in the

---

[10] For these early foundations, see e.g. Rashdall, *Universities*, i. 501 ff.

[11] See P. Glorieux, *Les Origines du Collège de Sorbonne* (Texts and Studies in the History of Mediaeval Education, no. viii, Notre Dame, Indiana, 1959); A. L. Gabriel, 'Robert de Sorbonne', *Revue de l'Université d'Ottawa*, 23 (1953), pp. 473 ff.

thirteenth and fourteenth centuries, a priority need to make provision for the longer-term scholar. Consequently, the English secular colleges were designed to give not a general arts education, but a diet of advanced arts and superior faculty studies, the exact scope of which varied according to the interests and predilections of the founder. In this regard, the early English colleges were similar to the Sorbonne, the European matrix of the purely graduate secular college. English collegiate history began in 1264 with the foundation of Merton College, Oxford, which must rank as the prototype of the English 'graduate' college of the pre-Reformation era.[12] It was followed by University College, Oxford, in *c.* 1280 and by Balliol in 1282. At Cambridge, the only thirteenth-century college, Peterhouse, was established by Hugh de Balsham, bishop of Ely, in 1284.[13]

---

[12] It is relevant to point out here that De Vaux College, founded at Salisbury by Bishop Bridport in 1262, has a tenuous claim to be regarded as 'the first university college in England': K. Edwards, 'College of De Vaux Salisbury', *Victoria History of the County of Wiltshire,* iii (ed. R. B. Pugh and E. Crittall, Oxford, 1956), 369 ff. at 371; see further A. F. Leach, *A History of Winchester College* (London, 1899), p. 86. An award of 1279 made between the chancellor and subdean of Salisbury Cathedral 'shows that most of the essentials of a *studium generale* or university then existed at Salisbury': Edwards, 'The Cathedral of Salisbury', *Victoria History of the County of Wiltshire,* iii (ed. R. B. Pugh and E. Crittall, Oxford, 1956), 156 ff. at 169 and *The English Secular Cathedrals in the Middle Ages,* ed. cit., p. 194. The nascent university was evidently not sustained, but De Vaux College remained until its dissolution in 1542, and it is known that throughout its history a fair proportion of its fellows took degrees at Oxford and elsewhere. For a detailed examination of this college, see Edwards, 'College of De Vaux Salisbury', op. cit., iii. 369–85.

[13] On the foundation of Merton, University and Balliol Colleges, see e.g. J. R. L. Highfield, 'The Early Colleges', *The History of the University of Oxford,* i. 225 ff., *passim*; H. W. Garrod, 'Merton College', *V. C. H. Oxon.* iii. 95 ff.; B. W. Henderson, *Merton College* (College Histories Series, London, 1899), ch. 1; A. Oswald, 'University College', *V. C. H. Oxon.* iii. 61 ff.; R. W. Hunt, 'Balliol College', ibid., iii. 82 ff. On University and Balliol Colleges, see further Reitzel, *The Founding of the Earliest Secular Colleges within the Universities of Paris and Oxford,* pp. 187–245. Although the scholars of John de Balliol were settled in Oxford before June 1266, the college dates as a legal corporation from the issue of the first statutes in 1282: on this point, see H. W. C. Davis, *A History of Balliol College* (2nd ed. by R. H. C. Davis and R. Hunt, Oxford, 1963), pp. 8–9. On the foundation of Peterhouse, see e.g. H. Butterfield, 'Peterhouse', *V. C. H. Camb.* iii. 334 ff.; Reitzel, op. cit., pp. 246–9; Rubin, *Charity and Community in Medieval Cambridge,* pp. 271–3.

It is clear, then, that English colleges and undergraduates[14] were relatively late bedfellows. As in the case of Paris University, students, in the early stages of English university development, lived a separate existence, wherever they could find accommodation compatible with their means, either in the halls of Oxford or in the hostels of Cambridge,[15] or in inns, or in private dwellings. This posed the major problem for the university authorities of both Oxford and Cambridge of how to discipline this academic population, distributed as it was throughout the town.[16] In the first half of the thirteenth century, the initial step taken towards solving this difficulty at both Universities was to ensure that every *bona fide* student had his name inscribed on the *matricula*, the roll of a regent master, whose ordinary lectures he was obliged to attend in the schools. In return, the master would protect, and be answerable for the conduct of, his charge.[17] But this contractual device proved

---

[14] Throughout this book the term 'undergraduate' is taken to mean a scholar who had not yet 'determined' as a bachelor.

[15] The most usual word for hall at Oxford was *aula*, although a range of other terms are found, including *hospicium*, *domus* and *introitus*. At Cambridge, *hospicium* was, at least in the fourteenth and fifteenth centuries, the normal appellation for hostel, the equivalent of the Oxford hall. In the thirteenth century, however, *domus* was used probably just as much as *hospicium* with reference to Cambridge hostels. *Aula* was commonly utilized at Cambridge as a less formal title than *collegium* for collegiate foundations: for example, *Aula Regis* (the King's Hall) and *Aula Trinitatis* (Trinity Hall). The situation is further complicated by the fact that at Oxford and Cambridge *domus* was sometimes applied to collegiate establishments in the late thirteenth and early fourteenth centuries before being superseded by *collegium* as the official term at both Universities. On this confusing terminology, see A. B. Emden, *An Oxford Hall in Medieval Times* (Oxford, 1927), pp. 43–5; see also the remarks of Hackett, *The Original Statutes of Cambridge University*, p. 86.

[16] Much information on disorder and disciplinary matters in medieval Oxford is given by Pantin, *Oxford Life in Oxford Archives*, chs. 1, 2, 6, 10.

[17] For the *matricula* arrangements at Oxford, see the statute of *a.* 1231 in Gibson, *Statuta Antiqua*, p. 82: and for later legislation on this theme, pp. 60–1, 83. For the equivalent legislation of the first half of the thirteenth century at Cambridge see Hackett, op. cit., pp. 210–11, with discussion, pp. 72–4: see also *Camb. Docs.*, i. 332–3, and the Old Proctor's Book (*Liber procuratoris antiquus*), CUL/COLL ADMIN 3, fo. 25. The Old Proctor's Book contains the official codex of the university statutes and seems to have been compiled in *c.* 1390–5: the statutes take up fos. 17–40v.

inadequate, for the lecture room was a poor disciplinary unit. The university establishments soon came to see that a more effective control could be maintained through the licensed halls or hostels where the students spent a good part of their time.[18] As the number of halls and hostels multiplied, so they came to house the majority of the undergraduates.[19] By this development, the worst excesses of disorder and criminality were eliminated. Nonetheless, the disciplining of the undergraduate population through the halls and hostels could not provide the final solution to the problems of student misconduct. The main disadvantage of the halls and hostels was that they were unendowed societies, with no security of tenure beyond the year for which the premises had been leased. They were, therefore, potentially unstable units, a situation worsened by an unedifying mercenary competition among their governing principals for the custom of the fee-paying undergraduates. Moreover, lacking the resources with which the colleges were able to erect their increasingly imposing buildings in the later medieval period, the insecure halls and hostels came to be overshadowed by comparison. When the colleges began to open their doors to paying students, the position of the halls and hostels became progressively less tenable.

Before the mainstream transference of the undergraduate population to the colleges had been set in motion, there were two exceptional and highly influential colleges which had housed a significant proportion of undergraduates either as fellows or as probationary fellows. It is apparent that the royal College of the King's Hall, Cambridge, whose origins, as the Society of the King's Scholars, date from *c*. 1317, and which became an endowed college in 1337, was the first English college to incorporate a

[18] See e.g. Pantin, op. cit., pp. 2–3.

[19] For halls and hostels, see Emden, *An Oxford Hall in Medieval Times;* W. A. Pantin, 'The Halls and Schools of medieval Oxford: an attempt at reconstruction', *Oxford Studies presented to Daniel Callus*, pp.31 ff.; H. P. Stokes, *The Mediaeval Hostels of the University of Cambridge* (C.A.S., Octavo Publications, xlix, 1924); R. Willis and J. W. Clark, *The Architectural History of the University of Cambridge and of the Colleges of Cambridge and Eton* (4 vols., Cambridge, 1886), i. xix–xxviii; Mullinger, *The University of Cambridge,* i. 217–21.

sizeable undergraduate element which, at the same time, formed an integral part of the institution.[20] As a college which accommodated an association of university scholars engaged in study from undergraduate to doctoral level, the King's Hall possessed more than half a century earlier a cardinal ingredient of New College, Oxford, which was founded in 1379, and which has often been designated the fount of the mixed collegiate ideal.[21] In other words, New College has, in the past, been singled out repeatedly as the foundation whereby the Mertonian 'graduate' college tradition was deflected into those channels which produced the mixed or consciously balanced societies characteristic of the sixteenth century, but the element of conscious balance apart, it is clear that, in fact, the King's Hall was the pristine example of the English secular college which enabled a scholar to pass through the entire educational gamut within the walls of the same institution: the distinctive type of English college of the pre-Reformation era.

Although the King's Hall and later New College were important practical examples of mixed undergraduate and graduate societies and undoubtedly helped to promote the institutional species which ultimately was to dominate their respective universities, the mass infiltration of the colleges by English undergraduates was, in the main, consequent upon social and economic pressures. As already indicated, the university authorities came to believe that the long-term solution to the matter of the governance of students was to house the undergraduates in the purpose-built colleges, where a more disciplined style of life could be enforced. This could not be achieved overnight. Economic pressures bearing upon the colleges, however, eventually led them to adopt measures which ended in their absorption of the undergraduate sector.[22] Inflationary trends of the late fifteenth and early sixteenth centuries motivated the colleges, whose revenues depended in substantial part upon fixed rents, to seek out novel ways of increasing their finances. One such

[20] See Cobban, *The King's Hall,* esp. pp. 50 ff.

[21] For the relative significance of the King's Hall and New College in English academic history, see the detailed discussion, ibid., ch. 2.

[22] On the transference of the undergraduates to the colleges, see conveniently Emden, op. cit., introductory.

means was to extend a cautious welcome to undergraduates. The heart-searchings involved may well be imagined. Nevertheless, financial interests prevailed over the exclusiveness of the fellows, especially when they realized that their incomes could be augmented with tutorial fees. Although lectures and academic exercises had certainly been staged in the Oxford halls from at least the fourteenth century, as they had indeed in the Oxford monastic colleges,[23] many of the halls and hostels of Oxford and Cambridge did not possess teaching facilities comparable to those of the colleges, lacking, as they did, not only permanency, but also a sufficiently large and long-tenured graduate teaching force. As a result, the secular colleges were able to attract a flow of undergraduates on the strength of the tutorial advantages they offered. With the establishment of endowed college-lectureships from the second half of the fifteenth century both in the older colleges and in the new foundations of the late-medieval period, teaching came to be centred in the colleges, a process which was virtually complete by the beginning of the reign of Elizabeth.[24] This will be the subject of a detailed appraisal in chapter 5.

By Elizabeth's reign, the colleges had emerged, to a lesser or greater extent, as self-contained teaching units, increasingly less reliant upon the increasingly moribund system of public instruction offered by the universities. A tardy effort was made to stem this decentralizing movement by regenerating English university teaching through the establishment of a body of salaried lecturers or professors who would be part of the university's teaching contingent rather than of that of the college network.[25] But despite these attempts to bolster the mechanism of public university instruction, the course of events had gone too far in favour of the colleges to be reversed. These efforts proved to be both too late and too little to prevent the colleges from becoming the central teaching

[23] For lectures and academic exercises in Oxford monastic colleges and in halls, see Cobban, 'Decentralized Teaching in the Medieval English Universities', art. cit., pp. 193–4, 199–200.

[24] On the decentralization of teaching in the secular colleges of the English universities, see Cobban, art. cit., and Cobban, *The Medieval Universities,* esp. pp. 141 ff.; also Curtis, *Oxford and Cambridge in Transition,* pp. 102–5.

[25] See Curtis, op. cit., pp. 101–2; Cobban, *The King's Hall,* pp. 81–2.

organs within Oxford and Cambridge, a position generally maintained right down to the twentieth century (when, however, there has been a perceptible shift of emphasis back towards the university sector).

From the fact that the majority of the undergraduate students of Oxford and Cambridge remained external to the secular colleges until the late fifteenth and early sixteenth centuries, it follows that until that period the colleges accommodated only a small proportion of the two academic populations. Although the matter of the numbers of those resident at the medieval English Universities is a problem incapable of definite resolution, it has been estimated that in the late fourteenth century Cambridge's academic population may have ranged between 400 and 700, while that of Oxford seems to have been in the region of 1,500.[26] In the fourteenth century, according to their statutes, the eight Cambridge colleges furnished a total of 137 fellowships, excluding headships, distributed as follows: Peterhouse 14; Michaelhouse 6; the King's Hall 32; Clare 19; Pembroke 24; Gonville 20; Trinity Hall 20; and Corpus Christi 2.[27] Except for those for the King's Hall, Michaelhouse, Corpus Christi and possibly Peterhouse, these statutory figures are misleading as to the actual numbers of fellows maintained. The number of fellows at Clare probably never exceeded 13; the usual number at Gonville appears to have been about 4, and at Trinity Hall, it was about the same or occasionally less; and in the fourteenth century, Pembroke had only about 6 fellows, and at the beginning of the fifteenth century, about 9.[28]

---

[26] See the estimates of Aston, Duncan and Evans, 'The Medieval Alumni of the University of Cambridge', art. cit., pp. 26–7.

[27] See the statutes of Peterhouse, Clare, Pembroke and Trinity Hall, *Camb. Docs.*, ii. 19–20, 129, 193, 417–18; see the statutes of Michaelhouse in A. E. Stamp, *Michaelhouse* (privately printed, Cambridge, 1924), p. 41, and in Mullinger, *The University of Cambridge*, i. 640–1, and the statutes of the King's Hall in Rouse Ball, *The King's Scholars and King's Hall*, p. 64. For Gonville and Corpus Christi, see P. Grierson, 'Gonville and Caius College', *V. C. H. Camb.* iii. 356 ff. at 357, and J. P. T. Bury, 'Corpus Christi College', *V. C. H. Camb.* iii. 371 ff. at 372.

[28] For numbers at Clare, see W. J. Harrison, 'Clare College', *V. C. H. Camb.* iii. 340 ff. at 342. Numbers at Gonville are discussed by Grierson, 'Gonville and Caius College', ibid., iii. 357. For the years between 1350 and 1400, the names

When these actual numbers are added to the relatively accurate statutory figures for the King's Hall, Michaelhouse, Corpus Christi and Peterhouse, the more reliable total is recorded of about 80 fellowships provided by the Cambridge colleges in the fourteenth century.[29] This is higher than the number of fellowships furnished by the Oxford colleges before 1379. It has been computed that, prior to the virtual doubling of the number of fellowships with the foundation of New College in 1379, the six secular colleges supplied a total of only about 63 graduate fellows.[30] As Oxford's population may have been two or three times the size of that of Cambridge, and since the Cambridge colleges harboured a larger number of fellowships, it would appear that the proportion of college fellows to university residents must have been greater at Cambridge than at Oxford. It would, therefore, seem valid to conclude that before 1379 the Cambridge colleges occupied a more prominent position within the *studium* than did their Oxford counterparts. This situation was apparently carried forward into the fifteenth century. By *c.* 1450, Cambridge's population may well have risen to about 1,300, while that of Oxford may have increased slightly to about 1,700.[31] Since the statutory number of college fellowships at Cambridge in the mid-fifteenth century was in the region of 225, and that of those at Oxford between 150 and 200,[32] it

of only about 18 fellows, including the masters, have been discovered: see C. N. L. Brooke, *A History of Gonville and Caius College* (The Boydell Press, Suffolk, 1985), p. 30. Details of numbers at Trinity Hall are given by C. W. Crawley, *Trinity Hall: The History of a Cambridge College 1350–1975* (Cambridge, 1976), p. 15, and 'Trinity Hall', *V. C. H. Camb.* iii. 362 ff. at 363; see also *Warren's Book* (ed. A. W. W. Dale, Cambridge, 1911), p. 1. For numbers at Pembroke, see A. Attwater, *Pembroke College, Cambridge* (ed. with an introduction and postscipt by S. C. Roberts, Cambridge, 1936), pp. 13, 15.

[29] Aston has advanced a maximum figure of 123 fellowships, compared with my figure of about 80: Aston et al., 'The Medieval Alumni of the University of Cambridge', p. 13 and n. 10. My figure is exclusive of heads of colleges, while that of Mr Aston is inclusive.

[30] Salter, *Medieval Oxford,* p. 97. The six secular Oxford colleges founded before 1379 were Merton, University College, Balliol, Exeter, Oriel and Queen's.

[31] Aston et al., 'The Medieval Alumni of the University of Cambridge', pp. 13, 19, 26.

[32] Ibid., p. 14.

is clear that, if the statutory numbers are given their full weight, the Cambridge colleges continued to maintain a proportionately larger place within the University than that held by the Oxford colleges at Oxford.

On the basis of computations made using the numbers found in the statutes, it would appear that the King's Hall accounted for just over a fifth of the total number of fellowships supplied by the Cambridge colleges in the fourteenth century, this royal college furnishing 32 out of 137 fellowships. But the real proportion, as evidenced by the figures given for the actual, lower number of fellowships, was about double, with the King's Hall supplying 32 or more from the revised total of about 80 fellowships. In the light of this, it would seem that the King's Hall was responsible for about 40 per cent of the Cambridge college fellowships of the fourteenth century. This is a very high percentage for a single college and is paralleled only by the performance of Merton College, Oxford. Since Merton made provision for 30 or more out of a total of about 63 fellowships before 1379,[33] it is apparent that the King's Hall and Merton each supplied just under half of the fellowships of their respective universities. From this, it is evident that the King's Hall was by far the largest and most important of the Cambridge colleges for well over a hundred years. Its position within the *studium* was not challenged until King's College did so in the second half of the fifteenth century.[34] Indeed, it has not been generally appreciated that, prior to the foundation of New College, Oxford, the King's Hall shared with Merton the distinction of being one of the two largest and most celebrated of all the English colleges.[35] Whereas

---

[33] Salter, op. cit., p. 97.

[34] Founded in 1441.

[35] The high regard in which the King's Hall was held in university circles is well brought out in Richard Parker's *History and Antiquities of the University of Cambridge,* completed in 1622. There it is recorded that in the King's Hall there were elderly fellows so noted for their gravity and wisdom that the college was looked upon as the oracle (*oraculum*) of the University. As Parker, himself a fellow of Caius, was writing less than eighty years after the dissolution of the King's Hall in 1546, it may be assumed that his comments embody something of the contemporary reputation enjoyed by the King's Hall within the medieval University: see the Latin text of Parker's *History,* first published by T. Hearne in his edition of J. Leland, *Collectanea,* v (Oxford, 1715), 185 ff. at 244;

Merton's reputation derived originally from its antiquity and its position as the prototype of the 'graduate' college of the pre-Reformation era and was sustained by its intellectual excellence in the fourteenth century, especially in the spheres of logic, physics and theology, the reputation of the King's Hall was based on its royal household origins, its size, and the special relationship it maintained with the king and the court, every warden and fellow being appointed directly by the crown — a unique feature in English academic history.[36]

The typical English medieval college was a self-governing community of fellows organized on democratic lines. In every college founded before 1500, with the exception of the King's Hall, Cambridge, the right of electing the warden, master, president, and provost was conferred by statute on the fellows themselves. Although the results of these elections usually required confirmation by an external authority, such as the bishop of the diocese or the university chancellor, where this was so, it was normally stipulated that the confirmation was to be of a nominal character.[37] Similarly, most codes of English college statutes make provision for the removal of an unsuitable master.[38] The details of this provision vary from code to code, but the basic point is that the constitutional machinery existed for this purpose, and could be set in motion by the fellows of the college. These inviolable statutory rights of election to the headship and this power of removal vested in the *comitia*, the collective body formed by all the members on the boards of the foundation, constituted two of the three indispensable preconditions of the self-governing English college society of the Middle Ages. The third was the right of co-optation of members.

In at least four of the English colleges, the French practice of vesting control of the patronage in an external authority, such as an

for translation, see R. Parker, *The History and Antiquities of the University of Cambridge* (London, 1721 (?)), p. 139; reproduced by E. Carter, *The History of the University of Cambridge* (London, 1753), p. 307.

[36] Cobban, *The King's Hall*, pp. 21, 148 ff.

[37] See, from numerous examples, the statutes of Michaelhouse in Stamp, *Michaelhouse*, p. 46, and the statutes of Trinity Hall in *Camb. Docs.*, ii. 421.

[38] See e.g. the statutes of Clare and Trinity Hall, *Camb. Docs.*, ii. 128–9, 426.

archbishop, a bishop, the head of a religious house, or a group of university officials, found, for a time, a pale reflection.[39] In the case of University College, Oxford, the original four masters were, by the statutes of 1280, placed under the care of the chancellor and the masters of the University, especially the masters of theology, who, with the chancellor, were to be principally concerned with the election to vacant fellowships. Moreover, the senior fellow, who served as head of the society, had to act in conjunction with an external master of arts. In 1292, the requirement for an external supervisory master was eliminated, but the college was to be under the government of the chancellor and masters of theology, who were to elect the new fellows. By 1311, however, the power to elect to fellowships had been vested in the college society, the university authorities retaining a right of veto. In the course of the fourteenth century, University College acquired a substantial degree of autonomy as outside restraints were significantly reduced.[40] The statutes of 1282 of Dervorguilla, widow of John de Balliol, placed the principal and scholars of Balliol College, Oxford, under the supervision of two external procurators (*procuratores*), a Franciscan friar and a secular master of arts, who were to confirm the election of the principal, to elect to vacancies, and generally, to administer the funds and property of the establishment.[41] Although their powers steadily diminished, the office of the external procurators, or 'rectors', as they came to be styled, persisted until the beginning of the sixteenth century, when, by the new statutes of 1507, it was abolished.[42] Similarly, in her first code of statutes, Mary de Valence,

---

[39] For Parisian influence on the Oxford colleges of the late thirteenth century, see J. R. L. Highfield, *The Early Rolls of Merton College, Oxford* (Oxf. Hist. Soc., new series, xviii, 1964), pp. 67–8.

[40] On the governmental situation at University College, see Rashdall, *Universities*, iii. 178; Oswald, 'University College', *V. C. H. Oxon.* iii. 61–2. The statutes of 1280 are printed in *Munimenta Academica*, ii. 780–3, and the statutes of 1311 in ibid., i. 87–91, and in *Mediaeval Archives*, 84–6.

[41] The statutes of 1282 are printed in *Statutes*, i. ch. 1, v–vii, and in *The Oxford Deeds of Balliol College* (ed. H. E. Salter, Oxford, 1913), pp. 277–9; see also R. W. Hunt, 'Balliol College', *V. C. H. Oxon.* iii. 82; H. W. C. Davis, *A History of Balliol College*, ed. cit., pp. 10 ff.

[42] The statutes of 1507 are printed in *Statutes*, i. ch. 1, 1 ff.; see also Mallet, *A History of the University of Oxford*, i. 103–4.

countess of Pembroke, subjected her Cambridge college to the authority of two annually elected external rectors with restricted powers of visitation and charged with the duty of admitting newly elected fellows. No trace of these rectors occurs in the later fourteenth-century code, and it is to be assumed that their powers had before then been transferred to the master and fellows of the college.[43] This situation was partly paralleled at Peterhouse, Cambridge, where the bishop of Ely, as founder, initially retained the patronage of the college for himself. In 1338, this was partly resigned to the master and fellows by Bishop Montacute, who nevertheless reserved to himself and to his successors the right of admitting scholars and of choosing the master from two candidates elected by the college.[44]

From these details, it is clear that what French influence there was on early English collegiate development was of a transitory character. It was so obviously unpopular that the Parisian 'external' attributes were soon discarded in favour of the indigenous Mertonian pattern of internal self-government, with full powers of co-optation of members vested in the fellows. In the broad context of the academic history of England in the pre-Reformation era, it is arguable that, with respect to patronage arrangements, the King's Hall, Cambridge, affords the one lasting parallel with the French colleges. From the foundation in *c.* 1317 of the Society of the King's Scholars, which became the endowed College of the King's Hall in 1337, to the dissolution of the college in 1546, the patronage lay entirely with the kings of England. This circumstance prevented evolution towards full corporate independence. Doubtless, the dual founders, Edward II and Edward III, were influenced by the 'external' arrangements of the Paris colleges. But the overriding consideration derived from the fact that the King's Hall was designed, at least in part, to serve the needs of the royal household,

---

[43] See Attwater, *Pembroke College, Cambridge*, p. 9; Rashdall, op. cit., iii. 305–6.

[44] Rashdall, op. cit., iii. 296–7. For the bishop of Ely's residual powers of patronage, see the statutes of 1344 in *Camb. Docs.*, ii. 60, 64–5; see also T. A. Walker, *Peterhouse* (College Histories Series, London, 1906), p. 49. The statutes of 1344 refer to earlier statutes, but these have not survived: see R. Lovatt, 'The Early Archives of Peterhouse', *Peterhouse Record* (1975–6), pp. 26 ff. at p. 34.

the court, and the various departments of government. If this objective were to be fulfilled, it was essential that the king should exercise a direct supervision over the appointment of collegiate personnel.

While ultimate sovereignty in most English medieval colleges resided in the fellows, acting together as a body or corporation, day-to-day administrative business was usually conducted jointly by the head of college and committees of elected fellows. In most collegiate societies, though not perhaps in all, the organization was so designed that the majority of fellows who stayed for any length of time at some point in their tenure would play a part, however small, in the running of college affairs. For example, the statutes of Queen's College, Oxford, enjoin that every fellow, the provost and the doctors in theology and canon law excepted, was to undertake the office of seneschal of the hall in weekly rotation.[45] A similar arrangement was in operation at New College, Oxford,[46] and also at King's College, Cambridge.[47] The 'democratic' involvement of the fellows of the King's Hall in collegiate government might not have been as extensive as that which prevailed in the average type of English college. But a detailed study of the annually elected committees of seneschals[48] reveals that, although they were weighted towards relatively senior members of this royal society, there was, throughout the history of the college, a healthy turnover of personnel which prevented the growth of oligarchical government.

Generally speaking, English colleges contrived to secure that the administrative burden in internal and external affairs fell with a distributed weight upon a broad section of the fellowship. Fellows in most English colleges were constitutionally involved in the governmental process from the start. The powers of the head of college were hedged around with effective checks and balances, and, in the main, the fellows seemed to acquiesce in this form of

[45] *Statutes*, i. ch. 4, 25.

[46] Ibid., i. ch. 5, 42.

[47] *Camb. Docs.*, ii. 533.

[48] See Cobban, *The King's Hall*, pp. 181–2.

contractual division of authority, worked out by the founder and developed and adjusted in the light of experience. Even if mundane collegiate business was the preserve of small committees of fellows, the majority consent of the fellowship, registered through a college meeting, was normally required for items of high expenditure, or matters of particular difficulty or delicacy which deeply affected the life of the society. The combination of the ultimate deterrent — the college meeting — and the operative principle of election to administrative office, ensured that a system of responsible government was firmly embedded in the constitutions of most of the English medieval colleges.

The pattern of collegiate development at Oxford and Cambridge makes for a notable comparison. In the late thirteenth and early fourteenth centuries, four Oxford colleges were founded: Merton (1264), University College (*c.* 1280), Balliol (1282) and Exeter (*c.* 1314). For some thirty years following the foundation of Peterhouse in 1284, Cambridge's only thirteenth-century college, no other college was established and no marked interest was seemingly taken in the University on the part of potential college founders. But in 1317, the situation was dramatically changed when Edward II settled his Society of the King's Scholars in Cambridge. The Society was, in effect, an extension or arm of Edward II's chapel royal established in the University of Cambridge. As such, it was the first royal colony of clerks to be located in the English Universities and constituted the initial institutional link forged between the latter and the royal household, a prestigious bond sustained down to the mid-sixteenth century.[49] After the settlement of the Society of the King's Scholars in Cambridge, the shape of collegiate expansion at both Universities was radically altered. At Oxford only two colleges, Oriel in 1324 and Queen's in 1341, were founded in the remainder of the first half of the fourteenth century. At Cambridge, on the other hand, no fewer than seven colleges were established between 1300 and 1352: Michaelhouse (1324); University or Clare Hall (1326); the King's Hall (1337); Pembroke Hall (1347); Gonville Hall (1349); Trinity Hall (1350); and Corpus Christi College (1352), for long more

---

[49] See ibid., ch. 1 and *passim.*

usually styled 'St Benet's College'.[50] It is apparent that the coming of royal patronage to Cambridge in the form of the King's Scholars was followed by a reappraisal of their attitude towards the Universities by those sections of society which produced the college founders and benefactors of fourteenth-century England. Whereas Oxford had hitherto drawn off much of the surplus wealth available for university purposes, now affluent, high-ranking members of the ministerial class, such as Hervey de Stanton, founder of Michaelhouse, ecclesiastics of the calibre of William Bateman, bishop of Norwich, papal judge and royal diplomat, and founder of Trinity Hall and second founder of Gonville Hall, and rich lay patrons, of whom Lady Clare and the countess of Pembroke are prominent examples, had all come to regard Cambridge as a sound 'investment' for the future, sealed with the stamp of royal approval.

There seems little doubt that one of the chief inspirations behind this new-found confidence in Cambridge University, expressed in the sudden flow of interest and material resources towards the *studium*, was the encouraging presence there of England's most thoroughly royal academic college of the medieval period. Until the foundation of King's College, Cambridge, in 1441, the King's Hall remained the only true royal establishment at either of the English Universities. Oriel (1324) and Queen's (1341) at Oxford cannot be reckoned royal foundations in a strict technical sense. (Oriel, founded by the chancery clerk, Adam de Brome, was later re-established with Edward II as nominal founder; and Queen's, founded by Robert de Eglesfield, chaplain to Queen Philippa, consort of Edward III, was placed under the patronage of the queens of England.) Moreover, the King's Hall was marked off from all other English colleges with royal associations by virtue of the fact that all of its fellows and wardens were crown appointees. This placed the King's Hall in a unique relationship with the king and the central government. Whereas the Capetian kings of France had,

---

[50] In the medieval period, Cambridge colleges were frequently referred to as 'halls'. 'Hall' was the translation of the Latin term *aula*, which was commonly used at Cambridge for 'college' as a less formal alternative to *collegium*. When 'college' eventually superseded 'hall' as the established nomenclature at Cambridge, Trinity Hall retained its medieval title to avoid a clash with Trinity College.

in the early fourteenth century, developed a system of annual grants to be paid to a chain of Parisian colleges, irrespective of the circumstances of their foundation,[51] the English kings seem to have concentrated their major collegiate benefactions on the King's Hall and King's College, with intermittent donations to other university colleges.

The foundation of New College, Oxford, by William of Wykeham in 1379 was something of a landmark in English collegiate history. In terms of scale, both in the number of fellowships and in the magnificence and layout of its buildings, the college surpassed all existing foundations.[52] As previously mentioned, the number of fellowships offered by the Oxford secular colleges was virtually doubled by the establishment of New College. It might be thought that Wykeham's foundation would have precipitated a major phase of collegiate expansion. But by 1400, Oxford had effectuated only seven secular colleges compared with the eight of Cambridge; and whereas Cambridge realized five new colleges in the fifteenth century, that is, Godshouse (1439), King's College (1441), Queens' College (1446), St Catharine's College (1473), and Jesus College (1497), Oxford achieved only the three colleges of Lincoln (1427), All Souls (1437/8), and Magdalen (1448), all of them in the first half of the century. It seems that Henry V had the intention, frustrated by his death, of founding a secular college for arts and theology, to be established in Oxford castle and supported from the revenues of alien priories. The

---

[51] See F. J. Pegues, 'Philanthropy and the Universities in France and England in the Later Middle Ages', *The Economic and Material Frame of the Mediaeval University* (Texts and Studies in the History of Mediaeval Education, no. xv, Notre Dame, Indiana, 1977),pp. 69 ff. at p. 72.

[52] Discussion of Wykeham as an educational innovator can be found e.g. in A. H. Smith, *New College, Oxford, and its Buildings* (Oxford, 1952); A. F. Leach, *A History of Winchester College;* H. Rashdall and R. S. Rait, *New College* (London, 1901); G. R. Potter, 'Education in the Fourteenth and Fifteenth Centuries', *Cambridge Medieval History,* viii (ed. C. W. Previté-Orton and Z. N. Brooke, 1936), pp. 688 ff.; C. P. McMahon, *Education in Fifteenth Century England,* reprinted from *The Johns Hopkins University Studies in Education,* no. 35 (Baltimore, 1947); A. H. M. Jones, 'New College', *V. C. H. Oxon.* iii. 144 ff. at 154–5; R. L. Storey, 'The Foundation and the Medieval College, 1379–1530', *New College Oxford 1379–1979* (ed. J. Buxton and P. Williams, Oxford, 1979), pp. 3 ff.

tentative evidence for this is contained in Thomas Gascoigne's *Loci e Libro Veritatum,* written between the early 1430s and *c.* 1457, and in John Rous's *Historia Regum Angliae,* completed between 1485 and 1491.[53] Rous states that he saw a reference to the royal plan in a documentary source at Oxford (*'in scriptis Oxoniae'*) when visiting the town as a boy. From such frugal details, there would appear to have been no organic connection between this projected Henrician college and the three Oxford colleges founded in the fifteenth century before 1450.

There can be little doubt that the taint of heresy weakened the secular collegiate movement in Oxford. As the main intellectual focus of Wyclifite doctrine in the late fourteenth century, Oxford came to be deeply implicated with heresy. Although stringent efforts were made to purge the University of its Wyclifite and Lollard associations, the stigma of heresy lingered there for much of the fifteenth century. Oxford's reputation as 'the University of heresies' (Archbishop Courtenay) seems to have redounded to the profit of Cambridge. Because of its relative freedom from the suspicion of heresy, fifteenth-century Cambridge was regarded as a sound prospect for collegiate enterprise, and was, to some extent, used to counter the heretical tendencies of Oxford. It is virtually certain, for example, that Oxford's involvement with heresy was one of the considerations which prompted Henry VI to choose Cambridge for the academic project that eventually became King's College.[54] The founders of Cambridge colleges later in the fifteenth century, those of Queens', St Catharine's and Jesus, appear to have shared in this objective of reinforcing Cambridge as a bastion of orthodoxy.[55]

A series of attempts was made, however, to restore Oxford's doctrinal respectability, the most important institutional response

[53] T. Gascoigne, *Loci e Libro Veritatum,* ed. cit., pp. 218–19; J. Rous, *Historia Regum Angliae* (1st ed. by T. Hearne, Oxford, 1716), p. 208.

[54] See Rashdall, op. cit., iii. 316; see also the letters patent of Henry VI of 10 July 1443 in *Camb. Docs.,* ii. 471, where the king's intention that the college should aid in the extirpation of heresy is stated.

[55] On this subject, see Cobban, 'Origins: Robert Wodelarke and St Catharine's', *St Catharine's College 1473–1973* (ed. E. E. Rich, Leeds, 1973), pp. 1 ff. at pp. 11 ff.

being the foundation of Lincoln College in 1427 by Richard Fleming, bishop of Lincoln. Previously, Fleming had been suspected by Archbishop Arundel, apparently without justification, of harbouring Lollard opinion.[56] Whatever the case, Fleming in later life was much preoccupied with the issue of heresy, and the principal motive for his foundation was the establishment of a seminary for the production of graduates in theology as an aid towards combating the heresies and errors in the church, an aim somewhat reminiscent of the original Dominican ideal.[57] Lincoln appears to have been the first English secular college to be concerned specifically with anti-heretical drives. The next Oxford foundation, All Souls, prescribed heresy as one of the crimes for which a fellow may be expelled.[58] But apart from this, the issue did not figure largely at All Souls or indeed at Magdalen, founded later in the century. The idea of the secular college as a vehicle for the suppression of heresy was given a wider application in fifteenth-century Cambridge. As indicated, the extirpation of heresy was one of the motives underlying the foundation of King's College;[59] St Catharine's was much concerned with the preservation of Christian orthodoxy, and the crime of heresy was placed first among the statutory reasons for which a fellow may be deprived of his

---

[56] See *Snappe's Formulary*, pp. 95–8; see also A. Clark, 'Lincoln College', *The Colleges of Oxford* (2nd ed., London, 1892), pp. 171 ff. at p. 171.

[57] See the prefatory note later prefixed to the code of statutes given in 1479/80 by Thomas Rotheram, bishop of Lincoln and later archbishop of York (Fleming's envisaged statutes were never executed), where it is emphasized that Fleming's foundation was designed 'pro destruendis haeresibus, et erroribus evellendis, plantandisque sacrae doctrinae seminariis . . .': *Statutes,* i. ch. 6, 11. Henry VI's charter of 13 October 1427 for Lincoln rather oddly refers only indirectly to the heresy issue: Lincoln College Archives, Charters I, Box no. 7, and *Statutes,* i. ch. 6, 4–6. The anti-heretical motive for the foundation is also given primacy in a composition between the college and a relative of the founder contained in the earliest surviving register: Lincoln College Archives, *Vetus Registrum 1472–1570,* fo. 19. See also G. F. Lytle, 'Universities as Religious Authorities in the later Middle Ages and Reformation', *Reform and Authority in the Medieval and Reformation Church* (ed. G. F. Lytle, Washington, 1981), pp. 69 ff. at p. 81.

[58] *Statutes,* i. ch. 7, 66.

[59] *Camb. Docs.,* ii. 471.

fellowship;[60] and at Queens' and Jesus Colleges there was an emphasis on the conservation of the purity of the faith.[61] In view of Oxford's damaging associations with heresy, it is surprising that its collegiate sector did not afford more overt expression to anti-heretical affirmation.

The Oxford colleges were more heavily subject to ecclesiastical influences than were those of Cambridge. Of the ten secular colleges founded at Oxford between the late thirteenth and the end of the fifteenth century, nine had ecclesiastical founders, comprising five bishops, two of Winchester (New College and Magdalen), one of Rochester (Merton),[62] one of Exeter (Exeter), and one of Lincoln (Lincoln); an archbishop of Canterbury (All Souls); an archbishop-elect of Rouen (University);[63] an Oxford rector and chancery clerk, who associated Edward II as co-founder (Oriel); and a chaplain in the household of Queen Philippa (Queen's). Only Balliol had a secular founder, in the person of John de Balliol, lord of Barnard Castle, and his widow Dervorguilla, who gave the college its first statutes in 1282. Of the thirteen Cambridge colleges established during the same period, only three had episcopal founders (Peterhouse, Trinity Hall and Jesus), and three were founded by rectors (Gonville, Godshouse and Queens'), although Queens' acquired, as later founders, Queen Margaret of Anjou and Queen Elizabeth Woodville, consorts of Henry VI and Edward IV respectively. The remainder had, as secular founders, three kings

[60] See the original statutes, St Catharine's Muniments, XL/10, fos. 12v, 13; Philpott, *Documents relating to St Catharine's College in the University of Cambridge*, pp. 24–5.

[61] With reference to Queens' (and its earlier prototypes), this point is discussed by E. F. Jacob, *The Fifteenth Century 1399–1485* (Oxford, 1961), pp. 671–2, and Mullinger, *The University of Cambridge*, i. 313–14. For Jesus, see e.g. A. Gray, *The Earliest Statutes of Jesus College, Cambridge* (Cambridge, 1935).

[62] Merton's founder, Walter de Merton, became bishop of Rochester in 1274, following a period of two years during which he had been not only chancellor of England but virtually its regent: Highfield, *The Early Rolls of Merton College, Oxford*, p. 29.

[63] William of Durham, who may be regarded as the founder of University College, was sometime archbishop-elect of Rouen: Rashdall, *Universities*, iii. 176.

(the King's Hall and King's College),[64] a chancellor of the exchequer of Edward II (Michaelhouse), a provost of King's College (St Catharine's),[65] two wealthy noblewomen (Clare and Pembroke), and a Cambridge guild (Corpus Christi), the only instance of a guild as a college founder.

The more-pronounced ecclesiastical aura surrounding the Oxford colleges was further reinforced by the fact that the majority of their founders, following the fashion of college founders at Paris and in several of the French provincial universities,[66] placed their colleges under ecclesiastical supervision. For example, the bishop of Lincoln was visitor at Oriel and Lincoln, the bishop of Exeter at Exeter, the bishop of Winchester at New College and Magdalen, the archbishop of York at Queen's, and the archbishop of Canterbury at All Souls.[67] At Merton, the visitor was at first the bishop of Winchester, but later the founder transferred the office to the archbishop of Canterbury.[68] This presents a striking contrast to the situation at Cambridge, where the normal practice was to vest the power of visitation not in an ecclesiastic, but in the chancellor or vice-chancellor of the University,[69] although at Peterhouse, the bishop of Ely, and at King's College, the bishop of Lincoln, served

---

[64] The three kings comprise Edward II and Edward III, who may be reckoned the co-founders of the King's Hall, and Henry VI, the founder of King's College.

[65] By founding St Catharine's while still provost of King's College, Robert Wodelarke established a notable English academic record, in so far as this furnishes the only example in medieval England of the head of one college who was simultaneously the founder of another: Cobban, 'Origins: Robert Wodelarke and St Catharine's', pp. 6–7.

[66] On French provincial colleges and ecclesiastical control, see Cobban, 'Episcopal Control in the Mediaeval Universities of Northern Europe', p. 16 and notes.

[67] Information derived from *Statutes*, i, ii, and supplemented by the articles on the colleges in *V. C. H. Oxon.* iii; see also H. M. Jewell, 'English Bishops as Educational Benefactors in the Later Fifteenth Century', *The Church, Politics and Patronage in the Fifteenth Century* (ed. R. B. Dobson, Gloucester, 1984), pp. 146 ff. at pp. 151–2.

[68] Garrod, 'Merton College', *V. C. H. Oxon.* iii. 103 and n. 47; Highfield, *The Early Rolls of Merton College, Oxford*, pp. 75–6.

[69] Information derived from *Camb. Docs.*, ii, iii.

as visitor.[70] Even Bishop Bateman of Norwich, founder of Trinity Hall and secondary founder of Gonville Hall, appointed the chancellor as visitor of both colleges.[71] Furthermore, in every case in which the chancellor, or vice-chancellor, was visitor, his right of intervention was so hedged around with checks and balances as to render it largely inoperative in all but the most abnormal of circumstances. From the very outset, the Cambridge colleges were fiercely jealous of their independent status. A comparative study of their statutes reveals that, in the ordinary way, the jurisdiction of the chancellor and of the bishop of Ely over secular college affairs was kept to the absolute minimum. It is true that the authority of either the chancellor or bishop might be occasionally invoked to help resolve a point of unusual constitutional complexity.[72] Exceptional circumstances apart, however, the Cambridge colleges remained consistently opposed to the intervention of university and ecclesiastical authorities in their affairs. This collegiate difference between Oxford and Cambridge with respect to outside intervention will be further considered in chapter 7, where the relationships between the English Universities and external authorities are examined.

The preponderance of ecclesiastical founders of colleges at Oxford helps to explain why the concept of founder's kin became a prominent feature of the Oxford scene and why, by contrast, it does not appear to have materialized at Cambridge.[73] Since ecclesiastics of means could not have direct heirs, they were expected to provide for their immediate relatives, who would be deprived of much of their inheritance if an ecclesiastic vested substantial resources in a collegiate foundation. In order to compensate for loss to his relatives, a founder could at least arrange for members of his kindred to be educated at the college as a primary preferential right. The

---

[70] For Peterhouse, see ibid., ii. 38; for King's, see J. Saltmarsh, 'King's College', *V. C. H. Camb.* iii. 376 ff. at 377.

[71] *Camb. Docs.*, ii. 231–2, 420–1.

[72] For such instances, see e.g. the statutes of Clare, Gonville Hall and Trinity Hall, ibid., ii. 124, 128–9, 137–8, 232, 421, 426.

[73] The central study of founder's kin is by G. D. Squibb, *Founder's Kin: Privilege and Pedigree* (Oxford, 1972).

practice of according preference to founder's kin among the statutory categories of those eligible for admission to a secular college was inaugurated by Walter de Merton. As originally conceived in *c.* 1262–4, Merton College was designed for the sole benefit of the founder's numerous nephews.[74] When the scheme outgrew this initial purpose, founder's kin were given first preference in all three codes of Mertonian statutes of 1264, 1270 and 1274.[75] Through the operation of founder's kin, Walter de Merton made arrangements for the instruction of a number of *parvuli*, needy and orphan children of his kindred (*de parentela*). They were to be taught in the elements of learning, and the most promising of them were to be advanced to the status of scholar. The *parvuli* remained the special care of the warden. They were treated as part of his household, but lived outside the college in rented hospices with their own instructors.[76] Provision was also made for kinsmen by Robert de Eglesfield, founder of Queen's College, where they were to share a preference with youths from places where the college owned property. If they progressed to the requisite level, they were to be preferred in the election to fellowships.[77] At New College, the founder, William of Wykeham, ascribed the first preference in the recruitment of scholars to founder's kin. Although they were required to be competent in grammar, they were to be admitted as full fellows on a non-probationary basis.[78] Following Wykeham's example, Archbishop Chichele, founder of All Souls College, gave first preference for entry to founder's kin, who were to be elected full fellows from the start, all other entrants having to serve a probationary year, during which they were called *scolares*.[79]

Not all ecclesiastics who gave of their wealth and energies as

[74] Highfield, 'The Early Colleges', *The History of the University of Oxford,* i. 246 and *The Early Rolls of Merton College, Oxford,* pp. 5–8.

[75] *Statutes,* i. ch. 2, 6 (code of 1264), 17 (code of 1270), 36 (code of 1274); see also Squibb, op. cit., pp.5–8.

[76] Highfield (ed)., *The Early Rolls of Merton College, Oxford,* p. 72.

[77] *Statutes,* i. ch. 4, 12; Squibb, op. cit., p. 8.

[78] *Statutes,* i. ch. 5, 5; Squibb, op. cit., pp. 8–9.

[79] *Statutes,* i. ch. 7, 21–2; Squibb, op. cit., pp. 9–10.

founders of Oxford colleges made arrangements for their kin. For example, Richard Fleming, bishop of Lincoln and founder of Lincoln College, contributed little to the endowment of his college from property which would otherwise have passed to his relations. He was therefore presumably under less pressure than were Merton, Eglesfield, Wykeham and Chichele to make special educational provision for kinsmen.[80] Similarly, William Waynflete, founder of Magdalen College, made no arrangements for founder's kin. In this instance, however, the reason may have been that he had few near relatives, and indeed none are mentioned in his will.[81] Nevertheless, between the late thirteenth century and *c.* 1500 a number of the Oxford colleges made elaborate provisions for founder's kin and were, to this degree, 'family' colleges. Moreover, some of them were able to extend their patronage beyond the obligations of kinship, and help their members secure ecclesiastical positions. In this manner, colleges could make a signal contribution to the employment of their graduates, and this was especially valuable when papal sources of patronage were dramatically reduced.

In this connection, the secular collegiate movement in Oxford *a.* 1450 cannot be seen as having been divorced from the need to alleviate the patronage crisis affecting the University between *c.* 1340 and *c.* 1430, during which period there appears to have been some decline in the number of graduates obtaining preferment within the Church.[82] As the centralized system of papal provisioning came under mounting lay attack in England and, as far as Oxford and Cambridge were concerned, virtually collapsed in the early years of the fifteenth century (Oxford appears to have sent its last roll of petitions for benefices to the papal curia in 1404), graduates of the English universities were bereft of a main source of patronage, the former papal patronage being divided among a myriad of indigenous lay and ecclesiastical patrons. The various expedients of the commons in parliament, the English clergy and

---

[80] Squibb, op. cit., p. 9.

[81] Ibid., p. 10.

[82] For this subject, see G. F. Lytle, 'Patronage Patterns and Oxford Colleges *c.* 1300–*c.* 1530', *The University in Society* (2 vols., ed. L. Stone, Princeton and London, 1975), i. 111 ff.

individual patrons to ameliorate the situation came to little.[83] Oxford and Cambridge had only a handful of livings at their disposal, and the galaxy of unendowed halls and hostels had no such patronage. But the number of available livings could be augmented through the medium of the colleges. The surest method was to increase the number of livings in the gift of colleges by making these livings an integral part of the endowment. This matter has been investigated by G.F. Lytle with respect to the Oxford colleges. The results of his survey may be briefly stated. At New College, for example, 13 or 14 advowsons were attached to the 21 manors given by Wykeham, and another 2 were separately granted.[84] An analysis of scholars of Queen's, New College, All Souls and Magdalen presented to first livings by a range of patrons over varying periods in the fourteenth and fifteenth centuries has revealed that in each case a substantial proportion were presented by the home college or its episcopal patron or visitor.[85] This suggests that some of the Oxford colleges were responding significantly to growing patronage problems. Moreover, graduates who owed a first promotion to their college and were subsequently advanced to high office, and especially those advanced to bishoprics, would often act as patrons for college members.[86] It needs to be stressed, however, that Lytle's thesis regarding the extent of the patronage crisis in England between c.1340 and c.1430 has not been universally accepted. In particular, it has been cogently challenged by T. H. Aston, who has analysed the preferment of graduates of both Oxford and Cambridge in the fourteenth and fifteenth centuries and has found that the rate of preferment was reasonably steady, and

---

[83] Ibid., i. 132–4.

[84] Ibid., i. 139; see also New College Archives, 9703, 9818.

[85] Between c. 1385 and c. 1450, New College, Winchester College and the visitor combined presented to 47.7 per cent of scholar's first livings: between 1451 and c. 1515 the figure was 39.8 per cent. The comparable figure for Queen's College between 1350 and 1500 was 55 per cent; for All Souls between 1420 and 1500 the figure was 20 per cent; and for Magdalen between 1450 and 1500 the figure was 32.3 per cent: see tables 3, 4, in Lytle, op. cit., i. 141, 142.

[86] Ibid., i. 142–6.

at times buoyant, throughout that period.[87] At the very least, Lytle has emphasized the value of academic colleges as sources of patronage irrespective of the state of the patronage crisis affecting English university graduates as a whole. This patronage capacity of the colleges helped to cement their rising position within the English Universities in the late medieval period. Their endowments and network of patronage connections underlined the solid potential of the colleges by comparison with the halls and hostels, many of which enjoyed only an ephemeral existence.

Apart from the preference for founder's kin operating in some of the Oxford colleges, a number of colleges in both Oxford and Cambridge restricted recruitment according to geographical predilections. These probably modified to some degree what was otherwise the general pattern of recruitment within the English Universities. In terms of recruitment, Oxford and Cambridge in the Middle Ages can be more properly described as regional rather than pronouncedly national universities. Although they drew students from virtually all parts of England, each had different regional concentrations.

In the period before 1500, Cambridge seems to have drawn its scholars mainly from the eastern and northern parts of England, the dioceses of Norwich, Lincoln, York, Ely and London supplying the greatest number.[88] In the fourteenth century, Cambridge recruited

---

[87] Aston et al., 'The Medieval Alumni of the University of Cambridge', pp. 68 ff., with main conclusions drawn, pp. 83–4; see also the interesting commentary on this patronage theme by B. Dobson, 'Oxford Graduates and the so-called Patronage Crisis of the later Middle Ages', *The Church in a Changing Society* (Commission Internationale d'Histoire Ecclésiastique Comparée, Swedish sub-commission of CIHEC: Publications of the Swedish Society of Church History, new series, 30, Uppsala, 1977), pp. 211 ff.; see further the cautionary discussion on the alleged 'crisis patronage' by R. N. Swanson, 'Universities, Graduates and Benefices in Later Medieval England', *Past and Present*, no. 106 (1985), pp. 28 ff., and M. C. Burson, 'Emden's *Registers* and the Prosopography of Medieval English Universities', *Medieval Prosopography*, 3 (1982), pp. 35 ff. at pp. 39–41.

[88] See the diocesan survey of 380 members of Cambridge who petitioned for papal graces in the second half of the fourteenth century by Emden, *B.R.U.C.*, pp. xxvi–xxvii; see also the analysis of 203 members of the King's Hall who may be assigned to counties on the basis of local surnames by Cobban, *The King's Hall*, pp. 157–60. The findings of this collegiate survey are compared with those of

predominantly from the group of eastern dioceses of Norwich, Ely and London, and from Lincoln diocese, and, to a far lesser extent, from the group of northern dioceses of York, Carlisle and Durham, although the intake from York diocese was significant.[89] Cambridge's recruitment in the fifteenth century, however, presents a somewhat altered pattern from that of the fourteenth century. In the fifteenth century, the three eastern dioceses of Norwich, Ely and London furnished markedly fewer scholars than in the preceding century. At the same time, recruitment from the three northern sees of York, Carlisle and Durham appears to have more than doubled.[90] This substantial increase from the northern dioceses was accompanied by perceptible rises in recruitment from the southern and western sees and from the dioceses of Coventry and Lichfield, although the intake from

Dr Emden's diocesan analysis of 380 scholars, a comparison which reveals broadly similar results: ibid., pp. 159–60. The most recent and most extensive recruitment analysis of members of Cambridge of known geographical provenance is that by Aston et al., 'The Medieval Alumni of the University of Cambridge', pp. 28 ff.

[89] An analysis by T. H. Aston and assistants of a sample of 469 Cambridge scholars in the fourteenth century of known geographical origins has revealed that 56 per cent of the total were recruited from the eastern dioceses of Norwich, Ely and London, with Norwich alone accounting for 39 per cent of scholars; Lincoln diocese, which straddled some eastern and midland counties, contributed 20 per cent; and the northern dioceses of York, Carlisle and Durham accounted for 15 per cent, with York supplying 13 per cent. By contrast, the diocese of Coventry and Lichfield provided only 3 per cent; the western dioceses of Hereford, Worcester, Bath and Wells, and Exeter 1 per cent; and the southern dioceses of Salisbury, Winchester, Chichester, Rochester and Canterbury 4 per cent. This sample was made up of 326 scholars without known collegiate associations and 143 scholars with college links. If these groupings are considered separately, the general pattern is similar, except that the colleges drew more scholars from the five southern sees than did the non-collegiate section of the University: details extracted from Aston et al., 'The Medieval Alumni of the University of Cambridge', pp. 28 ff.

[90] For fifteenth-century Cambridge T. H. Aston analysed a sample of 879 scholars of known geographical origins, 339 having no discoverable college connections. The eastern dioceses of Norwich, Ely and London furnished only 27 per cent of these 339 scholars, Norwich provided 13 per cent, and the northern sees of York, Carlisle and Durham yielded no less than 39 per cent, York accounting for 30 per cent: ibid., p. 30.

Lincoln diocese was smaller than in the fourteenth century.[91] It is clear that in the fifteenth century Cambridge was still mainly reliant upon the eastern and northern dioceses for its recruitment. In the non-collegiate sector, however, northerners may well then have outnumbered scholars from the eastern parts of the country. It is true that the recruitment in several Cambridge colleges in the fifteenth century, including that in Pembroke, the King's Hall, Clare, Michaelhouse and Peterhouse, reflected the increase in northern recruitment in the University at large.[92] But taking the colleges as a group, their intake from the northern dioceses in the fifteenth century was notably less than that of the non-collegiate area, while admissions to the colleges from southern sees was about double that of other quarters of the University.[93] However, it needs to be stressed that King's College alone, founded in 1441, made a major contribution to collegiate recruitment from southern dioceses.[94]

Oxford's pattern of recruitment was in many ways the reverse of that of Cambridge, and was similarly affected by collegiate preferences.[95] A sample analysis of non-collegiate scholars in the

[91] Lincoln's contribution fell from 20 per cent in the fourteenth century to 15 per cent in the fifteenth century: ibid.

[92] Ibid., p. 32.

[93] The collegiate intake from northern dioceses in the fifteenth century was about 25 per cent, as against the non-collegiate figure of 39 per cent. Admissions to colleges from southern sees was about 11 per cent, compared with 5 per cent from the non-collegiate area: ibid., pp. 32, 33.

[94] Of the entrants to King's College of known origins in the fifteenth century, 31 per cent derived from the southern and western regions, with a particularly strong intake from the dioceses of Salisbury and Winchester: ibid., p. 31.

[95] For details of Oxford's recruitment in the fifteenth century, see Aston et al., 'The Medieval Alumni of the University of Cambridge', pp. 33–4. For examples of regional preferences in English colleges, see *Camb. Docs.*, ii. 54–5 (Peterhouse), 132 (Clare), 232 (Gonville), 422 (Trinity Hall), 486 (King's); *Statutes*, i. ch. 2, 5, 10, 27 (Merton), ch. 4, 12 (Queen's), ch. 5, 6–7 (New College), ch. 6, 12–13 (Lincoln), ch. 7, 21 (All Souls). The original statutes of Exeter College of 26 April 1316 enacted that all the scholars were to originate from Exeter diocese: the statutes are printed in *The Register of Walter de Stapeldon, Bishop of Exeter, 1307–1326* (ed. F. C. Hingeston-Randolph, London and Exeter, 1892), pp. 304–8 at p. 304. Regional preferences may have had the injurious effect of concentrating the government of the college in the

fifteenth century whose dioceses of origins can be assigned reveals that the western dioceses of Hereford, Worcester, Bath and Wells and Exeter supplied the largest grouping, in contrast to the modest numbers which Cambridge recruited from these sees. The second highest intake in the Oxford sample came from the northern dioceses of Carlisle, Durham and York. The eastern sees of Norwich, Ely and London furnished only a small number of scholars, and this contrasts vividly with the substantial admissions to Cambridge from these regions.[96]

This notable representation of northern scholars in the English Universities may have owed something to the strong connection which existed throughout the fourteenth century between the cathedral chapter at York and the central government.[97] It has been shown that from the time of Edward I's chancellor, Robert Burnell, until early in the reign of Henry IV, a large proportion of the Yorkshiremen who had acquired during that period prebends or canonries in the chapter at York were royal clerks, many of whom

hands of a 'county clique': see e.g. R. H. Hodgkin, *Six Centuries of an Oxford College* (Oxford, 1949), p. 49. But regional ties also produced a galaxy of college benefactors from the areas of preference: see e.g. H. M. Jewell, ' "The Bringing up of Children in Good Learning and Manners": A Survey of Secular Educational Provision in the North of England, *c.* 1350–1550', *Northern History*, xviii (1982), pp. 1 ff. at pp. 13–16.

[96] The Oxford sample comprised 45 non-collegiate scholars. The western dioceses supplied 38 per cent of the sample, as compared with only 4 per cent of non-collegiate scholars at Cambridge. The northern dioceses provided 29 per cent of this sample, and this is approaching the order of magnitude of the 39 per cent recorded for Cambridge. The eastern sees furnished a mere 4 per cent of the Oxford sample, as against 27 per cent at Cambridge. Lincoln diocese yielded 11 per cent, Coventry and Lichfield accounted for 13 per cent, and the five southern sees for 4 per cent, the equivalent Cambridge percentages being 15, 10 and 5.

[97] See A. Hamilton Thompson, 'Cathedral Church of St Peter, York', *Victoria History of the County of Yorkshire*, iii (ed. W. Page, London, 1913), 375 ff.; see also Hamilton Thompson, 'The Medieval Chapter', *York Minster Historical Tracts 627–1927* (ed. A. Hamilton Thompson, London, 1927), no 13, and *The Register of William Greenfield, Archbishop of York (1306–1315)* (5 vols., ed. W. Brown and A. Hamilton Thompson, Surtees Soc., 1931–40), i (1931), xviii; see further Edwards, *English Secular Cathedrals in the Middle Ages,* pp. 85–6, and J. L. Grassi, 'Royal Clerks from the Archdiocese of York in the Fourteenth Century', *Northern History,* v (1970), pp. 12 ff.

held office in the chancery. The Yorkshire–central-government nexus was probably firmest in the reign of Edward II; but it persisted in a significant form until interrupted by Archbishop Scrope's rebellion in the early fifteenth century. This conspicuous deployment of so many Yorkshire clerks in royal administration in the fourteenth century must have encouraged a growing number of youths from Yorkshire to seek a university education in order to qualify for the ecclesiastical and governmental patronage so patently available to them. While career prospects for Yorkshire clerks in the royal service may have dipped in the early fifteenth century, admissions from the diocese of York to Oxford and Cambridge were maintained at a fairly steady rate throughout the remainder of the century.

As in the case of King's College at Cambridge, the largest of the Oxford colleges, New College, which drew heavily upon the dioceses of Salisbury and Winchester, must have made a substantial contribution to the representation of the southern region. A study by G.F. Lytle of a sample of 804 members of New College between *c.* 1400 and *c.* 1500 has demonstrated that 59 per cent were drawn from the five southern sees, 27 and 30 per cent coming from Salisbury and Winchester dioceses respectively.[98] This agrees well enough with the results of Aston's analysis of a much smaller sample of New College personnel.[99] The effect of the New College bias towards the southern parts of England on the representation of those parts at Oxford was reinforced to a lesser degree by southern contingents in several of the other Oxford colleges of the fifteenth century. It is probably true to say that the Oxford colleges, as a grouping, provided an identifiable corrective to the markedly low level of southern recruitment in the non-collegiate sphere.

For the sake of comprehensiveness, it needs to be added that Cambridge drew only about 1 per cent of its scholars from Wales, Scotland and Ireland, compared with the 6 per cent drawn by

[98] G. F. Lytle, 'The Social Origins of Oxford Students in the Late Middle Ages: New College, *c.* 1380–*c.* 1510', *The Universities in the Late Middle Ages* (ed. J. Ijsewijn and J. Paquet, Leuven University Press, 1978), pp. 426 ff., esp. pp. 427–31.

[99] Aston et al., 'The Medieval Alumni of the University of Cambridge', p. 33 and n. 63.

Oxford. Whereas the Welsh and Irish were sufficiently numerous at Oxford (the Scots were much less so) to establish their own halls, no such nationalist hostels appear to have materialized at Cambridge.[100] Neither University recruited extensively from continental Europe. Only about 2 per cent of scholars at Oxford and 1 per cent of those at Cambridge came from this source.[101] Of the continental scholars drawn to Cambridge, the majority were friars studying theology. In this connection, it is relevant to emphasize that only Paris, Oxford, Cambridge and Florence — from 1359 — and Bologna — from 1364 — had a right of promotion to the doctorate in theology,[102] so that the English Universities had a specific practical attraction. The friars apart, however, it is clear that the English Universities were rather insular institutions, Cambridge even more so than Oxford.

From this discussion of university and collegiate recruitment, it seems that Oxford and Cambridge in the period before 1500 were regional universities, Cambridge relying mainly upon the eastern and northern parts of England and Oxford recruiting largely from the western and northern dioceses. The intake from northern England rose significantly at Cambridge as between the fourteenth and fifteenth centuries. In both Universities, the colleges helped to modify the general pattern of recruitment, especially by increasing admissions from the southern region, which would otherwise have been minimally represented. That the south-east of the country, with its high concentration of wealth and population, was a low recruitment area for the English Universities is a finding which is both surprising and difficult to explain. It is known, however, that

---

[100] Ibid., p. 35. See further R. W. Hays, 'Welsh Students at Oxford and Cambridge Universities in the Middle Ages', *Welsh Hist. Rev.*, iv (1968–9), pp. 325 ff.: Hays gives a total of about 390 Welsh students at medieval Oxford (p. 326: listed pp. 355–60) and only 38 at Cambridge (listed p. 361). For Irish scholars, see M. H. Somers, *Irish Scholars in the Universities at Paris and Oxford before 1500* (unpublished Ph.D. thesis, The City University of New York, 1979), *passim*, and for the halls frequented by Irish scholars. p. 24. Aston (p. 35) has recorded a total of 315 Irish scholars at Oxford before 1500: Somers (p. 5) gives totals of 47 in the thirteenth century, 57 in the fourteenth century and 83 in the fifteenth century.

[101] Aston et al, 'The Medieval Alumni of the University of Cambridge', p. 35.

[102] See e.g. Cobban, *The Medieval Universities*, p. 71.

the Inns of Court and Chancery in London provided a powerful counter-attraction to Oxford and Cambridge. They were popular venues not only for those who sought to become professional practitioners of the common law, not taught formally at the English Universities, but also for members of the gentry and nobility who could acquire a training in the basics of the common law, allied to a more general education and the gaining of a range of social accomplishments.[103] The Inns of Court and Chancery, with their proximity to the capital's law courts and government departments, were in some ways more advantageously placed in terms of social contacts and patronage prospects than were the more-distant Universities. It is certainly possible that the Inns of Court and Chancery absorbed a proportion of students from London and the south-east who might otherwise have gravitated towards Oxford and Cambridge.[104]

II

THE HALLS AND HOSTELS

Although by 1500 the groundwork had been laid for the structural metamorphosis of the Universities of Oxford and Cambridge into federations of colleges, the colleges had by then advanced only part

[103] For the Inns of Court, see W. R. Prest, *The Inns of Court under Elizabeth I and the Early Stuarts 1590–1640* (London, 1972); see also J. H. Baker, 'The English Legal Profession, 1450–1550', *Lawyers in Early Modern Europe and America* (ed. W. Prest, London, 1981), pp. 16 ff., and P. Brand, 'Courtroom and Schoolroom: the Education of Lawyers in England prior to 1400', *Historical Research* (formerly *B.I.H.R.*), 60 (1987), pp. 147 ff.

[104] An analysis of the geographical origins of members of the Inns of Court between 1590 and 1639 shows that every English county was represented, along with a sizeable number of entrants from Ireland and Wales. The largest single group comprised Londoners, and these, combined with students from Middlesex, made up just over 11 per cent of the total: Prest, op. cit., pp. 32–3. Excluding native Londoners, 18.5 per cent of entrants in this same survey were recruited from the Home Counties, defined as Essex, Hertfordshire, Kent, Middlesex and Surrey: R. Findlay, *Population and Metropolis: The Demography of London 1580–1650* (Cambridge, 1981), table 3.5, p. 64. Although this survey is chronologically late for the present purpose, it may nevertheless be some pointer to the degree to which the Inns of Court recruited from London and the south-east in the pre-1500 period.

of the way towards acquiring a monopoly of undergraduate accommodation and teaching. With one or two exceptions, they had only recently begun to depart from their élitist postgraduate function within the academic community. It is apparent that before 1500 the halls of Oxford and the equivalent hostels of Cambridge typified for many the common university experience.[105] As previously stated, the university authorities, at some point in the thirteenth century, came to see that the halls and hostels could make a notable contribution to the extension of more-effective discipline over the undergraduate population.[106] Initially, halls and hostels had crystallized without reference to the university guild. Any mature member of the university, whether a master or a bachelor or occasionally even a maniciple,[107] could lease a house for a specified duration from a town landlord and establish a hall or hostel for scholars with himself as principal. At Cambridge, however, the principals were subject to regulation by the University by *c*. 1250, when it was enacted that a principal of a hostel had to give a guarantee either to the landlord or to the chancellor for the payment of the hostel's annual rent.[108] Similar legislation concerning the principals of Oxford halls dates from *c*. 1313, and was probably operative a good deal earlier.[109] This procedure, relating to annual renewal, was tantamount to official university recognition of the halls and hostels, whose principals were now rendered university agents accountable for the well-being and behaviour of the residents in their charge. It was rapidly realized that the exercise of discipline over scholars in the places where they lived was likely to be more

[105] For the main references concerning halls and hostels, see above, n. 19, and for their nomenclature, n. 15.

[106] See above, p. 118; also Pantin, *Oxford Life in Oxford Archives*, pp. 2–3.

[107] Although it is unlikely that many maniciples set up as principals, an Oxford statute of *a*. 1380 made it a punishable offence for any maniciple or other servant of scholars to hold a principalship: Gibson, *Statuta Antiqua*, pp. 182–3; see also Emden, *An Oxford Hall in Medieval Times*, p. 37.

[108] See Hackett, *The Original Statutes of Cambridge University*, pp. 214–15.

[109] Gibson, op. cit., pp. 78–81: this legislation also prohibited the tenure of more than one principalship (p. 81). On this legislation, see further Emden, op cit., pp. 22 ff.

efficacious than the transient control brought to bear by regent masters in the lecture rooms. For this reason, the burden of responsibility for undergraduate discipline, and for the supervision of a fair proportion of postgraduates was progressively shifted from the teaching corps to those who regulated the board and lodging of scholars in halls and hostels.

An Oxford statute of *a*. 1313 instituted an annual general inquiry into the behaviour of scholars who disturbed the peace of the University in various defined ways. The inquisition was to be conducted under the auspices of the chancellor, and the principals and manciples of the halls were to play a key role in the proceedings.[110] This is the earliest known instance of principals being utilized for the preservation of academic discipline as part of the formal university machinery. In 1313, Oxford principals and manciples of the halls were again prominent in the disciplinary sphere. In this case, they were statutorily required to furnish the chancellor or one of the proctors with the names of members of their hall who entered into associations likely to pose a threat to order, or who openly disturbed the peace, or who bore arms, or who practised the art of buckler-play, or who fomented discord between northerners and southerners, or who kept women in their chambers.[111] According to a late fourteenth-century Cambridge statute, the hostels were subject to a twice yearly visitation by the chancellor or vice-chancellor, assisted by the proctors and some of the masters and doctors of the University, the object of which was the investigation of the record of both the principals and the student residents. Recalcitrant principals could ultimately be removed, and scholars who had defied the principal's authority, or who were guilty of one or more of a series of named offences, and had refused to amend their ways, could be deprived of their scholarly status.[112] From this statute, it is clear that Cambridge principals were obliged to restrain scholars from excessive wandering abroad, were to see to it that they did not keep arms in their rooms, and were expected to ensure that they attended lectures, whether in the hostels or in the

---

[110] Gibson, op. cit., pp. 88–9; Emden, op. cit., pp. 28–9.

[111] Gibson, op. cit., pp. 110–11; Emden, op. cit., p. 29.

[112] *Camb. Docs.*, i. 316–17.

university schools, and that the appropriate lecture fees were paid. This responsibility for enforcing the payment of university lecture fees was likewise imposed upon the principals of the Oxford halls, or at least those of the artists, as is made manifest in a statute of 1333.[113]

These statutory instances disclose the extent to which the chancellors of Oxford and Cambridge had come, in the course of the thirteenth and fourteenth centuries, to rely upon the halls and hostels for the implementation of university discipline over the academic population. They realized that the capacity for discipline would clearly be maximized if as many scholars as possible were to be accommodated within houses controlled by the University. As a result, the axiom was formulated that residence in approved premises was an essential qualification for the rank of scholar. Residence in a hostel or college was made a statutory requirement for all scholars at Cambridge in the late fourteenth century.[114] This stipulation was echoed at Oxford in *c.* 1410,[115] and this *c.* 1410 measure was reinforced by a statute of Henry V in 1420.[116] The timing of these measures at Oxford probably owed something to the prevalence of Lollardy there and to the belief that religious error was prone to spread more rapidly among unattached and unsupervised scholars living in the town. In 1432, legislation was enacted at Oxford to enforce the graduate status of hall principals,[117] although it is likely that from the later thirteenth century the majority of principals had been graduates, even if some were of only bachelor status.[118]

The move at both Universities to eliminate scholars who had no intention of pursuing a serious academic course by making defined residence a mark of *bona fide* scholarly status was hitherto the most advanced device used by the Universities to deal with this long-

---

[113] Gibson, op. cit., pp. 131–2.

[114] *Camb. Docs.*, i. 317.

[115] Gibson, op. cit., p. 208.

[116] Ibid., pp. 226–7.

[117] Ibid., pp. 243–4: there seems to be no extant statutory provision for Cambridge on this matter before 1500.

[118] Emden, *An Oxford Hall in Medieval Times*, p. 37.

standing problem. These troublesome unattached scholars who continued to live in unlicensed rooms let by townspeople and who, under the cover of their position at the university, indulged in anti-social and criminal activities were at Oxford called 'chamberdeacons'. In the statute of *c.*1410 designed for their repression, the chamberdeacons are graphically described as 'sleeping by day and haunting taverns and brothels by night, intent on robbery and homicide'.[119] This description may be somewhat exaggerated and does not take account of those genuinely poor scholars who lived in the cheapest of lodgings because they could ill afford even the low-cost rates of living in a hall. There can be no doubt, however, that unattached scholars presented the university authorities with a disciplinary problem of some magnitude. The requirement at Oxford and Cambridge that all scholars be accommodated in either halls or colleges was not wholly effective immediately, and the process by which the majority of the university members were institutionalized extended well into the sixteenth century. At Oxford, it was still found to be necessary in 1512 for the chancellor, in conjunction with the heads of colleges and halls, to promulgate a decree to try to enforce chamberdeacons to move into their halls or colleges within eight days, under threat of banishment.[120] By the second half of the sixteenth century, however, the vexatious matter of unattached living had been largely brought under control and the worst excesses of student disorder curbed.

The mandatory residence of scholars in halls, hostels or colleges not only facilitated discipline but also nurtured the growth of lecturing and tutorial facilities in these communities as a supplement to the public instruction of the university schools. This development, which was to have the most profound effect upon the shape and character of the English Universities (it will be discussed in the next chapter), meant that increasingly in the late-medieval

---

[119] Gibson, *Statuta Aniqua*, p. 208; Emden, op. cit., pp. 30–1.

[120] See E. Russell, 'The Influx of Commoners into the University of Oxford before 1581: an optical illusion?', *E.H.R.*, xcii (1977), pp. 721 ff. at p. 731; see also Hammer, 'Oxford Town and Oxford University', *The History of the University of Oxford*, iii. 112.

period the halls of Oxford, the hostels of Cambridge and the secular colleges of both Universities had become not only the natural habitats of the vast majority of scholars, but also the locations of much of their educational life.

Given the ephemeral nature of many of the halls and hostels consequent upon their unendowed status, it is difficult to be in any way precise about either their total numbers or the numbers of halls and hostels operational in any given year. According to the list of Oxford halls drawn up in *c.* 1440–50 by John Rous, the Warwickshire antiquary and topographical pioneer, there were then some 65 halls (including 2 accounted from dubious entries). It also makes reference to a further 6 halls destroyed before his time and to 6 destroyed in the course of the construction of All Souls.[121] The chancellor's register contains 16 lists of cautions, the securities given by the principals of Oxford halls to the chancellor or his commissary to ensure the renewal of the principalship for the following year. These lists extend from 1436 to 1469, and, excluding the two obviously incomplete lists of 1457 and 1463, they provide annual numbers of halls ranging from 44 in 1468 to 70 in 1444, and they point to 58 as the average number of halls.[122] It is

---

[121] Rous's original list is not extant but several copies survive. The edition used here is that by A. Clark in '*Survey of the Antiquities of the City of Oxford*' *composed in 1661–6 by Anthony Wood*, i (Oxf. Hist. Soc., xv, 1889), 638–41. The copy used by Clark was probably written by Miles Windsor, who was admitted to Corpus Christi College, Oxford, in 1557 and died in 1624. A sixteenth-century copy of Rous's list by John Leland is edited by L. Toulmin Smith, *The Itinerary of John Leland in or about the years 1535–1543, Parts iv and v, with an Appendix of Extracts from Leland's Collectanea* (London, 1908), Appendix, at pp. 154–6. On the few differences between the copies of Leland and Windsor, see Aston, 'Oxford's Medieval Alumni', *Past and Present*, no. 74 (1977), pp. 3 ff. at p. 36. For the dating of Rous's list, see Aston, art. cit., pp. 37–8, and Aston, 'The Date of John Rous's list of the Colleges and Academical Halls of Oxford', *Oxoniensia*, xlii (1977), pp. 226 ff.

[122] Figures derived from hall lists in *Registrum Cancellarii*, i, ii, *passim*. A. B. Emden has published in tabular form the number of halls in each list of the chancellor's registers between 1436 and 1537, together with the list of John Rous: A. B. Emden, 'Oxford Academical Halls in the Later Middle Ages', *Medieval Learning and Literature: Essays presented to Richard William Hunt* (ed. J. J. G. Alexander and M. T. Gibson, Oxford, 1976), pp. 353 ff. at p. 355. I have accepted Mr Aston's slight revisions of Dr Emden's figures for the lists for 1444 and 1468: see Aston, 'Oxford's Medieval Alumni', p. 36, n. 50.

likely that this suppositional average errs on the side of conservatism, for these lists are not always complete, and, given Rous's enumeration of 65 halls in existence and 12 recently destroyed, it may well be that, in the fifteenth century, the average number of halls operational each year lay between 60 and 70.[123] Rous produced a similar list of colleges and hostels for Cambridge, probably compiled at about the same time as the Oxford list, that is, c. 1440–50.[124] Only 17 Cambridge hostels are itemized by Rous, for what appears to be one particular point in the mid-fifteenth century: 6 of the 17 are designated hostels for artists and 6 as hostels for legists. If this is at all representative of the extent of the hostel tally, then the annual number of Cambridge hostels, at least in the fifteenth century, would have stood at only about 25 per cent of that of the Oxford halls. Several attempts have been made to reconstruct lists of Cambridge hostels for the thirteenth to the sixteenth centuries, the most recent of which, by H.P. Stokes, yields a total of 136, although this reduces to 133 when erroneously included colleges, such as the King's Hall, Michaelhouse and Godshouse, are excluded.[125] Rous's list, however, seems to be the only one which furnishes a view of the hostels at one particular moment, and probably remains the best available guide as to the annual number.

While it is reasonably clear that the Cambridge hostels were far less numerous than the Oxford halls, there is evidence to suggest that at least some of them were of notably larger capacity than their Oxford equivalents. The Oxford halls were usually adapted middle-

---

[123] See the remarks of Aston, 'Oxford's Medieval Alumni', p. 38.

[124] John Leland's copy of Rous's list is edited by Toulmin Smith, *The Itinerary of John Leland*, p. 157.

[125] See Stokes, *The Mediaeval Hostels of the University of Cambridge*, pp. 60–106. Willis and Clark, *The Architectural History of the University of Cambridge and of the Colleges of Cambridge and Eton*, i. xxv–xxviii, gives a list of 27 hostels derived from the lists of Archbishop Matthew Parker, John Caius, Richard Parker and Thomas Fuller. Caius gives an account and a list of hostels in his *Historiae Cantabrigiensis Academiae*, pp. 46–53; Fuller in *The History of the University of Cambridge*, ed. cit., pp. 56–60, lists 34 hostels, and at p. 62 his editors printed Matthew Parker's list of hostels; Richard Parker's list of hostels is printed in *The History and Antiquities of the University of Cambridge*, pp. 28–32.

sized town houses, owned by corporate or individual landlords. From Dr W. A. Pantin's examination of the few academic halls of which any substantial structure remains, such as Tackley's Inn, Beam Hall and Bedel Hall, it can be seen that the typical Oxford hall in the fifteenth century probably consisted of a large hall, used for meals, lectures and social occasions, and a group of chambers, housing two, three or four students each, the total number of students per hall ranging from ten to thirty.[126] Dr Pantin's estimates for the capacities of nine halls (excluding the grammar halls) produce an average of 18.5 students per hall, and this is perhaps the best mean figure available.[127] Assuming that about 70 halls were operational each year in the fifteenth century, an average of 18.5 students per hall gives an aularian population of 1,295. If it is objected that the average of 18.5 students per hall is too high, on the grounds that the halls investigated by Dr Pantin may have been of above-average capacity, then a revised figure of 15 or 16 may be used and this still gives an estimate of over 1,000 for the hall population in fifteenth-century Oxford.[128]

The evidence does not exist for Cambridge that would allow the formulation of an average figure for the number of residents per hostel. R. Willis and J.W. Clark, in their monumental work *The Architectural History of the University of Cambridge and of the Colleges of Cambridge and Eton*, assumed, from the dimensions of the ground-plans of several of the Cambridge hostels, that they were generally of small capacity. But this is not the pattern which emerges on the basis of those few hostels for which there is some indication of residential numbers. For example, before the Society of the King's Scholars became the endowed College of the King's Hall in 1337, it was housed in rented premises after the manner of a

---

[126] Pantin, 'The Halls and Schools of medieval Oxford: an attempt at reconstruction', *passim*; see also Pantin, 'Tackley's Inn, Oxford', *Oxoniensia*, vii (1942), pp. 80 ff., and supplemented by J. Munby, 'J. C. Buckler, Tackley's Inn and Three Medieval Houses in Oxford', *Oxoniensia*, 43 (1978), pp. 123 ff.

[127] Pantin, 'The Halls and Schools of medieval Oxford', pp. 38 ff.; see also Aston, 'Oxford's Medieval Alumni', p. 39.

[128] See Aston's comments on Oxford's aularian population, art. cit., p. 7.

hostel community, albeit one uniquely supported from exchequer revenues:[129] the complement comprised a warden and 12 scholars in 1317, and this had increased to over 30 scholars by 1337.[130] If it is argued that this is a special case, it may be remarked that St Thomas' Hostel, acquired by Pembroke College from St John's Hospital in 1451, had no fewer than 34 scholars in 1457, each paying 8d. a term to the college for their lodging.[131] In 1490, the principal of St Augustine's Hostel paid £2 to King's College, which owned the hostel, on behalf of the 20 residents.[132] John Caius, writing early in Elizabeth's reign, states that Physwick Hostel had some 30 or 40 residents, an observation which refers in time to some point between its purchase by Gonville College in 1393 and its incorporation by Trinity College in 1546.[133] Moreover, the fact that one or two of the hostels possessed their own libraries (as did at least two of the Oxford halls), that St Thomas's and St Bernard's Hostels had chapels, that St Margaret's Hostel had an oratory and that St Bernard's had some kind of ornate gallery, indicates that several of the Cambridge hostels were substantial structures.[134] The hostels mentioned above were for artists, although King's Hostel for the King's Scholars was beginning to cater for a mixed academic

---

[129] In 1336, Edward III purchased for the King's Scholars a house from Robert de Croyland, rector of Oundle, which he assigned to them as part of the endowment of the King's Hall, founded in October 1337. The rented hostel inhabited by the King's Scholars before the grant of this house has not yet been identified, but it is possible that it was the same building: Cobban, *The King's Hall*, p. 10.

[130] Ibid., pp. 9, 17, 44, 123, n. 5: see also the profit and loss account for the King's Hall for 1342–3, which specifies exchequer maintenance allowance for the warden and 35 scholars for the year, ibid., p. 119.

[131] Attwater, *Pembroke College, Cambridge*, ed. cit., pp. 21–2.

[132] Stokes, *The Mediaeval Hostels of the University of Cambridge*, p. 62.

[133] See the translation of Caius's description of Physwick Hostel in Willis and Clark, op. cit., ii. 417, and in Stokes, op. cit., pp. 36–7: for the original, see Caius, *Historiae Cantabrigiensis Academiae*, p. 38. See also Brooke, *A History of Gonville and Caius College*, p. 28.

[134] On these features of Cambridge hostels, see e.g. Aston, 'The Medieval Alumni of the University of Cambridge', p. 17 and n. 22.

clientele on the eve of its transformation into a college in 1337.[135] Of the 6 legist hostels listed by Rous in *c.* 1440–50 reference is made to 4 of them by Archbishop Parker, who records that each accommodated between 80 and 100 residents in, it seems, the late fifteenth or early sixteenth centuries.[136] If 80 is taken as the complement for each of the 6 legist halls in the fifteenth century, and 20 to 40 for that of each of the other 11 hostels in Rous's list, then figures for the aularian population of Cambridge in the fifteenth century range from 700 to 920. This is not as far short of the comparable Oxford figure of 1,295 as might have been supposed from the relative paucity of Cambridge hostels.

Although a hall or hostel might change its academic category, it seems that, at any given time, halls and hostels were segregated into artist, legist, artist-theological, theological and grammarian, with perhaps the occasional hybrid.[137] The establishments for legists were probably mainly graduate in composition, although it was possible for students in late medieval Oxford and Cambridge to embark upon a law course without having an arts degree. In general, the legist houses, designed for the more mature student, may well have had a higher degree of comfort than the halls of the artists.[138] While many aularian theologians after graduation in arts continued to reside in what were predominantly artist houses, there were, nevertheless, a small number of halls and hostels where theologians formed a substantial proportion of the higher faculty membership.[139] Some of the Oxford halls came to be associated with national groupings or geographical regions. For example, Welshmen were especially prominent at St Edward, Brend, Gloucester, Haberdash, Hincksey (Hinxey), St George, Stock and Trillmill Halls; Irishmen at Aristotle, Heron (Eagle), Vine, Coventry and Beef Halls; scholars from south-west England at St

---

[135] Cobban, *The King's Hall*, p. 54.

[136] See Aston, 'The Medieval Alumni of the University of Cambridge', p. 17.

[137] See the comments of Pantin, 'The Halls and Schools of medieval Oxford', p. 37.

[138] Loc. cit.

[139] Aston, 'Oxford's Medieval Alumni', p. 20.

Edmund Hall, at least in the early fourteenth century; and northerners at Sparrow Hall.[140] Welsh, Irish and Scottish students were present at Cambridge in only small numbers, and no hostel is known to have been especially associated with these ethnic groupings. While halls and hostels were relied upon by the university authorities to maintain an effective level of discipline, this did not prevent a degree of violent feuding between rival establishments. For example, in 1452 the junior proctor at Oxford, Thomas Reynold, was fatally wounded when he intervened in a conflict between Peckwater Inn and St Edward Hall.[141] At Cambridge, St. Nicholas's and St Clement's Hostels in the late fifteenth and early sixteenth centuries were notable for their involvement in violent affrays with other hostels.[142]

The extent of feuding among opposing halls and hostels indicates some degree of identification between these institutions and their members. But the makeshift character of many of these houses, their tenurial instability, and their lack of resources, all combined to render them less attractive as long-term venues than the secular colleges, with their elaborate buildings arranged around courts and quadrangles, their imposing gate-towers and their general air of opulent permanency. The spacious collegiate environment was better suited to teaching and orderly living than the frequently cramped aularian conditions. More particularly, some halls and hostels became inoperative when swallowed up in college buildings. For example, as mentioned above, Rous records that six Oxford halls were destroyed to make way for the creation of All Souls College;[143] in the early sixteenth century, the foundation of Brasenose (1512) and Corpus Christi (1517) led to the

---

[140] Hays, 'Welsh Students at Oxford and Cambridge Universities in the Middle Ages', p. 330; also Catto, 'Citizens, Scholars and Masters', *The History of the University of Oxford*, i. 179; Somers, *Irish Scholars in the Universities at Paris and Oxford before 1500*, p. 24.

[141] See W. A. Pantin, 'Before Wolsey', *Essays in British History presented to Sir Keith Feiling* (ed. H. R. Trevor-Roper, London, 1964), pp. 29 ff. at pp. 53–4.

[142] Stokes, op. cit., pp. 40–1.

[143] See above, p. 150.

incorporation of some fourteen halls or hall sites;[144] and at Cambridge, Long Entry Hostel and the Hostel of the Holy Cross went towards the construction of Corpus Christi College (1352), as did Crouched Hostel in the case of King's College (1441).[145] The number of halls and hostels was further diminished through amalgamation. At Oxford, for instance, St Mary and Bedel Halls were merged, and Staple, Glasen and Black Halls were combined, as were Great White, Little White and Pery Halls.[146] Strictly speaking, this practice was contrary to the university statutes, but the letter of the law was deemed to have been satisfied if each constituent hall was rented in the name of a different master.

Many halls and hostels in the late medieval period lost their independent status when they were purchased or leased by a college. After colleges had generally begun to admit fee-paying undergraduates, a college would sometimes acquire one or more halls or hostels to be utilized as annexes for its undergraduate members where they could be taught by fellows of the college. By this means, colleges could obviate the difficulties inherent in the limitations of their existing buildings and in the restrictive nature of their statutes. At the same time, such an arrangement would not impinge too much upon the sensibilities of those fellows who were resistant to the transformation of their societies by an undergraduate intake.[147] Where colleges absorbed hostels in Cambridge, the college usually appointed an external principal,

---

[144] Emden, 'Oxford Academical Halls in the Later Middle Ages', p. 357; see also J. G. Milne, *The Early History of Corpus Christi College, Oxford* (Oxford, 1946), ch. 2.

[145] See Bury, 'Corpus Christi College', *V.C.H. Camb*. iii. 371, and Saltmarsh, 'King's College', ibid., iii. at 386.

[146] Pantin, 'The Halls and Schools of medieval Oxford', p. 35.

[147] On halls as undergraduate annexes for colleges, see Emden, *An Oxford Hall in Medieval Times*, pp. 237–8. Merton College used St Alban, Urban and Corner Halls for this undergraduate purpose, while Nun Hall was hired for the housing of the founder's kin: ibid., p. 237, and Highfield, 'The Early Colleges', *The History of the University of Oxford*, i. 228. At Cambridge, St Thomas's Hostel was acquired by Pembroke College, St Bernard's Hostel by Queens' College and Physwick Hostel by Gonville College for the accommodation of their younger members: e.g. Stokes, *The Mediaeval Hostels of the University of Cambridge*, pp. 34–7.

who would be a fellow and would continue in residence, and an internal principal would be elected by the inmates of the hostel, with the consent of the external principal.[148] At Oxford, this dualist pattern seems not to have taken root. There a fellow normally acted as the sole principal of a hall which was attached to his college. Sometimes, however, a college might acquire one or more halls or hostels primarily for investment purposes rather than for the logistic reason of isolating the college's undergraduates. For example, in the fourteenth and fifteenth centuries University College, Oxford, suffered periodic financial crises: to help alleviate the situation, the college tried to increase its income through extensive hall ownership.[149] Judging from those years the entries for which in the Bursars' Rolls are sufficiently copious and capable of unambiguous interpretation, the college seems to have made a modest profit from its aularian imperialism.[150] Similar considerations apply to Lincoln College, Oxford, which, in the late fifteenth and early sixteenth centuries, owned Laurence Hall and Staple Hall.[151] As with University College, so too at Lincoln the profit motive appears to have been the main reason for aularian enterprise.

In these various ways, the majority of halls and hostels lost their

---

[148] Stokes, op. cit., loc. cit.

[149] From the Bursars' Rolls, which itemize the rents received from the hall principals and the college expenditure on repairs, it appears that in 1381–2 University College possessed about a dozen halls; in 1383–4 and 1385–6 about 11; in 1407–8 about 6; in 1409–10 about 9; in 1416–17 and 1419–20 about 8; in 1439–40 about 6; in 1463–4 about 7; and a small colony of halls was still being maintained in the closing years of the fifteenth century: University College Archives, Bursars' Rolls, PYX EE Fasc. 1/1, 1/3, 1/5, 3/8, 3/10, 4/6a, 4/9, 6/11; PYX GG Fasc. 1/4, 2/11, 2/6.

[150] For example, in 1383–4, the surplus of income over expenditure on halls was £11 4s. 5½d.; in 1385–6, it was £16 19s. 4d.; in 1416–17, it was £7 19s. 10d.; and in 1419–20, it was £8 14s. 4d.; in 1463–4, however, a loss of £11 1s. 2½d. was made: ibid., PYX EE Fasc. 1/3, 1/5, 4/6a, 4/9: PYX GG Fasc. 1/4.

[151] In the Lincoln College Bursars' Books, there are entries for these halls from 1487–8 for rents and for repairs: Lincoln College Archives, Bursars' Books, i. p. 8 (of account for 1487 or 1488); ii. pp. 10, 35 (of account for late 1480s or early 1490s); pp. 9, 29, 31 (of account for 1495); pp. 12, 13, 49, 49v, 51 (of account for early sixteenth century: dating uncertain). Apart from the rents of 40s. a year obtained from the principals, rents were also received from lodgers to whom hall rooms had been let: e.g. ibid., ii. p. 16 (of account for *c.* 1513).

independent status and came to be progressively absorbed within the collegiate sphere. As unendowed societies with no estates, halls and hostels were particularly vulnerable to the price inflation of the late fifteenth and sixteenth centuries. This meant that they often lacked the resources to enable them to subsidise the board or commons of their members to the degree that was frequently realized in the colleges. At Oxford, the apparent decrease in the University's population for at least part of the fifteenth century — a decline exacerbated by repeated visitations of plague, which began in *c.* 1440 and persisted well into the sixteenth century — may have contributed to the aularian decline.[152] This decline must not, however, be either antedated or exaggerated. The available figures for the Oxford halls indicate that the aularian demise was a protracted business. In 1444, there were about 69 halls; in 1469, about 50; in 1501, about 31; in 1511, about 25; in 1514, about 12; and in 1552, about 8.[153] But even when the halls were a minority constituent of university life, as they were by the mid-sixteenth century, they still accommodated a large proportion of the academic population: the eight surviving Oxford halls accommodated more than 200 students in *c.* 1550; just under 450 scholars were housed in the thirteen colleges.[154] The position regarding the decline of the Cambridge hostels was summarized by John Caius. Caius testified that the majority of the hostels which he listed were in existence in the early sixteenth century, but that at the time of writing, in 1573, only nine remained, and that all of these were attached to colleges.[155] Beyond these directions given by this contemporary witness, it does not seem to be possible to chart the demise of the Cambridge hostels in more particular detail.

[152] *Registrum Cancellarii*, ii. 358.

[153] Cobban, *The Medieval Universities*, p. 141. The figures for aularian decline at Oxford derive largely from Dr Pantin's researches: see the detailed discussion by J. K. McConica in his review, *E.H.R.*, lxxxvii (1972), p. 124, of H. Kearney, *Scholars and Gentlemen: Universities and Society in Pre-Industrial Britain 1500–1700* (London, 1970). Kearney is misleading on the history of the halls and has an inadequate view of collegiate development.

[154] Cobban, op. cit., loc. cit.; Pantin, *Oxford Life in Oxford Archives*, p. 10.

[155] Caius, *Historiae Cantabrigiensis Academiae*, pp. 52–3; see also Willis and Clark, op. cit., i. xxii–xxiii.

Before *c.* 1500 the principals of halls and hostels formed an important grouping in university society, smaller but comparable in standing to the corps of college fellows. At Oxford, it has been reckoned that between 1434 and 1518 almost 80 principals of arts halls, or their graduate assistants, served as university proctors. And principals of artist halls were also prominent among the holders of a series of lesser university offices, including keeperships of loan-chests and collectorships of university rents. Of the principals of the legist halls, some practised in the chancellor's court, and some acted as episcopal or archidiaconal officials or commissaries.[156] Principalships were much sought after by college fellows. For example, an analysis of the fellows of Oriel College, Oxford, in *c.* 1460 reveals that almost half of them were at one time or another principals of halls, the majority of which were under the dominion of the college.[157] In the fifteenth century, at least eight Oxford principals became bishops, including John Morton, bishop of Ely and later archbishop of Canterbury, who had been admitted as principal of Peckwater Inn in 1452.[158]

That the Oxford halls and Cambridge hostels persisted as a significant force in English university life until far into the sixteenth century is a salutary reminder of the chronic state of potential instability which was so characteristic of the medieval universities. A state of entrenched permanence, derived from the rooting of the universities in a web of solid buildings and wealthy endowments, is a relatively late feature of univerity history, and, in this respect, the English Universities are no exceptions. Whilst the secular colleges in the fourteenth and fifteenth centuries played an influential intellectual role greatly disproportionate to their number and size, and whilst college fellowships were islands of stability and continuity in what were still partially 'disemboided' universities, it is apparent that, for many, the halls and hostels typified the life of medieval Oxford and Cambridge. By 1500, the colleges had made

---

[156] For this analysis of Oxford principals, see Emden, 'Oxford Academical Halls in the Later Middle Ages', pp. 360–5.

[157] Information derived from notes left by the late Dr Pantin. For examples of Oxford fellows holding principalships, see Emden, op. cit., pp. 360–1.

[158] Emden, op. cit., p. 363.

some headway towards transforming the Universities into federated collegiate structures. But they had by then by no means completed the absorption of the undergraduate population, and, with exceptions in the form of the King's Hall and New College, they were only in the process of converting into undergraduate teaching institutions. Moreover, although by 1500 the colleges were notable contributors to university life through the participation of their fellows in university assemblies and administration, they had not yet emerged as central governmental units. The movement whereby the relatively democratic rule of the regent masters was superseded by the oligarchic government of the heads of colleges was effected only in the course of the sixteenth century.

Given the lingering prominence of the halls and hostels until the early sixteenth century, it would not have been altogether clear to the contemporary observer at the close of the fifteenth century that within fifty years or so the essential character of the English Universities would be collegiate rather than aularian. The feature which ensured that the secular colleges would emerge as the key components of the English Universities was their acquisition, by the mid-sixteenth century, of a near-monopoly of teaching within Oxford and Cambridge. It is with the variety of teaching facilities which evolved in the medieval English universities that the next chapter is concerned.

Chapter 5

Teaching: University and Collegiate

The medieval universities were generally regarded as vocational institutions, providing a range of intellectual disciplines and techniques of direct community value.[1] They were not, in any specific sense, research centres, and they offered no research degrees or research positions analogous to those offered by modern universities. They were essentially designed as teaching academies, and were expected to produce concrete returns for investments in university concerns. Precious resources were not easily given by European benefactors for the support of non-utilitarian university enterprises.[2] Society's conception of educational utility is an ever-changing one, and twentieth-century notions of a utilitarian education are not necessarily in accord with those of the medieval period. The type of criticism advanced by some humanist scholars of the late fifteenth and sixteenth centuries regarding the alleged aridity and social irrelevance of much of the education of the preceding university age is historically unsound, and may well have been propagandist in intent.[3] There may be a degree of truth in the humanist contention that university education of the pre-humanist age was prone to the excesses of logical pedantry and to an immoderate adherence to Aristotle and his commentators. But a rigorous training in logic and disputational techniques was widely valued in medieval society as an appropriate groundwork for the

[1] See e.g. the reflections of F. M. Powicke, 'The Medieval University in Church and Society', *Ways of Medieval Life and Thought*, pp. 198 ff.

[2] Cobban, *The Medieval Universities*, p. 219.

[3] E.g. Rashdall, *Universities*, iii. 453–4; Curtis, *Oxford and Cambridge in Transition*, pp. 21–2, 65 ff.; K. Charlton, *Education in Renaissance England* (London and Toronto, 1965), pp. 65–6. See the cautionary remarks on these humanist criticisms by J. M. Fletcher, 'Change and resistance to change: a consideration of the development of English and German Universities during the sixteenth century', *History of Universities*, i. (1981), pp. 1 ff. at pp. 30–1.

oral and written demands of many areas of professional life. In this sense, the arts course was viewed as no less utilitarian and no less socially applicable than disciplines such as law, theology or medicine.[4]

In a legalistic society with a maze of competing rights and privileges conferred by a hierarchy of authorities and meticulously defended, there was almost limitless scope for the application of that dialectical adroitness fundamental not only to arts, but also to civil and canon law, and indeed to the other superior faculties. Whether the university graduate aimed to make his career within the governmental, judicial, ecclesiastical or academic arenas, his gaining a dialectical prowess was deemed to be a worthwhile preparation for the range of problems he was likely to encounter.[5] Thus, medieval university students had the satisfaction of pursuing what were considered to be socially relevant courses. However, they were innocent of the modern notion of the cultural divide maintained between the sciences and the arts. It is true that they were constantly aware of the polarity between classical and Christian learning, but they were not aware of two distinct cultures as exemplified by the sciences and the arts. Such a separatist view of areas of learning would have made little sense in medieval universities, where the course leading to the M.A. degree was an amalgam of arts and scientific and mathematical subjects, studied in easy conjunction. This absence of a false dichotomy between the arts and sciences ensured that medieval students avoided the premature compartmentalism which is a common university experience in the twentieth century.

As it did in the continental universities, public university instruction in medieval Oxford and Cambridge centred upon the lecture and the disputation. The lectures, which the English students in arts or in the higher faculties had to attend, were divided into ordinary, extraordinary and cursory lectures, although the exact relation between the two latter categories is not at all easy to

---

[4] See e.g. the comments of H. Perkin, 'The Changing Social Function of the University: A Historical Retrospect', *CRE-Information Quarterly*, art. cit., p. 121.

[5] Cobban, op. cit., pp. 219–20.

determine.[6] The distinction between ordinary, extraordinary and cursory lectures was based upon such criteria as the method of lecturing, the content of the lecture and the standing of the lecturer. Ordinary lectures, which were the official lectures prescribed by university statute, were delivered by the regent masters on every day assigned for lectures (*dies legibilis*) at the most favoured hours of the day, usually in the morning, and they seem to have lasted a minimum of one hour.[7] No competing lectures, for example, those of bachelors, were permitted during the hours reserved for ordinary lectures[8] in order to ensure that no counter-attractions would be mounted in opposition to the diet of official instruction provided in each faculty. In the domain of the ordinary lecture, the master was supreme. As a member of the teaching guild, a regent master at Oxford or Cambridge was an independent functionary and apart from in exceptional circumstances — for instance, those arising from suspicions of heretical involvement — he lectured without supervisory curbs. His task was not only to give a detailed exposition of the stipulated texts but also to deliver magisterial or definitive rulings on difficult points generated by the text itself (*quaestiones*)[9] or stemming from the glosses of commentators on the text.

The extent to which the lecturer dealt with the glossatorial literature at the expense of the basic text was a matter of balance and was left to his personal judgment, although there was often pressure from his students to give the glosses as much exposure as possible

---

[6] On ordinary and extraordinary lectures in arts at Oxford, see e.g. J. A. Weisheipl, 'Curriculum of the Faculty of Arts at Oxford in the early fourteenth century', *Mediaeval Studies*, xxvi (1964), pp. 143 ff., esp. pp. 150 ff.; for teaching arrangements in canon law at Oxford, see L. Boyle, 'The Curriculum of the Faculty of Canon Law at Oxford in the first half of the fourteenth century', *Oxford Studies presented to Daniel Callus*, pp. 135 ff.; on ordinary and extraordinary lectures at Cambridge, see Hackett, *The Original Statutes of Cambridge University*, pp. 133–8. For teaching in law faculties in medieval universities, see H. Coing, *Handbuch der Quellen und Literatur der neueren europäischen Privatrechtsgeschichte*, i (Munich, 1973), pp. 71–2.

[7] E.g. Hackett, op. cit., pp. 135–6; Gibson, *Statuta Antiqua*, pp. lxxxi, 45, 59.

[8] Hackett, op. cit., pp. 138, 200–1; Gibson, op. cit., pp. lxxxi, 56; Weisheipl, art. cit., p. 150.

[9] Weisheipl, art. cit., p. 151.

with the expectation of a lively commentary on and sometimes a challenge to the authoritative text. It is clear that the ordinary lectures frequently exceeded the function of the exposition of the text. Through the resolution of *quaestiones* — the problems raised by the text — and the critical analysis of its glosses, a regent master might disseminate ideas and open avenues of inquiry which far transcended the textual limits.[10]

Not much is known about the process of allocating the set books to the regent masters. Prior to the fifteenth century, the allocation was perhaps decided at special meetings of the masters of the faculty, although no records of such gatherings are extant.[11] However, judging from an Oxford statute of 1431 regulating the distribution of the set texts among the regents in arts,[12] it is probable that in the later medieval period statutory provision in such matters generally superseded any such informal meetings of regent masters.

Masters were usually confined to one course of ordinary lectures at a time. If, by any chance, the regent master was unable to complete the course and another master could not be found as a substitute, then, exceptionally, a bachelor might be charged with the task.[13] By 1231, at Oxford, all students, excluding bachelors who aimed to incept as masters within a year, were required to attend at least one ordinary lecture on each *dies legibilis*.[14] This requirement was reiterated in a statute of *a.* 1313, with the qualification that students might leave before the end of a lecture, so long as they remained until the master had completed his *quaestiones* and the *ordinacio*, the division of the text into sections.[15] A student

---

[10] See e.g. Fletcher, 'The Faculty of Arts', *The History of the University of Oxford*, i. 375–6; and on the sensitive balance maintained between adherence to the authoritative text and creative lines of independent thought generated by the text, see the discussion by J. Paquet, 'Aspects de l'université médiévale', *The Universities in the Late Middle Ages*, ed. cit., pp. 3 ff. at pp. 16–19.

[11] Fletcher, op. cit., p. 377.

[12] Gibson, op. cit., pp. 235–6; Pantin, *Oxford Life in Oxford Archives*, p. 34.

[13] Weisheipl, art. cit., p. 160; Gibson, op. cit., p. 193; Cobban, op. cit., p. 210.

[14] Gibson, op. cit., p. 107.

[15] Ibid., p. 24.

normally heard the lectures of the regent master upon whose roll (*matricula*) his name was inscribed, but he could attend lectures given by other masters of the faculty.[16] The parallel legislation at Cambridge of the first half of the thirteenth century was less exacting, and stipulated that a scholar need attend only three ordinary lectures a week.[17] This was more in conformity with the situation at Bologna and Paris than was the Oxford provision.[18]

The ordinary lectures were designed to cover the set texts, the knowledge and understanding of which were required for the acquisition of a degree in a given faculty. That is to say, they were *pro forma* lectures, the mainstay of the official curriculum. Lecturing in the English Universities, however, was not confined to the prescribed texts. Extraordinary lectures were delivered by masters on books which were not part of the formal course.[19] Such lectures could be given in any area of university learning at times which did not clash with the programme of ordinary lectures. They were sometimes delivered on a day not assigned to ordinary lectures (*dies non legibilis*), sometimes on a day specifically designated for extraordinary lectures and sometimes on a *dies legibilis* after the ordinary lectures were over. The extraordinary lecture was less formal and probably less rigorously constructed than the ordinary lecture. It served, however, an invigorating function by bringing before students a range of texts, which although peripheral to the curriculum, were in some cases at least of a stimulating and broadening nature.[20] Moreover, a text treated in extraordinary lectures might, at a future date, be promoted to being a text treated in the ordinary lectures, and vice versa. For example, in the Oxford faculty of canon law, Gratian's *Decretum*, which had been an ordinary text, had, by the beginning of the fourteenth century,

---

[16] Weisheipl, art. cit., pp. 149–50; Fletcher, 'The Faculty of Arts', p. 375.

[17] *Camb. Docs.*, i. 332–3, and the Old Proctor's Book (*Liber procuratoris antiquus*), CUL/COLL ADMIN 3, fo. 25; also the comments by Hackett, op. cit., pp. 72–4.

[18] Hackett, op. cit., p. 74.

[19] On extraordinary lectures, see e.g. ibid., p. 135.

[20] E.g. Fletcher, 'The Faculty of Arts', p. 378.

been reduced to the status of an extraordinary book; and the *Decretals*, which had previously been an extraordinary text, had become fully established as an ordinary book by 1333.[21]

Although extraordinary lectures were normally the preserve of regent masters, it is curious that in the early thirteenth-century Cambridge constitutions edited by Dr Hackett, bachelors as well as masters are prohibited from staging extraordinary lectures or disputations during the hours reserved for ordinary lectures and disputations.[22] In this instance, 'extraordinary' may be used in a blanket sense to embrace the lectures and disputations of bachelors which, at a later date, were described as 'cursory'.[23] The precise meaning of 'extraordinary' and 'cursory' has not been fully resolved, and there may have been a measure of interchangeability between the terms. But while masters could occasionally give cursory lectures,[24] this category was primarily associated with the functions of bachelors. As part of their training for teaching, bachelors in arts, studying for the M.A. degree, and bachelors in the superior faculties, preparing for doctoral degrees in theology, civil law, canon law or medicine, were required to deliver a series of lectures under the supervision of a master or doctor. These lectures, which were heard by undergraduates in arts and by younger bachelors in the superior faculties, were generally styled 'cursory', a term not wholly understood but which seems to indicate the mode of lecturing. Cursory lectures were conducted at a lower level of expertise than that required for ordinary lectures, and usually consisted of a straightforward reading, paraphrase and summary of a text, with little in the way of commentary.[25] As such, cursory lectures were a valuable supplement to the more advanced and more intricate ordinary lectures, for they helped the student to familiarize

---

[21] L. Boyle, 'The Curriculum of the Faculty of Canon Law at Oxford in the first half of the fourteenth century', pp. 148–9; also Boyle, 'Canon Law before 1380', *The History of the University of Oxford*, i. 531 ff. at p. 535.

[22] Hackett, op. cit., pp. 200–1.

[23] See ibid., p. 138.

[24] Weisheipl, 'Curriculum of the Faculty of Arts at Oxford in the early fourteenth century', p. 151; Hackett, op. cit., p. 133.

[25] See e.g. Fletcher, 'The Faculty of Arts', p. 386; Weisheipl, art. cit., p. 151.

himself with the basics of a text without becoming involved in the complexities of the formal lecture. This was especially important in the thirteenth and fourteenth centuries, when price levels for texts were beyond the reach of many students, and when library facilities were extremely limited. It is also of interest that, apart from performing their statutory cursory lectures, well-qualified bachelors in the faculty of canon law at both Oxford and Cambridge were, from the early fourteenth century, engaged to give a number of ordinary lectures in order to relieve the pressures on the teaching doctors arising from the increased lecturing load caused by the issuing of new collections of decretals.[26] At Oxford, such lectures were called 'quasi-ordinary' (*quasi ordinarie*),[27] the University being careful to underline the point that, while bachelors in canon law may on occasion have substituted as ordinary lecturers, they did not thereby acquire that official status.

In addition to their lecturing duties, the regent masters in the English Universities were expected to stage public disputations on days set aside for this purpose.[28] These disputations, which were governed by strict procedural rules and which were held on a 'disputable day' (*dies disputabilis*), are to be distinguished from the *quaestiones* conducted by the masters at the morning ordinary lectures, which were speculative explorations of textual difficulties and lacked the structured character of the disputation. The magisterial disputation may have evolved from these *quaestiones*, by their becoming in their mature state quite distinct from the ordinary lectures, being separately and publicly mounted.[29] In parallel with the division of their lectures into ordinary and extraordinary categories, the disputations of the regent masters were similarly classified — an early instance of this, and perhaps this is the earliest

---

[26] Boyle, 'The Curriculum of the Faculty of Canon Law', pp. 146–51; *Camb. Docs.*, i. 367–9.

[27] Boyle, 'The Curriculum of the Faculty of Canon Law', pp. 146–7.

[28] On disputations at Oxford, see Weisheipl, art. cit., pp. 176–85, and at Cambridge, Hackett, op. cit., pp. 138–42. Much information on disputations is afforded by A. G. Little and F. Pelster, *Oxford Theology and Theologians c. A.D. 1282–1302* (Oxf. Hist. Soc., xcvi, 1934), pp. 29 ff. and pp. 226 ff.

[29] See e.g. Hackett, op. cit., pp. 139, 140–1.

of all such classifications of disputations in medieval universities, is found in the Cambridge constitutions of the first half of the thirteenth century.[30] Like the ordinary lecture, an ordinary disputation was a public and formal occasion, and was conducted by a regent master in the university schools; and during the time that ordinary disputations were staged no extraordinary disputations could be held.[31] A regent master always presided at ordinary disputations and usually, though not in every case, gave his summing up or determination of the question disputed either immediately after the debate or a day or two later.[32]

Ordinary disputations were attended by masters and bachelors of the faculty, and, in arts, by undergraduates as well.[33] For the regent masters, the disputation was an opportunity to explore more deeply complex issues which could not be adequately treated within the ambit of the formal lecture; for participating bachelors, it afforded an essential part of the training necessary for their qualification as a master in arts or a doctor in one of the superior faculties; and for undergraduates in arts, it was a means whereby, first as spectators and later, when more experienced, as minor disputants, they could shape and extend their dialectical skills. In the faculty of arts two of the chief types of ordinary disputations were *de sophismatibus* or *de problemate*, which comprised logical matters, and *de quaestione*,

[30] Ibid., pp. 200–1, with Hackett's comment on the matter, pp. 138–9.

[31] The formal nature of ordinary disputations is emphasized in the Cambridge constitutions of the first half of the thirteenth century, which stipulated that the bedels were to visit the university schools during the hours of both ordinary lectures and disputations. Furthermore, the bedel of canon law and theology had the duty of ringing the bell as a signal for the first disputations in each faculty: Hackett, op. cit., pp. 206–7. At Oxford, the disputations of regent masters were proclaimed by the bedels in the university schools so that all bachelors and scholars, both secular and members of religious orders, had the opportunity to attend: Little and Pelster, op. cit., p. 230, and H. Rashdall, 'The Friars Preachers v. the University AD 1311–1313', *Collectanea*, ii., ed. cit., 240.

[32] On this difficult matter of the relationship between a formal disputation (*disputatio*) and the full summing up and ruling on the question disputed (*determinatio*), see Little and Pelster, op. cit., pp. 39–42.

[33] Hackett, op. cit., pp. 140–1; Little and Pelster, op. cit., p. 37, who, however, suggest that regent masters at Oxford did not frequently attend the ordinary disputations of another master.

which related to mathematics, natural science, metaphysics and other areas of *quadrivium* study.[34] Undergraduates of two years standing were expected to take an active part in the disputations *de sophismatibus*, whence they derived the appellation of 'sophisters'.[35] Extraordinary disputations were given by both masters and bachelors, although exceedingly little has been discovered about them in the English Universities or, indeed, in any European university of the medieval period.[36] It may be affirmed, however, as with the extraordinary and cursory lectures, that they were designed to supplement the regular teaching of the university schools and to provide practical disputational experience both for bachelors and undergraduates in arts and for bachelors in the higher faculties, who, in pursuance of their degree courses, would have to engage as opponents or respondents in the more stringent ordinary disputations.

Disputations held in association with the inception of masters and doctors were sometimes labelled 'solemn',[37] and this nomenclature was extended to the important category or extraordinary disputations known as 'quodlibetical' or 'disputations *de quolibet*'.[38] These latter disputations were celebrated occasions when any proposition, regardless of controversial import or contemporary association, could be debated. Such disputations, which often touched upon matters of current ecclesiastical or political concern, were prominently advertised happenings, were open to all comers and often involved many disputants. They were not bound by a fixed agenda, and anyone present might raise issues for debate. Disputations *de quolibet* provided a much-needed release for some of the intellectual frustration generated by an educational system so oriented towards reverence for authority. Although

[34] See Weisheipl, art. cit., p. 154.

[35] Gibson, *Statuta Antiqua*, p. lxxxix.

[36] Hackett, *The Original Statutes of Cambridge University*, p. 141 and n. 1; Little and Pelster, op. cit., p. 247.

[37] Little and Pelster, op. cit., pp. 37, 42 ff.

[38] On disputations *de quolibet*, see e.g. Leff, *Paris and Oxford Universities in the Thirteenth and Fourteenth Centuries*, pp. 171–3; J. Verger, *Les universités au moyen âge*, pp. 61–2.

quodlibetical disputations probably reached their most mature expression in theological faculties, they were also mounted in law, medicine and arts. They were being staged in theology at Cambridge by the early 1270s,[39] in theology at Oxford by the early 1280s[40] and in the arts faculty at Oxford in the fourteenth century.[41]

Prior to the evolution of teaching facilities in the halls and hostels and in the monastic and secular colleges in the later medieval period, this programme of lectures and disputations constituted the sole formal instructional diet within the English Universities, although informal academic exercises and tuition may well have been improvised by individual masters for the benefit of their students. In each faculty, study took the form of the critical evaluation and meticulous analysis of a prescribed corpus of texts, augmented by the material treated in extraordinary lectures and disputations. As ultimate truth was deemed to lie beyond the reach of human understanding, study had to be conducted according to the bounds set by the accepted authorities, the overriding authority being the Bible, against which all other texts were to be assessed.[42] This meant that, in general, university study operated within an *a priori* system of thought. In particular, dialectical inquiry — the basic analytical method applied to all areas of study and used to elucidate the meaning of textual points, to harmonize seeming contradictions and to adjudicate logically between differing interpretations of matters arising from a text — was subject to the constraints inherent in a framework of scholarship founded upon key authoritative sources. Logical analysis could certainly challenge and modify the rulings of authority; but it was extremely difficult to break away entirely from the given mould by positing counter theses based upon first principles. It is true that an outstanding scholar, while appearing to work within the parameters of accepted truths, could, by means of a profound and multi-faceted penetration of textual meanings, allied to the speculations of an original cast of

[39] Hackett, op. cit., p. 141, n. 2.

[40] Little and Pelster, op. cit., pp. 94–5.

[41] Weisheipl, art. cit., p. 183.

[42] See e.g. Leff, op. cit., p. 5.

mind, depart significantly from conventional wisdom and reach a position which far transcended the authoritative text which had provided the starting point for the inquiry. Even in the course of the ordinary disputations, and certainly in those *de quolibet*, the *pro* and *contra* of logical debate might well lead the participants into avenues of thought which were at odds with received authority; and the final summing up of a formal debate, the *determinatio*, might, on occasion, embody something akin to creative investigation. Nonetheless, teaching and learning in medieval Oxford and Cambridge, as in the continental universities, was, at the average level, an innately conservative process, wherein questioning was conducted as a form of training within an accepted intellectual framework. The mastery of a difficult discipline, the sharpening of the critical faculties, the gaining of an ability to expound logically, the careful digestion of approved knowledge: these were the features of university education as experienced by the majority of the academic population.[43] For the most part, the English Universities afforded a training designed rather to perpetuate a body of doctrine than to further independent avenues of inquiry.

Salaried lectureships had been progressively adopted in the universities of southern Europe in the course of the thirteenth and fourteenth centuries.[44] But in some of the northern universities, they were a late-medieval introduction, and Oxford and Cambridge were among the last to initiate endowed lectureships. The consequence of this was that for almost three centuries the English Universities relied heavily upon the 'necessary regency' system, an economical method of lecturer recruitment whereby every new master of arts or doctor in a superior faculty had to contract to teach for periods of one or two years, depending upon the particular faculty's regulations.[45] At Oxford, this teaching obligation was

---

[43] Cobban, *The Medieval Universities*, p. 167.

[44] See ibid., pp. 154–7.

[45] Gibson, *Statuta Antiqua*, p. 54. The term 'necessary regent' (*necessarius regens*) is used in an Oxford statute of 1438: ibid., p. 258. On the necessary regency in the faculty of arts at Oxford and its modifications in the fifteenth and early sixteenth centuries, see J. M. Fletcher, 'The Teaching of Arts at Oxford, 1400–1520', *Paedagogica Historica: International Journal of the History of Education*, vii (2) (Ghent, 1967), pp. 417 ff., esp. pp. 424–9; also, for the regency

sealed by an oath, while at Cambridge, a caution or pledge was required of the recently created master or doctor against the performance of his statutory teaching duties.[46] Although each new master in arts was contracted to teach for a specified duration, which was considerably shortened in the later medieval period,[47] those who had the requisite aptitude, motivation and financial resources commonly undertook study in one of the superior faculties after the final completion of their imposed teaching duties. While there was no objection to a master continuing to lecture in arts while studying in a higher faculty, the commitments of time made this conjunction difficult. The study of theology, law, or medicine, involving as they did the full round of ordinary and extraordinary lectures and disputations and other academic exercises, would not have afforded much time for the master in arts to continue ordinary lectures in the arts faculty on any regular basis. It seems that relatively few masters in arts were able to combine these lecturing and study functions in different faculties.[48] Because it was fairly frequent at Oxford and Cambridge for masters in arts to enrol in a superior faculty after the necessary regency period and to sever teaching connections with the arts faculty, a teaching bias was inevitably produced towards the younger and more inexperienced lecturer, a circumstance not always in the best interests of the student body. It is not suggested that the English Universities were entirely reliant on the necessary regency system for lecturer recruitment. There would always have been some lecturers who would elect to remain as university teachers for a

system in the sixteenth century, Fletcher, 'Change and resistance to change: a consideration of the development of English and German Universities during the sixteenth century', *History of Universities*, i (1981), pp. 10–11 (Oxford), 13 (Cambridge); Pantin, *Oxford Life in Oxford Archives*, p. 32. The necessary regency system is prescribed in the Cambridge constitutions of pre-1250, where a minimum teaching period of one year is imposed upon all newly created regent masters: Hackett, op. cit., pp. 198–201.

[46] See above, pp. 88–9.

[47] For the shortening of the necessary regency in arts at Oxford and for the frequency of dispensations to individual masters from this obligation, see Fletcher, 'The Teaching of Arts at Oxford, 1400–1500', pp. 424–7.

[48] See e.g. Cobban, *The Medieval Universities*, p. 212.

number of years, maintained in part by a college fellowship, or by an ecclesiastical benefice, or by membership of a religious order. Nonetheless, this pool of 'compulsory' regent masters supplied the principal source of university teachers in the English Universities until the later Middle Ages.

It is true that some advantages may have accrued from a teaching contingent of young and energetic lecturers who had to compete, on a kind of commercial basis, for student audiences, upon whose fees they partly or chiefly depended for their livelihood. The rates of remuneration, especially in arts, were not particularly attractive. It appears that lecture fees were customarily exacted in the English Universities in the thirteenth century. In 1333, lecture fees in the faculty of arts at Oxford were made compulsory because wealthier masters had apparently been waiving their right to fees, with the result that they were drawing audiences away from poorer masters, who had, of necessity, to exact fees and whose earnings were being put in jeopardy.[49] Nevertheless, even after lecture fees were rendered compulsory at both Universities, fee levels were decidedly modest. Many young regent masters who lacked either the inclination for further study or the financial support for the lengthy courses in the higher faculties, must have been easily enticed into seeking more lucrative employment outside the university when their contractual lecturing had been completed. It is evident that such a drain, at least of the abler lecturers, had a most damaging effect upon the continuity of university teaching experience.[50] This deficiency could be remedied only by the establishment of salaried lectureships as the most important single contribution towards the emergence of some degree of tenure for university teachers.

As already stated, in comparison to most of the other medieval universities, Oxford and Cambridge were surprisingly belated in

[49] On compulsory lecture-fees at Oxford in the early fourteenth century, see Gibson, op. cit., p. 47; *Munimenta Academica*, i. 128; also G. Post, 'Masters' Salaries and Student-Fees in the Mediaeval Universities', *Speculum*, vii (1932), pp. 181 ff. at p. 195. For the legislation of 1333, see Gibson, op. cit., pp. 131–2. Lecture fees at Oxford are discussed by Mallet, *A History of the University of Oxford*, i. 199.

[50] Cobban, 'Decentralized Teaching in the Medieval English Universities', p. 205.

coming to terms with the need for endowed lectureships, and these materialized in those two universities only towards the end of the fifteenth century. It is probable that the unplanned and sometimes precariously random nature of the university teaching force in England was at least one of the factors which underlay the growth of supplementary tutorial and lecturing facilities in the halls and hostels and in the monastic and secular colleges. Over a period of time, these additional teaching aids came to rival and then to eclipse the university instruction of the regent masters, so that by the mid-sixteenth century, teaching in Oxford and Cambridge was largely centred in the secular colleges and in the few surviving halls and hostels. This teaching revolution was neither planned nor co-ordinated. The consequence, however, was to be the transformation of medieval Oxford and Cambridge from Universities of a centripetal character to those of a centrifugal one,[51] and this devolutionary movement was of such fundamental import that it now needs to be examined in appropriate detail.

The growth of decentralized teaching in the medieval English Universities — a growth which so completely altered their nature — had a threefold institutional source. It was a combination of the tutorial and lecturing practices which evolved in the monastic colleges, in the halls and hostels and in the secular colleges. Facilities of this kind were apparently established first in the monastic colleges and in the unendowed halls and hostels, and it is highly probable that these facilities influenced the shape of the tutorial and lecturing arrangements of the secular colleges, which, by the time of the Reformation, had been rendered the primary teaching units in the English Universities. Most of the evidence for the nature of the teaching in monastic colleges and in halls is available for Oxford and it is to be assumed that broadly equivalent developments occurred in the monastic colleges and the hostels of Cambridge University.

Individual tutorial contracts, as distinct from institutional arrangements, are found to have existed soon after Oxford had emerged as a fully-fledged *studium generale*. In *c.* 1220, Ralph Neville, bishop of Chichester, had engaged Elias, a canon of St Frideswide's, to

[51] This theme is analysed in ibid., *passim*.

supervise the welfare of Thomas de Bosco, an arts student supported by the bishop as patron. The bishop supplied his protégé with money and materials, and received reports from the canon as intermediary.[52] Similar triangular arrangements involving a patron, student and supervisor, or tutor, followed the foundation, from the late thirteenth century onwards, of the Oxford colleges of the monastic orders. Evidence from Benedictine sources of the second half of the fourteenth century reveals that a monk in the home monastery would sometimes support, as patron, one or more secular students, and would engage a monk-scholar of their Oxford college to serve as a tutor with reference to financial and moral aspects. A few cases will illustrate the system.

For a number of years between *c*. 1360 and *c*. 1390 a Durham monk maintained at Oxford two secular scholars, who were placed under the supervision of a monk-scholar, probably a member of Durham College. On one occasion, the monk-patron sent the monk-scholar a mark towards the support of one of the students for the current term, and instructed him to reach agreement with the other student's hall principal that he be accommodated in the coming session at the rate of half commons. As these students were to return to Durham for vacations, it is likely that they were natives of that city. Another monk-patron of Durham, it seems, maintained a secular student, Thomas de S., at Oxford for about eight years. In another case, for some time between *c*. 1367 and *c*. 1388, the prior of Durham sent the son of a lay official to Oxford. He was to be placed under the general supervision of a monk-scholar, apparently of Durham College, who was to install the youth in a hall of artists at the rate of half commons, to control his finances, doling them out on his behalf according to need, and to satisfy himself as to his charge's moral and academic progress.[53] The

---

[52] See J. Boussard, 'Ralph Neville, Evêque de Chichester et Chancelier d'Angleterre d'après sa correspondance', *Revue Historique*, clxxvi (1935), pp. 217 ff. at p. 226 and n. 2; see also Pantin, 'The Conception of the Universities in England in the period of the Renaissance', *Les Universités Européennes du xive au xviii siècle*, p. 110.

[53] For these Durham cases, see *Oxford Formularies*, i. 233–4, 235–6, 238–9; also *Chapters of the English Black Monks 1215–1540* (3 vols., ed. W. A. Pantin, Camden Soc., 3rd ser., xlv, xlvii, liv, 1931–7), iii. 54.

directives given by the abbot of Glastonbury in *c.* 1365 to a monk-scholar for the supervision of a student at Oxford make it clear that responsibility for the youth was to be shared between the monk-scholar, as tutor, and a university master. Disciplinary matters might be the concern of either, but the student's finances were to be at the disposition of the monk-tutor, who, among other items, was responsible for the payment of his charge's hall account.[54]

From instances of this nature, it is apparent that the monastic establishments had devised a rudimentary kind of tutorial organization for the benefit of their secular pupils at Oxford. The system here unfolded was a wholly personal one, as yet devoid of a binding institutional context, the secular students living in academic halls and not with their monk-tutors in the monastic colleges. Moreover, the monk-tutor was involved with only two of the three components which formed the tutorial system as it was later formulated in the Oxford and Cambridge secular colleges. Academic instruction remained, it seems, in the hands of the secular masters in the University. It is symptomatic of the anomalous position of the secular student supported by a monastic patron that, when resident in a hall, control of his finances was vested in the external monk-tutor, while the finances of his co-aularians were probably entrusted to the principal of the hall or to one of his graduate assistants.

The support of and supervisory arrangements made for secular students was not the sole contribution made by the monastic colleges to the embryonic tutorial system. The monastic orders sent a regular stream of monk-students to their university colleges to study arts followed by theology. This had the consequence of creating, in the fourteenth century, mixed graduate and undergraduate societies at a time when, with one or two exceptions, the secular colleges were mainly postgraduate in composition. The mixed nature of the monastic colleges engendered opportunities for the growth of teaching facilities. In the fourteenth century, at the Oxford Benedictine foundation, Gloucester College, senior monks acted as moral tutors to the junior monks, and academic tuition was provided by visiting

[54] *Chapters of the English Black Monks*, iii. 54.

masters so that the movements of the monk-students about the town would be kept to the minimum. In addition, a senior monk at Gloucester College, who was to be a doctor of theology, was deputed, after the manner of a resident teaching master, to lecture in theology; and one of the monk-students was to lecture in philosophy to the junior members of the community. Internal disputations in both theology and philosophy were to be staged weekly in term-time, and also in vacations, if thought necessary. Despite there being this measure of collegiate teaching, students were nevertheless required to attend the ordinary lectures and disputations in the university schools.[55] It therefore seems probable that Gloucester College in the fourteenth century had moved towards the setting up of a collegiate system of tuition and lectures. This monastic academic framework was not wholly self-contained, as it relied upon complementary public university instruction and on a circle of visiting secular masters as tutors. Clearly, however, Gloucester College,and presumably other monastic colleges in the English Universities, furnished an early foretaste of a tutorial and lecture system, which would have served as a point of reference for the later teaching developments in the secular collegiate sphere.

The probable contribution of the monastic colleges to teaching facilities within the English Universities was further elaborated by that of the halls and hostels. It will be recalled that residence in a hostel or college was made compulsory for all scholars at Cambridge in the late fourteenth century, and that likewise at Oxford residence in a hall or college was made a statutory requirement in *c.* 1410, a provision reinforced by a statute of Henry V in 1420.[56] It is evident that in the English Universities until the late fifteenth and early sixteenth centuries the majority of undergraduates, and a fair proportion of graduates, were domiciled in the halls and hostels. In these circumstances of mandatory residence, the growth of internal teaching in the halls and hostels as a supplement to the public instruction of the university schools was a natural enough

---

[55] For teaching arrangements at Gloucester College, see ibid., ii. 55, 75; iii. 31. See also *The Letter Book of Robert Jospeh* (ed. H. Aveling and W. A. Pantin, Oxf. Hist. Soc., new ser., xix, 1967), pp. xviii-xxi.

[56] See above, p. 148.

development. A central feature of this was the hall lecture — the *lectura aularis* — given in the mornings by the hall principal or by one of his graduate aides. Aularian lectures of this type seem to date from the fourteenth century.[57] In the lengthy Oxford statute of 1409 which prescribes the procedure for determination, it is assumed that students on the point of qualifying as bachelors will have heard the appropriate college or hall lectures delivered by masters or bachelors:[58] and from this same statute, it may be inferred that the halls of the artists provided a staple diet of elementary logic and mathematics, supplemented here and there with texts of a more advanced character.[59] There is a record of 1424 of an Oxford principal engaging a master to lecture in his hall.[60] The Oxford *Register of Congregation 1448–1463* contains listings of numerous graces with references to hall lectures, many of them in canon and civil law.[61] And the Oxford aularian statutes (*statuta aularia*) of 1483–90 expected that morning lectures would be staged in the halls wherein masters and bachelors would expound the prescribed books as a supplement to the ordinary and extraordinary lectures of the university schools. The morning hall lecture was to be followed in the afternoon by a *recitatio* or repetition (also mentioned in the statute of 1409), a revision exercise at which students were catechized in the subject of the day's hall lecture. Such academic exercises were augmented by regular discussion groups and disputations in which the students were the main participants.[62]

These statutes clearly show that, in the fifteenth century, aularian teaching was making an important contribution to the Oxford arts

---

[57] Pantin, *Oxford Life in Oxford Archives*, p. 36.

[58] Gibson, *Statuta Antiqua*, p. 200.

[59] Ibid., 200–1.

[60] Emden, *An Oxford Hall in Medieval Times*, p. 196; H. E. Salter, 'An Oxford Hall in 1424', *Essays in History presented to R. L. Poole* (ed. H. W. C. Davis, Oxford, 1927), pp. 421 ff. at pp. 429–30.

[61] *The Register of Congregation 1448–1463*, pp. 49, 75, 80, 86, 184, 336.

[62] See the *statuta aularia* printed in Gibson, *Statuta Antiqua*, pp. 574 ff. at pp. 579–80; see also the comments of Emden, op. cit., p. 208.

course and that, as such, it was subjected to university control. Moreover, although hall teaching was essentially an aid to public university instruction, in certain circumstances the University seems to have accepted attendance at lectures in a hall as a substitute for attendance at the official ordinary lectures. For example, when Robert Harlow supplicated for his bachelor's degree in November 1449, he successfully offered a period of hall lectures in place of some of the ordinary lectures.[63] From this, and other graces, it is also known that hall teaching continued throughout vacations.

These late fifteenth-century aularian statutes are not, however, very informative on the hall tutorial system. They point to its existence when they are making regulations for corporal punishment. It was enacted that every scholar who was under a master, tutor, or creditor (*sub magistro, tutore aut creditore*) and who had been guilty of a statutory breach either was to undergo corporal correction on Saturday evenings or was to pay a fine. The punishment was to be administered by the hall principal, notwithstanding the claim of the student's 'master, tutor, curator or creditor' that the fault had already been corrected, or that he was about to do so.[64] The assumption in the *statuta aularia* is that every hall undergraduate would have a tutor, who would sometimes be the principal himself. Apart from that of disciplinary supervision, however, the tutor's functions are undefined. However, there is evidence — for one Oxford hall — that shows that in 1424 control of the student's finances was an essential part of a hall tutor's business. In this case, John Arundel, who was principal probably of St Mildred Hall near Exeter College, and later bishop of Chichester, controlled the finances of those undergraduates who looked upon him as their tutor; and he accounted for their money term by term as it was expended piecemeal on their behalf.[65] Presumably, Arundel received the money for his charges from parents or

---

[63] *The Register of Congregation*, p. 47.

[64] Gibson, op. cit., p. 587; Emden, op. cit., p. 209.

[65] See Salter, 'An Oxford Hall in 1424', pp. 421 ff., and Emden, op. cit., p. 193. It is likely that law scholars living in a hall, who would often be of more mature years than the artists, would normally exercise a personal control over their expenditure.

guardians, who would have entered into contractual arrangements with the principal.

The evidence for this Oxford hall in 1424 and the *statuta aularia* taken together do not prove conclusively that individual hall tutors supervised in an academic sense as they did in a moral and disciplinary one. Nevertheless, it is highly probable that those masters and bachelors who were engaged to give hall lectures also acted as tutors, supervised *recitationes* and disputations and provided a measure of individual tuition. Whatever the extent of that individual tuition, the halls certainly advanced the financial and disciplinary aspects of guardianship. And with the monastic colleges, they were pioneers of institutional lectures and the disputational type of exercise conceived of as adjuncts to public university instruction. As such, they provided ever-present models for the collegiate teaching and tutorial practices which grew up and became dominant in the later medieval period.

It was emphasized in the previous chapter that the main aim behind the foundation of the English secular colleges was to make available support for students capable of study beyond a first degree and that, exceptional institutions apart, they remained largely postgraduate in character until the later medieval period. In the majority of the early secular colleges of Oxford and Cambridge, however, there were arrangements whereby the senior members would aid and teach younger colleagues who were incorporated fellows possessed of at least an arts degree. For example, the statutes of 1270 of Merton College, Oxford, the prototype of the English 'graduate' college, prescribe that teachers are to be selected from the more advanced fellows to help the younger ones in their studies and to look after their moral welfare.[66] Similar provisions were enacted at Peterhouse, Cambridge.[67] These supervisory arrangements, however, were so informal that they scarcely amounted to a system, and they embraced only fellows of graduate status. There is no suggestion, at this juncture, that the younger fellows vested control of their finances in the hands of senior colleagues, and, consequently there is no trace in the early stages of

[66] See the Merton statutes of 1270 in *Statutes*, i. ch. 2, 12.

[67] *Camb. Docs.*, ii. 12.

English secular collegiate development of the financial-control aspect of the tutorial system.[68] What is here displayed is the simplest kind of tutorial organization — informal, unpaid, and confined solely to members of the college. There is no evidence that in the secular colleges of the late thirteenth and fourteenth centuries there existed the internal lectures found in the contemporary monastic colleges.

The royal college of the King's Hall, Cambridge, whose origins date from *c.* 1317 and which became an endowed collegiate institution in 1337, was certainly the earliest English college to house a substantial intake of undergraduates who, as fellows, were fully incorporated members of the foundation.[69] As a college which accommodated university scholars at all levels, from undergraduates in arts to doctors in the superior faculties, the King's Hall was the archetype of the secular English college of mixed academic proportions. This invalidates the claim often made that the meticulously planned New College, Oxford, founded in 1379, more than half a century after the King's Hall, was the pioneer of the mixed collegiate pattern, and thereby marked the decisive break from the 'graduate' collegiate norm inaugurated by Merton College in the late thirteenth century.[70] The model inaugurated at the King's Hall of the mixed collegiate society where undergraduates, studying for the B.A., shared a life in common with those preparing for the M.A. and for degrees in the superior faculties was the model which has characterized the college scene at Oxford and Cambridge from its general realization in the Tudor era down to the twentieth century. In addition to the King's Hall and New College, which were so patently untypical of English secular colleges of the late thirteenth and fourteenth centuries with respect

---

[68] Cobban, 'The King's Hall, Cambridge and English medieval collegiate history', *Authority and Power: Studies on Medieval Law and Government presented to Walter Ullmann on his seventieth birthday* (ed. B. Tierney and P. Linehan, Cambridge, 1980), pp. 183 ff. at p. 185.

[69] See Cobban, *The King's Hall*, esp. pp. 50 ff.

[70] The educational significance of the King's Hall and New College in English academic history is assessed at some length in ibid., ch. 2. For the many and often exaggerated claims for Wykeham as an educational innovator, see the references in ch. 4, n. 52 above.

to their significant undergraduate elements, some account needs to be taken of those other pre-fifteenth-century colleges for which claims of an undergraduate presence have been entertained.

There was evidently an idea current among founders of English colleges of the medieval period that some provision ought to be made for charitable grammar teaching in collegiate establishments.[71] But this seems to have been a subsidiary aim, and if the various codes of statutes are compared, one is left in no uncertainty as to where the priorities lay. The overall impression derived is that the provisions concerning the instruction of poor youths were often tagged on as a sort of afterthought or as a conventional sop to charity. For it is always stressed that these 'grammar' clauses were to apply only if the funds of the college would allow, a condition which presupposes that the grammar instruction of poor scholars was to be readily sacrificed to the needs of the graduate members of the college. For example, the Peterhouse statutes enact that two or three grammar students are to be supported by the charity of the college in so far as the finances of the foundation will permit. On evidence of good progress, they might be made scholars: if not, they were to be removed from the college.[72] A similar example is contained in the statutes of 1359 of Clare College, Cambridge.[73] With the exception of the rather special arrangements at Merton, which will be discussed below,[74] these 'colonies' of grammar youths were not incorporated, but remained apart from the society, after the manner of charitable appendages. Given that the majority of English medieval colleges could not afford to maintain even the statutory complements of fellows, and given the monetary priorities, it may be understood that these 'grammar schools' would have been insignificant and, in some cases, the statutory provision would have remained largely or wholly inoperative. The extreme instance is perhaps that of Queen's College, Oxford, where although the founder's statutes provided for the

[71] On 'grammar colonies' in English secular colleges, see Cobban, *The King's Hall*, pp. 50–2 and notes.

[72] *Camb. Docs.*, ii. 24–6.

[73] Ibid., ii. 140–1.

[74] See below, pp. 184, 191–2.

maintenance and instruction of poor boys up to the number of seventy-two,[75] the actual number of poor boys amounted to only a handful before 1500.[76] The elaborate provision made by the founder, Robert de Eglesfield, for the teaching of poor boys in grammar, singing, logic and philosophy, and for the staging of a regular round of disputations,[77] is of considerable interest. In the event, however, this plan for charitable teaching at Queen's was, as has been noted, only minimally realized.

There is a possibility that, before the foundation of the King's Hall, three of the Oxford secular colleges and one of the monastic colleges had maintained a few undergraduate members as distinct from charity grammar boys. Dervorguilla's statutes for Balliol of 1282 clearly imply, though they do not state, that youths who had not yet taken a bachelor's degree in arts might be admitted to study for the master's degree.[78] But it is probable that students in arts entering Balliol would have had at least two years' standing in the University — that is to say, they would be sophists. Internal disputations (*sophismata*) were to be held every fortnight, and those scholars who were shortly to determine as bachelors in the university schools were to practise their exercises among the college fellows.[79] Similarly, Walter of Stapeldon's statutes of 1316 for Exeter College made specific provision for the reception of sophists or undergraduates of two years' standing. As the statutory complement was only thirteen, later increased to fifteen, and as the sophist qualification for entry was a minimum one,[80] the number of

---

[75] *Statutes*, i. ch. 4, 30.

[76] R. H. Hodgkin, 'The Queen's College', *V.C.H. Oxon.* iii. 132 ff. at 132.

[77] *Statutes*, i. ch. 4, 15, 30.

[78] Ibid., i. ch. 1, v-vii; *Oxford Balliol Deeds*, pp. 277-9.

[79] *Statutes*, i. ch. 1, vi.

[80] Concerning the qualifications and election of the thirteen scholars, see the original statutes of Exeter College of 26 April 1316 printed in *The Register of Walter de Stapeldon, Bishop of Exeter, 1307-1326*, ed. cit., pp. 304-8 at p. 304. The foundation of Exeter College, or Stapeldon Hall, as it was for long commonly styled, is discussed in considerable detail by M. Buck, *Politics, Finance and the Church in the Reign of Edward II: Walter Stapeldon Treasurer of England* (Cambridge, 1983), ch. 5. The complement of fellows was raised from

undergraduates must have been few at any given time.[81] Exeter seems to have been a graduate society which occasionally afforded entrance to advanced undergraduates on the point of 'determining' as bachelors. More convincing is Merton's claim to an undergraduate contingent. Taken together, the evidence concerning the boys of Walter de Merton's kin and that concerning those falling into the categories known as the 'poor secondary scholars' and the 'portionists', a later category from *c.* 1380, seems to point to the fact that, although these groups of students were not incorporated undergraduate fellows after the manner of those of the King's Hall and New College and although most were housed outside the college, they nevertheless partook of an undergraduate character, and were apparently regulated by a form of tutorial organization.[82] Finally, the situation at Canterbury College, the Benedictine college founded by the archbishop of Canterbury, Simon Islip, in 1363 as a mixed community of monks and secular fellows, should also be mentioned in this 'undergraduate' context. By 1370, the college had been converted into a predominantly monastic society; by 1384, however, arrangements had been made for the maintenance of five poor secular undergraduates, who were to assist in the chapel and who were to act as servitors to the monk-fellows.[83] Having gained a competence in grammar, these poor scholars were to study arts, and one or two of them might even proceed to civil law. They were to be supported for seven years, and they were expected to enter the ranks of the secular clergy or a religious order. It is specifically stated in the statutes of 1384 that these secular scholars were not to be, in any sense, fellows of the

---

13 to 15 in 1404, but there seems to have been no further increase before 1500: R. W. Southern, 'Exeter College', *V.C.H. Oxon.* iii. 107 ff. at 108.

[81] E.g. it is known that on 20 November 1420 the college comprised 6 masters, 4 bachelors, 2 sophists and a chaplain, two more sophists being elected within the next few days: Southern, 'Exeter College', p. 108.

[82] See below, pp. 191–2.

[83] For these secular undergraduates, see Archbishop Courtenay's statutes of 16 January 1384 for Canterbury College in *Canterbury College Oxford* (3 vols., ed. W. A. Pantin, Oxf. Hist. Soc., new ser., vi-viii, 1946–50), iii (1950), 179; see also Pantin, 'Before Wolsey', *Essays in British History presented to Sir Keith Feiling*, p. 56.

college: they were the beneficiaries of monastic charity and were possessed of no other status. All the same, it is of considerable interest to find a secular undergraduate colony, however small, in an Oxford monastic college.

It would seem reasonable to conclude that, prior to the foundation of New College, several English colleges made a gesture towards undergraduate intake — but, except in one case, with little of consequence materializing. Merton indeed admitted categories of scholars who were allied to undergraduates, and clearly the significance of this should not be minimized. It is only at the King's Hall, Cambridge, however, that there existed an undergraduate element on a considerable scale and only there were the undergraduates, from the start, incorporated fellows, as they were to be later in the century at New College.

Fundamental to William of Wykeham's educational programme for New College was his insistence that all his scholars be soundly based in grammar before proceeding to arts and the higher reaches of study.[84] It was to this end that he founded, in 1382, his complementary grammar school of Winchester, which was to serve as a 'feeder' for his Oxford college. Winchester, framed for seventy scholars of grammar, was the largest endowed grammar school yet realized in England, and, of the pre-Reformation schools, it was to be rivalled in size and importance only by Henry VI's Eton (1440) and by Cardinal Wolsey's Ipswich (1528).[85] In the later fourteenth century, there was evidently, in educated circles, concern about declining grammatical standards. This decline was caused partly, it seems, by a shortage of masters of arts to teach in grammar schools,[86] and was reflected in, for example, the deteriorating level of the productions of some of the late fourteenth-century Oxford

---

[84] *Statutes*, i ch. 5, 5–6.

[85] See e.g. Orme, *English Schools in the Middle Ages*, pp. 187–8. For the history of Winchester College, see Leach, *A History of Winchester College*; T. F. Kirby, *Annals of Winchester College, from its foundation in the year 1382* (London, 1892), who prints the foundation charter of 1382 and the statutes of 1400 at pp. 455 ff.; and *Winchester College: Sixth-Centenary Essays* (ed. R. Custance, Oxford, 1982).

[86] Orme, op. cit., p. 151.

grammarians.[87] This languishing of grammar may have contributed to the growing number of first-year Oxford students who could not cope adequately with the Latin instructional diet. The Winchester–New College nexus obviated this weakness by ensuring that students bound for New College had a thorough grasp of grammar, which Wykeham, in his foundation charter of 20 October 1382 for Winchester, reputed the foundation, door and fount of all other arts and sciences.[88] This need to shore up a grammatical decline in the English Universities of the later medieval period was to be a continuing problem. Attempts to raise the level of grammatical expertise found expression, for example, in fifteenth-century institutions such as Godshouse, Cambridge (1439), conceived as a training college for grammar masters,[89] the twin enterprise of Eton and King's College, Cambridge, in the 1440s, and Magdalen College school, founded at Oxford by 1480.

The stress laid by Wykeham upon a sound grounding in grammar as a necessary preliminary to entry to his Oxford college received an equally proper emphasis in the statutes of the King's Hall.[90] The King's Hall stemmed, as we have seen, from an extension of the chapel royal set in the University of Cambridge. A considerable proportion of the undergraduates who entered the college in the fourteenth and early fifteenth centuries were the products of the grammar school of the chapel royal, many of them boys and clerks of the chapel itself or the sons of household and court officials.[91] There existed between the King's Hall and the

---

[87] See R. W. Hunt, 'Oxford Grammar Masters in the Middle Ages', *Studies presented to Daniel Callus*, pp. 163 ff. at pp. 185–7.

[88] The relevant extract from the foundation charter is printed by M. E. C. Walcott, *William of Wykeham and his Colleges* (Winchester and London, 1852), p. 122.

[89] On Godshouse, see A. H. Lloyd, *The Early History of Christ's College, Cambridge* (Cambridge, 1934); Cobban, *The King's Hall*, pp. 79–80; and see below, pp. 196–8.

[90] See the statutes of the King's Hall printed by Rouse Ball, *The King's Scholars and King's Hall*, p. 67: the original statutes are no longer extant. The specific statutory extract is given by Cobban, *The King's Hall*, p. 59.

[91] See Cobban, op. cit., chs. 1, 2.

court a type of complementary academic relationship: namely, the household grammar school served the King's Hall as a 'feeder' institution, in which young boys of noble lineage or with high court connections were given a basic grammatical training before going up to the royal college to embark upon the arts course at Cambridge University. There is here the essence of Wykeham's conception. For although the court–King's Hall nexus never embodied that measure of conscious balance which characterized the Winchester–New College scheme and was never regulated by a rigorous statutory control, it stands out as an influential model for the association between a university college and a grammar school, albeit that the latter was of a rarefied kind, devoid of independent institutional status.[92]

It is perhaps misguided to seek a single model for Wykeham's grandiose project. Rather, the Winchester–New College scheme is an eclectic product deriving inspiration from a variety of sources.[93] Walter of Stapeldon's achieved foundation of Exeter College, Oxford, and his proposed endowed grammar scholarships in the Hospital of St John, Exeter, carried into effect by his successor as bishop of Exeter, John Grandisson, might be said to have prefigured Wykeham's idea, although there existed no organic linkage between Stapeldon's educational enterprises.[94] The contention of A.F. Leach that one of Wykeham's models may have been provided by De Vaux College, founded at Salisbury by Bishop Bridport in 1262 and not dissolved until 1542, with its alleged, but now disproven, institutional link with Oxford, would appear to carry little conviction.[95] It has been rightly stressed that, in the compilation of his lengthy code of statutes, Wykeham borrowed

---

[92] Ibid., p. 63.

[93] On Wykeham's possible models, see Leach, *A History of Winchester College*, pp. 77 ff.; A. W. Parry, *Education in England in the Middle Ages* (London, 1920), pp. 191–3; Cobban, *The King's Hall*, pp. 63–5.

[94] See Leach, op. cit., pp. 84–5; Orme, *English Schools in the Middle Ages*, pp. 182–3; Buck, *Politics, Finance and the Church in the Reign of Edward II*, pp. 112–13.

[95] See Leach, op. cit., pp. 86–7, and the counter arguments of Edwards, 'College of De Vaux Salisbury', *Victoria History of the County of Wiltshire*, iii. 372.

heavily from sections in those of Merton and Queen's College, Oxford.[96] In particular, Wykeham seems to have imbibed something of the largeness of conception of Robert de Eglesfield, who so lamentably failed to translate his vision into reality. Furthermore, it may be suggested that Wykeham was influenced by the scale and magnificence of some of the Paris colleges, notably Navarre, founded by Joan, queen of France, in 1304 as a mixed undergraduate–graduate society for seventy scholars in grammar, arts and theology.[97] As already indicated, however, the prominent indigenous example of a university college and linked grammatical 'feeder' was the King's Hall, Cambridge, and the chapel royal, whence it had sprung.

Wykeham was intimately associated with this royal Cambridge college over a number of years. The king alone, as founder, remained the legal visitor to the college. This meant that the visitatorial duty in practice devolved upon the holder of the office of lord chancellor,[98] a position held by Wykeham between 1367 and 1371. There is good evidence that both as lord chancellor and as keeper of the privy seal from 1363 to 1367 Wykeham was sometimes in charge of royal business relating to the college.[99] Moreover, as every fellow of the King's Hall was appointed directly by the crown under writ of privy seal,[100] Wykeham would have been involved closely with the personnel of the college when keeper of the privy seal. Thus, whether as head of a department through which passed all the writs of appointment to vacant King's Hall fellowships, or as lord chancellor and actual visitor to the college, Wykeham, an educationalist who would have had an obvious interest in one of the two largest colleges in England, had excellent

[96] See the discussion by Leach, op. cit., pp. 78 ff.

[97] Leach, *Educational Charters and Documents 598–1909* (Cambridge, 1911), pp. xxxiv-xxxv.

[98] On this point, see R. Phillimore, *The Ecclesiastical Law of the Church of England* (2nd ed., London, 1895), ii. 1452; also Cobban, *The King's Hall*, pp. 64, 102.

[99] See King's Hall Accounts, ii. fos. 72, 122. The 26 volumes of King's Hall Accounts are deposited in the Muniment Room of Trinity College, Cambridge, 0. 13. 1. – 0. 13. 26. See also Cobban, op. cit., pp. 64–5.

[100] Cobban, op. cit., pp. 150 ff.

opportunities to make a detailed first-hand appraisal of this royal Cambridge foundation. There would, therefore, seem to be good reasons for suggesting that the King's Hall was one of Wykeham's principal English models. With the exception of the New College salaried tutorial system, it is clear that the main points of Wykeham's educational programme had already been embodied in this Cambridge college from the early part of the fourteenth century.

The mixed academic composition of the King's Hall may well have encouraged the early growth of teaching facilities. Whatever the case, the unusually copious records of the King's Hall, comprising twenty-six volumes of accounts — the longest single series of paper collegiate records in England — augmented by a substantial corpus of material from the royal exchequer bearing upon the college, yield no positive references to tutorial or lecturing activities in the fourteenth century. The first development in this matter of collegiate teaching which can be definitely established, leaving aside the special instance of Merton College to be discussed below,[101] is the salaried tutorial system devised by William of Wykeham for New College towards the close of the fourteenth century. This system involved the setting aside of a sum of 100s. from college funds as payment for fellows or scholars who were to act as tutors (*informatores*) to younger fellows or scholars during their first three years of residence.[102] Neither in the New College statutes nor in the domestic records of the late fourteenth and fifteenth centuries is there any indication that these tutorial facilities were extended to students who were not college members.

An examination of the New College Bursars' and Receipt Rolls to 1500 reveals that instruction by fellows of the college, as *informatores*, was accorded only to fellows and scholars on the foundation.[103] It seems that in most years four, five, or six fellows were engaged as tutors, although in 1406–7 the number rose to

---

[101] See below, p. 191–2.

[102] *Statutes*, i. ch. 5, pp. 54.

[103] I have consulted all the New College Bursars' and Receipt Rolls between 1376–7 and 1498–9: details of these records are given by F. W. Steer, *The Archives of New College, Oxford* (Phillimore, London and Chichester, 1974).

ten.[104] Teaching commitments varied widely. A fellow taught one, two, or several scholars for part of a term, for one or more terms, or for the whole year. In the records for 1414–15, an insight is given into the number of scholars taught: in the first term, there were 26; in the second term, 24; in the third term, 11; and in the fourth term, 15.[105] Between 1406–7 and 1498–9, the money made available from college funds ranged, in most years, from £4 to £5. And the average payment to a teaching fellow was 1s. 3d. per scholar per term. There is nothing to show that the finances of Wykeham's tutees were controlled by the fellows or senior scholars who acted as their tutors. Finally, it seems, from the cumulative data of the New College Bursars' and Receipt Rolls, that Wykeham's *informatores* should be taken in the sense of tutors, and not of lecturers, as is sometimes suggested.[106] It is interesting that *informator* appears not to have had the same meaning everywhere in Oxford collegiate records. For example, at Merton and Oriel in the late fifteenth and early sixteenth centuries, the *informatores* seem not to have been concerned with academic instruction but with seeing that the newly elected college bachelors were kept informed of their duties and that they carried out the college rules.[107] From the New College records, however, it is manifest that the functions of the *informator* were of an academic nature.

It might be expected that in such a large college, with so many undergraduates and bachelors studying in arts, internal lectures would have evolved at New College by 1500. Neither the statutes nor the Bursars' Rolls substantiate this expectation. The statutes, however, prescribe a fulsome regime of weekly disputations for the undergraduates and bachelors in arts. Undergraduates were to dispute once a week during term time, and bachelors normally twice a week, and, at certain periods, once a week. As at Balliol and

---

[104] New College Archives, Bursars' Rolls, 7365(33).

[105] Ibid., 7385(53).

[106] See e.g. Curtis, *Oxford and Cambridge in Transition*, pp. 102–3, 284, n. G, who is inclined to construe *informatores* as college lecturers.

[107] *Registrum Annalium Collegii Mertonensis, 1483–1521* (ed. H. E. Salter, Oxf. Hist. Soc., lxxvi, 1923), pp. 47, 97; *The Dean's Register of Oriel, 1446–1661* (ed. G. C. Richards and H. E. Salter, Oxf. Hist. Soc., lxxxiv, 1926), p. 48.

other colleges, those about to determine as bachelors were required to rehearse the subject of their public disputations by giving it at least three public airings in the college hall. Disputations were also staged for the civilians, canonists and theologians.[108]

The temptation to exaggerate Wykeham's contribution to the construction of the collegiate tutorial system must be resisted. In effect, Wykeham merely formalized and buttressed by payment the informal and unremunerative tutorial practices to be found in the earlier secular colleges, the whole enterprise being still confined to members of the foundation. If the tutorial system had been developed, it would have been necessary to have opened up college teaching to commoners who were not foundation members. However, from the evidence of the New College Bursars' and Receipt Rolls of between 1376-7 and 1498-9 and the *Liber Senescalli Aulae 1397-1418*[109] a commoner undergraduate intake does not appear to have been a feature of New College before 1500. The New College domestic records contain numerous entries for casual visitors and for guests, as well as many references to visiting officials, such as university bedels, estate bailiffs, and tradesmen of various kinds. But throughout, there is no indication of academic commoners at New College in the medieval period, although they were present from the 1390s at Winchester College.[110]

In any review of early teaching arrangements in the colleges of the medieval English Universities, the role of Merton College in devising forms of tutorial organization for its non-graduate personnel must be considered. The college did not admit undergraduates in arts as fellows but it did provide an education in the elements of the arts course for specially selected groups of youthful scholars. Walter de Merton's *parvuli*, needy and orphan children of the founder's kin, were treated as part of the warden's household, although they lived outside the college in rented

---

[108] *Statutes*, i. ch. 5, 56-8.

[109] New College Archives, Bursars' Rolls, 7711(1) – 7459(136); 5527.

[110] See Leach, *A History of Winchester College*, ch. 8; Kirby, *Annals of Winchester College*, pp. 122 ff.; G. F. Lytle, 'Patronage and the Election of Winchester Scholars during the late Middle Ages and Renaissance', *Winchester College: Sixth-Centenary Essays*, pp. 167 ff. at p. 172.

hospices with their own instructors.[111] In the separate rolls which survive for these *pueri de genere fundatoris* in the fourteenth and fifteenth centuries, there are records of expenses for commons and the other necessities of daily living, for the rent of the hospice and for the salary of their grammar masters.[112] In an entry for 1459–60, one of these rolls[113] lists the individual expenses of Thomas Lee, a scholar of the founder's kin, and the roll ends with the statement that it was compiled during the sub-wardenship of John Yonge, who is also described as Lee's *creditor*, one of the several words used to designate a tutor in the later Middle Ages. This would indicate that control of Lee's finances was vested in the sub-warden as tutor. And the cumulative evidence of the rolls suggests that a kind of tutorial system was in operation involving grammar masters, sub-wardens and perhaps one or two fellows of the college. Although boys of the founder's kin remained, in a sense, external to the college and were eligible for election as scholars only upon becoming bachelors of arts,[114] their status approximated to that of an undergraduate, and they were given a measure of academic, financial and moral supervision. Similar considerations apply to Merton's other category of external scholars, *scolares in villa degentes*, the poor secondary scholars, who seem to have studied grammar under a master and, at times, under one or two of the college fellows; and also to their successors from *c.*1380, the poor scholars or portionists of John Wylyot, who engaged in the study of arts under the supervision of a bachelor fellow.[115] While Merton's categories of tutees are not fully comparable to the incorporated undergraduates of the King's Hall and of New College, these tutorial developments are distinctive enough to merit close attention.

---

[111] Highfield, *The Early Rolls of Merton College, Oxford*, p. 72.

[112] E.g. Merton College Archives, Rolls for Founder's Kin, 3973e, 3973f, 3974, 3974d, 3974e, 3976, 4116.

[113] Ibid., 4117.

[114] See the discussion by Cobban, *The King's Hall*, p. 51, n. 4.

[115] On the *scolares in villa* and Wylyot's portionists, see Highfield, *The Early Rolls of Merton College, Oxford*, pp. 72–4.

The Merton statutes are silent on undergraduate instruction and indeed on any type of teaching. But the college register, dating from 1483 to 1521, shows that, by this time, regular disputations, lectures and revision exercises were being held in the college primarily for the benefit of the bachelors of arts.[116] It is unlikely that this amounted to a comprehensive educational regime for the Mertonian bachelors. Presumably, however, it would have been extensive enough to offset deficiencies in the system of university instruction. Just how far these forms of teaching were functioning prior to the period of the college register is problematical.

If the tutorial system elaborated at New College were to progress, college teaching would have to be extended to embrace commoners who were not foundation members. It is not clear that the King's Hall ever possessed a salaried tutorial scheme in the Wykehamite sense. Nonetheless, there is sustained evidence that from the 1430s the college made tutorial facilities available to private pupils who were introduced from outside and who did not have fellowship status. Moreover, it is established that those fellows who acted as tutors to pupils of this kind were also responsible to the college administration for the expenses incurred by their charges.[117]

The evidence for these conclusions is contained in a series of entries in the King's Hall Accounts extending from the 1430s to the opening of the sixteenth century wherein seventeen different fellows settled with the seneschals or administrative officers of the college for sums due for commons and sizings (extra commons) for themselves and for their pupils (*pupilli*).[118] The King's Hall entries point to a situation in which several of the fellows stood in the relation of *in loco parentis* to a number of pupils for whose finances they had assumed responsibility.[119] Analysis of the data reveals that at least 4 of the 17 fellows who acted as tutors supervised two or more pupils at a time; but that the retention of a single pupil was a

---

[116] *Registrum Annalium Collegii Mertonensis, 1483–1521*, pp. 24–5, 408–9, 466–7.

[117] Cobban, *The King's Hall*, pp. 67 ff.

[118] King's Hall Accounts, ix. fos. 29v, 44, 92v; xiii. fo. 19v; xv. fo. 118; xvi. fo. 115v; xix. fos. 17, 17v; xx. fo. 15v.

[119] For an analysis of the fellow-tutors, see Cobban, op. cit., pp. 67–71.

more usual pattern. Some of the fellow-tutors took charge of pupils for several years. Mostly, however, individual fellows retained pupils for parts of one or two academic sessions. Although 11 of the 17 tutors held office at one time or another as college seneschals, only 3 of them acted as tutors in years of administrative office, which suggests that tutoring was an absorbing business. The majority of the fellow-tutors held degrees in arts or in law, the main academic concentrations in the King's Hall.

It is unlikely that the reception of pupils for tuition at the King's Hall had as yet assumed the shape of a regular system. For the admission of these undergraduate commoners (strictly speaking, semi-commoners) was not a fixed feature of college policy: systematic provision was not made for the planned entry of a quota of pupils each year. The intermittent nature of the entries for pupils indicates that the initiative lay with the individual fellow, who might desire to enlarge his income with tutorial fees, rather than with the college as a corporate body.[120] From later analogy, it is likely that a fellow-tutor made a private contract with a parent or guardian, who committed the pupil to his care and handed over a sum of money to be expended on the pupil's behalf over the agreed period.[121] That contractual documentation of this type would be of a private and not of a collegiate kind explains why copies of such contracts are not inscribed in the King's Hall Accounts.

The situation here displayed implies that every graduate fellow of the King's Hall was a potential tutor, and that tutoring work was geared to an open competitive market with no attempt yet made to restrict tutorial functions to several fellows designated by the

---

[120] See Cobban, 'Decentralized Teaching in the Medieval English Universities', p. 197.

[121] For details of a contract, drawn up in a chancery deed and made between a tutor and his pupil at Brasenose College, Oxford, in 1567, see J. K. McConica, 'Elizabethan Oxford: The Collegiate Society', *The History of the University of Oxford*, iii (*The Collegiate University*, ed. J. McConica, Oxford, 1986), 645 ff. at 694. For contractual arrangements of this kind in Oxford colleges in the seventeenth century, see e.g. G. H. Wakeling, *Brasenose College Quatercentenary Monographs* (Oxf. Hist. Soc., liii, 1909), ii. part i, no. xi, 14; see also H. V. F. Somerset, 'An Account Book of an Oxford Undergraduate in the years 1619–1622', *Oxoniensia*, xxii (1957), pp. 85 ff.; and Curtis, *Oxford and Cambridge in Transition*, p. 79.

governing body of the college. Post-Reformation parallels at Gonville and Caius College, Cambridge, and at Trinity College, Cambridge, reveal that, in the second half of the sixteenth century, any fellow might act as a tutor with only one or two students under his direction.[122] Essentially, this evidences continuity with the elastic tutorial practices operated at the King's Hall from at least the 1430s. For the English secular colleges, this King's Hall material supplies some of the earliest known evidence concerning that form of tutorial organization which encompassed undergraduates introduced into the college and taught by a number of fellow-tutors, who also regulated the finances of their pupils. It is possible that there were similar tutorial births in English secular colleges before that at the King's Hall in the early fifteenth century. But the many sets of college records examined have not yielded much concrete information on this elusive topic, with the exception, discussed above, of the rather special tutorial circumstances prevailing at Merton College.

The admission of undergraduate commoners for tutorial purposes at the King's Hall was an event of primary academic import. It can no longer be asserted that the entry of undergraduate commoners was an innovation of William Waynflete's Magdalen College, Oxford, founded in 1448, where the founder's statutes of 1479/80 made allowance for the admission of up to twenty commoners, who were to be the sons of nobles or other worthy persons and were to live in college at their own expense under the direction of a tutor.[123] Whatever impact Waynflete's 'commoner' provisions may have had on later collegiate life, there can be no doubt that undergraduate commoners formed part of the complement of the King's Hall at least some fifty years previously.

---

[122] See J. Venn, *Biographical History of Gonville and Caius College 1349–1897* (3 vols., Cambridge, 1897–1901), iii. 251–2; W. W. Rouse Ball, *Cambridge Papers* (London, 1918), ch. 2, esp. pp. 31–6; D. A. Winstanley, *Unreformed Cambridge* (Cambridge, 1935), pp. 267–8.

[123] *Statutes*, ii. ch. 8, 60: the commoners were to be *sub tutela et regimine creditorum vulgariter* creancers *nuncupatorum*. J. McConica takes the view that Waynflete's provision for commoners has to be seen 'more in light of a late medieval prelate's magnificence and hospitality . . . than as an academic innovation': McConica, 'The Rise of the Undergraduate College', *The History of the*

Moreover, from Magdalen's internal records of the fifteenth century, it seems that before *c.* 1500 undergraduate commoners were not resident in the college in any numbers (those that were probably included John Colet, the humanist scholar and re-founder of St Paul's School, London, Richard Foxe, the future bishop of Winchester and founder of the humanist haven Corpus Christi College, Oxford, and Robert Whittinton, the distinguished grammarian).[124]

The growth of tutorial facilities in the colleges paved the way for the emergence of the college lectureship. A sign of things to come is found in the Oxford statute of 1409 which enacted that those about to determine as bachelors were to have heard appropriate lectures given in the colleges or halls.[125] It is difficult to say if lectures were being delivered in any Oxford college as early as 1409. As previously indicated, it seems that Wykeham's *informatores* at New College should be taken in the sense of tutors rather than lecturers. Whether or not there were lectures in secular colleges by 1409, as there were in the monastic colleges and unendowed halls, the earliest concrete evidence of the college lecture concerns the Cambridge college of Godshouse, which possessed its own lecturer or reader (*lector*) probably from its foundation in 1439.

Godshouse, later re-founded as Christ's College, was initially an exceptional type of college.[126] According to the founder, William Byngham, the *raison d'être* for the college was the alleviation of the famine of grammar masters in the country and in the English Universities by the training of undergraduates for the degree of master of grammar with a view to their becoming teachers in

University of Oxford, iii (*The Collegiate University,* ed. J. McConica, Oxford, 1986), 1 ff. at 7.

[124] This conclusion concerning the paucity of commoners is derived from an analysis of the Magdalen College Archives, Bursars' Book, 1476/7–86, and the *Libri Computi* for 1481–8 and 1490–1510. J. R. Bloxam's notes on Magdalen commoners between 1460 and 1600 are of some assistance: Magdalen College Library, D. 7. 10.

[125] Gibson, *Statuta Antiqua,* p. 200.

[126] On Godshouse, see Lloyd, *The Early History of Christ's College, Cambridge,* and Cobban, *The King's Hall,* pp. 79–80.

England's languishing grammar schools.[127] Their training was entrusted to a lecturer elected by the college.[128] In additon to lecturing in grammar, the *lector* was required to give a number of lectures in logic and philosophy and to hear two or three disputations a week in logic, philosophy or grammar.[129] While the founder intended the Godshouse *lector* to cover subjects in the arts course over and above grammar, the primary aim was to prepare undergraduates for the degree of master of grammar and not for the arts degree. Because of the peculiar grammatical needs of Godshouse, the provision of a specialist *lector* was a *sine qua non* if the purpose of the foundation were to be fulfilled. Judging from an indenture of *c.* 1451, however, by which Ralph Barton was hired as the Godshouse *lector*, [130] the emphasis seems to have moved away from grammar and towards the arts course proper. It is made clear that logic and philosophy were to be his first concern. Subjects such as grammar, rhetoric and oratory were to be lectured upon only according to student need. This would indicate that the central objective of the college had not proved sufficiently attractive, and that adaptations had been necessary which allowed students to read for arts degrees. Indeed, a high percentage of those members of Godshouse for whom degree patterns can be discovered ultimately acquired theology degrees,[131] which implies that they had earlier taken the M.A. degree. Thus, from the available evidence, it would

---

[127] Lloyd, op. cit., pp. 12, 38, 40; see also *Early Statutes of Christ's College, Cambridge with the statutes of the prior foundation of God's House* (ed. H. Rackham, privately printed, Cambridge, 1927), introduction, p. i. Newly elected undergraduate fellows were to apply themselves to sophistry and logic for two or three years, at the end of which time, they were to turn to an intensive study of the subtler and deeper parts of grammar with a view to acquiring the degree of master of grammar. After this, they were bound to accept suitable positions in grammar schools built within the previous forty years: see statutes in Rackham, op. cit., pp. 24, 26 (with transl. pp. 25, 27).

[128] Rackham, op. cit., pp. 22, 24 (with transl. pp. 23, 25).

[129] Ibid., p. 28 (with transl. p. 29); see also D. R. Leader, 'Teaching in Tudor Cambridge', *History of Education*, 13 (1984), pp. 105 ff. at p. 113.

[130] See Lloyd, op. cit., pp. 134–6, 375–7.

[131] See A. B. Cobban, 'The Medieval Cambridge Colleges: a Quantitative Study of Higher Degrees to *c.* 1500', *History of Education*, 9 (1980), pp. 1 ff. at p. 9.

appear that the first known endowed college lectureship in the English Universities started life as a specialist post in grammar, set within a general arts framework, but soon broadened out into a plenary arts lectureship, thereby frustrating the will of the founder. It is not clear whether this lectureship was continuously or only intermittently filled before 1500.[132]

An extensive lecture programme was mounted at King's College, the next Cambridge college to be founded after Godshouse. From 1456, the King's account books record regular payments to the fellows for termly lectures given for the benefit of members of the college, ranging from the youngest scholars to those studying at various levels in the higher faculties.[133] Lectures were most commonly delivered in civil and canon law and theology, and lectures in medicine and astronomy are occasionally itemized.[134] After those for the early 1470s, there are no further entries for lectures in the college accounts for the remainder of the fifteenth century. A college order of 14 June 1483,[135] however, confirms that lectures continued to be given. By this edict, lectures were to be given in the college hall in the morning between the hours of six and eight, and those attending lectures were to submit each week to the vice-provost or to one of the deans a written précis of the lectures delivered. Entries for payments to lecturers resume on a regular basis in the college accounts of the sixteenth century. These lectures at King's College were confined to college residents. They were not of a permanent or endowed nature, but were given on an *ad hoc* basis and were financed by a combination of college funds and fees exacted from the hearers. An attempt to establish a permanent and

---

[132] See Leader, art. cit., p. 113.

[133] See King's College Archives, Mundum Books, iii (1456–9), fos. 22, 22v, 23, 23v, 24, 24v, 80–81v, 99–100v, 101; Mundum Books, v (1467–9), fos. 67v, 124, 124v; Mundum Books, vi (1469–74), fo. 47.

[134] For lectures in theology, see King's College Archives, Mundum Books, iii. fos. 23, 24v, 99, 99v; iv. fos. 67v, 124v; vi. fo. 67; for lectures in civil law, Mundum Books, iii. fo. 100v; iv. fos. 67v, 124v; vi. fo. 47; for lectures in canon law, Mundum Books, iii. fos. 81v, 100v; iv. fos. 67v, 124v; for lectures in astronomy and medicine, Mundum Books, iii. 81v, 100v.

[135] This is printed by J. E. T. Rogers, *A History of Agriculture and Prices in England*, iii (1882), 741; see also Leader, art. cit., p. 114.

public lectureship in theology at Queens' College, Cambridge, was made by Queen Margaret of Anjou in 1447.[136] The outcome of this is unknown. In 1472, however, a lectureship in theology at Queens' was endowed by the will of a benefactress, Dame Alice Wyche.[137] It was operational by 1484–5, according to the earliest extant account for Queens',[138] and functioned on a regular basis subsequently.[139]

However interesting the early instances of endowed lectureships at the Cambridge colleges of Godshouse and Queens' are, they were not perhaps as influential as those established at Magdalen College, Oxford, where, by the statutes of 1479/80, provision was made for three lectureships: one in theology, and the other two in natural and moral philosophy respectively. All three lecture courses were to be free and open to the entire university, including members of the religious orders.[140] It may well be that these lectureships were instituted a shade earlier than the statutes of 1479/80, for the Magdalen College Bursars' Book of 1476/7–86 records payments for three lecturers, beginning apparently in *c*. 1476–7.[141] In addition, records of lecturers in logic appear regularly from 1481–2. There are annual entries for the stipends of the three statutory lecturers in the Magdalen *Libri Computi* for 1481–8 and for 1490–1510.[142] In some

---

[136] See Margaret of Anjou's petition to Henry VI concerning the foundation of Queens' College in W. G. Searle, *History of the Queens' College of Saint Margaret and Saint Bernard in the University of Cambridge, 1446–1560* (2 vols., Cambridge, 1867–71), i (1867), 15–16.

[137] Searle, op. cit., i. 80–1.

[138] Queens' College Archives, Journale, i (1484–1518), fo. 23. (Queens' College Archives are now deposited in Cambridge University Library.)

[139] See e.g. ibid., i. fos. 47, 51v, 57, 81, 97, 116, 131v, 141. See also J. Twigg, *A History of Queens' College, Cambridge, 1448–1986* (The Boydell Press, Suffolk, 1987), p. 75.

[140] *Statutes*, ii. ch. 8, 47–9. See recently V. Davis, 'William Waynflete and the Educational Revolution of the Fifteenth Century', *People, Politics and Community in the Later Middle Ages* (ed. J. Rosenthal and C. Richmond, Gloucester, 1987), pp. 40 ff. at p. 50.

[141] Magdalen College Archives, Bursars' Book, 1476/7–86, fo. 5.

[142] Magdalen College Archives, *Libri Computi*, 1481–8, fos. 13v, 16, 43, 69v, 98v, 116, 141v, 173v; *Libri Computi*, 1490–1510, fos. 5v, 15v, 24, 38, 59v–60, 77, 92.

years, the lectures in theology and philosophy were shared between two lecturers, although a single *lector* for all three subjects was the more usual pattern. In logic, however, two or three lecturers might be employed annually. From 1484–5, the surnames of the lecturers were normally recorded, and it is clear that there was a fair measure of continuity in lecturer personnel. The stipends of the *lectores* in the Magdalen records correspond to the statutory rates. The theology *lector* was the most highly paid at £10 per annum, and the philosophy lecturers received £6 13s. 4d. each. The stipend of the logic lecturer, who is not specified in the statutes, was £5 a year.

There are also in the Magdalen statutes detailed regulations for the holding of college disputations in arts and theology.[143] The arts disputations were to be staged by the bachelors in arts, and, if there was a shortage of bachelors, the regent masters in arts were to lend assistance; and the lecturers in philosophy were to give of their expertise to these exercises. Theological disputations were prescribed for all the scholars of theology in the college, and they were to be supervised by the lecturer in theology. During vacations, further disputations in arts were to be performed, and cursory lectures were to be mounted by the bachelors in arts. As stipendiary payments were not involved, entries for disputations do not normally occur in the college's internal records. But in Magdalen College's *Register A 1480–92*, there is an interesting item concerning two disputations, one in moral philosophy and the other in theology, presented in the presence and by order of Richard III during his visit to Oxford University and to Magdalen College in July 1483. The names of the disputants are given, and it is recorded that they were all handsomely rewarded by the king.[144]

In the last decade of the fifteenth century, shortly after the launching of college lectures at Magdalen College, Oxford, an endowed lectureship in canon law was instituted at the King's Hall, Cambridge. This was the product of a legacy of £70 bequeathed to

---

[143] *Statutes*, ii. ch. 8, 34–5.

[144] Magdalen College Archives, *Register A 1480–92*, fo. 27v. See also R. C. Hairsine, 'Oxford University and the Life and Legend of Richard III', *Richard III Crown and People* (ed. J. Petre, Richard III Society, London, 1985), pp. 307 ff. at pp. 308–10.

the King's Hall by Robert Bellamy, D.Cn.L., a fellow of the college from 1464–5 until his death in 1492.[145] By the terms of his will, this sum was to be invested for the creation of an annual rent for the endowment of a permanent lectureship in canon law. The lectureship was to be of a semi-public nature. Bellamy stipulated that it was to be free and open to the fellows of the college and to all other poor clerks studying in Cambridge University, but that scholars outside the college with sufficient means were to be excluded, unless by special permission of the lecturer. The first known Bellamy lecturer was master Collett, a fellow of the college, who received a stipend of 20s. in 1502–3 for his lectures delivered in the term of the Annunciation of the Blessed Virgin Mary.[146] In the same year, an identical payment was made to another fellow, Ralph Cantrell, for his lectures in the term ending at the feast of St John Baptist.[147] The names of the subsequent Bellamy lecturers are not recorded, although the rents for their stipends kept flowing in until receipts ceased in 1528–9. It is likely that the lectureship was discontinued from this year, but, if not, it would have been abolished under the terms of the royal injunctions of 1535 which suppressed the study of canon law at the English Universities.

The evolution of tutorial and lecturing facilities in the halls and colleges made the undergraduate population less reliant upon the ordinary lectures of regent masters. (At Oxford, however, until at least the mid-sixteenth century, students were still required to be present at public lectures,[148] and at Cambridge, the chancellor, William Cecil, decreed in 1562 that all members of colleges were to attend the appropriate university lectures.[149]) As a result, the regency system, which had been the core of university teaching from the inception of the English Universities, gradually fell into abeyance. The entrenchment of the endowed college lectureship must have dealt a severe blow to university teaching, even though

---

[145] On the Bellamy lectureship, see Cobban, *The King's Hall*, pp. 77–9, 82.

[146] King's Hall Accounts, xx. fo. 36v.

[147] Ibid., xx. fo. 60v.

[148] Pantin, *Oxford Life in Oxford Archives*, p. 36.

[149] Leader, 'Teaching in Tudor Cambridge', pp. 111–12.

the full impact was delayed until well into the sixteenth century. Following the Magdalen and the King's Hall pattern, subsequent college lectureships were mostly, though not always, of a public or semi-public nature, and were held either by fellows of the college to which the lectureship was attached or by others from outside appointed to give a specific course of lectures at an agreed salary. After the influential Magdalen precedent, the statutes of every new foundation at the English Universities, with the extremely interesting exception of St Catharine's College, Cambridge, made provision for lectures,[150] and, at the same time, most of the older colleges revised their constitutions to keep abreast with this academic revolution. The exception among the new colleges, St Catharine's, which opened in 1473, was, during its initial phase of life, an entirely graduate community, specializing in philosophy and theology: in the late fifteenth and sixteenth centuries, it did not employ the services of a college lecturer.[151]

The degree to which the colleges catered for undergraduates before *c.* 1500 must not be exaggerated, in view of the fact that the halls and hostels were significant teaching forces in the second half of the fifteenth century, and remained so well into the first half of the sixteenth century. In the course of the sixteenth century, however, the colleges became the principal and most sought-after resorts for the student population.[152] The royal seal of approval was

---

[150] See the statutes of Corpus Christi, Oxford, of 1517 and of Cardinal College of *c.* 1527, *Statutes*, ii. ch. 10, 48–54, ch. 11, 71–2; the statutes of Christ's College, Cambridge, of 1506 and of Magdalene of 1553–4, *Camb. Docs.*, iii. 201–2, 351–2, and the Edward VI statutes of Trinity College, Cambridge, of 1552, p. 41 (Trinity College Library, 0. 6. 7.); also the discussion of the Nicholas West statutes of Jesus College, Cambridge, of *c.* 1516–17 with reference to lectureships by J. G. Sikes and F. Jones, 'Jesus College', *V.C.H. Camb.* iii. 421 ff. at 422; and for lecturers at St John's College, Cambridge, E. Miller, *Portrait of a College* (Cambridge, 1961), pp. 12–13.

[151] See Cobban, 'Origins: Robert Wodelarke and St Catharine's', *St Catharine's College 1473–1973*, pp. 30–1 and *passim*.

[152] See J. E. A. Dawson, 'The Foundation of Christ Church, Oxford and Trinity College, Cambridge in 1546', *B.I.H.R.*, lvii (1984), pp. 208 ff. The author seems to imply (p. 215) that the system of collegiate instruction was largely a sixteenth-century development, whereas it had a much longer pedigree and reached its apogee in that century.

set upon the colleges as the major teaching units within the English Universities by Henry VIII's foundation in 1546 of the magnificently conceived Trinity College, Cambridge, and Christ Church, Oxford, whose heads were to be royal appointments. These colleges were designed in part to give a further boost to humanist learning in Oxford and Cambridge and in part to increase monarchical control over the Universities. By the reign of Elizabeth, the colleges were well on the way to becoming self-contained teaching corporations, making it possible for a scholar to pass through the whole educational spectrum within the same institution, provided only that his progress was not impeded by statutory restriction. That is to say, a student of good ability in a college of maximum academic choice might have entered qualified only in the rudiments of grammar and emerged up to twenty years or so later as a doctor in one of the superior faculties. All this would have been achieved without much practical need for the public instruction of the university schools, even if attendance was still supposed to be obligatory. As a consequence of this development, lecturer stability in the English Universities was achieved largely through the medium of the secular colleges as the main foci for endowed teaching.

This collegial teaching advance was effected despite the restructuring of the lecturing capacity of Oxford and Cambridge by means of the introduction of a number of salaried positions in the course of the late fifteenth and first half of the sixteenth centuries. The attempted regeneration of university instruction was not really efficacious in the longer-term,[153] and the college lectureship emerged as the chief institutional means whereby Oxford and Cambridge were transformed into decentralized universities based upon the collegiate unit.[154] The decentralizing movement was more diffused in England than at Paris University, where a comparable

---

[153] On this restructuring movement, see Leader, art. cit., pp. 105–112, and Leader, 'Professorships and Academic Reform at Cambridge: 1488–1520', *Sixteenth Century Journal*, 14 (1983), pp. 215 ff.; Curtis, *Oxford and Cambridge in Transition*, p. 101 and notes; Cobban, *The King's Hall*, pp. 81–2.

[154] Cobban, 'Decentralized Teaching in the Medieval English Universities', p. 205.

revolution occurred.[155] Teaching at Paris came to be concentrated in a number of the larger colleges. The smaller colleges and the unendowed hospices were required to send their students to these wealthier colleges, which alone could afford to sustain the full range of lecture courses. At Oxford and Cambridge, however, most of the colleges endeavoured to organize nuclear teaching, which might on occasion be augmented by drawing upon the aid of colleges of the more affluent type. In general, the English Universities circumvented the two-tier collegiate system of Paris, where the majority of colleges came to be educationally reliant upon a number of their opulent neighbours.

As we have seen, a late effort was set on foot to halt the decentralization of teaching in the English Universities by extending university instruction through the establishment of a corps of salaried lecturers or professors (the terms being interchangeable in this context): this more stable method of lecturer recruitment would it was supposed eventually supersede the ailing necessary regency system. The earliest known intention to create a salaried lectureship in the English Universities was that expressed by John, duke of Bedford, who, in 1432, informed the then chancellor of Oxford that he planned to institute a lectureship in arts.[156] This never materialized, and after John's death his brother, Humphrey, duke of Gloucester, who was such a notable benefactor to the University, failed to put his brother's promise into effect.[157] In 1453, the Oxford congregation considered the possibility of establishing salaried lectureships in arts,[158] but no further action was taken. And in 1482, Edward IV agreed to endow a lectureship in theology,[159] but the king died before the project could be implemented. In the event, the first successful attempt to establish a

---

[155] Cobban, *The Medieval Universities*, pp. 131–2.

[156] For letters sent by Oxford University to the Duke of Bedford on this matter, see *Epistolae Academicae Oxoniensis*, i. 81–2, 94–5, 106–7.

[157] See the letters sent by Oxford University urging the Duke of Gloucester to carry out his brother's intention ibid., i. 83, 107–8, 139–140.

[158] *The Register of Congregation 1448–1463*, p. 153.

[159] For the letter sent to Edward IV by Oxford University giving thanks for the lectureship in theology, see *Epistolae Academicae Oxoniensis*, ii. 478–9.

salaried lectureship was launched at Cambridge in 1488, when three lectureships were instituted in the classical authors, logic and philosophy. Each lecturer or professor was to receive £1 6s. 8d. per term.[160] These lectureships were put on a firmer financial basis by Sir Robert Rede, chief justice of common pleas, who, in his will of *c.* 1519, made an endowment of £4 per annum for each of the three lectureships.[161] The first endowed university lectureships in a superior faculty, in this case theology or divinity, were set in motion by Lady Margaret Beaufort, who, in December 1496 and March 1497, obtained from her son, Henry VII, licence to inaugurate professorships in theology at both Oxford and Cambridge. After several years of negotiations about these two chairs of divinity, during which some lectures had been given, the positions were permanently established in 1502 or 1503.[162] The first Lady Margaret professor at Cambridge was John Fisher, and Erasmus occupied the chair from 1511–14. In the second decade of the sixteenth century, Greek lectures were officially sponsored in Oxford and Cambridge, although there may have been sporadic Greek lecturing in both Universities from the late fifteenth century.[163] By his will of 18 October 1524, Thomas Linacre, the humanist scholar and founding president of the College of Physicians, made arrangements for two endowed lectureships in medicine at Oxford and one at Cambridge.[164] The Cambridge

---

[160] *Camb. Docs.*, i. 361; see also Leader, 'Teaching in Tudor Cambridge', p. 106, and Leader, 'Professorships and Academic Reform at Cambridge: 1448–1520', p. 218.

[161] For more details, see e.g. Leader, 'Teaching in Tudor Cambridge', p. 106, and Leader, 'Professorships and Academic Reform at Cambridge', p. 223.

[162] On the Lady Margaret professorships in theology, see Mullinger, *The University of Cambridge*, i. 435–6; Mallet, *A History of the University of Oxford*, i. 409; Leader, 'Teaching in Tudor Cambridge', p. 108; *Epistolae Academicae Oxoniensis*, ii. 645–6; Gibson, *Statuta Antiqua*, pp. 300 ff.; G. D. Duncan, 'Public Lectures and Professorial Chairs', *The History of the University of Oxford*, iii (*The Collegiate University*, ed. J. McConica, Oxford, 1986), 335 ff. at 347–52; and Dyer, *The Privileges of the University of Cambridge*, i. 103.

[163] J. K. McConica, *English Humanists and Reformation Politics*, pp. 80, 83; Leader, 'Teaching in Tudor Cambridge', pp. 108–9; Cobban, *The King's Hall*, p. 83.

[164] See J. M. Fletcher, 'Linacre's Lands and Lectureships', *Linacre Studies: Essays on the Life and Works of Thomas Linacre c. 1460–1524* (ed. F. Maddison, M.

lectureship was probably operational, at St John's College, by the mid-1520s, and one of the Oxford lectureships, at Merton College, by 1559.[165]

The climax to the revival of university teaching came with the foundation at Oxford and Cambridge of Henry VIII's regius professorships of divinity, civil law, medicine (physic), Hebrew, and Greek, each with a stipend of £40 per annum, and functioning by at least 1542.[166] This movement to bolster public instruction in the English Universities continued into the seventeenth century, with, for example, Sir Henry Savile's provision for professorships in geometry and astronomy at Oxford in 1619, the endowment of chairs in history by William Camden at Oxford in 1622 and by Fulke Greville at Cambridge in 1627, and Archbishop Laud's chair in Arabic at Oxford.[167] But despite these attempts to regenerate university teaching, extending in an intensive form from the late fifteenth to the mid-sixteenth centuries and in a lesser vein down to the seventeenth century, the colleges sustained their growing appeal as the principal centres of instruction. Not only was it more convenient for students to receive their education within the walls of the institution which provided them with board and lodging, but also individual college tutors were sometimes equipped to offer an alternative range of studies to that of the official curriculum, including subjects such as history, geography, various modern developments in mathematics, astronomy, cosmography and

Pelling and C. Webster, Oxford, 1977), pp. 107 ff., esp. pp. 128–47; A. McLean, *Humanism and the Rise of Science in Tudor England* (London, 1972), p. 189; Leader, 'Teaching in Tudor Cambridge', p. 109.

[165] Fletcher, op. cit., pp. 136, 146.

[166] For the phased history of these professorships, the changing methods by which they were financed, and the appropriateness of the term 'regius', see F. D. Logan, 'The Origins of the So-Called Regius Professorships: an aspect of the Renaissance in Oxford and Cambridge', *Renaissance and Renewal in Christian History* (Studies in Church History, 14, ed. D. Baker, Oxford, 1977), pp. 271 ff.; see also Leader, 'Teaching in Tudor Cambridge', pp. 110-11.

[167] Curtis, *Oxford and Cambridge in Transition*, p. 102; K. Sharpe, 'The Foundation of the Chairs of History at Oxford and Cambridge: an episode in Jacobean politics', *History of Universities*, ii (1982), pp. 127 ff.

navigation.[168] These unofficial courses had a special attraction for the sons of aristocratic and gentry families who flooded into the English Universities in the sixteenth and seventeenth centuries. Many of these students from elevated social backgrounds were not primarily interested in obtaining a degree, wishing only to follow palatable lines of study with a contemporary application. To that extent, some of the colleges were now taking upon themselves a mantle exclusively worn until then by the Inns of Court, which for long had catered for the wider educational interests of entrants who were not destined for professional careers as common lawyers.[169]

When the colleges had introduced tutorial and lecturing arrangements, there had initially been no conscious desire to compete aggressively with the teaching of the university schools. However, what had been conceived as only supplementary to the basic round of university lectures and disputational exercises expanded gradually to the point where it first rivalled and then eclipsed the apparatus of university instruction. The latter was left in a somewhat moribund state, and the injection of endowed lectureships or professorships proved to be only a temporary palliative and not a lasting cure.

It has been seen that the emergence of decentralized teaching in the English Universities had tripartite origins. It was a combination of the tutorial and lecturing forms which crystallized in the monastic colleges, in the halls and hostels, and in the secular colleges. It would appear that such teaching aids were born first in the monastic colleges, and then in the halls and hostels; and it is probable that these helped to mould the tutorial and lecturing forms of the secular colleges, which were recognizably the main teaching venues within Oxford and Cambridge by the mid-sixteenth century. The constituent parts, the colleges, from the sixteenth century, were rendered more significant than the universities, the

---

[168] Curtis contrasts the official and unofficial curricula in Oxford and Cambridge between the accession of Queen Elizabeth in 1558 and the outbreak of the civil war in 1642: see ibid., esp. ch. 4, and for the range of subjects taught by college tutors, see pp. 107 ff. Some of Curtis's conclusions have been challenged, as exaggerated, by K. Charlton, *Education in Renaissance England* (London and Toronto, 1965), pp. 145 ff.

[169] See above, p. 145.

corporations, although the latter, through their chancellors and the masters and doctors of the various faculties, continued to function as the degree-awarding bodies. The metamorphosis of the 'graduate' college into a mixed undergraduate-graduate teaching society, ministering to the needs of scholars from primary arts to doctoral level, was a lengthy transition. And although it was related to, among other factors, the economic and social forces involved in the decline of the halls and hostels, colleges such as the King's Hall, Cambridge, and New College, Oxford, nevertheless made notable individual contributions to it, before that decline, as early influential prototypes of that kind of balanced collegiate society characteristic of the English Universities from the Reformation period to the twentieth century. It is apparent that the Cambridge colleges were no less innovative than their Oxford counterparts with respect to the evolution of teaching practices: and, from several points of view, Cambridge harboured, in the royal college of the King's Hall, an institution unique in English academic history. Having examined the teaching mechanisms within the medieval English Universities, attention will now be focused upon their main academic concentrations before *c*. 1500.

Chapter 6

Academic Concentrations

I
THE DISTRIBUTION OF STUDIES

Quantitative analyses of academic personnel of both Oxford and Cambridge, employing a computerized investigation of data where a manual approach would scarcely be feasible, have, in recent years, enabled overall assumptions to be made about the relative order of magnitude of the disciplines pursued in the medieval English Universities as a whole and in their component parts — the colleges, halls and hostels.[1] The late Dr A.B. Emden's *Biographical Register of the University of Oxford to A.D. 1500* and his companion volume, *A Biographical Register of the University of Cambridge to 1500*, together with his manuscript addenda, have furnished the basic data for such exercises. The computerized breakdown of this material, according to a range of relevant categories, allows different methods of presenting the numerical conclusions. Mr T.H. Aston, the former Director of the multi-volume, *The History of the University of Oxford*, has advanced many of his statistical findings, for both Oxford and Cambridge, in terms of total numbers or percentages over a century or longer chronological span: for example, the total number of university theologians produced before *c.* 1500 or the percentage output of theologians by a college over one or more

---

[1] See Aston, 'Oxford's Medieval Alumni' and Aston, Duncan and Evans, 'The Medieval Alumni of the University of Cambridge'; also Cobban, 'The Medieval Cambridge Colleges: a Quantitative Study of Higher Degrees to *c.* 1500', and Cobban, 'Theology and Law in the Medieval Colleges of Oxford and Cambridge', *B.J.R.L.*, lxv (1982), pp. 57 ff. See further the discussion of quantitative work in this field by Burson, 'Emden's *Registers* and the Prosopography of Medieval English Universities', art. cit., pp. 35 ff.

centuries.[2] The method which I have formerly used and which I employ in this chapter is the 'generational' approach. By this is meant that print-out was acquired of the names of all known members of Oxford and Cambridge colleges, halls and hostels up to *c.* 1500, along with their known degrees or at least their areas of study.[3] This material was processed for every institution by date of member residence using generations of twenty years. The results, in so far as the evidence will permit, give an insight into the higher faculty mix of the scholars of a specified institution in a selected generation of twenty years. In this mode of reckoning, many scholars fall within more than one generation. These, and their degrees or areas of study, have been included in each generation in which they occur, so that a 'moving' generational profile or series of snapshots of the known superior faculty concentrations in each generation is achieved. By contrast, Mr Aston, in his investigations, has counted scholars only once, according to the generation in which they first appear. This has the effect of ironing out overlap, making possible the compilation of straightforward totals or percentages over a given time scale. There are, however, some advantages to be gained through the 'generational' approach, especially when monitoring the distribution of studies within the units of the university as opposed to the university as a whole. Whatever the balance of advantages is, both methods are valid and complementary, and when each independently seems to confirm major trends, some satisfaction may be derived from this form of quantitative investigation.

The limitations inherent in this type of quantitative analysis stem from the inadequacies of the source material for the biographical profiles of the personnel of medieval Oxford and Cambridge. Before the sixteenth century, it is not possible to make more than the broadest of estimates for the changing dimensions of English university populations. For it was not until 1544 at Cambridge and

---

[2] Articles by Aston in previous note.

[3] This computerized data for Oxford and Cambridge, which is basic material for this chapter and which I have analysed manually, was obtained through my association with *The History of the University of Oxford* Project, to whose former Director, Mr T. H. Aston, I am indebted.

1565 at Oxford that matriculation registers were instituted, and these, despite their omissions and defects, provide at least a profitable starting point for the computation of overall admissions to the Universities.[4] Although, at both Universities, students from the early thirteenth century were required to have their names on the *matricula* (the roll of a regent master) in order to qualify as a *bona fide* scholar,[5] no such rolls have survived. It is probable that this practice had fallen into abeyance by the fifteenth century, when the principals of halls and hostels were made responsible for their scholars without, apparently, having to maintain official university registers.[6] One or two colleges, such as New College from *c.* 1400 and Magdalen College from *c.* 1480, kept authoritative lists of admissions.[7] The majority of colleges, however, seem not to have compiled official lists. But partial or, exceptionally, as in the case of the King's Hall, Cambridge, near complete annual lists[8] may be reconstructed from the entries in account books or bursars' rolls. The unendowed halls and hostels have left no convenient lists of personnel, and membership of these establishments can only be determined on a random basis, from incidental references in a variety of indirect sources. Moreover, degree lists for both

---

[4] For the Cambridge matriculation registers, see Peek and Hall, *The Archives of the University of Cambridge*, pp. 30–1: there is a gap in the registers between 1590 and 1601. On the first matriculation register for Oxford, covering the years 1565 to 1615, see Pantin, *Oxford Life in Oxford Archives*, pp. 3–4: L. Stone, 'The Size and Composition of the Oxford Student Body 1580–1910', *The University in Society*, i. 3 ff. at 12–15, discusses the merits and defects of the Oxford matriculation registers as historical sources.

[5] For the *matricula* provisions at Oxford, see the statute of *a.* 1231 in Gibson, *Statuta Antiqua*, p. 82, and for the later legislation on this subject, pp. 60–1, 83; for the equivalent arrangements at Cambridge, see *Camb. Docs.*, i. 332–3, and the Old Proctor's Book (*Liber procuratoris antiquus*), CUL/COLL ADMIN 3, fo. 25.

[6] See *The Register of Congregation 1448–1463*, p. xxx.

[7] See *The Registrum Primum* alias *Liber Albus* (*c.* 1400–*c.*1480), New College Archives, 9654; *Register A 1480—92*, Magdalen College Archives.

[8] Lists of fellows for most years may be compiled for the King's Hall from the twenty-six volumes of accounts, extending from 1337 to 1544, and supplemented by the substantial body of exchequer material relating to the college.

Universities survive only from the fifteenth century. Although a statute of 1347 for Oxford lays the responsibility for recording degrees upon the proctors,[9] the earliest extant degree lists occur, for several years, in the register of congregation of the mid-fifteenth century.[10] For Cambridge, the series of proctors' accounts, beginning in 1454, are the first records to contain significant data on degrees.[11] Because of the uneven distribution of sources for information about degrees and areas of study over the three hundred years before 1500, much more information on these matters is available for quantitative analysis for the fourteenth and fifteenth centuries than for the thirteenth century. It is probable that scholars who acquired a degree in a higher faculty were more likely to have information about them recorded than many of those studying arts, especially at B.A. level, or than those who remained for a number of years without taking a degree of any kind. It also seems to be the case that scholars attached to colleges are more prominently represented in the records than those who lived in unendowed premises.[12]

Because of all these problems and biases in the sources, it is clear that those entered in Dr Emden's *Biographical Registers* formed a very small proportion — at the most optimistic between one fifth and one quarter — of total admissions to the English Universities before 1500.[13] Given the restricted and variable nature of the samples involved in this type of quantitative exercise, the resultant propositions concerning the academic shape of medieval Oxford and Cambridge may be advanced in only the broadest of terms. Nevertheless, the degree of measurement that has been achieved has allowed the replacement of the intuitive generalizations of previous generations of historians of universities by rather firmer

---

[9] Gibson, *Statuta Antiqua*, p. 150.

[10] See the distribution of degree lists in *The Register of Congregation*, pp. xiii-xv.

[11] The proctors' accounts for 1454–1488 and for 1488–1511 are printed in *Grace Book A* and *Grace Book B Part i*.

[12] See the comments of Aston et al., 'The Medieval Alumni of the University of Cambridge', p. 11.

[13] See Aston, 'Oxford's Medieval Alumni', p. 5.

conclusions, resting, in some areas, upon an often substantial corpus of distilled numerical or biographical data.[14] Making full allowances for the deficiencies in the basic material, it is still worthwhile to hazard quantitative judgments relating to the distribution of scholars engaged in higher faculty studies both within the universities as entire institutions and within their collegiate sectors — the developing areas of academic significance. The conclusions derived from this kind of analysis help to reveal at least the relative order of magnitude of the various study areas, and the extent to which the colleges either conformed with or deviated from the main directional trends in the growth or decline in size of those study areas in the English Universities before 1500, especially with regard to theology and law, the most prominent subjects apart from arts.

Over the three centuries between 1200 and 1500, theology was the largest single faculty at Oxford, accounting for 2,104 scholars out of a total of 4,614 scholars known to have studied for or definitely to have taken a degree in a higher faculty.[15] The leading position attained by the theology faculty is not perhaps surprising. A high premium was placed upon a qualification in theology for senior ecclesiastical careers in the thirteenth and first part of the fourteenth centuries. Thereafter a degree in law became equally important to one in theology, and in the fifteenth century patently more so. Allied to this consideration there is the fact of the pervasive presence of regulars, numbering 2,568, of whom 1,287 studied in the higher faculties, 1,169 of them in the faculty of theology.[16] The Oxford regulars comprised members of no fewer than five monastic orders — by far the largest grouping being the Benedictines, followed at some distance by the Cistercians — the Premonstratensian and Austin canons, who supplied small numbers, and members of the four orders of friars — the

[14] For recent continental examples of quantitative work relating to medieval universities, see J. Verger, 'Les comptes de l'université d'Avignon, 1430–1512', *The Universities in the Late Middle Ages*, ed. cit., pp. 190 ff.; E. Mornet, '*Pauperes scolares*. Essai sur la condition matérielle des étudiants scandinaves dans les universités aux xive et xve siècles', *Le Moyen Age*, lxxxiv (1978), pp. 53 ff.

[15] Aston, 'Oxford's Medieval Alumni', pp. 8, 10.

[16] Ibid., pp. 8, 11, 17.

Dominicans, the Franciscans, the Austins and the Carmelites —, who collectively provided 1,556 members of the community of regulars compared with 871 monks and 141 regular canons.[17] For most of the thirteenth century, Oxford theologians, it seems, followed in the intellectual wake of those of Paris, but by the 1280s, Oxford masters were making contributions to theological debates on a par with those made by their Parisian colleagues. Oxford's markedly original theological phase was inaugurated by Duns Scotus towards the close of the thirteenth century and reached its zenith in the first half of the fourteenth century.[18] The intellectual distinction which this generated, combined with the fact that only Paris, Oxford and Cambridge, from their origins, Florence, from 1359, and Bologna, from 1364, had the right to promote to the doctoral degree in theology,[19] made Oxford, and indeed Cambridge, attract a migratory stream of continental friars, and this influx was accentuated when Paris University fell into one of its recurrent states of disorder.[20]

If, for reasons of this kind, theology was the largest single faculty, it was so only if civil and canon law are treated as separate faculties for this reckoning. Disregarding those who studied both laws, it is likely that civilians outnumbered canonists by just over a third,[21] and, taken together, civilians and canonists probably outstripped theologians by a not inconsiderable margin, there being at least 2,359 lawyers, compared with 2,104 theologians.[22] In terms of single faculties, however, theology predominated. Theology and law had strikingly different levels of participation as between regulars and seculars. Whereas about nine-tenths of the regulars engaged in theology and only about one tenth in law, just under

[17] Ibid., pp. 16–17.

[18] See the arguments of J. I. Catto, 'Theology and Theologians 1220–1320', *The History of the University of Oxford*, i. 471 ff., especially 504–17.

[19] Cobban, *The Medieval Universities*, pp. 70–1.

[20] See Aston et al., 'The Medieval Alumni of the University of Cambridge', pp. 35–6, and the references, p. 36, n. 69.

[21] Aston, 'Oxford's Medieval Alumni', p. 11.

[22] Ibid., p. 10.

three-tenths of the seculars were theologians and just over two-thirds were lawyers, that is, either civilians or canonists or both.[23] While theology was, on available evidence, the largest single faculty for seculars, as it was, overwhelmingly for regulars, it was so by an extremely narrow margin over civil law, the numbers being 935 theologians as against 920 civilians.[24] Clearly, more fulsome data might well necessitate a revision of this picture of the relative positions of the faculties of theology and civil law, the leading study areas for secular scholars. Medicine, the remaining higher faculty, was numerically rather insignificant before 1500 with only 157 recorded scholars, some of whom also studied in the faculties of theology, civil law and canon law.[25]

Having determined that theology and law were the largest higher study areas in the University of Oxford as a whole, the higher faculty mix within the collegiate sector will now be examined and compared. (Although some halls are known to have been especially associated with particular disciplines,[26] biographical data for membership of halls is too sparse to make quantitative analysis on any scale a feasible proposition for the aularian sector.)

It is apparent that the Oxford colleges absorbed only a relatively small proportion of the total academic population.[27] Nevertheless, from the grandiose foundation of New College in 1379, this was an increasing proportion and it included, along with the company of hall principals and mendicant orders, some of the ablest and most influential members of the University. The position of theology in the Oxford secular colleges, taken as a group, solidly mirrors its position as the primary faculty. In all but two of the ten colleges founded between the late thirteenth century and 1500, theology

---

[23] Ibid., p. 11.

[24] Loc. cit.

[25] Ibid., p. 10.

[26] See above, chapter 4, p. 154; also Pantin, 'The Halls and Schools of medieval Oxford: an attempt at reconstruction', *Oxford Studies presented to Daniel Callus*, pp. 36–7.

[27] See Salter, *Medieval Oxford*, p. 97; Pantin, *Oxford Life in Oxford Archives*, p. 21; Aston, 'Oxford's Medieval Alumni', pp. 4–5, 7.

was the dominant area of study.[28] But whereas on the university plane, theologians held only the narrowest of leads over civil lawyers and were outnumbered by civilians and canonists combined, in the majority of the secular colleges theologians were, in the thirteenth and fourteenth centuries, numerically superior to all lawyers: in the earliest phase of collegiate development, in the late thirteenth century, about four-fifths of the members of secular colleges were theologians and only about a fifth were lawyers; in the fourteenth century, well over half of the college members were theologians and about two-fifths were lawyers. However, in the fifteenth century, the college theologians fell to between two-fifths and a half of college members, while lawyers now accounted for just over a half.[29]

These century-based proportions conceal, however, the extent to which theology predominated in eight of the ten secular colleges, for the figures embrace from the late fourteenth century the sizeable legal complements first of New College and later of All Souls. Taking the eight secular colleges of Merton, Balliol, University, Exeter, Oriel, Queen's, Lincoln and Magdalen, and reckoning the number of theologians in each college on a century basis, the average percentage of collegiate theologians would seem to be in the region of 70 per cent.[30] This tallies well with the results obtained when the superior faculty composition is analysed for every college not on a century basis but by generations of twenty years each. Quantitative investigation by generations reveals that in the eight specified colleges theology substantially led over all other disciplines, and that civil and canon law were minority subjects, achieving periodically a modest importance.[31] From this, it is

---

[28] My own findings in this regard, to be published in vol. 2 of *The History of the University of Oxford*, are in close conformity with those of Aston, 'Oxford's Medieval Alumni', p. 13, although, as explained at the beginning of this chapter, our methods of approach are different.

[29] Aston, 'Oxford's Medieval Alumni', p. 13; Cobban, 'Theology and Law in the Medieval Colleges of Oxford and Cambridge', p. 60.

[30] Derived from the figures given by Aston, art. cit., p. 13.

[31] Conclusions based upon the 'generational' approach employed in my contribution to vol. 2 of *The History of the University of Oxford*.

evident that while the Oxford secular colleges did indeed reinforce the standing of theology as the largest single faculty, the collegiate differential between theology and law was patently divergent from that which prevailed for seculars in the University as a whole. This theological concentration in the colleges was in broad conformity with the statutory provisions of the founders.[32] This is a timely reminder of the lack of co-ordinated educational planning in Oxford University, whose intellectual development, like that of any medieval university, was liable to be affected by the individual academic predilections of wealthy benefactors.

On occasion, however, the will of the collegiate benefactor could be circumvented and, in the case of two Oxford colleges, this had considerable consequences for the matter of theological preference. William of Wykeham had designed New College, founded in 1379, for a warden and seventy fellows or scholars, augmented by ten priests and three clerks for the chapel and sixteen boy choristers.[33] Ten of his fellows were to study civil law and ten canon law, and elaborate regulations were prescribed for the maintenance of these quotas; two were to be permitted to study medicine, provided that a university regent existed in this discipline; and two were to be allowed to specialize in astronomy, although there was no such separate degree at Oxford. From Wykeham's statutory arrangements, it is evident that the majority of the fellows were expected to study arts before proceeding to theology. The abundant publications on Wykeham and New College have assumed that the academic proportions within the medieval college were in general accord with the statutory blueprint.[34] The sixth centenary commemorative volume of 1979 on New College has not dissented from this view.[35]

---

[32] The statutes of the ten secular colleges founded at Oxford before 1500 are given in *Statutes*, i, ii.

[33] For the statutory composition of New College, see ibid., i. ch. 5, 2–4.

[34] From many examples, this is the assumption in G. H. Moberly, *Life of William of Wykeham* (Winchester and London, 1887), ch. 9; also in the section on New College in Rashdall, *Universities*, iii. 213–23, and in Rashdall and Rait, *New College*.

[35] Storey, 'The Foundation and the Medieval College, 1379–1530', *New College Oxford 1379–1979*, pp. 4, 20, 22.

TABLE 1

Number of Oxford scholars of New College, All Souls, Lincoln and Magdalen known to have engaged in civil law or both laws, canon law, and theology in each generation between 1380 and 1499.

College	Generation	Civil law or both laws	Canon law	Theology
New	1380–99	53	–	22
(1379)	1400–19	64	4	31
	1420–39	64	9	33
	1440–59	71	3	37
	1460–79	71	4	27
	1480–99	80	5	28
Lincoln	1420–39	3	2	10
(1427)	1440–59	3	3	16
	1460–79	5	1	20
	1480–99	5	2	28
All Souls	1420–39	20	4	4
(1437/8)	1440–59	43	7	7
	1460–79	47	4	6
	1480–99	63	4	10
Magdalen	1440–59	1	1	11
(1448)	1460–79	7	2	29
	1480–99	27	4	51

However, computerized analysis of New College members whose higher faculty study is known, by generations of twenty years and extending from 1380 to 1499, has revealed a very different picture. As may be seen from table 1, the ratio of civilians or those engaged in both laws to theologians was approximately 2:1 between 1380 and 1459; and between 1460 and 1499, the ratio was in the region of 3:1.[36] These findings are strikingly contrary to the statutory quotas, wherein civil lawyers were to compose only one seventh of the fellowship. It is true that in every generation the proportion of members whose area of graduate study is known was less than half of the sample. Nevertheless, since the number of civilians and those who studied both laws is consistently and demonstrably higher than the number of theologians, a matter of considerable import is here uncovered. It may well be that the turnover in lawyers was more rapid than was the case with theologians. Whatever the case, the data certainly indicates that the college permitted, and did so from its first two decades of life, a substantially larger complement of civilians or students in both laws than was allowed for in the statutory provisions. In his list of Oxford colleges and halls of *c.* 1440–50, John Rous categorized New College as a centre for theology and law.[37] It would now seem to be more accurate to describe it as a focus for law, with theology as the supportive branch of study. Indeed, New College, between 1380 and 1500, and All Souls, from the late 1430s, were overwhelmingly the main collegiate sources for civil lawyers in Oxford. By contrast, New College's output of canonists, as is apparent from table 1, fell far short of the statutory provision for ten at any one time. The table also shows that the output of canonists from All Souls was similarly low.[38] While the canon law proportions are augmented when those who studied both laws are included, nonetheless, the production of unadulterated canonists from the principal legal colleges of late medieval Oxford is not at all impressive.

The distortion in favour of law of the statutory provisions at

---

[36] Statistics derived from my contribution to vol. 2 of *The History of the University of Oxford*. In percentage terms, theology, in each of the twenty-year generations between 1380 and 1499, accounted successively for only 29, 30, 30, 32, 26 and 24 per cent of the recorded graduate members.

[37] See the copy of Rous's list ed. by Clark, '*Survey of the Antiquities of the City of Oxford*' composed in 1661–6 by Anthony Wood, i. 638–41: the description of New College is given at p. 638.

[38] T. H. Aston reckoned that only about 5 per cent of the lawyers produced by New College before 1500 were canonists. The comparable figure for All Souls was 8 per cent: Aston, 'Oxford's Medieval Alumni', p. 15.

New College which made itself manifest during even the first twenty years of the college's existence is made all the more tantalizing by the fact that the founder, not himself a university graduate, was actively concerned with his foundation, albeit at a distance, until his death in 1404.[39] The earliest extant statutes, of 1400, were not the first to be issued, and it is clear that they embody a good deal of collective experience, the outgrowth of an initial period of trial and error.[40] There are strong indications that some of Wykeham's original statutes had not been universally obeyed by the fellowship. But the subversion of the fundamental statutory balance between theology and law was of such major concern that it is difficult to understand why the founder, during his lifetime, and the wardens of New College, from the late fourteenth century, acquiesced in this radical departure from the projected academic plan. The observation may be advanced, however, that when New College was founded a degree in civil or canon law or in both was arguably more pertinent than a qualification in theology to a successful career in ecclesiastical administration, and that secular government had long preferred graduates in law.[41] That New College fell victim to utilitarian career pressures, which tended to emphasize law at the expense of theology, is a reasonable conclusion to draw from the quantitative evidence. If indeed New College experienced a volte-face in the balance of its study areas in response to the clamour of worldly inducements, that situation appears to have been repeated in only one of the other Oxford colleges where the promotion of theological study had been prescribed by the founder as a primary aim.

[39] E.g. Moberly, op. cit., ch. 9; Storey, 'The Foundation and the Medieval College, 1379–1530', pp. 8–9.

[40] Moberly, op. cit., p. 203; R. Lowth, *The Life of William of Wykeham* (2nd ed., London, 1759), pp. 189–90.

[41] E.g. R. L. Storey, 'Diocesan Administration in the Fifteenth Century', *St Anthony's Hall Publications*, no. 16 (1959), pp. 3 ff. at p. 22; also J. R. Lander, *Conflict and Stability in Fifteenth-Century England* (London, 1969), p. 125; and further J. A. Brundage, 'English-Trained Canonists in the Middle Ages: A Statistical Analysis of a Social Group', *Law-Making and Law-Makers in British History: Papers presented to the Edinburgh Legal History Conference 1977* (Royal Historical Society Studies in History Series, London, 1980), pp. 64 ff. at pp. 74–8.

All Souls College, founded by Archbishop Henry Chichele in 1437 or 1438, may be regarded as Oxford's legal parallel to New College. In the statutes of 1443, the original complement of twenty fellows was increased to forty, of whom twenty-four were to be artists who might proceed to theology, and sixteen were to be jurists embracing both civil and canon law.[42] It was also prescribed that every fellow who was a master of arts must take priest's orders within two years of completing his necessary regency and that every bachelor of civil law who did not take a doctoral degree within five years must proceed to the priesthood.[43] When the higher faculty studies pursued by members of All Souls between the 1430s and 1499 are analysed, however, the resultant pattern is intriguingly divergent. As table 1 demonstrates, the ratio of civilians or those engaged in both laws to theologians was 5:1 before 1439; 6:1 in the generation 1440–59; 8:1 in the generation 1460–79; and 6:1 in the generation 1480–99.[44] For this analysis, information concerning higher faculty studies is known for about half of the members in each generational sample. As at New College, it is probable that the turnover in civilians was more rapid than for theologians, but it is clear that civil law was the dominant discipline at All Souls. This is a startling finding, and could in no wise have been predicted from the statutes, since they enjoined that the number of theologians was always to exceed that of lawyers by a third. Thus, New College and All Souls were consistently, and by a massive lead, the most prominent colleges for civil law in Oxford before 1500, no college having been specifically and successfully founded for legal studies at Oxford in the medieval period.

As in the case of New College, the explanation of the statutory upset at All Souls may lie in the higher vocational value of law. That is, the lucrative career advantages of law over theology may have caused a substantial deflection from the constitution of All Souls as

[42] *Statutes*, i. ch. 7, 12.

[43] Ibid., i. ch. 7, 39–40.

[44] Figures from my contribution to vol. 2 of *The History of the University of Oxford*. In percentage terms, theologians, in each of these generations, constituted respectively only 14, 12, 10 and 12 per cent of the total recorded graduates.

envisaged by Archbishop Chichele.[45] It is somewhat puzzling that worldly prelates of the stamp of Wykeham and Chichele, the latter of whom was a notable ecclesiastical lawyer and a civil-law graduate of New College, had not, at the planning stage, orientated their foundations more generously towards the legal requirements of the age. Apart from the elaborate chantry motives underlying the foundation of their colleges, it is apparent that both founders were more concerned with university education as a utilitarian training for professional service than as a means of promoting disinterested scholarship. Given this motivation, it is difficult to understand why they tried to accord to the discipline of theology a special eminence just when civil and canon law degrees were acquiring such a high vocational value.

While New College and All Souls took a different academic path from that designated by their founders, such discrepancies were not much reflected in the secular colleges of pre-fifteenth-century vintage, which generally maintained their primacy in theology through to 1500, although Queen's harboured a noticeable number of civil lawyers in the three generations between 1380 and 1439.[46] Lincoln (1427) and Magdalen (1448), which, with All Souls, formed the sum total of Oxford's college foundations of fifteenth-century origin, were both predominantly theological preserves. Table 1 charts the analysis of the discernible higher degrees or study areas of the members of Lincoln by generations between its foundation and 1499. It can be seen just how heavily this endorses

---

[45] On Chichele's motivation for All Souls, see *Statutes*, i. ch. 7, 11–12; and the foundation charter of Henry VI ibid., i. ch 7, 4; also E. F. Jacob, *Archbishop Henry Chichele* (London and Edinburgh, 1967), p. 79; *The Register of Henry Chichele, Archbishop of Canterbury 1414–1443* (4 vols., ed. E. F. Jacob, Canterbury and York Society, 1937–47), i. liii-liv. Chichele's magnificent foundation gift to the college of 369 volumes ascribes more emphasis to theology and canon law than to civil law. The collection breaks down as follows: theology (105), canon law (100), civil law (89), philosophy (17), logic (8), astronomy and astrology (18), medicine (22), and 10 volumes which do not fit these disciplinary categories: see N. R. Ker, 'Oxford College Libraries before 1500', *The Universities in the Late Middle Ages*, ed. cit., pp. 293 ff. at p. 304.

[46] This point and the following statistics for Lincoln and Magdalen are derived from my contribution to vol. 2 of *The History of the University of Oxford*.

the theological character of the society as depicted in the statutes.[47] It is interesting, however, that in each generation there were a small number of fellows with either separate civil law degrees or degrees in both laws. According to the statutes only one fellow at a time might study canon law,[48] and nowhere is there mention of civil law. At Magdalen, theology was the principal area of study, in conformity with the statutes.[49] As may be seen from table 1, this concentration was qualified over the fifteenth century as degrees in civil and canon law or in both laws made increasing inroads.[50] Since the statutes permitted only two or three fellows to study canon or civil law, and then only by special licence,[51] it is clear that there was some relaxation in favour of law in the application of the statutes.

It is evident, then, that the secular colleges of medieval Oxford helped to reinforce the position of theology as the largest higher faculty. Just as the proportion of seculars engaged in theology in the colleges was substantially greater than that in the University as a whole, so the number of collegiate lawyers was proportionately far smaller than that of non-collegiate lawyers, the secular colleges catering only minimally for law. If statutory intentions had everywhere been observed to the letter, this imbalance would have been ever more pronounced. Before the sixteenth century, there was a multiplicity of halls at Oxford where lawyers appear to have constituted the main academic grouping; and prior to *c.* 1500, it seems, the halls were more important venues for legal studies than were the colleges.[52] The theological concentration in the secular

[47] *Statutes*, i. ch. 6, 17, 19.

[48] Ibid., i. ch. 6, 20.

[49] Ibid., ii. ch. 8, 5–6, 16–17.

[50] As a percentage, theology, in the generations 1440–59, 1460–79 and 1480–99, amounted to 85, 73 and 55 per cent of the recorded graduate members: the corresponding percentages for law degrees of all kinds were 15, 23 and 34 per cent.

[51] *Statutes*, ii. ch. 8, 6.

[52] According to the list of Oxford halls drawn up *c.* 1440–50 by John Rous, there were 34 halls for legists: see Rous's list ed. by Clark, op. cit., i. 638–41. Dr Emden has published, in tabular form, the number of halls in each list of the chancellor's registers between 1436 and 1537, together with that of Rous:

colleges was firmly complemented by the five monastic colleges: Gloucester (1283–91), Durham (*c.* 1289) and Canterbury (1361), the three Benedictine colleges; St Mary's (1435), the college of the Austin Canons; and St Bernard's (1437), the Cistercian college. The theological focus within the University was further concentrated by a number of halls where this discipline was the principal study.[53]

The secular colleges of medieval Cambridge each made a broadly similar contribution to the overall academic shape of the University, although there are some differences in emphasis. Mr Aston has estimated that in the late fourteenth century theology was the largest faculty at Cambridge, and that the mendicants formed by far its major constituent. Secular theologians made up perhaps only a quarter of the theological total, and this represents a mere 10 per cent of recorded secular scholars.[54] Law probably accounted for up to a third or even more of the seculars, and about half of the secular scholars did not progress beyond arts.[55] The proportions for law and arts were, it seems, much the same at the close of the fifteenth century.[56] But with the increase in the number of secular scholars, allied to the non-expansion of the number of regulars, the size of the faculty of theology must have been reduced, and with it the influential position of the regulars, especially of the mendicants, within the University. Between the late fourteenth and late fifteenth centuries, the percentage of all scholars engaged in theology may have fallen from about 40 per cent, of whom three-quarters were regulars, to about 15 per cent, of whom only about half were regulars. This decline in the size of the faculty of theology, together with the consequent diminution of the position of the orders of friars, was one of the most profound circumstances

Emden, 'Oxford Academical Halls in the Later Middle Ages', *Medieval Learning and Literature: Essays presented to Richard William Hunt*, p. 355.

[53] Aston, 'Oxford's Medieval Alumni', pp. 19, 20.

[54] Aston, Duncan and Evans, 'The Medieval Alumni of the University of Cambridge', pp. 57 ff. and especially p. 61.

[55] Ibid., pp. 58–9.

[56] Ibid., pp. 61–3.

affecting the character and ethos of Cambridge in the late medieval period.

When theology was clearly the foremost faculty at Cambridge in the fourteenth century, the eight secular colleges founded before 1400, taken as a group, certainly reflected this situation. The position is set out in table 2 in the form of statistics, obtained for each college, which express the average collegiate percentage output of those engaged in theological study, or of holders of degrees in theology, for every generation of twenty years over the period 1300 to 1399. As can be seen from table 2, the three leading colleges for theology were Michaelhouse, Gonville and Pembroke, although for Michaelhouse the samples in each generation are rather low. Corpus Christi and Clare were of middling importance for theology, and Peterhouse had an even smaller, but still significant, theological concentration. At the bottom of the theological league table stood the King's Hall and Trinity Hall. The statistics in table 2 reveal that six of the Cambridge secular colleges, if Peterhouse is included, were notable for theology. In general, however, they did not reach the high-level concentrations of theologians which were to be found in most of the Oxford colleges of the same period. Nevertheless, given that only about 10 per cent of recorded seculars were engaged in theology in the University in the late fourteenth century, the collective contribution of the Cambridge secular colleges to the pool of secular theologians must have been substantial. This point is further underlined by the consideration that none of the Cambridge hostels is known to have been particularly associated with theologians, whereas at Oxford ten or so of the halls had high concentrations of theologians among their membership.[57]

While lawyers were only marginally accommodated by the Oxford colleges before the foundation of New College, the

---

[57] Although the material for the Cambridge hostels is fragmentary and only a small number of scholars may be confidently assigned to hostels, my calculations indicate that out of a total of about 30 hostels, identifiable at different times between 1300 and 1500, in only 4 of them is there definite evidence of theologians, the collective yield being 29, with the number of theologians per hostel ranging from 1 to 4. For concentrations of theologians at Oxford halls, see Aston, 'Oxford's Medieval Alumni', p. 20.

TABLE 2

Average collegiate percentage output per generation of twenty years of the Cambridge secular colleges over the period 1300–1399*

Theologians	%	Civilians	%	Canonists	%
Michaelhouse	89	King's Hall	49	Peterhouse	39
Gonville	54	Peterhouse	29	King's Hall	19
Pembroke	45	Clare	16	Clare	18
Corpus Christi	40	Gonville	10	Corpus Christi	14
Clare	39	Trinity Hall	7	Trinity Hall	13
Peterhouse	22	Pembroke	7	Pembroke	12
King's Hall	5	Corpus Christi	4	Gonville	8
Trinity Hall	0	Michaelhouse	0	Michaelhouse	3

Average collegiate percentage output per generation of twenty years of the Cambridge secular colleges over the period 1400–1499*

Theologians	%	Civilians	%	Canonists	%
Queens'	97	King's Hall	52	King's Hall	41
Godshouse	94	King's College	16	King's College	21
St Catharine's	88	Trinity Hall	14	Peterhouse	11
Corpus Christi	82	Peterhouse	6	Trinity Hall	11
Michaelhouse	79	Pembroke	6	Pembroke	5
Pembroke	78	Clare	6	Corpus Christi	5
Clare	76	Gonville	5	Clare	5
Jesus	75	Corpus Christi	4	Gonville	4
Gonville	71	Jesus	2	Michaelhouse	2
Peterhouse	59	Queens'	2	St Catharine's	2
King's College	51	Godshouse	2	Jesus	1
King's Hall	20	Michaelhouse	0	Queens'	1
Trinity Hall	0	St Catharine's	0	Godshouse	1

*Scholars who studied in both laws have been reckoned separately as civilians and canonists.

Cambridge secular colleges before *c.* 1400 were, as is clear from table 2, moderately important legal centres. The three most significant colleges in this regard were the King's Hall, Peterhouse and Clare. The King's Hall, whose statutes do not specify the academic regime,[58] produced more civil lawyers than any other college. Peterhouse was decisively the leading college for canon law, and Clare was almost equally divided between the laws. Of the remaining colleges, Trinity Hall, Pembroke, and Corpus Christi produced small numbers of civilians, Michaelhouse was wholly uninvolved with civil law and Corpus Christi, Trinity Hall, Pembroke, Gonville and Michaelhouse had minor colonies of canonists. From the data, it is apparent that, as remarked above, the Cambridge secular colleges in the fourteenth century assumed a greater prominence as legal institutions than did their Oxford equivalents. Before the foundation of New College, the King's Hall was, with Merton, one of the two largest colleges in the English Universities,[59] and this tended to accentuate the degree to which the King's Hall was a legal focus within the University. Indeed, over the fourteenth and fifteenth centuries, the King's Hall produced just over a fifth of all university civilians.[60] This is a striking percentage output for an individual college, especially in a period when the colleges were still in the process of establishing themselves as major constituents of the Universities.

The collegiate landscape in fifteenth-century Cambridge reveals important academic changes, characterized by a contraction in law and a concomitant expansion in theological study. It is certainly the case that the King's Hall and Trinity Hall sustained their role as legal centres. Table 2 demonstrates that the output of civilians at the King's Hall marginally increased and that that of canonists doubled.[61] In the fifteenth century, Trinity Hall's contribution of

[58] Printed in Rouse Ball, *The King's Scholars and King's Hall*, appendix 1.

[59] Cobban, *The King's Hall*, pp. 45–6.

[60] The average generational contribution of the King's Hall to total university civilian output was 22 per cent. See Cobban, 'The Medieval Cambridge Colleges: a Quantitative Study of Higher Degrees to *c.* 1500', where table 2 demonstrates the King's Hall's share in university civilians in each generation between 1320 and 1499.

[61] Over the entire period from the early fourteenth century to 1499, however, the college's average contribution to university canonist production was only 11

canon lawyers was slightly reduced. Taking the fourteenth and fifteenth centuries together, Trinity Hall had a near equal concentration of civilians and canonists, the latter only narrowly exceeding the former. Of the new foundations of the fifteenth century, King's College was the only one significant for law. It was more prominent for canonists than for civilians. Table 2 demonstrates that between its foundation in the 1440s and the end of the century it was second only to the King's Hall in respect of both canon and civil law.[62] As at New College and All Souls, there was at King's College a serious discrepancy with regard to the legal fellowship between the statutory numbers and those found to have existed. For in contrast to the numbers listed in table 2, the statutes of the early 1440s prescribe that the majority of the seventy fellows or scholars are to study theology, a mere four being allowed to follow canon law and only two to engage in civil law.[63]

Apart from the King's Hall, Trinity Hall and Michaelhouse, of the Cambridge colleges founded before 1400, Peterhouse, Clare, Pembroke, Gonville and Corpus Christi all exhibited parallel academic trends in the fifteenth century. That is to say, their production of lawyers was noticeably curtailed, very substantially so at Peterhouse and Clare, and the theological element was increased dramatically, as is evidenced by the data in table 2. Paradoxically, Michaelhouse, an overwhelmingly theological college,[64] actually experienced a measurable reduction in the number of its theologians in the fifteenth century. The King's Hall, which among Cambridge colleges rested near the base of the theological ladder, increased its contingent of theologians considerably in the fifteenth century. Trinity Hall, loyal to its

per cent, which is half the corresponding civilian average: see Cobban, art. cit., p. 8, where table 4 depicts the King's Hall's share in university canonists in each generation between 1320 and 1499.

[62] King's College appears to have produced only four civilians in its first generation, between the 1440s and 1459: see ibid., p. 2, table 1.

[63] *Camb. Docs.*, ii. 482–4.

[64] Hervey de Stanton's statutes for Michaelhouse are printed by Stamp, *Michaelhouse*, p. 42.

statutes,[65] remained exclusively a college for law. This intensification of theology in the old-established colleges was complemented by the heavy theological composition of the new secular foundations of the fifteenth century, Queens', Godshouse, St Catharine's, Jesus and King's. As in the fourteenth so in the fifteenth century, the contribution of the Cambridge hostels to the maintenance of theologians seems to have been insignificant.

This emphasis upon theology by the majority of the secular colleges in the English Universities of the later medieval period is an arresting fact. It seems to conflict with the contemporary consensus which, from the second half of the fourteenth century, valued a training in law as the optimum requirement for an ecclesiastically or politically useful career. While the magnetic attraction of law manifested itself at New College and All Souls, causing a marked deflection from the statutory intent, at Cambridge in the fifteenth century the legal constituent was notably diluted in the majority of the old-established colleges, and of the new foundations, only King's College was at all a resort for academic lawyers.

It may be supposed that the increasingly supportive role of the Cambridge colleges in the theological sphere was one of the factors which lessened the dominance of the mendicants within the theological faculty in the fifteenth century. As at Paris and Oxford so at Cambridge, and for similar reasons, there had been inter mittent disputes between the ubiquitous mendicants and the seculars,[66] and while there may not have been any outstandingly large conflict in the fifteenth century, the gradual loosening of the mendicants' grip on the faculty of theology must have been an objective of the Cambridge seculars, as it was on the part of their continental colleagues. By *c.* 1500, a theological faculty more evenly apportioned between regulars and seculars was apparently realized;[67] and it is reasonable to conclude that the colleges were to some

---

[65] *Camb. Docs.*, ii. 417–18. Trinity Hall was the only college in the medieval English Universities wholly confined to law: see Crawley, *Trinity Hall: the History of a Cambridge College 1350–1975*, ch. 1.

[66] See Roach, 'The University of Cambridge', *V.C.H. Camb.* iii. 153–4.

[67] Aston et al., 'The Medieval Alumni of the University of Cambridge', pp. 62–3.

degree instrumental in redressing this balance. But the need to combat the mendicants' dominance within the faculty of theology was probably not the primary motive underlying the theological upsurge in the Cambridge colleges in the fifteenth century. What appears to be detectable in fifteenth-century Cambridge is, in some measure, a collective collegiate response to the encroaching tide of legal studies in the English Universities and, at the same time, a positive affirmation of theological orthodoxy.

In late-medieval England, the Church had become immoderately legalistic, with an ever-expanding maze of courts and officials to implement the diocesan work of bishops, who were often non-resident dignitaries. The Universities were expected to provide the army of law graduates needed to serve this complex ecclesiastical machine. The number of secular theologians who obtained promotion to a high position within the fifteenth-century Church was limited, and only a small proportion of the bishops were theological graduates.[68] However competently the Church might conduct itself in external legal forms, there was no shortage of critics to argue that this was accomplished at the expense of an acceptable level of spirituality. For example, the Dominican theologian and preacher John Bromyard, who was probably acting chancellor of Cambridge University in 1382, and the preacher Thomas Wymbledon, who is perhaps to be identified with the fellow of Merton College of that name in the 1380s, repeatedly lamented the neglect of theology in the English Universities for the lucrative pursuit of law.[69] Similarly, Thomas Gascoigne, the Oxford chancellor in the early 1440s, was a stringent critic of a system which seemed openly to prefer legal dexterity to religious zeal, which served to turn out priests trained more to give a legal

---

[68] See Storey's analysis of the fifteenth-century episcopal bench, 'Diocesan Administration in the Fifteenth Century', art. cit.

[69] On Bromyard and Wymbledon, see G. R. Owst, *Preaching in Medieval England* (Cambridge, 1926), pp. 32–3; also Emden, *B.R.U.C.*, p. 96, and *B.R.U.O.*, iii. 2120. The pull of law was also felt in the faculties of arts, in the sense that in the later medieval period a fair number of arts students migrated to law before completing the arts course. For the situation at Oxford, see J. M. Fletcher, 'Inter-Faculty Disputes in Late Medieval Oxford', *From Ockham to Wyclif* (Studies in Church History, Subsidia 5, 1987), pp. 331 ff. at pp. 338, 339.

ruling than a spiritual lead.[70] Arising from judgments of this kind, the common assertion was that the dearth of men of spiritual capacity within the Church was the principal cause of contemporary social evils in fifteenth-century England. Some of the commentators who were disturbed by what they saw as the excessive worldliness which permeated the ecclesiastical hierarchy looked to the Universities for the genesis of a spiritual regeneration by means of which the ills of society were to be ameliorated. Were not Oxford and Cambridge the 'eyes and blazing lights of the kingdom?', 'the mother, lantern and well of the clergy?'.[71] By a return to the discipline of theology, the Universities, they thought, had the capability to propagate values of a spiritually uplifting nature that would counteract the morally deleterious effects of a prevalent legal materialism.

The collegiate movement in fifteenth-century Cambridge was in some ways a reflection of this type of argument. It has been seen that in the fifteenth century the majority of the Cambridge colleges founded before 1400 had raised their theological and reduced their legal numbers. In parallel fashion, a rigorous contraction of law, or its virtual or complete exclusion, and a paramount emphasis on theology were characteristics of the statutes of the new colleges of the fifteenth century. Although there was a measure of modification of the statutes at King's College in favour of law, theology, in practice, remained the largest single area of study there. The statistics given for Queens', St Catharine's and Jesus have confirmed that the high statutory concentration on theology was actually realized in these colleges. Godshouse, founded in 1439, stands somewhat apart from the collegiate norm, having been designed, as was explained in the previous chapter, to train undergraduates for the degree of master of grammar, preparatory to their acceptance of teaching posts in English grammar schools.[72] This academic intention did not, apparently,

---

[70] T. Gascoigne, *Loci e Libro Veritatum*, ed. cit., p. 202. On the state of the English clergy in the later Middle Ages, see P. Heath, *English Parish Clergy on the Eve of the Reformation* (London and Toronto, 1969).

[71] *Epistolae Academicae Oxoniensis*, i. 157, 294.

[72] See above, chapter 5, pp. 196–8.

engender much support and adaptations were introduced to permit students to read for arts degrees. An analysis of those members of Godshouse in the fifteenth century whose academic attainments can be discerned proves that a fair percentage progressed beyond arts, and eventually acquired theology degrees.[73] St Catharine's College, a society of student-priests with an exclusive study regime of philosophy and theology, was probably the most complete embodiment of the conservative educational ethos geared to the advancement of theology and the rejection of utilitarian and especially legal values.[74] In terms of the activities of its personnel, St Catharine's and the other 'high theology' colleges of fifteenth-century Cambridge could, by definition, make only a limited practical impact in this direction. What was equally important was to transform the climate of educational opinion, to make an institutional gesture towards the way that university education needed to be oriented if graduates of the right calibre, and in adequate numbers, were to be produced to raise the 'spiritual average' of the clergy and, by extension, the spiritual norm throughout society. In the event, this collegiate attempt to arrest the engulfing spread of legal studies by a theological reversion centred in the colleges did not survive into the sixteenth century. It fell victim both to the driving legal requirements of the Tudor state and to the powerful alternative of humanist education.

It will be apparent from the above that St Catharine's College, Cambridge, founded by Robert Wodelarke,[75] was an exceptional type of institution, and it is desirable here to expand upon some of its salient features.[76] The extremely conservative nature of St Catharine's is underlined by its almost exclusively graduate

---

[73] Loc. cit.

[74] On St Catharine's and the educational philosophy of the founder, see Cobban, 'Origins: Robert Wodelarke and St Catharine's', *St Catharine's College 1473–1973*, ed. cit., pp. 1 ff.

[75] Details of Wodelarke's career are given by Emden, *B.R.U.C.*, pp. 645–6; see also C. Hardwick, 'Robert Woodlark, founder and first Master of St Catharine's Hall', *C.A.S., Communications*, i (1850–9), no. xxxvii, pp. 329 ff., and N. Moore, 'Robert Wodelarke', *The Dictionary of National Biography*, xxi (Oxford, 1917–), p. 748.

[76] For this subject, see ibid. and Cobban, *The Medieval Universities*, pp. 226–9.

composition during the initial phase of its being. The original statutes prescribe that the fellows were to be of M.A. status or, failing this, were to be selected from among the better bachelors of arts. All the fellows were to be at least in deacon's orders, and preferably they were to be priests.[77] And the master of the college was required to be a graduate in theology.[78] The studies of the fellows were to be strictly limited to philosophy and theology, there being no statutory concession whatsoever in favour of the disciplines of civil or canon law or medicine. The master was to swear not to permit any fellow to pursue a course of study other than in philosophy and theology,[79] and the fellows themselves were to swear never to agree to one of their number studying outside the two prescribed disciplines.[80] Quantitative analysis of the known personnel of St Catharine's between its inception in 1473 and 1500 has shown that the fellowship was indeed overwhelmingly theological — one or two of the known fellows were canonists, but none engaged in civil law or medicine.[81] St Catharine's, the twelfth college to be founded in Cambridge, was the antithesis of the type of collegiate society which was evolving by the late fifteenth century. That is to say, Robert Wodelarke set his face against the trend towards the college of mixed undergraduate and graduate composition. St Catharine's was conceived wholly in the Mertonian 'graduate' image. Undergraduates had no place in Wodelarke's original scheme: commoners admitted to the college to study philosophy and theology were to be of graduate status.[82] There is nothing to suggest that Wodelarke envisaged his foundation as a teaching establishment. Although weekly disputations in philosophy and theology were laid down by

[77] See the original statutes, St Catharine's Muniments, XL/10, fo. 6v; Philpott, *Documents relating to St Catharine's College in the University of Cambridge*, p. 16.

[78] Ibid., XL/10, fo. 3; Philpott, p. 12.

[79] Ibid., XL/10, fo. 5v; Philpott, p. 15.

[80] Ibid., XL/10, fo. 7v; Philpott, p. 18.

[81] See table 2.

[82] On the graduate commoners at St Catharine's, see Cobban, 'Origins: Robert Wodelarke and St Catharine's', pp. 18–20, 30–1.

statute,[83] there is no evidence of college lectureships at St Catharine's in the late fifteenth century.

It would therefore seem legitimate to describe the college of Wodelarke's design as a small conservative community following an outworn Mertonian 'graduate' tradition and standing apart from the exciting movement which was then transforming teaching patterns within the English Universities. As a result, St. Catharine's might appear to have occupied an anomalous and almost irrelevant position in late medieval university society. However, the college gave clear expression to a significant educational move against contemporary utilitarian concerns. Wodelarke and some of his fellow college founders at Cambridge were convinced of the necessity of providing an institutional antidote to the materialism of society, in the promotion of which, as they saw it, the Universities were so obviously implicated. Robert Wodelarke's collegiate conception is probably best regarded as the central focus or set piece of a more general movement in fifteenth-century Cambridge characterized by a partial return to a contemplative, quasi-monastic ideal. This ideal had at its core the spurning of an educational philosophy geared to serving the lucrative career-structure of late medieval England.

This particular English example is a distinctive illustration of the perennial conflict between the utilitarian and non-utilitarian conceptions of education the appreciation of which is so fundamental to a balanced understanding of European academic development. This fifteenth-century collegiate movement in Cambridge was one of those recurrent, if short-lived endeavours, designed to qualify the vocational emphasis which usually predominated at the average educational level. Whether a university can successfully or purposefully function on a purely professionally oriented diet was a problem which much engaged the minds of Wodelarke and his circle — as much as it has those of later generations. As provost of King's College and twice chancellor of Cambridge University, Wodelarke was better placed than most to understand the forces of change at work in the English Universities. Nevertheless, in formulating the St Catharine's project, he patently

---

[83] Statutes, St Cath. Mun., XL/10, fo. 7; Philpott, p. 17.

refused to swim with the tide and deliberately turned away from all that seemed to be progressive in the academic landscape. It is true that his vision of contemplative and introspective university study, centring entirely on the speculative pursuits of philosophy and theology, had insufficient substance to withstand the increasing involvement of the English Universities in the professional concerns of the world. The irresistible ebb and flow of university–society supply and demand militated against the longevity of the kind of educational ideal which Wodelarke and his associates were attempting to translate into practice. This is not, however, a good enough reason to dismiss their efforts as of no account. Every generation benefits from those who strive to keep alive educational notions whose concerns transcend the immediately consumable and who try to prevent the canon of utility from acquiring uncontested permanency. Robert Wodelarke's ideal may seem in retrospect both negative and forlorn; but given the circumstances of the time — the apparently crumbling fabric of society, the misappropriation of educational talent and learning commonly prostituted for money — it assumes a more positive and challenging aspect.

The Oxford collegiate scene does not seem to have manifested such a concerted reaction against the acceleration in the growth of legal studies as was exhibited in Cambridge. This may stem in part from the circumstance that law did not feature as largely in the fourteenth-century Oxford colleges as it did in those of Cambridge of the same period. But even when it had become apparent that New College and All Souls were developing into major legal centres, there was no obvious theological reaction. Indeed, as has been seen, both of the mainly theological colleges — Lincoln and Magdalen — contained a fair representation of legal fellows. Of the three new Oxford colleges of the fifteenth century, Lincoln was the most theological in complexion: envisaged as a rather introspective society of student-priests, it was similar, in some ways, to St Catharine's College, Cambridge. However, the establishment of Lincoln College was not so much a reaction against the position of law in the University as an attempt to reassert the orthodoxy of Oxford after the traumatic ravages of Wyclifism.[84] Despite the

[84] See above, chapter 4, p. 132.

cogent efforts made to cleanse the University of its Wyclifite and Lollard proclivities, the taint of heresy lingered at Oxford throughout the fifteenth century. Richard Fleming, the founder of Lincoln, was deeply concerned about the heretical threat, and the chief motive behind his college enterprise was the desire to erect a seminary for the nurturing of graduates in theology who would make a contribution towards the elimination of heretical errors in the Church.

As mentioned in chapter 4, Lincoln seems to have been the earliest English secular college with a specific concern for wrestling with the problems of heresy.[85] Apart from in Lincoln, however, the theme of the combating of heresy is not prominently represented in the new collegiate foundations at Oxford in the fifteenth century.[86] It appears that the notion of the secular college as an instrument in the fight against heresy was more extensively deployed in fifteenth-century Cambridge: the need to combat heresy was a principal *raison d'être* for the foundation of King's College;[87] at St Catharine's, proof of heresy was placed first among the statutory reasons for which a fellow may be removed;[88] and at Queens' and Jesus Colleges, there was a pronounced emphasis upon the guardianship of Christian orthodoxy.[89] The stress laid by Cambridge University in general and by a number of Cambridge colleges in particular upon the suppression of heretical sentiment, together with the lingering traces of heresy at Oxford, helped to attract to Cambridge a proportion of the royal and aristocratic patronage which might otherwise have gone to Oxford. Although the Cambridge secular colleges had a necessarily circumscribed role in the counteraction of

---

[85] Loc. cit.

[86] In the All Souls statutes, heresy is itemized as one of the crimes for which a fellow may be removed, but it does not seem to have been a major preoccupation of the founder: *Statutes*, i. ch. 7, 66.

[87] *Camb. Docs.*, ii. 471.

[88] Statutes, St Cath. Mun., XL/10, fos. 12v, 13; Philpott, pp. 24–5.

[89] For this point with reference to Queens' (and its earlier versions), see Jacob, *The Fifteenth Century 1399–1485*, pp. 671–2, and Mullinger, *The University of Cambridge*, i. 313–14. For Jesus, see e.g. Gray, *The Earliest Statutes of Jesus College, Cambridge*.

heresy in contemporary society, a founder might at least take all anticipatory steps to ensure that his college was not used to subsidize fellows with heretical inclinations, as had clearly occurred at Oxford, Merton College in the late fourteenth century being a case in point.[90] In view of adverse reactions to Oxford's involvement in Wyclifite and Lollard doctrines and the urgent need to project an image of orthodoxy, it is worthy of remark that the Oxford colleges in the fifteenth century did not make efforts even more stringent than those made by their Cambridge equivalents to root out heretical opinion. It may be concluded that while a primary concern of the secular colleges in fifteenth-century Cambridge was the curtailment of the proliferation of legal studies by maximizing the number of fellowships available in theology, among the new foundations at any rate, the heresy issue was also a prominent if secondary consideration. This collegiate defence against heretical tenets must have proved invaluable in strengthening even further the reputation of Cambridge University, which already obtained in influential circles, as a bulwark of orthodoxy.

From this analysis of the academic concentrations in the secular colleges, it appears that they were rather conservative study areas within Oxford and Cambridge before *c.* 1500; and that they were not typical of the level of secular involvement in legal disciplines in these Universities at large. The investigation has revealed how extensive were the concentrations of theologians in the majority of the secular colleges, these concentrations being of a higher order of magnitude at Oxford than at Cambridge in the fourteenth century but with Cambridge colleges achieving a theological parity in the fifteenth century. Whereas law was more prominent in the Cambridge colleges in the fourteenth century than in those of Oxford, in the fifteenth century the situation was somewhat altered: New College and All Souls emerged as prolific legal centres at Oxford, and at Cambridge law proportions in most colleges either were scaled down or, in the new foundations, were minimal or negligible. It is of considerable importance that, in the fifteenth

---

[90] M. Aston, 'Lollardy and Sedition, 1381–1431', *Lollards and Reformers: Images and Literacy in Late Medieval Religion* (London, 1984), pp. 1 ff. at pp. 22–3.

century, some of the Cambridge colleges tended to develop along rarefied theological channels. This movement, with St Catharine's College as the most extreme representative, embodied an educational concept wedded to the rejection of mundane values, especially those derived from legal materialism. In the event, this movement was relatively short-lived. But the entrenchment of theology in so many of the colleges of the English Universities through to *c.* 1500 may well have acted as a brake upon academic innovation and, in particular, may have helped to slow down the speed with which Oxford and Cambridge came to terms with the impulses of continental humanism. These quantitative findings have, moreover, reinforced the need for caution when dealing with college statutes. The degree of discrepancy between statutory intent regarding the distribution of studies and their actual distribution may vary from a minor deflection to a distortion on such a scale as to necessitate quite a major reassessment of academic trends in the history of the English Universities.

One of the most intriguing findings derived from the analysis of the personnel of medieval Oxford and Cambridge is that there was an impressively large number of scholars who engaged in civil law. At Oxford between *c.* 1200 and *c.* 1500 there were 932 known civilians as compared with 711 canonists and 716 who studied both laws.[91] At Cambridge in the same period, the civilians were not so prominent, even allowing for the fact that Cambridge was the lesser university, and here the canonists were probably more numerous. Nevertheless, Cambridge produced 523 known civilians and 220 scholars in both laws.[92] In collegiate terms, it has been established that the King's Hall at Cambridge and New College and All Souls at Oxford were the most important institutions for the production of civilians before 1500. It is surprising that in the medieval English Universities only one college, Trinity Hall, Cambridge, was founded solely for the promotion of civil and canon law; and analysis of its known scholars shows that all of them indeed pursued

---

[91] Aston, 'Oxford's Medieval Alumni', p. 11.

[92] See C. T. Allmand, 'The Civil Lawyers', *Profession, Vocation, and Culture in Later Medieval England* (ed. C. H. Clough, Liverpool, 1982), pp. 155 ff. at p. 172, n. 1.

a legal course.[93] Interestingly, an attempt was made to found an Oxford college specializing in civil and canon law, by John of Winwick from Huyton in Lancashire, who was keeper of the privy seal betwen 1355 and 1360. This intention, however, was never implemented.[94] Again, a plan was mooted by royal commissioners, when visiting the Universities in 1549, to convert All Souls into a college entirely given over to civil law. This was to be achieved by transferring the legists from New College to All Souls and the artists from the latter to the former.[95] Nothing came of this proposal. At about the same time, a few years after the dissolution of the King's Hall in 1546, a similar plan was launched to create a civil-law college at Cambridge by the merging of Trinity Hall and Clare College. Although this project was pursued by Edward VI's commissioners, the new college did not, in the event, materialize.[96] Because the fellowship of Trinity Hall was of very slender proportions throughout the medieval period, the King's Hall was certainly the most important legal centre in Cambridge, especially for civil law, producing, over the fourteenth and fifteenth centuries, just over a fifth of all university civilians and just over a tenth of university canonists.[97]

The prolific output of civil lawyers from the English Universities implies that there were adequate career opportunities for civilians in a country geared to the English common law. In the thirteenth century, civil law was not much in evidence in England. This is probably to be linked with the reaction against the excesses of power displayed by the Angevin kings, notably Henry II and John,

---

[93] See table 2 above, p. 226.

[94] On this abortive attempt, see Highfield, 'The Early Colleges', *The History of the University of Oxford*, i. 229–30.

[95] For this plan, see J. K. McConica, 'The Social Relations of Tudor Oxford', *T.R.H.S.*, 5th ser., 27 (1977), pp. 115 ff. at p. 117; Curtis, *Oxford and Cambridge in Transition 1558–1642*, p. 158.

[96] McConica, art. cit., p. 117; Curtis, op. cit., pp. 158–9; Crawley, *Trinity Hall: the History of a Cambridge College 1350–1975*, pp. 52–3.

[97] See Cobban, 'The Medieval Cambridge Colleges: a Quantitative Study of Higher Degrees to *c*. 1500', pp. 4, 8; also Cobban, 'Theology and Law in the Medieval Colleges of Oxford and Cambridge', pp. 69–70.

who had attempted to utilize the authoritarian principles inherent in the Roman or civil law to accentuate the prerogatives of kingship. Nevertheless, while the civil law, from this standpoint, was regarded as antithetical to the common law, there were some openings for notaries and their civil-law procedures in the thirteenth century and appreciably more in the fourteenth century. They were employed in ecclesiastical courts, in private and mercantile business and, to some degree, in departments of secular government.[98] The Anglo–French war, extending from the 1330s to the mid-fifteenth century, greatly multiplied the career outlets for English civil lawyers. They were required, for example, to assist in formulating and in drafting complex treaty arrangements, which raised matters of law on the international plane far transcending the narrow limits of the common law.[99]

From the second half of the fourteenth century, English civil lawyers found a further expression for their talents when a new emphasis was placed upon the courts of admiralty and chivalry, which, from some points of view, served the purpose of international tribunals, especially important during the Hundred Years War. The court of admiralty was concerned mainly with maritime conflicts and piracy, and the court of chivalry with cases arising from breaches of the law of arms, for instance, armorial disputes, ransoms and occasionally treason. These courts operated according to legal principles which were derived ultimately from the Roman law and were therefore suitable environments for civil lawyers.[100] It may also be said that, in parallel with a phase of the Anglo–French war, the Great Schism, which lasted from 1378 to 1417, further expanded England's diplomatic activity and afforded much scope for the involvement of civil lawyers at various levels. In addition, civil lawyers figured conspicuously in the administration of the equitable jurisdiction of the chancellor's court, which was conceived as a judicial supplement to the common law, providing

---

[98] See the study by C. R. Cheney, *Notaries Public in England in the Thirteenth and Fourteenth Centuries* (Oxford, 1972), *passim*.

[99] See e.g. Allmand, op. cit., p. 157.

[100] On these courts, see conveniently ibid., p. 156; see also G. D. Squibb, *The High Court of Chivalry* (Oxford, 1959).

rulings in cases which could not be dealt with adequately under the common law. This system of equity, significant from the late fourteenth century, became extensive in the fifteenth and early sixteenth centuries. It was an important arena wherein civil lawyers could bring a modifying influence to bear upon the operation of English law.[101]

There existed, apart from these natural avenues for the deployment of civil lawyers, avenues that opened up because of the vested interest that the English monarchy had in the discreet cultivation of the Roman law, with its concomitant theories appropriate to theocratic kingship.[102] In his *De Laudibus Legum Anglie*, Sir John Fortescue makes a pointed reference to those English kings who had attempted to assert the primacy of civil law over the English common law so that they might rule regally over a subject people.[103] Generally speaking, with the ever-present example before them of the French monarchy, with its pronouncedly theocratic features, English kings had to a lesser or greater degree according to circumstances essayed to harness to their support Romanist governmental principles and to claim the more 'mystical' attributes of kingship. Edward II's *imitatio regis Francorum*, the episode pertaining to the king's unsuccessful efforts to obtain papal approval for the use at the English coronation of the supposedly miraculous oil of Thomas Becket,[104] is an apt illustration of the latter point. So far as the English Universities were concerned, it seems clear that successive English kings came to regard the King's Hall, their own exclusive university possession, as a college whose primary function was the production of civil-law graduates, who would constitute a corps of legally trained 'king's men'. In furtherance of this objective, English kings, including

---

[101] For the system of equity and the scope which it afforded to civil lawyers, see the summary discussion by Allmand, op. cit., pp. 156–7.

[102] For the conflicting feudal and theocratic elements of English kingship, see W. Ullmann, *Principles of Government and Politics in the Middle Ages* (2nd ed., London, 1966), pp. 150 ff.

[103] *De Laudibus Legum Anglie* (ed. S. B. Chrimes, Cambridge, 1942), pp. 79–80.

[104] W. Ullmann, 'Thomas Becket's Miraculous Oil', *Journal of Theological Studies*, viii (1957), pp. 129 ff.

Edward II, Edward III and Henry VI, sought to stimulate civilian studies at the college by grants of civil-law texts and commentaries, Henry VI in 1435 making the largest single bequest — 77 volumes, of which 28 related to civil law.[105] Evidently, under direct royal patronage and encouragement, the King's Hall was designed to play a leading part in the renaissance and perpetuation of civil-law studies in the English Universities in the medieval period.[106] Civil law never succeeded in supplanting English common law, though it presented a serious challenge for a time in the sixteenth century. By ensuring the continuation of the study of civil law at the Universities, through such institutions as the King's Hall, over which it had a direct control, the English monarchy appears to have been striving not only to assure a ready supply of trained civilians for practical employment, but also to engender a climate of thought which would be generally receptive to the accentuation of the more theocratic aspects of kingship.

In this connection, it has to be remembered that the functions of the English chapel royal, in contrast to those of the chapels royal in some regions of continental Europe, for example, in Germany and Sicily, were primarily ecclesiastical and liturgical.[107] Judging from the account of William Say, dean of the chapel royal in the reign of Henry VI, the institution was, it seems, designed mainly to service the religious needs of the king and queen, and of their immediate entourage.[108] There would therefore appear to be firm grounds for the conclusion that in England the chapel royal did not constitute a

---

[105] Cobban, *The King's Hall*, pp. 247, 256–7.

[106] Analysis of an almost complete library catalogue of the King's Hall of 1391, in conjunction with four extant lending lists, reveals that in the late fourteenth century about half of the entire library stock was composed of books on civil law, comprising basic texts and an impressive spread of commentaries by the glossators and post-glossators of the Roman law. When the King's Hall library material is compared with the surviving library lists of Cambridge University and its colleges for the medieval period, the conclusions emerge that the ratio of civil-law volumes to the total stock is elsewhere much smaller than at the King's Hall, and that the range of jurist commentaries is in no wise comparable: see ibid., pp. 247–54.

[107] *Liber regie capelle* (ed. W. Ullmann, Henry Bradshaw Society, xcii, Cambridge, 1959), pp. 7–8; Cobban, *The King's Hall*, p. 19.

[108] *Liber regie capelle*, p. 8.

special training area for clerks destined for office in the Church or for governmental service. Hence, English kings had perforce to rely upon a variety of sources for the recruitment of personnel; and within the university context, that academic offshoot of the chapel royal, the King's Hall, in which civil-law studies predominated, must have been among the most prominent of these sources. This is not to deny that other centres productive of civil lawyers, such as New College, All Souls College and, on a lesser scale, Trinity Hall, were of singular importance for the purposes of royal recruitment. The distinguishing feature of the King's Hall, however, was that the fellows were the King's Scholars. They were directly appointed by and removable by the king,[109] and, in a very real sense, formed a royal reservoir of potential servants of the crown: over the personnel of other colleges with legal concentrations, the king exercised no direct or comparable measure of control.

II

THE HUMANIST IMPACT

The traditional curriculum was to some degree modified by the onset of humanist learning. Humanist infiltration of the English Universities should not, however, be exaggerated. It was a gradual process which began in a superficial and piecemeal manner in the

---

[109] Cobban, *The King's Hall*, pp. 65, 103, 150-1, 155. The King's Hall fellows were appointed individually by writ of privy seal. These writs have survived in some quantity from before the late fifteenth century and they are analysed ibid., pp. 151–4. The writs are deposited in P.R.O. Exchequer Accounts, King's Remembrancer, E101 class: from many examples, see E101/348/4/5/12/16/17. Writs have not been found for the period between the late fifteenth century and the dissolution of the college in 1546. Fortunately, there are two pieces of evidence which prove that direct appointment by the crown continued until 1546. The first is a document of 13 August 1541 recording a composition made between the college and Thomas Pylson, fellow, in which mention is made of Pylson's appointment by letters of privy seal: King's Hall Cabinet, Trinity College Muniment Room, no. 144. The second fragment of evidence is Archbishop Parker's testimony to the effect that the master and fellows of the King's Hall continued to be appointed by the crown until the dissolution of the college: M. Parker, *De Antiquitate Britannicae Ecclesiae* (ed. S. Drake, London, 1729), p. xxvii, lines 45–6.

second half of the fifteenth century and became more entrenched and institutionalized in the course of the sixteenth century.[110] The humanist impact was probably greatest within the arts faculties of Oxford and Cambridge. But even in arts, the most flexible of the faculties, humane elements had, by *c.* 1600, constituted only a minority ingredient of the curriculum.[111] In general, the English Universities incorporated those aspects of continental humanism which were most compatible with the inherited corpus of learning. That is, Oxford and Cambridge absorbed humanist features into the mainstream of English intellectual life without effecting a major deflection of traditional intellectual horizons. For this reason, the English Universities cannot be reckoned to have been humanist centres comparable in importance with many of the contemporary universities in continental Europe.

Humanist interests are detectable at Oxford earlier in the fifteenth century than at Cambridge.[112] Before humanism became anchored in the form of endowed lectureships or in collegiate foundations with humanist leanings, it was advanced at Oxford through the individual efforts of influential patrons such as Duke Humphrey, brother of Henry V, and John Tiptoft, Earl of Worcester; through visiting Italian and Greek scholars and secretaries; and through a series of Oxford scholars who travelled in Italy and attended the schools of the celebrated humanists, notably that of Guarino da Verona at Ferrara.[113] Duke Humphrey played a

[110] See e.g. R. Weiss, *Humanism in England during the Fifteenth Century*, and McConica, *English Humanists and Reformation Politics*, ch. 4.

[111] See the argument of J. M. Fletcher, 'Change and resistance to change: a consideration of the development of English and German Universities during the sixteenth century', art. cit., pp. 1 ff.

[112] See e.g. Weiss, op. cit., especially chs. 4, 8–12.

[113] Weiss, op. cit., *passim*; D. Hay, 'England and the Humanities in the Fifteenth Century', *Itinerarium Italicum: the profile of the Italian Renaissance in the mirror of its European transformations: dedicated to Paul Oskar Kristeller on the occasion of his seventieth birthday* (ed. H. A. Oberman and T. A. Brady, Jr., Leiden, 1975, Studies in Medieval and Reformation Thought, 14), pp. 305 ff.; R. J. Mitchell, 'English Law Students at Bologna in the Fifteenth Century', *E.H.R.*, li (1936), pp. 270 ff.; 'English Students at Padua, 1460–1475', *T.R.H.S.*, 4th ser., xix (1936), pp. 101 ff.; and 'English Students at Ferrara in the Fifteenth Century', *Italian Studies*, i (1937), pp. 74 ff.

key role in the advancement of humanist interests in England in the 1430s and 1440s until his death in 1447. He employed Italian humanists such as Tito Livio Frulovisi and Antonio Beccaria as secretaries; he commissioned Latin translations from the Greek of seminal works, including Plato's *Republic* and Aristotle's *Politics* by Pier Candido Decembrio and Leonardo Bruni respectively; and he secured many valuable books for his library through his written contacts with scholars in Italy.[114] His bequest of just under 300 manuscripts to Oxford University, which were received in instalments between 1435 and 1450, was a powerful stimulus to humane studies within the University. For his splendid library included not only modern editions of classical works in common circulation, but also copies of recently discovered classical texts, as well as a range of works by Italian authors, including Petrarch, Boccaccio and Salutati.[115] Although Duke Humphrey had intended all of his books for Oxford, a proportion of them found their way into King's College, Cambridge,[116] where they were less accessible than they would have been had they been deposited in a more-central university collection. Duke Humphrey's patronage activities were complemented on a large scale by John Tiptoft, Earl of Worcester,[117] who had read arts at Oxford and had amassed a considerable library on his Italian journeys. Part of this collection, which was scattered after his execution in 1470, probably came to rest in both Oxford and Cambridge, although much uncertainty surrounds this matter.[118]

Until the last two or three decades of the fifteenth century, most humanist enterprises in England were conducted on the level of the individual scholar who had developed an amateur interest in humane pursuits, commonly with the aim of enhancing aspects of established learning. For in fifteenth-century England, humanism

---

[114] See Weiss, op. cit., chs. 3, 4.

[115] Hay, op cit., pp. 329–30.

[116] Ibid., p. 329; Weiss, op. cit., p. 67, n. 4.

[117] On Tiptoft, see Weiss, op. cit., pp. 112–22; R. J. Mitchell, *John Tiptoft* (London, 1938).

[118] Weiss, op. cit., p. 118.

was not seen as an alternative culture: it was viewed as a storehouse, from which elements might be extracted and either applied to current philosophy, theology or grammar, or used to raise standards of Latinity in diplomatic, university or private correspondence.[119] That is, scholars in the English Universities in the fifteenth century tended to regard humanism as subsidiary to their inherited framework of studies, more a means to an end than a complex body of thought and attitudes which needs to be systematically explored. Although the value of Greek texts for a whole range of disciplines had been fully appreciated from the twelfth century, very few English scholars were fluent readers in that language: the rest had to rely primarily upon Latin translations. The situation did not change significantly in the fifteenth century: access to classical and contemporary humanist literature was still mainly by means of Latin. Knowledge of Greek in England appears to have been generally extended through the scribal activities of a band of Greek visitors in the third and fourth quarters of the fifteenth century, among whose ranks were Emanuel of Constantinople, George Hermonymos and John Serbopoulos.[120] Towards the end of the century, a coterie of scholars had emerged in the English Universities capable of reading texts in the original Greek and of teaching the language to at least a modest standard. For most of the fifteenth century, however, the majority of patrons and scholars assimilated Greek texts only in Latin versions.

The enterprises of patrons of the stamp of Duke Humphrey and John Tiptoft were supplemented by the individual efforts of a number of scholars who travelled to Italy to sample the schools of the humanist teachers, especially that of Guarino da Verona at Ferrara.[121] Among the English scholars from Oxford who did so were Robert Fleming, nephew of Richard Fleming (founder of Lincoln College) and dean of Lincoln cathedral in 1452; William Grey, chancellor of Oxford University in 1440 or 1441 and later bishop of Ely; and John Free who pursued humane studies with an

---

[119] See Weiss's conclusions ibid., pp. 179–83.

[120] Ibid., ch. 9; and the cautionary remarks of Hay, op. cit., p. 361.

[121] See Weiss, op. cit., chs, 6, 7, and the articles by Mitchell cited above in n. 113.

almost professional dedication.[122] Among those from Cambridge who did so was John Gunthorpe, later warden of the King's Hall, dean of the chapel royal, a diplomatist, keeper of the privy seal and a holder of numerous ecclesiastical offices. He achieved a command of Greek and built up a considerable collection of humanist texts, many of which came to be housed in Jesus College, Cambridge, in the sixteenth century.[123] Despite the valuable direct contacts which these scholars made with humanists in Italy and the impressive progress made in Greek studies, on their return to England no permanent focus for humanist endeavour was established by them. If sustained advances were to be achieved and consolidated, it was necessary that Latin and Greek humanism be embodied in an institutional frame within the Universities. This development will be discussed below.

Consideration also needs to be given to the fact that there were Italian and English teachers of humane studies in Oxford and Cambridge for some time before endowed lectureships were founded in this field. The Italian humanist Cornelio Vitelli of Cortona, who was probably praelector at New College in the period 1482–7 and who, on a subsequent visit to Oxford, in 1490, rented a room at Exeter College until 1492, is likely to have taught Greek in Oxford on a private basis.[124] He may even have been a temporary lecturer, in view of the description of him as 'orator', which may imply a position as *lector*.[125] It is conceivable that Vitelli taught Greek to William Grocyn, reader in theology at Magdalen College from 1483 until 1487. When Grocyn returned to Oxford after a period of study in Florence, he rented a room at Exeter

---

[122] See Weiss's high estimate of Free, op. cit., pp. 111–12: on the other hand, Hay, op. cit., p. 332, remarks that Free's death 'was hardly an intellectual catastrophe'.

[123] On Gunthorpe's career, see Cobban, *The King's Hall*, p. 287; Emden, *B.R.U.C.*, pp. 275–7, and Weiss, op. cit., pp. 122–7.

[124] See the arguments of C. H. Clough, 'Thomas Linacre, Cornelio Vitelli, and Humanistic Studies at Oxford', *Linacre Studies: Essays on the Life and Works of Thomas Linacre c. 1460–1524*, ed. cit., pp. 1 ff., with main conclusions, pp. 21–2.

[125] Magdalen College Archives, Bursars' Book 1490–99, fo. 17; see also Clough, op. cit., pp. 11–12.

College from 1491 to 1493. During this time, he appears to have given informal classes in humane studies, including Greek.[126] It is also known that Stefano Surigone, a humanist scholar and Latin poet from Milan, lectured at Oxford on aspects of Latin humanism at some point between 1454 and 1464, and possibly also between 1465 and 1471, and it is possible that he taught Greek informally.[127] It is of some remark that at Cambridge, where humanist endeavour in the fifteenth century is but sparsely recorded, the Italian humanist and *poeta* Caius Auberinus was employed both as a letter writer and as a university lecturer. In the former capacity, he was active from 1483–4,[128] and as a lecturer intermittently from 1492–3 or earlier until at least 1503–4.[129] Auberinus lectured on classical subjects, including the *Comedies* of Terence, during term times and in vacations. He was paid for the lectures delivered, but there is no suggestion that he held a permanent endowed lectureship. It is also known that John Doget, who became provost of King's College, Cambridge, in 1499, was heavily involved in humanist pursuits, and composed a commentary on Plato's *Phaedo* at some point between 1473 and 1486, in which he strove to emphasize those elements in Platonic thought which bore a close affinity with Christian doctrine.[130] There is no evidence, however, that Doget gave official lectures on the new learning in the University. The presence in Cambridge in *c.* 1478 of the Italian Franciscan Lorenzo Traversagni, commonly known as Lorenzo da Savona, is a further indication of humanist interests in the University in the last quarter of the fifteenth century. Although Lorenzo was hired to lecture on theology, he possessed humanist leanings and produced, during his stay in Cambridge, a humanist treatise on rhetoric.[131]

[126] Clough, op. cit., p. 22.

[127] Weiss, op. cit., pp. 138–40, 153; Clough, op. cit., p. 10.

[128] *Grace Book A*, pp. 185, 198; *Grace Book B Part i*, pp. 10, 29, 50, 63, 64, 87, 88, 96, 104, 119–21, 136–8, 171–3, 183–4, 193–5.

[129] *Grace Book B Part i*, pp. 44, 51, 138, 159, 175, 196; on Auberinus as a Cambridge lecturer, see Warton, *The History of English Poetry*, ii. 553.

[130] On Doget, see Weiss, *Humanism in England*, pp. 164–7.

[131] Weiss, op. cit., pp. 162–3.

From the admittedly random evidence available, it would appear that interest in humanism was manifested later at Cambridge than at Oxford. Whereas it was clearly visible at Oxford by the middle of the fifteenth century, it is detectable at Cambridge only from the 1470s. Cambridge did not benefit to the same degree as Oxford from patrons of humanism of the stature of Duke Humphrey and John Tiptoft, and this difference may in part account for the slower rate at which Cambridge responded to the humanist challenge. An additional circumstance which may have impeded an earlier reception of humanist learning at Cambridge was the relative strength of the conservative reaction, previously mentioned, in favour of the more traditional brand of theology institutionalized in several of the Cambridge colleges in the fifteenth century.

Perhaps the most enduring humanist achievement in the English Universities in the fifteenth century was the evolution of high standards in the teaching of Latin grammar as a necessary groundwork for all Latin humanist enterprises. This was largely an Oxford movement in its origins, and it was particularly associated with the school which William Waynflete, founder of Magdalen, attached to his college.[132] As an experienced schoolteacher, Waynflete was disturbed by declining levels of competence in grammar in the English academic world, as before him had been William of Wykeham and William Byngham, the founder of Godshouse, the Cambridge training college for grammar masters. As in the case of his predecessors, Waynflete was keenly alive to the dangers of students proceeding to the arts course without a firm grasp of Latin grammar and literature. But Waynflete's concern went beyond the conventional instruction of grammar. His foundation, Magdalen school, was to be a focal point for that type of humane teaching of grammar grounded in the classical authors that was pioneered by grammarians of Renaissance Italy of the

---

[132] See Hay, 'England and the Humanities in the Fifteenth Century', p. 361. For the contribution of New College graduates to the raising of grammatical standards in the late fifteenth and early sixteenth centuries, see G. F. Lytle, 'A University Mentality in the later Middle Ages: The Pragmatism, Humanism, and Orthodoxy of New College, Oxford', *Genèse et Débuts du Grand Schisme d'Occident 1362–1394* (Colloques Internationaux du Centre National de la Recherche Scientifique, no. 586, Paris, 1980), pp. 201 ff.

calibre of Lorenzo Valla (1407–57) and Niccolò Perotto (1429–80), the works of both of whom exercised a considerable influence in England.

The first headmaster of Magdalen school was John Anwykyll, who had studied grammar at Cambridge in the mid-1470s and was appointed to this post in *c.* 1481.[133] The influence of Valla and Perotto was reflected in his *Compendium totius Grammaticae*, published in Oxford in 1483, and the Latin examples in his compilation of *Vulgaria* — model sentences in Latin and English — were taken from the plays of Terence. Anwykyll was the first of an influential group of humanist grammarians who taught or studied at Magdalen school in the last quarter of the fifteenth and early sixteenth centuries. Besides Anwykyll, this group included John Stanbridge, John Holt, Robert Whittinton, William Lily, Thomas Wolsey, and probably John Colet and Thomas More. From Magdalen school, the movement of humanist grammar fanned outwards, and by the mid-sixteenth century classical studies predominated in the curricula of England's main grammar schools. The institutionalization of the grammatical aspect of Latin humanism at Magdalen provided an important stimulus to humanist studies in Oxford at large, and must have been a point of reference for the founders of Corpus Christi and Cardinal College, both of which incorporated Latin and Greek humanism. Indeed, to note the connection in terms of personnel, Magdalen furnished Corpus with its first president, John Claymond, and its first reader in Greek, Edward Wotton; and Thomas Wolsey, the founder of Cardinal College, had himself been a teacher of grammar at Magdalen school in 1497–8.[134]

It is somewhat ironical that while Cambridge was the slower of the English Universities in awakening to humane learning, it was Cambridge which established the first lectureship specifically launched to promote humanist studies. This lectureship was one of

---

[133] On grammar and grammar masters at Magdalen College school in the fifteenth century, see *The Register of St Mary Magdalen College, Oxford* (7 vols., ed. J. R. Bloxam, Oxford, 1853–85), iii. 7–70; R. S. Stanier, *Magdalen School* (2nd. ed., Oxford, 1958), pp. 25–65; Orme, *English Schools in the Middle Ages*, especially pp. 107–11.

[134] Orme, op. cit., p. 201.

the three salaried university lectureships instituted at Cambridge in 1488.[135] It was placed on a firm endowed footing by the terms of the will of Sir Robert Rede of *c.* 1519.[136] The lectureship was designed for students in the initial two years of the arts course. It was to be concerned with the nebulously defined *libri humanitatis*, and its institution clearly represented an attempt to inject into the arts faculty a heightened awareness of the classical authors and of contemporary humanist literature. At both Universities, Greek may have been taught sporadically from the late fifteenth century. Regular lectureships, however, seem to date only from the second decade of the sixteenth century. When he was Lady Margaret professor of divinity at Cambridge, Erasmus, for a fee, taught Greek at Queens' College in 1511.[137] The first public lecturer in Greek in Cambridge University was probably Richard Croke, who was appointed by the university chancellor, John Fisher, in *c.* 1518 and commenced his duties in 1519. Temporary teaching in Greek took place at Oxford in 1512. The first permanent lectureship in Greek, however, was instituted by Bishop Foxe when he established public lectureships in Greek, Latin and rhetoric at Corpus Christi College in 1517, although the Greek lectureship did not in fact come into being until a few years later.[138]

At Oxford, Foxe's Corpus Christi College (1517) and Wolsey's Cardinal College (1525, refounded as King Henry VIII's College in 1532, and finally as Christ Church in 1546) and at Cambridge, Christ's College (refounded from Godshouse in 1505 by Lady Margaret Beaufort, with the guiding assistance of John Fisher) and St John's College (1511, founded by Lady Margaret, aided by Fisher) were all in varying degrees humanist centres. These colleges furnished much of the institutional support for the new learning in

---

[135] *Camb. Docs.*, i. 361; see also above, chapter 5, pp. 204–5.

[136] For details, see e.g. Leader, 'Teaching in Tudor Cambridge', p. 106, and 'Professorships and Academic Reform at Cambridge: 1488–1520', p. 218.

[137] See e.g. Leader, 'Teaching in Tudor Cambridge', p. 108.

[138] For Croke, see ibid., pp. 108–9; McConica, *English Humanists and Reformation Politics*, p. 80. On teaching Greek at Oxford in 1512, see McConica, op. cit., p. 83. For the public lectureships at Corpus Christi College, see ibid., pp. 80, 82, and *Statutes*, ii. ch. 10, 48–54.

the English Universities in the first half of the sixteenth century, and this support was bolstered at Cambridge by the foundation of Trinity College in 1546.

The first visitation of the English Universities initiated by the Tudor state occurred in 1535, when Thomas Cromwell sent his agents to inquire into the condition of Oxford and Cambridge. The broad consequence of this visitation was an endorsement of humanist learning. The study of canon law was to be suppressed, along with all commentaries on the *Sentences* of Peter Lombard, and a number of humanist commentators on Aristotle's logic were advocated as replacements for the traditional medieval authorities.[139] Moreover, at Cambridge the colleges were to maintain, at their own expense, two daily public lectures in Greek and Latin, and the University was to support a public lecture in either Greek or Hebrew.[140] As a result of this, Greek and Hebrew university lectureships were rapidly instituted, the Hebrew lectureship being financed from 1535 until 1539 by funds derived from the suppression of a mathematical lectureship.'[141] The directive on college lectureships is known to have been carried out at least in some instances. Gonville and Christ's, both of which had

---

[139] On the royal injunctions of 1535 issued in connection with the visitations, see Logan, 'The Origins of the So-Called Regius Professorships: an aspect of the Renaissance in Oxford and Cambridge', art. cit., p. 273; Fletcher, 'Change and resistance to change: a consideration of the development of English and German Universities during the sixteenth century', pp. 26–7; Mallet, *A History of the University of Oxford*, ii. 62–3; *The Statutes of Sir Walter Mildmay for Emmanual College* (ed. F. Stubbings, Cambridge, 1983), pp. 4–5. Only the royal injunctions of 1535, which are undated but appear to belong to the beginning of October, and which were issued to Cambridge University after Cromwell, already chancellor of the University, had been appointed visitor, have survived; and these are summarized in Cooper, *Annals*, i. 375, and in Mullinger, *The University of Cambridge*, i. 630. It is assumed here that the Oxford injunctions were essentially the same as those directed to Cambridge. Additional injunctions, of 22 October 1535, were issued for Cambridge by Dr Thomas Leigh, one of Cromwell's chief visitatorial agents: for these, see Cooper, op. cit., i. 376.

[140] The directive on collegiate lectureships was included in the royal injunctions of 1535, Cooper, op. cit., i. 375: the provision regarding university lectureships was contained in the additional injunctions of Dr Leigh, ibid., i. 376.

[141] See conveniently Leader, 'Teaching in Tudor Cambridge', p. 110.

already been maintaining a Latin lecture, now established one in Greek.[142] Queens' and King's both originated Greek lectureships shortly after the visitation, and by the 1540s, King's also had a lectureship in Hebrew'.[143] The King's Hall followed (and exceeded) the terms of the command given to the University and not that specifically issued to the colleges. That is, it instituted public lectures in Greek and Hebrew, in addition to the Latin lectures already being supported, and these were delivered in the university schools at the college's expense.[144] These new lectureships maintained by the King's Hall appear to have come into operation immediately after the visitation of Dr Thomas Leigh, one of Cromwell's chief inquisitors, in 1535,[145] and they were still functioning at the time of the last extant college account, 1543–4.[146]

No official record of the Oxford visitation survives, but it seems that the royal visitors established or confirmed public lectures in Greek or Latin or in both Greek and Latin at New College, All Souls, Magdalen, Merton and Queen's.[147] It is apparent that by the mid-sixteenth century Oxford and Cambridge were fairly well served by endowed lectureships in humanist subjects. This does not mean, however, that humanism had deeply infiltrated the curricular fabric before 1550. On the contrary, in so far as such a movement can be assessed, it seems that the humanist impact on the English

---

[142] See J. Simon, *Education and Society in Tudor England* (Cambridge, 1966), p. 201, n. 2; Leader, art. cit., p. 117.

[143] See Leader, art. cit., p. 118. At King's, payments for a Greek lecturer are recorded in King's College Archieves, Mundum Books, xi (1535–46), in the account for 1535–7 (not foliated); payments for a Hebrew lecturer are recorded in the accounts for 1544–5 and 1545–6 (not foliated).

[144] Cobban, *The King's Hall*, pp. 84–5.

[145] King's Hall Accounts, xxv. fo. 45v (1535–6): 'Item pro lectura ex iniuncto commissarii regis xiiis iiiid; item pro lecturis hebraica et greca in scolis publicis viiis iiiid'.

[146] Ibid., xxvi. fo. 124v. For further references to these lectureships, see Cobban, *The King's Hall*, p. 85, notes 3–6.

[147] Mallet, *A History of the University of Oxford*, ii. 62–3; Pantin, *Oxford Life in Oxford Archives*, p. 37.

Universities was seldom profound and, in many areas of study, only marginal.

It is abundantly clear from the above discussion that the onset of humane learning in the English Universities was belated and that its limited assimilation was a gradual process. There existed no humanist programme *per se* for the systematic reform of teaching at Oxford and Cambridge, only a piecemeal implementation of aspects of the new learning. This is perhaps more intelligible in view of the fact that humanist scholars in England were themselves much divided as to what the desirable amount of curricular reform was. Some humanists advocated the wholesale rejection of the contemporary curriculum; others sought only to alter, and to diversify within, the existing framework; and yet others proposed the establishment of humanist-oriented institutions entirely outside the orbit of the Universities.[148] In the event, the English Universities resisted pressures for radical humanist reform; and, in the course of the sixteenth century, the structure and content of the curricula in arts, theology, civil law and medicine were subject only to modest adjustments.[149] Canon law was phased out after its suppression under the terms of the royal injunctions of 1535; Greek was introduced for bachelors of arts proceeding to the M.A., although it was not apparently made compulsory at either University until the second half of the sixteenth century;[150] and the teaching of Hebrew was instituted for the especial benefit of masters of arts studying theology.[151] At both Universities in the sixteenth century, a range of humanist texts were incorporated into the arts course, in particular texts dealing with grammar, rhetoric and

---

[148] See e.g. Fletcher, 'Change and resistance to change: a consideration of the development of English and German Universities during the sixteenth century', p. 2. For some of the alternative humanist academies projected, see Charlton, *Education in Renaissance England*, pp. 154–7; Curtis, *Oxford and Cambridge in Transition 1558–1642*, pp. 65–8; and R. O'Day, *Education and Society 1500–1800: The Social Foundations of Education in early Modern Britain* (London and New York, 1982), pp. 88–9.

[149] See the comments of McConica, 'The Social Relations of Tudor Oxford', p. 132.

[150] Fletcher, art. cit., pp. 9, 11.

[151] For the situation at Oxford, see Gibson, *Statuta Antiqua*, p. 408.

mathematics.[152] Aristotelian material remained a staple in the field of logic. There was here, however, a different emphasis, in the sense that attempts were made to set Aristotelian logic within a more recognizably humanist context. Aristotelian logic in the late medieval English Universities may have tended to be over concerned with arid esoteric technicalities, and humanist influence seems to have had some success in modifying the extent of that concern. Efforts were made to divest training in logic of pedantic excesses, to render it less a series of technical exercises, and to direct it more consciously towards equipping a scholar for involvement in public affairs.[153]

Apart from making the limited curricular adaptations of the kind indicated above — the introduction of new texts in selected areas and some changes of emphasis arising from humanist criteria — it is clear that the English Universities responded with a conservative caution to the thrust of the humanist movement. In this respect, they contrasted sharply with, for example, most of the contemporary German universities, where the curricula were radically transformed. One possible point of explanation of this difference may derive from the fact that the German universities tended to be relatively small and much dependent on the local secular authority, whether an individual ruler or a municipality.[154] In these circumstances, it was patently easier to initiate planned and more-trenchant humanist reform than it was in the English Universities, which, until well into the sixteenth century, experienced little royal intervention beyond benign intervention in matters concerning privileges and the maintenance of law and order.[155] In the absence of a strong external directive regarding the

---

[152] Fletcher, art. cit., pp. 10, 12–13. L. Jardine seems to argue for a substantial measure of humanist curricular reform at Cambridge. While reform may have been more marked than at Oxford, the main lines of the traditional curriculum remained intact: see the discussion of Jardine, 'Humanism and the Sixteenth Century Cambridge Arts Course', *History of Education*, 4 (1975), pp. 16 ff.

[153] See the complex discussion by McConica, 'Humanism and Aristotle in Tudor Oxford', *E.H.R.*, xciv (1979), pp. 291 ff.

[154] Fletcher, art. cit., p. 26; Cobban, *The Medieval Universities*, pp. 119–20.

[155] See the comments of Fletcher, art. cit., p. 26.

implementation of a humanist programme of reform, the English Universities did not emulate the pace of curricular change of many of their continental counterparts. It is with the relations between the Universities of Oxford and Cambridge and external authorities that the following chapter is concerned.

Chapter 7

Relations with the Municipal and Ecclesiastical Authorities

I

The Universities and the Town

It was almost inevitable that when the populations of the nascent English Universities expanded to significant proportions in the course of the thirteenth century conflicts would ensue between the Universities and the municipalities of Oxford and Cambridge, as rival corporations, and between individual members of the academic and urban communities. The tensions which arose had a twofold origin. They derived from the privileged position of university members as clerks, and from the increasing jurisdictional role of the chancellors in the legal, social and economic life of the citizenry. At Oxford, the clerical status of the scholars was dramatically underlined in the award of the papal legate of June 1214 whereby the burgesses not only were required to take upon themselves the burdens itemized above in chapter 2,[1] but were bound to uphold the immunity of the scholars from arrest by the agents of secular justice. This was a very clear statement that the Oxford scholars formed a privileged estate within the town and were subject not to the ordinary processes of lay jurisdiction, but to clerical authority as represented externally, at the diocesan and provincial levels, by the bishop of Lincoln and the archbishop of Canterbury, and internally,

---

[1] See above, pp. 45–6. For the version of the award of 25 June 1214, collated with that of 20 June 1214, see *Mediaeval Archives*, i. 2–4, and *Munimenta Academica*, i. 1–4.

for most purposes, by the chancellor's court, which was deemed to function according to delegated episcopal powers. There is nothing comparable to this papal award for Cambridge. It may be assumed, however, that the inception of the Cambridge chancellorship, probably by *c.* 1222 and certainly by 1225,[2] marked the full recognition of the protected clerical status of the body of Cambridge scholars within Ely diocese and Canterbury province.

The award of the papal legate of 1214 for Oxford and the recognition of Cambridge as an academic corporation in 1233 by the papacy[3] made a major contribution towards ensuring the survival of the infant Universities. But their emergence as privileged institutions set in the heart of their respective towns provoked ambivalent responses from the burgesses. The coming of the English Universities could have been welcomed by the citizenry as a stimulus to the urban economy. The inflow of a large concourse of masters and students, who initially had to live and work in rented accommodation, was of obvious benefit to both the private and institutional landlord,[4] as well as to a range of service occupations, such as parchment-dealers, bookbinders, illuminators, stationers and retailers of necessary provisions. When halls and hostels and the later colleges and other purpose-built university structures materialized, employment opportunities were enhanced in Oxford and Cambridge, and in the surrounding districts, for builders and allied tradesmen, and for a variety of communal servants, including bedels, butlers, cooks, bakers, brewers, barbers, laundresses, book-bearers and gardeners. However, despite these economic benefits accruing to the citizens, the privileges accorded to the Universities by successive English kings, beginning with Henry III,[5] combined

---

[2] For the inception of the Cambridge chancellorship, see above. p. 57.

[3] *Register Gregory IX,* ed. cit., i. 779, no. 1389.

[4] In Oxford, by *c.* 1300, local religious houses were very prominent among the landlords who provided accommodation for scholars, the other categories of landlord being private citizens, clergy beneficed in the Oxford region and university bedels: see Catto, 'Citizens, Scholars and Masters', *The History of the University of Oxford,* i. 164.

[5] For the royal charters of privileges given to Oxford University up to *c.* 1500, see Kibre, *Scholarly Privileges in the Middle Ages,* pp. 268–324; and some of the charters granted to Cambridge from the reign of Henry III to that of James I are printed by Dyer, *The Privileges of the University of Cambridge,* i. 5–53. For

with the already substantial privilege of clerical immunity, created a climate of resentment which led to the eruption of periodic clashes between townsmen and scholars, in which the latter generally gained, through royal intervention, at the expense of the former.

The powers of the English university chancellor, previously described,[6] embracing degrees of civil, criminal and spiritual jurisdiction, had been accumulated piecemeal by means of a series of royal charters and papal grants. By the fourteenth century, the Oxford and Cambridge chancellors had gained a multifarious authority unsurpassed elsewhere among universities of the medieval period. They had acquired cognizance of all civil suits between scholars and townsmen, with the exception of freehold matters, and of all criminal cases between scholars and citizens arising within Oxford and Cambridge, apart from cases of murder and maiming, which were reserved for the royal judiciary. From 1406, even this limitation was removed in the case of lay servants and other dependants of Oxford scholars (including members of privileged trades such as stationers, parchment-dealers and bookbinders), who, when accused of these serious crimes, could now be tried by a special court presided over by the university steward, who was appointed by the chancellor.[7] This judicial presence of the English chancellors in the lives of the townspeople was further extended by the array of penalties which the chancellors could employ to enforce the decisions of their courts, and which could be imposed upon members of the university and citizenry alike. These punishments comprised fines, expulsion from the town and suburbs for a limited duration, long-term banishment and, within specified restrictions, the sentence of excommunication. In addition to their being so empowered in civil and criminal cases, the chancellors were

examples of royal letters of protection for the chancellor and masters and for the maintenance of their privileges, see those of 24 March 1327 and 14 December 1335, CUL/UA, Luard, nos. 25, 28.

[6] See above, pp. 66 ff.

[7] See the royal charter of 1406 in *Mediaeval Archives*, i. 231–4. In 1407, the mayor and bailiffs tried to secure the revocation of this charter, and they seem to have obtained some modifications, but the privilege of 1406 was confirmed by a royal charter of 1461: see the comments of J. Cooper, 'Medieval Oxford', *V.C.H. Oxon.* iv. 57.

empowered to investigate immorality within the town, with special reference to brothels and prostitution, on the assumption that immoral behaviour was often associated with disturbances of the peace and so merited the closest supervision. The final area of intervention in the lives of the citizens was the major involvement which the chancellors had in the economic business of the university towns. From 1355 at Oxford and from 1382 at Cambridge, the chancellors, after previous stages of limited participation, gained decisive control of the operation of market trading in the university towns and their suburbs through custody of the assize of bread, wine and ale, the supervision of weights and measures, and the regulation of other matters relating to the disciplined conduct of urban commerce. These powers in the economic field, as with those in the judicial and moral fields, were underpinned with an arsenal of appropriate penalties for townspeople who infringed the market regulations. Despite the disaffection of the citizens that resulted from the dominance of the Oxford and Cambridge chancellors in their business lives, there is no convincing evidence that the chancellors exercised their control to the disadvantage of those engaged in market trading.[8]

The emergence of the English Universities as formidable forces in urban affairs was a palpable curb on the independence of the mayors, bailiffs and burgesses. Although on many issues — for instance, the joint assessment of rents of accommodation inhabited by scholars — co-operation between representatives of the university and the town was the norm, the course of their relations was punctuated by a series of violent conflicts, which would sometimes assume the character of pitched battles. At Oxford in 1248, a fracas led to the murder of a Scottish scholar. The University called for a cessation of lectures, the bishop of Lincoln, Robert Grosseteste, imposed a ban of excommunication on the perpetrators of the act and, as a result of the king's intervention, the municipality was fined eighty marks.[9] Henry III, following the settlement of this matter, attempted to

[8] See Salter, *Medieval Oxford*, p. 57; Catto, 'Citizens, Scholars and Masters', p. 163.

[9] See Kibre, op. cit., pp. 274–5 and p. 275, n. 34; Mallet, *A History of the University of Oxford*, i. 38.

establish the principle that if any resident of Oxford was found guilty of the murder of, or of having done an injury to, a scholar, then the whole lay community of the town would admit communal responsibility and suffer the subsequent punishment; and that if the bailiffs of the town were found to be culpable, they were to be held individually responsible and in addition to their share in any collective penalty levied on the townspeople, were to bear an appropriate punishment.[10] Similar arrangements were formulated for Cambridge in the same year.[11] In 1255, further efforts were made by Henry III to safeguard the Oxford scholars from the attacks of the townspeople. Four aldermen and eight burgesses were to act as deputies to the mayor and bailiffs in matters involving breaches of the peace. They were to have the power to prosecute malefactors, disturbers of the peace and vagabonds, as well as those who sheltered the criminal fraternity.[12] The measures of 1248 and 1255 certainly refined the mechanisms for the maintenance of law and order, but outbreaks of violence between scholars and citizens continued to occur with some regularity. A particularly serious clash, in which a scholar and a citizen were killed, occurred in 1297-8. Those responsible for the death of the scholar were excommunicated by the bishop of Lincoln, and the town was ordered by the king's justices to pay £200 in damages to the University.[13]

By far the most dramatic instance of armed warfare to sully the streets of Oxford was the riot of St Scholastica's Day of 1355. This bloody affray, which lasted for three days and of which contrary town and university accounts survive, began as a tavern brawl involving a group of scholars. It developed into a series of major

[10] Kibre, op. cit., p. 275; the royal charter of 29 May 1248 is printed in *Mediaeval Archives*, i. 18-19, and in *Munimenta Academica*, ii. 777-9 (a confirmation of 1268).

[11] Kibre, op. cit., p. 275.

[12] The royal charter of 18 June 1255 is printed in *Mediaeval Archives*, i. 19-21.

[13] Salter discusses the riots of 1297-8 in detail and prints ten associated documents in *Mediaeval Archives*, i. 43-81; the final concord of 22 September 1298 containing the terms of the settlement made between the scholars and burgesses is printed in *Munimenta Academica*, i. 67-9.

confrontations between scholars and townspeople, the townspeople being sometimes reinforced by bands of countrymen drafted into Oxford for this purpose. During the protracted struggles, many on both sides were wounded and some were killed, and a number of houses and academic halls were sacked.[14] Following a royal inquiry into the riot, several of Oxford's leading townsmen were imprisoned in the Tower of London and both University and town had to surrender their privileges to the king. However, the town's privileges were then returned with reductions, while those of the University were significantly increased.[15] Indeed, the settlement in favour of the University in the aftermath of the St Scholastica's Day riot set the seal upon the clear ascendancy of the University in civic affairs, in some respects right down to the nineteenth century. The accumulated legal powers of the chancellor as they affected the citizens were confirmed and enhanced, and he was given overall responsibility for market trading,[16] as has been described above. The bishop of Lincoln imposed an interdict on the town for a year[17] and a subsequent penance to the effect that every year on St Scholastica's Day the mayor, bailiffs and sixty citizens were to attend a mass at St Mary's Church for the souls of those scholars and others killed in the rioting.[18] This annual ceremony continued, in an amended form, until 1825.

Although it resulted in the confirmation of the civic ascendancy of the University, the St Scholastica's Day riot did not end conflict between town and gown. Rivalry and strife continued to darken

---

[14] Much of the documentation pertaining to the St Scholastica's Day riot is printed, with a brief introduction, in J. E. T. Rogers, *Oxford City Documents 1268-1665* (Oxf. Hist. Soc., xviii, 1891), pp. 245–68, and in *Mediaeval Archives*, i. 148–60; see also Pantin, *Oxford Life in Oxford Archives*, pp. 99–104, and Mallet, *A History of the University of Oxford*, i. 160–2.

[15] Pantin, op. cit., p. 101.

[16] See the royal charter of 27 June 1355 for Oxford University printed in *Mediaeval Archives*, i. 152–7.

[17] See the material relating to the raising of the interdict printed in *Oxford City Documents*, pp. 259–60, 261–6.

[18] See the indenture of 14 May 1357 made between the university chancellor and the mayor and corporation of Oxford printed in *Mediaeval Archives*, i. 168–9.

relations between citizens and academics for centuries to come. The St Scholastica's Day riot was, however, the last of the extreme bloody encounters, subsequent quarrels being mostly resolved by less violent means, with readier recourse to litigation and government appeals.[19] The level of violent feuding was undoubtedly reduced when the majority of scholars became subject to the relatively strict discipline of collegiate living, although this was not standardized for undergraduates until the sixteenth century.

The Oxford pattern of violent conflict between scholars and citizens was reproduced in similar vein at Cambridge. The frequency of brawls between the scholars and citizens at Cambridge in the thirteenth century is indicated by the fact that there was a series of judicial inquiries into the matter.[20] By a charter of Henry III of 22 February 1268, modelled on one of 1255 granted to Oxford, the town's role in the maintenance of law and order was delineated: two aldermen and four senior burgesses, assisted by two sworn men in each parish, were to aid the mayor and bailiffs in the keeping of the peace for the benefit of both clerks and laymen.[21] The University complained that these functions were incompetently performed, and in April 1270, an agreement was negotiated by the Lord Edward, the heir to the throne, whereby the responsibility for upholding law and order was made a joint concern of the University and the town.[22] Under this scheme, ten burgesses — seven from the town and three from the suburbs — were to be elected annually, along with five scholars from the English counties, three from Scotland, two from Wales and three from Ireland, and together they were charged with keeping the peace. The scholars were to assist the burgesses in arresting offenders, whether clerical or lay. Elected masters were to compile registers of the principals and inmates of the hostels so that lawless residents might be more easily identified and punished; persistent lawbreakers were to be expelled

[19] On this topic, see Pantin, op. cit., p. 102.

[20] E.g. *Annals*, i. 45, 48.

[21] Ibid., i. 50–1.

[22] Ibid., i. 52–3; Dyer, *The Privileges of the University of Cambridge*, i. 66–7; see also the copy in CUL/UA, Luard, no. 3.

from the University and town of Cambridge and the assistance of the king and council was to be invoked in cases of difficulty; and both clerks and burgesses were to swear to uphold the privileges of the University.

However, these constructive arrangements failed to stem dissension in Cambridge between scholars and townspeople. In 1304, a dispute occurred in which townsmen stormed a number of hostels and assaulted several of the scholars.[23] In 1322, a serious affray erupted, in the course of which townsmen were directed by the mayor and bailiffs to attack colleges, hostels and inns occupied by scholars, some of whom were injured and others removed to prison. During these attacks, many books and effects were seized, a priest was killed and writs concerning the privileges of the University were destroyed. After the University had threatened to disperse, the king ordered that the mayor, four of the bailiffs and 319 other persons were to be brought to justice for their part in the proceedings.[24] Further violent scenes occurred in 1371 when scholars broke into townspeople's houses and assaulted the owners, and when a number of bailiffs were severely beaten by an armed group which included scholars and a local rector.[25]

It is clear that a long history of endemic conflict had preceded the most disruptive episode in the relations between Cambridge scholars and townspeople, namely, the riotous events which took place in June 1381 during the Peasants' Revolt.[26] The local form which the upheaval assumed in Cambridge was characterized by an

[23] *Annals*, i. 70.

[24] Ibid., i. 79–80; see also A. C. Chibnall, *Richard de Badew and the University of Cambridge 1315–1340* (Cambridge, 1963), pp. 10–11. The mayor and all the senior burgesses appear to have been involved in the rioting.

[25] *Annals*, i. 110–11.

[26] These events and their aftermath are set out in detail in ibid., i. 120–4; Cam, 'The City of Cambridge', *V.C.H. Camb.* iii. 8–12; *The Peasants' Revolt of 1381* (ed. R. B. Dobson, Macmillan History in Depth Series, London, 1970), pp. 239–42. See also the account in the Parliamentary Rolls, *Rotuli Parliamentorum 1278–1503* (6 vols., Record Commission, London, 1783: index vol. 1832), iii. 107–9. For the disturbed state of Cambridge as early as December 1380, see A. Harding, 'The Revolt against the Justices', *The English Rising of 1381* (ed. R. H. Hilton and T. H. Aston, Cambridge, 1984), pp. 165 ff. at p. 167.

alliance between the mayor and burgesses and rebels from the county, who combined to attack university and college property and personnel, as well as the priory of Barnwell, although the mayor later claimed that he had been coerced into leading the assault on the priory. Among the many acts of pillage were the destruction of the house of William Wigmore, a university bedel; the raiding of Corpus Christi College and the taking away or burning of its muniments, probably done because the college was, it seems, the third largest landowner in the town[27] and the collector of unpopular rents;[28] the attacks on the houses of various burgesses, including that of Roger of Harleston, who was a member of parliament for Cambridgeshire from 1376, a justice of the peace for both shire and borough, a commissioner for implementing the Statute of Labourers and a poll-tax commissioner;[29] the rifling of the university chest in St Mary's Church and the burning of its archival contents; the plundering of the house of the Carmelite friars on the site of the later Queens' College, wherein another chest belonging to the University was seized; and, as already mentioned, the assault on Barnwell Priory by a force drawn from the town and county, and indeed from other counties, and led by the mayor with the declared object of asserting the customary rights of driftway and pasture in the meadows which the prior had fenced off and planted with trees.[30] According to the account in the parliamentary roll, the mayor, bailiffs and burgesses compelled the University and its colleges to renounce all of their royal privileges, to agree to abide by the ancient customs of the borough and to abandon all legal processes against the burgesses.[31] The University and colleges were required to surrender their charters of privileges and other deeds, which were then burned in the market-place as a symbolical

---

[27] Cam, 'The City of Cambridge', *V.C.H. Camb.* iii. 10, n. 38.

[28] Fuller, *The History of the University of Cambridge*, ed. cit., p. 115.

[29] On Roger of Harleston, see Cam, 'The City of Cambridge', in op. cit., iii. 10; also Maitland, *Township and Borough*, pp. 63, 126, 128–9.

[30] Cam, 'The City of Cambridge', in op. cit., iii. 11; also Mairland, op cit., pp. 192–3.

[31] *Rotuli Parliamentorum*, iii. 108; *The Peasants' Revolt of 1381*, p. 241; *Annals*, i. 121.

expression of the destruction of the legal chains which had allegedly oppressed the citizenry for the best part of two centuries.[32]

It is undoubted that the University lost a quantity of archival material in the sequence of violent events which engulfed the town between 15 and 17 June 1381. But the extent of this loss, though serious, should not be exaggerated. The detailed inventory of the contents of the University's common chest compiled in 1420 by master William Rysley, who may have been one of the proctors, lists some forty royal charters of pre-1381 vintage;[33] and more than thirty royal charters, letters and mandates, and a quantity of ecclesiastical and other records, all dating from before 1381, are still extant in the archives of Cambridge University.[34] It is therefore clear that while a smaller quantity of archival material survives for Cambridge University than for Oxford, the difference cannot be attributed entirely to the traumatic happenings of June 1381.

The risings in Cambridge were suppressed by an armed band under the command of the bishop of Norwich, and a series of judicial commissions were instituted to deal with the injuries suffered by the University, the prior of Barnwell and other individuals who had sustained damage or loss, and to inquire into the trespasses, felonies and treasons perpetrated by the rebels.[35] It seems that only one burgess was hanged,[36] but the ex-mayor, Edmund Lister, and bailiffs had to answer before parliament in

---

[32] *Rotuli Parliamentorum*, iii. 106–7, 108; *The Peasants' Revolt of 1381*, pp. 241–2; *Annals*, i. 121.

[33] See the printed edition of Rysley's catalogue in C. P. Hall, 'William Rysley's Catalogue of the Cambridge University Muniments, compiled in 1420', *Transactions of the Cambridge Bibliographical Society*, iv (1965), pp. 85 ff. at pp. 91–2; for the original, see *Registrum Librorum*, CUL/UA, COLL ADMIN 4, fos. 9–14 at fos. 9–9v.

[34] Peek and Hall, *The Archives of the University of Cambridge*, pp. 24–5.

[35] Cam, 'The City of Cambridge', in op. cit., iii. 11; for Richard II's commission of 10 August 1381 authorizing the Cambridge chancellor and others to inquire into the damage to university property and the destruction or theft of university muniments, see CUL/UA, Luard, no. 54.

[36] This was John Giboun, who had led the mob which invaded St Mary's Church and rifled the university chest.

December 1381.[37] The renunciation of privileges, which had been wrested by threats from the University and colleges, was declared null and void by parliamentary authority, and the mayor and bailiffs were ordered to surrender the liberties of the town into the hands of the king.[38] These liberties were restored to the mayor and bailiffs by a royal charter of 1 May 1382, with the exception of those which related to the regulation of market trading.[39] By a royal charter of 17 February 1382, the king, with the assent of parliament, had transferred the custody of the assize of bread, wine and ale, and the oversight of weights and measures in Cambridge and its suburbs, from the jurisdiction of the town to that of the chancellor of the University, together with all the punitive apparatus necessary for enforcement.[40] In this respect, the outcome of the disturbances in Cambridge in 1381 paralleled that at Oxford following the St Scholastica's Day riot in 1355. And just as Oxford University achieved a commanding dominance in civic affairs after 1355, so Cambridge University attained an undisputed leverage in the borough after 1381.

Being consumers and being situated as they were, the English Universities had an obvious concern for environmental conditions in their own town and suburbs, embracing standards of hygiene and the cleansing and paving of the streets. Between the late thirteenth and mid-fourteenth centuries, Oxford University brought strong pressure to bear upon the town corporation to attempt a number of salutary improvements. Among the proposals of reform were that the butchers' shambles should be relocated; that the skinners should practise their trade outside the walls (a point won in 1339); that livestock should not be kept in town dwellings; that the streets should be properly cleaned; that only clean water should be used in baking and brewing; and that conditions within the town prison should be improved, with separate accommodation being provided

---

[37] Cam, 'The City of Cambridge', in op. cit., iii. 12.

[38] Ibid.

[39] *Annals,* i. 125–6.

[40] Ibid., i. 124–5.

for women.[41] By the royal charter of 27 June 1355, issued after the riot of St Scholastica's Day, the chancellor was given ultimate responsibility for the cleansing of the streets and the maintenance of paving, with authority to impose ecclesiastical censures on those members of the town who defaulted in these matters.[42] The addition of this environmental function to the already heavy burdens of the chancellorship implies that the town's record in the area of public hygiene and essential street repairs had been indifferent or negligent.

At Cambridge, the chancellor does not seem to have been charged at any time before 1500 with the overriding responsibility for urban cleanliness or for street maintenance or for both. By the royal charter of 1268, the mayor and bailiffs, in conjunction with two sworn burgesses in each street, were to ensure that Cambridge was effectively cleaned, drained and paved.[43] In 1330 and 1351, the University petitioned parliament with the complaint that the mayor and bailiffs had neglected their public-hygiene duties,[44] and from 1391, the chancellor was associated with the mayor and bailiffs in jointly carrying out their functions.[45] The chancellor's power in this regard was further strengthened in 1459 when, at the supplication of Robert Wodelarke, provost of King's College and chancellor of the University, he was given parliamentary authority

---

[41] On these proposed reforms, see Catto, 'Citizens, Scholars and Masters', *The History of the University of Oxford*, i. 166.

[42] See the royal charter of 27 June 1355 printed in *Mediaeval Archives*, i. 152–7 at 155.

[43] See the royal charter of 22 February 1268 in *Annals*, i. 50–1 at 51.

[44] Ibid., i. 85, 102.

[45] Ibid., i. 140. The chancellor and the mayor were to enforce the provisions of 'The Statute of Cambridge', which was the statute enacted at the Cambridge Parliament of 1388 empowering stringent measures to be taken to purge London and other towns and boroughs within the realm of all unhygienic nuisances, which might cause infectious diseases among the inhabitants and the travelling population: see ibid., i. 134. It is probable that this legislation was prompted by the impact which the insalubrious state of Cambridge had made on the members of the parliament held in the town in 1388. The enactment of 1388 has been described as the 'first urban sanitary act' in English history: see e.g. C. Platt, *The English Medieval Town* (London, 1976), p. 70.

to inquire into all manner of nuisances such as dung, refuse and intestines and carcases of animals deposited in alleys, streets, ditches and rivers and in other places within his jurisdiction, as well as all kinds of obstructions in gutters, watercourses and sewers.[46] This was clearly designed as a necessary check on the degree to which the mayor and bailiffs had carried out their cleaning and sanitary obligations. Co-operation between the chancellor and the mayor and bailiffs in this area of public health continued into the sixteenth century, and was given detailed expression in an indenture of 1503 in which the University and the town corporation registered agreement to what was, in effect, a code of sanitary or environmental conduct.[47]

Through their courts, the English university chancellors came to exercise jurisdiction not only over all members of the academic community and over townspeople involved with scholars in most categories of criminal and civil cases, but also over an ever-expanding army of 'privileged persons', who comprised dependants of scholars and members of trades which serviced the Universities.[48] In this respect, the English Universities were following continental practice as pioneered at Bologna and Paris. At Bologna, stationers, illuminators, bookbinders, scribes and money-changers were among the groups subject to university rectorial jurisdiction;[49] and at Paris, scholarly privilege was extended by Innocent IV in 1245 to the common servitors of the university,[50] a class which, in the second half of the fourteenth century, is known to have embraced booksellers, scribes, illuminators, parchment-dealers and bedels.[51] The Oxford chancellor clearly claimed jurisdiction over university

---

[46] *Annals*, i. 209.

[47] See the indenture of 1503 printed in ibid., i. 260–70 at 268.

[48] See above, the references in chapter 3, p. 67, n. 12.

[49] See the statutes of the law students of Bologna of 1317 in *Archiv für Literatur-und Kirchengeschichte*, iii. 266–7, 279–81, and in *Statuti delle università e dei collegi dello studio bolognese*, ed. cit., pp. 20–1, 59.

[50] *Chartularium*, i. no. 141.

[51] Ibid., iii. nos. 1346, 1348; see also Kibre, *Scholarly Privileges in the Middle Ages*, p. 162.

servants such as bedels from early in the thirteenth century,[52] but categories of 'privileged persons' seem to have been first officially defined by Edward I in a charter of 1290. Here, the non-academic personnel who are to be subject to the chancellor's court and are to be exempt from borough jurisdiction as long as they remain within the precincts of the University are given as the servants of the scholars, bedels, parchment-dealers, illuminators, scribes and barbers, and any others who wore the livery or robes of clerks.[53] By the mid-fifteenth century, according to an agreement of 1458 made between the University and the town corporation, the above list of 'privileged persons' had been enlarged to include the university bellringer, caterers, manciples, spencers, cooks, launderers, poor children attached to scholars and clerks within the precincts of the University, common carriers, and messengers in the employ of scholars.[54] When it is considered that the relatives and households of those falling into certain categories of 'privileged persons' were also held to share this protected status, the impressive size of the University's extended family within the borough is graphically underscored.

This situation regarding 'privileged persons' was paralleled at Cambridge. A royal charter of 10 December 1383 unambiguously established the chancellor's jurisdiction over all university servants and over those of individual masters and scholars.[55] The number of 'privileged persons' was augmented by an award of 11 July 1502,

---

[52] When Adam, the university bedel, drowned himself in the Cherwell at some time between 1241 and 1247, the chancellor, John of Taunton, declared his chattels forfeit as the direct consequence of its being a case of suicide, which came within the jurisdiction of his court: see *Snappe's Formulary*, pp. 320–1. Although the king's judges were uncertain about the validity of the chancellor's action in this case, they observed that parchment-dealers and scribes were subject to the chancellor's court: see Lawrence, 'The University in State and Church', *The History of the University of Oxford*, i. 141, nn. 2, 5.

[53] See the inspeximus of 11 March 1315 of the charter of Edward I of 1290 printed in *Mediaeval Archives*, i. 88–94 at 92; see also Underwood, 'The structure and operation of the Oxford Chancellor's court, from the sixteenth to the early eighteenth century', *Journal of the Society of Archivists*, vi (1978), p. 19.

[54] *Epistolae Academicae Oxoniensis*, ii. 344–5; also Underwood, art. cit., p. 19.

[55] The charter is printed by Dyer, *The Privileges of the University of Cambridge*, i. 86–8.

made between the University and the town, in which it is stipulated
that manciples, cooks, butlers and launderers of all colleges and
hostels, the university bedels and all apothecaries, physicians,
surgeons, stationers, illuminators, scribes, parchment-dealers and
bookbinders are to have the privileges of scholars, as long as they
continue in their several occupations.[56] In the year of this award,
some seventy persons, it appears, enjoyed this privileged status.[57]
The dimensions which the regiment of 'privileged persons' came to
assume at both Oxford and Cambridge inevitably brought conflict
with the town; for, as with the scholars, 'privileged persons'
escaped many of the duties and impositions which fell on their
fellow townspeople, and were exempt, in many important respects,
from the jurisdiction of the borough courts. A grievance which
particularly rankled was that a townsman could enrol as a scholar's
servant merely nominally, so as to acquire the status of 'privileged
person' and gain the protection of the chancellor's court.[58] This was
sometimes a device to shield him from current enemies in the
town,[59] and an insurance that all legal cases in which he might
become entangled would be tried in the university court.
Alternatively, a townsman might, it seems, seek to become a
'privileged person' in order to use the chancellor's court to effect a
speedier and cheaper recovery of debts than could normally be
obtained in extra-university courts.[60] Even if a townsman was not
prepared to go to such lengths, he had available to him a murky
custom whereby an outstanding debt was ceded as a legal fiction to a
member of the university so that the matter might be dealt with in
the chancellor's court.[61] The town corporations inveighed against
such malpractices, and the phenomenon of 'privileged persons' was
for centuries the subject of intermittent review by and compromise

[56] Ibid., i. 97–8.

[57] Peek and Hall, *The Archives of the University of Cambridge*, p. 58.

[58] See Salter's remarks in *Registrum Cancellarii*, p. xxxi.

[59] Ibid., p. xxxiii.

[60] Ibid., p. xxxiii; see also Underwood, art. cit., p. 20.

[61] Ibid., pp. xxxiv–xxxv.

between the Universities and the citizenries of Oxford and Cambridge.

One of the stormiest periods in Cambridge town–gown relations occurred during the mayoralty of the infamous John Bilneye.[62] This arch-enemy of the University had been a clerk of the chapel royal and, by this route, had become a fellow of the King's Hall in 1382. He appears to have taken an M.A. degree by 1388–9, but he relinquished academic life in *c*. 1400 and embarked upon a long trouble-filled career in Cambridge municipal politics. He served as mayor in 1406–7, 1414–15, 1416–17 and 1433–4, and was a member of parliament for Cambridge in 1415, 1417 and 1419. By 1415, a bitter dispute had erupted between Bilneye and the University over his refusal to permit the conversion of one of his houses into a hostel for scholars. The altercation generated extreme behaviour by both parties, and a group of scholars attacked Bilneye's house and threatened to kill him. The original dispute fanned out into a wrangle of vast proportions which necessitated an appeal to the king's council. The outcome was that Bilneye was excommunicated. In 1420, the University published a schedule of twenty-five articles of complaint summarizing the points at issue,[63] and accusing Bilneye of everything from perjury to threatening resistance to the chancellor's authority with a hundred armed men. Although allowance has to be made for propagandist excesses on the University's part, the burden of guilt seems to have lain with Bilneye and the municipal authorities.

While there were numerous areas of tension which frequently gave rise to frayed relations between the English Universities and their town corporations, it would perhaps be misleading to suggest that conflict was the natural state of affairs. The broad framework of their relations was one of co-operation at all levels, since, despite the many disputes, the university chancellors and the mayors and bailiffs were often made jointly responsible for the conduct of public business. At Oxford, the mayor's court was sometimes staged in

---

[62] For Bilneye, see Emden, *B.R.U.C.*, p. 62; J. M. Gray, *Biographical Notes on the Mayors of Cambridge* (reprinted from *Cambridge Chronicle*, Cambridge, 1921), pp. 16–17.

[63] *Annals*, i. 164–6.

Hinxey Hall, and the coroners occasionally held their proceedings in the chapel of New College.[64] Whatever resentments were provoked by the encroachment of the jurisdictional powers of the English chancellors on the affairs of the boroughs of Oxford and Cambridge, the scholars formed a captive band of consumers and the many townspeople who depended directly or indirectly on them for their livelihood consequently had a vested interest in the stability of the academic population. Moreover, it must not be assumed that the periodic conflicts between scholars and townspeople accounted for most of the violence in medieval Oxford and Cambridge. Serious riots involving northern and southern scholars in both Universities were a common feature of academic life down to the sixteenth century. Feuds of this nature occurred at Oxford in 1252, 1258, 1267, 1273, 1303, 1314, 1319, 1334, 1385, 1388 and 1389, periodically throughout the fifteenth century, and as late as 1506 and 1587.[65] While it is not possible to document inter-scholastic conflict at Cambridge in comparable detail, it is clear that the major riot of 1260, in which townsmen participated, began as a clash between northern and southern scholars.[66]

In some of the conflicts in the English university towns, there was no sharp demarcation in the composition of the battling groups between scholars and townspeople, the rival parties sometimes being composed of mixed gangs of members of the university and of the town. It is also noteworthy that the records of murders and affrays in the Oxford coroners' rolls, mainly of the late thirteenth and fourteenth centuries, indicate that these acts were more frequent between scholars than between scholars and townspeople, and that violent deaths among the latter were more often the result of acts perpetrated by other citizens, or by strangers having no fixed residence in Oxford, than by scholars.[67]

---

[64] Catto, 'Citizens, Scholars and Masters', *The History of the University of Oxford*, i. 168.

[65] Kibre, *The Nations in the Mediaeval Universities*, pp. 163–6.

[66] *Annals*, i. 48, where the year 1261 is incorrectly given for 1260.

[67] For the inquests of coroners at Oxford, see *Records of Mediaeval Oxford* (ed. H. E. Salter, Oxford, 1917), pp. 3–56, and *Oxford City Documents*, pp.150–74.

From this, it is apparent that the city of Oxford would have been a violent place in the fourteenth century even without the presence of the University.[68] In the broad perspective of the medieval universities, it would seem that the scholars of Oxford and Cambridge maintained a more effective level of co-operation with their citizen hosts than was achieved in some of the continental universities, especially those of a strong cosmopolitan character, where relations with the citizenry tended to be excessively turbulent. This was one respect in which the relative insularity of the English Universities may have proved advantageous.

II

THE UNIVERSITIES AND THE CHURCH

As institutions within the diocese, Oxford and Cambridge Universities were subject to the ordinary jurisdiction of the bishops of Lincoln and Ely respectively, and to the metropolitan jurisdiction of the archbishop of Canterbury. However, the relations of the English Universities with the ecclesiastical powers over three centuries cannot be considered in isolation; they must be seen as part of the general European pattern of such relations.

For university–episcopal relations in the Middle Ages, an analogy might be profitably borrowed from the annals of British history, and a distinction made between an early, embittered, 'imperial' era and a succeeding, more-constructive, 'commonwealth' phase.[69] The late medieval episcopate, or 'commonwealth' bishops as they may be termed, had come to accept the principle that the core of a

---

[68] See the conclusions of C. I. Hammer, Jr., 'Patterns of Homicide in a Medieval University Town: Fourteenth-Century Oxford', *Past and Present,* no. 78 (1978), pp. 3 ff. at p. 16: 'The presence of the university was felt in regard to crime as to other aspects of Oxford life, but here its impact should not be exaggerated'.

[69] For the substance of this paragraph, see Cobban, 'Episcopal Control in the Mediaeval Universities of Northern Europe', art. cit., p. 2; also Cobban, *The Medieval Universities,* pp. 75–6.

university was its autonomy. It was generally recognized that although the university might continue to function under the tenuous sway of an external authority the academic guild was an autonomous legal entity, standing outside the ecclesiastical structure. Within these terms of reference, it was the duty of the episcopate to nurse its university offspring towards maturity and full corporate independence. For example, it is hard to imagine that the fifteenth-century Scottish Universities could have survived at all without the sustained and enlightened treatment which they received at the hands of their episcopal sponsors. In the thirteenth and fourteenth centuries, however, episcopal authority was all too often channelled in a direction antithetical to the growth of university independence. This turbulent 'imperial' era was characterized by an episcopal outlook which tended to classify the north European universities as near ecclesiastical 'colonies', almost as the physical possessions of the local bishops and their representatives. The universities were not regarded as evolved organisms: rather they were viewed as natural ecclesiastical appendages, as the highest form of educational vehicle yet to emerge under the auspices of the Church. As such, they were to be integrated into the existing ecclesiastical structure and subjected to a permanent ecclesiastical tutelage. This dependent and static role cast for the universities was one wholly at odds with the ideas and aspirations of the guilds of masters and the associated scholars. For this reason, much of the history of university–episcopal relations is concerned with the complexities and stormy difficulties inherent in the slow transition from the 'imperial' to the 'commonwealth' phase.

All over northern Europe a *modus vivendi* had to be worked out between the academic guilds and the external ecclesiastical powers. The compromises achieved depended upon many factors, arranged in any one instance in one of a number of permutations: the university's date of origin, its size, geographical location and constitutional form, the statesmanlike qualities of the individuals involved, some or all of these factors might go towards determining the final outcome in any given case. Paris University provides both the earliest and the most dramatic example in European history of the struggle for university autonomy in the face of ecclesiastical domination.[70] In this instance, the pivotal point of ecclesiastical control was the authority claimed by the chancellor of the cathedral of Notre Dame, as an external official set above the masters' guild and acting as the delegate of the bishop of Paris, to grant or to withhold the teaching licence, without which no master could legitimately teach. After a prolonged conflict, marked by much bitterness and protracted litigation, the bull of Pope Gregory IX of 1231, *Parens Scientiarum*,[71] effectively stopped the attempt of the bishop and chancellor to gain dominance over the masters' guild, allowing a smoother growth towards the corporate independence of the university. Developments at Paris formed the key point of reference for the masters of Oxford and Cambridge in their own drive for emancipation from ecclesiastical tutelage. There was, however, a fundamental difference between the English and the Parisian situation. Originally, the chancellors of Oxford and Cambridge were regarded as the officials of the bishops of Lincoln and Ely, wielding delegated episcopal jurisdiction. But at an early stage in the thirteenth century, the chancellors of the English Universities were transformed into the elected heads of their magisterial guilds. From being episcopal officers set over and apart from the newly evolved Universities, the chancellors were now reckoned members of the masters' guilds and the personifications of their thrust for autonomous status. It is this identification of the English chancellors with the interests and objectives of the magisterial guilds which decisively differentiated them from their Parisian counterpart. Whereas the Paris chancellor had an uncertain affinity with the masters' guild and often seemed a barrier to notions of guild independence, the English chancellors were the embodiment of their universities in their negotiations with the external authorities.

It will be recalled that the Oxford chancellorship, which had a shadowy existence prior to 1209, was more firmly established in the years immediately following the legatine award of 1214 — certainly

---

[70] For the achievement of independence by the masters' guild at Paris from the powers of the bishop of Paris and the chancellor of Notre Dame Cathedral, see e.g. Cobban, *The Medieval Universities*, pp. 76–84.

[71] *Chartularium*, i. no. 79.

by August 1216 and probably by September 1215[72] — and that the Cambridge chancellorship was instituted by June 1225 at the latest, and perhaps as early as *c*. 1222.[73] At Oxford, there was initially an ambiguous phase, during which the bishop of Lincoln was unwilling to concede a full recognition to the designation and status of chancellor, because, by implication, it derogated from his own authority. The evidence for this is a statement made in 1295 by Oliver Sutton, bishop of Lincoln, to the effect that one of his predecessors, Hugh of Wells, had forbidden Robert Grosseteste, probably chancellor at some point between 1214 and 1216, to use the term 'chancellor' (*cancellarius*), allowing him to use only 'master of the schools' (*magister scolarum*).[74] This clash over the title to be accorded to the head of the masters' guild is an early indication of the lengthy jurisdictional sparring which centred on the University's claim to the independent standing of the chancellor. There is no evidence that the inception of the Cambridge chancellorship provoked a similar level of dispute over nomenclature with the then current bishop of Ely. The circumstances surrounding the institution of the chancellor's office at Cambridge, however, were rather different from those which existed at Oxford. The chancellorship had evolved piecemeal at Oxford and eventually presented the bishop of Lincoln with something of a *fait accompli*, in which he gradually acquiesced. It is to be supposed that at Cambridge the office was planned in imitation of that of Oxford, and that the bishop of Ely from the start gave his sanction to a development with which he would have been closely associated, given the intimate links between the embryonic University and the episcopal authority.[75] But while Cambridge's chancellorship was inaugurated amid harmonious relations between the University and the bishop of Ely, the fundamental issues regarding the method by which the chancellor was to be appointed and the ultimate position of the chancellor and

[72] See above, chapter 2, p. 48.

[73] See above, chapter 2, p. 57.

[74] *The Rolls and Register of Bishop Oliver Sutton, 1280–1299*, ed. cit., v. 60.

[75] See the comments of Hackett, *The Original Statutes of Cambridge University*, pp. 48, 59–60.

the University within the diocese that figured so prominently in Oxford's struggle for autonomous status were equally implicit in Cambridge's jurisdictional subjection to the see of Ely.

In the thirteenth and fourteenth centuries, the bishops of Lincoln and Ely generally shared the 'imperial' attitudes towards universities which, as outlined above, were common among the north European episcopate of the period: the English Universities, like any other ecclesiastical corporation within the diocese, had necessarily to submit to episcopal jurisdiction. There was no clear understanding by the bishops of Lincoln and Ely that the Universities would gravitate towards an antonomous status incompatible with ecclesiastical dominion. From the episcopal standpoint, it was clear that Oxford and Cambridge were to be absorbed into the ecclesiastical hierarchy of institutions and denied a natural progression towards independent corporate being. While the chancellors of the English Universities had emerged as the *de facto* heads of their Universities and had a growing practical jurisdictional authority, the ultimate episcopal position was that the chancellors exercised their powers only as a result of a commission from the bishop.[76] It is true that the bishops of Lincoln and Ely did not excessively intervene in the daily administration of the Universities of Oxford and Cambridge, but this practical abnegation did not nullify their legal right to do so. As the chancellors were the vicegerents of their diocesans, the bishops claimed it to be within their legal rights to supersede the chancellors' jurisdiction at any moment of their choosing. They were determined that none of their episcopal rights should lapse, and this entailed a constant vigilance so that unacceptable precedents were not established by the moves of the chancellors and regent masters. For these reasons, the bishops of Lincoln and Ely were insistent that they should continue to receive appeals directly

---

[76] For the Oxford situation, see e.g. Rashdall, *Universities*, iii. 114, and Lawrence, 'The University in State and Church', *The History of the University of Oxford*, i. 98; for Cambridge, see Peacock, *Observations on the Statutes of the University of Cambridge*, pp. 17–18 and 18, n. 4. In the Ely episcopal registers, prior to the late fourteenth century, the bishops repeatedly used the possessive form *universitatis nostre Cantebr'* (of *our* University of Cambridge): the registers are deposited in Cambridge University Archives.

from the chancellors' courts, and that they were entitled to carry out visitations of the Universities as of any institutions within the diocese.

These attitudes were increasingly antithetical to the aspirations of the chancellors and magisterial guilds of Oxford and Cambridge, who aimed to make their Universities as independent of ecclesiastical jurisdiction as Paris had become by the third decade of the thirteenth century. They sought entire freedom to elect their own officials, and to convert the *de facto* powers of the chancellors into a *de iure* authority, fully and universally recognized. In every way, the Universities considered that they had outgrown diocesan jurisdiction: they were to be treated no longer as ecclesiastical colonies, but as sovereign guilds — regulated by their own statutes, customs and privileges, and answerable only to secular government.

Six or even seven out of the nine bishops of Lincoln who occupied the see between 1209 and 1362 had previously been masters at Oxford, and two of them, Robert Grosseteste and Oliver Sutton, had passed the greater part of their adult lives in the University, Grosseteste having been one of its earliest chancellors.[77] Former association with the University did not, however, temper the attitudes of these Oxonians when they ascended to the bishopric of Lincoln: and all of them, in varying measure, adopted towards the University a hard paternalistic stance, designed to safeguard the rights of their episcopal office. It has been mentioned that in *c*.1214 the bishop of Lincoln, Hugh of Wells, would not permit Robert Grosseteste to use the title of 'chancellor' as this pertained to a cathedral dignitary, such as already existed in Lincoln Cathedral. When Grosseteste himself became bishop, he showed no inclination to make concessions to the University's aspirations for autonomy. He confirmed his right as bishop to control the granting of the teaching licence through the agency of the chancellor, he attempted to influence teaching arrangements in theology, and he opposed the University's own use of a common seal.[78] Grosseteste's successor as bishop, Henry of Lexington, continued this aggressive stance

---

[77] Lawrence, 'The University in State and Church', p. 99.

[78] Ibid., pp. 100–2. Rashdall's statement that 'so long as the see of Lincoln was filled by Robert Grosseteste – the most distinguished son that the infant

towards the University's claims to independence. In 1255, he obtained papal confirmation of his spiritual jurisdiction over all clerks in the town of Oxford,[79] and in 1257, he challenged the right of the University to make statutes binding on all of its members — a fundamental attack on the concept of guild autonomy.[80] His successor, Richard Gravesend, appears to have been more flexible in his dealings with the University; and when he was exiled following his support for Simon de Montfort and participation in the rebellion of 1264–5, the University was, for a period, free from episcopal restraint, and had the opportunity to reinforce its claims to independence.[81] However, the situation changed dramatically when Oliver Sutton succeeded Gravesend in 1280; and until the end of his episcopate in 1299 university–episcopal relations were strained by sharp jurisdictional feuding over the powers of chancellor and bishop in university affairs.

Sutton had been a regent master in arts at Oxford and had also studied canon and civil law. On becoming bishop of Lincoln, he meticulously applied in his diocesan administration and in his heavy handed tussles with the University the knowledge he had acquired by his legal training.[82] The three main areas of dispute during his episcopate centred on Sutton's claim to possess the right as bishop to subject the University to visitation, to receive appeals from the chancellor's court without hindrance from the chancellor and masters, and to control the appointment of the chancellor by insisting upon episcopal confirmation of the chancellor-elect. As

university had yet produced – almost unbroken harmony prevailed between the university and the diocesan', *Universities,* iii. 115, is in need of modification.

[79] *Snappe's Formulary,* p. 300.

[80] Lawrence, 'The University in State and Church', p. 105; Rashdall, *Universities,* iii. 116–17.

[81] Lawrence, 'The University in State and Church', p. 106; Rashdall, op. cit., iii. 118.

[82] For Sutton's career and disputes with Oxford University, see R. M. T. Hill, 'Oliver Sutton, Bishop of Lincoln, and the University of Oxford', *T.R.H.S.,* 4th ser., xxxi (1949), pp. 1 ff., and Hill's introduction to *The Rolls and Register of Bishop Oliver Sutton 1280–1299,* iii (1952), especially pp. xiii–xxiii, lxiv–lxxvii; also Hill, *Oliver Sutton* (Lincoln Minster Pamphlets, no. 4, 1950), especially pp. 3–5, 28–32. See further Lawrence, 'The University in State and Church', pp. 106–11, and Rashdall, op. cit., iii. 118 ff.

soon as Sutton became bishop, he denied the validity of a number of university customs, and in 1280, Oxford's sovereign body was moved to assert as legitimate rights the following four practices, allegedly based on immemorial custom: that a scholar could cite a lay defendant before the chancellor; that the chancellor had probate of the wills of all scholars who die within the University; that the right to investigate the moral failings of masters and scholars belonged to the regent masters; and that no master or scholar could be forced to plead in any court except that of the chancellor, with respect to contracts entered into within or without the University.[83]

A few months after his enthronement in 1281, Sutton tried to carry out a visitation of the University and met with vociferous opposition. He pressed on, however, and sought to enforce the penalties prescribed by canon law against a group of masters and scholars guilty of moral offences. The chancellor, Henry of Staunton, intervened and asserted that the right of visitation and correction of university members belonged to the chancellor alone, the bishop's role being confined to the hearing of such appeals as were permitted to go forward by the University. The wrangle was eventually submitted to the judgment of the archbishop of Canterbury, and Sutton had to make a few concessions, without which there was a danger that the University might have dispersed. Sutton again provoked much dissension, by his claim to exercise a direct appellate jurisdiction over the chancellor's court. The matter was highlighted by the case of Robert Baldock, a master of arts of the University, who had been deprived of his lodging by a decision of the chancellor's court. Baldock appealed to the bishop, and the chancellor retaliated by suspending the master's teaching licence.[84] Sutton intervened to aid Baldock, although with what success is unknown, for the final outcome of the dispute is cloaked in obscurity. The case reveals the entrenched attitudes of both parties. The University could not deny the ultimate right of appeal to the diocesan. It could, however, try to curtail the frequency with which it was exercised by insisting that appeals against decisions of the

[83] Gibson, *Statuta Antiqua,* pp. 96–7.

[84] *The Rolls and Register of Bishop Oliver Sutton,* v. 50–1.

chancellor's court should first be heard by the congregation of regents, then by the sovereign body — the congregation of regents and non-regents — and only in the final resort by the bishop.[85] In this way, the University sought to maintain as much legal autonomy as possible *vis-à-vis* its own members. From the bishop's standpoint, however, the loss of legitimate appeals was a detraction from the rights of the see of Lincoln and had to be resisted.

Probably the most serious matter for dispute with the University involving Sutton and his successors came to be the question of the method of appointment of the chancellor: that is to say, whether the University had the right to elect its own chancellor or only the right to nominate a candidate for presentation to the bishop, who would then make the actual appointment. Sutton regarded the university chancellorship as an office within the diocese just like the headship of any other ecclesiastical corporation.[86] The masters' guild might 'nominate' a candidate, but it was for the bishop to accept or reject the nominee according to the bishop's own judgment. The masters' guild, on the other hand, claimed the right to elect the chancellor, who, at the most, would be automatically confirmed in his office by the bishop. Moreover, the University asserted that the chancellor-elect should not be required to appear before the bishop in person: if necessary, at all, the confirmation should be done without delay, as soon as representatives informed him of the name of the master elected. These points remained at issue throughout Sutton's episcopate, and in those of his successors until the third quarter of the fourteenth century. Much shadow-boxing was indulged in by both parties over the appointment of the chancellor. Matters, however, took a sombre turn in 1350 when Bishop John Gynwell refused to confirm the election of William of Polmorva as chancellor. The University appealed to the archbishop of Canterbury, who ordered Gynwell to confirm the election. The bishop would not comply, and Archbishop Islip himself had to

[85] For this procedure, referred to by Sutton in 1290, see *Snappe's Formulary*, p. 46: for the regulation of appeals according to the university statutes, see Gibson, op. cit., pp. 91–5.

[86] See the comments of Hill, *The Rolls and Register of Bishop Oliver Sutton*, iii. p. lxix.

effect the confirmation.[87] When Bishop John Buckingham confirmed the election of William Courtenay as chancellor in 1367 he stated that he would not confirm any future chancellor unless that chancellor-elect appeared before him in person.[88] The University responded by turning to the papacy for assistance. In 1367, it obtained a privilege from Urban V, which, after so many years of intermittent, acrimonious struggle, dispensed with the need for episcopal confirmation of the chancellor-elect.[89] When Courtenay was succeeded by Adam Tonworth as chancellor in 1369, it would found that the papal privilege had not quashed the need for the bishop's commission of jurisdiction to be given to the new chancellor. This omission was remedied by a second privilege from Urban V, of 10 February 1370, which dispensed with the need for the bishop's commission as well as for his confirmation.[90] It may be said, therefore, that from 1370 Oxford University was exempt from the jurisdiction of the bishop of Lincoln.

Exemption from the jurisdiction of the bishop of Lincoln did not mean that the University of Oxford had a complete exemption from all ecclesiastical authority, for it was still subject to the metropolitan jurisdiction of the archbishop of Canterbury. However, by a bull of Boniface IX of 13 June 1395, the University claimed to have acquired a full emancipation from all ecclesiastical jurisdiction, including that of the archbishop of Canterbury.[91] Pressures to obtain such a bull had come mainly from the arts faculty, and the assistance of William Courtenay, archbishop of Canterbury, had been successfully solicited.[92] The exact circumstances surrounding

---

[87] Lawrence, 'The University in State and Church', pp. 111–12; Rashdall, op. cit., iii. 124; *Snappe's Formulary*, pp. 44–5.

[88] *Snappe's Formulary*, pp. 85–6.

[89] *Cal. Papal Registers* (Papal Letters), iv (1362–96), p. 66; the text is given in full in *Munimenta Academica*, i. 228–30 (the date is incorrectly stated as 1368).

[90] *Snappe's Formulary*, p. 83. For Bishop Buckingham's direction first to the archdeacon of Oxford's official on 4 May 1369 and then to the official of the bishop of Lichfield on 23 June 1369 to cite Adam Tonworth for acting as chancellor without due confirmation, see ibid., pp. 86–9.

[91] The bull of Boniface IX is printed ibid., pp. 144–6.

[92] Gibson, 'The University of Oxford', *V.C.H. Oxon.* iii, 1 ff. at 13; Rashdall, op. cit., iii. 128.

the acquisition of this bull are not entirely clear: and in a convocation held at St Paul's, London, in February 1397, it was renounced by representatives of Oxford's faculties of civil and canon law as a privilege which had been improperly obtained, and with the implication that it was a forgery.[93] In the following month, Richard II instructed the chancellor and masters, under threat of loss of their privileges, to make a public renunciation of the alleged exemption on the grounds that such an exemption would be a derogation of the rights of the crown and of archiepiscopal authority;[94] and in June of the same year, the king asserted that the right of visitation of the University belonged to the archbishop of Canterbury.[95] The matter of archiepiscopal visitation had come to the foreground with the appointment of Thomas Arundel as archbishop of Canterbury in 1396, his enthronement taking place on 18 February 1397.[96] Arundel was determined to assert archiepiscopal control over Oxford University and to carry out a thorough visitation in order to eradicate all lingering traces of Wyclifite and Lollard doctrines.[97] Although Wyclif had left the University in 1381 for his benefice at Lutterworth in Leicestershire, where he had died in 1384, Oxford was disturbed by heretical sentiment for about thirty years.

Wyclif's writings, both during his Oxford career and in his final three years at Lutterworth, constitute a devastating indictment of the entire ecclesiastical order.[98] His view of the real, though invisible church, as restricted to the elect — those in a state of grace

---

[93] *Snappe's Formulary,* pp. 104, 146–51.

[94] Ibid., pp. 104, 153–5.

[95] Ibid., pp. 104, 155–6.

[96] M. Aston, *Thomas Arundel* (Oxford, 1967), p. 229.

[97] E.g. ibid., pp. 375–6; Green, *A History of Oxford University,* p. 4.

[98] For Wyclif's doctrines, see e.g. G. Leff, *Heresy in the Later Middle Ages: the relation of heterodoxy to dissent c.1250–c.1450* (2 vols., Manchester, 1967), ii. ch. 7; K. B. McFarlane, *John Wycliffe and the Beginnings of English Nonconformity* (London, 1952), especially ch. 4; A. Kenny, *Wyclif* (Oxford, 1985); the essays by A. Kenny, M. Keen, N. Kretzmann, A. Hudson and G. Leff in *Wyclif in his Times* (ed. A. Kenny, Oxford, 1986); M. J. Wilks, 'The early Oxford Wyclif: Papalist or Nominalist?', *Studies in Church History,* v (1969), pp. 69 ff.

and predestined for salvation — was contrasted with the visible church as then established, which, for Wyclif, was an unreal church, rooted in a false authority. Because a proportion of those who governed the existing church must belong to the legion of the damned and, without grace, were unqualified to exercise dominion, the logical step was to reject the whole ecclesiastical hierarchy and to advocate the disestablishment and disendowment of the Church. Wyclif's thesis concerning predestination, which he refined from the works of a series of writers stretching back to St Augustine, also encompassed the papal office, which he regarded as, at the very least, unnecessary: he denied that the pope was the vicar of Christ, and argued that a pope who tolerated Church endowments was the Antichrist. When to notions of this kind were added his denial of transubstantiation and his promotion of the vernacular translation of the Bible, the cumulative force of Wyclif's onslaught on the late fourteenth-century Church is starkly evident. Wyclif was differentiated from most critics of the Church by the fact that, whereas the majority of those who denounced ecclesiastical abuses were prepared to accept the ultimate authority of the Church, Wyclif opposed that authority by direct appeal to the Bible and to his own philosophical and theological tenets. The extreme nature of his views brought Wyclif into conflict with the ecclesiastical hierarchy. In 1377, Pope Gregory XI condemned eighteen of his propositions, and ordered the chancellor of the University to suppress Wyclif's heresies in Oxford and to deliver him to the archbishop of Canterbury for examination.[99] In the event, the University compromised on the issue and Wyclif escaped with only warnings from the English episcopate.[100] At a provincial synod of May 1382, William Courtenay, archbishop of Canterbury, condemned twenty-four of Wyclif's propositions. The decree was published throughout the province of Canterbury and at Oxford,[101] although Wyclif had already left for Lutterworth, where he continued his venomous outpourings against the Church.

At the time of Arundel's enthronement as archbishop of

[99] McFarlane, op. cit., pp. 79-80; Gibson, 'The University of Oxford', p. 12.

[100] McFarlane, op. cit., pp. 81-2.

[101] Ibid., pp. 105 ff.; Gibson, 'The University of Oxford', p. 12.

Canterbury in 1397, Wyclif's writings were still circulating in Oxford. The University continued to harbour pockets of scholars who were sympathetic to Wyclif's views or to those of the Lollards, who acknowledged Wyclif as their inspirational source.[102] Merton housed a group of such sympathizers. Among the Lollards who were detained by the king at Beaumaris Castle in May 1395 were three fellows of the college, while another fellow was arrested at Bristol for defending Wyclif's doctrines on the Eucharist.[103] Arundel considered that he had strong grounds for making a visitation of the University so that all heretical sentiment might be expunged. His immediate plans in this direction had to be shelved when he was forced into exile in 1397. He returned in 1399 as one of the staunchest supporters of the Lancastrian regime of Henry IV, and, as archbishop of Canterbury, set out from 1407 to purge Oxford of heresy. He commanded that a strict watch be kept on the contents of disputations; and he established two boards of twelve members each, one for Oxford and one for Cambridge, to examine all Wyclifite and Lollard literature for evidence of heresy — a venture which must rank as one of the earliest instances of institutionalized censorship in England.[104] The Oxford board finally produced a list of 267 heresies in 1411.[105] In June of that year, five persons were appointed to administer an oath, to all members of the University, that they would disclaim the errors and heresies uncovered.[106] These steps were the prelude to an attempt by Arundel to realize his fixed purpose of carrying through a visitation of the University. This visitation he set in motion in the course of August 1411 amid the fiercest opposition and rioting from part of

---

[102] Leff's assertion that the Lollards 'after 1382 had no part in the life of Oxford' would appear to be an exaggeration: Leff, *Paris and Oxford Universities in the Thirteenth and Fourteenth Centuries*, p. 308.

[103] Aston, 'Lollardy and Sedition, 1381–1431', *Lollards and Reformers: Images and Literacy in Late Medieval Religion*, pp. 22–3; also Green, *A History of Oxford University*, pp. 17–18.

[104] Gibsón, 'The University of Oxford', p.13; *Snappe's Formulary*, pp. 99–100, 115, 118–19.

[105] *Snappe's Formulary*, pp. 128–30.

[106] Ibid., pp. 156–8.

the academic population.[107] Much confusion surrounds this event: it appears, however, that only a limited visitation was ever effected. The University's resistance to Arundel seems to have been due not so much to a defence of Wyclifite and Lollard opinion, although some members had a vested interest in this defence, as to the claim to immunity from archiepiscopal jurisdiction grounded in the disputed bull of Boniface IX of 1395.[108] The conflict between the University and Arundel was resolved through the mediation of Prince Henry, the future Henry V, and the University was obliged, for the present, to acknowledge the archbishop's right of visitation and to accept the revocation of the bull of Boniface IX which was ordered by Pope John XXIII in November 1411.[109] Eventually, the University acquired exemption from all ecclesiastical authority by a bull of Sixtus IV of 1479, and this was endorsed by a later bull, of Pope Innocent VIII.[110]

By contrast with Oxford's troubled situation, Cambridge University's dealings with the diocesan bishop of Ely and the archbishop of Canterbury were relatively pacific. Although the issues which had so perturbed Oxford and its ecclesiastical powers, such as the method of appointing the chancellor, the vexatious matter of appeals and the right of visitation, were common to Cambridge, they appear to have been contested with less heat and

---

[107] For a detailed account of Arundel's visitation, see ibid., pp. 101–15; see also Mallet, *A History of the University of Oxford*, i. 238–9. There seems to be little doubt that Arundel's exaggerated notion of the heretical problem at Oxford and his insensitivity on the issue of academic freedom helped to inflame the situation to the point of crisis: see R. G. Davies, 'Thomas Arundel as Archbishop of Canterbury 1396–1414', *J. Eccles. Hist.*, xxiv (1973), pp. 9 ff. at p. 19.

[108] Pantin, *Oxford Life in Oxford Archives*, p. 71; *Snappe's Formulary*, p. 114.

[109] For the submission of the University to Archbishop Arundel on 22 November 1411, and for the revocation of the bull of Boniface IX by John XXIII on 20 November 1411, see *Snappe's Formulary*, pp. 174–5, 176–9; for the University's letter of January 1412 to Arundel announcing that the bull of John XXIII had been published in the University, see ibid., pp. 179–80.

[110] The bull of Sixtus IV of 1479 is printed by Wood, *The History and Antiquities of the University of Oxford*, i. 632–5; for a paraphrase of the bull of Innocent VIII, contained in a summary of university privileges of between 1484 and 1523, see *Mediaeval Archives*, i. 360.

readier compromise. On the question of appeals, Cambridge had worked out an amicable *modus vivendi* with the bishop of Ely by 1264. In that year, Hugh de Balsham, bishop of Ely, conceded to the University the privilege whereby appeals were to proceed from the chancellor's court to the university assemblies, and only then to the bishop.[111] This was precisely the procedure for appeals which the Oxford masters advocated seventeen years later in their dispute with Bishop Sutton. It must not be supposed, however, that there were no further points of contention with the bishop of Ely concerning the jurisdiction of the chancellor's court after this appeals settlement of 1264. As late as 1392, the bishop claimed the right to remove to his court certain cases pending before the chancellor, an attempt which was quashed by order of Richard II.[112] Nevertheless, conflict in this area of appeals and in other disputed cases was not at Cambridge either as frequent or as intense as it was at Oxford. A similar comparison may be drawn in respect of the issue of episcopal or archiepiscopal visitation of the University. For example, Thomas Arundel, as archbishop of Canterbury, realized a thorough visitation of Cambridge University in September 1401, satisfying himself, among many other items, that the University was not a hotbed of heretical opinion. The visitation was achieved with the full co-operation of the chancellor and masters, and if there was opposition to the visitation, it was noticeably muted.[113] The contrast between Arundel's orderly and peaceful Cambridge visitation of 1401 and his turbulent and only half-completed visitation of Oxford in 1411 could not be more marked.

As at Oxford, so at Cambridge, much of the argument surrounding university autonomy came to focus upon the claim of the diocesan (in Cambridge's case, the bishop of Ely) to possess the right to confirm the election of the chancellor-elect. But this became a bone of contention very late on at Cambridge. Whereas Oxford obtained papal dispensation from the need for episcopal confirmation of the newly elected chancellor in 1367/70 after protracted wrangles over this matter extending from the thirteenth

[111] Hackett, *The Original Statutes of Cambridge University*, pp. 223–4.

[112] Rashdall, *Universities*, iii. 281.

[113] See the account of Arundel's visitation of 1401 in *Annals*, i. 147.

century, at Cambridge the issue seems to have come to prominence only from 1374. In that year, John de Donwich (Dunwich) was elected chancellor for a second time, and was confirmed by the new and extremely youthful bishop of Ely, Thomas Arundel, but without appearing in person and without taking the oath of canonical obedience.[114] In August of the same year, Donwich was cited by Nicholas Roos, the bishop's official, to render the oath of obedience to the bishop on pain of censure and deprivation. This was refused, and the case led to a suit in the court of Canterbury, where, eventually, judgment was given in favour of the bishop.[115] Donwich's successor, William Gotham, was confirmed as chancellor in 1376: there is no record of difficulties with this confirmation or of the exaction from Gotham of an oath of obedience. In 1378, however, when Arundel's own official, Richard Scrope, was elected chancellor, the bishop stated that although he would not insist on the oath of obedience on this occasion, he would reserve the right to exact it from Scrope's successors. The next chancellor, Eudo la Zouche, obtained a similar dispensation in 1380, because of his noble status. However, both John Burgh in 1384 and Richard Maycent in 1386 were required to take the oath of obedience.[116] Arundel appears to have experienced no further opposition over the canonical oath before he left the see of Ely for the archbishopric of York in 1388. The last chancellor to be confirmed by the bishop and to render the oath of obedience was Richard Billingford, who was confirmed by Bishop John Fordham in 1400.[117] In 1401, the need of the chancellor-elect of Cambridge University to be confirmed by the bishop of Ely was dispensed with by a bull of Boniface IX[118]: Cambridge had achieved the exemption from diocesan jurisdiction which Oxford had acquired some thirty years previously.

[114] Ibid., i. 112.

[115] For details of this affair, see Aston, *Thomas Arundel*, pp. 28–30.

[116] For the cases of Gotham, Scrope, la Zouche, Burgh, and Maycent, see ibid., pp. 31–2; see also *Annals*, i. 116–17, 118, 128.

[117] *Annals*, i. 146.

[118] *Cal. Papal Registers (Papal Letters)*, v (1396–1404), pp. 370–1.

In this matter of Cambridge University and diocesan jurisdiction, it needs to be affirmed that the royal college of the King's Hall occupied, as in so many other respects, a somewhat anomalous position. As an institution within Ely diocese, the King's Hall and the King's Scholars were subject to ordinary diocesan regulation concerning such business as the appropriation of churches, or the licensing of individual fellows to choose their own confessors, to say mass within the college or to erect private oratories.[119] However, the King's Hall and its Scholars appear to have been exempt from the visitatorial powers of Ely and Canterbury during the time that the University as a whole and its several colleges were subject to episcopal and archiepiscopal visitation. As founder, the king served as sole visitor to the college, a duty which devolved in practice upon the holder of the office of the royal chancellor.[120] And in matters of a non-spiritual nature the king jealously guarded his rights against encroachment by the ecclesiastical authorities. This is splendidly illustrated by the letters patent of 14 July 1383[121] whereby the king commissioned Thomas Arundel, bishop of Ely, to visit the King's Hall in order to investigate the alleged abuses which had arisen during the unhappy wardenship of Simon Neylond.[122] The document makes it unequivocally plain that Arundel was to act not in his capacity as bishop, but as king's commissioner, wielding delegated royal powers.[123] The jurisdictional rights over the King's Hall and the King's Scholars, held solely by the crown, are further

---

[119] Cobban, *The King's Hall*, pp. 100–1. For instances of licences allowed to individual King's Scholars, see the Register of Thomas de l'Isle, bishop of Ely, 1345–61, CUL/UA, EDR, G/1/1, fos. 9v, 38v, 42v, and the Register of Thomas Arundel, bishop of Ely, 1374–88, CUL/UA, EDR, G/1/2, fo. 5v.

[120] On this point, see Phillimore, *The Ecclesiastical Law of the Church of England*, ed. cit., ii. 1452; also Cobban, op. cit., p. 102.

[121] See the Register of Thomas Arundel, fo. 106v.

[122] Warden of the King's Hall from 6 October 1377 until his removal on 19 May 1385.

[123] Arundel was to visit: 'custodem, scolares et ministros eiusdem collegii in propria persona vestra nomine nostro ac iure regio . . .': the Register of Thomas Arundel, fo. 106v. See also Cobban, op. cit., p. 102.

protected in a later passage where it is stipulated that Arundel was not to presume to exercise any ordinary jurisdiction over the college, its warden, scholars, or 'ministers': nor was that visitation to be treated in any way as a precedent.[124] In conjunction with the fact that there is no other recorded instance of a visitation of the King's Hall by a bishop of Ely, this evidence points to the conclusion that throughout its life the King's Hall remained the exclusive concern of the crown: that the bishop's jurisdiction did not extend over it except in respect of the kind of diocesan business itemized above.

Moreover, the available evidence strongly suggests that the King's Hall and its Scholars were exempt from the metropolitan visitation of the archbishop of Canterbury.[125] This is negatively demonstrated by an entry in Arundel's Canterbury register concerning the archiepiscopal visitation of the University in 1401.[126] On this occasion, Arundel first visited the chancellor and the University in person, and then the several colleges were visited by commissaries. Of the eight Cambridge colleges, only two — Corpus Christi and the King's Hall — were not visited. C. H. Cooper has acutely drawn attention to the fact that in this year the master of Corpus, Richard Billingford, was also chancellor of the University.[127] Consequently, it may very well be that the archbishop considered that, through his personal visitation and questioning of its master, the college had been vicariously visited. In the case of the King's Hall, however, the explanation would appear to be that the college was not visited simply because it was exempt from archiepiscopal jurisdiction.

---

[124] Ibid. It seems that in Ely 'as in other dioceses, separate visitation records were kept and have not survived': D. M. Owen, 'Ely Diocesan Records', *Studies in Church History*, i (1964), pp. 176 ff. at p. 177. The fact that Arundel's commission concerning the King's Hall is to be found in his register tends to emphasize that this was an exceptional type of episcopal visitation.

[125] On this topic, see Cobban, op. cit., pp. 103–4.

[126] The entry is printed by I. J. Churchill, *Canterbury Administration* (2 vols., London, 1933), ii. 152.

[127] *Annals*, i. 147, n. 1.

As far as can be determined, the King's Hall never acquired a formal bull of exemption from ecclesiastical visitation. Perhaps the explanation of its status in respect of ecclesiastical authority is to be sought in its origins. Because the King's Hall evolved from a detachment of the chapel royal set in the University of Cambridge, it is reasonable to suppose that it gained by transmission the privileges and immunities of that body, of which it was the academic offshoot. From the *Liber regie capelle* and the Black Book of Edward IV, it is known that members of the chapel and the household of the monarch were exempt from episcopal and archiepiscopal jurisdiction, being directly subject to the jurisdiction of the dean of chapel.[128] When Edward II established his chapel 'colony' in Cambridge, it was most probably endowed *a priori* with the same exemptions from ecclesiastical authority as those belonging to the chapel as a whole. These would have been automatically transferred to the college founded by Edward III. Throughout the period in which the Universities and their colleges lay within the episcopal and archiepiscopal orbit, the King's Hall would appear to have been the only college at either University to have enjoyed this immunity from ecclesiastical supervision. In 1445 Henry VI obtained a bull from Eugenius IV granting to his Cambridge foundation, King's College, exemption from the ecclesiastical jurisdictions of Ely and Canterbury and placing the college under the visitatorial powers of the bishop of Lincoln.[129] But this exemption was inexplicably acquired when the University and its colleges were already exempt from the jurisdiction of Ely and Canterbury. This being so, the case of King's College in no way detracts from the uniqueness of the King's Hall in respect of ecclesiastical immunity.

It is ironical that in the year in which Cambridge University was effectively exempted from diocesan jurisdiction, 1401, the University was the recipient of a metropolitan visitation by Archbishop Arundel. As previously indicated, this was carried

[128] See *Liber regie capelle*, ed. cit., p. 15; also A. R. Myers, *The Household of Edward IV* (Manchester, 1959), p. 134.

[129] See J. Saltmarsh, 'King's College', *V.C.H. Camb.* iii. 377.

through with the compliance of the chancellor and masters. The visitation, however, would have strengthened the gathering conviction at Cambridge in the early part of the fifteenth century that university autonomy was incompatible with submission to external ecclesiastical dominion, and that the exemption from episcopal jurisdiction won in 1401 must be crowned with the nullification of archiepiscopal control.

It is true that the issue of university emancipation was fought at Cambridge with less sustained urgency than at Oxford. In this connection, one or two observations may be advanced. It has been argued in chapter 4 that the Oxford colleges were more heavily subject to ecclesiastical influences than were their Cambridge equivalents, of which seven had secular founders, and in which there was generally maintained a policy of allowing beyond what was absolutely necessary only strictly limited intervention on the part of both the chancellor and the bishop of Ely.[130] It seems clear that the ecclesiastical impact from diverse quarters must have been an ever-present reality to the fellows of the Oxford colleges, a fair number of whom were also regent masters in the University and would themselves have been involved in the drive for autonomy. At Cambridge, on the other hand, the practical manifestations of ecclesiastical control can scarcely have made much impression upon the daily lives of the college fellows. And this collegiate distinction between Oxford and Cambridge may have some bearing upon the different intensities with which the contest for autonomy was conducted at the English Universities. The relative slowness of the emancipation movement at Cambridge may not have been entirely or at all the result of lethargy or a lack of initiative on the part of the Cambridge masters. If the collegiate evidence is anything to go by, it seems probable that the issue of ecclesiastical jurisdiction assumed a more theoretical complexion at Cambridge than it did at Oxford. This being so, the Cambridge masters had no impelling, insupportable grievances to provide them with reasons for combating the lenient and distant powers of Ely and Canterbury. On the other hand, Cambridge in the fifteenth century was emerging as a university of some European consequence. An

[130] For this subject, see above, p. 135.

293

illustration of Cambridge's growing reputation is the revealing fact that during the Council of Constance the cardinals in 1417 took the trouble to send a special letter to the University to inform it of their choice of a new pontiff: as far as is known, there was no corresponding announcement to Oxford University.[131] As a university now prominent upon the European stage, Cambridge could not afford to lag behind in this matter of university independence, even if there was no question of its having to be liberated from a crushing burden of ecclesiastical dominance. It is consequently very understandable that in the early fifteenth century the Cambridge masters should have aspired to a final definition of the position of the University with respect to all ecclesiastical authority.

This final definition was achieved as a result of the Barnwell Process of 1430. In July 1430, Pope Martin V delegated the prior of Barnwell and John Depyng, canon of Lincoln, to investigate the University's claim to exemption from all ecclesiastical jurisdiction.[132] In the event, the prior conducted the inquiry on his own and delivered his judgment in favour of the University. This was confirmed by a bull of Pope Eugenius IV of September 1433 whereby the University was declared to be exempt from all episcopal and archiepiscopal jurisdiction.[133]

A number of historians have argued that, while the issue of ecclesiastical exemption was not absolutely settled until the Barnwell Process, Cambridge University had been granted a theoretical exemption from all ecclesiastical authority by the papal

---

[131] For an analysis of this topic, see W. Ullmann, 'The University of Cambridge and the Great Schism', *Journal of Theological Studies,* ix (1958), pp. 53 ff. at pp. 65 ff.: an edition of the cardinals' letter is given at pp. 75 ff.

[132] *Annals,* i. 182.

[133] Ibid., i. 183, 185. For the original documentation connected with the Barnwell Process, see *Processus Barnwellensis ex mandato Martini Papae V cum bullis Johannis XXII et Bonifacii IX,* dated 10 October 1430, CUL/UA, Luard, no. 108; a printed translation is given by Heywood, *Collection of Statutes for the University and the Colleges of Cambridge,* pp. 181 ff. For the confirmatory bull of Eugenius IV of 18 September 1433, see the copy preserved in CUL/UA, luard, no. 114; see also *Cal. Papal Registers* (Papal Letters), viii (1427–47), pp. 484–5.

award of John XXII of 9 June 1318.[134] But there is nothing in the text of this papal letter which could possibly be construed as supporting evidence for this interpretation. The apostolic letter of 9 June 1318 confirmed for Cambridge all the rights and privileges inherent in the status of *studium generale* as then understood. In the language of the award, the *studium* was to enjoy all the rights of a legitimately constituted university (*universitas legitime ordinata*).[135] These are not further defined. One may suppose, however, that contemporaries would have fully comprehended the nature and extent of rights commonly pertaining to every legally established *studium generale*.[136] But the relationship of European *studia generalia* with external bodies, whether episcopal, archiepiscopal, civic, regal, or imperial, were so diverse that they could not be reduced to a simple formula, and could not possibly be deduced from the general phrase *universitas legitime ordinata*. The situation regarding continental universities such as Salamanca and Avignon, to take only two from many examples,[137] clearly demonstrates that

[134] For this bull of John XXII and Cambridge's legal status, see above, chapter 2, pp. 59 ff. Commenting upon the award of Pope John XXII, J. Lamb, the Cambridge historian, wrote: 'The University acquired a full exemption from the ecclesiastical and spiritual power of the bishop of the diocese, and of the archbishop of the province; and these powers as far as members of the University were concerned, were vested in the chancellor or rector of that body. This privilege was, however, constantly disputed': *A Collection of Letters, Statutes and other Documents from the manuscript library of Corpus Christi College illustrative of the history of the University of Cambridge* (ed. J. Lamb, London, 1838), introductory remarks, p. xviii. Dr Lamb's commentary has been printed by C. H. Cooper and paraphrased by J. B. Mullinger: *Annals*, i. 77, and Mullinger, *The University of Cambridge*, i. 145–6. The same conclusion is expressed by J. P. C. Roach in his article on the University of Cambridge: Roach, 'The University of Cambridge', *VC.H. Camb.* iii. 154. Rashdall, in his discussion of the award, does not draw attention to the point of ecclesiastical exemption.

[135] See the edition of the text by Cobban, 'Edward II, Pope John XXII and the University of Cambridge', art. cit., pp. 76–8.

[136] Apart from the *ius ubique docendi*, the theoretical academic concept frequently violated in practice, the most important of these rights was the privilege of dispensation from residence in their living for beneficed clergy in order that they may attend a *studium generale* for a specified duration. On the *ius ubique docendi*, see above, chapter 1, pp. 4–6.

[137] Cobban, *The King's Hall*, pp. 107–8.

freedom from episcopal or archiepiscopal authority was not a right inherent in the fourteenth-century concept of a *studium generale*. For this exemption, a university required an express papal award. Therefore, in the case of Cambridge, that there was ecclesiastical exemption cannot be inferred from the fact that there was a confirmation of rights common to every fully constituted *studium generale*.

Nor is it in any way possible to extract a meaning of ecclesiastical exemption from that clause in the award of John XXII which confirms all previous papal or royal privileges and indults. There is no papal award to the Univerity of the thirteenth or fourteenth centuries from which an exemption could (or can) be inferred. The likelihood is that the 'papal privileges' of the award were those granted to the University by Gregory IX in 1233,[138] this being the earliest known papal recognition of the University. Likewise, an examination of all royal grants made to the University before 1318 leads to the same conclusion.

It is nevertheless true that the award of John XXII was dramatically associated with the Barnwell Process. The letter was solemnly produced by the University in 1430 during the legal proceedings in the chapter-house at Barnwell. It was presented as documentary evidence of papal confirmation of the alleged bulls of Honorius I and of Sergius I.[139] By this association, it became an important exhibit in the University's claim to exemption from ecclesiastical jurisdiction, which rested upon the twin bases of custom and the fabricated papal awards of the seventh century.[140] It

---

[138] *Register Gregory IX,* i. 779, no. 1389.

[139] The alleged bulls of Honorius I of 624 and of Sergius I of 689 are preserved in Cambridge University Archives: CUL/UA, Luard, no. 115. They are reproduced in the Cambridge *Historiola* in *Thomae Sprotti Chronica,* ed. cit., pp. 253, 255, and are printed by Dyer, *Privileges,* i. 58–60.

[140] The award of John XXII was presented in a public instrument on 9 October 1430 in the chapter-house at Barnwell along with the bull of Boniface IX of 1401, the forged bulls, and other statutes and muniments. This written evidence was furnished as documentary proof of Cambridge's claim to exemption from all ecclesiastical authority: *Processus Barnwellensis,* and for translation Heywood, *Collection of Statutes,* pp. 181 ff., especially pp. 196–205. In its petition to Pope Martin V, the University claimed that the chancellor '. . . has usually exercised ecclesiastical and spiritual jurisdiction in taking cognisance and of deciding causes and matters which relate . . . to members of the University':

was alleged that the original bulls of Honorius and Sergius had been lost but that the University possessed accurate copies.[141] These forgeries purport to confer on the University a full exemption from the ecclesiastical powers of any archbishop, bishop or archdeacon, or of any of their officials. These bulls formed the core of the Univerity's case for exemption from ecclesiastical control. Accepting the validity of these bulls and acknowledging the chancellor's customary exercise of ecclesiastical and spiritual jurisdiction, the prior upheld the University's claim to independence.

In this matter of Cambridge's exemption from ecclesiastical jurisdiction, it is evident that the apostolic letter of 1318 has acquired significance only by a deliberate and false historical association.[142] For it is apparent that the Cambridge masters could link the phrase in the letter confirming all former papal awards with the forged bulls of Honorius and Sergius. It is not known when these forgeries were perpetrated, but a reasonable guess would be the first quarter of the fifteenth century in the years immediately following Archbishop Arundel's metropolitan visitation of the University. However this may be, it is clear that the later construction placed by the Cambridge masters upon the letter of 1318, linking it with the forged papal bulls at the time of the Barnwell Process, could not possibly have been placed upon it by

this petition is reported in *Processus Barnwellensis;* see also Heywood, op. cit., pp. 184–6. This claim was incorporated in the third article delivered by William Wraby, proctor, representing the University before the prior of Barnwell as papal delegate. The other proctors were Ralph Duckworth, M.A., John Athill (atte Hille) and William Gull (Heywood, p. 182, gives 'Tull'), and the chancellor was John Holbroke. The claim was further reinforced by the testimony of John Dynne, the first and oldest of the seven witnesses furnished by the University. This witness, aged seventy-nine, claimed that when archbishops or bishops of Ely came to Cambridge they 'totally superseded and omitted the use and exercise of ecclesiastical jurisdiction at the request of the chancellor of the University for the time being, as far as regarded the persons who were subject to the said chancellor': *Processus Barnwellensis;* Heywood, op. cit., p. 193.

[141] Information contained in the University's petition to Martin V: *Processus Barnwellensis;* Heywood, op. cit., p. 186.

[142] Cobban, *The King's Hall,* p. 111.

Edward II, Pope John XXII, or the corporation of masters in June 1318.

If Cambridge was more laggard than Oxford in seeking emancipation from ecclesiastical tutelage, then it is at first sight surprising that it achieved a complete exemption, papally confirmed in 1433, some forty-six years before Oxford unequivocally received a similar exemption in 1479, the exemption granted by Boniface IX in 1395 having been hotly contested in England and subsequently revoked by the papacy in 1411. The explanation would seem to lie in the deeper involvement of Oxford with heresy. It is true that Cambridge University was not entirely innocent of Wyclifite and Lollard opinion. Lollard debates, which included the topic of the use of images in worship, were, apparently, held at Cambridge in the 1390s.[143] Yet although Cambridge did not remain wholly untouched by the spread of heretical ideas (it would have been remarkable had it done so), it nevertheless maintained a broad orthodoxy in the late fourteenth and fifteenth centuries.[144] This circumstance had the effect of increasing the flow of influential patronage towards Cambridge in the late medieval period. And it also partly explains why a complete ecclesiastical exemption was realized earlier at Cambridge than at Oxford. Because of the persistent traces of heresy at Oxford, the continuation of the custodial role of the Church over the University was thought necessary. If it was reckoned, however, that heresy had been extinguished at Oxford when complete exemption was granted in 1479, the assumption was manifestly misplaced. Heretical thought was still a problem which disturbed the University in the final two decades of the fifteenth century, as was agonisingly evidenced by John Russell, bishop of Lincoln.[145]

The protracted struggle between the Oxford adherents of Wyclifite and Lollard doctrines and the authorities of Church and State illustrates the ultimate constraints which were placed upon freedom of thought in the medieval English Universities. For the purposes of intellectual training, a good deal of latitude was

---

[143] Aston, 'Lollard Women Priests?', *Lollards and Reformers,* pp. 49 ff. at p. 55.

[144] J. A. F. Thomson, *The Later Lollards 1414–1520* (Oxford, 1965), pp. 213–14.

[145] Ibid., p. 218.

permitted. Because of the adversarial nature of the disputation, propositions of a radical import were frequently advanced. As long as this was seen to be an essential part of the teaching process, the matter was of no consequence. But an entirely different situation arose when university lecturers used their positions consistently to publicize views which were disruptive of the status quo. The ecclesiastical and secular authorities expected the Universities to conform to the broad spectrum of orthodox opinion. The high degree of autonomy which Oxford and Cambridge enjoyed was conditional upon their continuance as intellectual supports for the established norms of Church and State. In this sense, the masters of Oxford and Cambridge were to contribute to the stability of the social order. The Wyclifite episode at Oxford and the repression which followed underline the vulnerability of an English medieval university to external interference when the tolerated limits of dissension were deemed to have been breached. Attention will now turn, in chapter 8, from the external relations of the English Universities and towards their internal composition, and will take the form of an analysis of the component sections of the academic populations of Oxford and Cambridge as they evolved over three centuries.

Chapter 8

The Academic Community

It is generally true to say that far more can be discovered about the endowed personnel of the English academic community than about those who lived in unendowed circumstances. This is so because stabilized living in permanent institutions in a medieval university was normally more productive of archival material than was the case with transient residence. For this reason, the problems of determining the social status and conditions of life of the mass of students and masters domiciled in the unendowed halls and hostels and, before attachment to a hall, hostel or college became compulsory, in private lodgings in the houses of townspeople or in taverns are among the most intractable of the problems inherent in the study of the English academic community in the Middle Ages. Other such problems — those relating to the changing dimensions of the populations of the English Universities in the later medieval period and to the geographical areas of recruitment — have been explored in chapters 3 and 4 respectively, and need not be further examined here.

It may be asked whether the typical English medieval undergraduate was materially poor in any appreciable sense, and whether there were provisions at Oxford and Cambridge to ensure that student poverty was not an insuperable obstacle to academic achievement. One of the chief sources for material to illumine these matters is the substantial body of model student letters found in the formularies and writing manuals of the professional *dictatores*, who practised and taught *dictamen*, the art of composing letters and formal documents.[1] While the majority of these student letters are

---

[1] On student letters, see the seminal study by C. H. Haskins, *Studies in Mediaeval Culture* (Cambridge, 1929), ch. 1; see also the collection of model letters of the Oxford *dictatores*, many of which relate to students, *Oxford Formularies*, ii. 331–450.

not originals, being models framed by the practitioners of *dictamen*, their stereotyped contents presumably broadly represent the kind of problems confronting the average student. The most persistent theme coursing through these letters is the lack of money,[2] from which numerous related hardships are said to stem. With much rhetorical embellishment, the letters complain that students often suffer from a shortage of food, heat, clothes, bedding, books, parchment, and so on, and that they are frequently ill, are sometimes robbed and are commonly exposed to the avaricious malpractices of townspeople, with whom conflict might ensue, leading to a legal imbroglio and punishment.[3] It can scarcely be denied that the English medieval student was subject to levels of discomfort and insecurity deemed to be insupportable by present-day standards, but caution is required before accepting this letter evidence at face value. In particular, the plea of student poverty has too often been admitted without a proper consideration of relevant mitigating circumstances. Because student letters repeatedly emphasize the shortage of money, it should not necessarily be assumed that the majority of students were poverty-stricken or anything like it. A student who wrote such a letter might be the victim of one of the recurrent scarcities of coin which afflicted medieval English society;[4] and if a shortfall in the availability of coin coincided with years of bad harvests and sharply rising prices, the student might well be financially embarrassed for a period, but not, in any real sense, reduced to the level of poverty.[5] There are, however, more immediate factors which might account for a temporary lack of ready cash. It sometimes arose from the unwillingness of parents or guardians to supply more money until the student had put a curb upon financial extravagance and had cultivated sounder budgeting habits; or it may be that reports of

---

[2] Haskins, op. cit., pp. 7–14 and notes.

[3] On the frequency of student imprisonment, see e.g. the situation at the medieval University of Paris in Kibre, *Scholarly Privileges in the Middle Ages*, chs. 4, 5, 6.

[4] See E. F. Jacob, 'English University Clerks in the later Middle Ages: the Problem of Maintenance', *B.J.R.L.*, xxix (1946), pp. 304 ff. at p. 306.

[5] See the comments of Cobban, *The Medieval Universities*, p. 197.

misconduct or unsatisfactory academic progress had caused relatives or patrons to hold back further instalments of monetary assistance; or problems at home may have led to a hiatus in the sending of much-needed cash;[6] or an arts student, who lived in an Oxford hall or a Cambridge hostel, might be held on a tight financial rein by the principal to whom a parent or guardian had entrusted the undergraduate's allowance.[7]

It is, then, reasonable to suppose that while the main feature of student letters is the plea for money, the periodic shortage of ready cash does not imply a state of grinding poverty for the majority of undergraduates. Many of them had reserves at a distance, from which they could draw to alleviate a temporary monetary crisis. The view that the average English medieval student lived on the margins of poverty is not one which accords with the ascertainable data. It is almost certain that before 1500 the majority of students, both in England and on the Continent, were of intermediate social status.[8] Oxford and Cambridge recruited, in the rural area, from the lesser gentry, from the wealthier peasant and yeoman class and from the sons of the officials of village and manorial society, including stewards, bailiffs and reeves; in the urban sector, they recruited from merchant and artisan families and from the families of lesser and greater property-owners; and from both urban and rural areas, they recruited from the sons of government officials at all levels.[9] Before 1500, a small proportion of students were of noble birth, and these will be discussed below. But, by comparison with the notable contingents of privileged nobles at the universities of southern Europe or in the late medieval German Universities, the aristocratic involvement in pre-sixteenth-century Oxford and

[6] For examples of reasons for monetary delay, see Haskins, op. cit., pp. 14 ff.; Jacob, art. cit., p. 307, prints a letter in which money is denied because of ill-conduct; also in *Oxford Formularies*, ii. 360–1.

[7] Jacob, art. cit., pp. 306–7; also Salter, 'An Oxford Hall in 1424', *Essays in History presented to R. L. Poole*, p. 422. The more-mature students of law probably managed their own finances.

[8] See the remarks of Rashdall, *Universities*, iii. 408, and Cobban, op. cit., p. 198.

[9] See the useful comments of Aston et al., 'The Medieval Alumni of the University of Cambridge', pp. 50–1.

Cambridge was insufficient to qualify, to any marked degree, the mainly middling social derivation of the academic population.

It is undeniable, however, that there were at the English Universities genuinely poor scholars, as there were at those of continental Europe.[10] Poor scholars were probably to be found most commonly among the younger members of arts faculties. For this reason, colonies of poor scholars seem to have been more numerous in the universities of northern Europe than in those of southern Europe, where the faculties of arts were smaller and the students more affluent.[11] From sample investigations, embracing the Universities of Paris between 1425 and 1494, Vienna between 1377 and 1413, Leipzig between 1409 and 1430 and Freiburg between 1508 and 1514, it would appear that the proportion of the academic community which can be classified as 'poor students' (*pauperes*) ranged from about 17 to 25 per cent.[12] Here, it needs to be borne in mind that 'poverty' was a matter of definition, the criteria for which varied from university to university.[13] The poverty threshold would have been higher in universities with a significant intake of students from elevated backgrounds than in the universities with a uniformly lower social mix.

In the English Universities, as elsewhere, the term 'poor scholar' is encountered as a stereotype in college records, implying no more

[10] For the concept of student poverty, see the valuable studies of J. Paquet, 'L'universitaire "pauvre" au moyen âge: problèmes, documentation, questions de méthode', *The Universities in the Late Middle Ages*, ed. cit., pp. 399 ff.; 'Recherches sur l'universitaire "pauvre" au moyen âge, *Revue belge de philologie et d'histoire*, lvi (1978), pp. 301 ff.; 'Coût des études, pauvreté et labeur: fonctions et métiers d'étudiants au moyen âge', *History of Universities*, ii (1982), pp. 15 ff.

[11] E.g. Verger, *Les universités au moyen âge*, pp. 173–4.

[12] For the Paris, Vienna and Leipzig investigation, see A. L. Gabriel, 'The English-German Nation at the University of Paris from 1425–1494', *Garlandia: Studies in the History of the Mediaeval University* (Notre Dame, Indiana, 1969), pp. 167 ff. at pp. 176, 186–7; for the Freiburg investigation, see J. M. Fletcher, 'Wealth and Poverty in the Medieval German Universities', *Europe in the Late Middle Ages* (ed. J. R. Hale, J. R. L. Highfield and B. Smalley, London, 1965), pp. 410 ff. at p. 433.

[13] For the various criteria governing student poverty, see Paquet, 'Recherches sur l'universitaire "pauvre" au moyen âge', pp. 306–18.

than a scholar who is unable to support himself for the duration of a lengthy course of study without some measure of financial assistance.[14] 'Income ceilings' were prescribed in the statutes of most English colleges of the fourteenth and fifteenth centuries. These stipulated the maximum personal income compatible with the retention of a fellowship, and they demonstrate that a substantial proportion of fellows were expected to succeed to property or to ecclesiastical livings.[15] It was clearly assumed that most college fellows would have a source of independent income. By means of 'income ceilings', however, founders sought to ensure that provision would be made for scholars of modest resources, and not for those who already had sufficient finances to sustain them through the lengthy courses of study leading to the M.A. or to degrees in the superior faculties. Balliol College, Oxford, was founded expressly for 'poor scholars';[16] and New College, All Souls and Magdalen at Oxford, and King's College at Cambridge, were said to be founded for 'poor and indigent scholars'.[17] Despite this terminology, all these colleges were, in fact, designed for scholars of average means, who could not be described as 'poor' according to any literal interpretation of that word. At New College, fellows who were unable to meet the heavy degree expenses, and had no friend or colleague to assist them financially, might receive supplementary allowances, making it possible for them to obtain the degree.[18] However, such fellows cannot be categorized as 'poverty-stricken': they lacked only the money necessary for the attainment of their degrees. That the phrase 'poor and indigent scholars' had a somewhat elastic interpretation may be deduced from the results of an analysis of the social origins of 937 scholars at New College between *c*. 1380 and *c*. 1500. It was found that 61.4

[14] See Rashdall, op. cit., iii. 411; also J. A. W. Bennett, *Chaucer at Oxford and at Cambridge* (Oxford, 1974), p. 117.

[15] For detailed information on 'income ceilings', see Cobban, *The King's Hall*, p. 146, n. 1.

[16] *Oxford Balliol Deeds*, p. 280.

[17] *Statutes*, i. ch. 5, 1; i. ch. 7, 11; ii. ch. 8, 5; *Camb. Docs.*, ii. 481.

[18] *Statutes*, i. ch. 5, 51–3; see also R. S. Rait, *Life in the Medieval University* (Cambridge, 1912), p. 76.

per cent of these scholars were recruited from the families of rural smallholders, 21.7 per cent from the middle to upper ranks of urban society and 12.5 per cent from the gentry. Only 0.1 per cent came from a background of serfdom and only 0.1 per cent from families of urban labourers.[19]

Some founders of English colleges had the intention of making provision for the instruction of poor youths in grammar. If these poor students made good academic progress, they might be promoted to the status of scholar and gain full membership of the society. Such arrangements were made at Peterhouse and Clare College, Cambridge, and at Merton and Queen's College, Oxford. But the case of Merton apart, it is doubtful whether these statutory objectives amounted to very much in practice. For a long time in these colleges, precious resources could ill be spared from the primary role of maintaining the complement of fellows, and there was therefore, during that time, generally only a minimal revenue for charitable purposes.[20]

Overall, there seems to have been little in the way of effective formal provision for genuinely poor scholars on the part of either the university or college authorities. Perforce, they mostly had to subsist on the margins of the academic community. Cambridge's fourteenth-century statutes decreed that regent masters were to make no difficulties about admitting scholars to the University who could convincingly swear to their impoverished condition.[21] This implies, though the statutes did not so state, that dispensations from certain fees would be conceded to such entrants. Apart from meagre institutional assistance, there were other possible avenues by which poor scholars could improve their material lot. They might become casual labourers within the university precincts. The accounts of the King's Hall, Cambridge, for example, record

---

[19] G. F. Lytle, 'The Social Origins of Oxford Students in the Late Middle Ages: New College, *c*. 1380 – *c*. 1510', *The Universities in the Late Middle Ages*, p. 432; also Lytle, *Oxford Students and English Society: c.1300–c.1510* (unpublished Ph.D. thesis, Princeton University, 1976), p. 156.

[20] For the provision of instruction of poor youths in grammar at Peterhouse, Clare, Merton and Queen's, see above, ch. 5, pp. 182–3, 184, 191–2; see also Paquet, 'Recherches sur l'universitaire "pauvre" au moyen âge', pp. 327–8.

[21] *Camb. Docs.*, i. 332.

frequent payments for poor scholars who worked in the college garden, and at Merton College, Oxford, poor scholars assisted in the construction of the new library between 1373 and 1378.[22] Poor scholars would sometimes engage as servants to wealthier scholars or to university masters.[23] Alternatively, they might become attached to a hall, hostel or college, where, in return for the performance of menial duties, such as waiting at table, they would receive a substantial reduction in the cost of board and lodging there.[24] In the aularian statutes *(statuta aularia)* for the Oxford halls of 1483–90, students of this type are described as 'batellers'.[25] The same term was used at Oriel College, Oxford, in the early sixteenth century, although in this instance its exact significance is not entirely clear.[26]

Extremely poor scholars could be granted begging licences by the chancellor, a practice initially made acceptable through the mendicity of the friars.[27] Begging was probably thought less appropriate in the later medieval period, when residence in an approved establishment was made compulsory for all *bona fide* scholars. Nevertheless, licences to beg continued to be granted through to the sixteenth century,[28] and English kings from Richard II to Henry VIII attempted by legislation to ensure that only

---

[22] See e.g. King's Hall Accounts, iii. fo. 96; xxvi. fo. 180; Garrod, 'Merton College', *V.C.H. Oxon.* iii. 101.

[23] Cobban, *The Medieval Universities*, p. 199; Rashdall, *Universities*, iii. 405–8; Paquet, 'Recherches sur l'universitaire "pauvre" au moyen âge', pp. 325–6, 340. For a survey of poor scholars as servants in medieval universities, see Paquet, 'Coût des études, pauvreté et labeur: fonctions et métiers d'étudiants au moyen âge', pp. 23–9.

[24] Emden, *A Oxford Hall in Medieval Times*, p. 211.

[25] *Statuta Antiqua*, p. 584.

[26] W. A. Pantin, 'Oriel College and St Mary Hall', *V.C.H. Oxon.* iii. 119 ff. at p. 120.

[27] On the subject of student begging, see Rashdall, op. cit., iii. 406–7, and Paquet, 'Coût des études, pauvreté et labeur: fonctions et métiers d'étudiants au moyen âge', pp. 29–30.

[28] See e.g. *Registrum Cancellarii*, ii. 40, for begging licences granted to two poor scholars of Aristotle Hall in 1461.

formally licensed students would be permitted to beg without fear of prosecution.[29] Because of the alleged association between unbridled begging and lawlessness, the English monarchy and the university authorities combined to reduce the number of student-beggars to a controlled minimum.

Apart from the limited provision made for poor scholars by college founders, they were the object of charitable concern by a wide spectrum of benefactors. For example, the wife of Edward I, Queen Eleanor of Castile, who died in 1290, left in her will 100 marks for poor scholars of Cambridge;[30] Robert Winchelsey, archbishop of Canterbury, apparently supported poor scholars at both Oxford and Cambridge between 1294 and 1313;[31] Reginald de la Lee, a former university bedel, by his will of 1294, left his house to 'the community of poor scholars', and also made a gift to his parish church, St Mary the Virgin, for an annual distribution of bread to a hundred poor scholars;[32] and by his will of 1500, Cardinal Morton, a law graduate of Oxford who became bishop of Ely, archbishop of Canterbury between 1478 and 1500, chancellor of Oxford between 1495 and 1500, and chancellor of Cambridge between 1499 and 1500, donated £128 3s. 8d. per annum for twenty years for the support of at least thirty poor scholars, two-thirds of whom were to study at Oxford and the remainder at Cambridge. The Morton scholars were placed in a variety of colleges and halls, and control of the finances for their maintenance was vested in the warden of Canterbury College, Oxford.[33]

---

[29] Paquet, 'Coût des études . . .', p. 30.

[30] *Annals*, i. 62; Fuller, *The History of the University of Cambridge*, p. 130.

[31] J. H. Denton, *Robert Winchelsey and the Crown 1294–1313* (Cambridge, 1980), pp. 13, 25.

[32] Aston and Faith, 'The Endowments of the University and Colleges to *circa* 1348', *The History of the University of Oxford*, i. 272; *Mediaeval Archives*, i. 302.

[33] For Morton's legacy and payments to his endowed scholars between 1501–2 and 1508, see Pantin, *Canterbury College Oxford*, iii. 227 ff.; for Morton's career, see Emden, *B.R.U.O.*, ii. 1318–20, and *B.R.U.C.*, pp. 412–14. For examples of grants or scholarships for university students made by the testamentary disposition of continental benefactors, see P. Trio, 'Financing of University Students in the Middle Ages: A New Orientation', *History of Universities*, iv (1984), pp. 1 ff. at pp. 4–10.

Opportunities were available for poor scholars to negotiate loans, but chronically poor students would not have possessed the means to meet the high rates of interest charged by the Jewish money-lenders of Oxford and Cambridge in the thirteenth century.[34] Likewise, it is difficult to see how the loan-chest system at Oxford and Cambridge could have done much to alleviate the poverty of the poorest scholars; for, in order to secure a loan in this way, a pledge of an item of property, such as plate or a book, was required whose value was in excess of the sum to be borrowed. In these circumstances, it is probable that only wealthier scholars and the university masters would have been in a position to avail themselves of this facility.[35] It is true that poor scholars could interrupt their studies and return to Oxford and Cambridge when their finances improved. However, this option became less realistic when a more sedentary pattern of life, with fixed terms, more-sophisticated techniques of instruction and an obligatory attachment to a university residence, was progressively established. At Oxford and Cambridge, the university terms had crystallized by 1250 and remained basically the same through to 1500.[36] There were three terms, although the summer term was divided into two parts. The session extended from early October to July, with a Christmas,

---

[34] Roth, *The Jews of Medieval Oxford*, pp. 126–50; see also Catto, 'Citizens, Scholars and Masters', *The History of the University of Oxford*, i. 172, and Aston and Faith, 'The Endowments of the University and Colleges to *circa* 1348', ibid., i. 274–5. Roth (p. 130) takes the view that Jewish interest rates in Oxford were not excessive: they were fixed by royal edict in 1233, 1244, 1248 and 1268 at a maximum of 2d. in the pound weekly, equivalent to 43⅓ per cent per annum. Roth (pp. 130–1) is unaware of a limitation on the rate chargeable at Cambridge.

[35] For Oxford's loan-chest system, see Aston and Faith, op. cit., pp. 274–87, and G. Pollard, 'The Loan Chests', *The Register of Congregation 1448–1463*, appendix iii, pp. 418–20; for Cambridge, see Pollard, 'Mediaeval loan-chests at Cambridge', pp. 133 ff., and Rubin, *Charity and Community in Medieval Cambridge*, pp. 282–8. For the extent to which Exeter College, Oxford, in a period of financial difficulty in the fifteenth century, relied upon frequent loans from both college and university chests as well as from past and present fellows and from citizens of Oxford, see A. F. Butcher, 'The Economy of Exeter College, 1400–1500', *Oxoniensia*, 44 (1979), pp. 38 ff. at pp. 41–5.

[36] See *Statuta Antiqua*, p. 55, and Hackett, *The Original Statutes of Cambridge University*, pp. 200–3; also Catto, op. cit., p. 173.

Easter and long summer vacation. It is likely that a high proportion of undergraduates left Oxford and Cambridge for at least the long vacation. Poor scholars, however, had to balance with special care the expenses of the journey to and from home against the costs of remaining in the university town throughout the summer. Finally, among the aids haphazardly available to poor scholars must be mentioned the arrangements at Oxford and Cambridge whereby students who could not afford to take a degree could determine as bachelors, or even incept as masters, under the aegis of richer scholars, who would bear the burden of the collective expenses.[37] It is impossible to say with what frequency and comprehensiveness this device was employed. It is an interesting example of the kind of expediency resorted to in universities lacking an overall policy for dealing with the problem of student poverty.

The later medieval universities, having learned from the accumulated experience of the past, were more prone from the start to adopt a systematic approach to the problem of student poverty. The German Universities, for example, made deliberate efforts to deal understandingly and generously with all students who could plead genuine poverty. They were therein often treated as a class apart, worthy of special consideration at every stage in their academic careers.[38] Towards this end, the arts faculties in several of the German Universities made statutory dispensations in favour of

[37] This practice is not wholly understood and there are apparent contradictions in the available evidence: see the discussion by Rashdall, *Universities*, iii. 144–5 and 144, n. 2; Fletcher, 'The Faculty of Arts', *The History of the University of Oxford*, i. 383–4; and for the situation at Paris, G. C. Boyce, *The English-German Nation in the University of Paris during the Middle Ages* (Bruges, 1927), pp. 96–100 and appendix ii, pp. 184–5, and Mornet, 'Pauperes scolares. Essai sur la condition matérielle des étudiants scandinaves dans les universités aux xive et xve siècles', p. 70, n. 45. See also the remarks of Paquet, 'Recherches sur l'universitaire "pauvre" au moyen âge', pp. 342–3. For instances at Oxford of scholars who determined for others (*pro aliis*), see *The Register of Congregation 1448–1463*, pp. 26, 172, 240, 289, 392.

[38] Fletcher, 'Wealth and Poverty in the Medieval German Universities', *Europe in the Late Middle Ages*, pp. 410, 423 ff., and Fletcher, *The Liber Taxatorum of Poor Students at the University of Freiburg im Breisgau* (Texts and Studies in the History of Mediaeval Education, no. xii, Notre Dame, Indiana, 1969), p. 5: this valuable document reveals the detailed manner in which the statutory provisions relating to poor scholars were implemented at Freiburg.

poor scholars from fees for matriculation, lectures and official exercises, from the regulations governing academic dress and from obligatory residence in university accommodation.[39] Some universities, including Freiburg, Erfurt and Vienna, provided low-rate hostels for poor scholars.[40] So far as degree fees were concerned, universities might require of exempted scholars an undertaking that they would reimburse their faculty of study when their incomes allowed. A few instances of such repayment have been recorded.[41]

In the German Universities, the criterion of poverty was usually a defined low-income ceiling, which varied from centre to centre. At Ingolstadt, the student was obliged to furnish letters from his home town testifying to his poverty.[42] In general, the case of a scholar classified as 'poor' was kept under periodic review, and his financial obligations were altered according to changing circumstances.[43] From evidence of this kind, it is clear that in one group of universities of the late medieval period a sophisticated mechanism was in operation to cope systematically with the problem of genuine student poverty. However, along with other old-established universities, Oxford and Cambridge had no such co-ordinated or uniform method of alleviating academic hardship, only a number of palliatives and *ad hoc* measures, which, however, in combination, may have had some palpable, if necessarily random, impact.

[39] Fletcher, 'Wealth and Poverty in the Medieval German Universities', pp. 423 ff.; see also the discussion by Paquet of poor scholars and the problem of fees in a selection of medieval universities, 'Coût des études . . .', pp. 18–21.

[40] Fletcher, 'Wealth and Poverty in the Medieval German Universities', pp. 425–6; Rashdall, op. cit., iii. 405–6. Rashdall (p. 406, n. 1) draws attention to one Oxford hall which was apparently designed as a house for poor scholars.

[41] For the situation at Freiburg, see Fletcher, op. cit., pp. 431, 434–5, and *The Liber Taxatorum*, pp. 6–7.

[42] Fletcher, op. cit., pp. 424–5; Stelling-Michaud, 'L'histoire des universités au moyen âge et à la renaissance au cours des vingt-cinq dernières années', pp. 119–20. For the diverse forms of proof sought by medieval universities in order to establish the condition of student poverty, see Paquet, 'Recherches sur l'universitaire "pauvre" au moyen âge', pp. 328–35.

[43] For the procedure at Freiburg, see Fletcher, op. cit., pp. 433–4, and *The Liber Taxatorum*, p. 6. At Paris, poor scholars were also expected to repay dispensed fees if future circumstances would allow: Boyce, op. cit., pp. 166–7.

Evidence for the nature and extent of undergraduate expenses in the medieval English Universities is decidedly sparse. Consequently, an inestimable value is to be placed on the tutorial accounts of 1424 of John Arundel, who was, it seems, principal of St Mildred Hall, Oxford, near Exeter College; for these have survived and possess illuminating detail.[44] From these accounts, Dr A. B. Emden reckoned that an undergraduate in the first term of his third year would have incurred an expenditure in the region of 16s. 4½d., which covered the cost of his board, clothes and entertainment, lecture fees, room rent, the cost of candles, payments to hall servants and to the university bedel, the cost of a book, and the cost of a journey home.[45] Dr Emden concluded that if allowance is made for the cost of the journey to Oxford, in addition to that of the journey home, then the sum of £3 13s. 4d. would have been enough to defray all the necessary expenses of an undergraduate during the third year of his residence in an Oxford hall in the early fifteenth century.[46] This is inexpensive living. Even so, E. F. Jacob estimated that in 1450 the total expenditure of an economically minded undergraduate domiciled in an Oxford hall need have been no more than about £2 10s. a year.[47] A more recent calculation, which takes cognizance of the evidence for the maintenance of scholars of the founder's kin at Merton as well as of Arundel's accounts, has projected that a sum in the region of £2 12s. 6d. would have been enough to meet all of an Oxford undergraduate's annual expenses, including two journeys home, in the second half of the fifteenth century.[48]

---

[44] For these accounts, see Salter, 'An Oxford Hall in 1424', *Essays in History presented to R. I. Poole*, pp. 421 ff., and Emden, *An Oxford Hall in Medieval Times*, pp. 192–6; see also J. M. Fletcher and C. A. Upton, 'The Cost of undergraduate study at Oxford in the Fifteenth Century: the evidence of the Merton College "Founder's Kin"', *History of Education*, 14 (1985), pp. 1 ff. at pp. 3–4, 10–11.

[45] Emden, op. cit., p. 194.

[46] Loc. cit.

[47] Jacob, 'English University Clerks in the later Middle Ages: the Problem of Maintenance', p. 312.

[48] Fletcher and Upton, art. cit., p. 16.

What is especially noteworthy in Arundel's accounts is that the basic charge for weekly board was about 6½d., and in one instance less, and this works out at under 1d. a day.[49] This corresponds with the experience of the grammarian, Robert Whittinton, who, in his *Vulgaria* of 1520, looked back to his own student days, at the end of the fifteenth century, when it was possible to live competently at a commons rate of 7d. a week.[50] In 1424, the year of Arundel's tutorial accounts, the average weekly sum charged to each fellow of the King's Hall, Cambridge, was 1s. 9¾d., just over 3d. a day.[51] This year's charges seem to have been fairly representative, since, over the period 1382–3 to 1443–4, the average charge for commons was 1s. 8¼d. per week.[52] It will be recalled that a proportion of the King's Hall fellows were of undergraduate status: these were charged the same rate for basic commons as their more advanced colleagues. If the figures furnished for the Oxford hall in 1424 were at all typical, then the average commons rate at the King's Hall for undergraduate fellows was approximately three times that normally levied in halls or hostels of the period. This conclusion would doubtless have to be amended in the case of the halls of the legists, where boarding rates were significantly higher than in establishments designed for the majority of the less mature students. It is almost certainly true that the cost of a fellow's maintenance in the King's Hall was well above the average level in other English colleges,[53] and hence the comparison with hall rates is somewhat inflated. Nevertheless, a commons rate ranging from less than 1d. to just under 3d. a day probably represents the parameters of daily expenditure on basic food and drink for most undergraduates at Oxford and Cambridge in the later fourteenth and fifteenth centuries. As this period saw a general fall in the price

[49] Emden, op. cit., p. 194.

[50] Ibid., p. 195.

[51] Cobban, *The King's Hall*, table 5 (pullout), column 16 (opposite p. 126).

[52] Ibid., p. 139.

[53] Ibid., pp. 140–1.

of consumables compared with the steep rise from the late twelfth to the early fourteenth centuries,[54] it may be tentatively deduced that the standard of living of the average scholar rose in the later Middle Ages. From the evidence of a number of inventories of Oxford scholars of the mid-fifteenth century, it seems that all but the poorest could by then afford a range of clothing, items of bedding, spoons, knives, candlesticks, a pair of bellows, one or two books, and musical instruments.[55]

At the other end of the social scale from the poor scholar and the average undergraduate of modest means was the wealthy nobleman. Members of the aristocracy had been present from an early date in the universities of southern Europe, which for long were more closely identified with the fabric of aristocratic life than were universities in the northern latitudes.[56] In general, sons of the nobility did not enter the English Universities on any scale before the latter half of the fifteenth century. The reasons for the belated aristocratic adoption of Oxford and Cambridge are not entirely clear. Certainly, the piecemeal incorporation of humanist studies rendered the Universities more enticing foci to that class, which had hitherto not been much attracted to the type of intellectual fare on offer at Oxford and Cambridge. Of particular relevance here is the influence of the Platonic notion embodied in the *Republic*, available in England in Latin translation from the mid-fifteenth century,[57] that those who aspire to government must be functionally qualified for that task. As an idea, this proved to be powerfully influential. In combination with the increasingly complex nature of governmental

---

[54] See e.g. E. H. Phelps Brown and S. V. Hopkins, 'Seven Centuries of the Prices of Consumables, compared with Builders' Wage-rates', *Economica*, new series, 23 (1956), pp. 296 ff., with relevant conclusion on p. 305; reprinted in *Essays in Economic History* (2 vols., ed. E. M. Carus-Wilson, London, 1954–62), ii. 168 ff.

[55] *Registrum Cancellarii*, i. 83–4, 160–1, 321, 352.

[56] Cobban, *The Medieval Universities*, p. 201.

[57] The Latin translation of Pier Candido Decembrio, dedicated to Humphrey, Duke of Gloucester: see Weiss, *Humanism in England during the Fifteenth Century*, pp. 54–9.

processes under the Yorkists and Tudors, this Platonic conception played a part in encouraging members of aristocratic families to seek some form of educational training at one of the English Universities or more usually at one of the Inns of Court in London.[58] That participation in government ought to be earned by means of either a broadly based education or the acquisition of the skills of a relevant discipline was a theme common to many humanist scholars, including Erasmus, Sir Thomas More and Sir Thomas Elyot.[59] Indeed, as worked out in his *Utopia*, More was prepared to take the argument to its logical conclusion by advocating that an aristocracy of merit should replace an hereditary aristocracy as England's governing force. This was too radical a view for the consumption of sixteenth-century English society, where power was still rooted largely in landed wealth; and most humanist writers adopted the compromise position that an enlarged aristocracy of merit should at least coexist with an hereditary aristocracy.[60] It was against such a backcloth that Oxford and Cambridge began to attract significant numbers of recruits from aristocratic families.

The influx of sons of the nobility was probably greatest at Oxford between the late sixteenth century and the 1630s, after which there was a notable decline in the remainder of the century.[61] Nevertheless, even in the fourteenth and fifteenth centuries, and in even smaller numbers in the thirteenth, students of noble birth were present in the English Universities, and these, in a variety of ways, seem to have exercised an influence consonant with their status, if disproportionate to their number. It has been reckoned that between 1307 and 1485, at least 88 members of 42 noble families attended the English Universities — 69 at Oxford and 19 at

---

[58] See e.g. Curtis, *Oxford and Cambridge in Transition 1558–1642*, ch. 3, especially pp. 63–76.

[59] See F. Caspari, *Humanism and the Social Order in Tudor England* (Chicago, 1954), pp. 46–9 (Erasmus), 58–75 (More), 76–109 (Elyot).

[60] Ibid., pp. 58–75.

[61] L. Stone, 'The Size and Composition of the Oxford Student Body 1580–1910', *The University in Society*, i. 46–7.

Cambridge,[62] and some of them acquired degrees at both.[63] Of the 88 scions of the nobility who entered the Universities, 51 received their experience of university life in the fourteenth century compared with 37 in the fifteenth century.[64] Cambridge's 19 noble scholars were distributed almost equally over the two centuries, while Oxford had rather more in the fourteenth than in the fifteenth century.[65] Although a minority of university trained aristocrats embarked upon secular occupations, as landowners, knights or courtiers, most of the noble intake followed solid ecclesiastical careers, 15 becoming bishops in the fourteenth century and 16 in the fifteenth century.[66] While some noble students did not either obtain or seek a degree, the majority acquired one or more degrees, mainly in the fields of arts and law, with theology a distant

---

[62] For noble youths at Oxford in the thirteenth century, see N. Orme, *From Childhood to Chivalry: The Education of the English Kings and Aristocracy 1066–1530* (London and New York, 1984), pp. 67, 70. For the analysis of noble entrants between 1307 and 1485, see J. T. Rosenthal, 'The Universities and the Medieval English Nobility', *History of Education Quarterly*, 9 (1969), pp. 415 ff. at p. 416. Rosenthal's distribution of noble scholars gives a ratio of 3.5:1 as between Oxford and Cambridge, and this accords well with a sample investigation of the paternal status of students in the medieval English Universities, which yields, for noble recruits, a ratio of 4:1: J. A. Brundage, 'English-Trained Canonists in the Middle Ages: A Statistical Analysis of a Social Group', *Law-Making and Law-Makers in British History: Papers presented to the Edinburgh Legal History Conference 1977*, p. 69. Brundage (p. 69) quotes 1.3 per cent as pertaining to the Cambridge sample, whereas, according to his table 4, this pertains to a combined Oxford and Cambridge sample.

[63] Rosenthal, art. cit., pp. 416–17. For example, Thomas Cobham held an M.A. degree from Paris, a D.Cn.L. degree from Oxford and a D.Th. degree from Cambridge by 1314; and Robert FitzHugh, who, in the early fifteenth century, became warden of the King's Hall, chancellor of Cambridge and bishop of London, obtained the degree of D.Th. from both Oxford and Cambridge: Emden, *B.R.U.O.*, i. 450–1; *B.R.U.C.*, pp. 231–2.

[64] Rosenthal, art. cit., p. 417.

[65] Ibid., pp. 417–18.

[66] Ibid., pp. 418–19. Rosenthal is here in broad agreement with the conclusion of J. H. Hexter, *Reappraisals in History* (New York, Harper Torchbooks, 1963), p. 54: 'that except for such as were planning careers in or through the Church, English gentlemen did not ordinarily go to Oxford or Cambridge in the later Middle Ages'.

third.[67] Several nobles went on from Oxford and Cambridge to study in continental universities, where some accumulated further degrees. For instance, Thomas Cobham in the late thirteenth or early fourteenth century took an M.A. at Paris in addition to his D.Cn.L. from Oxford and his D.Th. from Cambridge,[68] and Philip Beauchamp attained the degree of D.C.L. at Bologna in 1369.[69] A total of 15 of the noble scholars became university chancellors, 11 of them at Oxford and 4 at Cambridge, and all but 5 of these 15 also became bishops:[70] William Courtenay and Henry Beaufort, later Cardinal Beaufort, held the chancellorship at Oxford for only a brief period; Robert FitzHugh retained the office at Cambridge from 1423 to 1428; and Eudo la Zouche was the Cambridge chancellor on at least three separate occasions.[71] Members of the nobility also served the Universities as proctors and in diplomatic capacities.

The members of the nobility in the English Universities did not, before *c*. 1500, form a highly privileged élite after the manner of the contingents of nobles in, for example, the German Universities, where, in return for extra financial contributions and influential political support, members of the nobility were accorded a series of privileges and exemptions.[72] It may well be that there was some relaxation of academic requirements for noble scholars at Oxford and Cambridge in the second half of the fifteenth century.[73] Nevertheless, any degree of preferential treatment of noble scholars

---

[67] Rosenthal has summarized the situation of nobles known to have taken degrees between 1307 and 1485 as follows: arts 42; law 38; and theology 12: ibid., p. 419.

[68] Emden, *B.R.U.O.*, i. 450–1.

[69] Ibid., i. 136–7. Rosenthal, art. cit., p. 421, gives the date of Philip Beauchamp's D.C.L. degree at Bologna as 1460 instead of 1369.

[70] Rosenthal, art. cit., p. 424.

[71] For William Courtenay, Henry Beaufort, Robert FitzHugh and Eudo la Zouche, see Emden, *B.R.U.O.*, i. 502–4, 139–42; *B.R.U.C.*, pp. 231–2, 358.

[72] On the position of members of the nobility in German Universities, see Fletcher, 'Wealth and Poverty in the Medieval German Universities', pp. 410–13. For the general impact of the aristocracy on the medieval universities, mainly those of southern Europe, see Verger, *Les universités au moyen âge*, pp. 176–87.

[73] Rosenthal, art. cit., pp. 427–8; Orme, *From Childhood to Chivalry*, p. 69.

in the English Universities was not on a scale comparable with that lavished upon noble scholars in continental universities.

The residential patterns of English noble scholars are not comprehensively known. Several of them clearly had individual tutors and servants and presumably lived in some style. For instance, Thomas de Segrave, son of Sir John de Segrave, had, as private tutor at Cambridge, Richard de Aston, who, in 1312, at the request of Sir John, had been granted leave of absence from his ecclesiastical living to study in a university and to act as tutor to Thomas;[74] and in 1351, Thomas de Percy, fifth son of Henry, second baron Percy of Alnwick, was a scholar in arts at Oxford studying under William de Blythe.[75] A number of noble scholars were attached to a college or hall or inn for at least part of their residence at university. Whether or not members of the nobility were bound to live in a college, hall or hostel when that became obligatory at both Universities is a matter which cannot be easily determined.

In contrast to the members of the nobility in several of the continental universities, nobles at Oxford and Cambridge before 1500 were not, taken as a group, conspicuous benefactors.[76] No college was founded by the son of a noble family who attended one or both of the English Universities, although Clare College and Pembroke College, Cambridge, were instituted respectively by Elizabeth de Burgh — Lady Clare and granddaughter of Edward I — and by Mary de Valence, the widowed countess of Pembroke; and Balliol College, Oxford, had, as its effective second founder, Lady Dervorguilla of Galloway in Scotland. Apart from these foundations, and a few sizeable bequests, such as that of Thomas Cobham for the establishment of a university library in Oxford, and the valuable manuscript donations of Humphrey, duke of Gloucester, and John Tiptoft, earl of Worcester,[77] the benefactions made by members of the nobility were unspectacular,

---

[74] For Richard de Aston, see Emden, *B.R.U.O.*, i. 68.

[75] For William de Blythe and Thomas de Percy, see ibid., i. 207; iii. 1462.

[76] See the discussion by Rosenthal, art. cit., pp. 428–31.

[77] For the bequests of Thomas Cobham, Duke Humphrey and John Tiptoft, see above, chapter 3, pp. 82–3, and chapter 6, p. 245.

taking the form of numerous small gifts of manuscripts, or items of plate, or capital for the foundation of loan-chests, or contributions towards building enterprises.

In general, the English Universities were only lightly patronized by the nobility before *c.* 1500, and mainly as convenient venues for younger sons destined for an ecclesiastical career, or for those members of noble families interested in aspects of the humanist learning sporadically taking root at Oxford and Cambridge in the fifteenth century. The majority of noble scholars appear to have had a serious academic purpose, and, in terms of both high university offices held and successful careers pursued, their record of achievement is reasonably impressive. While it was not until the later sixteenth and early seventeenth centuries that the English nobility most fully exploited the potential of the Universities, resulting in their transformation into highly stratified institutions, it is clear that the origins of this aristocratic penetration may be traced to the later medieval period.[78]

The endowed personnel of the English Universities comprised the communities of monks and friars, the fellows of the secular colleges and, from the late fifteenth century, the holders of salaried lectureships or chairs, who, in most cases, would also have been college fellows. At Oxford, a monastic presence was firmly established from the late thirteenth century, and five colleges for monks were founded between the 1280s and 1437. The first three colleges were Benedictine foundations, that is, Gloucester (1283–91), Durham (*c.* 1289) and Canterbury (1361), and these were supplemented in 1435 by St Mary's College for the Austin Canons and in 1437 by St Bernard's College for the Cistercians. Although the four orders of friars — the Dominicans, the Franciscans, the Austins and the Carmelites — supplied by far the largest number of regulars before *c.* 1500, with a recorded total of 1,556, the monastic orders and the regular canons together

---

[78] This conclusion, which specifically concerns the nobility, seems to accord with that reached by Aston et al., 'The Medieval Alumni of the University of Cambridge', p. 85, who argue that 'the pronounced upper-class invasion of the universities in the Elizabethan period and after' had its origin in the later Middle Ages: this 'upper-class invasion' appears to refer to the upper ranks of the gentry and the nobility combined.

furnished about two-thirds of that number, with recorded totals of 871 and 141 respectively.[79] The regulars were evidently an important numerical constituent of Oxford's academic population, and, taking the thirteenth, fourteenth and fifteenth centuries together, they accounted for 17 per cent of the University's total recorded alumni.[80] In contrast to Oxford, Cambridge had only a small monastic representation which was vastly outnumbered by members of the four orders of friars: in the period before 1500, monks and regular canons combined amounted to only 206, compared with 1,136 recorded friars.[81] Whereas Oxford had five monastic colleges, Cambridge realized only one, Buckingham College, inaugurated for Benedictines in the 1470s.[82] Prior to this, a hostel had been acquired in 1340 for the Benedictine monks of Ely studying in Cambridge. In 1428, property was obtained for the use of Benedictines pursuing theology and canon law, and this community, which had become known as 'Monk's Place' by 1472, was the origin of Buckingham College.[83] The regular canons had a house in Cambridge, and they also had a centre at the adjacent Barnwell Abbey. The number of them involved in university study was small, however. As at Oxford, even with a recorded total of only 84, the number of Benedictines at Cambridge far outstripped that of any of the other orders of monks and regular canons.[84]

It must not be supposed that the regulars and seculars were entirely segregated communities. At Oxford, the three Benedictine colleges admitted varying proportions of seculars. Gloucester

---

[79] Aston, 'Oxford's Medieval Alumni', p. 17.

[80] Loc. cit.

[81] Aston et al., 'The Medieval Alumni of the University of Cambridge', p. 55. On the sites of the communities of friars at Cambridge, see Brooke, 'The Churches of Medieval Cambridge', *History, Society and the Churches: Essays in Honour of Owen Chadwick*, pp. 60–1, 73–4.

[82] For Buckingham College, see Ellis and Salzman, 'Religious Houses', *V.C.H. Camb.* ii. 312. Buckingham College was the predecessor of Magdalene College, founded in 1542.

[83] Ibid., ii. 207.

[84] Aston et al., 'The Medieval Alumni of the University of Cambridge', p. 55.

College had a group of 7 known seculars in the fifteenth century.[85] Durham and Canterbury were in effect mixed societies, Canterbury having at least 47 seculars, compared with 111 monks, between its foundation in 1361 and 1500, and Durham harbouring 82 seculars, compared with 91 monks, between *c.* 1381 and 1500.[86] The secular colleges did not appreciably reciprocate by admitting significant numbers of regulars, although records of monks in colleges in the fifteenth century are occasionally found. For example, 6 Benedictines lived as pensioners in Gonville College, Cambridge, beteen 1480 and 1499;[87] and at Cambridge, a number of monks seem to have resided in secular hostels because of the inadequacy of the monastic accommodation in the University.

The majority of endowed college fellows at Oxford and Cambridge were engaged in advanced courses of study and were undoubtedly well-appointed members of the academic population. By wider community criteria, however, they did not stand particularly high in the economic hierarchy. A fellowship would have allowed basic needs to be satisfied to an acceptable level and have provided extra communal comforts to add a savour to the austere regime of daily life. But for those fellows primarily dependent upon the revenues of a fellowship, the standard of living was of a decidedly middling order.[88]

In addition to the use of a room or rooms and an annual set of livery or its monetary equivalent, the fellows in English colleges were normally allocated a weekly allowance from college funds to cover the cost of their board or commons. Many colleges geared this allowance system to a sliding scale with stipulated minima and maxima rates and regulated according to fluctuations in grain prices. The system was so designed as to cover most of the costs of a

[85] Aston, 'Oxford's Medieval Alumni', p. 18.

[86] Loc. cit.

[87] Aston et al., 'The Medieval Alumni of the University of Cambridge', pp. 54–5.

[88] For the economic standing of the fellows of the King's Hall, see Cobban, *The King's Hall*, ch. 4, and for the condition of New College fellows, see Lytle's unpublished thesis, *Oxford Students and English Society: c.1300–c.1510*, pp. 82–4.

fellow's basic food and drink requirements, even in years of particularly high prices of wheat and malt barley, the staple grains used in the collegiate diet.[89] The standard maintenance allowance for commons in most fourteenth-century English colleges, including the magnificently conceived New College, Oxford, was 1s. per fellow per week.[90] The uppermost of the prescribed limits of the sliding scale varied from college to college. At Oriel College, for example, the stipulated maximum limit of 1s. 3d. was to come into force when a quarter of wheat was selling at 10s. or more in Oxford or the surrounding district.[91] William of Wykeham, on the other hand, prescribed that the commons rate for his New College fellows might be increased to 1s. 4d. in times of scarcity; and, in the event of the bushel of wheat fetching more than 2s. in Oxford or neighbouring markets, the commons limit was to be advanced to 1s. 6d.[92] Similar arrangements were made for King's College, Cambridge, in the mid-fifteenth century. There, the commons allowance was to rise from the basic rate of 1s. 4d. a week to 1s. 5d. or 1s. 6d. in years of bad harvest, with an ultimate ceiling of 1s. 8d. when the bushel of wheat was selling at 2s. or more in the Cambridge area.[93] The situation was not so liberal at Peterhouse, where the bishop of Ely, John Alcock, inserted in 1489 an ordinance in the statutes to the effect that the fellows were to have no more than 1s. 2d. per week for their commons, although this might be marginally increased in years of lean harvest.[94] At the King's Hall, Cambridge, the statutes prescribed a flat commons rate of 1s. 2d. per fellow per week and this was paid out of the royal exchequer. In contrast to most other colleges, there was no sliding scale in operation, and this meant that the fellows in this exceptional college

---

[89] See Cobban, *The King's Hall*, pp. 139–41.

[90] See e.g. the statutes of 1359 for Clare College, Cambridge, in *Camb. Docs.*, ii. 135; the statutes of Michaelhouse in Stamp, *Michaelhouse*, p. 43, and the statutes of Oriel and New College in *Statutes*, i. ch. 3, 7; ch. 5, 38–9.

[91] *Statutes*, i. ch. 3, 15.

[92] Ibid., i. ch. 5, 38–9.

[93] *Camb. Docs.*, ii. 527–8.

[94] Ibid., ii. 48–9.

almost invariably had to make a contribution from their own resources in order to meet the costs of weekly commons.[95]

The case of the King's Hall apart, however, it is clear that collegiate maintenance was generally designed to relieve each fellow of the necessity of drawing overmuch upon his private means for the satisfaction of his basic living requirements. However, it has to be assumed that a college fellow would have had some independent source of income. At the very least, he would have needed this in order to defray the expenses of any luxury items of food and drink ordered over and above his basic commons. In some colleges, in times of scarcity and soaring food prices, when college funds would not stretch to cover the abnormally high commons rate entailed, each fellow would have been expected to make contributions from his private income during the period of crisis.[96] Such an arrangement also existed in some of the Paris colleges: for example, it was given statutory force at the fourteenth-century Ave Maria College.[97]

In the absence of much concrete data, one can only speculate about the sources of private revenue of English college fellows. Those fellows who were also regent masters would have derived an income from teaching in the university schools; and, in the later medieval period, there were opportunities, though these were limited, for fellows to augment their incomes with tutorial fees in at least some of the English colleges. A proportion of college fellows would have realized an income from benefices — held concurrently with their fellowships — whose value was less than the prescribed statutory maximum, which was commonly fixed at £5 and occasionally at £4 or £6 13s. 4d.[98] Exemptions from the statutory

---

[95] Cobban, *The King's Hall*, pp. 129, 141: see also King's Hall statutes in Rouse Ball, *The King's Scholars and King's Hall*, p. 69.

[96] Cobban, *The Medieval Universities*, pp. 204–5.

[97] A. L. Gabriel, *Student Life in Ave Maria College, Mediaeval Paris* (Publications in mediaeval studies, xiv, Notre Dame, Indiana, 1955), pp. 361–2.

[98] For 'income ceilings' prescribed as compatible with the retention of fellowships in English and Parisian colleges, see Cobban, *The King's Hall*, p. 146, n. 1. Whereas founders of English colleges stipulated fairly uniform allowable rates of income applicable to all fellows, founders of French colleges, often fixed a scale of statutory rates graded according to academic standing:

income-limits were given, but with what frequency it is not easy to determine. Finally, as in the case of undergraduate students, younger fellows would probably have been able to command financial aid from relatives or patrons. The overall position appears to be that the generality of fellows did not possess much in the way of private income, a situation reinforced by the 'income ceilings' prescribed by several colleges of the fourteenth and fifteenth centuries. It is nevertheless likely that few fellows were entirely dependent upon the bounty of the founder. And in some of the wealthier colleges, a larger reserve of private income was probably required than in the poorer ones. This seems to have been the case at New College, Oxford,[99] and it was certainly true of the King's Hall, Cambridge, which offered a level of material comfort midway between that of the average type of college of the fourteenth and fifteenth centuries and the more luxurious standards of aristocratic households of the period towards which it undoubtedly gravitated.

As already indicated, the commons allowance system in the King's Hall was not geared to a sliding scale. The fellows were each allocated a flat rate of 1s. 2d. per week by direct exchequer grant, and they had to find the remainder from their own resources. Between 1382–3 and 1443–4, the average charge levied on the King's Hall fellows for their weekly commons ranged from 1s. 2½d. to 2s. 3½d. each and gives an average of 1s. 8¼d. each per week over the whole period,[100] which is a high maintenance rate, equivalent to a luxury level in most English colleges. The King's Hall fellows had to find each week from their own means the difference between the flat rate commons allowance of 1s. 2d. each and the actual amount charged for commons and sizings, the latter being the extra items ordered over and above basic commons. In the selected period, 1382–3 to 1443–4, the average King's Hall fellow had to pay sums ranging from about 7¾d. to 1s. 1¼d. per week, that is, from about

Gabriel, 'The College System in the Fourteenth-Century Universities', *The Forward Movement of the Fourteenth Century*, p. 90.

[99] See Lytle's unpublished thesis, *Oxford Students and English Society: c.1300–c.1510*, p. 84.

[100] Cobban, *The King's Hall*, p. 139 and table 5 (pullout), column 16 (opposite p. 126).

£1. 14s. to £3 per annum.[101] These sums have been 'corrected' by means of a price index constructed from the prices which the college had to pay for wheat and malt barley over the same period,[102] and consequently a view of the range of average expenditure is obtained when fluctuations due to major price variations have been 'ironed out'. It is abundantly clear that in this *collège de luxe* it was necessary for a fellow to have a source of substantial income merely in order to defray his bills for essential board, and that such a source was even more necessary if he was to participate to the full in communal collegiate life. Given that, in addition to his heavy combined expenditure on commons and sizings, the King's Hall fellow had to meet a variety of miscellaneous expenses — including lecture and degree fees, the cost of the occasional text, travelling costs, the cost of the maintenance of guests in college and, in some instances, of a private servant,[103] and an exceptional outlay on feast days — it is probable that the average fellow would have tended to spend the greater part of his allowable income each year. This was set at £6 13s. 4d. if derived from an ecclesiastical benefice, and £5 if derived from temporal possessions, pensions, or other secular revenues.[104]

The exclusive nature of the King's Hall is all the more apparent when it is taken into account that, over and above his steep maintenance costs, every fellow upon first entry was required to pay burdensome admission charges. There is no mention of entrance dues in the statutes of 1380. From the annual accounts, however, it is clear that upon admission each new fellow was bound to make three separate payments to the college. First, each new fellow had to provide a breakfast or feast for all the members of the college, rated at a monetary equivalent of 20s.;[105] next, he was required to make a contribution of 20s. towards a plate fund, from which the college could draw for the purchase of new items of plate and for repairs to

[101] Ibid., pp. 135, 137.

[102] Ibid., pp. 134 ff.

[103] For private servants of fellows, see ibid., pp. 242–4.

[104] Ibid., pp. 145–6.

[105] E.g. King's Hall Accounts, v. fos. 163, 183; vi. fos. 104v, 140; vii. fos. 1v, 111v; viii. fos. 1v, 18v, 40; ix. fos. 1v, 148v; x. fo. 82v.

existing stock;[106] and finally, he had to pay 4d. towards the fitting out, maintenance and running costs of the college boat.[107] In all, therefore, admission charges amounted to the very sizeable sum of £2 0s. 4d. When it is noted that the annual wage of the King's Hall butler was in most years only £1 6s. 8d.,[108] or that the wages of numerous categories of skilled tradesmen of the late fourteenth and fifteenth centuries ranged from about 3d. to 6d. a day, the large size of these entrance dues may be discerned. From evidence provided by college statutes, it would appear that the custom of exacting entrance charges from new fellows was not widespread in English colleges, and was associated with Cambridge rather than with Oxford.[109] An examination of English college statutes from the late thirteenth to the seventeenth century reveals that only in three codes, those of Peterhouse, the King's Hall and Michaelhouse, are entrance dues specified. At Peterhouse, a fellow had to supply himself with a surplice within three months and, without delay, had to present a mazer cup and a silver spoon to the society;[110] and at Michaelhouse, the new fellow was obliged to have a white surplice and to give the college a silver spoon, a mazer cup and a napkin and cloth for the fellows' table.[111] It is surprising to find no trace of admission dues in any Oxford code before the seventeenth century. As in the case of the King's Hall, it is possible that any exaction of entrance charges which did exist before then and was not statutory belonged to the body of customary arrangements which had grown up after the founder's death and were never embodied in statutory form. It is of some interest that the levying of admission dues was fairly common among the fourteenth-century Paris colleges. For example, the founder of the Ave Maria College (1339) enacted that

---

[106] E.g. ibid., iv. fo. 137; v. fos. 113, 130; vi. fos. 15, 99, 140; vii. fos. 69v, 111v; viii. fos. 18v, 40, 87v; ix. fos. 93v, 148v; x. fos. 1v, 28v.

[107] E.g. ibid., v. fo. 130; vi. fos. 15v, 140; vii. fo. 1v; viii. fos. 18v, 87v; ix. fos. 93v, 148v; xi. fos. 1v, 61v.

[108] Cobban, *The King's Hall*, pp. 138, 236.

[109] Ibid., p. 137, n. 1.

[110] *Camb. Docs.*, ii. 6.

[111] Stamp, *Michaelhouse*, p. 29.

new entrants should bring with them their own linen, towels, and items necessary for their beds;[112] and at the colleges of Boncour (1337) and Dainville (1380), new members had to provide their own bed furnishings.[113]

While the colleges were designed principally for the support of their communities of fellows, they came in the later medieval period to harbour an increasing quota of commoners, who, collectively, formed an important and invigorating sector of the academic population. Before the undergraduate commoners began to permeate the English colleges in the fifteenth century,[114] the normal type of academic commoner was of mature years and often of graduate status.[115] Most English colleges seem to have made provision for a number of residents who were not a charge on the foundation. There were those who may be described appropriately as 'ex-fellow pensioners' — fellows who had vacated their fellowships but continued to live in college, paying for their board and lodging. And there were those who were residents who had never at any time been on the foundation and who were admitted to the college either as commoners, taking full commons, or as semi-commoners, who paid only half of the commons rate for board of a lower standard. The division of the commoner population of the King's Hall into distinct gradings, commoner and semi-commoner, affords proof that the origins of the stratified commoner system are to be placed at least as early as the first half of the fourteenth century.[116]

The terminology for these academic commoners, often described in a blanket sense as *extranei* or foreigners, is diverse to the point of confusion. Among the terms most commonly found are *commensales, commorantes, communarii* (and *semicommunarii*),

---

[112] Gabriel, *Student Life in Ave Maria College, Mediaeval Paris*, p. 94 and statute no. 88, pp. 349–50.

[113] Ibid., p. 94, n. 6.

[114] See above, chapter 5, pp. 193–6.

[115] Cobban, *The Medieval Universities*, p. 145; see also the remarks of Salter, *Medieval Oxford*, p. 100.

[116] Cobban, *The King's Hall*, p. 275.

batellarii, sojournants, and *per(h)endinantes.*[117] This last term, *per(h)endinantes,* is the one most commonly used in Cambridge college statutes of the fourteenth and fifteenth centuries to denote lodgers.[118] By contrast, it is not found in the Oxford codes of the same period. The first use at Cambridge of *pensionarius* in place of *per(h)endinans* is in the statutes of Christ's College of 1505,[119] and henceforth in the sixteenth-century codes *pensionarii* and *commensales* are the terms usually found.[120] It is probable that it was

[117] At University College, Oxford, the terms *commensales* and *commorantes* were used: Oswald, 'University College', *V.C.H. Oxon.* iii. 63. At Oriel, lodgers were known as *commorantes* in the fifteenth century and *commensales, communarii* or *batellarii* in the sixteenth century: Pantin, 'Oriel College and St Mary Hall', ibid., iii. 120; see also the references cited in *The Dean's Register of Oriel, 1446–1661,* pp. 51, 56, 61–2, and for *commorantes,* see *Oriel College Records* (ed. C. L. Shadwell and H. E. Salter, Oxf. Hist. Soc., lxxxv, 1926), pp. 52, 55–6. Rooms were let to *commorantes* at Canterbury College: Rashdall, *Universities,* iii. 213, n. 1. At Exeter and Queen's, *communarii* and *commensales* were the terms employed: Salter, *Medieval Oxford,* p. 100. Among the *commensales* of Queen's in the late fourteenth century were John Wyclif, Nicholas Hereford and John Trevisa: R. H. Hodgkin, *Six Centuries of an Oxford College,* pp. 27–38. The *communarii* of Merton College had a peculiar standing. They appear to have been youths who were maintained for several years in return for the performance of specified duties. These *communarii* were therefore a charge upon the finances of Merton whereas elsewhere they were usually a source of income: *Registrum Annalium Collegii Mertonensis 1483–1521,* pp. xv–xvii. At Eton College, the *commensals* were privileged commoners who were given free tuition provided that they had paid for their board and lodging: H. C. Maxwell-Lyte, *A History of Eton College 1440–1910* (4th ed., London, 1911), p. 19: an analysis of the statutory provisions regarding *commensals* is given, appendix A, p. 582. At the King's Hall, Cambridge, commoners were referred to variously as *commensales, sojournants, commorantes, communarii* (and *semicommunarii*) and *per(h)endinantes*: Cobban, *The King's Hall,* pp. 260–1.

[118] See e.g. the statutes of Peterhouse, *Camb. Docs.,* ii. 27, and the statutes of Queens', ibid., iii. 37.

[119] Ibid., iii. 208. The term *pensionarius* was used in the first quarter of the sixteenth century in the earliest extant Bursar's Book of Gonville Hall: see *Computus Book of Gonville Hall* (c.1423–c.1523), Gonville and Caius College MS. 365, pp. 74, 83; see also J. Venn, *Early Collegiate Life* (Cambridge, 1913), pp. 68–9, and Venn, *Gonville and Caius College* (College Histories Series, London, 1910), p. 30.

[120] From many examples, see the statutes of Clare of 1551, *Camb. Docs.,* ii. 164; also the Edwardian statutes of Trinity College, Cambridge, of 1552, Trinity College Library, 0. 6. 7., cap. xvi, pp. 20–1. However, *perendinant* was

the prevalence of the designation *pensionarius* among the Cambridge colleges of the sixteenth century which led to its post-Reformation adoption to describe that class of undergraduate commoners who were not on the foundation.[121]

It is not always easy to be precise about the exact significance of the terminological usage in any given case. Our knowledge of these lodgers does not, in many instances, extend beyond their surnames, their periods of residence, and the rates charged for commons.[122] Of those who are identifiable, a fair number were beneficed clergy who had obtained episcopal leave to attend a university, whether named or not, for a specified duration. Examples from the King's Hall of commoners with study permits, which were tantamount to ecclesiastical scholarships, include dominus Hugo (Hugh) Wymundeswold, who was granted permission to study at a university for one year on 26 September 1344 and resided as a commoner during 1344–5; Thomas Barbur, vicar of Kenninghall, Norfolk, who was granted licence to study at Cambridge on 11 May 1411 and lived as a semi-commoner for parts of 1439–40; and Robert Ayscogh, canon of Sarum, prebendary of Charminster and Bere, and rector of Campsall, Yorkshire, who obtained leave of absence for three years on 8 March 1456 in the midst of his periods of residence as a commoner, which are recorded for 1447–50, 1451–3, 1454–5, 1457–9 and 1460–1.[123] Commoners of this type often took either an advanced degree in arts or a degree in a superior faculty. Some commoners, however, came to university not to

sometimes retained as a sectional heading in the statutes: see e.g. the early sixteenth-century statutes of Jesus College, *Camb. Docs.*, iii. 120–1.

[121] The equivalent of the Oxford undergraduate 'commoner'. On the post-Reformation pensioner at Cambridge, see D. A. Winstanley, *Unreformed Cambridge*, pp. 200–1.

[122] An account of commoners and semi-commoners at the King's Hall is given by Cobban, *The King's Hall*, especially pp. 273–9.

[123] For Wymundeswold, see Emden, *B.R.U.O.*, iii. 2121, and King's Hall Accounts, i. fo. 91v; for Barbur, see Emden, *B.R.U.C.*, pp. 35–6, and King's Hall Accounts, ix. fo. 106v; for Ayscogh, see Emden, *B.R.U.C.*, p. 27, and King's Hall Accounts, xi. fos. 17v, 48v, 74v, 101v, 133v; xii. fos. 13, 74v, 103v; xiii. fo. 20.

acquire an additional degree, but to enjoy a refresher regime of study in a congenial atmosphere. For instance, Peter Irford alias Beverley was a commoner at Pembroke College, Cambridge, in 1438. By this date, he had accumulated the degrees of M.A., B.Th. and D.Th., had held a variety of ecclesiastical positions and seems to have experienced periods of non-residence for university study.[124] It is probable that his stay in Pembroke was unrelated to any particular course of study and was more in the nature of a convenient interlude between different sections of a busy career. Judging from the pattern of their careers, some mature commoners appear to have attended university with the express intention of maximizing their chances of acquiring a good ecclesiastical living. For example, dominus John Clerevaus, charged as a commoner at the King's Hall between 1363–4 and 1365–6, attained the degree of B.Cn.L. and was rector of Banham, Norfolk, in 1371; and Thomas Martyn(s), a King's Hall commoner in 1491–2, 1493–4 and 1495–6, was admitted as rector of Papworth St Agnes, Cambridgeshire, in 1497.[125] Relatives or friends of college fellows sometimes boarded for brief spells as commoners, and here the purpose would have been social rather than academic.[126]

As indicated earlier in this chapter, some commoners of noble lineage attended colleges before 1500. At the King's Hall some of the noble commoners already held ecclesiastical offices upon admission to the college. These included Gilbert, rector of Halsall, Lancashire; Richard Moresby, with diverse rectorships to his credit; and John and William, the natural sons of the earl of Huntingdon, both of whom were rectors at the time of their entry, and who were accounted for as commoners in 1440–1 and 1441–2.[127] Other

---

[124] Emden, *B.R.U.C.*, p. 328; see also Attwater, *Pembroke College, Cambridge*, pp. 20–1.

[125] For Clerevaus, see King's Hall Accounts, ii. fos. 81, 129, and Emden, *B.R.U.C.*, p. 138; for Martyn(s), see King's Hall Accounts, xvii. fo. 17v; xviii. fos. 139, 166v; xix. fos. 41v, and Emden, *B.R.U.C.*, p. 394.

[126] Cobban, *The King's Hall*, p. 278.

[127] Ibid., p. 276; Emden, *B.R.U.C.*, pp. 282, 322, 410; King's Hall Accounts, ix. fos. 161v, 162; x. fo. 13v.

commoners of noble lineage evidently did not hold an ecclesiastical position upon admission to this royal establishment. These included William Bardolf, brother of Thomas, fifth Lord Bardolf, and one of the *nobiles* on the Colville roll, the Cambridge University roll of petitions for benefices sent to the papal curia in *c.* 1390, who was charged as a commoner between 1387–8 and 1389–90;[128] and Sir Henry Huntingdon, who succeeded to the earldom of Huntingdon and the dukedom of Exeter in 1447, and was a commoner from 1439–40 to 1441–2.[129] At Gonville College, Cambridge, John de Ufford, the third son of Robert, earl of Suffolk, entered as an undergraduate commoner or pensioner in *c.* 1350, aged only about nine years, and, despite his youth, obtained a papal dispensation to enable him to hold various ecclesiastical livings; and between 1490 and 1500, John de la Pole, son of the second duke of Suffolk, when rector of Barrowby in Lincolnshire resided in Gonville as a pensioner, and during this time proceeded to degrees in civil and canon law.[130] Henry Beaufort, the second illegitimate son of John of Gaunt, duke of Lancaster, and future cardinal and chancellor of Oxford University and of England, was present as a commoner at Peterhouse in 1388–9 and at Queen's College, Oxford, between 1390 and 1393.[131] University College, Oxford, though catering mainly for mature commoners, in impressive numbers, received at intervals a few noble undergraduate commoners, such as Robert Hungerford, later Lord Hungerford and Moleyns, resident for three terms in 1437–8 under the care of his tutor, master John Chedworth; and John Tiptoft, the future earl of Worcester and humanist patron, resident between 1440–1 and 1443–4 with his

---

[128] King's Hall Accounts, iii. fos. 19, 43, 74v; see also Emden, *B.R.U.C.*, p. 36, and E. F. Jacob, 'Petitions for Benefices from English Universities during the Great Schism', *T.R.H.S.*, 4th ser., xxvii (1945), pp. 41 ff. at p. 58.

[129] King's Hall Accounts, ix. fos. 106v, 162; x. fo. 13v; see also *B.R.U.C.*, p. 321.

[130] *B.R.U.C.*, pp. 180–1, 603.

[131] Ibid., p. 46; T. A. Walker, *A Biographical Register of Peterhouse Men, Part i 1284–1574* (Cambridge, 1927), pp. 23–4. Beaufort was charged 20s. for his room at Peterhouse in 1388–9: Peterhouse Archives, Computus Roll for 1388–9.

tutor, master John Hurley.[132] Oriel College hosted as a commoner between 1409 and 1412 William Scrope, who was the son of Stephen, second Lord Scrope of Masham, and subsequently lived as a commoner at Queen's College from 1420 to 1426.[133] And John Lowe, of noble birth, resided in Lincoln College as a commoner in 1455–6 when archdeacon of Rochester.[134]

The King's Hall, Cambridge, absorbed an impressively large number of commoners. The King's Hall Accounts record that between 1337 and 1500 no fewer than 120 full commoners, including 52 ex-fellows, resided in the college; and that in the same period, about 100 semi-commoners lived in the college, the majority of them in the fifteenth century.[135] The size of the commoner population of University College, Oxford, approached that of the commoner population of the King's Hall. The names of at least 187 commoners are recorded in the University College Bursars' Rolls for the period between 1385–6 and 1495–6.[136] It is to be supposed that these totals for commoners at the King's Hall and University College were unusually large for their respective universities and that their colonies of collegiate commoners would normally have been much smaller. The Treasurers' Accounts of Oriel for 1409–15 and 1450–82 yield at least 30 commoners; and the two Bursars' Books of Lincoln for the fifteenth century, beginning in 1455, indicate the presence of about a dozen commoners. By contrast, the Bursars' and Receipt Rolls of New College from 1376–7 to 1500 and the three Bursars' Books of All Souls of the

---

[132] For Hungerford and Tiptoft, see Emden, *B.R.U.O.*, ii. 985; iii. 1877–9. Hungerford was aged about 9 or 10 when living in college; Tiptoft was aged between 13 and 16. See also Orme, *From Childhood to Chivalry*, p. 71.

[133] Oriel College Archives, *Treasurers' Accounts*, i (1409–15), pp. 39, 85; see also *B.R.U.O.*, iii. 1660–1.

[134] Lincoln College Archives, Bursars' Books, i. p. 13 (of account for 1455): see also *B.R.U.O.*, ii. 1169.

[135] Cobban, *The King's Hall*, pp. 273–4.

[136] Cobban, 'The King's Hall, Cambridge, and English medieval collegiate history', *Authority and Power: Studies on Medieval Law and Government*, p. 189. The magnificent series of Bursars' Rolls of University College begins in 1381–2.

second half of the fifteenth century supply no evidence of commoners beyond short-stay guests and casual visitors, including university bedels, bailiffs, and tradesmen.

The reasons for the differing collegiate attitudes towards commoners are not easy to elucidate. Generally speaking, all colleges were suitably wary about the admission of academic commoners. Most codes of college statutes place a cautious emphasis upon the trustworthiness of potential commoners. In 1566, the founder of St John's College, Oxford, Sir Thomas White, reduced the quota of statutory commoners from 16 to 12 because 'inconvenyence cometh by borders in my colledge'.[137] Although this concern about outsiders is similarly reflected in the King's Hall statutes,[138] the college was clearly not deterred from admitting a strikingly large concourse of commoners and semi-commoners. It is understandable that college authorities had to guard against the entry of commoners who might prove to be a financial burden or who might introduce dissension into the college. These fears were evidently not always groundless. That the commoner intake could be at least a temporary financial drag upon a college may be illustrated from the situation at the King's Hall, where, by 1454–5, the arrears of 11 commoners owing for commons, sizings, room-rents and servants amounted to £63 3s. 10¼d., with individual debts ranging from 4s. 10¼d. to £24 9s. 3½d.[139] It was probably because of financial difficulties of this kind that the King's Hall markedly curtailed commoner admission in the second half of the fifteenth century, and this curtailment culminated

---

[137] For the statutory evidence, see e.g. the statutes of Michaelhouse, Stamp, *Michaelhouse*, p. 44; the statutes of Peterhouse, Clare and King's, *Camb. Docs.*, ii. 27, 136–7, 534–6; the statutes of Merton, Balliol, Oriel, Queen's and New College, *Statutes*, i. ch. 2, 13 (1270), 26 (1274); i. ch. 1, 20; i. ch. 3, 8; i. ch. 4, 18; i. ch. 5, 43. For Sir Thomas White's statement, see W. H. Stevenson and H. E. Salter, *The Early History of St John's College Oxford* (Oxf. Hist. Soc., new ser., i, 1939), p. 421.

[138] See the statutes in Rouse Ball, *The King's Scholars and King's Hall*, p. 66.

[139] See the entries for arrears of John Derby, Richard Lyes, John Whyte, Richard Moresby, John Bank, Robert Fereby, Stephen Close, Robert Ayscogh, Adam Copyndale, William Alnewyk and Thomas Wilton in King's Hall Accounts, xii. fos. 26–8; also Cobban, *The King's Hall*, p. 273.

in the virtual demise of commoner admission there in the first half of the sixteenth century.[140]

It is sometimes asserted that the English colleges looked on pre-Reformation commoners as a means of augmenting their revenues.[141] The profit motive behind the maintenance of commoners was doubtless a real one in the English Universities, just as it was at Paris. But from the limited evidence available on the workings of the commoner system at colleges such as the King's Hall and Queen's, it seems unlikely that much financial benefit was in fact realized.[142] The efficiency with which commoner arrangements were administered may have varied from college to college. On balance, however, it would appear that the admission of mature commoners was not a lucrative practice, yielding at most only a marginal profit. In the course of time considerations other than money came to prevail. Some college founders came to see that good advantage was to be derived from a cautious diversification of the college complement. A moderate degree of intellectual and social contact with more mobile associates of like-minded interests could only have a broadening and salutary effect upon the fellows. For reasons of this kind, Robert Wodelarke intended that commoners should form from the beginning in the 1470s an integral part of his college of St Catharine's, Cambridge.[143]

The diversity of the commoner population at the English Universities can best be illustrated by the social and intellectual mix which may be glimpsed in several of the medieval colleges.[144] As previously mentioned, University College, Oxford, possessed an

---

[140] Cobban, op. cit., pp. 274, 275.

[141] See e.g. the remarks of Carr, *University College*, p. 19, and for Paris colleges, Gabriel, 'The College System in the Fourteenth-Century Universities', *The Forward Movement of the Fourteenth Century*, p. 93.

[142] See Cobban, *The King's Hall*, pp. 272–3, and Hodgkin, *Six Centuries of an Oxford College*, p. 28, n. 1.

[143] See Cobban, 'Origins: Robert Wodelarke and St Catharine's', *St Catharine's College 1473–1973*, pp. 18–20.

[144] The following analysis has been derived from University College Archives, Bursars' Rolls, 1385–6–c.1494–5, PYX EE Fasc. 1/5 – PYX GG Fasc. 2/6; Oriel College Archives, *Treasurers' Accounts*, i (1409–15), pp. 39, 85, 126, 158, 192; ii (1450–82), pp. 1, 15, 55, 67, 83, 97, 111, 127, 159, 173, 189,

exceedingly large number of commoners. The names of at least 187
are recorded for the period between 1385–6 and *c*. 1495–6, and they
remained for periods extending from under a year to eighteen years.
Of these commoners, 12 were ex-fellows of University College,
and 5 were former masters of the college; 10 were ex-fellows of
Merton and 2 were subsequently fellows of that college; 6 were ex-
fellows of New College; 2 were ex-fellows of Queen's; 1 was an ex-
fellow of Oriel and 1 probably of Exeter. Two of the commoners,
Robert FitzHugh and Christopher Urswick, later became wardens
of the King's Hall;[145] and 5 were ex-principals of Oxford halls.
During the time that they were commoners of University College,
at least 52 were rectors, 11 were secular canons, 10 were
Augustinian canons, 5 were vicars, 2 were archdeacons and 2 were
Cistercian monks; and there was 1 Benedictine monk and 1
Premonstratensian abbot. In the realm of university administration,
6 of the commoners had acted as procters, and 5 did so during their
residence in University College; and 2 acted as chancellor's
commissaries. Four of the commoners were later to become
bishops, and these included Richard Fleming, the founder of
Lincoln College. Of the Oriel commoners recorded as having
studied there between 1409 and 1415 and between 1450 and 1482,
at least 12 were ex-fellows of the college; 3 were ex-fellows of other
colleges; 5 were ex-principals of halls and one other probably was;
and 2 were ex-commoners of external colleges. Moreover, 2 of the
commoners, Thomas Lentwardyn and Thomas Hawkins, who
were both ex-fellows, later became provosts of Oriel,[146] 1
commoner became a fellow of the college and another a warden of
Merton. Oriel commoner, Robert Gilbert, subsequently became

269, 291, 315, 339, 363, 409, 421, 440, 490, 570 (the Oriel commoners were
much reduced in number towards the end of the fifteenth century and very few
are recorded in *Treasurers' Accounts*, iii. (1482–1515); Lincoln College
Archives, Bursars' Books, i. p. 13 (of account for 1455), p. 11 (of account for
1476), p. 11 (of account for 1477); ii. p. 8 (of account for 1495). These
documentary sources are complemented by Emden, *B.R.U.O.* and *B.R.U.C.*

[145] For FitzHugh and Urswick, see Cobban, *The King's Hall*, pp. 284–5, and
B.R.U.C., pp. 231–2, 605–6.

[146] *B.R.U.O.*, ii. 891–2, 1131–2.

dean of the chapel royal, and then, in 1436, bishop of London,[147] and a galaxy of the Oriel commoners were archdeacons, rectors, canons or prebendaries either during their residence in college or in later years. The colony of Lincoln College commoners, the composition of which has been reconstructed from the records of a few years in the second half of the fifteenth century, embraced 3 ex-fellows, 2 of Lincoln and 1 of Merton; 1 ex-commoner of University College; 1 ex-principal of a hall; and John Tristrope, an ex-fellow of Lincoln, who was appointed rector of the college a few years after his sojourn there as a commoner.[148] As in the case of Oriel and University College, Lincoln harboured commoners who were archdeacons, rectors, canons or prebendaries either during or after their residence in the college. One of the most distinguished of these was Richard Cordon, D.C.L. by 1430, who died in his rooms as a commoner of Lincoln in 1452 when still archdeacon of Rochester. He had previously been advocate of the court of Canterbury and advocate of the papal consistory during the pontificate of Martin IV, and had held a variety of rectorships, canonries and prebendaries.[149]

It has been stated above that ex-fellows constituted about a quarter of the known full commoners and semi-commoners at the King's Hall, that is, 52 out of over 200 commoners identifiable between 1337 and 1500. An analysis of the ex-fellow pensioners of the King's Hall yields a number of conclusions which are of general interest for this elusive topic.[150] Most of the ex-fellows had vacated their fellowships upon promotion to benefices, and some of them were subsequently granted an episcopal licence to study at university for a stipulated period. Ex-fellow pensioners of this study-type were resident in the college for the greater part of each year when pursuing degree courses. Other ex-fellows, during the time that they were King's Hall pensioners and living in the college,

---

[147] Ibid., ii. 766–7.

[148] For Tristrope, see ibid., iii. 1908–9; see also V. H. H. Green, *The Commonwealth of Lincoln College 1427–1977* (Oxford, 1979), pp. 31–2.

[149] *B.R.U.O.*, i. 486–7; see also Green, op. cit., p. 19.

[150] See Cobban, *The King's Hall*, pp. 266–8.

participated in diocesan administration in such capacities as episcopal chancellors or vicars general, and as archdeacons or their officials. Limited conclusions may be reached as to how ex-fellow pensioners who held benefices apportioned their time between the college and their charges. It has been found that beneficed ex-fellow pensioners did not neglect their livings by excessive residence in the college: time and energies were divided irregularly between the King's Hall and ecclesiastical livings and, in some instances, the pensionership served as a base in the period between the tenure of successive benefices. For the majority of ex-fellows, life as a pensioner or commoner was not an end in itself. It was regarded either as a means by which a former fellow might be conveniently housed while continuing his studies or as affording an attractive lodging place, retained for intermittent use by those actively engaged in ecclesiastical administration.

Of the 52 ex-fellow pensioners present in the King's Hall between 1337 and 1500, no fewer than 33 retained one or more private servants, who were charged at the rate of half commons;[151] and of the 68 full commoners who had never been fellows, 21 maintained servants.[152] It is clear that a prolonged stay in the King's Hall must have been a rather expensive business for ex-fellows and for the other categories of commoners. From the rates levied on commoners, it may be calculated that a commoner who paid the full commons rate and who resided for a year would have incurred a bill of about £5 for his commons alone.[153] To this must be added an allowance for extra commons (sizings), which might range in cost from ¼d. to 1s. or more per week. If the rounded sum of 6d. is adopted as representing an average weekly expenditure on extra commons, this means that about £1 6s. would have been spent on sizings per annum. Moreover, if a commoner retained a servant at the rate of half commons, the cost of maintenance of this servant for

---

[151] Ibid., p. 270: the term *famulus* was the one usually employed to denote a private servant but *garcio* and *clericus* are occasionally found.

[152] Ibid., p. 279.

[153] For this and the following calculations concerning commoners' expenses, see ibid., p. 271.

the year would have been about £2 3s. 4d.[154] Finally, to these expenses must be added the rent of his room or rooms. Rents ranged from 6s. 8d. or 10s. for a single room to 13s. 4d. for a set of two chambers, one of which would probably have been a small study area. Since 13s. 4d. was the most usual charge for full commoners, this may be taken as the average rent. These estimated sums for expenditure give a total of £9 2s. 8d. per annum, and this indicates very roughly that the maintenance costs for a full commoner in the King's Hall was in the region of 3s. 6d. a week. A comparison between these sums and those deduced for the average King's Hall fellow, whose board and lodging were subsidized, discloses that the maintenance expenditure for a commoner was substantially larger than that for a fellow. Given that the average King's Hall fellow almost certainly had to spend a good deal more on his basic requirements than was general among fellows of medieval English colleges, it may be assumed that the expenditure levels of King's Hall commoners were untypically high. Nevertheless, the difference in amount between commoner and fellow expenditure at the King's Hall is perhaps a representative pointer to that which obtained in the majority of the medieval colleges of Oxford and Cambridge.

Judging from the rates charged for the rooms of commoners elsewhere, the King's Hall rentals of 6s. 8d., 10s. and 13s. 4d., assessed presumably on the basis of the number, size and quality of the rooms, were moderate.[155] For example, when John Wyclif and Nicholas of Hereford lived as *commensales* at Queen's College, Oxford, in the latter half of the fourteenth century, they were charged 20s. for their rooms;[156] at Oriel, the Treasurers' Accounts of the fifteenth century indicate that the most usual room-rent was 13s. 4d. per annum, with a few rents at 10s. and 20s., the last being

---

[154] For the purposes of this calculation 10d. has been selected as the average rate for half commons.

[155] Cobban, *The King's Hall*, pp. 268–9.

[156] Wyclif paid 40s. for two rooms in 1365–6; and in 1374–5 and 1380–1 he paid 20s. Nicholas of Hereford paid 20s. for a room in 1380–1, and one 'Britell' paid a room-rent of 20s. in 1374–5: see J. R. Magrath, *The Queen's College* (2 vols., Oxford, 1921), i. 122 and notes, and Hodgkin, 'The Queen's College', *V.C.H. Oxon.* iii. 133.

the annual rent charged to Thomas Gascoigne for more than twenty years, after which, in 1449, he was granted a rent-free room for life;[157] at University College, the Bursars' Rolls of the late fourteenth and fifteenth centuries record room-rents varying from 6s. 8d. to 20s.; at Lincoln College, the two Bursars' Books of the second half of the fifteenth century yield room-rents ranging from 6s. 8d. to 16s.; and, in a general survey of Oxford *commensales*, H.E. Salter cites as typical room-rents ones of 10s., 13s. 4d., 16s. and 20s.[158]

It is clear that there were opportunities for the promotion of commoners to the ranks of the fellows. At the King's Hall, for example, at least four of the fellows before 1500 had previously been commoners in the college, and a further four fellows had been semi-commoners;[159] and at St Catharine's College, Cambridge, two of the commoners or *commensales* who had entered the college when it first opened in November 1473 were later promoted to fellowships, and it is probable that these were not isolated cases at St Catharine's.[160] As already mentioned, there are dramatic instances of commoners, such as Thomas Lentwardyn of Oriel and John Tristrope of Lincoln, becoming heads of their colleges in subsequent years,[161] although it needs to be added that both Lentwardyn and Tristrope had been fellows of their colleges before their period as commoners. However, while a degree of academic mobility existed for members of the commoner class, it is doubtful whether promotions to fellowships occurred on a significant scale. They appear to have been occasional happenings, making sporadic breaches in the rather solid wall dividing foundation fellows from the motley assembly of tolerated lodgers.

The study of the mature commoner population of the medieval English Universities, and of those of the universities of continental

---

[157] *The Dean's Register of Oriel, 1446–1661*, p. 370.

[158] Salter, *Medieval Oxford*, p. 100.

[159] Cobban, *The King's Hall*, pp. 263–4.

[160] Cobban, 'Origins: Robert Wodelarke and St Catharine's', *St Catharine's College 1473–1973*, p. 20.

[161] See above, pp. 334, 335.

Europe, is an important area for further research. For contact with this variegated class formed one of the principal means by which college fellows were enabled to interact intellectually and socially with representatives from differing sections of extra-university society. It is apparent that any analysis of the medieval academic community in the English Universities which failed to take due notice of this elusive category of personnel would not do justice to the rich diversity of that community before 1500.[162] This fluid commoner grouping on the academic margins requires further detailed and co-ordinated research if its place within the university framework is to be fully evaluated.

In previous chapters, mention has been made of the principal common servants of the English Universities: bedels, registrars, chaplains and librarians, as well as other 'privileged persons', such as stationers, illuminators, scribes, parchment-dealers and bookbinders, who were regarded as members of the extended academic community.[163] To these must be added the company of college and hall servants, who became a distinctive element within the university population in the later medieval period. Judging from the impressive lists of servants prescribed by founders of English colleges, it would seem that the average English fellow enjoyed service facilities superior to those of his Parisian counterpart. Whereas the typical Paris college of the fourteenth century often provided only one or two servants for the entire complement of fellows, in England all but the poorest of colleges furnished a range of domestics, who relieved the fellows of most of the essential internal chores and maximized the time available for academic concerns.[164] For example, the King's Hall's earliest account, of 1337–8, reveals that the regular staff then comprised a butler, a cook, a laundress, a barber and one other servant, who probably

---

[162] E. Russell, 'The Influx of Commoners into the University of Oxford before 1581: an optical illusion?', art. cit., recognizes the presence of commoners *a. 1500*, but she appears to underestimate both their numbers and their significance quite seriously.

[163] See above, chapter 3, pp. 90–5 and chapter 7, pp. 269–72.

[164] Cobban, *The King's Hall*, p. 231; for the corps of servants at Lincoln College, see Green, *The Commonwealth of Lincoln College 1427–1977*, pp. 95, 231–4.

filled the office of baker.[165] By 1347–8, a servant who combined the functions of baker and brewer had emerged as a permanent employee.[166] From c.1472–3, however, and until the dissolution of the college, separate bakers and brewers were regularly engaged each year.[167] An undercook and underbaker made their appearance in the second half of the fourteenth century.[168] The position of janitor emerged between 1492 and 1495, and was subsequently combined with the office of barber.[169]

The most colourful college functionary was the book-bearer (*portitor* or *lator librorum*), a servant hired to carry the fellows' books to and from the university schools. This position was instituted at the King's Hall in 1356–7.[170] The office was a fairly regular one in the fourteenth and early fifteenth centuries. It became less so later in the fifteenth century and the tasks of the book-bearer were occasionally fulfilled by other members of the domestic staff, for instance, by the baker in 1443–4 and by the barber in 1449–50.[171] From the academic character of the college, it may be surmised that book-bearing arrangements were particularly necessary at the King's Hall because of the emphasis placed there upon legal studies. As there seems to have been a strong obligation on students taking courses in law to possess copies of a proportion of the bulky set texts (although this was not stipulated in the Cambridge statutes, as it was in the Oxford ones[172]), it may be deemed likely that the provision of transport facilities for books between the college and the lecture rooms was a much-appreicated luxury. The office of book-bearer is found to have existed in at least three other colleges,

---

[165] King's Hall Accounts, i. fo. 8v.

[166] Ibid., i. fo. 117v.

[167] Cobban, op. cit., p. 231.

[168] Loc. cit.

[169] King's Hall Accounts, xvii. fo. 11v; xviii. fo 162; xix. fos. 12v, 117v, 160.

[170] Ibid., ii. fo. 12, where a quarterly payment of 3s. is recorded as having been made to Hugo Bukbereher.

[171] Ibid., x. fo. 62; xi. fo. 71v.

[172] Gibson, *Statuta Antiqua*, pp. 43, 44, 46.

all of which were prominent legal centres. Stipends for book-bearers were recorded in the Bursars' and Receipt Rolls of New College from the late fourteenth century, and the office was prescribed in the statutes of All Souls College, Oxford, where it was combined with that of gardener, and in the statutes of King's College, Cambridge.[173]

It was common for colleges to engage staff annually for the permanent domestic offices by means of formal written agreements.[174] Sometimes these agreements furnish details of the liveries supplied. A high proportion of the college servants seem to have been liveried on a differential basis according to status, butlers usually occupying the first rank in the sartorial hierarchy.[175] College laundresses were generally non-liveried servants who were not permitted to reside on the premises. Most medieval codes of college statutes affirm that, as far as is possible, all domestics employed within the precincts of the college are to be males.[176] Where a laundress had to be hired, elaborate precautions were to be taken to ensure that personal contacts with the fellows were kept to an absolute minimum. In the statutes of New College, All Souls, and King's College, it is specifically stated that the laundress is to live in the town.[177] Taking wages only into consideration, laundresses tended to be among the highest paid of the college servants, their stipends presumably containing an assessed monetary equivalent for the college board and lodging, from the enjoyment of which they were precluded by reason of their sex. At the King's Hall, the annual wage of the laundress varied from 10s. to 20s. between 1337–8 and 1399–1400, and between 1401 and c. 1465, the

---

[173] New College Archives, Bursars' and Receipt Rolls, 7711(1), 7330(2), 7332(4), 7336(8); *Statutes*, i. ch. 7, 58–9; *Camb. Docs.*, ii. 596.

[174] For examples of these agreements (*conventiones*), see King's Hall Accounts, vii. fos. 10v, 81v; xii. fo. 137v; xiii. fo. 112v; xv. fo. 72v.

[175] For the liveries of the domestic staff at the King's Hall, see Cobban, *The King's Hall*, pp. 233–5.

[176] See e.g. the statutes of Merton (1270 and 1274), Oriel and New College in *Statutes*, i. ch. 2, 19–20, 36–7; i. ch. 3, 15; i. ch. 5, 94; also the statutes of King's in *Camb. Docs.*, ii. 596.

[177] *Statutes*, i. ch. 5, 94; i. ch. 7, 58; *Camb. Docs.*, ii. 596.

rate was fixed at 20s. In 1466–7, the stipend was raised to 25s. It was augmented to 26s. 8d. in 1475–6 and was stabilized at this level until the mid-sixteenth century.[178] At Merton, the laundress was paid 20s. or 21s. 8d. a year in the fifteenth century,[179] and at New College, the laundress was hired at 26s. 8d. a year in 1381–2 and 1383–5, and at the princely rate of 40s. a year in 1390–1.[180] Although the stipend of the laundress at Lincoln College was only 13s. 4d. in the late fifteenth century, it had increased dramatically to 36s. by 1574.[181] In strictly cash terms, these wage levels brought laundresses into the remunerative range of senior college servants, and they are indicative of the value which English colleges attached to a regime of cleanliness among their residents.

College domestic staff had to be versatile and prepared on occasion to fill a gap as the need arose. The intermittent book-bearing activites of the barber and baker at the King's Hall have been observed above, and in 1486–7, the barber had to step in to fill the office of butler for a year.[182] Moreover, servants were sometimes called upon to transact external college business. In 1468–9, for example, the King's Hall barber journeyed to London on behalf of the college, and in 1505–6, the barber was dispatched to purchase wheat for the college in place of one of the contracting seneschals, who were the fellows with responsibility for making contracts for the bulk procurement of provisions.[183] At Lincoln College, Oxford, the manciple or steward would sometimes ride with the

---

[178] For these wage rates of the laundress, see Cobban, op. cit., p. 233.

[179] For payments to laundresses in the early fifteenth century, see Merton College Archives, Bursars' Rolls, 3727, 3737, 3750; for payments in the late fifteenth century, see J. M. Fletcher and C. A. Upton, ' "Monastic enclave" or "open society"? A consideration of the role of women in the life of an Oxford college community in the early Tudor period', *History of Education*, 16 (1987), pp. 1 ff. at pp. 6–7.

[180] New College Archives, Bursars' and Receipt Rolls, 7330(2), 7332(4), 7336(8).

[181] Lincoln College Archives, Bursars' Books, i. p. 26 (of account for 1487–8); Green, *The Commonwealth of Lincoln College 1427–1977*, p. 233, n. 6.

[182] King's Hall Accounts, xviii. fo. 12v.

[183] Ibid., xiv. fo. 6; xx. fo. 127.

bursar to inspect college estates, would deliver missives to the college visitors, and would collect rents from college tenants.[184]

While some of the unmarried domestic staff were boarded in the college, married servants and ex-servants who lived in the town were not uncommonly housed as tenants in college property. Illustration of this may be made from the extremely copious records of the King's Hall. Towards the middle of the fifteenth century, the college acquired a series of tenements situated in the Cambridge parish of All Saints in Jewry.[185] For the next eighty years or so, these properties were rented out to a variety of townspeople and to a number of the college's domestic servants, among whom butlers, bakers, brewers, cooks and laundresses were much in evidence. Thomas Kelsay and his wife, baker and laundress to the King's Hall, inhabited one of these tenements for some years; and in 1457-8, John Gylmyn, who ceased to serve as the King's Hall butler in that year, leased one of the holdings for a twelve-year period at an annual rent of 40s.[186] In this manner, some colleges became both employers and landlords to members of their domestic staff.

Because of the dearth of material relating to the internal economies of halls and hostels, not much information is available on the common servants of these unendowed institutions. It may be deduced, however, that manciples and cooks stood at the apex of the hierarchy of servants. Manciples or stewards were responsible for provisioning the halls and hostels, and they also appear to have kept account books, although none have yet come to light.[187] A few of the manciples were scholars but mostly they were townspeople.[188] It seems that instances occurred of Oxford manciples setting up as principals of halls, a trend which prompted a

---

[184] Green, op. cit., p. 231.

[185] Cobban, *The King's Hall*, pp. 240-1.

[186] For Kelsay and his wife, see King's Hall Accounts, xix. fos. 132, 157v; for Gylmyn, see ibid., xii. fo. 85v.

[187] *Registrum Cancellarii*, i. 187.

[188] Catto, 'Citizens, Scholars and Masters', *The History of the University of Oxford*, i. 182; on manciples, see Bennett, *Chaucer at Oxford and at Cambridge*, pp. 103-5.

statute of *a*.1380 making it an offence for any manciple or other servant of scholars to occupy a principalship.[189] This legislation may have been hastened by the murky reputation for lawlessness which manciples, as a class, had hitherto acquired. The evidence of the Oxford coroners' rolls of the fourteenth century, which record cases of manciples involved in robbery, assault and murder, suggests that their unsavoury image was not wholly without substance.[190] Manciples were also commonly suspected of creaming off supplies purchased for hall communities for the purpose of private retail in the town. By an early statute of *a*.1313, Oxford attempted to prohibit this practice,[191] although it is difficult to estimate the degree of success achieved. Whatever the case, the reputation of manciples appears to have improved somewhat in the fifteenth century, in the sense that they were then less obviously associated with major crime.

One important component of the academic population remains to be considered. This section comprised those who were involved in what may be called the area of 'university extension'. This can be defined as that area of university study which catered for students who attended university not in order to follow an official degree course, but in order to undertake a practical training in preparation for a particular line of employment. The subjects taught under this umbrella were closely allied to *dictamen* and its specialist offshoot, the *ars notaria*. *Dictamen (ars dictaminis* or *ars dictandi*) was the art of letter-writing, the art of drafting all types of official documents according to rigorous procedural rules. It became an indispensable training for clerks in papal, imperial, royal and episcopal service, and for those employed in genteel and noble households.[192] The *ars notaria*, which evolved from *dictamen*, embraced a series of skills specifically related to the professional needs of the craft of the

[189] *Statuta Antiqua*, pp. 182–3; see also Emden, *An Oxford Hall in Medieval Times*, p. 37.

[190] *Records of Mediaeval Oxford*, ed. cit., pp. 13, 19, 22, 23, 55–6.

[191] *Statuta Antiqua*, p. 153; see also Emden, op. cit., p. 41.

[192] On *dictamen* and its practitioners, the *dictatores*, see Haskins, *Studies in Mediaeval Culture*, chs. i, vi, ix; see also Cobban, *The Medieval Universities*, pp. 221–2.

notary, and was in heavy demand in those regions of Europe where the civil law prevailed.[193] *Dictamen* was raised to a position of primacy in the arts faculties of some of the Italian Universities in the thirteenth century, although there is no evidence that it achieved a separate faculty status in this group of universities. It is, however, strong witness to the close relationship which existed between the Italian Universities and the professional needs of society that the *ars notaria* attained a separate, quasi-faculty standing, first at Bologna by 1250, and then at other Italian *studia* later in the century.[194] The *ars notaria* was not taught in England in any formal sense, and neither the *ars dictandi* nor the *ars notaria* developed separate faculty organization at Oxford or Cambridge. Nevertheless, something akin to these disciplines, an adulterated and semi-official form of them, was taught at Oxford. English society did not create a demand for notaries in any way comparable to that created on the Continent. Civil law, viewed as in some measure antagonistic to the common law, was not widely utilized in thirteenth-century England, though it was afforded more outlets in the fourteenth and fifteenth centuries. Although notarial opportunities were limited in England, notaries were to be found there in the thirteenth century and they were present in some numbers in the fourteenth century.[195] They were employed, for example, to apply civil-law procedures in ecclesiastical courts, in mercantile business and in a range of governmental departments; they were attached to some university colleges, including King's College, Cambridge, and New College and Magdalen College, Oxford, to attest their formal documentation and to authenticate their admissions;[196] and, from

---

[193] For the teaching of *dictamen* and the *ars notaria* in Italy and France, see Paetow, *The Arts Course at Medieval Universities*, pp. 67 ff.

[194] Loc. cit.

[195] See Cheney, *Notaries Public in England in the Thirteenth and Fourteenth Centuries*, *passim*.

[196] For King's College, see the statutes in *Camb. Docs.*, ii. 497, 503, 515, and the series of *Libri Protocollorum* in King's College Archives. In 1448, Henry VI, on behalf of King's, obtained a papal bull which conceded to the provost and his successors the right to create notaries, and until the Reformation, the notaries at the college were usually actual or former fellows: see T. Brocklebank, 'Notaries Public in King's College, Cambridge', *C.A.S., Communications*, iii

the late fifteenth century, the Oxford registrar was required to be a notary.[197] It is of considerable interest that, from an early date, Oxford University provided a training in subjects which bore a close affinity to elements of *dictamen* and of the work of the professional notary.

The earliest reference to *dictamen* at Oxford occurs in a university statute of *a*. 1313 relating to grammar, which reveals that a knowledge of *dictamen* was a necessary qualification for a teacher of grammar.[198] A statute of 1432 gives an important insight into the teaching of the 'useful subjects' at Oxford.[199] The purpose of the statute was disciplinary: it was framed in order to impose a stricter control over students learning the art of writing, the *ars dictandi*, French, the composition of deeds and procedural routine in the English courts.[200] It is improbable that students of this kind were engaged upon the arts course proper, for they are described as 'scholars competent only in grammar' (*scolares competenter in gramatica solummodo*). The implication here is that Oxford accepted students who went to university for a wholly utilitarian regime of study — one that would fit them for a business career. The subjects listed in this statute of 1432 indicate that such students were given a cram course of study in at least some of the practical elements which were constituents of *dictamen* and the *ars notaria*, although at a simplified and less integrated level. It is not to be supposed that the Oxford instruction was concerned with the professional requirements of the notary public as such. It would, however, have

---

(1864–76), pp. 47 ff.; for New College, see New College Archives, *The Registrum Primum* alias *Liber Albus* (*c*.1400–*c*.1480), 9654, *passim*, and also the notarial instrument of 14 December 1402, 9468; for Magdalen College, see Magdalen College Archives, *Register A 1480–92*, *passim*.

[197] *Statuta Antiqua*, p. 285.

[198] Ibid., p. 20. Business studies at Oxford are discussed by Cobban, *The Medieval Universities*, pp. 222–5, and Orme, *English Schools in the Middle Ages*, pp. 75–7, 190.

[199] *Statuta Antiqua*, p. 240.

[200] Loc. cit. See H. G. Richardson, 'Business Training in Medieval Oxford', *A.H.R.*, xlvi (1940–1), pp. 259 ff. at p. 259; see also Richardson, 'An Oxford Teacher of the Fifteenth Century', *B.J.R.L.*, xxiii (1939), pp. 436 ff.

grounded the student in legal principles and familiarized him with selected procedures of notarial practice.[201] It seems that subjects of this nature were taught in a rudimentary form at Oxford from the early part of the thirteenth century — from the reign of John, there has survived a legal formulary pertaining to the drafting of letters and other documents — and it is likely that business training of this kind was sustained at Oxford until it faded out in the course of the fifteenth century, for reasons which are not altogether intelligible.

By the beginning of the reign of Henry III, there was at Oxford a colony of teachers who specialized in the 'useful subjects' — those considered to have a direct application to the practical problems of business administration.[202] The teachers of these courses, which covered the drafting of charters, wills and letters, conveyancing, the keeping of accounts, court practice and heraldry, did not necessarily possess a degree.[203] Nevertheless, they set up their schools in the town of Oxford, and they were subject to the jurisdiction of the university authorities, who thereby gave an explicit recognition to the system of university extension. Among the foremost of these teachers was Thomas Sampson, who taught in Oxford from *c*. 1350 to 1409. Judging from his extant formularies of model letters and deeds, he seems to have been primarily a practitioner of *dictamen*, although the teaching of accountancy and conveyancing was also included in his repertoire. A certain Simon O. and William Kingsmill were among the noted teachers in the Sampson mould in early fifteenth-century Oxford. As indicated above, it is probable that many of the youthful students who attended these practical courses had at no time intended to take a degree. A few of the

---

[201] See Cheney, op. cit., p. 78. On similarities between Italian notarial manuals and the subject-matter taught at Oxford, see J. J. Murphy, 'Rhetoric in Fourteenth-Century Oxford', *Medium Aevum*, xxxiv (1965), pp. 1 ff. at pp. 15–17. On vocational training of this nature, see generally I. Hajnal, *L'Enseignement de l'écriture aux universités médiévales* (2nd ed., L. Mezey, Budapest, 1959), ch. v; also Hajnal, 'A propos de l'enseignement de l'écriture dans les universités médiévales', *Scriptorium*, xi (1957), pp. 3 ff.

[202] Richardson, 'Business Training in Medieval Oxford', p. 275; also W. A. Pantin, 'A Medieval Treatise on Letter-Writing, with examples, from the Rylands Latin MS. 394', *B.J.R.L.*, xiii (1929), pp. 326 ff.

[203] Richardson, art. cit., p. 261; *Statuta Antiqua*, pp. 169, 172.

students, however, may have been refugees from the arts course who had come to grief, cut their losses and settled for a less exacting but 'useful' course of study. One of Sampson's letters mentions a boy who transferred from the arts course in order to learn a range of practical disciplines preparatory to entering aristocratic service.[204] The object of this type of utilitarian study at Oxford was not to turn out a finished product. It was to lay a necessary foundation for the many facets of a business career. It was a training which might be compressed into no more than six months[205] and it would have been of an intensive character throughout its duration.

It is apparent, then, that from the early thirteenth century to the mid-fifteenth century there were to be found in operation at Oxford what were in effect university extension courses, which formed a meeting-ground between the more strictly academic concerns of the University and the affairs of the wider world. There is nothing comparable known for Cambridge. But there is evidence that instruction in some features of business life was given by grammar masters in several of England's grammar schools.[206] The phasing out of these utilitarian courses at Oxford in *c*. 1450 may in part be explained by reference to the competition offered by the Inns of Court in London, which mounted teaching in a variety of business subjects, and conceivably on a more co-ordinated basis than that which obtained at Oxford.[207] It is unlikely that Oxford stood alone among the universities of northern Europe with regard to the promotion of business studies,[208] and much about these fringe areas of medieval university life probably remains to be elucidated.

In conclusion, it may be affirmed that the academic populations of Oxford and Cambridge were more stratified in 1500 than they had been in the thirteenth century. On the socio-economic scale, they ranged from the genuinely poor scholar at one end to the

---

[204] *Oxford Formularies*, ii. 407.

[205] Ibid., ii. 372.

[206] Orme, *English Schools in the Middle Ages*, pp. 77–8.

[207] Ibid., p. 77.

[208] Cobban, *The Medieval Universities*, p. 225; also Hajnal, *L'Enseignement de l'écriture aux universités médiévales*, ed. cit., p. 177.

growing and influential aristocratic contingent at the other. This social and economic differentiation clearly undermined the potential for unified action in the face of external encroachment; and it may help to explain the comparative ease with which the English Universities were brought under monarchical control during the sixteenth and seventeenth centuries. While bearing in mind this degree of stratification, it is nonetheless true that before 1500 the average undergraduate at Oxford and Cambridge was from the middle orders of society: he could usually call upon the monetary aid of parents or other relatives, or of guardians or patrons, to sustain him through his university course and to stop him falling into desperate financial straits. In so far as student poverty is concerned, the English Universities failed to evolve a systematic policy for dealing with the problem of the minority of genuinely poor scholars and relied mainly upon a variety of expedients for the mitigation of hardship. These devices must have functioned on a fairly random basis, however, and by no means may it be supposed that poverty was never an ultimate barrier to the scholar of ability. In the endowed sector of the English Universities, college fellowships of the pre-1500 era were designed in the main for the support of scholars of proven merit and limited financial means. Although a private source of income appears to have been necessary, fellows were usually required to vacate their positions when their incomes exceeded a level, always a moderate one, prescribed by their college's statutes: and while exceptions occurred, and statutory provisions were sometimes disregarded, fellowships were generally reserved for scholars of intermediate economic status. Fellowships were not yet conceived of as lucrative posts, held for life irrespective of academic achievement or personal finances. In regard to the other inhabitants of the Universities, there can be little doubt that the jostling army of mature commoners, extending from the struggling semi-commoner to the affluent scion of the aristocracy, combined with the limited number of undergraduate commoners who made their appearance in colleges in the fifteenth century, added a rich vein to the academic populations of Oxford and Cambridge, and especially to the quality of collegiate life, both socially and intellectually. When this commoner element is taken in conjunction with the communities of friars and monks, the clientele

349

for business studies and the heterogeneous range of common servants of the university and domestic staffs of the colleges, halls and hostels, who were nearly all recruited locally and who enjoyed the status of 'privileged persons', something of the diversity of the academic scene in the English Universities may be savoured. Further aspects of undergraduate and postgraduate life in Oxford and Cambridge in the medieval period will be explored in the next, complementary chapter.

Chapter 9

Student Academic and Social Life

The social framework within which students in the medieval English Universities pursued their university careers can only be partly reconstructed. For the medieval period there is nothing approximating to the intimacy of a student diary or a tutor's report, and the majority of letters which have survived are of a stereotyped character. From a diversity of sources, it is nevertheless possible to reconstitute something of the world of the undergraduate students and their postgraduate seniors. In the academic sphere, matters such as university entry ages, wastage rates, examination methods and facilities for study can all to some extent be illuminated. Similarly, there are many aspects of the student's social environment for which there is evidence, though the amounts vary. These include forms of discipline, styles of dress, entertainments and recreational activities, the place of women in the university context and the ever-present menace of plague. The vital role of patronage in the advancement of students and the quantitative analysis of their subsequent careers are areas of research which are yielding interesting, though tentative, results. Using these disparate elements, a composite view of the life of students in the medieval English Universities has been essayed in this chapter. In the preceding chapter, facets of the lives of undergraduates and postgraduates have inevitably been looked at in connection with the discussion of the academic community, for example, expenditure patterns at university, and discussion of these will not be here repeated.

The average age at which students in the Middle Ages entered the English Universities and those of the rest of northern Europe has probably been usually assessed at too low a level.[1] Confusion has arisen because groups of young boys of about eight to fifteen years

[1] See the discussion by Cobban, *The Medieval Universities*, pp. 207-9.

old are sometimes found to have been resident in university towns. Not all of these youths, however, were engaged upon the arts course. A proportion of them came to the university town in the first instance to master Latin grammar, which they did in order to prepare themselves for the university arts course.[2] They received their instruction either in grammar schools operating within the town or in one of the colleges, as at Paris in the fourteenth and fifteenth centuries.[3] Those youths who showed little aptitude for academic study were weeded out at the pre-university stage. But if soundly based in grammar, it was possible for students of thirteen or fourteen to be enrolled in arts faculties. The statutes of 1215 granted to Paris by Robert de Courçon stated that no one was to begin lecturing in arts before his twenty-first year and before he had studied in arts for at least six years.[4] This gives a possible starting age in arts of fourteen or even younger. The statutes of the English-German nation at Paris of 1252 required those determining in arts, the equivalent of taking the B.A. degree, to be nineteen years or more and to have studied arts for four or five years.[5] This implies a minimum commencement age of fourteen. These are only static insights, and it has to be borne in mind that the length of courses varied from university to university and within the same university at different times.[6] There was also a tendency for the duration of arts courses to contract in the later medieval period.[7] All these variables add considerably to the difficulties involved in assessing the entry ages for the arts faculties.

[2] See e.g. Jacob, 'English University Clerks in the later Middle Ages: the Problem of Maintenance', p. 308; see also Gabriel, 'Preparatory Teaching in the Parisian Colleges during the Fourteenth Century', *Garlandia: Studies in the History of the Mediaeval University,* pp. 97 ff.

[3] At the Ave Maria College in Paris, grammar students were admitted in their eighth or ninth year: Gabriel, op. cit., p. 98.

[4] *Chartularium*, i. no. 20.

[5] Ibid., i. no. 202.

[6] At Paris University, for example, the minimum age for determination as a bachelor was, in the fourteenth century, reduced to the completion of the fourteenth year: Gabriel, op. cit., p. 100.

[7] Rashdall, *Universities*, i. 462–4 and notes.

Oxford statutes of before the sixteenth century do not prescribe a minimum entry age. The Cambridge statutes of the mid-thirteenth century are also silent on this point. The late fourteenth-century statutes, however, stipulate fourteen as the admission threshold.[8] Supplementary information may be garnered from college statutes, where entry ages are occasionally prescribed. The statutes of 1380 of the King's Hall, Cambridge, which admitted undergraduate fellows from the early fourteenth century, fixed the minimum age of admission at fourteen, which mirrors the university statutes.[9] At New College, Oxford, the youngest undergraduates were not to be admitted until they had completed their fifteenth year.[10] But these are statutory minima, and the average age would have been somewhat higher. Indeed, an analysis of New College entrants has shown that the average age was about seventeen over the fifteenth century.[11] Taking the available evidence together, it would seem that fourteen was generally adopted as the minimum entry age at Oxford and Cambridge. The actual admission ages of undergraduates varied a good deal more than they do in the twentieth century, fifteen to seventeen probably being the age of entry in arts for the majority of students in the medieval English Universities. The absence of formal entrance examinations and the relaxed nature of the admissions process help to account for this diversity in the entry ages in arts.

It is not easy to generalize about the academic level which students had attained when admitted to Oxford and Cambridge. Since lectures and disputations were given in Latin, it would have been necessary for the aspiring student to have a good grasp of written and spoken Latin and perhaps a rudimentary knowledge of logical problems. Apart from pre-eminent establishments such as Winchester and Eton, which were designed as 'feeder' schools for the universities, most schools were not specifically geared to

---

[8] *Camb. Docs.*, i 337.

[9] See the statutes in Rouse Ball, *The King's Scholars and King's Hall*, p. 67; also Cobban, *The King's Hall*, p. 59.

[10] *Statutes*, i. ch. 5, 7.

[11] Lytle, *Oxford Students and English Society: c.1300-c.1510* (unpublished Ph.D. thesis), pp. 189, 190.

university entrance. Although much illuminating work has been completed on English medieval schools,[12] it does not seem possible to assign a significant proportion of university students to particular schools the nature and standard of whose teaching can be assessed. It is probable that undergraduate entrants to colleges were more closely assessed than were those who entered the university to live in halls or hostels or in private lodgings: colleges tended to be rigorously selective in their admissions, and would often conduct what was tantamount to their own oral examinations.[13] As it was only from the late fifteenth and early sixteenth centuries that the colleges became general venues for undergraduates, university freshmen before 1500 would have exhibited marked variations of age, of social background, of educational experience and of academic levels reached.

The lack of an admissions policy, and consequently of systematic screening at entry, was one of the important factors underlying the student wastage rate in the English Universities. Several reasons may be advanced to explain the fact that a seemingly large number of students failed to complete the degree course in arts. Some genuinely poor scholars who had exhausted all possible sources of aid would have had no alternative but to terminate their studies before having acquired a degree. Sometimes, the reason for withdrawal lay in the attitude to study, a matter articulated in the statutes of New College, which cite the loss of desire for study as one of the reasons for which a college place might be forfeited.[14] This 'loss of desire' may mean either disenchantment with academic study or an inability to measure up to the demands of the course. If a proportion of New College undergraduates who had had the distinct advantage of a preparatory Winchester education experienced difficulties in coping with the arts course, then it may

---

[12] See e.g. Orme, *English Schools in the Middle Ages;* J. H. Moran, 'Education and Learning in the City of York 1300–1560', *St Anthony's Hall Publications,* no. 55 (1979), pp. 1 ff., and 'Literacy and Education in Northern England, 1350–1550: A Methodological Inquiry', *Northern History,* xvii (1981), pp. 1 ff.

[13] Rashdall, op. cit., iii. 342; for a particular instance of a college oral examination at the point of admission, see the statutes of the King's Hall in Rouse Ball, op. cit., p. 67.

[14] *Statutes,* i. ch. 5, 64; also Jones, 'New College', *V.C.H. Oxon.* iii. 158.

be appreciated how heavy the pressures would have been on students from schools less oriented towards the university curriculum. The disadvantages possessed by youths who had received much of their education informally, at the hands of local clergy, are manifest.

Given that the average student was capable of following and benefiting from his course and that he had the finances requisite for survival, his chances of realizing a degree were fair. Much of the student wastage, the rate of which was incomparably higher than would be condoned in a modern university, occurred in the early stages of the course of studies, when undergraduate numbers were inflated by students insufficiently prepared for the stringencies of academic life. As there was no artificial cushioning in the medieval English Universities to help a student to overcome a lack of aptitude or ability, students with these failings were fairly naturally excised. Whatever intellectual prodding individual masters may have given, Oxford and Cambridge, as institutions, did not admit a collective responsibility for coaxing unsatisfactory students towards a degree. The study regime was hard, the standards exacting, and the student was expected to apply himself with the appropriate dedication or else suffer the consequences of his failure to do so.

Although the English student was not required to sit formal written examinations, he was nonetheless assessed at every juncture of his undergraduate career and in subsequent courses in the superior faculties. It could be argued that, if all the procedures were observed, a degree from Oxford and Cambridge was awarded on the basis of a total and continuous assessment of a scholar's performance. In accordance with the mileage principle, the student had to attend the prescribed lectures and, through probing oral examinations, to satisfy the teaching masters of the faculty that he possessed a detailed knowledge and understanding of the stipulated texts. In addition, the student had to project himself as a potential master of his craft by the phased assimilation of a series of complex academic exercises specified for different points in the course. However, against the full panoply of statutory degree requirements, has to be reckoned the fact that dispensations or graces were obtainable whereby students might proceed to a degree without fulfilling all the regulations to the letter, a practice that was, it seems, extensive in the English Universities in the fifteenth century.[15] Uncertainty about the ease and frequency with which dispensations were granted compounds the problem of trying to relate medieval to twentieth-century degree criteria. The fact that students might interrupt their studies because of domestic pressures and resume university life at some future date is a further circumstance which makes comparison with modern degree procedures a troublesome exercise. Nevertheless, the impression gained is that the degree procedure — designed as it was to produce graduates versed in the rigours of Aristotelian logic and attuned to the exactitude of thought and fine intellectual distinctions of the disputation, conducted throughout as it was in a foreign language and involving as it did examination by prolonged practical and oral assessment — was, by any set of educational standards, one of innate difficulty.

The absence of matriculation registers and comprehensive degree lists precludes any kind of reliable quantification of student wastage on a university-wide basis. However, useful figures are available for New College, Oxford, where students were carefully assessed at the point of admission. A. H. M. Jones has reckoned that of the 1,350 scholars who passed through the college between 1386 and 1547 about a third left prematurely, many not having taken any degree, and these are additional to the 254 scholars who died in the college, 124 of them while still undergraduates.[16] G. F. Lytle has estimated that the wastage rate at New College, excluding deaths, between *c*. 1390 and *c*. 1510 was in the order of 35 per cent,[17] and this accords closely with Jones' conclusion. R. L. Storey's computations concerning New College personnel admitted between 1386 and 1540 yield a similar pattern of high student wastage. He has concluded that one in ten entrants died within his first four years, before acquiring a degree, that one in seven scholars, who at entry had to undertake to remain for at least five years, left before completing the two years necessary for election as a fellow, and that one in seven fellows departed in his first two years, without taking a

---

[15] See *The Register of Congregation 1448–1463*, pp. xxi–xxii and *passim*.

[16] Jones, op. cit., p. 158.

[17] Lytle, *Oxford Students and English Society: c.1300–c.1510*, pp. 191, 192.

degree.[18] This alarming rate of wastage at New College — caused by academic failure, inadequate motivation and death — would almost certainly have been surpassed for students who lived in the less stable and less comfortable environments of the halls and hostels or in rooms rented from townspeople.

Although the high student wastage level seems to have been a serious and continuous problem in the medieval English Universities, some qualifications need to be made. There were always a number of students who had come up to Oxford and Cambridge with no intention of taking a degree: they had merely wished to experience a measure of university study prior to pursuing a predetermined line of employment, or to moving on to one of the Inns of Court or Chancery in London. Moreover, at least some of those who had intended to take a degree but had had to abandon their studies mid-course were probably able to capitalize upon their period at university. Even a spell at university unrewarded by a degree would have carried some weight in the employment stakes.[19] Students of this type, in company with those who had successfully graduated, often secured from the principals of halls or hostels or from college heads or regent masters testimonial letters designed to influence a prospective employer or patron. Oxford formularies of the late fourteenth and fifteenth centuries contain model testimonial letters of this kind.[20]

If the average student of limited means opted to study beyond a first degree, he had to obtain either a college fellowship or both a supporting benefice and an episcopal licence to attend a university. Since the colleges could cater for only a proportion of graduates, there was the fiercest competition among university personnel for benefices. In the fourteenth century, the English Universities, in unison with those of continental Europe, became heavily dependent upon the operation of international papal patronage for the supply of ecclesiastical livings needed to assuage the graduate demand for benefices. Indeed, such was the keenness of the competition for

[18] Storey, 'The Foundation and the Medieval College, 1379–1530', *New College Oxford 1379–1979*, pp. 17–18.

[19] See e.g. Lytle, op cit., p. 191.

[20] *Oxford Formularies*, ii, 400–1, 465–6.

benefices that some students would begin to negotiate ecclesiastical livings during their undergraduate career. Individual scholars had the right to petition the papal curia for benefices, and Oxford formularies contain letters from the university to the papacy seeking benefices on behalf of particular members.[21]

It became customary, however, for universities in the fourteenth century to send to the papal curia collective rolls of petitions of scholars requesting benefices either for immediate occupation or reserved for a future date.[22] The earliest university rolls of petitions seem to have been those sent from Paris and Oxford in the first quarter of the fourteenth century, Oxford beginning with petitions for fellows of Merton in 1317 and burgeoning into fully-fledged rolls by at least 1335.[23] The first traceable list of Cambridge petitioners belongs to 1331, though previous rolls may well have been compiled.[24] Rolls were not sent as a matter of routine. They were dispatched irregularly, often on special occasions, such as the accession of a new pope.[25] The form of these rolls varied considerably. At Paris, the officially sponsored rolls were largely concerned with the petitions of masters and doctors, although these were sometimes supplemented by semi-official rolls representing other sectional interests, for example, those of bachelors of theology, canon law and arts.[26] Oxford and Cambridge combined

---

[21] Ibid., i. 29–31; ii. 395–6.

[22] On this subject, see D. E. R. Watt, 'University Clerks and Rolls of Petitions for Benefices', *Speculum,* xxxiv (1959), pp. 213 ff.; E. F. Jacob, 'Petitions for Benefices from English Universities during the Great Schism', art. cit., pp. 41 ff., and 'On the promotion of English University Clerks during the later Middle Ages', *J. Eccles. Hist.,* i (1950), pp. 172 ff.; A. H. Lloyd, 'Notes on Cambridge Clerks petitioning for Benefices, 1370–1399', *B.I.H.R.,* 20 (1943–5), pp. 75 ff. On papal provisioning in general, see G. Barraclough, *Papal Provisions* (Oxford, 1935).

[23] Jacob, 'Petitions for Benefices from English Universities during the Great Schism', p. 44; Lawrence, 'The University in State and Church', *The History of the University of Oxford,* i. 125; Rashdall, *Universities,* i. 555, n. 1; Emden, *B.R.U.O.,* i. xxxvi.

[24] Emden, *B.R.U.C.,* p. xxiv.

[25] Rashdall, *Universities,* i. 555, was mistaken in his assumption that the Paris rolls were annual events.

[26] Cobban, *The Medieval Universities,* p. 216.

the petitions of doctors, masters, bachelors and advanced students on one roll, usually set out in order of seniority from the doctors of theology downwards.[27] The hierarchical character of the Parisian and English rolls contrasts with the more democratically organized rolls of the German and French provincial universities, where the petitions of bachelors and advanced undergraduates tended to occupy a more prominent position.[28] By the early fifteenth century, there was a marked decline in the number of rolls submitted to the papal curia, and Oxford's final roll was probably dispatched in 1404.[29] The reduction in the quantity of rolls sent to the papacy was in part a manifestation of a wider reaction against the international system of papal patronage or provisioning, which was increasingly thought of as incompatible with the concept of the sovereign state; and the pontificate of Eugenius IV(1431–39) saw the virtual demise of collective petitioning by universities.

The university rolls of petitions for benefices had to compete with the rolls of influential lay and ecclesiastical personages. In England, the Universities also had to take account of the Statute of Provisors. First issued in 1351, and reissued in a more stringent version in 1390, this statute curbed the workings of papal patronage in the country and made the sending of rolls a matter of accelerating difficulty.[30] It has to be recognized that a favourable response from the papacy did not necessarily imply an immediate possession of a benefice. The transfer had to be implemented by the local patron, and this often led to long delays or to even non-compliance with the papal letter which the petitioner had received and which was designed to initiate the process.[31] It is probable, however, that a fair proportion of English university scholars ultimately obtained a

---

[27] Ibid.

[28] Ibid.

[29] Lytle, 'Patronage Patterns and Oxford Colleges *c*.1300–*c*.1530', *The University in Society*, i 128.

[30] See e.g. Jacob, 'English University Clerks in the later Middle Ages: the Problem of Maintenance', pp. 319–20.

[31] See the remarks of Jacob, 'Petitions for Benefices from English Universities during the Great Schism', p. 42.

concrete return from these collective petitions, even if the benefice or position of first preference was not secured.[32]

The assertion that papal patronage was a significant force in the lives of English graduates is supported by G. F. Lytle's analysis of a limited sample of the careers of Oxford scholars in the fifteenth century. This investigation found that between 1301 and 1350 about 48 per cent of the graduates who had ecclesiastical careers had received at least one living as a result of papal patronage; and that about 26 per cent of the graduates acquired their first benefice from this source, although between 1351 and 1400 the percentages reduced to 40 and 16 respectively, doubtless reflecting the diminishing efficacy of papal provisioning in the late fourteenth century.[33] With the phasing out of direct papal patronage for English graduates in the early fifteenth century, Oxford and Cambridge scholars had to rely increasingly upon the traditional range of indigenous patrons, including the crown, the episcopacy, members of the nobility and upper gentry, university colleges and religious orders. No single patronage source came to occupy the predominant role which papal provisions had performed in the fourteenth century. But combined they responded to the patronage need, and the number of presentations to livings made to graduates throughout the fifteenth century was, it seems, well maintained.[34] By these means, papal withdrawal from the realm of patronage in fifteenth-century England was substantially offset.

The life of the student in the English Universities was conducted without the therapeutic aid of many licensed recreations.[35] Oxford

---

[32] Ibid.

[33] Lytle, 'Patronage Patterns and Oxford Colleges *c.1300–c.*1530', p. 128, and his unpublished thesis, *Oxford Students and English Society: c. 1300–c.1510*, p. 284.

[34] See Lytle's thesis for discussion of indigenous patronage sources, pp. 281 ff., with main conclusion on p. 312.

[35] On this subject, see Rashdall, *Universities*, iii. 419 ff., and Cobban, *The Medieval Universities*, pp. 212–13. The obligation on the student to live a sober and moral life is a prominent theme of a fifteenth-century Latin verse educational treatise by Goswin Kempgyn de Nussia, a master of arts of Erfurt University and law graduate of Cologne, which was written to serve as a guiding handbook for the new university entrant: *Goswin Kempgyn de Nussia Trivita studentium: Eine Einführung in das Universitätsstudentium aus dem 15. Jahrhundert* (ed. M. Bernhard, *Münchener Beiträge zur Mediävistik und Renaissance-Forschung*, xxvi, Munich, 1976).

and Cambridge, in conformity with the generality of northern European universities, tended to mirror the negative ecclesiastical denial of bodily pleasures and sought to inhibit organized levity. This puritanical attitude was fuelled by the serious disciplinary problems with which the English Universities had to cope. But it may also be argued that the university authorities over-reacted in areas which were peripheral to those which gave rise to significant disorder. For example, many codes of college statutes were forceful in their prohibition of the keeping of pets and of manifold forms of gambling. At Peterhouse, the statutes of 1344 forbade scholars to keep dogs or birds, and specifically falcons, because the ensuing commotion was said to distract from study; and dice and chess were suppressed, except in special circumstances, lest study be disrupted and conflict arise. Chess was also forbidden in the near contemporary statutes of Queen's College, Oxford, of 1340. The pets prohibited by the statutes of New College, Oxford, of 1400 included hawks, dogs, ferrets and birds of prey; and by these statutes dice, chess and all forms of gambling were disallowed, as was the jocund practice of shaving beards on the eve of the inception of masters in arts. The statutes of All Souls College of 1443 repeated the New College strictures regarding hawks, dogs, ferrets and birds of prey, but whereas dice and other types of gambling were proscribed, chess was not, and this is a pointer to the growing tolerance of chess that developed in the course of the fifteenth century. By the statutes of King's College, Cambridge, of the early 1440s, a veritable menagerie of pets was banned, the ban embracing dogs, ferrets, birds, monkeys, bears, wolves and stags, and nets for hawking or fishing were also banned. Dice and all gambling activities which might lead to monetary loss, were outlawed, but chess, it seems, was permitted. Magdalen College, Oxford, in the statutes of 1479/80, added singing birds to the proscribed array of hawks, dogs and ferrets, and cards were specified along with dice among the prohibited games, although chess was, it seems, acceptable. In the opening years of the sixteenth century, the statutes of Christ's College, Cambridge, likewise made no reference to chess when they forbade, except at Christmas, games of cards and knucklebones, as well as the keeping of dogs and birds of prey. The statutes of Corpus Christi College, Oxford, of 1517 debarred dogs, ferrets, hunting and singing birds, dice and cards. But they contained one noticeable relaxation in that they permitted handball in the college garden for the sake of bodily and mental health.[36] While the generality of collegiate regulations on birds, animals and gambling were framed to prevent rowdy behaviour and diversions from study, the statutes of Queen's College, Oxford, of 1340 defined the problem in rather different terms. In common with so many colleges, Queen's placed a ban upon hunting birds and dogs, and extended this to cover all animals, including a stable of horses, and gave as the primary reason for these measures the need to maintain the purity of the air for the efficacy of study.[37] In addition, the Queen's statutes outlawed the use of all musical instruments in college, except on special occasions, on the grounds that music-making engendered levity and was prejudicial to learning.[38]

The aularian statutes of 1483–90 for the Oxford halls were similarly inimical to many student diversions, and they particularly prohibited dice, board-games, handball and 'sword and buckler play',[39] a type of fencing which was fashionable in London circles and popular among highwaymen.[40] It is of interest, however, that the aularian statutes were alive to the desirability of harmless communal exercise. The principals of halls were encouraged to send their students, as a group, to some appropriate spot for outdoor recreation.[41] This is an important nugget of information, for recognition by university authorities of the need for bodily exercise

---

[36] For the Cambridge statutory regulations relating to pets and games at Peterhouse, King's College and Christ's College, see *Camb. Docs.,* i. 29–30 (Peterhouse), ii. 542 (King's), iii. 197–8 (Christ's). For Oxford regulations on pets and games at Queen's, New College, All Souls, Magdalen and Corpus Christi, see *Statutes,* i. ch. 4, 18 (Queen's), ch 5, 48 (New College), ch. 7, 44–5 (All Souls), ii. ch. 8, 42 (Magdalen), ch. 10, 68, 69 (Corpus Christi).

[37] *Statutes,* i. ch. 4, 19.

[38] Ibid., ch. 4, 18.

[39] *Statuta Antiqua,* p. 576; also Emden, *An Oxford Hall in Medieval Times,* pp. 204–5.

[40] Catto, 'Citizens, Scholars and Masters', *The History of the University of Oxford,* i. 183.

[41] *Statuta Antiqua,* p. 577; Emden, op. cit., p. 205.

is infrequently found in the sources used for the study of medieval universities. One rare instance of the advocacy of therapeutic exercise is found in a fourteenth-century treatise in the form of a letter from a physician of Valencia to his two sons studying at Toulouse. The treatise gives elaborate instructions on dict, personal hygiene and physical exercise, all deemed to be essential for the maintenance of student health.[42] It is evident, however, that the English Universities did not assume responsibility for facilitating the recreational activities of their students beyond the marginal type of measure indicated in the Oxford aularian statutes and in those of Corpus Christi College, Oxford. There were no organized sports facilities at Oxford or Cambridge and, so far as is known, no inter-collegiate or inter-hall games were staged. It was accepted that students could not be altogether prevented from joining in the sports of the town and the surrounding area, and some would have participated in bear-baiting, in hunting with dogs and birds, in fishing and in dancing in the streets and fields.[43]

The repressive attitudes of the university authorities towards non-academic activities produced an inevitable reaction and accentuated, in a section of the student population, already strong libertarian tendencies, which manifested themselves in the excesses of drunkenness, gambling, immorality, disorder and crime that were common to all medieval universities.[44] Although university, college and aularian statutes attempted to prevent students from patronizing taverns and brothels[45] and from carrying arms in the town,[46] their effectiveness in this regard was decidedly limited. The

[42] The letter is printed by L. Thorndike, *University Records and Life in the Middle Ages* (Records of Civilisation, no. xxxviii, New York, 1944: repr. Octagon Books, New York, 1971), pp. 154–60.

[43] Catto, 'Citizens, Scholars and Masters', p. 184; Bennett, *Chaucer at Oxford and Cambridge*, p. 48.

[44] For selected cases, see Rashdall, op. cit., iii. 427 ff.

[45] *Statuta Antiqua*, pp. 152 (university), 575–6 (halls); *Statutes*, i. ch. 4, 19 (Queen's), ch. 5, 47 (New College), ch. 7, 43 (All Souls), ii. ch. 8, 41 (Magdalen); *Camb. Docs.*, ii. 31 (Peterhouse), iii. 197 (Christ's); statutes of the King's Hall in Rouse Ball, *The King's Scholars and King's Hall*, p. 66.

[46] *Statuta Antiqua*, pp. 81 (university), 578 (halls); *Statutes*, i. ch. 5, 46 (New College), ch. 7, 41 (All Souls), ii. ch. 8, 70 (Magdalen), ii. ch. 10, 67 (Corpus

frequenting of taverns and the consequent drunkenness were firmly associated with the bearing of weapons and the perpetration of serious crimes, as cases outlined in the Oxford coroners' rolls vividly exemplify.[47]

Prostitution was a perennial problem in the university towns, and repeated legislative attempts were made to drive prostitutes out of Oxford and Cambridge. In 1317 and 1327, the king conceded to Cambridge University that no 'common woman' would be allowed to dwell in the town or suburbs and, at the promptings of the chancellor, the mayor and bailiffs were to order, four times a year or more frequently, the departure of all such women within a specified period.[48] In 1459, the chancellor was given powers to banish prostitutes for a distance of over four miles from Cambridge.[49] In 1461, Edward IV granted to the Oxford chancellor the authority to banish prostitutes to places over ten miles from Oxford.[50] The evidence of the Oxford chancellor's register of between 1434 and 1469 reveals that prostitutes were punished by imprisonment, banishment, fines or the pillory, or by a combination of these means.[51] In 1443–4, the chancellor, Thomas Gascoigne, concluded a major drive against prostitution in Oxford.[52] It is noteworthy that many of the prostitutes ordered to leave the town were married women, and all the indications are that the chancellor had to deal with an organized network of prostitution on some scale. There are instances of Oxford scholars themselves being involved in the promotion of prostitution. For example, in 1444, Hugh Sadler, a scholar in priest's orders, came before the chancellor's court on

Christi); *Camb. Docs.*, i. 320 (university), ii. 31 (Peterhouse), 539 (King's); statutes of the King's Hall in Rouse Ball, op. cit., p. 68.

[47] E.g. *Records of Mediaeval Oxford*, pp. 8, 16–17.

[48] *Annals*, i. 76, 83.

[49] Ibid., i. 209–10.

[50] *Mediaeval Archives*, i. 251–2.

[51] *Registrum Cancellarii*, i. xvii–xix; for the use of the pillory in the punishment of a prostitute, see ibid., i 332–3.

[52] Ibid., i. 92–9.

charges of disrupting the peace and furthering prostitution. This same scholar, in company with others, was alleged to have had improper relations with the nuns of nearby Godstow nunnery.[53] At best, the university authorities succeeded only in curbing prostitution. The problem proved intractable, and was worsened by the negative policy of the Universities towards student leisure pursuits. By striving to suppress *joie de vivre* and *camaraderie* instead of channelling this loose energy into a relaxing and innocent form, the English university and collegiate establishments made a collective error of judgment which had injurious effects upon their academic populations.

The progressive extension of university discipline over the academic communities of Oxford and Cambridge, initially by means of matriculation rolls, subsequently through halls and hostels and finally through the agency of the colleges, has been explored in chapter 4. This broad interpretative theme need not be further elaborated, but it is of some interest to consider the specific ways by which order was enforced within this evolving disciplinary scene. From the thirteenth century, the chancellors of Oxford and Cambridge had widespread disciplinary powers over both scholars and an ever increasing section of the citizenry.[54] At the hands of the chancellors of the English Universities, scholars could be deprived of their degrees or prevented from taking them, or, if a regent master, forbidden to teach. Scholars could also be fined, expelled permanently or for a specified duration and made to suffer short terms of imprisonment and, in certain instances, even excommunication. Our knowledge of the internal code of discipline in the Oxford halls must be derived largely from the aularian statutes of 1483–90. These statutes show that, overwhelmingly, the main form of punishment was the imposition of fines, arranged in a hierarchical system.[55] A few examples will illustrate the diversity of offences for which fines were exacted as well as affording precious insights into facets of hall life. No such body of statutes survive for the Cambridge hostels.

---

[53] Catto, 'Citizens, Scholars and Masters', pp. 184–5; *Registrum Cancellarii*, i. 97.

[54] See above, chapter 3, pp. 69 ff.

[55] See the remarks of Emden, *An Oxford Hall in Medieval Times*, pp. 201–2.

According to the Oxford aularian statutes,[56] scholars were fined for obstinately voicing a heretical opinion, for unseemly behaviour at meals, for detracting from the reputation of the hall or disclosing confidential matters, for consorting with persons of ill-repute, for participating in forbidden games, for climbing in and out of hall after the closure of the main gate or for spending a night away from the hall without permission or leaving Oxford without authorization. A multitude of fines were concerned with offences relating to the annoyance of fellow students, and to the fomenting of disorder within the hall. Under threat of fine, no student was to create discord by making odious comparisons between different countries or classes of the community or between different faculties. The carrying of weapons was wholly forbidden unless they were being carried just before or immediately after a journey. A student was fined not only for possessing weapons, but also for lending them to another or for depositing them secretly with any person in the town. Fines were imposed for bringing an unsheathed knife to table and for striking another student with a fist, a stone or any other instrument, the penalty being doubled if blood was shed, and, if the offence was repeated, the perpetrator was to be expelled. The section in the statutes dealing with studies was designed mainly to ensure the application of students and the observance of the university regulations concerning academic courses, the various measures being underpinned by an armoury of fines. Of particular note is the requirement that only Latin is to be spoken within the precincts of the hall, except on feast occasions and principal festivals.[57] This stipulation is commonly found in college statutes.[58] At Peterhouse, Cambridge, and at Oriel and Queen's, Oxford, French was permitted as an alternative.[59]

---

[56] For the following statutory points pertaining to scholars in halls, see *Statuta Antiqua*, pp. 574–83; see also Emden, op. cit., ch. 9.

[57] *Statuta Antiqua*, p. 579.

[58] *Statutes*, i. ch. 2, 26 (Merton), ch. 5, 41 (New College), ch. 7, 35 (All Souls) ii. ch. 8, 45 (Magdalen), ch. 9, 24–5 (Brasenose); *Camb. Docs.*, ii. 531 (King's), iii. 113–14 (Jesus), 178 (Christ's).

[59] *Camb. Docs.*, ii. 31 (Peterhouse); *Statutes*, i. ch. 3, 8 (Oriel), ch. 4, 14 (Queen's).

The aularian statutes pertaining to institutional meals reveal that not all of the halls were equipped to provide meals, and arrangements had to be made for students in halls that were not so equipped to eat in neighbouring establishments where lectures were also given in their faculty, their permanent hall being used mainly for sleeping purposes.[60] Just how extensive this system of complementary halls was is unknown. A series of fines and forfeitures of food was attached to unpunctuality or over-lengthy sessions at hall meals.[61] By the late fifteenth century, the two main meals in both colleges and halls consisted of dinner at about 10 or 11 a.m. and supper at about 5 p.m. Breakfast was becoming more popular but was still optional, and it was customary to be served a measure of beer before retiring for the night.[62] The aularian statutes tended to inculcate a proper respect for the fabric of the hall on the part of its inhabitants. Students were fined for disturbing the rushes and straw which formed the floor coverings, for spilling things upon or cutting the table-cloths and for defacing tables, walls, doors or windows, and all breakages of windows or furniture were to be repaired at the expense of the malefactors.[63]

Respect for the surroundings of the hall was to be encouraged by imposing fines for running across the grass or trampling upon plants and by ordering students to work in the garden according to need, failure to do so resulting in a fine.[64] On the hygiene front, students were fined if they washed their hands in the well-bucket.[65] In the recreational sphere, students were forbidden gambling, handball, swordplay and the keeping of sporting dogs, ferrets, hawks and other small birds under penalty of a fine.[66] This entire apparatus of fines was extended to the domestic staff in order to

[60] *Statuta Antiqua*, p. 581.

[61] For the statutory section on meals, see ibid., pp. 580–2.

[62] Emden, op. cit., p. 211; Rashdall, *Universities,* iii. 401–4.

[63] *Statuta Antiqua,* p. 582.

[64] Ibid., pp. 582–3.

[65] Ibid., p. 583.

[66] Loc. cit.

ensure high standards of punctuality and hygiene, and impartial service to all members of the hall.[67]

From the standpoint of discipline, these aularian statutes differ markedly from most codes of college statutes. Whereas fining was the usual method of discipline in the halls, and by the early fifteenth century was regarded by the Oxford university authorities as one of the most effective deterrents in the drive against disturbers of the peace,[68] the system of fines was used only lightly in the colleges. They are prescribed on a limited basis in the Brasenose College statutes of 1521 for internal feuding and for late attendance or disorderly conduct at lectures.[69] It is known that for part of the fourteenth century the King's Hall, Cambridge, had been governed by a code of statutory fines. It appears that the system had been abandoned by 1380, for there are no provisions for fines in the earliest statutes of that year, and the college accounts shed no further light on the matter.[70] Apart from occasional instances of fines and the ultimate deterrent of expulsion, the principal disciplinary means employed in the colleges was the deprivation of commons or meals for varying lengths of time appropriate to the offence.[71] The persistency with which withdrawal of commons was prescribed as a penalty in English colleges down to the sixteenth century suggests that this was a fairly efficacious means of discipline. One further mode of correction, which came into use in colleges and halls in the later medieval period, was corporal punishment. In the Oxford aularian statutes, it was laid down that corporal punishment was to be administered publicly by the principals of halls on Saturday evenings to offending younger students for whom this might be thought more suitable than fines.[72] It may be assumed that poor grammar-boys maintained as

[67] Ibid., pp. 583–4.

[68] Ibid., p. 204.

[69] *Statutes*, ii. ch. 9, 16, 25–6.

[70] Cobban, *The King's Hall*, pp. 176–7.

[71] *Statutes*, i. ch. 5, 41, 42–3, 44, 47, 49, 58, 59–60, 100 (New College), ch. 7, 35, 38, 41, 44, 45, 50, 59 (All Souls), ii. ch. 8, 36, 43 (Magdalen), ch. 10, 64, 68, 69, 100 (Corpus Christi); *Camb. Docs.*, ii. 556 (King's).

[72] *Statuta Antiqua*, p. 587.

an act of charity by colleges were subject to correction by the birch, as were grammar-boys everywhere throughout England. This was certainly the case at Queen's College, Oxford.[73]

The first traceable reference to corporal punishment for scholars or fellows of a college occurs in the statutes of King's College, Cambridge, of the early 1440s which prescribe that scholars and junior fellows may be beaten, at the discretion of the provost and dean, for the commission of more serious offences. The statutes of Magdalen College, Oxford, of 1479/80 allow for the physical correction of the demies, who were young scholars on the foundation in receipt of half of the fellows' allowance for commons. The punishment was to be carried out by the grammar master in the school attached to the college. At Christ's College, Cambridge, the statutes of 1505 authorize corporal punishment, as an alternative to a fine, for scholars of pre-adult age for transgressions such as lateness or absence from divine office or failure to meet academic obligations, the age of adulthood not, however, being defined. Younger scholars were subjected to a strict regime at Brasenose College, where, according to the statutes of 1521, they could be beaten for disorderly conduct in lecture-rooms or for unpunctuality or for absence from divine service.[74] The maximum age considered suitable for corporal punishment was specified in the statutes of Cardinal College of *c.* 1525–27, where the founder, Thomas Wolsey, fixed it at twenty years.[75] Dr Caius, in his statutes for Gonville and Caius College of 1572, stipulated eighteen as the uppermost age for physical correction.[76]

[73] *Statutes*, i. ch. 4, 30.

[74] For corporal punishment at King's College and Christ's, see *Camb. Docs*, ii. 556 (King's), iii. 191 (Christ's). For corporal punishment at Magdalen and Brasenose, see *Statutes*, ii. ch. 8, 76–7 (Magdalen), ch. 9, 16, 19 (Brasenose). See also McConica, 'Elizabethan Oxford: The Collegiate Society', *The History of the University of Oxford*, iii. 654. For the extension of corporal punishment to Corpus Christi College, Oxford, in the early sixteenth century, see ibid., iii. 654–5. W. W. Rouse Ball, *Cambridge Papers*, p. 198, suggests that corporal punishment was constantly inflicted on non-adults in the medieval English Universities in lieu of fines: this, however, is largely speculative for the thirteenth and fourteenth centuries.

[75] *Statutes*, ii. ch. 11, 70.

[76] *Camb. Docs.*, ii. 271.

The available evidence on flogging in the English Universities would seem to establish that this method of discipline was operational in the halls by the late fifteenth century, and was presumably so from an earlier period, and had also made a tentative appearance in one or two of the colleges in the course of that century. There is no doubt that corporal punishment blossomed as a major disciplinary force in the sixteenth-century colleges. This development may be linked with a fall in the average age of entrants to colleges in the sixteenth century: that is, what was thought appropriate in England's schools was now considered suitable for the generality of the younger members of a college community. The adoption of corporal punishment by many English colleges over the fifteenth and sixteenth centuries was paralleled among the Parisian colleges. And it is likely that the austere disciplinary regimes of some of the collegiate establishments of Paris, that of the College of Montaigu being the most extreme,[77] may have had a considerable influence upon the character of life in the English colleges.

Before 1500, the English Universities were rather haphazard in their promotion of academic dress as a measure of social control.[78] For the mass of undergraduates, who were not associated with colleges, distinctive or uniform dress was not much prescribed before the sixteenth century, though they were obligated to wear decent clerical garb. Since notions of clerical dress for undergraduates were elastic and admitted of many variants and colours, sombre black not being imposed until the sixteenth century, non-collegiate undergraduate dress was fashioned for almost three hundred years in a medley of styles and hues.[79] In the medieval period, the university statutes laid more emphasis upon the attire of graduates than upon that of undergraduates — upon the academic garb of the doctors, masters and bachelors in the

---

[77] Rashdall, *Universities,* iii. 369, 412–13.

[78] For Oxford academic dress, see W. N. Hargreaves-Mawdsley, *A History of Academical Dress in Europe until the end of the eighteenth century* (Oxford, 1963), pp. 60–106, and for Cambridge, pp. 107–37. This book is a detailed reference work rather than an interpretative study.

[79] See e.g. the remarks of Catto, 'Citizens, Scholars and Masters', p. 155; Rashdall, op. cit., iii. 387.

different faculties.[80] The shape and cut of academic costumes, and not their colour, were the distinguishing features of graduate robes,[81] and, as with undergraduate dress, a riot of colours prevailed before more sober standards of apparel were introduced in the sixteenth century.[82]

In the fourteenth and fifteenth centuries, the robes of masters of arts and of doctors in the superior faculties were lined or trimmed with fur according to what was prescribed for each rank within each faculty. As a result, the type of fur or lining used on a gown or hood is often an indication of the status of the scholar. By a university statute of 1414, bachelors of arts at Cambridge were forbidden adornments of fur or silk on their gowns, and unless of noble birth, in which case more precious furs might be used, were allowed only budge or lamb's wool on their hoods.[83] Among the varieties of fur used in English academic costume are miniver, lamb's wool or budge, rabbit, marten, wolf, fox, wild cat and popel, which is of uncertain derivation but may well be squirrel's fur; and among the lining fabrics used are silk, satin and freize.[84] The attractiveness of the robes of the senior members of the Universities was a source of temptation to the undergraduates, and Oxford found it necessary in 1432 to legislate against the wearing by non-graduates of linings or furs appropriate to masters and noblemen.[85] In 1490, it was enacted that non-graduates were not to use headdresses pertaining to the status of master.[86] In the fifteenth century, the English Universities allowed special concessions in dress to scholars of noble birth, the earliest instances occurring in a statute of 1414 at Cambridge and of

---

[80] L. H. D. Buxton and S. Gibson, *Oxford University Ceremonies* (Oxford, 1935), p. 20.

[81] Hargreaves-Mawdsley, op. cit., p. 6.

[82] Buxton and Gibson, op. cit., pp. 22–4.

[83] *Camb. Docs.*, i. 402; for the fur trimmings and linings given to King's Hall fellows for their robes and hoods, see Cobban *The King's Hall*, pp. 198–9.

[84] Buxton and Gibson, op. cit., p. 21. On 'popel', see the discussion by Cobban, op. cit., p. 198 and notes 6–9.

[85] *Statuta Antiqua*, pp. 239–40.

[86] Ibid., p. 297.

1490 at Oxford.[87] With the heavy influx of members of the nobility in the post-Reformation period, the dress of noble scholars became more elaborate from Elizabeth's reign down to the eighteenth century.[88]

Academic populations throughout Europe were keenly alive to the contemporary fashions of the wealthy laity. It serves as a reminder of the youth of many of the teaching masters in the English Universities to note that an Oxford statute of *a.*1313 was required to prevent masters of any faculty from delivering ordinary lectures while shod in excessively fashionable footwear.[89] In 1342, the archbishop of Canterbury issued from a London council a constitution condemning the extravagance in the dress and appearance of university students and clergy alike. These extravagances included such features as hair which was long and effeminate or curled and powdered, shoes chequered with red and green, cloaks edged with expensive furs, fingers bejewelled with rings, and costly and elaborately decorated girdles from which hung long knives after the manner of swords.[90] In parallel with the sporadic university regulations on dress, many of the colleges devised a livery for their members in the sense that they imposed a tunic of clerical cut, and of uniform material and colour, with distinguishing traits according to academic status. Liveries were prescribed at Queen's, New College and Corpus Christi College, Oxford, and at Gonville, Trinity Hall, the King's Hall and King's College, Cambridge.[91] At Queen's, the fellows wore outer garments of a purple colour in memory of the blood of Christ.[92] In

---

[87] *Annals,* i. 157; *Statuta Antiqua,* p. 297; Hargreaves-Mawdsley, op. cit., pp. 92, 128.

[88] Hargreaves-Mawdsley, op. cit., pp. 92–5, 128–30.

[89] *Statuta Antiqua,* p. 57.

[90] *Annals,* i. 94–5.

[91] *Statutes,* i. ch. 4, 14, 16 (Queen's), ch. 5, 45–6 (New College), ii. ch. 10, 84–5 (Corpus Christi); *Camb. Docs.,* ii. 229–30 (Gonville), 419 (Trinity Hall), 538–9 (King's), and the King's Hall statutes in Rouse Ball, *The King's Scholars and King's Hall,* p. 68.

[92] *Statutes,* i. ch. 4, 14; Hargreaves-Mawdsley, op. cit., p. 101. Rashdall, *Universities,* iii. p. 387, erroneously states that the Queen's livery was blood-red: the prescribed statutory colour is purple.

the first half of the fourteenth century, the tunics and tabards of the fellows of the King's Hall were of a blue or bluish-grey colour. Nothing is known positively of the colour in the second half of the century, but in a royal wardrobe list of 1444 it is recorded that all the fellows, graduate and non-graduate, received lengths of blue material for their robes.[93] That this blue livery was royal livery is proved by the wording of the letters patent of Henry VI of 19 November 1448. Here, it is reported that since robes had not been delivered for two or three years, it was necessary that new sets be issued so that the fellows might be decently attired in clerical habit of the royal livery according to their academic rank.[94] It is clear that the King's Hall fellows alone wore the royal livery in the English Universities. Before the sixteenth century, the only body of undergraduates at Oxford and Cambridge to be garbed in a specific uniform were those who were members of colleges with recognizable liveries.

While English university regulations adopted a generally repressive stance towards recreational activities, some relaxation occurred during the principal festivals of the ecclesiastical year, and especially on the feast of St Nicholas on 6 December, at Christmas and on the feast of the Holy Innocents on 28 December. Halls and colleges indulged their younger members by permitting a temporary inversion of authority, ritualized in the election of a lord of misrule or a Christmas king or a king of the beans, and accompanied by all manner of revelries. At Merton College, Oxford, the king of the beans, *rex fabarum* or *rex regni fabarum*, was a fellow elected to preside over the festivities of the Christmas period, holding office from 19 November until Candlemas.[95] Oxford formularies contain mock correspondence between rival Christmas kings. A letter of 5 December 1432 purports to come

---

[93] Cobban, *The King's Hall*, pp. 199–200: *blodius* or *blodeus* is here the adjective translated as blue and *glaucus* as bluish grey.

[94] King's Hall Cabinet, no. 104 (Trinity College Muniment Room); *Cal. Pat. R.*, 1446–1452, pp. 206–7.

[95] See E. K. Chambers, *The Mediaeval Stage* (2 vols., Oxford, 1903), i. 407–8; H. H. Henson, 'The "Rex Natalicus" ', *Collectanea*, i (ed. C. R. L. Fletcher, Oxf. Hist. Soc., v, 1885), pp. 39 ff. at pp. 41–2; *Registrum Annalium Collegii Mertonensis, 1483–1521,* pp. xviii–xix

from King Balthasar of Hinxey Hall and was addressed to the 'pretended' principal of Greek Hall.[96] In a similar vein, a letter in a late fourteenth-century formulary now at Corpus Christi College, Cambridge, is allegedly sent by Balthasar, son of Jove, to John, 'the surburban king of the most sordid neighbourhood of Stockwell Street'.[97] Something akin to the rituals of boy-bishops occurred at New College, Oxford, where boys officiated at services on the feast of the Holy Innocents, and at King's College, Cambridge, where boys presided over services on the feast of St Nicholas.[98] Boy-bishops also feature in the accounts of Magdalen College, Oxford, from the late fifteenth century.[99] The evidence for minstrel entertainments in university colleges dates largely from the late fifteenth century.[100] However, it is known that at Cambridge, Peterhouse received two visits from a company of players in 1388–9,[101] and the voluminous accounts of the King's Hall prove conclusively that from the first half of the fourteenth century minstrels were frequent performers in at least one English college. The King's Hall material concerning minstrelsy is so unusually copious that it merits some detailed consideration.

The royal household character of the King's Hall is nowhere better reflected than in the prominent place occupied by minstrel entertainments in the life of the college.[102] References to minstrels

---

[96] *Oxford Formularies,* ii. 439.

[97] Loc. cit.

[98] *Statutes,* i. ch. 5, 69; *Camb. Docs.,* ii. 569. On boy-bishops, see K. Young, *The Drama of the Medieval Church* (2 vols., Oxford, 1933), i. 106–11, and Chambers, *The Mediaeval Stage,* i. 336 ff.

[99] See extracts from the Magdalen accounts in Chambers, op. cit., ii. 248–70; on boy-bishops at Madgdalen, see R. S. Stanier, *Magdalen School: A History of Magdalen College School, Oxford* (Oxf. Hist. Soc., new ser., iii, 1940) pp. 50–1.

[100] See the assembled evidence for the appearance of minstrals in the Oxford colleges in R. E. Alton (ed.), 'The academic drama in Oxford: extracts from the records of four colleges', *Malone Society Collections,* v (Oxford, 1960), pp. 29 ff. at pp. 40 ff., and G. C. Moore Smith (ed.), 'The academic drama at Cambridge: extracts from college records', *Malone Society Collections,* ii. pt. ii (Oxford, 1923), pp. 150 ff.

[101] See Lovatt, 'The Early Archives of Peterhouse', p. 36.

[102] For this theme, see Cobban, *The King's Hall,* pp. 222–7.

in the King's Hall accounts extend from 1342–3 to the final extant account, of 1543–4.[103] They reveal that individual minstrels or small groups of minstrels visited the college regularly on the days of the main ecclesiastical festivals. They were especially common on the feasts of the Epiphany, the Purification of the Blessed Virgin Mary, Easter, All Saints, Christmas and Holy Innocents' Day, and on 5 May, the occasion of the exequies of the founder of the Society of the King's Scholars, Edward II. An impressively wide compass of medieval minstrelsy is covered by the diversity of the terms used. Those which most often occur are *ioculator*, *iugulator*, *me(i)ne(i)strallus*, *mimus*, *histrio*, *lusor*, *ludens*, *tripudians*, *fistulator*, *buccinator*, *tubicens*, *wayt* and *pleyar*. It is notoriously difficult to distinguish medieval categories of entertainers or to identify each with a specific form of dramatic performance.[104] There is a measure of agreement, however, that some of the terms listed above may be broadly taken to denote professional or semi-professional actors, as long as these are taken to be 'actors' in a rather imprecise sense.[105] There can be little doubt that *fistulator* (piper), *buccinator* and *tubicens* (trumpeters) were specialist musical performers. The *tripudiantes* who appear in the King's Hall accounts were almost certainly entertainers connected with the staging of *tripudia* or revels in the Cambridge churches of Great St Mary's and All Saints in Jewry on the days of their respective dedications.[106] The *wayts* of the accounts were most probably troupes of minstrels in the service of the

[103] See, from a multitude of reference, King's Hall Accounts, i. fos. 58v, 146v; ii. fos. 3v, 149v; iii. fos. 7, 59; iv. fos. 21, 43; v. fos. 26, 117; vi. fos. 19, 125v; vii. fos. 7, 115v; ix fos. 37, 66; x. fos. 33, 88; xi. fos. 39, 156; xii. fo. 131; xiv. fo. 6; xv. fos. 94, 112; xvi. fos. 10, 91; xvii fo. 58; xviii. fo. 104; xix. fo. 187v; xx. fos. 127, 164; xxi. fos. 8, 137; xxii. fos. 18, 74; xxiv. fos. 40v, 117v; xxv. fos. 1v, 119v; xxvi. fos. 39v, 180v.

[104] Chambers, *The Mediaeval Stage*, ii. 230–3.

[105] G. Wickham, *Early English Stages 1300 to 1660* (2 vols., London and New York, 1963), i. 185; Alton (ed.), 'The academic drama in Oxford', *Malone Society Collections*, v. 35.

[106] E.g. King's Hall Accounts, iv. fo. 128; v. fos. 92, 117, 170v; vi. fos. 19, 125v; vii. fo. 115v; xv. fos. 94, 138: for an explanation of the term *tripudia*, see Chambers, op. cit., i. 275. In 1400, players of the city staged a *tripudium* in Winchester College: D. Keene, *Winchester Studies 2: Survey of Medieval Winchester*, i. pt. i (Oxford, 1985), p. 393.

municipal corporation,[107] and were apparently synonymous with the *histriones ville*, who are mentioned with great regularity in the college records. Apart from the visits of small and presumably unattached groups of itinerant minstrels, the college received visits from parish, municipal, royal and noble troupes of entertainers. These included the folk players of All Saints Parish, Cambridge, the town minstrels, who would have formed a liveried body licensed by the corporation of Cambridge, the king's household minstrels, the queen's minstrels, troupes maintained by the earl of Salisbury, the duke of Norfolk and the duke of Exeter, and in 1342, a local group attached to Richard de Goldynton, a King's Hall commoner and a future chancellor of the University.[108] On occasion, individual performers from aristocratic or royal households were received. In 1468-9, for instance, an entertainment was given by a *mimus* of the duchess of York;[109] and in 1532-3, the college expended 2s. 6d. for the services of the king's conjurer (*prestigiator regis*), perhaps identifiable with '*braunden the kyngs jogular*', on whom 2s. 11d. was spent two years later.[110]

---

[107] King's Hall Accounts, xx. fos. 69v, 127; xxi. fo. 8; xxii. fo. 18; xxiii. fo. 6; xxiv. fo. 1v; xxvi. fo. 39v. See the remarks of Chambers, op. cit., i. 51.

[108] For the folk players of All Saints parish, see King's Hall Accounts, i. fo. 59. C. R. Baskervill, 'Dramatic Aspects of medieval folk festivals in England', *Studies in Philology*, xvii (1920), pp. 19 ff. at p. 82, cites this entry as one of the earliest known instances of a medieval institution opening its doors to folk players. For the town minstrels, see King's Hall Accounts, iv. fos. 43, 92, 93, 110v, 128; v. fo. 170v; ix. fo. 7; xi. fo. 39. Cambridge is not included in Chambers' list of corporations which had their own bands of minstrels: Chambers, op. cit., i. 51. But the evidence of the King's Hall Accounts shows that Cambridge possessed its own troupe of minstrels from at least as early as 1394-5. For the king's household minstrels, see King's Hall Accounts, ix. fo. 7; x. fo. 33; xxiv. fo. 40v; xxv. fos. 45v, 119v. In 1500-1, a troupe of the king's musicians gave a performance in the college: ibid., xix. fo. 187v. For the queen's minstrels, the troupes of the earl of Salisbury, the duke of Norfolk and the duke of Exeter, see ibid., x. fo. 88; x. fo. 33; xi. fos. 39, 156. For Goldynton's minstrels, see ibid., i. fo. 70v. Goldynton was charged as a King's Hall commoner in 1340-1 and 1341-2, ibid., i. fos. 48, 60. Goldynton is not included in a list of chancellors in *V.C.H. Camb.* iii. 331-3, but ought to be inserted between Thomas de Northwood (1344) and John de Crakhall (1346-8): on this point see Emden, *B.R.U.C.*, p. 264.

[109] King's Hall Accounts, xiv. fo. 6v.

[110] Ibid., xxiv, fo. 117v; xxv. fo. 1v.

The most lavish feasts of the year involving minstrels at the King's Hall took place over the Christmas period, and the feast held on Holy Innocents' Day was especially splendid. At this festival, the company of fellows and commoners was augmented by the invited presence of townsmen, university dignitaries, tenants of the college and their wives, friars and other assorted guests. The expenditure incurred was often considerable. In 1468–9, the entertainment bill for performers and guests came to £2 2s. 9d.[111] The scale and range of minstrel diversions in the King's Hall savoured of the royal court, from which it derived. Undergraduates who were King's Hall fellows must have been privy to organized entertainments far in excess of what was available to the majority of their undergraduate colleagues in the English Universities.

Evidence for the presentation of fully-fledged plays in English university colleges dates from the late fifteenth and early sixteenth centuries.[112] At Oxford, religious dramas were performed with some regularity at Magdalen College from 1486 onwards; plays were staged at Cardinal College in 1530, at Brasenose in c.1542 and possibly at Christ Church in c.1546.[113] At Cambridge, the King's Hall presented comedies by Terence in 1510–11 and 1516–17. On the second of these occasions, the performance was given by the pupils assigned to the vice-warden as tutor, and these productions rank among the earliest of classical Latin plays in English colleges.[114] At St John's College, the *Plutus* of Aristophanes was rendered in Greek in 1536; and a play is known to have been staged at Christ's College in 1545.[115] The university authorities appear to have grudgingly tolerated dramatic presentations in colleges and halls,

---

[111] Ibid., xiv. fo. 6.

[112] For early plays in English colleges, see F. S. Boas, *University Drama in the Tudor Age* (Oxford, 1914), ch. 1. On plays at the English Universities in the post-Reformation era and the association with immorality, see the brief discussion by V. H. H. Green, *The Universities* (Pelican Books, 1969), pp. 307–8.

[113] Chambers, op. cit., ii. 195.

[114] King's Hall Accounts, xxi. fo. 137; xxvi. fo. 180v; see also Cobban, *The King's Hall*, p. 228.

[115] Chambers, op. cit., ii. 195.

and particularly those by classical authors, on the grounds that their educational value might outweigh the attendant frivolity and dangers to the soul alleged by disciplinarians to be inherent in play production. Since women were not permitted to participate in these performances, male students had to impersonate female characters. In the accounts of Magdalen College, Oxford, for 1518–19, there is an entry for expenses for women's hair for the use of students in connection with a college play.[116]

Attitudes towards women on the part of the English university authorities were permeated by the belief that women and universities should be kept apart as much as was conveniently possible. One of the few elevated roles open to women in the university sphere was that of benefactress, whether as foundress of a college or of a loan-chest or by making testamentary provision for the support of poor scholars. In the towns of Oxford and Cambridge, women indirectly served the university communities through their involvement in retail trades, especially as ale-sellers, and in their capacity as landladies,[117] before compulsory student residence in a college, hall or hostel reduced the opportunities in this direction. The colleges, however, allowed little scope for the employment of women. Many sets of college statutes, such as those of Merton, Oriel, New College and All Souls, Oxford, and King's College, Cambridge, declared that all servants were to be males because the proximity of women might provoke sexual immorality.[118] The only exception to this prohibition was that, failing the availability of a male launderer, a laundress might be employed, as long as certain conditions were met. For example, at New College, All Souls and King's College, it was specifically stated that the laundress must reside in the town, and under no circumstances in the college, and she was to be of such an age that

---

[116] This entry is reproduced in Boas, op. cit., p. 3.

[117] See Aston and Faith, 'The Endowments of the University and Colleges to *circa* 1348', *The History of the University of Oxford*, i. 282, n. 2.

[118] *Statutes*, i. ch. 2, 19–20, 36–7 (Merton), ch. 3, 15 (Oriel), ch. 5, 94 (New College), ch. 7, 58 (All Souls); *Camb. Docs.*, ii. 596 (King's). For a discussion of some of the statutory evidence, see Fletcher and Upton, '"Monastic enclave" or "open society"?', art. cit., pp. 2–3.

any suspicion of impropriety would be allayed.[119] It was stipulated at Peterhouse, King's, New College and All Souls that all clothes were to be transmitted from the fellows to the laundress by means of an intermediary servant and were to be similarly returned.[120] The Peterhouse statutes added a further prohibition on possible physical contact between fellows and laundress by forbidding laundresses, and particularly young ones, from entering the room of a scholar for the purpose of washing his head.[121]

Some colleges were prepared to afford facilities to female visitors, though those that were afforded were severely limited. For instance, a scholar at Peterhouse might meet a female relative or other reputable woman in the hall or some other public place, with another scholar or a college servant acting as a chaperon, the meeting to be kept as brief as possible lest the scholar be led by temptation to commit an evil act.[122] At Christ's College, Cambridge, a woman was permitted to enter a fellow's chamber at times of illness, and on no other occasion, with the approval of the master of the college or his deputy.[123] At Corpus Christi College, Oxford, a mother or sister was allowed to visit a member of the college in his room, but only the president might receive a female guest outside this restricted category.[124] It is exceedingly clear that the statutes of the English colleges embodied the view of woman as sexual temptress, a sinful being from whom the fellows must be shielded. While prostitution could only be curbed and not eradicated in the town, at least the colleges set out to provide the environmental framework for the life of purity deemed by founders to be fitting for unmarried scholars who, in theory at any rate, were wedded to the pursuit of learning.

Not all colleges were equally exclusive of contact with women.

---

[119] *Statutes*, i. ch. 5, 94, ch. 7, 58; *Camb. Docs.*, ii. 596.

[120] *Camb. Docs.*, ii. 30, 596; *Statutes*, i. ch. 5, 94, ch. 7, 58.

[121] *Camb. Docs.*, ii. 30.

[122] Loc. cit.

[123] Ibid., iii. 197.

[124] *Statutes*, ii. ch. 10, 79.

The King's Hall statutes do not exclude women, and indeed do not refer to them in any way. Whether this silence is significant or not, the King's Hall accounts reveal that the college was associated with women, through the 'hocking' activities of the women of the Cambridge parish of All Saints in Jewry, in which it was situated.[125] 'Hock-tide' was a term applicable to the Monday and Tuesday following the second Sunday after Easter.[126] On Hock Monday, the parish women roamed the streets 'hocking' or 'capturing' members of the public with ropes for the purpose of exacting forfeits, usually in the form of money. On Tuesday, it was the turn of the men. The funds raised in this manner were put to the use of the parish. The King's Hall accounts for 1480–1 and 1483–4 itemize sums paid out to 'gaggles of women' without actually mentioning the Hock-tide season.[127] These entries are similar to those for a series of years in the 1530s which specify that the payments were made to the women on Hock-Monday.[128] Such payments were presumably contributions by the King's Hall towards this annual parish event. Some of the expenditure incurred may have been used to provide refreshment for the wives in the college. Analogous evidence elsewhere confirms that it was customary for the parish to supply a meal for the women when the day's collecting was over.[129] In 1483–4, a portion of the King's Hall's payments went specifically towards expenses on behalf of the women,[130] suggesting that the college provided a meal for the women as a charitable act. Whether or not the fellows of the King's Hall actually participated in the general merriment which accompanied 'hocking' frolics is a matter which the impersonal business records of the college do not choose to elucidate. At the

---

[125] See Cobban, *The King's Hall*, pp. 229–30.

[126] On Hock-tide and 'hocking', see Chambers, op. cit., i. 155–8; J. Brand, *Observations on Popular Antiquities* (2 vols., revised by H. Ellis, London, 1813), i. 156 ff. at p. 161, n. *d*; S. Denne, 'Memoir on Hokeday', *Archaeologia*, vii (1785), pp. 244 ff.

[127] King's Hall Accounts, xvi, fos. 33v, 107.

[128] Ibid., xxiv. fos. 73v, 117v; xxv. fos. 1v, 25, 81v, 119v.

[129] Brand, op. cit., i. 164, n. *k*.

[130] King's Hall Accounts, xvi. fo. 107.

very least, the association of the King's Hall with the parish women in a less than sober vein is an arresting counter to the typical emphasis in the statutes upon the avoidance of contact with members of the opposite sex.

The educational experiences of the majority of undergraduates at medieval Oxford and Cambridge were centred largely upon the lecture and disputational programmes and only to a limited extent upon the direct usage of books. As mentioned in chapter 3, there is no clear evidence that the *exemplar-pecia* system, which made available to scholars multiple copies of parts of basic texts, commentaries and disputations, was at Oxford extended beyond the faculties of civil and canon law and theology to encompass texts used in the arts faculty; and there is no definite proof that at Cambridge the system functioned at all.[131] University libraries were slow to materialize. At Oxford, the library set in motion by the bequest of Thomas Cobham in *c.* 1320 was not fully operational until 1412,[132] and was limited by legislation in that year to graduates.[133] At Cambridge, the library, which was functioning in the first half of the fifteenth century, was restricted by a statute of *c.* 1490 to graduates and to those accompanied by graduates.[134] Just as university libraries were not designed with undergraduates in mind, so college libraries would have been beyond the reach of most undergraduates before *c.* 1500. Only in a very few colleges, such as the King's Hall and New College, which had significant undergraduate numbers from the fourteenth century, were college libraries available to younger members of the academic community, although even here access probably had to be arranged through graduate fellows. It may be assumed that a few books would have been kept in most halls and hostels.[135] There were those books belonging to the principals and their graduate assistants, some of

---

[131] See above, chapter 3, pp. 95–6.

[132] See above, chapter 3, pp. 82–3.

[133] *Statuta Antiqua*, p. 218.

[134] *Camb. Docs.*, i. 403.

[135] Ker, 'Oxford College Libraries before 1500', *The Universities in the Late Middle Ages*, p. 293.

which were possibly made accessible to undergraduates; occasional donations of books to halls and hostels are recorded; and at least two of the Oxford halls had recognizable libraries.[136] Thus, English undergraduates were, it seems, ill served by institutional libraries, yet few could afford to build up a private collection. So far as the evidence will allow, it can be asserted that book-ownership among secular scholars before 1500 was of a low order. Only about 10 per cent of recorded seculars at Oxford are known to have owned books, the corresponding Cambridge figure being about 9 per cent.[137] Since the incidence of book-ownership was substantially greater among scholars in the superior faculties than among those of no recorded higher faculty,[138] the impression is confirmed that undergraduates in arts would have owned very few books and, in the absence of good access to libraries, were heavily dependent upon oral forms of instruction.

For graduates who were college fellows, collegiate libraries came to have an increasing importance in the later medieval period. The earliest English colleges seem originally to have kept their books in chests, then in a room set aside as a makeshift library and subsequently in purpose-built libraries. While all colleges had library collections from an early stage, the first substantial planned college library was probably that constructed by Merton between 1373 and 1378 to supersede the previous library arrangements.[139] It appears that New College was the earliest college to incorporate a library as part of the original design.[140] It was conceived on a generous scale and the founder, William of Wykeham, had

---

[136] Ibid., p. 293, n. 2, and Aston et al., 'The Medieval Alumni of the University of Cambridge', p. 17.

[137] Aston, 'Oxford's Medieval Alumni', p. 34; Aston et al., 'The Medieval Alumni of The University of Cambridge', p. 65.

[138] Loc. cit.

[139] Highfield, 'The Early Colleges', *The History of the University of Oxford*, i. 257; Aston, 'External Administration and Resources of Merton College to *circa* 1348', ibid., i. 311 ff. at 312, n. 2; P. Morgan, *Oxford Libraries outside the Bodleian* (Oxford, 1974), p. 80.

[140] R. W. Hunt, 'The Medieval Library', *New College Oxford 1379–1979*, pp. 317 ff. at p. 317.

endowed it with a total of 246 volumes by *c.* 1400,[141] by *c.*1500, the library stock had risen to more than 650 books, at a conservative estimate.[142] It is not possible to furnish a definitive evaluation of the relative sizes of English college libraries. But the surviving catalogues and lists of donors afford some perspective on this topic.

Of the Oxford colleges, Magdalen, New College, Merton and All Souls probably had the largest libraries before 1500, ranging from a stock of about 400 at All Souls to more than 800 at Magdalen.[143] Balliol, Oriel, and Lincoln appear to have had lesser but still adequate libraries.[144] By contrast, the slender amount of data concerning the pre-1500 libraries of University College, Queen's and Exeter suggests that they were of only modest proportions.

[141] Ibid., p. 319.

[142] Hunt, ibid., p. 324, lists 345 volumes received by New College between 1400 and 1500, excluding those given by the founder (246) and by William Rede, bishop of Chichester (*c.* 65), which, when included, would yield a total of about 656 volumes. For Rede's bequest, see ibid., pp. 320–1, and Ker, 'Oxford College Libraries before 1500', p. 303, n. 45.

[143] It is said that Bishop Waynflete, the founder of Magdalen College in 1448, gave about 800 books to the college in 1480: Ker, 'Oxford College Libraries before 1500', p. 305. Merton may have had about 500 books by 1372, and this collection was augmented by the gifts of forty or so donors between 1375 and 1500: ibid., pp. 296, 303. Archbishop Chichele gave 369 volumes to his college of All Souls as a magnificent foundation gift in *c.* 1438, and this was supplemented in 1440 by a bequest of 27 books from Henry VI from the royal exchequer: ibid., p. 304, and *Records of All Souls Library 1437–1600* (Oxford Bibliographical Society, new series, xvi, 1971), pp. 1–2, 3–14. See also R. Weiss, 'Henry VI and the library of All Souls College', *E.H.R.*, lvii (1942), pp. 102 ff. For the list of books of All Souls of *c.* 1440, see E. F. Jacob, 'An early book list of All Souls College', printed as an appendix to 'The two lives of Archbishop Chichele', *B.J.R.L.*, xvi (1932), pp. 428 ff. at pp. 469–81.

[144] Balliol had about 150 volumes by 1375, and these were enriched by the valuable collection of books of William Grey, the humanist scholar and bishop of Ely, which he left to the college on his death in 1478 and most of which still remain at Balliol: Ker, 'Oxford College Libraries before 1500', pp. 296, 303, 305. An incomplete library catalogue of 1375 indicates that there were more than 100 books at Oriel by that year: ibid., p. 296 and n. 14. The library catalogue of Lincoln College of 1474 implies a total of 135 volumes, although the catalogue omits more than 40 works known to have been in the library before 1474; ibid., p. 304, n. 54, and Green, *The Commonwealth of Lincoln College 1427–1977*, pp. 34, 674.

Similar variations in the size of collegiate collections are found at Cambridge. A not entirely complete library catalogue of the King's Hall of 1391 yields a total of 101 volumes.[145] This is only about one third of the 302 books recorded at Peterhouse in 1418.[146] From the evidence of book lists or lists of donations or inventories, it appears that the pre-1500 libraries of Corpus Christi, Clare, King's, Pembroke and Gonville Hall possessed stocks of between 100 and 200 books. It has been reckoned, however, that in the early sixteenth century Gonville may have owned a substantially increased stock of more than 300 volumes.[147] The lengthy catalogue for Queens' of 1472, which enumerates 224 volumes, indicates that

---

[145] Cobban, *The King's Hall*, p. 249. This catalogue was printed by C. E. Sayle, 'King's Hall Library', *Proceedings of the C.A.S.*, xxiv (old series, no. lxxii, 1921–2), pp. 54 ff. at pp. 64–7.

[146] See Willis and Clark, *The Architectural History of the University of Cambridge and of the Colleges of Cambridge and Eton*, iii. 403.

[147] The earliest book list for Corpus Christi College of *c*. 1376 gives a total of 55 volumes, and this had been increased to 131 by 1439: the list is printed by M. R. James, *A Descriptive Catalogue of the Manuscripts in the Library of Corpus Christi College, Cambridge*, i (Cambridge, 1912, pp. ix–xi. The catalogue of 76 books bequeathed in 1439 to Corpus by Thomas Markaunt, fellow of Corpus from 1413–14 until his death in 1439, is printed by M. R. James, 'Catalogue of Thomas Markaunt's library from MS. C.C.C. 232', *C.A.S.*, octavo series, no. xxxii, 1899, pp. 1 ff. at pp. 76–82. From an inventory and a supplementary list of donations, it seems that Clare had amassed 166 volumes by *c*. 1440: the inventory and list of donations are printed by R. W. Hunt, 'Medieval Inventories of Clare College Library', *Transactions of the Cambridge Bibliographical Society*, i (1950), pp. 105 ff. at pp. 110–18. The earliest surviving library catalogue of King's College, of *c*. 1452, lists 175 items: the catalogue is printed by M. R. James, *A Descriptive Catalogue of the Manuscripts other than Oriental in the Library of King's College, Cambridge* (Cambridge, 1895), pp. 72–83; see also the examination of fifteenth-century wills containing bequests of books to King's College by A.N.L. Munby, 'Notes on King's College Library in the fifteenth century', *Transactions of the Cambridge Bibliographical Society*, i (1951), pp. 280 ff. From an incomplete list of donations, extending from 1347 to 1487, Pembroke would appear to have possessed at least 158 books: see M. R. James, *A Descriptive Catalogue of the Manuscripts in the Library of Pembroke College, Cambridge* (Cambridge, 1905), pp. xiii–xvii; also G. E. Corrie, 'A list of books presented to Pembroke College, Cambridge, by different donors during the fourteenth and fifteenth centuries', *C.A.S., Communications*, ii (1860–4), no. iii, pp. 11 ff. For the Gonville library, see Brooke, *A History of Gonville and Caius College*, pp. 33–5.

this was one of the largest libraries in fifteenth-century Cambridge.[148] From these occasional insights, it seems that the Cambridge college libraries before 1500 did not emulate the largest of those of Oxford, such as Magdalen, Merton, New College and All Souls. In general, they appear to have been of an intermediate size and of a serviceable character.

All college libraries at Oxford and Cambridge seem to have divided their books into a chained or reference department, to which each graduate fellow would normally have had a key, and a lending or circulating section.[149] At the King's Hall in 1391, only about one-fifth of the books were chained.[150] This proportion is about the same as that found at the Paris college of the Sorbonne in 1338.[151] It is apparent that the King's Hall library was overwhelmingly a borrowing one. Likewise, at Merton the chained books were much less numerous than those that were for lending.[152] At Peterhouse, on the other hand, just under half of the 302 books listed in 1418 were chained.[153]

Books were borrowed by college fellows from the circulating categories of libraries by means of an annual *electio* or selection. They were retained for a year or sometimes longer. For example, at New College and All Souls, scholars of civil and canon law might

---

[148] This catalogue is printed by W. G. Searle, 'Catalogue of the library of Queens' College in 1472', *C.A.S., Communications*, ii (1864), no. xv, pp. 165 ff. at pp. 168–81.

[149] See e.g. Ker, 'Oxford College Libraries before 1500', p. 294, and Morgan, *Oxford Libraries outside the Bodleian*, p. x.

[150] Cobban, *The King's Hall*, p. 249.

[151] The catalogue of the Sorbonne of 1338 records 1,722 books, of which 330 are described as 'chained' (*cathenati*): F. M. Powicke, *The Medieval Books of Merton College* (Oxford, 1931), p. 9.

[152] Ibid., pp. 7–8; B. H. Streeter, *The Chained Library* (London, 1931), p. 8. For a valuable analysis of the distribution of philosophy books among the fellows of Merton in 1372 and 1375, see N. R. Ker, 'The Books of Philosophy distributed at Merton College in 1372 and 1375', *Books, Collectors and Libraries: Studies in the Medieval Heritage* (ed. A. G. Watson, London and Ronceverte, 1985), pp. 331 ff.

[153] Willis and Clark, op. cit., iii. 403; Streeter, op. cit., p. 8.

borrow a set of texts for the duration of their studies, provided that they did not already own these works.[154] Wykeham's statutes for New College enacted that only those books which remained after the fellows had made their selection were to be chained in the library.[155] The essence of this enactment was incorporated in the statutes of King's College, Cambridge.[156] In the statutes of All Souls of 1443, however, it is decreed that the fellows may select from only those books left over after the removal of the books to be chained.[157] This procedure is a notable reversal of the practice at New College, and it is repeated with variations in the statutes of Magdalen, Brasenose, Corpus Christi and Cardinal College, Oxford.[158] The King's Hall statutes are silent on library arrangements. From the fact that the chained books in the catalogue of 1391 are indicated in the margin by the abbreviation *cath* (i.e. *cathenati* or 'chained') against each such volume, it seems that here also it was customary to make a definite choice of books for the reference department prior to the selection of books by the fellows.[159] The distinction between the chained and circulating categories appears to have been maintained in most college libraries down to *c.* 1500. In the course of the sixteenth century, however, the circulating sections fell progressively into desuetude. The reasons for this are not wholly understood. But the increasing tendency of donors to stipulate that their books be kept permanently chained and the decisions of many colleges to augment the reference areas at the expense of the lending sections are two of

---

[154] *Statutes*, i. ch. 5, 98 (New College), ch. 7, 55 (All Souls).

[155] Ibid., i. ch. 5, 98.

[156] *Camb. Docs.*, ii. 601–2.

[157] *Statutes*, i. ch. 7, 54–5.

[158] Ibid., ii. ch. 8, 61 (Magdalen), ch. 9, 35 (Brasenose), ch. 10, 90 (Corpus Christi), ch. 11, 112 (Cardinal College). For the chained and circulating sections of Oxford college libraries in the sixteenth century, see Ker, 'Oxford College Libraries in the Sixteenth Century', *Books, Collectors and Libraries*, ed. cit., pp. 379 ff. at pp. 383–6.

[159] Cobban, *The King's Hall*, p. 250.

the factors which led to the phasing out of the circulating collections in the sixteenth century.[160]

Information concerning the borrowing habits of fellows in medieval English colleges is exceedingly elusive. It is indeed fortunate that the accounts of the King's Hall contain parts of four illuminating library lending lists. One of these belongs to 1386–7, one to some date between 1385 and 1391, the third to 1390–1 and the fourth to 1392–3.[161] These record the name of the fellow to whom the book was loaned, the author, the *incipit* or opening words of the second folio, and, in the case of the second of these lists, the monetary value placed upon the book. No borrowing dates are specified and, apart from the liability for the payment of the assessed price of the book in the event of loss or damage, no pledge seems to have been exacted. The list for 1386–7 records that 80 volumes were distributed among the warden and 22 fellows so that the warden and one of the fellows had 11 each, two had 7, one had 5, two had 4, three had 3, nine had 2, and the remaining four fellows 1 each. The second list is briefer and records the distribution of books among the warden and seven fellows. In this instance, the warden had 6 books, two of the fellows had 2, and the rest 1 volume apiece. With the exception of a few medical treatises and the occasional volume on grammar, logic, or theology, the majority of the books borrowed were the basic texts on civil and canon law or commentaries upon the same. The diversity concerning the number of volumes borrowed per fellow indicates that books might be borrowed according to immediate academic need and that no rigid limitation was placed upon the number or type of volumes that could be borrowed by one fellow. Nor was borrowing restricted to the books of a fellow's current faculty. In the lending list of 1386–7, it is recorded that Simon Godrich, B.C.L., had taken out eleven

---

[160] For donors who stipulated that their gifts of books be chained in the library, see instances at Merton and Corpus in the sixteenth century, Ker, 'Oxford College Libraries in the Sixteenth Century', p. 385; and for the transfer of two classical texts from the circulating to the reference section of the library of All Souls, see Ker, 'Oxford College Libraries before 1500', p. 306.

[161] The first, third and fourth of these lists are printed by Sayle, art. cit., pp. 62–3, 67–8, 69–70: the second list was missed by Sayle and is to be found in the King's Hall Accounts, iii. fo. 104.

volumes, of which seven were parts of the Digest and the Code, one was a commentary of Azo and three were medical texts. In the same list, it is stated that William Waltham, B.C.L., had borrowed two medical works in addition to three of the 'extraordinary' books of the Code.[162] Occasionally, it seems, a volume normally in the chained category might be borrowed. Two such instances have been detected at the King's Hall, and one similar relaxation at Merton.[163] In 1372, a total of 137 volumes, characterized as philosophical, were distributed among twenty-two fellows of Merton so that three received 8, and the others 7, 5, or 4; and in 1375 a collection of 134 volumes, likewise pertaining to philosophy, were distributed among fifteen fellows so that one received 12, and the rest 8, 9, or 10. The result of these distributions at Merton was that each fellow was provided with as full an allocation of Aristotelian texts and commentaries on Aristotle, especially those of Averroes, as the means of the college would allow.[164]

If these details concerning the workings of the lending sections of the libraries of the King's Hall and Merton are in any way representative, it would seem that English college fellows were well served by their college libraries. They appear to have had direct access to at least a proportion of the key texts for the purposes of private study. To this extent, graduate fellows who were studying for advanced degrees would have been much more book-oriented and less vulnerably dependent upon the formal teaching programmes than were the mass of the undergraduate population.

Among the circumstances which threatened the continuity of academic study in the medieval English Universities was the recurrent menace of plague. It is likely that the scholars of Oxford and Cambridge suffered less than some other parts of the population, for the diet and living conditions of all but the poorest of scholars in the fourteenth and fifteenth centuries were probably above the average for the populace at large. It may also be advanced

---

[162] The 'extraordinary' books of the Code are books x–xii.

[163] For details, see Cobban, *The King's Hall*, p. 250, and Powicke, *The Medieval Books of Merton College*, p. 11.

[164] See Ker, 'The Books of Philosophy distributed at Merton College in 1372 and 1375', pp. 333–4.

that the university community, being for the most part relatively youthful, ought to have had a good natural resistance to disease.[165] The overall effects of the Black Death on the English Universities cannot be assessed statistically since the necessary data is unavailable. There are estimates of the injury done to Oxford's population from visitations of plague which derive from the fourteenth and fifteenth centuries.[166] But these are so exaggerated that they can form no useful basis for demographic calculation. From an investigation of the mortality rate appertaining to a sample of 87 theologians known to have been resident in Oxford in the decade before the Black Death of 1348–9, W. J. Courtenay has concluded that this catastrophic visitation of plague had only a small impact on Oxford's academic population.[167] Although this analysis is of interest, it is obviously too circumscribed to make Courtenay's general conclusion anything more than speculative. There is some contemporary evidence that the town of Cambridge was severely affected by the Black Death in 1349 and by the later visitation of 1361–2.[168] But, as in the case of Oxford, there is little specific evidence on the extent to which the university population was affected. It is certain that sixteen of the fellows of the King's Hall were victims of the Black Death in 1349, and that during the visitation of 1361–2, the warden, Thomas Powys, and eight of the fellows died.[169] There is no means of knowing, however, whether this incidence of mortality was typical of all areas of the University.

In the fourteenth century, it was apparently not yet common for college communities at either Oxford or Cambridge to take evasive action by leaving the university town for a rural retreat for the duration of a plague visitation. The fact that plague epidemics of the fourteenth century embraced wide regions of the countryside as

---

[165] See the arguments of W. J. Courtenay, 'The Effect of the Black Death on English Higher Education', *Speculum*, 55 (1980), pp. 696 ff. at p. 703.

[166] See e.g. P. Ziegler, *The Black Death* (London, 1969), pp. 140–1.

[167] Courtenay, art. cit., p. 702.

[168] F. A. Gasquet, *The Black Death of 1348 and 1349* (2nd ed., London, 1908), p. 157; Ziegler, op. cit., p. 172.

[169] Cobban, *The King's Hall*, p. 221.

well as the towns[170] would have lessened the incentive for organized evacuation. In the course of the fifteenth century, however, the pattern of plague outbreaks in England begun to assume a predominantly urban character so that a country sanctuary then became an objective for those who were in a position to move to areas of comparative safety.[171] At Oxford, the fellows of Merton had plague retreats in the Oxfordshire villages of Cuxham and Islip;[172] Magdalen fellows migrated to havens at Ewelme and Witney in Oxfordshire, at Wallingford in Berkshire and at Brackley in Northamptonshire;[173] and Lincoln College utilized a series of houses in villages in Oxfordshire and Buckinghamshire for this purpose.[174] It is unclear whether at Cambridge the fellows of the King's Hall migrated to safe retreats collectively or individually. Whatever the case, in plague years in the early sixteenth century significant numbers of fellows left the college for unspecified ports of call, lengths of absence varying from a few weeks to five months.[175] English college fellows in retreat would normally have been able to draw an allowance for their commons during their self-imposed exile from the university town.[176] Sometimes fellows were joined by members of the domestic staff.[177]

---

[170] J. M. W. Bean, 'Plague, population and economic decline in England in the later middle ages', *Econ. Hist. Rev.*, 2nd ser., xv (1962–3), pp. 423 ff. at pp. 430–1.

[171] Ibid., pp. 430–1.

[172] See P. D. A. Harvey, *A Medieval Oxfordshire Village, Cuxham 1240 to 1400* (Oxford, 1965), p. 91; also C. Creighton, *A History of Epidemics in Britain*, i (Cambridge, 1891), p. 283.

[173] N. Denholm-Young, 'Magdalen College', *V.C.H. Oxon.* iii. 193 ff. at 195.

[174] Green, *The Commonwealth of Lincoln College 1427–1977*, pp. 120 ff.

[175] Cobban, *The King's Hall*, pp. 221–2. In 1505–6, 1517–18, 1520–1 and 1525–6, 5, 17, 11 and 6 fellows respectively absented themselves from the college because of plague: King's Hall Accounts, xx. fo. 149; xxii. fos. 37v, 133v; xxiii. fo. 168v.

[176] In 1513–14, the King's Hall fellow John Barow was provided with commons for five months' absence because of plague: King's Hall Accounts, xxi. fo. 68v; see also Green, op. cit., pp. 120, 121, 122 and notes.

[177] E.g. Green, op. cit., pp. 121, 122.

The Oxford register of congregation covering the years 1448 to 1463 records instances of graces or dispensations granted to scholars arising from the interruptions to degree courses caused by pestilence. These graces usually took the form of allowing time spent at Cambridge or at some other university to count towards the statutory requirements for the Oxford degree.[178] Dispensations were normally granted to individual scholars. In 1452, however, because of disruptions caused by plague, all of the scholars of the Oxford faculty of arts were permitted to reckon twelve ordinary lectures as if they were the complete number of lectures statutorily required for one term.[179] The frequency of these dispensations suggests that a very considerable dislocation of studies had become woven into the pattern of Oxford life and legislation by the middle of the fifteenth century. The records of the King's Hall provide an intriguing insight into the extent to which Cambridge was subjected to repeated visitations of plague or sweating sickness, with all the attendant miseries of interrupted studies, suffering and death which are so poignantly brought home to us in the Cambridge letters of Erasmus.[180] References to plague or sweating sickness are found in the King's Hall accounts of 1498-9, 1499-1500, 1500-1, 1502-3, 1505-6, 1508-9, 1513-14, 1516-17, 1517-18, 1520-1 and 1525-6.[181] The accounts of Lincoln College

---

[178] For example, in 1449, Peter Talbot, a scholar of the arts faculty, was allowed to reckon two terms and three long vacations spent in Cambridge because of plague as the equivalent of one full term of his Oxford course: *The Register of Congregation 1448–1463*, p. 44. In 1453, William Brown, B.A., was allowed to reckon one year spent studying in arts outside Oxford as the equivalent of a full year at Oxford University: ibid., p. 159. In 1455, it was conceded to Thomas Horn, a scholar of the arts faculty, that he could regard two long vacations and several small vacations as a substitute for the terms he spent outside Oxford because of pestilence: ibid., pp. 221–2. In 1463, Robert Isam was dispensed for the year in which he was prevented from hearing ordinary lectures in the faculty of civil law during a plague hiatus: ibid., p. 389.

[179] *The Register of Congregation 1448–1463*, p. 102.

[180] Much information on sweating sickness or the English sweat will be found in Creighton, *A History of Epidemics in Britain*, i. 237–81. The Cambridge letters of Erasmus have been translated and edited by D.F.S. Thomson and H. C. Porter, *Erasmus and Cambridge* (Toronto, 1963).

[181] King's Hall Accounts, xix. fos. 143v, 177, 207; xx. fos. 59, 149, 212v; xxi. fo. 68v; xxii. fos. 37v, 133v, xxiii. fo. 160v, xxvi. fo. 172v.

display a similar frequency of epidemic disease in Oxford in the early sixteenth century.[182] The periodic and traumatic advent of plague and other diseases of the fever variety ensured that the university communities could not evade that outlook of morbidity and preoccupation with death which permeated later medieval England and which is such a notable feature of the literature and art of the age. The extent to which so many of the English colleges incorporated chantry arrangements is a powerful reminder of this funereal climate of thought.

If the threat and actuality of plague and associated diseases unsettled the tenor of English academic life from the mid-fourteenth century onwards, at least Oxford and Cambridge were spared the aggravations arising from the machinations of student power. In the northern European universities, student power did not materialize, as it did in southern Europe, as a serious challenge to the dominance of the teaching masters. In this connection, one or two general points may be offered by way of explanation.[183] At Oxford and Cambridge, the arts faculties occupied a larger position within the university than they did in many of the universities of southern Europe, where they were sometimes mere adjuncts to legal studies or to medicine. Much of the university effort in England went into training young men, for the majority of whom the B.A. degree was the academic ceiling. In terms of maturity and wordly experiences, these adolescents were ill-equipped to organize and spearhead movements of student militancy. The average English student was less politically and legally sophisticated than his southern fellows. The product of a middling to lower social background, he was likely to view the university as one of the few means of career advancement. These circumstances, allied to his tender years, would have predisposed the average student at Oxford and Cambridge to accept the hierarchical assumptions upon which the university was based, and to acquiesce, albeit with the reluctance of youth, in the disciplinary codes imposed by the magisterial guilds on their undergraduate populations. By contrast,

---

[182] Green, op. cit., pp. 119–22.

[183] For the substance of this paragraph, see Cobban, 'Medieval Student Power', pp. 60–4.

many of the southern students were recruited from wealthy backgrounds, and a good number were of noble origin. A sizeable proportion of them were in their twenties or even older, and some came straight to university from holding positions of responsibility in society. Students of this type had a more legalistic, contractual view of university life than was prevalent in England. In the southern environment, students were accustomed to regard the universities and lecturing staffs as agencies to be used and hired so as best to serve the students' own convenience and future professional interests. This kind of thinking would have struck few chords in the English students, who accepted their role as academic apprentices. They did not claim to possess that full professional status, on a par with extra-university professions, which was vociferously claimed by their southern counterparts.

Moreover, at Oxford and Cambridge, the masters' guilds afforded paternalistic protection to the undergraduate population, and this sheltered the students from many of the dangers to which their fellows were exposed in southern Europe. This greatly lessened the motivation for student power enterprise. Added to this magisterial protection, the sustained support given to Oxford and Cambridge by the English monarchy from the thirteenth century created a relative security which tended to work against the development of student militancy. Finally, Oxford and Cambridge did not harbour large colonies of foreign students. And it was the presence of groupings of foreign scholars in the cosmopolitan universities of southern Europe which was the chief spur for the emergence of defensive student organizations or guilds. In many instances, these guilds had gone on to acquire in the affairs of university government either the controlling voice or at least a substantial measure of participation therein. Student unrest at the English Universities took the negative form of street violence, whether between rival gangs of students or between students and townspeople. There is no evidence that it was ever channelled into seeking participatory powers in university government.

In an earlier part of this chapter, some attention was given to the sources of patronage for English scholars by whose agency they could hope to be launched upon a successful career. It now remains to attempt a broad picture of the types of career pursued by scholars of Oxford and Cambridge before *c*.1500. Only a proportion of the careers of known graduates can be traced. Furthermore, the unquantifiable number of students who attended university for a time without taking a degree may have followed occupations which, for the most part, have gone unrecorded. But within these limitations it is possible to draw tentative conclusions concerning the deployment of university alumni in English society.

It is apparent that the Church at all levels and in all its manifestations was a principal employer for university-trained personnel. At the topmost rungs of the ecclesiastical hierarchy, the offices of bishops and deans of secular cathedrals, Oxford's contribution far outstripped that of Cambridge. Between 1216 and 1499, Oxford supplied 57 per cent of English bishops, compared with the 10 per cent provided by Cambridge.[184] In the last forty years of the fifteenth century, Cambridge's count of bishops significantly improved, there being in that period 16 appointments for Cambridge by comparison with 31 for Oxford.[185] Nevertheless, over three centuries, Cambridge's contribution to the episcopate was assuredly mediocre, and the episcopal bench was unmistakably something of an Oxford stronghold.[186] Of the Oxford and Cambridge appointees to English bishoprics, those who were legists led the field ahead of those who were theologians, with artists and those of unknown discipline lagging far behind. Of the lawyers, those with degrees in civil law predominated over those with degrees in canon law or with degrees in both laws.[187] It is, however, interesting that in the fifteenth century the number of theologians promoted to bishoprics was significant, 33 Oxford theologians compared with 50 legists and 10 Cambridge

---

[184] Aston, 'Oxford's Medieval Alumni', pp. 27–8.

[185] Aston et al., 'The Medieval Alumni of the University of Cambridge', p. 69.

[186] On the Oxford dominance of the episcopate in the fifteenth century, see J. T. Rosenthal, 'The Training of an Elite Group: English Bishops in the Fifteenth Century', *Transactions of the American Philosophical Society*, new series, lx (1970), pt. 5, pp. 5 ff. at pp. 14–15.

[187] Aston, 'Oxford's Medieval Alumni', p. 28, and Aston et al., 'The Medieval Alumni of the University of Cambridge', p. 70.

theologians compared with 18 legists and one artist.[188] The increase in theologians may be attributed in part to Henry VI's penchant for theology and theologians. Between 1443 and 1461, during Henry's adult years as king, 16 of the 25 bishops promoted to the episcopate were theologians, the preference for lawyers being restored under the Yorkists from 1461 and maintained by Henry VII.[189]

The disparity in numbers as between the promotion of Oxford and Cambridge graduates to bishoprics was mirrored with respect to deanships of secular cathedrals. Between 1307 and 1499, no fewer than 58 per cent of decanal appointments went to Oxford alumni and only 10 per cent to Cambridge men. As in the case of the bishops, deans who were legists prevailed heavily over those who were theologians.[190] Oxford and Cambridge alumni made a major contribution to the ranks of the senior offices of English secular cathedrals below the position of dean, these offices comprising those of treasurer, precentor, chancellor and sub-dean, and they were also prominent among the prebendaries of cathedrals and diocesan archdeacons.[191] Moreover, large numbers of Oxford and Cambridge men obtained preferment in the lesser ecclesiastical sphere as rectors, vicars, chaplains and chantry priests and as members of collegiate churches. From an analysis of the entries in A.B. Emden's Cambridge biographical register, it is apparent that about one third of Cambridge's secular alumni acquired this type of lesser preferment.[192]

---

[188] Aston et al., 'The Medieval Alumni of the University of Cambridge', p. 70. Rosenthal, art. cit., p. 14, draws attention to the importance of theology as a training for the episcopate in the fifteenth century, but he exaggerates the number of theologians, as compared with legists, who become bishops.

[189] See R. G. Davies, 'The Episcopate', *Profession, Vocation and Culture in Later Medieval England*, pp. 51 ff. at pp. 57, 61.

[190] Aston, 'Oxford's Medieval Alumni', p. 28, and Aston et al., 'The Medieval Alumni of the University of Cambridge', pp. 69–70. In the former article, it is stated that 60 per cent of all deans appointed between 1307 and 1499 were Oxford alumni: the revised figure of 58 per cent is given in the latter article.

[191] Aston et al., 'The Medieval Alumni of the University of Cambridge', pp. 70–6.

[192] Ibid., p. 77.

The communities of monks and friars in the English Universities made an impressive contribution to the governance of their orders as measured by the number who became heads of religious houses or provincials within their order. Oxford yielded 605 heads of houses or provincials, compared with Cambridge's total of 253, which, given that Cambridge was numerically the smaller university, is a sizeable figure.[193] This was a high return on the investment which the regular orders had made in sending some of their ablest members to be educated in the English Universities.

Apart from the Church or a career as a schoolteacher, the main avenues of employment for Oxford and Cambridge alumni, including the regulars, were in posts associated with royal, episcopal, noble and papal service.[194] The available statistics suggest, however, that the assimilation of personnel from the English Universities into these areas before c. 1500 was not as extensive as might be supposed.[195] As with bishoprics and deanships, lawyers were prominent in these four career areas, civil lawyers and graduates in both laws being more so than canonists. It should be mentioned, however, that in the fifteenth century Cambridge theologians were noticeably represented in the royal household, among officers of state and king's clerks and in the diplomatic service. Another career avenue which attracted a steady, though modest, flow of graduates was that of notary public.[196]

---

[193] On this subject, see ibid., pp. 67–8, and Aston, 'Oxford's Medieval Alumni', pp. 28–9.

[194] See Aston, 'Oxford's Medieval Alumni', pp. 29–30, and Aston et al., 'The Medieval Alumni of the University of Cambridge', pp. 80–2: there is also much information in J. Dunbabin, 'Careers and Vocations', *The History of the History of Oxford*, i. 565 ff.

[195] The obtainable percentages of Oxford seculars who attained positions in one or more of these four career areas were 26, 16 and 8 in the thirteenth, fourteenth and fifteenth centuries respectively, the comparable percentages for regulars being 15, 11 and 7. At Cambridge, taking the three centuries together, only 11 per cent of seculars and 5 per cent of regulars are known to have found placements in these spheres of employment: Aston, 'Oxford's Medieval Alumni', pp. 29–30, and Aston et al., 'The Medieval Alumni of the University of Cambridge', pp. 80–2.

[196] Almost 2 per cent of all recorded Oxford alumni followed this career, as did just under 1 per cent of Cambridge personnel: Aston, 'Oxford's Medieval Alumni', pp. 30–1, and Aston et al., 'The Medieval Alumni of the University of Cambridge', p. 82.

While this kind of employment had a natural appeal to graduates in civil law or in both laws, arts graduates were not excluded, and a good few cases of artists who became notaries without acquiring a law degree are found among Cambridge alumni.

Against the broad career pattern of the medieval English Universities, it is instructive to look at the output of two particular colleges. The multifarious career activities of the fellows of the King's Hall, which had an especially close relationship with the king and the royal household, defy neat classification.[197] It is not possible to estimate with any precision how many of the King's Hall fellows came to be directly employed in the service of the crown. The indications are, however, that the proportion was fairly substantial. King's Hall fellows were employed in the chancery, the exchequer, the king's council and the diplomatic arena; they were employed in the queen's household, as royal bailiffs and keepers of the forest, and as judicial commissioners; at least three held the office of master of the rolls; one was a keeper of the privy seal; another a king's secretary; and one rose to the position of keeper of the great seal of England. The wardens of the Kings' Hall followed a similar galaxy of distinguished careers in government and the royal household. They are discovered as king's secretaries, keepers of the privy seal, royal councillors, deans of the chapel royal, king's and queen's chaplains, queen's secretaries, king's almoners, clerks of parliament, chancery clerks, barons of the exchequer and royal diplomats. In addition, two of the wardens became bishops, and of these, Geoffrey Blythe was also lord president of the council of Wales.[198]

In terms of ecclesiastical offices held, the fellowship of the King's Hall produced 3 bishops, at least 21 archdeacons — some of whom retained two or more archdeaconries at a time — 10 bishop's officials, 3 archdeacon's officials, an archiepiscopal secretary, 2 episcopal chancellors, an episcopal chaplain and a number of bishop's commissaries and vicars general.[199] An analysis of more

[197] For a discussion of the careers of King's Hall fellows, see Cobban, *The King's Hall*, pp. 290–9 and notes.

[198] For an analysis of the careers of the wardens of the King's Hall, see ibid., pp. 281–90 and notes.

[199] Ibid., p. 393 and notes.

than 1,600 ecclesiastical livings held by King's Hall fellows between 1317 and 1500, these livings comprising mainly rectorships, vicarages, deaneries, canonries and prebends, has established that when they are grouped according to dioceses, and when these groups are ranked in order of size, the Lincoln, London, Norwich, York, Sarum and Ely groups occupy the first six places.[200] With the exception of Sarum, this diocesan concentration is the same as that for the geographical recruitment of fellows, which has been analysed for the period 1317 to 1443.[201] While these were the main concentrations, reflecting the bias one would expect to find in England's eastern university, it is clear that the King's Hall fellows found livings in every diocese of England with the possible exception of Carlisle.

An analysis of the subsequent careers of New College men who were fellows between 1386 and 1547 shows that 312 became beneficed clergymen (the majority of whom remained as rectors or vicars throughout their lives), 80 returned to teach at Winchester, 70 attained positions within royal, aristocratic and episcopal households, 40 became schoolmasters outside Winchester, 22 practised as common lawyers and 20 as lawyers in ecclesiastical courts and 13 entered religious orders.[202] Given the size of New College and its importance as a major legal focus in Oxford, the proportion of its fellows who entered royal, noble and episcopal service over such a lengthy time-span is not perhaps as large as might have been expected. And when it is considered that 254 members of New College had died while still at university, and that no fewer that 533 had left college without proceeding to any recorded employment,[203] the decidedly slender tally of those who scaled the higher echelons of Church and State is further underlined. Whatever success rates individual colleges had in placing a proportion of their members in the most prestigious areas of

---

[200] For this analysis, see ibid., pp. 293–4.

[201] Ibid., pp. 157–60.

[202] See G. F. Lytle, 'The Careers of Oxford Students in the Later Middle Ages', *Rebirth, Reform and Resilience*, ed. cit., pp. 213 ff. at p. 221.

[203] Loc. cit.

A. The decorated initial 'I' in this fourteenth-century commentary on Aristotle represents Bishop Robert Grosseteste, an early chancellor of Oxford and the most original and influential of the thirteenth-century Oxford scholars who worked on Aristotelian scientific and mathematical material: Merton College MS. 289, fo. 101r. (By kind permission of The Warden and Fellows of Merton College, Oxford. Photograph: The Bodleian Library, Oxford.)

B. Edward III grants privileges to the University of Oxford in
1375: Oxford University Archives, *Registrum A*, fo. 17r. (By
kind permission of The Bodleian Library, Oxford.)

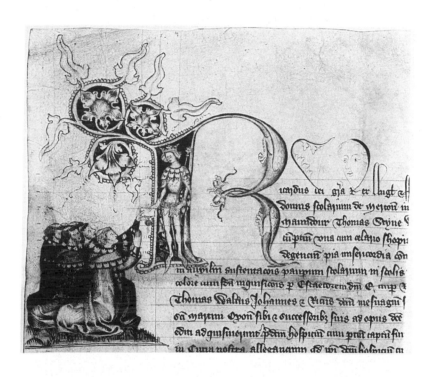

C. Charter of Richard II of 1380 granting land in Oxford to Merton College. The fellows kneel before the king to receive the charter: Merton College Archives, Charter 370. (By kind permission of The Warden and Fellows of Merton College, Oxford. Photograph: The Bodleian Library, Oxford.)

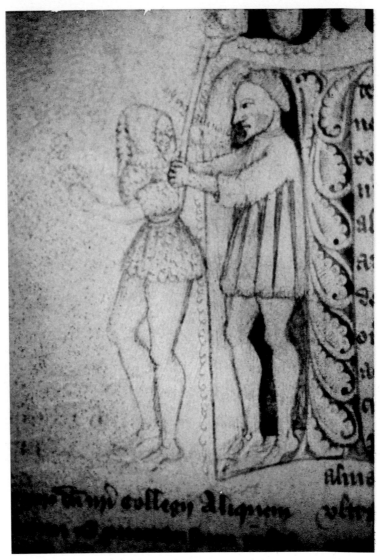

D. The decorated initial 'I' from a copy of the statutes of New
College, Oxford, of *c.* 1400 depicts the porter ejecting a
student who is not a member of New College with the words,
'non intrabis hic' ('you shall not enter here'): New College
Archives, 3584. (By kind permission of The Warden and
Fellows of New College, Oxford. Photograph: Miss E. A.
Danbury.)

E. The initial 'R' shows Thomas Arundel, as Archbishop of
Canterbury, seated in his pastoral chair surrounded by four
Benedictine monks: Bodleian MS. Laud. Misc. 165, fo. 5r.
Arundel attempted to purge Oxford University of its Wycli-
fite and Lollard heresies in the early fifteenth century despite
much opposition from a section of the academic population.
(By kind permission of The Bodleian Library, Oxford.)

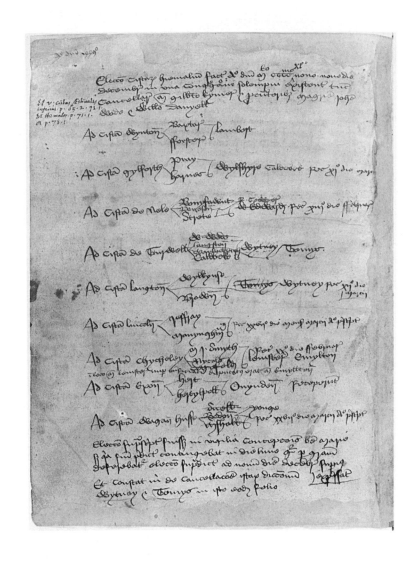

F. The election of keepers of loan-chests at Oxford in 1449: Oxford University Archives, *Registrum Aa*, fo. 6v. (By kind permission of The Bodleian Library, Oxford.)

G. A view of New College, Oxford, with its associated member-
ship and warden Thomas Chaundler, *c.* 1463: New College
MS. 288, fo. 3v. (By kind permission of The Warden and
Fellows of New College, Oxford. Photograph: The Bodleian
Library, Oxford.)

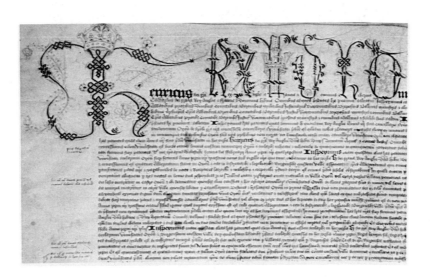

H.   Letters Patent of Henry VII of 1 March 1487 containing an
     inspeximus and confirmation of grants to Oxford University.
     This is the earliest decorated royal grant in the University's
     possession: Oxford University Archives, LBXX. (By kind
     permission of The Bodleian Library, Oxford.)

I. The illuminated initial 'E' of the Charter of Edward I of 1291/2
confirming the privileges of Cambridge University: Cambridge
University Archives, Luard, no. 7*. (By kind permission of
The Syndics of Cambridge University Library.)

J. Letters Patent of Edward III of 19 September 1343 augmenting the Cambridge chancellor's jurisdiction within the town. A bedel with his staff of office stands behind the kneeling chancellor: Cambridge University Archives, Luard, no. 33A. (By kind permission of The Syndics of Cambridge University Library.)

K. Full-page illumination of St Christopher from the Old Proctor's Book, *c.* 1390, fo. 6r: Cambridge University Archives,
Liber procuratoris antiquus, COLL ADMIN 3. (By kind permission of The Syndics of Cambridge University Library.)

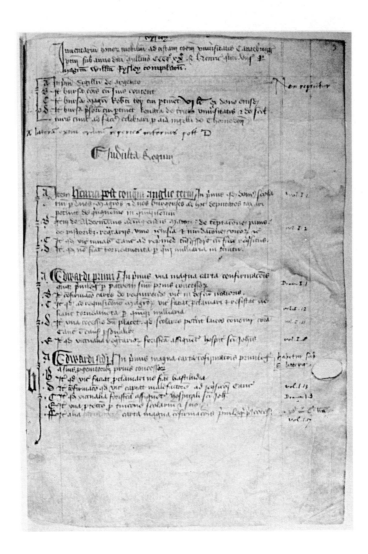

L. Inventory of the Cambridge University Archives compiled by
    William Rysley in 1420: *Registrum Librorum*, fo. 9r, Cam-
    bridge University Archives, COLL ADMIN 4. (By kind
    permission of The Syndics of Cambridge University Library.)

M. Charter of Henry VI of 16 March 1446 in favour of King's
College, Cambridge. Illumination of William Abel contain-
ing an early representation of the Lords and Commons of
Parliament, who are supporting the king's petition to the
Virgin Mary on behalf of his new foundation: King's College
Archives, A 20. (By kind permission of The Provost and
Scholars of King's College, Cambridge.)

N.   Petition of 20 May 1448 from Pembroke College, Cambridge, to Henry VI seeking financial assistance: Pembroke Muniments, College Box A 19. (By kind permission of The Master and Fellows of Pembroke College, Cambridge.)

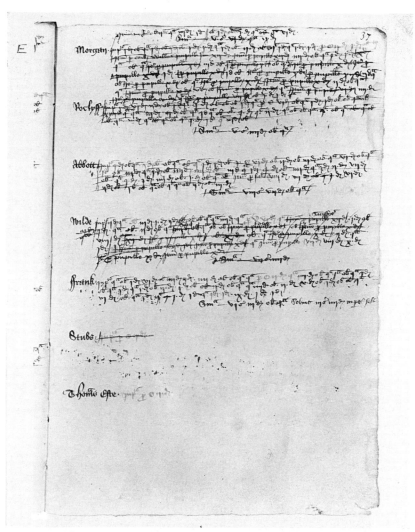

O. Evidence for the tutorial system at the King's Hall, Cambridge. The expenses incurred in 1460–1 by Richard Morgan and William Wilde, fellows of the college, for the pupils (*pupilli*) or undergraduate commoners in their care. The *pupilli* were charged at the rate of half commons, normally about 10d. a week: Trinity College Archives, King's Hall Accounts, xiii. fo. 19r. (By kind permission of The Master and Fellows of Trinity College, Cambridge.)

P. Exemplification (in book form) of Letters Patent of Henry VII of 1 May 1506 for Christ's College, Cambridge. The illuminated initial 'H' contains the arms of Henry VII: Christ's College Archives, CC/M/Found/1. (By kind permission of The Master and Fellows of Christ's College, Cambridge.)

employment, it is clear that a sizeable section of collegiate personnel was destined for the myriad positions which came under the umbrella heading of lesser ecclesiastical preferment.

While medieval Oxford and Cambridge tolerated a wastage rate which would be unacceptable by twentieth-century criteria, they nonetheless seem to have succeeded in providing the necessary manpower for the manifold needs of secular and ecclesiastical government and administration. University personnel penetrated at all levels. They are prominent among the principal officers of state, king's councillors, bishops, deans of cathedrals and heads of religious houses, royal clerks in the various governmental departments, diplomats, judges in both secular and ecclesiastical courts, members of parliament, the senior officials, canons and prebendaries of cathedrals, archdeacon's and bishop's officials, and functionaries within aristocratic households. Lower down the employment scale, they are much in evidence among the ranks of notaries public, schoolmasters, the parish clergy, chantry priests and domestic chaplains. In certain areas, graduate status seems to have become almost a *sine qua non* by 1500, for example, among the senior officers of the secular cathedrals; and, in the later medieval period, graduates were becoming increasingly common among the parish clergy, although not always with improving results.[204] Over the three centuries to *c.* 1500, the English Universities had come to acquire an indispensable role in buttressing the fabric of England's political, administrative, legal and ecclesiastical structures, and in playing that role they were deemed to be responding to the utilitarian demands of society.

---

[204] See P. Heath, *English Parish Clergy on the Eve of the Reformation*, pp. 35–6, 81–2.

Conclusion

It is an arresting fact that medieval England, a country of modest size and population, made such a prominent contribution to the early phase of European university development. Oxford, which had crystallized as a university towards the close of the twelfth century, belonged to the primary group of universities, ranking alongside Bologna, Paris and Montpellier. Cambridge, which materialized as a university shortly after 1209, may be reckoned a member of the secondary tide of university foundations. Indeed, by c. 1209, there were only six or seven centres outside England which could be accorded the designation of universities. It is abundantly clear that Cambridge can no longer be regarded as a mere derivative or insubstantial version of Oxford. Even in the thirteenth century, Cambridge's degree of indigenous evolution is a striking feature. Whether from the standpoint of organizational growth, or of legal status, or of the innovative nature of its collegiate development, of which perhaps the King's Hall is the foremost representative, or of its powers of attraction of notable scholars, the University of Cambridge proved itself over the thirteenth and fourteenth centuries to be a significant addition to Europe's expanding family of universities. By the early fifteenth century, Cambridge, although still numerically smaller than Oxford, appears to have acquired a European renown as a university of the first rank. In the late fifteenth and early sixteenth centuries, Cambridge came close to rivalling Oxford in terms of size, and it had probably achieved a complete parity with Oxford by c.1600. The sustained support given to the English Universities throughout the medieval period by the monarchy, which converted Oxford and Cambridge into highly privileged corporations, is not easy to find a parallel for anywhere in continental Europe. Nor was the position of the English chancellor exactly reproduced elsewhere in Europe. The chancellors of Oxford and Cambridge exercised a far more extensive

400

authority — spiritual, civil and criminal — than that exercised by their continental counterparts, and as the dominant forces within the university towns and the surrounding areas they had no equal among Europe's university heads.

As late as *c.* 1500, the English Universities were far from wealthy corporations, Cambridge being even less wealthy than Oxford. Without fixed and predictable financing, long-term academic planning was seldom possible, and haphazard growth was the hallmark of English university development in the medieval period. The paucity of resources for long delayed the emergence of purpose-designed buildings, with the result that before the fifteenth century much university life and business, outside the sphere of the colleges, was conducted within hired and temporary accommodation. Even in the fifteenth century, university building was a prolonged and vexatious matter, and often had to be financed by public subscription. For most of the time that the English Universities functioned in scattered groups of rented premises their government and administration lay chiefly in the hands of the lecturing staff, with only a minimal assistance from non-academic officials. By 1500, when the Universities were to some degree concentrated in permanent structures, an embryonic administrative class was in being as a minor satellite to the teaching masters. After three centuries of development, the English Universities were still regarded primarily as academic guilds. As teaching institutions of the magisterial type, it would have been inconceivable to them that administrative employees could serve in any other capacity than as university servants. In the medieval period, Oxford and Cambridge were spared the inflated administrative bureaucracy and all the accompanying paraphernalia considered by some to be necessary for the functioning of the modern university. This can only have had a salutary effect on the intellectual life of the teaching masters and students alike. One of the central strengths of the medieval English Universities was indeed the fact that they were essentially academic occasions wherein administrative concerns were relegated to a suitably supportive role.

Sovereignty within the English Universities had initially been located in the congregation of regents. By the early fourteenth century, it had come to be vested in the regents and non-regents combined, comprising the masters and doctors in all of the faculties. The regents, however, continued to conduct the routine business of the Universities and, in many ways, they formed the hub of government down to the sixteenth century. Since the regents of the arts faculty had a numerical preponderance among the regents at both Oxford and Cambridge, young and inexperienced teachers would often have figured on university governing bodies. Some of these youthful masters would have no permanent stake in the future of their university, for in the absence of tenured contracts and of salaried lectureships, which emerged in England only from the late fifteenth century, a lifelong career in university teaching was a minority objective. Thus, the quality of university government was prone to suffer from a less than desirable degree of continuity in experienced personnel. But at least the English Universities before the sixteenth century were democratically organized institutions, as defined in terms of government by the regents and non-regents. During the sixteenth and seventeenth centuries this democratic character was eroded in favour of a more oligarchical structure, with power concentrated in the heads of the colleges, who were expected to comply with the authoritarian demands of the Tudor and Stuart monarchy. For long, the arts faculties at Oxford and Cambridge were the most advanced in organizational terms. Whereas the superior faculties at Paris had been motivated to develop their internal cohesion and structural hierarchy from the second half of the thirteenth century, the higher faculties in the English Universities remained institutionally weak right through to the fifteenth century. Magisterial nations were reproduced in the English Universities, in imitation of Paris, as sub-divisions of the faculty of arts. For a period in the thirteenth century they were officially acknowledged at Oxford. Although the Parisian nations remained a significant force in university affairs until at least the mid-fifteenth century, the Oxford nations had been stifled as official units by the last quarter of the thirteenth century. In contrast to the nations at Paris, Bologna and other continental universities, the nations of Oxford and Cambridge had never been deeply rooted in either a governmental or an academic sense. Since there was an insufficiently large cosmopolitan population to accord the nations an importance as defensive groupings for students of widely divergent ethnic origins, they were fairly rapidly phased out as irrelevancies on the university scene.

By 1500, the English Universities had moved some way towards the federated collegiate structures which they progressively became in the course of the sixteenth and seventeenth centuries. The absorption of the undergraduate population by the colleges, however, was not substantially advanced until the first half of the sixteenth century. Colleges such as the King's Hall, Cambridge, and New College, Oxford, which admitted undergraduates from the fourteenth century, were exceptional in this regard. The colleges before 1500 made a disproportionate contribution to their universities through the intellectual distinction of their fellows and the prominent role of the latter in university assemblies and in administrative offices. But for the majority of undergraduates and a good number of graduates the unendowed Oxford hall or Cambridge hostel would have provided the normal university experience well into the sixteenth century. This is a timely reminder of the potentially unstable nature of much university accommodation even as late as *c.* 1500 and of the fact that this was so despite the palpable progress which had been made towards purpose-designed buildings at both Universities in the fifteenth century.

While the secular colleges had not emerged as the key governmental units within their universities by *c.* 1500, a good deal of the groundwork had been laid for their transformation from being mainly graduate preserves into being the central teaching venues for undergraduates, which has remained their principal *raison d'être* from the sixteenth to the twentieth centuries. The conversion of the English Universities into decentralized teaching institutions had tripartite origins, and was a combination of the tutorial and lecturing forms which had evolved first in the monastic colleges, then in the halls and hostels and eventually in the secular colleges. Attempts to regenerate the public system of university instruction by the regent masters achieved only a limited success. Inexorably, teaching within the Universities came to be concentrated in the colleges, leaving such centralized university instruction as remained in an atrophied state. Salaried lectureships were a late phenomenon at Oxford and Cambridge by comparison with the universities of continental Europe. They made a tentative appearance in both the collegiate and university domain from the late fifteenth century. This meant that for almost three hundred years the English Universities had to depend for lecturer recruitment upon the 'necessary regency' system, an economical but ultimately unsatisfactory means of furnishing a force of teaching masters. From this point of view, the English Universities must be accounted extremely laggard in coming to terms with the concept of the endowed lectureship. This was certainly a contributory factor which enabled the advance of the colleges as more attractive teaching centres than the lecture halls of the regent masters. It was the eventual entrenchment of lecturing and tutorial provision in the colleges which converted Oxford and Cambridge from being teaching institutions of a centripetal character to being teaching institutions of a centrifugal one.

Over the three centuries before 1500, theology was the largest of the superior faculties at Oxford, although if the faculties of civil and canon law are taken together they outstripped theology by a considerable margin. However, in all but two of the ten Oxford secular colleges theology was the dominant area of study, New College and All Souls emerging as the most important collegiate centres for law in striking contradiction to the intentions of their founders. It may be estimated that about nine-tenths of Oxford regulars engaged in theology and one-tenth in law, whereas of the seculars who progressed beyond arts, about three-tenths were theologians and just over two-thirds were lawyers. It is manifest that the theological concentration in the secular colleges was not generally representative of the level of secular involvement in theology or in civil and canon law in Oxford University at large. While law probably accounted for up to a third or even more of the Cambridge seculars, about a half of whom did not progress beyond arts, theology was certainly the largest of the superior faculties in the late fourteenth century, the mendicants being by far its largest constituent. The eight secular colleges founded before 1400, taken as a group, mirrored the primacy of theology in the university sector, although they afforded more scope to law than did the Oxford colleges, the King's Hall having an exceptional importance in this sphere as the most significant legal centre at either University. By

1500, however, the size of the Cambridge faculty of theology had been reduced, and with it the influential position of the regulars within the University. Between the late fourteenth century and 1500, the percentage of scholars engaged in theology at Cambridge may well fallen from about 40 per cent, of whom three-quarters were regulars, to about 15 per cent, of whom about half were regulars. While this is a notable transformation in the academic concentrations within the University, the collegiate scene in fifteenth-century Cambridge ran counter to this trend. It was characterized by a contraction in law and a concomitant expansion in the number of fellowships made available for theology. This collegiate development appears to have been the result of a concerted effort to stem the engulfing tide of legal studies, with the aim of promoting a less materialistic form of scholarship, based upon theological values, that would spearhead a spiritual revival within society at large. In the event, the enterprise proved to be ephemeral. It is nonetheless interesting to uncover an institutionalized endeavour at Cambridge to keep alive educational notions which transcended the short-term and the immediately consumable, no comparable venture being discernible at Oxford.

One of the most crucial findings of the analysis of the personnel of medieval Oxford and Cambridge concerns the large number of scholars who engaged in civil law. Between *c.* 1200 and *c.* 1500, Oxford produced 932 known civilians as compared with 711 canonists and 716 who studied in both laws. In the same period, Cambridge yielded 523 known civilians and 220 scholars in both laws. It has been established that, in the collegiate sector, the King's Hall at Cambridge and New College and All Souls at Oxford were the most prolific institutions for the production of civilians before 1500. Indeed, the King's Hall was responsible for just over a fifth of all Cambridge's civilians over the fourteenth and fifteenth centuries. This growing emphasis upon civil law was a consequence of the expanding career opportunities for civil lawyers from the early fourteenth century. But the production of civilians was also encouraged by the English monarchy so as to create a climate of thought which would be receptive to the accentuation of the prerogative powers of kingship. The King's Hall, the exclusive university possession of the crown, was regarded as the college *par excellence* whose primary function was the output of civil law graduates or graduates in both laws who would constitute a corps of legally trained 'king's men' and who could be expected to be favourably disposed towards the more theocratic aspects of monarchy. As such, the King's Hall was designed to play a cardinal role in the revival of civil-law studies in England in the fourteenth and fifteenth centuries. The extent to which Richard II, who embodied in extreme measure an exalted and rigid view of royal prerogative power, recruited civil lawyers from the two Universities, and especially from Cambridge, caused concern that an attempt was being made to challenge some facets of the English common law. Suspicions of this kind were again aroused under the Tudor monarchy and in the reign of James I. These fears were not realized and there was much benign interaction between the two systems of law. Oxford and Cambridge did not formally encompass the common law, but throughout the medieval period they made a sterling contribution to the perpetuation in England of the internationally based civil and canon law, a preoccupation which forged enriching links with the wider European community.

The traditional curriculum of the English Universities was partially modified by the impact of humanist learning. This modification was a gradual process. It was superficial and piecemeal in the second half of the fifteenth century and only put down deeper, institutionalized roots in the course of the sixteenth century. Humanist influence was probably at its most extensive in the arts faculties of Oxford and Cambridge. In general, the English Universities incorporated, it seems, only those ingredients of continental humanism deemed to be compatible with the corpus of inherited learning. This being so, selected humanist features were absorbed into the main lines of English intellectual life without effecting major deflections from established intellectual horizons. For this reason, Oxford and Cambridge cannot be considered to have been humanist centres on a par with the many contemporary German universities where the curricula were radically reoriented according to humanist criteria.

In the ecclesiastical sphere, Cambridge University remained relatively free of Wyclifite and Lollard heresy, which had ensnared a coterie of Oxford scholars in the late fourteenth and fifteenth centuries. Just as the establishment of the King's Hall — an extension of the royal household set in Cambridge in the early fourteenth century — had attracted a flow of lay patronage to the University, so the lingering taint of heresy at Oxford caused a further transference of influential patronage to Cambridge in the later medieval period. Cambridge's intake rose appreciably in the fifteenth century, and by 1500, the University's population was well on the way to achieving parity with that of Oxford. The most notable response to the heretical threat in Oxford was the foundation of Lincoln College in 1427 as a bastion of orthodoxy within the University. It was the earliest secular college designed to combat the heretical problem. The collegiate drive against heresy provided by Lincoln was not vigorously maintained; and the heretical issue did not figure largely at All Souls and Magdalen, the other new colleges of the fifteenth century. The notion of the secular college as the vehicle for the suppression of heresy was given a wider scope in fifteenth-century Cambridge. At King's, Queens', St Catharine's and Jesus, there was an emphasis on the conservation and purity of the faith which surpassed anything to be found at Oxford. The longevity of heretical sentiment at Oxford may help to explain why Cambridge achieved a complete exemption from ecclesiastical authority, papally confirmed in 1433, some forty-six years before Oxford's similar emancipation in 1479. In this regard, it may also be remarked that ecclesiastical influence was of a stronger and more pervasive character at Oxford than at Cambridge, and that relations between Oxford University and the bishop of Lincoln were stormier than those which prevailed between Cambridge University and the bishop of Ely. For reasons of this kind, Cambridge came to be regarded by the ecclesiastical authorities as the sounder of the English Universities; as an institution which could be safely exempted from episcopal and archiepiscopal jurisdiction at an earlier date than its errant Oxford counterpart.

While there were many areas of tension between the English Universities and their respective town corporations, it would be an exaggeration to suggest that conflict was the norm. Behind the numerous disputes there existed a broad framework of co-operation, and the university chancellors and the mayors and bailiffs were often made jointly responsible for the conduct of public business. Moreover, it must not be too readily assumed that the periodic conflicts between scholars and townspeople accounted for most of the violent activity in medieval Oxford and Cambridge. The evidence for Oxford, at any rate, indicates that serious incidents were more frequent among scholars than between scholars and townspeople; and that violent deaths among the latter were more often caused by other citizens or by strangers than by scholars of the University. It seems clear that the academic personnel of Oxford and Cambridge maintained a more impressive *modus vivendi* with the citizenry than was realized in many of the continental universities, with their more cosmopolitan academic populations. The relative insularity of the English universities was, from this point of view, a signal advantage.

The university populations of Oxford and Cambridge were markedly more stratified by 1500 than they had been in the early thirteenth century. They ranged from poor scholars at one end of the spectrum to an aristocratic grouping at the other, and they incorporated a large and variegated mature commoner class. The resultant reduction in academic cohesion towards 1500 may well have made it easier to bring the Universities into the orbit of monarchical control in the sixteenth and seventeenth centuries. The average English undergraduate appears to have been of middling to comparatively low social origins. For the minority of genuinely poor scholars, there was no systematic plan for coping with their disadvantaged state, only a variety of expedients which had a random efficacy. Before 1500, college fellowships were not unduly lucrative, and a small private income was probably necessary in most cases. Fellowships in the English medieval colleges were not sinecures designed to furnish a life-long support irrespective of academic achievement or level of income. While exceptions are to be found, fellowships seem to have been responsibly deployed in the interests of scholars of slender means and of proven ability, and they were subject to stringent conditions governing their tenure and vacation. By the close of the fifteenth century, the aristocratic influx was only beginning to assume the significant proportions which it attained in the sixteenth and seventeenth centuries. In the later medieval period, the nobility tended to categorize the Universities as convenient venues for younger sons, who were most likely destined for an ecclesiastical career, or for those members of the family whose interests were oriented towards elements of humanist learning. Most of the noble scholars at Oxford and Cambridge appear to have had a serious academic intention and in terms of university offices held and careers pursued their record of achievement is substantial. It is apparent that this aristocratic presence in the English Universities, which was eventually to transform Oxford and Cambridge into communities of a highly privileged character, had already taken firm root by the beginning of the Tudor age.

Contrary to popular belief, the average entry age to medieval Oxford and Cambridge was probably of the order of fifteen to seventeen years. The English Universities had nothing approximating to an admissions policy, although oral investigations were conducted by some of the colleges, and wastage rates were incomparably higher than would be acceptable in a twentieth-century university. By any educational standards, the academic regime was one of innate difficulty and required a high measure of intellectual dexterity and sustained powers of application. Students had to cope with teaching in a foreign language, they had to wrestle with the intricacies of abstruse texts, they had to master a series of complex practical exercises prescribed for different stages of degree courses and they had to weather probing oral examinations which amounted to a continuous assessment of a scholar's performance. Questioning at the undergraduate level was conducted as a form of training within an accepted overall framework, and the measured absorption of an approved corpus of knowledge rather than the promotion of independent lines of thought was a central feature of the arts course in the English Universities, as it was throughout Europe. The undergraduate learning experience in medieval Oxford and Cambridge was based largely upon the pivotal mechanisms of the lecture and the disputation and only minimally upon direct access to books, from which many undergraduates were excluded because of the high cost of manuscripts. Members of the superior faculties were much more book-oriented and, apart from book ownership, they had greater access to college and university library collections.

English students often began to negotiate for subsequent careers at an early stage in their university studies and, until the late fourteenth century, the centralized system of papal provisioning was one of the principal means by which an ecclesiastical position might be secured. With the demise of papal provisioning in the early fifteenth century, the vacuum was filled by a variety of indigenous sources, including the crown, the episcopacy, the nobility, the upper gentry, university colleges and the religious orders. Taken together, these diverse avenues served the English Universities well throughout the fifteenth century, and the increase of indigenous at the expense of alien patronage probably worked to the ultimate benefit of the English academic community.

There were few licensed recreations for English students in the medieval period, and only occasional appreciation by the university authorities of the desirability of bodily exercise as a counter to the rigours of the academic regime. The repressive outlook of the university authorities towards non-academic activities probably exacerbated the student disorder which the measures that it gave rise to were designed to contain. The exceedingly negative attitude displayed towards women that is found in university and college statutes and the attempt to exclude them as far as was possible from all contact with scholars, except where absolutely necessary and then under the most stringent of conditions, must have aggravated the perennial problem of student involvement in the thriving prostitution which stalked the streets of Oxford and Cambridge. The English Universities evolved widespread disciplinary powers for maintaining some degree of law and order within their communities and within the town. At the hands of the English chancellors, scholars could be deprived of their degrees or prevented from taking them, and regent masters could be forbidden to teach. Scholars could be fined, or expelled permanently or for a limited duration, or they could be imprisoned or even excommunicated. Within the colleges, fellows might be expelled for grave offences, and for lesser misdemeanours, they could be deprived of commons or fined. In the halls and hostels, the main form of discipline was the imposition of fines, arranged in a hierarchical system, supplemented, at least in the Oxford halls by the late fifteenth century, by corporal punishment. This latter type of discipline was

410

used in a few colleges from the 1440s, and it became a major method of collegial correction in the sixteenth century. Academic dress was not used much as a means of social control in the medieval English Universities. For the majority of undergraduates, there was no distinctive or uniform dress. Only the minority of undergraduates who were members of colleges, and who would have worn a college livery, were subject to a strict conformity in garb. University regulations concerning dress applied mainly to scholars in the superior faculties, and the shape and cut rather than the colour was the distinguishing feature of academic attire before the sixteenth century. The differential modes of dress employed in the medieval English Universities did little to enhance community cohesiveness.

While English university regulations adopted a repressive stance towards recreational activity, some relaxation was permitted on the principal festivals of the ecclesiastical year. This reached an apogee during the Christmas period, when all manner of rituals associated with the inversion of authority, and embodied in the election of Christmas kings, lords of misrule, kings of the beans and boy-bishops, were staged in colleges and halls. The evidence for minstrel entertainments in English university colleges dates largely from the late fifteenth century, although they are recorded as having taken place at Peterhouse in 1388–9; and at the King's Hall, Cambridge, diverse categories of minstrels were frequent performers from their first appearance in 1342–3 until 1543–4, two years before its dissolution. By the 1530s and 1540s, play production was a fairly common feature of many of the English colleges, and the university authorities appear to have tolerated, though grudgingly, dramatic presentations in colleges and halls, especially of classical plays, because of their ascertainable educational value.

The continuity of academic study in medieval Oxford and Cambridge was frequently threatened from the mid-fourteenth century by the menace of plague. The overall impact of the Black Death on the English Universities cannot be assessed statistically. It is likely, however, that scholars, as a group, suffered less than some other sections of the population, for the diet and living conditions of all but the poorest of scholars were probably above the average for the populace at large. It was not yet common in the fourteenth century for college fellowships at Oxford and Cambridge to take

411

evasive action by leaving the university town for a rural sanctuary for the duration of a plague visitation. From the mid-fifteenth century, however, a country retreat became a desired objective for several of the English colleges, and they established comfortable havens of this kind. If epidemic diseases appreciably disturbed the tenor of English academic life, at least Oxford and Cambridge were untroubled by the aggravation of the student power phenomenon, which was such a disruptive force in many of the universities of southern Europe.

Despite the high wastage rate, it would appear that the English Universities were relatively successful in the three centuries before 1500 in furnishing the requisite personnel for the myriad needs of secular and ecclesiastical government and administration. University graduates penetrated the hierarchies of Church and State at all levels, from the highest to the comparatively humble, and by the late fifteenth century, graduates seem to have had a near monopoly in a range of employment areas. By their concentration upon the Roman and canon law, however, the English Universities precluded themselves from making a vocational contribution to domains served by the indigenous common law. Professional training in the common law came to be concentrated in the Inns of Court in London, which Sir John Fortescue described in the fifteenth century as the capital's *studium pupplicum*. As part of their training, common-law students required easy access to the law courts at Westminster, and this told against the Universities as centres for the common law. The medieval English Universities were deemed to be responding, with this notable exception, to the utilitarian demands of their society, evidencing a symbiosis which was even more pronounced in the fourteenth and fifteenth than in the thirteenth century.

The approbation given to the utilitarian stamp of English university education is amply demonstrated by the confidence displayed towards Oxford and Cambridge by English monarchs over three centuries in the form of expansive privileges and royal protection, and by the heavy investment in the collegiate sphere by a succession of kings, queens, bishops and lesser ecclesiastics, and wealthy members of the laity. This university–society nexus presupposed that medieval Oxford and Cambridge generally acquiesced in the hierarchical assumptions upon which society was constructed. They viewed themselves primarily as service institutions for the bolstering of the existing political, legal, ecclesiastical and social apparatus rather than as agencies for the promotion of radical challenge. In this way, the English Universities contributed to the stability of the established order, the Wyclifite phase at Oxford being an exceptional episode. At the same time, the Universities enabled a considerable degree of social mobility on the part of graduate personnel from middling to comparatively humble backgrounds. Between *c.* 1200 and *c.* 1500, Oxford and Cambridge undoubtedly established themselves as crucial institutions in the life of the nation, as the 'eyes and blazing lights of the kingdom' according to a graphic fifteenth-century evaluation. But while, as corporations, they built up a high degree of autonomy and projected their separate identities within society, the English Universities were, in the final analysis, reliant upon the support of the crown and the papacy, and this measure of patronage prevented their realization as a wholly independent estate within the realm.

Bibliography

ORIGINAL SOURCES

Oxford University and Colleges

The surviving archives of the University of Oxford before 1500 have now virtually all been published in a series of volumes of the *Oxford Historical Society*: they are itemized under the section on printed sources for Oxford. In 1931, Strickland Gibson published his fine edition of the medieval statutes as *Statuta Antiqua Universitatis Oxoniensis* (Oxford, 1931), and this needs to be taken in conjunction with G. Pollard, 'The Oldest Statute Book of the University', *The Bodleian Library Record*, viii (1969), pp. 69 ff. Except in a few instances, references to Oxford University Archives are to the more easily accessible, printed editions.

Bodleian MS. Laud. Misc. 165.
Letters Patent of 1 March 1487, Oxford University Archives, LBXX.
All Souls College Archives, Bursars' Books, for 1450–1, *c.* 1495, and 1497–8, Bodleian MSS. D.D. b. 29.
Lincoln College Archives, Bursars' Books, i, ii.
Lincoln College Archives, Charters I, Box no. 7.
Lincoln College Archives, *Vetus Registrum 1472–1570*.
Magdalen College Archives, Bursars' Books, 1476/7–86, 1490–99.
Magdalen College Archives, *Libri Computi*, for 1481–8 and 1490–1510.
Magdalen College Archives, *Register A 1480–92*.
Magdalen commoners between 1460 and 1600: notes by J. R. Bloxam, Magdalen College Library, D. 7. 10.
Merton College Archives, Bursars' Rolls, 3727, 3737, 3750.
Merton College Archives, Rolls for Founder's Kin, 3973e, 3973f,

3974, 3974d, 3974e, 3976, 4116, 4117.

Merton College Archives, Charter 370.

Merton College MS. 289.

New College MS. 288.

New College Archives, Bursars' and Receipt Rolls, 1376–7–1498–9, 7711 (1)–7459 (136): a guide to these Rolls and their rather unpredictable reference numbers is provided by F. W. Steer, *The Archives of New College, Oxford* (London and Chichester, 1974).

New College Archives, Statutes of *c.* 1400, 3584.

New College Archives, *Liber Senescalli Aulae*, i (1397–1418), 5527.

New College Archives, *The Registrum Primum* alias *Liber Albus* (*c.* 1400–*c.* 1480), 9468, 9654.

New College Archives, Wykeham's endowments of college advowsons, 9703, 9818.

Oriel College Archives, *Treasurers' Accounts*, i (1409–15), ii (1450–82), iii (1482–1515).

University College Archives, Bursars' Rolls, PYX EE Fasc. 1/5 - PYX GG Fasc. 2/6; PYX EE Fasc. 1/1, 1/3, 3/8, 3/10, 4/6a, 4/9, 6/11; PYX GG Fasc. 2/11.

Cambridge University and Colleges

Agreement of April 1270 negotiated by the Lord Edward concerning the joint responsibility of the University and the town for the maintenance of law and order, CUL/UA, Luard, no. 3.

Apostolic Letter of 9 June 1318 addressed to the University of Cambridge, Vatican Register of John XXII, lxviii, fo. 66, no. 1230.

Bull of Eugenius IV of 18 September 1433, CUL/UA, Luard, no. 114.

Charter of Henry III of 7 February 1266, CUL/UA, Luard, no. 1.

Charter of Edward I of 1291/2, CUL/UA, Luard, no. 7*.

Charter of Edward III of 24 March 1327, CUL/UA, Luard, no. 25.

Charter of Edward III of 14 December 1335, CUL/UA, Luard, no. 28.

Letters Patent of Edward III of 19 September 1343, CUL/UA, Luard, no. 33a.

Commission of Richard II of 10 August 1381 authorizing an

inquiry into damage to university property and the destruction or theft of university muniments, CUL/UA, Luard, no. 54.

Old Proctor's Book (*Liber procuratoris antiquus*), CUL/COLL ADMIN 3.

Processus Barnwellensis ex mandato Martini Papae V cum bullis Johannis XXII et Bonifacii IX of 10 October 1430, CUL/UA, Luard, no. 108.

Register of Thomas de l'Isle, bishop of Ely, 1345–61, CUL/UA, EDR, G/1/1.

Register of Thomas Arundel, bishop of Ely, 1374–88, CUL/UA, EDR, G/1/2.

Registrum Librorum, CUL/UA, COLL ADMIN 4.

Spurious bulls of Honorius I of 624 and of Sergius I of 689, CUL/UA, Luard, no. 115.

Computus Book of Gonville Hall (*c.* 1423–*c.* 1523), Gonville and Caius MS. 365.

Christ's College Archives, Exemplification (in book form) of Letters Patent of Henry VII of 1 May 1506, CC/M/Found/1.

King's College Archives, *Libri Protocollorum*.

King's College Archives, Mundum Books, iii, iv, v, vi, xi.

King's College Archives, Charter of Henry VI of 16 March 1446, A 20.

King's Hall Accounts, i–xxvi, Muniment Room of Trinity College, 0. 13. 1. – 0. 13.26.

King's Hall Cabinet, Muniment Room of Trinity College, nos. 104, 144.

Pembroke Muniments, petition from Pembroke to Henry VI of 20 May 1448, College Box A 19.

Peterhouse Archives, Computus Roll of 1388–9.

Queens' College Archives, Journale, i (1484–1518) (deposited in CUA).

St Catharine's College Muniments, XL/10.

The paper statutes of Trinity College of 8 November 1552, Trinity College Library, 0. 6. 7.

Public Record Office

P.R.O. Exchequer Accounts, King's Remembrancer, E101 class: E101/348/4/5/12/16/17.

Printed Sources

Oxford University and Colleges

Canterbury College Oxford (3 vols., ed. W.A. Pantin, Oxf. Hist. Soc., new ser., vi–viii, 1946–50).

(The) Dean's Register of Oriel, 1446–1661 (ed. G. C. Richards and H. E. Salter, Oxf. Hist. Soc., lxxxiv, 1926).

(The) Early Rolls of Merton College, Oxford (ed. J. R. L. Highfield, Oxf. Hist. Soc., new ser., xviii, 1964).

Epistolae Academicae Oxoniensis (2 vols., ed. H. Anstey, Oxf. Hist. Soc., xxxv–vi, 1898).

Formularies which bear on the History of Oxford c.1204–1420 (2 vols., ed.H. E. Salter, W. A. Pantin and H. G. Richardson, Oxf. Hist. Soc., new ser., iv–v, 1942).

(The) Mediaeval Archives of the University of Oxford (2 vols., ed. H. E. Salter, Oxf. Hist. Soc., lxx, lxxiii, 1917–19).

Munimenta Academica: Documents illustrative of Academical Life and Studies at Oxford (2 vols., Rolls Series, ed. H. Anstey, 1868).

Oriel College Records (ed. C. L. Shadwell and H. E. Salter, Oxf. Hist. Soc., lxxxv, 1926).

Oseney Annals, *Annales Monastici* (4 vols., Rolls Series, ed. H. R. Luard, London, 1864–9).

Oxford City Documents 1268–1665 (ed. J. E. T. Rogers, Oxf. Hist. Soc., xviii, 1891).

(The) Oxford Deeds of Balliol College (ed. H. E. Salter, Oxford, 1913).

Records of All Souls Library 1437–1600 (Oxford Bibliographical Society, new series, xvi, 1971).

Records of Mediaeval Oxford (ed. H. E. Salter, Oxford, 1917).

(The) Register of Congregation 1448–1463 (ed. W. A. Pantin and W. T. Mitchell, Oxf. Hist. Soc., new ser., xxii, 1972).

(The) Register of St Mary Magdalen College, Oxford (7 vols., ed. J. R. Bloxam, Oxford, 1853–85).

Registrum Annalium Collegii Mertonensis, 1483–1521 (ed. H. E. Salter, Oxf. Hist. Soc., lxxvi, 1923).

Registrum Cancellarii Oxoniensis 1434–1469 (2 vols., ed. H. E. Salter, Oxf. Hist. Soc., xciii–iv, 1932).

Bibliography

Snappe's Formulary and other records (ed. H. E. Salter, Oxf. Hist. Soc., lxxx, 1924).

Statuta Antiqua Universitatis Oxoniensis (ed. S. Gibson, Oxford, 1931).

Statutes of the Colleges of Oxford (3 vols., ed. by the Queen's Commissioners, Oxford and London, 1853).

'Survey of the Antiquities of the City of Oxford' composed in 1661–6 by Anthony Wood, i (ed. A. Clark, Oxf. Hist. Soc., xv, 1889).

'The academic drama in Oxford: extracts from the records of four colleges', *Malone Society Collections*, v (ed. R. E. Alton, Oxford, 1960), pp. 29 ff.

Twyne, B. *Antiquitatis Academiae Oxoniensis Apologia* (Oxford, 1608).

Vindiciae Antiquitatis Academiae Oxoniensis (ed. T. Hearne, Oxford, 1730).

Wood, A. *The History and Antiquities of the University of Oxford* (2 vols. in 3, ed. J. Gutch, 1792–6).

Cambridge University and Colleges

Annals of Cambridge (ed. C. H. Cooper, 4 vols., Cambridge, 1842–53).

Caius, J. *De Antiquitate Cantabrigiensis Academiae* (London, 1568). *Historiae Cantabrigiensis Academiae ab urbe condita, Liber primus* (London, 1574).

Cantalupe, N. *Historiola de Antiquitate et Origine Universitatis Cantabrigiensis* appended to *Thomae Sprotti Chronica* (ed. T. Hearne, Oxford, 1719).

(A) Collection of Letters, Statutes and other Documents from the manuscript library of Corpus Christi College illustrative of the history of the University of Cambridge (ed. J. Lamb, London, 1838).

Collection of Statutes for the University and Colleges of Cambridge (ed. J. Heywood, London, 1840).

Documents relating to St Catharine's College in the University of Cambridge (ed. H. Philpott, Cambridge, 1861).

Documents relating to the University and Colleges of Cambridge (3 vols., ed. by the Queen's Commissioners, London, 1852).

Early Statutes of Christ's College, Cambridge with the statutes of the prior foundation of God's House (ed. H. Rackham, privately printed, Cambridge, 1927).

Fuller, T. *The History of the University of Cambridge from the Conquest to the year 1634* (ed. M. Prickett and T. Wright, London and Cambridge, 1840).

Grace Book A (ed. S. M. Leathes, *C.A.S.*, Luard Memorial Series, i, Cambridge 1897).

Grace Book B Part i (ed. M. Bateson, *C.A.S.*, Luard Memorial Series, ii, Cambridge, 1903).

Hackett, M. B. *The Original Statutes of Cambridge University: The Text and its History* (Cambridge, 1970).

(The) Privileges of the University of Cambridge (ed. G. Dyer, 2 vols., London, 1824).

(The) Statutes of Sir Walter Mildmay for Emmanual College (ed. F. Stubbings, Cambridge, 1983).

'The academic drama at Cambridge: extracts from college records', *Malone Society Collections*, ii. pt. ii (ed. G. C. Moore Smith, Oxford, 1923), pp. 150 ff.

Warren's Book (ed. A. W. W. Dale, Cambridge, 1911).

Miscellaneous

Alexandri Neckam De Naturis Rerum Libri Duo (Rolls Series, ed. T. Wright, London, 1863).

Alfred the Great: Asser's Life of King Alfred and other contemporary sources (transl. and introduction and notes by S. Keynes and M. Lapidge, Penguin Books, 1983).

Annals of Winchester College, from its foundation in the year 1382 (ed. T. F. Kirby, London, 1892).

Archiv für Literatur und Kirchengeschichte des Mittelalters (ed. H. Denifle and F. Ehrle, iii, Berlin, 1887).

Asser. *Life of King Alfred together with the Annals of Saint Neots* (ed. W. H. Stevenson, Oxford, 1904): new impression by D. Whitelock, Oxford, 1959.

Bede. *Ecclesiastical History of the English Nation* (Everyman's Library, 1958).

Bulaeus, C. E. *Historia Universitatis Parisiensis* (6 vols., Paris, 1665–73).

Calendar of Close Rolls, preserved in the Public Record Office.

Calendar of Entries in the Papal Registers, relating to Great Britain and Ireland: Papal Letters, 1198–1492.

Calendar of Patent Rolls, preserved in the Public Record Office.

Camden, W. *Britannia* (4th ed., London, 1600).

Chapters of the English Black Monks 1215–1540 (3 vols., ed. W. A. Pantin, Camden Soc., 3rd ser., xlv, xlvii, liv, 1931–7).

Chartularium Universitatis Parisiensis (4 vols., ed. H. Denifle and E. Chatelain, Paris, 1889–97).

Chronicles of the reign of Stephen, Henry II and Richard I (3 vols., Rolls Series, ed. R. Howlett, London, 1884–6).

Chronicon Abbatiae de Evesham ad annum 1418 (Rolls Series, ed. W. D. Macray, London, 1863).

Curia Regis Rolls, preserved in the Public Record Office.

Educational Charters and Documents 598–1909 (ed. A. F. Leach, Cambridge, 1911).

FitzStephen, W. *Descriptio Londoniae* in *Materials for the History of Thomas Becket* (7 vols., Rolls Series, ed. J. C. Robertson and J. B. Sheppard, London, 1875–85), iii (1877).

Fortescue, Sir John. *De Laudibus Legum Anglie* (ed. S. B. Chrimes, Cambridge, 1942).

Gascoigne, T. *Loci e Libro Veritatum* (ed. J. E. T. Rogers, Oxford, 1881).

Geoffrey of Monmouth. *(The) History of the Kings of Britain* (transl. with an introduction by L. Thorpe, Penguin Books, 1966).

Gervase of Canterbury. *Actus Pontificum Cantuariensis Ecclesiae, The Historical Works of Gervase of Canterbury* (2 vols., Rolls Series, ed. W. Stubbs, London, 1879–80).

Giraldi Cambrensis Opera (8 vols., Rolls Series, ed. J. S. Brewer and others, London, 1861–91).

Goswin Kempgyn de Nussia Trivita studentium: Eine Einführung in das Universitätsstudentium aus dem 15. Jahrhundert (ed. M. Bernhard, Münchener Beitrage zur Mediävistik und Renaissance-Forschung, xxvi, Munich, 1976).

Historia Diplomatica Friderici II (7 vols., ed. J. L. A. Huillard-Bréholles, Paris, 1852–61).

(The) Historia Regum Britanniae of Geoffrey of Monmouth (ed. A. Griscom, London, 1929).

(The) Itinerary of John Leland in or about the years 1535–1543, Parts iv and v, with an Appendix of Extracts from Leland's Collectanea (ed. L. Toulmin Smith, London, 1908).

Leland, J. *Collectanea*, v (ed. T. Hearne, Oxford, 1715).

(The) Letter Book of Robert Joseph (ed. H. Aveling and W. A. Pantin, Oxf. Hist. Soc., new ser., xix, 1967).

(The) Letters of Pope Innocent III (1198–1216) concerning England and Wales (ed. C. R. Cheney and M. G. Cheney, Oxford, 1967).

(The) Liber Pauperum of Vacarius (ed. F. de Zuluetta, Selden Soc., 44, London, 1927).

Liber regie capelle (ed. W. Ullmann, Henry Bradshaw Society, xcii, Cambridge, 1959).

(The) Liber Taxatorum of Poor Students at the University of Freiburg im Breisgau (ed. J. M. Fletcher, Texts and Studies in the History of Mediaeval Education, no. xii, Notre Dame, Indiana, 1969).

Metalogicon (ed. C. C. J. Webb, Oxford, 1929).

(The) Metalogicon of John of Salisbury (transl. D. D. McGarry, Berkeley and Los Angeles, 1955).

Parker, M. *De Antiquitate Britannicae Ecclesiae* (ed. S. Drake, London, 1729).

Pipe Roll Society (New Ser., ed. D. M. Stenton), iii (1927), v (1928), vi (1929), vii (1930), ix (1932).

Polychronicon Ranulphi Higden Monachi Cestrensis (9vols., Rolls Series, ed. C. Babington and J. R. Lumby, London, 1865–86).

Register Gregory IX (ed. L. Auvray, Paris, 1896).

(The) Register of Henry Chichele, Archbishop of Canterbury 1414–1443 (4 vols., ed. E. F. Jacob, Canterbury and York Society, 1937–47).

(The) Register of Walter de Stapeldon, Bishop of Exeter, 1307–1326 (ed. F. C. Hingeston-Randolph, London and Exeter, 1892).

(The) Register of William Greenfield, Archbishop of York (1306–1315) (5 vols., ed. W. Brown and A. H. Thompson, Surtees Soc., 1931–40).

(Les) Registres d'Innocent IV (3 vols., ed. E. Berger, Paris, 1884–97).

(Les) Registres de Nicolas IV (9 Fascs., ed. E. Langlois, Paris, 1881–93).

Roger of Wendover. *Flores Historiarum* (Rolls Series, 3 vols., ed. H. G. Hewlett, London, 1886–9).

Bibliography

(The) Rolls and Register of Bishop Oliver Sutton, 1280–1299 (7 vols., ed. R. M. T. Hill, Lincoln Record Society, 1948–75).

Rotuli Parliamentorum 1278–1503 (6 vols., Record Commission, London, 1783: index vol. 1832).

Rous, J. *Historia Regum Angliae* (1st ed., T. Hearne, Oxford, 1716; 2nd ed., T. Hearne, Oxford, 1745).

Rymer, T. *Foedera*, ii (ed. A. Clarke, London, 1818).

Sarti, M. *De Claris Archigymnasii Bononiensis Professoribus a saeculo xi usque ad saeculum xiv* (Bologna, 1769–72).

Statuti delle università e dei collegi dello studio bolognese (ed. C. Malagola, Bologna, 1888).

(Les) Statuts et Privilèges des Universités francaises depuis leur fondation jusqu'en 1789 (3 vols., ed. M. Fournier, Paris, 1890–2).

The Peasants' Revolt of 1381 (ed. R. B. Dobson, Macmillan History in Depth Series, London, 1970).

University Records and Life in the Middle Ages (ed. L. Thorndike, Records of Civilisation, no. xxxviii, New York, 1944: reprinted Octagon Books, New York, 1971).

Vetus Liber Archidiaconi Eliensis (ed. C. L. Feltoe and E. H. Minns, C. A. S., Octavo Publications, xlviii, 1917).

William Harrison's Description of England AD 1577–1587 (ed. from the first two editions of Holinshed's chronicle, AD 1577, 1587, by F. J. Furnivall, New Shakespeare Society, series vi, i, London, 1877).

Secondary Works

Allmand, C. T. 'The Civil Lawyers', *Profession, Vocation, and Culture in Later Medieval England* (ed. C. H. Clough, Liverpool, 1982), pp. 155 ff.

Aston, M. *Thomas Arundel* (Oxford, 1967).
  'Lollardy and Sedition, 1381–1431', *Lollards and Reformers: Images and Literacy in Late Medieval Religion* (London, 1984), pp. 1 ff.
  'Lollard Women Priests?', ibid., pp. 49 ff.

Aston, T. H. 'Oxford's Medieval Alumni', *Past and Present*, no. 74 (1977), pp. 3 ff.

423

'The Date of John Rous's list of the Colleges and Academical Halls of Oxford', *Oxoniensia*, xlii (1977), pp. 226 ff.

'The External Administration and Resources of Merton College to *circa* 1348', *The History of the University of Oxford*, i (*The Early Oxford Schools*, ed. J. I. Catto, Oxford, 1984), 311 ff.

Aston, T. H., G. D. Duncan and T. A. R. Evans. 'The Medieval Alumni of the University of Cambridge', *Past and Present*, no. 86 (1980), pp. 9 ff.

Aston, T. H., and R. Faith. 'The Endowments of the University and Colleges to *circa* 1348', *The History of the University of Oxford*, i *(The Early Oxford Schools*, ed. J. I. Catto, Oxford, 1984), 265 ff.

Attwater, A. *Pembroke College, Cambridge* (ed. with an introduction and postscript by S. C. Roberts, Cambridge, 1936).

Baker, J. H. 'The English Legal Profession, 1450–1550', *Lawyers in Early Modern Europe and America* (ed. W. Prest, London, 1981), pp. 16 ff.

'The Inns of Court and Chancery as Voluntary Associations', *The Legal Profession and the Common Law: Historical Essays* (London and Ronceverte, 1986), pp. 45 ff.

Baldwin, J. W. 'Masters at Paris from 1179 to 1215: A Social Perspective', *Renaissance and Renewal in the Twelfth Century* (ed. R. L. Benson and G. Constable, with C. D. Lanham, Oxford, 1982), pp. 138 ff.

Barraclough, G. *Papal Provisions* (Oxford, 1935).

Barton, J. L. 'The Study of Civil Law before 1380', *The History of the University of Oxford*, i *(The Early Oxford Schools*, ed. J. I. Catto, Oxford, 1984), 519 ff.

Baskervill, C. R. 'Dramatic Aspects of medieval folk festivals in England', *Studies in Philology*, xvii (1920), pp. 19 ff.

Bean, J. M. W. 'Plague, population and economic decline in England in the later middle ages', *Econ. Hist. Rev.*, 2nd ser., xv (1962–3), pp. 423 ff.

Bennett, J. A. W. *Chaucer at Oxford and at Cambridge* (Oxford, 1974).

Boas, F. S. *University Drama in the Tudor Age* (Oxford, 1914).

Bolgar, R. R. *The Classical Heritage and its Beneficiaries from the Carolingian Age to the end of the Renaissance* (New York, 1964).

Boussard, J. 'Ralph Neville, Evêque de Chichester et Chancelier d'Angleterre d'après sa correspondance', *Revue Historique*, clxxvi (1935), pp. 217 ff.

Boyce, G. C. *The English-German Nation in the University of Paris during the Middle Ages* (Bruges, 1927).

Boyle, L. 'The Curriculum of the Faculty of Canon Law at Oxford in the first half of the fourteenth century', *Oxford Studies presented to Daniel Callus* (Oxf. Hist. Soc., new ser., xvi, 1964), pp. 135 ff.

'Canon Law before 1380', *The History of the University of Oxford*, i (*The Early Oxford Schools*, ed. J. I. Catto, Oxford, 1984), 531 ff.

Brand, J. *Observations on Popular Antiquities* (2 vols., revised by H. Ellis, London, 1813).

Brand, P. 'Courtroom and Schoolroom: the Education of Lawyers in England prior to 1400', *Historical Research* (formerly *B.I.H.R.*), 60 (1987), pp. 147 ff.

Brocklebank, T. 'Notaries Public in King's College, Cambridge', *C.A.S., Communications*, iii (1864–76), pp. 47 ff.

Brooke, C. N. L. *A History of Gonville and Caius College* (The Boydell Press, Suffolk, 1985).

'The Churches of Medieval Cambridge', *History, Society and the Churches: Essays in Honour of Owen Chadwick* (ed. D. Beales and G. Best, Cambridge, 1985), pp. 49 ff.

Brooke, C. N. L., and G. Keir. *London 800–1216: the Shaping of a City* (London, 1975)

Brundage, J. A. 'English-Trained Canonists in the Middle Ages: A Statistical Analysis of a Social Group', *Law-Making and Law-Makers in British History: Papers presented to the Edinburgh Legal History Conference 1977* (Royal Historical Society Studies in History Series, London, 1980), pp. 64 ff.

Buck, M. *Politics, Finance and the Church in the Reign of Edward II: Walter Stapeldon Treasurer of England* (Cambridge, 1983).

Burson, M. C. 'Emden's *Registers* and the Prosopography of Medieval English Universities', *Medieval Prosopography*, 3 (1982), pp. 35 ff.

Bury, J. P. T. 'Corpus Christi College', *V.C.H. Camb.* iii (ed. J. P. C. Roach, Oxford, 1959), 371 ff.

Butcher, A. F. 'The Economy of Exeter College, 1400–1500', *Oxoniensia*, 44 (1979), pp. 38 ff.

Butterfield, H. 'Peterhouse', *V.C.H. Camb.* iii (ed. J. P. C. Roach, Oxford, 1959), 334 ff.

Buxton, L. H. D., and S. Gibson. *Oxford University Ceremonies* (Oxford, 1935).

Callus, D. A., (ed.). *Robert Grosseteste: Scholar and Bishop* (Oxford, 1955).

Cam, H. M. 'The City of Cambridge', *V.C.H. Camb.* iii (ed. J. P. C. Roach, Oxford, 1959), 1 ff.

Carr, W. *University College* (College Histories Series, London, 1902).

Carter, E. *The History of the University of Cambridge* (London, 1753).

Carus-Wilson, E. M., (ed.). *Essays in Economic History* (2 vols., London, 1954–62).

Caspari, F. *Humanism and the Social Order in Tudor England* (Chicago, 1954).

Catto, J. I. 'Citizens, Scholars and Masters', *The History of the University of Oxford*, i (*The Early Oxford Schools*, ed. J. I. Catto, Oxford, 1984), 151 ff.

'Theology and Theologians 1220–1320', ibid., 471 ff.

Chambers, E. K. *The Mediaeval Stage* (2 vols., Oxford, 1903).

Charlton, K. *Education in Renaissance England* (London and Toronto, 1965).

Cheney, C. R. *Notaries Public in England in the Thirteenth and Fourteenth Centuries* (Oxford, 1972).

Cheney, M. G. 'Master Geoffrey de Lucy, an early chancellor of the University of Oxford', *E.H.R.*, lxxxii (1967), pp. 750 ff.

Chibnall, A. C. *Richard de Badew and the University of Cambridge 1315–1340* (Cambridge, 1963).

Churchill, I. J. *Canterbury Administration* (2 vols., London, 1933).

Clark, A. 'Lincoln College', *The Colleges of Oxford* (2nd ed., London, 1892), pp. 171 ff.

Clarke, M. L. *Higher Education in the Ancient World* (London, 1971).

Classen, P. 'Die ältesten Universitäts-reformen und Universitästsgründungen des Mittelalters', *Heidelberger Jahrbücher*, xii

(1968), pp. 72 ff.

Clough, C. H. 'Thomas Linacre, Cornelio Vitelli, and Humanistic Studies at Oxford', *Linacre Studies: Essays on the Life and Works of Thomas Linacre c.1460–1524* (ed. F. Maddison, M. Pelling and C. Webster, Oxford, 1977), pp. 1 ff.

Cobban, A. B. 'Edward II, Pope John XXII and the University of Cambridge', *B.J.R.L.*, xlvii (1964), pp. 49 ff.

The King's Hall within the University of Cambridge in the Later Middle Ages (Cambridge Studies in Medieval Life and Thought, third ser., vol. 1, Cambridge, 1969).

'Episcopal Control in the Mediaeval Universities of Northern Europe', *Studies in Church History*, v (Leiden, 1969), pp. 1 ff.

'Medieval Student Power', *Past and Present*, no. 53 (1971), pp. 28 ff.

'Origins: Roberts Wodelarke and St Catharine's', *St Catharine's College 1473–1973* (ed. E. E. Rich, Leeds, 1973), pp. 1 ff.

The Medieval Universities: their development and organization (London, 1975).

'Decentralized Teaching in the Medieval English Universities', *History of Education*, 5 (1976), pp. 193 ff.

'The King's Hall, Cambridge and English medieval collegiate history', *Authority and Power: Studies on Medieval Law and Government presented to Walter Ullmann on his seventieth birthday* (ed. B. Tierney and P. Linehan, Cambridge, 1980), pp. 183 ff.

'The Medieval Cambridge Colleges: a Quantitative Study of Higher Degrees to *c.* 1500', *History of Education*, 9 (1980), pp. 1 ff.

'Theology and Law in the Medieval Colleges of Oxford and Cambridge', *B.J.R.L.*, lxv (1982), pp. 57 ff.

Coing, H. *Handbuch der Quellen und Literatur der neueren europäischen Privatrechtsgeschichte*, i (Munich, 1973).

Cooper, J. 'Medieval Oxford', *V.C.H. Oxon.* iv (ed. A. Crossley, Oxford, 1979), 3 ff.

Corrie, G. E. 'A list of books presented to Pembroke College, Cambridge, by different donors during the fourteenth and fifteenth centuries', *C.A.S., Communications*, ii (1860–4), no. iii. pp. 11 ff.

Courtenay, W. J. 'The Effect of the Black Death on English Higher

Education', *Speculum*, 55 (1980), pp. 696 ff.

Crawley, C. W. 'Trinity Hall', *V. C. H. Camb.* iii (ed. J. P. C. Roach, Oxford, 1959), 362 ff.

  Trinity Hall: The History of a Cambridge College 1350–1975 (Cambridge, 1976).

Creighton, C. *A History of Epidemics in Britain*, i (Cambridge, 1891).

Curtis, M. H. *Oxford and Cambridge in Transition 1558–1642* (Oxford, 1959).

Custance, R., (ed.). *Winchester College: Sixth-Centenary Essays* (Oxford, 1982).

Davies, R. G. 'Thomas Arundel as Archbishop of Canterbury 1396–1414', *J. Eccles. Hist.*, xxiv (1973), pp. 9 ff.

  'The Episcopate', *Profession, Vocation and Culture in Later Medieval England* (ed. C. H. Clough, Liverpool, 1982), pp. 51 ff.

Davis, H. W. C. *A History of Balliol College* (2nd ed. by R. H. C. Davis and R. Hunt, Oxford, 1963).

Davis, V. 'William Waynflete and the Educational Revolution of the Fifteenth Century', *People, Politics and Community in the Later Middle Ages* (ed. J. Rosenthal and C. Richmond, Gloucester, 1987), pp. 40 ff.

Dawson, J. E. A. 'The Foundation of Christ Church, Oxford and Trinity College, Cambridge in 1546', *B.I.H.R.*, lvii (1984), pp. 208 ff.

Delhaye, P. 'L'organisation scolaire au xiie siècle', *Traditio*, v (1947), pp. 211 ff.

Denholm-Young, N. 'Magdalen College', *V.C.H. Oxon*, iii (ed. H. E. Salter and M. D. Lobel, London, 1954), 193 ff.

Denifle, H. *Die Entstehung der Universitäten des Mittelalters bis 1400* (Berlin, 1885).

Denley, P. 'Recent Studies in Italian Universities of the Middle Ages and Renaissance', *History of Universities*, i (1981), pp. 193 ff.

Denne, S. 'Memoir on Hokeday', *Archaeologia*, vii (1785), pp. 244 ff.

Denton, J. H. *Robert Winchelsey and the Crown 1294–1313* (Cambridge, 1980).

Destrez, J. *La Pecia dans les manuscrits universitaires du xiiie et du xive*

siècle (Paris, 1935).

D.Irsay, S. *Histoire des universités françaises et étrangères des origines à nos jours* (2 vols., Paris, 1933–5).

Dobson, B. 'Oxford Graduates and the so-called Patronage Crisis of the later Middle Ages', *The Church in a Changing Society* (Commission Internationale d'Histoire Ecclésiastique Comparée, Swedish sub-commission of CIHEC: Publications of the Swedish Society of Church History, new ser., 30, Uppsala, 1977), pp. 211 ff.

Dunbabin, J. 'Careers and Vocations', *The History of the University of Oxford*, i (*The Early Oxford Schools*, ed. J. I. Catto, Oxford, 1984), 565 ff.

Duncan, G. D. 'The Heads of Houses and Religious Change in Tudor Oxford 1547–1558', *Oxoniensia*, 45 (1980), pp. 226 ff.

'Public Lectures and Professorial Chairs', *The History of the University of Oxford*, iii (*The Collegiate University*, ed. J. McConica, Oxford, 1986), 335 ff.

Edwards, K. 'The Cathedral of Salisbury', *V.C.H. Wiltshire*, iii (ed. R. B. Pugh and E. Crittall, Oxford, 1956), pp. 156 ff.

'College of De Vaux Salisbury', *V.C.H. Wiltshire*, iii (ed. R. B. Pugh and E. Crittall, Oxford, 1956), 369 ff.

English Secular Cathedrals in the Middle Ages (2nd ed., Manchester, 1967).

Ellis, D. M. B., and L. F. Salzman. 'Religious Houses', *V.C.H. Camb.* ii (ed. L. F. Salzman, London, 1948), 197 ff.

Emden, A. B. *An Oxford Hall in Medieval Times* (Oxford, 1927).

A Biographical Register of the University of Oxford to A.D. 1500 (3 vols., Oxford, 1957–9).

'The remuneration of the medieval proctors of the University of Oxford', *Oxoniensia*, xxvi/vii (1961/2), pp. 202 ff.

A Biographical Register of the University of Cambridge to 1500 (Cambridge, 1963).

'Northerners and Southerners in the Organization of the University to 1509', *Oxford Studies presented to Daniel Callus* (Oxf. Hist. Soc., new ser., xvi, 1964), pp. 1 ff.

'Oxford Academical Halls in the Later Middle Ages', *Medieval Learning and Literature: Essays presented to Richard William Hunt* (ed. J. J. G. Alexander and M. T. Gibson, Oxford, 1976), pp.

353 ff.

Ermini, G. 'Concetto di "Studium Generale" ', *Archivio Giuridico*, cxxvii (1942), pp. 3 ff.

Findlay, R. *Population and Metropolis: The Demography of London 1580–1650* (Cambridge, 1981).

Fletcher, J. M. 'Wealth and Poverty in the Medieval German Universities', *Europe in the Late Middle Ages* (ed. J. R. Hale, J. R. L. Highfield and B. Smalley, London, 1965), pp. 410 ff.

'The Teaching of Arts at Oxford, 1400–1520', *Paedagogica Historica: International Journal of the History of Education*, vii (2) (Ghent, 1967), pp. 417 ff.

'Linacre's Lands and Lectureships', *Linacre Studies: Essays on the Life and Works of Thomas Linacre c. 1460–1524* (ed. F. Maddison, M. Pelling and C. Webster, Oxford, 1977), pp. 107 ff.

'Change and resistance to change: a consideration of the development of English and German Universities during the sixteenth century', *History of Universities*, i (1981), pp. 1 ff.

'University Migrations in the Late Middle Ages, with particular reference to the Stamford Secession', *Rebirth, Reform and Resilience: Universities in Transition 1300–1700* (ed. J. M. Kittelson and P. J. Transue, Columbus, Ohio, 1984), pp. 163 ff.

'The Faculty of Arts', *The History of the University of Oxford*, i (*The Early Oxford Schools*, ed. J. I. Catto, Oxford, 1984), 369 ff.

'Inter-Faculty Disputes in Late Medieval Oxford', *From Ockham to Wyclif* (Studies in Church History, Subsidia 5, 1987), pp. 331 ff.

Fletcher, J. M., and C. A. Upton. 'The Cost of undergraduate study at Oxford in the Fifteenth Century: the evidence of the Merton College "Founder's Kin" ', *History of Education*, 14 (1985), pp. 1 ff.

' "Monastic enclave" or "open society"? A consideration of the role of women in the life of an Oxford college community in the early Tudor period', *History of Education*, 16 (1987), pp. 1 ff.

Gabriel, A. L. 'Robert de Sorbonne', *Revue de l'Université d'Ottawa*,

23 (1953), pp. 473 ff.

Student Life in Ave Maria College, Mediaeval Paris (Publications in mediaeval studies, xiv, Notre Dame, Indiana, 1955).

'The College System in the Fourteenth-Century Universities', *The Forward Movement of the Fourteenth Century* (ed. F. L. Utley, Ohio, 1961), pp. 79 ff.

'Motivation of the Founders of Mediaeval Colleges', *Beiträge zum Berufsbewusstsein des mittelalterlichen Menschen* (Miscellanea Mediaevalia, 3, 1964), pp. 61 ff.

The Mediaeval Universities of Pécs and Pozsony (Frankfurt am Main, 1969).

'Preparatory Teaching in the Parisian Colleges during the Fourteenth Century', *Garlandia: Studies in the History of the Mediaeval University* (Notre Dame, Indiana, 1969). pp. 97 ff.

'The English-German Nation at the University of Paris from 1425–1494', ibid., pp. 167 ff.

Garrod, H. W. 'Merton College', *V.C.H. Oxon.* iii (ed. H. E. Salter and M. D. Lobel, London, 1954), 95 ff.

Gasquet, F. A. *The Black Death of 1348 and 1349* (2nd ed., London, 1908).

Gibson, S. 'The University of Oxford', *V.C.H. Oxon.* iii (ed. H. E. Salter and M. D. Lobel, London, 1954), 1 ff.

Glorieux, P. *Les Origines du Collège de Sorbonne* (Texts and Studies in the History of Mediaeval Education, no. viii, Notre Dame, Indiana, 1959).

Gransden, A. *Historical Writing in England c. 550–c. 1307* (London, 1974).

Historical Writing in England c. 1307 to the Early Sixteenth Century (London, 1982)

Grassi, J. L. 'Royal Clerks from the Archdiocese of York in the Fourteenth Century', *Northern History*, v (1970), pp. 12 ff.

Gray, A. *The Earliest Statutes of Jesus College, Cambridge* (Cambridge, 1935).

Gray, J. M. *Biographical Notes on the Mayors of Cambridge* (reprinted from *Cambridge Chronicle*, Cambridge, 1921).

Green, V. H. H. *The Universities* (Pelican Books, 1969).

A History of Oxford University (London, 1974).

The Commonwealth of Lincoln College 1427–1977 (Oxford, 1979).

Grierson, P. 'Gonville and Caius College', *V.C.H. Camb.* iii (ed. J. P. C. Roach, Oxford, 1959), pp. 356 ff.

Hackett, M. B. *The Original Statutes of Cambridge University: The Text and its History* (Cambridge, 1970).

'The University as a Corporate Body', *The History of the University of Oxford*, i (*The Early Oxford Schools*, ed. J. I. Catto, Oxford, 1984), 37 ff.

Hairsine, R. C. 'Oxford University and the Life and Legend of Richard III', *Richard III Crown and People* (ed. J. Petre, Richard III Society, London, 1985), pp. 307 ff.

Hajnal, I. 'A propos de l'enseignement de l'écriture dans les universités médiévales', *Scriptorium*, xi (1957), pp. 3 ff.

L'Enseignement de l'écriture aux universités médiévales (2nd ed., L. Mezey, Budapest, 1959).

Hall, C. P. 'William Rysley's Catalogue of the Cambridge University Muniments, compiled in 1420', *Transactions of the Cambridge Bibliographical Society*, iv (1965), pp. 85 ff.

Hammer, C. I., Jr. 'Patterns of Homicide in a Medieval University Town: Fourteenth-Century Oxford', *Past and Present*, no. 78 (1978), pp. 3 ff.

'Oxford Town and Oxford University', *The History of the University of Oxford*, iii (*The Collegiate University*, ed. J. McConica, Oxford, 1986), 69 ff.

Harding, A. 'The Revolt against the Justices', *The English Rising of 1381* (ed. R. H. Hilton and T. H. Aston, Cambridge, 1984), pp. 165 ff.

Hardwick, C. 'Robert Woodlark, founder and first Master of St Catharine's Hall', *C.A.S., Communications*, i (1850–9), no. xxxvii, pp. 329 ff.

Hargreaves-Mawdsley, W. N. *A History of Academical Dress in Europe until the end of the eighteenth century* (Oxford, 1963).

Harrison, F.Ll. 'The Eton Choirbook', *Annales Musicologiques*, i (1953), pp. 151 ff.

Harrison, W. J. 'Clare College', *V.C.H. Camb.* iii (ed. J. P. C. Roach, Oxford, 1959), 340 ff.

Harvey, P. D. A. *A Medieval Oxfordshire Village, Cuxham 1240 to 1400* (Oxford, 1965).

Haskins, C. H. *The Rise of Universities* (New York, 1923).

Studies in the History of Mediaeval Science (New York, 1924: reprinted 1960).

Renaissance of the Twelfth Century (Cambridge, Mass., 1927).

Studies in Mediaeval Culture (Cambridge, 1929).

Haskins, G. L. 'The University of Oxford and the "ius ubique docendi" ', *E.H.R., lvi* (1941), pp. 281 ff.

Hay, D. 'England and the Humanities in the Fifteenth Century', *Itinerarium Italicum: the profile of the Italian renaissance in the mirror of its European transformations: dedicated to Paul Oskar Kristeller on the occasion of his seventieth birthday* (ed. H. A. Oberman and T. A. Brady, Jr., Leiden, 1975, Studies in Medieval and Reformation Thought, 14), pp. 305 ff.

Hays, R. W. 'Welsh Students at Oxford and Cambridge Universities in the Middle Ages', *Welsh Hist. Rev.,* iv (1968–9), pp. 325 ff.

Heath, P. *English Parish Clergy on the Eve of the Reformation* (London and Toronto, 1969).

Henderson, B. W. *Merton College* (College Histories Series, London, 1899).

Henson, H. H. 'The "Rex Natalicus" ', *Collectanea,* i (ed. C. R. L. Fletcher, Oxf. Hist. Soc., v, 1885), pp. 39 ff.

Hexter, J. W. *Reappraisals in History* (New York, Harper Torchbooks, 1963).

Highfield, J. R. L. 'The Early Colleges', *The History of the University of Oxford,* i (*The Early Oxford Schools,* ed. J. I. Catto, Oxford, 1984), 225 ff.

Hill, R. M. T. 'Oliver Sutton, Bishop of Lincoln, and the University of Oxford', *T.R.H.S.,* 4th ser., xxxi (1949), pp. 1 ff.

Oliver Sutton (Lincoln Minster Pamphlets, no. 4, 1950).

Hodgkin, R. H. *Six Centuries of an Oxford College* (Oxford, 1949).

'The Queen's College', *V.C.H. Oxon.* iii (ed. H. E. Salter and M. D. Lobel, London, 1954), 132 ff.

Holland, T. E. 'The University of Oxford in the Twelfth Century', *Collectanea,* ii (ed. M. Burrows, Oxf. Hist. Soc., xvi, 1890), 137 ff.

Huber, V. A. *The English Universities* (transl. and ed. by F. W. Newman, London, 1843).

Hudson, A. 'Wycliffism in Oxford 1381–1411', *Wyclif in his Times* (ed. A. Kenny, Oxford, 1986), pp. 67 ff.

Hunt, R. W. 'English Learning in the late Twelfth Century', *T.R.H.S.*, 4th ser., xix (1936), pp. 19 ff.

'Medieval Inventories of Clare College Library', *Transactions of the Cambridge Bibliographical Society*, i (1950), pp. 105 ff.

'Balliol College', *V.C.H. Oxon.* iii (ed. H. E. Salter and M. D. Lobel, London, 1954), 82 ff.

'Oxford Grammar Masters in the Middle Ages', *Studies presented to Daniel Callus* (Oxf. Hist. Soc., new ser., xvi, 1964), pp. 163 ff.

'The Medieval Library', *New College Oxford 1379–1979* (ed. J. Buxton and P. Williams, Oxford, 1979), pp. 317 ff.

Jacob, E. F. 'An early book list of All Souls College', printed as an appendix to 'The two lives of Archbishop Chichele', *B.J.R.L.*, xvi (1932), pp. 428 ff.

'Petitions for Benefices from English Universities during the Great Schism', *T.R.H.S.*, 4th ser., xxvii (1945), pp. 41 ff.

'English University Clerks in the later Middle Ages: the Problem of Maintenance', *B.J.R.L.*, xxix (1946), pp. 304 ff.

'On the promotion of English University Clerks during the later Middle Ages', *J. Eccles. Hist.*, i (1950), pp. 172 ff.

The Fifteenth Century 1399–1485 (Oxford, 1961).

Archbishop Henry Chichele (London and Edinburgh, 1967).

James, M. R. *A Descriptive Catalogue of the Manuscripts other than Oriental in the Library of King's College, Cambridge* (Cambridge, 1895).

'Catalogue of Thomas Markaunt's library from MS. C. C. C. 232', *C.A.S.*, octavo ser., no. xxxii, 1899, pp. 1 ff.

A Descriptive Catalogue of the Manuscripts in the Library of Pembroke College, Cambridge (Cambridge, 1905).

A Descriptive Catalogue of the Manuscripts in the Library of Corpus Christi College, Cambridge, i (Cambridge, 1912).

Jardine, L. 'Humanism and the Sixteenth Century Cambridge Arts Course', *History of Education*, 4 (1975), pp. 16 ff.

Jewell, H. M. ' "The Bringing up of Children in Good Learning and Manners": A Survey of Secular Educational Provision in the North of England, c. 1350–1550', *Northern History*, xviii

(1982), pp. 1 ff.

'English Bishops as Educational Benefactors in the Later Fifteenth Century', *The Church, Politics and Patronage in the Fifteenth Century* (ed. R. B. Dobson, Gloucester, 1984), pp. 146 ff.

Jones, A. H. M. 'New College', *V.C.H. Oxon.* iii (ed. H. E. Salter and M. D. Lobel, London, 1954), 144 ff.

Kearney, H. *Scholars and Gentlemen: Universities and Society in Pre-Industrial Britain 1500–1700* (London, 1970).

Keene, D. *Winchester Studies 2: Survey of Medieval Winchester*, i. pt. i (Oxford, 1985).

Kendrick, T. D. *British Antiquity* (London, 1950).

Kenny, A. *Wyclif* (Oxford, 1985).

Ker, N. R. *Records of All Souls College Library 1437–1600* (Oxford Bibliographical Society, new ser., xvi, 1971).

'Oxford College Libraries before 1500', *The Universities in the Late Middle Ages* (ed. J. Ijsewijn and J. Paquet, Leuven University Press, 1978), pp. 293 ff.

'The Books of Philosophy distributed at Merton College in 1372 and 1375', *Books, Collectors and Libraries: Studies in the Medieval Heritage* (ed. A. G. Watson, London and Ronceverte, 1985), pp. 331 ff.

'Oxford College Libraries in the Sixteenth Century', ibid., pp. 379 ff.

Kibre, P. *The Nations in the Mediaeval Universities* (Mediaeval Academy of America, Cambridge, Mass., 1948).

'Scholarly Privileges: Their Roman Origins and Medieval Expression', *A.H.R.*, lix (1954), pp. 543 ff.

Scholarly Privileges in the Middle Ages (Mediaeval Academy of America, London, 1961).

Knowles, D. *The Evolution of Medieval Thought* (London, 1962).

Lander, J. R. *Conflict and Stability in Fifteenth-Century England* (London, 1969).

Laurie, S. S. *Lectures on the Rise and Early Constitution of Universities* (London, 1886).

Lawrence, C. H. 'The Origins of the Chancellorship at Oxford', *Oxoniensia*, xli (1976), pp. 316 ff.

'The University in State and Church', *The History of the*

University of Oxford, i (*The Early Oxford Schools*, ed. J. I, Catto, Oxford, 1984), 97 ff.

Leach, A. F. *A History of Winchester College* (London, 1899).

'Stamford University', *V.C.H. Lincoln*, ii (ed. W. Page, London, 1906), pp. 471 ff.

Leader, D. R. 'Professorships and Academic Reform at Cambridge: 1488–1520', *Sixteenth Century Journal*, 14 (1983), pp. 215 ff.

'Teaching in Tudor Cambridge', *History of Education*, 13 (1984), pp. 105 ff.

Lees, B. A. *Alfred the Great* (New York and London, 1915).

Leff, G. *Heresy in the Later Middle Ages: the relation of heterodoxy to dissent c. 1250–c. 1450* (2 vols., Manchester, 1967).

Paris and Oxford Universities in the Thirteenth and Fourteenth Centuries (New York, 1968).

Lesne, E. 'Les écoles de la fin du viiie siècle à la fin du xiie', *Histoire de la propriété ecclésiastique en France*, v (Lille, 1940).

Little, A. G. and F. Pelster. *Oxford Theology and Theologians c. A.D. 1282–1302* (Oxf. Hist. Soc., xcvi, 1934).

Lloyd, A. H. *The Early History of Christ's College, Cambridge* (Cambridge, 1934).

'Notes on Cambridge Clerks petitioning for Benefices, 1370–1399', *B.I.H.R.*, 20 (1943–5), pp. 75 ff.

Logan, F. D. 'The Origins of the So-Called Regius Professorships: an aspect of the Renaissance in Oxford and Cambridge', *Renaissance and Renewal in Christian History* (Studies in Church History, 14, ed. D. Baker, Oxford, 1977), pp. 271 ff.

Lovatt, R. 'The Early Archives of Peterhouse', *Peterhouse Record* (1975–6), pp. 26 ff.

Lowth, R. *The Life of William of Wykeham* (2nd ed., London, 1759).

Lytle, G. F. 'Patronage Patterns and Oxford Colleges *c.*1300–*c.*1530', *The University in Society* (2 vols., ed. L. Stone, Princeton and London, 1975), i. 111 ff.

Oxford Students and English Society: c.1300–c.1510 (unpublished Ph.D. thesis, Princeton University, 1976).

'The Social Origins of Oxford Students in the Late Middle Ages: New College, *c.*1380–*c.*1510', *The Universities in the Late*

Middle Ages (ed. J. Ijsewijn and J. Paquet, Leuven University Press, 1978), pp. 426 ff.

'A University Mentality in the later Middle Ages: The Pragmatism, Humanism, and Orthodoxy of New College, Oxford', *Genèse et Débuts du Grand Schisme d'Occident 1362–1394* (Colloques Internationaux du Centre National de la Recherche Scientifique, no. 586, Paris, 1980), pp. 201 ff.

'Universities as Religious Authorities in the later Middle Ages and Reformation', *Reform and Authority in the Medieval and Reformation Church* (ed. G. F. Lytle, Washington, 1981), pp. 69 ff.

'Patronage and the Election of Winchester Scholars during the late Middle Ages and Renaissance', *Winchester College: Sixth-Centenary Essays* (ed. R. Custance, Oxford, 1982), pp. 167 ff.

'The Careers of Oxford Students in the Later Middle Ages', *Rebirth, Reform and Resilience: Universities in Transition 1300–1700* (ed. J. M. Kittelson and P. J. Transue, Columbus, Ohio, 1984), pp. 213 ff.

MacDougall, H. A. *Racial Myths in English History* (Montreal and Hanover, New Hampshire, 1982).

McConica, J. K. *English Humanists and Reformation Politics* (Oxford, 1965).

'The Social Relations of Tudor Oxford', *T.R.H.S.*, 5th ser., 27 (1977), pp. 115 ff.

'Humanism and Aristotle in Tudor Oxford', *E.H.R.*, xciv (1979), pp. 291 ff.

'The Rise of the Undergraduate College', *The History of the University of Oxford*, iii (*The Collegiate University*, ed. J. McConica, Oxford, 1986), 1 ff.

'Elizabethan Oxford: The Collegiate Society', *The History of the University of Oxford*, iii (*The Collegiate University*, ed. J. McConica, Oxford, 1986), 645 ff.

McFarlane, K. B. *John Wycliffe and the Beginnings of English Nonconformity* (London, 1952).

McKisack, M. *Medieval History in the Tudor Age* (Oxford, 1971).

McLean, A. *Humanism and the Rise of Science in Tudor England* (London, 1972).

McMahon, C. P. *Education in Fifteenth Century England*, reprinted from *The Johns Hopkins University Studies in Education*, no. 35 (Baltimore, 1947).

Magrath, J. R. *The Queen's College* (2 vols., Oxford, 1921).

Maitland, F. W. *Township and Borough* (Cambridge, 1898).

Makdisi, G. *The Rise of Colleges: Institutions of Learning in Islam and the West* (Edinburgh, 1981).

Mallet, C. E. *A History of the University of Oxford* (3 vols., London, 1924–7).

Martin, J. 'Classicism and Style in Latin Literature', *Renaissance and Renewal in the Twelfth Century* (ed. R. L. Benson and G. Constable, with C. D. Lanham, Oxford, 1982), pp. 537 ff.

Maxwell-Lyte, H. C. *A History of the University of Oxford* (London, 1886).

A History of Eton College 1440–1910 (4th ed., London, 1911).

Michaud-Quantin, P. 'Collectivités médiévales et institutions antiques', *Miscellanea Mediaevalia*, i (ed. P. Wiepert, Berlin, 1962).

Universitas: expressions du movement communautaire dans le moyen âge latin (L'Eglise et l'Etat au Moyen Age, 13, Paris, 1970).

Miller, E. *Portrait of a College* (Cambridge, 1961).

Milne, J. G. *The Early History of Corpus Christi College, Oxford* (Oxford, 1946).

Mitchell, R. J. 'English Law Students at Bologna in the Fifteenth Century', *E.H.R.*, li (1936), pp. 270 ff.

'English Students at Padua, 1460–1475', *T.R.H.S.*, 4th ser., xix (1936), pp. 101 ff.

'English Students at Ferrara in the Fifteenth Century', *Italian Studies*, i (1937), pp. 74 ff.

John Tiptoft (London, 1938).

Moberly, G. H. *Life of William of Wykeham* (Winchester and London, 1887).

Moore, N. 'Robert Wodelarke', *The Dictionary of National Biography*, xxi (Oxford, 1917–), p. 748.

Moran, J. H. 'Education and Learning in the City of York 1300–1560', *St Anthony's Hall Publications*, no. 55 (1979), pp. 1 ff.

'Literacy and Education in Northern England, 1350–1550: A Methodological Inquiry', *Northern History*, xvii (1981), pp. 1 ff.

Morgan, P. *Oxford Libraries outside the Bodleian* (Oxford, 1974).

Mornet, E. '*Pauperes scolares*. Essai sur la condition matérielle des étudiants scandinaves dans les universités aux xive et xve siècles', *Le Moyen Age*, lxxxiv (1978), pp. 53 ff.

Morris, C. *The Discovery of the Individual 1050–1200* (Church History Outlines 5, London, 1972).

Mullinger, J. B. *The University of Cambridge* (3 vols., Cambridge, 1873–1911).

Munby, A. N. L. 'Notes on King's College Library in the fifteenth century', *Transactions of the Cambridge Bibliographical Society*, i (1951), pp. 280 ff.

Munby, J. 'J. C. Buckler, Tackley's Inn and Three Medieval Houses in Oxford', *Oxoniensia*, 43 (1978), pp. 123 ff.

Murphy, J. J. 'Rhetoric in Fourteenth-Century Oxford', *Medium Aevum*, xxxiv (1965), pp. 1 ff.

Myers, A. R. *The Household of Edward IV* (Manchester, 1959).

O'Day, R. *Education and Society 1500–1800: The Social Foundations of Education in early Modern Britain* (London and New York, 1982).

Orme, N. *English Schools in the Middle Ages* (London, 1973).
From Childhood to Chivalry: The Education of the English Kings and Aristocracy 1066–1530 (London and New York, 1984).

Oswald, A. 'University College', *V.C.H. Oxon.* iii (ed. H. E. Salter and M. D. Lobel, London, 1954), 61 ff.

Owen, D. M. 'Ely Diocesan Records', *Studies in Church History*, i (1964), pp. 176 ff.

Owst, G. R. *Preaching in Medieval England* (Cambridge, 1926).

Paetow, L. J. *The Arts Course at Medieval Universities* (Illinois University Studies, iii, no. 7, Urbana-Champaign, 1910).

Pantin, W. A. 'A Medieval Treatise on Letter-Writing, with examples, from the Rylands Latin MS. 394', *B.J.R.L.*, xiii (1929), pp. 326 ff.
'Tackley's Inn, Oxford', *Oxoniensia*, vii (1942), pp. 80 ff.
'Oriel College and St Mary Hall', *V.C.H. Oxon.* iii (ed. H. E. Salter and M. D. Lobel, London, 1954), 119 ff.
'Before Wolsey', *Essays in British History presented to Sir Keith Feiling* (ed. H. R. Trevor-Roper, London, 1964), pp. 29 ff.
'The Halls and Schools of medieval Oxford: an attempt at

reconstruction', *Oxford Studies presented to Daniel Callus* (Oxf. Hist. Soc., new ser., xvi, 1964), pp. 31 ff.

'The Conception of the Universities in England in the period of the Renaissance', *Les Universités Européennes du xive au xviiie siècle* (L'Institut d'Histoire de la Faculté des Lettres de l'Université de Genève, 4, Geneva, 1967), pp. 101 ff.

Oxford Life in Oxford Archives (Oxford, 1972).

Paquet, J. 'Aspects de l'université médiévale', *The Universities in the Late Middle Ages* (ed. J. Ijsewijn and J. Paquet, Leuven University Press, 1978), pp. 3 ff.

'L'universitaire "pauvre" au moyen âge: problèmes, documentation, questions de méthode', ibid., 399 ff.

'Recherches sur l'universitaire "pauvre" au moyen âge', *Revue belge de philologie et d'histoire*, lvi (1978), pp. 301 ff.

'Coût des études, pauvreté et labeur: fonctions et métiers d'étudiants au moyen âge', *History of Universities*, ii (1982), pp. 15 ff.

Paré, G., A. Brunet and P. Tremblay. *La renaissance du xiie siècle: les écoles et l'enseignement* (Paris and Ottawa, 1933).

Parker, J. *The Early History of Oxford 727–1100* (Oxf. Hist. Soc., 1885).

Parker, R. *The History and Antiquities of the University of Cambridge* (London, 1721 (?)).

Parry, A. W. *Education in England in the Middle Ages* (London, 1920).

Peacock, G. *Observations on the Statutes of the University of Cambridge* (London, 1841).

Peek, H. E. and C. P. Hall. *The Archives of the University of Cambridge* (Cambridge, 1962).

Pegues, F. J. 'Philanthropy and the Universities in France and England in the Later Middle Ages', *The Economic and Material Frame of the Mediaeval University* (Texts and Studies in the History of Mediaeval Education, no. xv, Notre Dame, Indiana, 1977), pp. 69 ff.

Perkin, H. 'The Changing Social Function of the University: A Historical Retrospect', *CRE-Information Quarterly*, new ser., no. 62 (1983), pp. 117 ff.

Phelps Brown, E. H. and S. V. Hopkins. 'Seven Centuries of the

Prices of Consumables, compared with Builders' Wage-rates', *Economica*, new ser., 23 (1956), pp. 296 ff.

Phillimore, R. *The Ecclesiastical Law of the Church of England* (2nd ed., London, 1895).

Platt, C. *The English Medieval Town* (London, 1976).

Pollard, G. 'Mediaeval loan-chests at Cambridge', *B.I.H.R.*, xvii (1939–40), pp. 113 ff.

'The University and the Book Trade in Medieval Oxford', *Beiträge zum Berufsbewusstsein des mittelalterlichen Menschen* (Miscellanea Mediaevalia, 3, 1964), pp. 336 ff.

'The Oldest Statute Book of the University', *The Bodleian Library Record*, viii (1968), pp. 69 ff.

'The Legatine Award to Oxford in 1214 and Robert Grosteste', *Oxoniensia*, xxxix (1975), pp. 62 ff.

'The *pecia* system in the medieval universities', *Medieval Scribes, Manuscripts and Libraries: Essays presented to N. R. Ker* (ed. M. B. Parkes and A. G. Watson, London, 1978), pp. 145 ff.

Post, G. 'Masters' Salaries and Student-Fees in the Mediaeval Universities', *Speculum*, vii (1932), pp. 181 ff.

'Parisian Masters as a Corporation, 1200–1246', *Speculum*, ix (1934), pp. 421 ff.

Potter, G. R. 'Education in the Fourteenth and Fifteenth Centuries', *Cambridge Medieval History*, viii (ed. C. W. Previté-Orton and Z. N. Brooke, 1936), pp. 688 ff.

Powicke, F. M. *The Medieval Books of Merton College* (Oxford, 1931).

Ways of Medieval Life and Thought (London, 1949).

Prest, W. R. *The Inns of Court under Elizabeth I and the Early Stuarts 1590–1640* (London, 1972).

Rait, R. S. *Life in the Medieval University* (Cambridge, 1912).

Rashdall, H. 'The Friars Preachers v. the University AD 1311–1313', *Collectanea*, ii (ed. M. Burrows, Oxf. Hist. Soc., xvi, 1890), 193 ff.

The Universities of Europe in the Middle Ages (3 vols., 2nd ed., F. M. Powicke and A. B. Emden, Oxford, 1936).

Rashdall, H., and R. S. Rait. *New College* (London, 1901).

Reitzel, J. M. *The Founding of the Earliest Secular Colleges within the Universities of Paris and Oxford* (unpublished Ph.D. thesis,

Brown University, 1971).

Richardson, H. G. 'An Oxford Teacher of the Fifteenth Century', *B.J.R.L.*, xxiii (1939), pp. 436 ff.

'Business Training in Medieval Oxford', *A.H.R.*, xlvi (1940–1), pp. 259 ff.

'The Schools of Northampton in the Twelfth Century', *E.H.R.*, lvi (1941), pp. 595 ff.

Ridder-Symoens, H. de. 'La migration académique des hommes et des idées en Europe, xiiie–xviiie siècles', *CRE-Information Quarterly*, new ser., no. 62 (1983), pp. 69 ff.

Roach, J. P. C. 'The University of Cambridge', *V.C.H. Camb.* iii (ed. J. P. C. Roach, Oxford, 1959), 150 ff.

Rogers, J. E. T. *A History of Agriculture and Prices in England* (7 vols., Oxford, 1866–1902).

Rosenthal, J. T. 'The Universities and the Medieval English Nobility', *History of Education Quarterly*, 9 (1969), pp. 415 ff.

'The Training of an Elite Group: English Bishops in the Fifteenth Century', *Transactions of the American Philosophical Society*, new ser., lx (1970), pt. 5, pp. 5 ff.

Rossi, G. ' "Universitas Scolarium" e Commune', *Studi e memorie per la storia dell'università di Bologna*, new ser., i (Bologna, 1956), pp. 173 ff.

Roth, C. *The Jews of Medieval Oxford* (Oxf. Hist. Soc., new ser., ix, 1951).

Rouse Ball, W. W. *The King's Scholars and King's Hall* (privately printed, Cambridge, 1917).

Cambridge Papers (London, 1918).

Rowse, A. L. *Oxford in the History of the Nation* (London, 1975).

Rubin, M. *Charity and Community in Medieval Cambridge* (Cambridge Studies in Medieval Life and Thought, fourth ser., vol. 4, Cambridge, 1987).

Russell, E. 'The Influx of Commoners into the University of Oxford before 1581: an optical illusion?', *E.H.R.*, xcii (1977), pp. 721 ff.

Russell, J. C. 'Richard of Bardney's Account of Robert Grosseteste's Early and Middle Life', *Medievalia et Humanistica*, ii (1943), pp. 45 ff.

Salter, H. E. 'Geoffrey of Monmouth and Oxford', *E.H.R.*, xxxiv

(1919), pp. 382 ff.

'The Beginning of Cambridge University', *E.H.R.*, xxxvi (1921), pp. 419 ff.

'The Stamford Crisis', *E.H.R.*, xxxvii (1922), pp. 249 ff.

'An Oxford Hall in 1424', *Essays in History presented to R.L. Poole* (ed. H. W. C. Davis, Oxford, 1927), pp. 421 ff.

'The medieval University of Oxford', *History*, xiv (1929–30), pp. 57 ff.

Medieval Oxford (Oxf. Hist. Soc., c, 1936).

Saltmarsh, J. 'King's College', *V.C.H. Camb.* iii (ed. J. P. C. Roach, Oxford, 1959), 376 ff.

Salzman, L. F. *English Trade in the Middle Ages* (Oxford, 1931).

San Martín, J. *La Antigua Universidad de Palencia* (Madrid, 1942).

Sayle, C. E. 'King's Hall Library', *Proceedings of the C.A.S.*, xxiv (old ser., no. lxxii, 1921–2), pp. 54 ff.

Scarth, A. J. *Aspects of the History and Organisation of the French Provincial Universities of Orleans, Angers, Avignon and Cahors, from their Origins to c. 1450* (unpublished Ph.D. thesis, Liverpool University, 1979).

Searle, W. G. 'Catalogue of the library of Queens' College in 1472', *C.A.S., Communications*, ii (1864), no. xv, pp. 165 ff.

History of the Queen's College of Saint Margaret and Saint Bernard in the University of Cambridge, 1446–1560 (2 vols., Cambridge, 1867–71).

Sharpe, K. 'The Foundation of the Chairs of History at Oxford and Cambridge: an episode in Jacobean politics', *History of Universities*, ii (1982), pp. 127 ff.

Sheehan, M. W. 'The Religious Orders 1220–1370', *The History of the University of Oxford*, i (*The Early Oxford Schools*, ed. J. I. Catto, Oxford, 1984), 193 ff.

Sikes, J. G. and F. Jones. 'Jesus College', *V.C.H. Camb.* iii (ed. J. P. C. Roach, Oxford, 1959), 421 ff.

Simon, J. *Education and Society in Tudor England* (Cambridge, 1966).

Smith, A. H. *New College, Oxford, and its Buildings* (Oxford, 1952).

Smith, C. E. S. *The University of Toulouse in the Middle Ages* (Milwaukee, Wisconsin, 1958).

Somers, M. H. *Irish Scholars in the Universities at Paris and Oxford before 1500* (unpublished Ph.D. thesis, The City University of

New York, 1979).

Somerset, H. V. F. 'An Account Book of an Oxford Undergraduate in the years 1619–1622', *Oxoniensia*, xxii (1957), pp. 85 ff.

Southern, R.W. 'Exeter College', *V.C.H. Oxon.* iii (ed. H. E. Salter and M. D. Lobel, London, 1954), 107 ff.

(ed.). *Essays in Medieval History* (London, 1968).

Medieval Humanism and other Studies (Oxford, 1970).

'Master Vacarius and the Beginning of an English Academic Tradition', *Medieval Learning and Literature: Essays presented to R. W. Hunt* (ed. J. J. G. Alexander and M. T. Gibson, Oxford, 1976), pp. 257 ff.

'The Schools of Paris and the School of Chartres', *Renaissance and Renewal in the Twelfth Century* (ed. R. L. Benson and G. Constable, with C. D. Lanham, Oxford, 1982), pp. 113 ff.

'From Schools to University', *The History of the University of Oxford*, i (*The Early Oxford Schools*, ed. J. I, Catto, Oxford, 1984), 1 ff.

Robert Grosseteste: The Growth of an English Mind in Medieval Europe (Oxford, 1986).

Squibb, G. D. *The High Court of Chivalry* (Oxford, 1959).

Founder's Kin: Privilege and Pedigree (Oxford, 1972).

Stamp, A. E. *Michaelhouse* (privately printed, Cambridge, 1924).

Stanier, R. S. *Magdalen School: A History of Magdalen College School, Oxford* (Oxf. Hist. Soc., new ser., iii, 1940).

Magdalen School (2nd ed., Oxford, 1958).

Steer, F. W. *The Archives of New College, Oxford* (Phillimore, London and Chichester, 1974).

Stein, P. 'Vacarius and the Civil Law', *Church and Government in the Middle Ages: Essays presented to C. R. Cheney* (ed. C. N. L. Brooke, D. E. Luscombe, G. H. Martin and D. Owen, Cambridge, 1976), pp. 119 ff.

Stelling-Michaud, S. 'L'histoire des universités au moyen âge et à la renaissance au cours des vingt-cinq dernières années', *XIe Congrès International des Sciences Historiques, Rapports*, i (Stockholm, 1960).

Stevenson, W. H. and H. E. Salter. *The Early History of St John's College Oxford* (Oxf. Hist. Soc., new ser., i. 1939).

Stokes, H. P. *The Chaplains and the Chapel of the University of Cambridge 1256–1568* (*C.A.S.*., Octavo Publications, xli, 1906).

'Early University Property', *Proceedings of the C.A.S.*, xiii (new ser., vii, 1908–9), pp. 164 ff.

The Esquire Bedells of the University of Cambridge from the 13th century to the 20th century (*C.A.S.*, Octavo Publications, xlv, 1911).

The Mediaeval Hostels of the University of Cambridge (*C.A.S.*, Octavo Publications, xlix, 1924).

Stone, L. 'The Size and Composition of the Oxford Student Body 1580–1910', *The University in Society* (2 vols., ed. L. Stone, Princeton and London, 1975), i. 3 ff.

Storey, R. L. 'Diocesan Administration in the Fifteenth Century', *St Anthony's Hall Publications*, no. 16 (1959), pp. 3 ff.

'The Foundation and the Medieval College, 1379–1530', *New College Oxford 1379–1979* (ed. J. Buxton and P. Williams, Oxford, 1979), pp. 3 ff.

Strasser, M. W. 'The Educational Philosophy of the First Universities', *The University World, A Synoptic View of Higher Education in the Middle Ages and Renaissance* (ed. D. Radcliffe-Umstead, Pittsburgh, 1973), pp. 1 ff.

Streeter, B. H. *The Chained Library* (London, 1931).

Swanson, R. N. 'Universities, Graduates and Benefices in Later Medieval England', *Past and Present*, no. 106 (1985), pp. 28 ff.

Taylor, J. *The Universal Chronicle of Ranulf Higden* (Oxford, 1966).

Thompson, A. H. 'Cathedral Church of St Peter, York', *V.C.H. Yorkshire*, iii (ed. W. Page, London, 1913), 375 ff.

'The Medieval Chapter', *York Minster Historical Tracts 627–1927* (ed. A. H. Thompson, London, 1927), no. 13.

Thomson, D. F. S. and H. C. Porter. *Erasmus and Cambridge* (Toronto, 1963).

Thomson, J. A. F. *The Later Lollards 1414–1520* (Oxford, 1965).

Thomson, R. M. 'England and the Twelfth-Century Renaissance', *Past and Present*, no. 101 (1983), pp. 3 ff.

Torraca, F., et al. *Storia della Università di Napoli* (Naples, 1924).

Trio, P. 'Financing of University Students in the Middle Ages: A New Orientation', *History of Universities*, iv (1984), pp. 1 ff.

Twigg, J. *A History of Queen's College, Cambridge, 1448–1986* (The Boydell Press, Suffolk, 1987).

Ullmann, W. 'Honorius III and the Prohibition of Legal Studies', *Juridical Review*, lx (1948), pp. 177 ff.

'Thomas Becket's Miraculous Oil', *Journal of Theological Studies*, viii (1957), pp. 129 ff.

'The University of Cambridge and the Great Schism', *Journal of Theological Studies*, ix (1958), pp. 53 ff.

'The Decline of the Chancellor's Authority in Medieval Cambridge: a Rediscovered Statute', *Historical Journal*, i (1958), pp. 176 ff.

Principles of Government and Politics in the Middle Ages (2nd ed., London, 1966).

Underwood, M. 'The structure and operation of the Oxford Chancellor's court, from the sixteenth to the early eighteenth century', *Journal of the Society of Archivists*, vi(1978), pp. 18 ff.

Venn, J. *Biographical History of Gonville and Caius College 1349–1897* (3 vols., Cambridge, 1897–1901).

Gonville and Caius College (College Histories Series, London, 1910).

Early Collegiate Life (Cambridge, 1913).

Verger, J. 'The University of Paris at the End of the Hundred Years War', *Universities in Politics: Case Studies from the Late Middle Ages and Early Modern Period* (ed. J. W. Baldwin and R. A. Goldthwaite, Baltimore, 1972), pp. 47 ff.

Les universités au moyen âge (Paris, 1973).

'Les comptes de l'université d'Avignon, 1430–1512', *The Universities in the Late Middle Ages* (ed. J. Ijsewijn and J. Paquet, Leuven University Press, 1978), pp. 190 ff.

'Des Ecoles à l'Université: la mutation institutionelle', *La France de Philippe Auguste: Le Temps des Mutations* (Colloques internationaux CNRS, no. 602, Paris, 1980), pp. 817 ff.

Wagner, D. L. (ed.). *The Seven Liberal Arts in the Middle Ages* (Indiana, 1983).

Wakeling, G. H. *Brasenose College Quatercentenary Monographs* (Oxf. Hist. Soc., liii, 1909).

Walcott, M. E. C. *William of Wykeham and his Colleges* (Winchester and London, 1852).

Walford, C. *Fairs, past and present* (London, 1883).

Walker, T. A. *Peterhouse* (College Histories Series, London, 1906).
A Biographical Register of Peterhouse Men, Part i 1284–1574 (Cambridge, 1927).

Warton, T. *The History of English Poetry* (3 vols., ed. R. Price, 1840).

Watt, D. E. R. 'University Clerks and Rolls of Petitions for Benefices', *Speculum*, xxxiv(1959), pp. 213 ff.

Weisheipl, J. A. 'Curriculum of the Faculty of Arts at Oxford in the early fourteenth century', *Mediaeval Studies*, xxvi (1964), pp. 143 ff.
'Science in the Thirteenth Century', *The History of the University of Oxford*, i (*The Early Oxford Schools*, ed. J. I. Catto, Oxford, 1984), 435 ff.

Weiss, R. 'Henry VI and the library of All Souls College', *E.H.R.*, lvii (1942), pp. 102 ff.
Humanism in England during the Fifteenth Century (2nd ed., Oxford, 1957).

Wickham, G. *Early English Stages 1300 to 1660* (2 vols., London and New York, 1963).

Wilks, M. J. 'The Early Oxford Wyclif: Papalist or Nominalist?', *Studies in Church History*, v (1969), pp. 69 ff.

Williamson, J. B. 'Unrest in Medieval Universities', *The University World, A Synoptic View of Higher Education in the Middle Ages and Renaissance* (ed. D. Radcliff-Umstead, Pittsburgh, 1973), pp. 56 ff.

Willis, R., and J. W. Clark. *The Architectural History of the University of Cambridge and of the Colleges of Cambridge and Eton* (4 vols., Cambridge, 1886).

Winstanley, D. A. *Unreformed Cambridge* (Cambridge, 1935).

Young, K. *The Drama of the Medieval Church* (2 vols., Oxford, 1933).

Ziegler, P. *The Black Death* (London, 1969).

Index